Understanding Medical Coding:

A Comprehensive Guide

Sandra L. Johnson, CMA

Delmar Publishers

an International Thomson Publishing company I(T)P®

Albany • Bonn • Boston • Cincinnati • Detroit • London • Madrid
Melbourne • Mexico City • New York • Pacific Grove • Paris • San Francisco
Singapore • Tokyo • Toronto • Washington

Delmar Staff
Publisher: Susan Simpfenderfer
Acquisitions Editor: Marlene McHugh Pratt
Developmental Editor: Jill Rembetski
Production Manager: Linda Helfrich
Art and Design Coordinator: Rich Killar
Editorial Assistant: Maria Perretta

COPYRIGHT © 2000

an International Thomson Publishing company I(T)P®

By Delmar Publishers
an International Thomson Publishing Company, Inc.

The ITP logo is a trademark under license.

Printed in United States of America

For more information, contact:

Delmar Publishers
3 Columbia Circle, Box 15015
Albany, New York 12212-5015

International Thomson Publishing Europe
Berkshire House
168-173 High Holborn
London, WC1V7AA
United Kingdom

Nelson ITP, Australia
102 Dodds Street
South Melbourne,
Victoria, 3205 Australia

Nelson Canada
1120 Birchmont Road
Scarborough, Ontario
M1K 5G4, Canada

International Thomson Publishing France
Tour Maine-Montparnasse
33 Avenue du Maine
75755 Paris Cedex 15, France

International Thomson Editores
Seneca 53
Colonia Polanco
11560 Mexico D. F. Mexico

International Thomson Publishing GmbH
Königswinterer Straße 418
53227 Bonn
Germany

International Thomson Publishing Asia
60 Albert Street
#15-01 Albert Complex
Singapore 189969

International Thomson Publishing Japan
Hirakawa-cho Kyowa Building, 3F
2-2-1 Hirakawa-cho, Chiyoda-ku,
Tokyo 102, Japan

ITE Spain/ Paraninfo
Calle Magallanes, 25
28015-Madrid, España

2 3 4 5 6 7 8 9 10 XXX 05 04 03 02 01 00 99

Library of Congress Cataloging-in-Publication Data

Understanding medical coding : a comprehensive guide / [edited by] Sandra R. Johnson.
    p.   cm.
    Includes bibliographical references and index.
    ISBN 0-7668-0104-7
    1. Nosology—Code numbers. I. Johnson, Sandra R. (CMA)
    [DNLM: 1. Terminology. 2. Disease—classification. W 15 U55 1999]
    RB115. U525 1999
    616′.001′48—dc21
    DNLM/DLC
    for Library of Congress   98-21887
                                       CIP

Contributors

Gay Boughton-Barnes, CPC, MPC
Coding and Reimbursement Manager
Oklahoma Heart Institute
Tulsa, OK
Module 7, Cardiology
Module 12, Reimbursement and Auditing/Appeals

Kathryn Cianciolo, MA, RRA, CCS, CCS-P
Consultant
Wankesha, WI
Module 5, Integumentary System

Linda French, CMA-C
Instructor
Simi Adult School and Career Institute
Simi Valley, CA
Module 8, OB/GYN

Nancy Heldt, CCS
Coding Supervisor
Florida Hospital
Winter Park Tech
Winter Park, FL
Module 4, Anesthesia/General Surgery

Sandra L. Johnson, CMA
Medical Assistant Instructor
Ivy Tech State College
Sellersburg, IN
Introduction
Module 10, Billing and Collections
Module 11, Filing the Claim Form

Marie A. Moisio, MA, RRA
Assistant Professor
Northern Michigan University
Marquette, MI
Module 3, Primary Care

Amy C. Morgan, RRA
Consultant
Asheville, NC
Module 8, OB/GYN

Julie Orloff, RMA, CMA, CPT
Program Coordinator
Medical Assisting/Medical Coding Specialist
National School of Technology
North Miami Beach, FL
Module 9, Radiology, Pathology, and Laboratory

Eugene Richard, RRA, CCS, CCS-P
Vice President
Health Systems Management Network
Belen, NM
Module 6, Orthopedics

Lois M. Smith, RN, CMA
Department Chair
Medical Assisting and Allied Health
Arapahoe Community College
Littleton, CO
Module 2, CPT Coding: Evaluation & Management

Karen S. Scott, MEd, RRA
Assistant Professor
Health Information Management
University of Tennessee, Memphis
Memphis, TN
Module 1, ICD-9-CM

Contents

MODULE 2 CPT CODING: EVALUATION AND MANAGEMENT 79

Lois M. Smith, RN, CMA

MODULE 3 PRIMARY CARE   125

Marie A. Moisio, MA, RRA

MODULE 4 ANESTHESIA/GENERAL SURGERY   163

Nancy Heldt, CCS

MODULE 12 REIMBURSEMENT AND AUDITING/APPEALS   429

Gay Boughton-Barnes, CPC, MPC

Preface

As the new millennium approaches, health care delivery systems will continue to be one of the major topics in our society as managed care organizations remain a strong force in the health care industry. Outpatient services and home treatment will continue to be the most popular method of medical care. As a result, the demand for qualified coders and billers in hospitals, physician offices, ambulatory care centers, and specialty clinics will increase. Training in coding, billing, reimbursement, and collections will be mandatory. Vocational and technical schools and community colleges must be prepared to supply skilled individuals to meet this employment demand. *Understanding Medical Coding: A Comprehensive Guide* is designed to address coding issues within specific content areas.

CONTENT

Understanding Medical Coding contains twelve modules, each written by a professional employed in a health care facility and/or educational institution. This textbook is designed to broaden coding knowledge and enhance coding skills by addressing specific coding issues within a particular area. It can be utilized by vocational schools, community colleges and career programs in training medical assistants, medical billers and coders. It is also useful for onsite training facilities to increase expertise of coding personnel.

Module 1 discusses ICD-9-CM, includes an overview of diagnostic coding, and provides a preview of ICD-10, due for release in the year 2001. Modules 2 through 9 are written sequentially to follow the organization of the CPT code book. Module 2 begins with CPT, in particular, Evaluation and Management coding. Primary care follows in Module 3 with its relationship to Evaluation/Management coding as well as the Medicine section. Modules 3 through 9 introduce specialty coding in anesthesia and surgery, the integumentary system, orthopedics, cardiology, OB/GYN, radiology, laboratory and pathology. The remaining modules focus on claim form instruction, billing and collection practices, and reimbursement guidelines, including the audit and appeals process.

KEY FEATURES

Each module contains the following learning aids to challenge learners:

Key Terms. Important terms are listed alphabetically at the beginning of each module. The key term is bolded when introduced within the context with the definition included.

Learning Objectives. Goals are listed at the beginning of each module. These objectives will address those concepts the learner should understand and they allow immediate feedback on progress.

Practice Exercises. Exercises utilizing both CPT and ICD-9-CM codes are included to challenge the learner's knowledge and application of the material presented and to facilitate problem solving.

Coding Tips. Each module includes advice to coding complex situations unique to medical specialties.

Summary. Each module summarizes content covered and highlights main points.

The modules also include current references, a listing of key resources, and organizations and associations pertinent to the chapter topic that will direct the learner to additional information for a particular specialty.

A glossary is also included at the end of the textbook to give a complete listing of all key terms for a quick and handy reference.

ACKNOWLEDGMENTS

Many people are to be recognized for their participation and involvement in this text. In 1996, at the American Association of Medical Assistants National Convention in Philadelphia, Pennsylvania, Delmar Publishers assembled a focus group of medical assistant educators and practitioners to address the need for a more advanced text on medical coding. This discussion led to the development of *Understanding Medical Coding*.

The contributors of each module, as well as the reviewers, played a major role in the development of this textbook. Individual authors sharing their expertise and working on tight schedules provided exemplary results. The comments and suggestions of the reviewers helped to finalize those chapters into text material. All are to be commended for their hard work, diligence, and dedication to this project. Reviewers include:

Beth Bowman, MPA, RRA
Health Information Management
College of Allied Health Sciences
The University of TN, Memphis
Memphis, TN

Juanita R. Bryant, CMA-A/C
Instructor
Sierra College
Rocklin, CA

Michelle Green, MPS, RRA, CMA
Associate Professor
Alfred State College
Alfred, NY

Eva I. Irwin
IVY Tech State College
Indianapolis, IN

Heather Sydney Joyner, RRA
Coding Instructor
Central Piedmont Community
   College
Charlotte, NC

Harriette Laronge, CMA
Program Director & Instructor
Medical Assisting & Coder Specialist
Sarasota County Technical College
Sarasota, FL

Elizabeth J. Miller, BA, MA, ART
Principal, EJM Associates
Seattle, WA

Karen Jody Smith, MS, RRA
Health Information Management
School of Allied Health Professions
St. Louis University
St. Louis, MO

I personally want to thank Jill Rembetski, Developmental Editor, for her direction and patience with me on this project. It has been an experience that has allowed me to develop new skills and work with many new people from whom I have learned much. I want to thank my husband, Bruce, for his encouragement to accept this new challenge, and his patience throughout the project. In particular, I want to acknowledge Pam Burton, my colleague, for her willingness to help me in any possible capacity, especially in setting priorities, meeting deadlines, and the offering of her computer knowledge and skills. Special recognition must be given to my friend and former co-worker, Cathy Allen, who remains at my beck and call to keep me current on the day-to-day changes in the health care setting. And I must thank my "boss," Deb Rowles, for allowing the time, flexibility, and support I needed at each stage of this project.

Introduction

Sandra Johnson

WHAT IS CODING?

Coding is defined as the translation of diagnoses, procedures, services, and supplies into numeric and/or alphanumeric components for statistical reporting and reimbursement purposes. Coding occurs when a medical term is cross-referenced into a three-, four-, or five-digit alphanumeric or numeric code. Coders abstract information from a patient record to assign the correct code(s).

Knowledge of medical terminology is required to describe accurately the patient's reason for the encounter, which is the diagnosis, symptom or complaint. Specific terms are also required to describe accurately surgical procedures, diagnostic tests and medical services provided to the patient. With the passage of the Medicare Catastrophic Coverage Act of 1988, the Health Care Financing Administration (HCFA) mandated the use of ICD-9-CM codes to report diagnoses and the treatment and HCPCS codes for services and supplies provided relative to those diagnoses.

WHAT IS FRAUD AND ABUSE?

To accurately assign codes, there must be an understanding of fraud and abuse and the rules of confidentiality. The Health Insurance Portability & Accountability Act of 1996 defines fraud as "knowingly and willfully executing, or attempting to execute, a scheme or artifact: 1) to defraud any health care benefit program; or, 2) to obtain, by false or fraudulent pretenses, representing, or promising, any of the money or property owned by or under the custody or control of a health care benefit program." Some examples of fraudulent activities are:

- coding to a higher level of service to increase revenue.
- billing for services, equipment or procedures that were never provided.
- receiving rebates or any type of compensation for referrals.
- misrepresenting a diagnosis to increase revenue.

Insurance abuse is not to be confused with fraud. Insurance abuse is defined as activities that are inconsistent with accepted business practices. Some examples of abuse are:

- overcharging for services, equipment or procedures.
- submitting claims for services that are not medically necessary for the treatment of a patient.
- violating participating provider agreements with insurance companies.
- improper billing practices.

The Health Insurance Portability & Accountability Act of 1996 establishes a formal link between government programs and the private insurance companies in an effort to provide recognition and penalties for submission of fraudulent claims. Penalties include a $10,000 fine per claim form when an individual knowingly and willfully misrepresents information submitted to result in greater payment or benefits, plus three times the fraudulent claim amount.

There are also civil penalties for fraudulent claims and coding errors contained in the Omnibus Budget Reconciliation Act of 1987 (OBRA 1987). OBRA penalizes the health care provider for errors made by coders in the amount of $2,000 fine per violation (a single coding error), an assessment in lieu of damages of up to twice the amount of the error submitted on the claim, and exclusion from Medicare and Medicaid programs for up to five years.

To avoid legal implications and ramifications, follow these rules:

■ Keep current with coding and billing practices. Purchase new code books annually. Update encounter forms, charge tickets, and computer programs yearly as well.
■ Know and understand coding rules and use them correctly.
■ Code only what is documented in the medical record. If there is a question or confusion, ask for clarification.
■ Develop and follow a coding compliance program.

TOOLS OF THE TRADE

When it comes to coding and billing, the proper tools are essential for optimal reimbursement. Be sure the following resources are available in the workplace. These include:

■ current ICD-9-CM manual (issued every October)
■ current CPT manual (issued every January)
■ current HCPCS manual (issued every January)
■ medical dictionary
■ carrier bulletins and newsletters

TYPES OF CODING

In 1983, Medicare created HCPCS (pronounced "hick picks"), the Health Care Financing Administration Common Procedural Coding System. HCPCS codes are required when reporting services and procedures provided to Medicare and Medicaid beneficiaries. HCPCS is a three-level coding system:

> Level I—CPT
> Level II—National Codes
> Level III—Local Codes

Level I—CPT Codes

The *Physicians' Current Procedural Terminology*, Fourth Edition (CPT), published by the American Medical Association, is a listing of descriptive terms with codes for reporting medical services and procedures performed by health care providers. CPT provides uniformity in accurately describing medical, surgical, and diagnostic services for effective communication among physicians, patients and third-party payers. CPT was introduced in 1966, and has undergone editing and modification to the current 1999 revision. The greatest change in CPT, having a major impact on coders, occurred in 1992 when "evaluation and management" services were created. This CPT section requires practitioners to make a decision as to level of service for offices, hospitals, nursing home services, etc.

It contains over 9000 different descriptions of services and procedures. Because CPT codes are updated annually, Appendix B of the CPT book summarizes the changes since the previous edition including additions and deletions essential for updating computer programs and/or encounter forms used in the facility.

The CPT Manual is referred to today as a volume reflecting the year of publication. (For example, CPT-99.) This textbook will refer to this procedural coding manual as CPT.

Modifiers

Appendix A of the CPT book contains a complete list of modifiers. A modifier is a two-digit code added to the main CPT code indicating the procedure has been altered by a specific circumstance. Or an alternative modifier may be used instead that begins with 099.

> CPT example: Procedure: Biopsy of right breast, needle core
> CPT code: 19100

The code 19100 indicates a unilateral procedure. To indicate a bilateral procedure, the modifier -50 would be added to the CPT code. Example: 19100-50; or the alternative code could be used, 09950.

Level II—National Codes

Level II consists of alphanumeric "national codes" supplied by the federal government. These codes supplement CPT codes enabling providers to report non-physician services such as durable medical equipment, ambulance services, supplies and medications, particularly injectable drugs. When billing Medicare and Medicaid for supplies and medications, avoid using CPT code 99070 (supplies and materials provided by the physician over and above those usually included with the office visit or other services). Level II codes list supplies and medications, especially injectable drugs, in more detail.

> Examples of Level II codes:
> Injection, dimenhydrinate, up to 50 mg J1240
> Elastic bandage (Ace) A4460

Modifiers

Level II also contains modifiers which are either alphanumeric or letters that can be used with all levels of HCPCS codes.

> Examples: -LT—used to identify procedures performed on the left side of
>   the body.
> -RR—used to identify durable medical equipment to be rented.

A listing of HCPCS Level II codes is available for purchase as an individual publication updated annually.

Level III—Local Codes

Level III codes are called "local codes" and are supplied by regional Medicare Part B carriers. They are reported for specific procedures or services to be submitted to government payers such as Medicare, Medicaid or CHAMPUS/CHAMPVA for which there is no national code. These five-digit alphanumeric codes use the letters S, and W through Z. Each local Medicare carrier may create local codes as the need dictates, obtaining HCFA approval before implementation. The Medicare carrier is responsible for providing a listing of local codes.

ICD-9-CM Codes

The International Classification of Diseases, Ninth Revision, Clinical Modification (ICD-9-CM) is a modification of ICD-9, which was created by the World Health Organization (WHO) based in Geneva, Switzerland. Since 1979, ICD-9-CM has provided a diagnostic coding system for the compilation and reporting of morbidity and mortality statistics for reimbursement purposes in the United States. It allows for the reporting of conditions, injuries and traumas along with complications and circumstances occurring with the illness or injury. It also provides the reason for patient care.

The ICD-9-CM contains three volumes. All health care facilities utilize Volume 1 (Tabular List of Diseases) and Volume 2 (Alphabetic Index to Disease) to report diagnoses. Hospitals use Volume 3 to report inpatient procedures (CPT is used to report procedures performed in physician offices, ambulatory care centers, and hospital outpatient departments).

ICD-9-CM requires assignment of the most specific code to represent the problem being treated by the provider. This means the primary diagnosis should be the one for the condition indicated within the medical record as the primary reason the patient sought medical care in an outpatient or office setting, or the principal diagnosis in an inpatient setting.

ICD-9-CM serves three major functions for insurance purposes. It

1. It justifies procedures and services rendered by the physician.
2. It assists in establishing medical necessity for services and procedures performed by the physician.
3. It serves as an indicator in measuring the quality of health care delivered by the physician provider.

CONCLUSION

The ultimate goal in coding is to present a clear picture of medical procedures and services performed (CPT codes), correlating the diagnosis, symptom, complaint, or condition (ICD-9-CM codes), thus establishing the medical necessity required for third-party reimbursement.

Continuing education is a must for medical billers and coders. Staying current and up-to-date on all billing and coding regulations is mandatory.

One example is HCFA's enforcement of new Evaluation and Management Documentation Guidelines, being developed jointly by HCFA and the American Medical Association (AMA). These guidelines will clearly outline documentation required in a patient's medical record for the CPT code submitted on the claim form, giving requirements for specific levels of service. The goal is to provide consistency and uniformity in medical record documentation for evaluation and management services. Many delays have occurred as the AMA and HCFA continue to review and test the new guidelines. Billers and coders must keep abreast of these changes for final approval of these guidelines and their enforcement.

And the new millennium will bring a new challenge to coders: ICD-10. Scheduled to replace ICD-9 in 2001, ICD-10 will be a major change that will require extensive training throughout the United States for all persons involved in the coding and billing process. Module 1 of this text presents an overview of ICD-10.

Module 1
ICD-9-CM

Karen Scott, MEd, RRA

KEY TERMS

AHA
AHIMA
Alphabetic Index
Category
Certification
Compliance
Cooperating Parties
DRG
Etiology
HCFA
ICD-10-CM
ICD-10-PCS
Main Term
NCHS
Primary (First) Diagnosis
Principal Diagnosis
Prospective Payment
RBRVS
Sequencing
Subcategory
Subclassification
Tabular List
Transient

LEARNING OBJECTIVES

Upon successful completion of this module, you should be able to:
1. Follow ICD-9-CM rules and regulations and code accurately.
2. Utilize *Coding Clinic for ICD-9-CM* and other resources appropriately.
3. Identify the correct principal and primary diagnoses.
4. Select instances in which V codes and E codes are appropriate and assign the correct codes in those circumstances.
5. Utilize resources including books, the Internet, and available organizations to increase coding accuracy.
6. Describe the ICD-10-CM coding system.

INTRODUCTION

The best way to use this module is to have the ICD-9-CM code book out while reviewing the material. Work through the examples as the information is discussed to have a thorough understanding of the material as it is presented.

X is used in this chapter to show that varying fourth and fifth digits may be used, depending on the specific diagnosis. For example, 250.XX shows that the diabetes category of 250 is used with appropriate fourth and fifth digits to further identify the type and manifestations of the disease.

HISTORY AND USAGE OF ICD-9-CM

ICD-9-CM stands for *International Classification of Diseases, Ninth Revision, Clinical Modification*. It is used for coding and classifying diagnoses and procedures by a numerical system. Classifying diseases by their cause has been done in various forms for many years, even as far back as the Greek civilization.

The ICD system has been around for many years and as the "ninth revision" implies, it has been updated many times to reflect changes in medicine. The ICD-9 classification was developed and is updated by the World Health Organization (WHO). It was modified by the

United States in the 1970s to provide greater specificity for use in classifying both diseases and procedures for hospital and physician usage. This modification is called ICD-9-CM.

ICD-9-CM was not developed for use as a reimbursement system, even though it is now the basis for hospital reimbursement within the **DRG** system. It was designed for statistical collection. It is a classification system, which means diagnoses and procedures are grouped together into various classes.

The ICD-9-CM code book is updated every year with changes effective October 1 of that year. It is essential that code books and coding software be updated yearly with the revisions. Many code books come in a loose-leaf version with updates provided at an extra charge.

The Cooperating Parties

There are four agencies known as the **cooperating parties** that have the responsibility for maintaining and updating ICD-9-CM. These are the American Hospital Association (**AHA**), the National Center for Health Statistics (**NCHS**), the Health Care Financing Administration (**HCFA**) and the American Health Information Management Association (**AHIMA**). Each agency has varying responsibilities as shown in Table 1–1.

The ICD-9-CM Coordination and Maintenance Committee, made up of various federal ICD-9-CM users, serves as an advisory committee to the cooperating parties.

Coding Clinic for ICD-9-CM

The *Coding Clinic for ICD-9-CM* is a quarterly publication published by the AHA. It is considered to be the official publication for ICD-9-CM coding guidelines and advice from the four cooperating parties. The advice given is to be followed by coders in all settings, including physician office, clinic, outpatient and hospital inpatient coding. Coders should regularly review this publication for information regarding ICD-9-CM coding. Many publishers have included references to specific official coding guidelines in their coding publications. Several sections of this module include guidelines reprinted from *Coding Clinic* to further illustrate concepts.

Sequencing Diagnosis Codes

Several of the official coding guidelines in this module refer to sequencing guidelines. **Sequencing** refers to the selection of the appropriate first diagnosis for the

TABLE 1–1	**Responsibilities of the Cooperating Parties for ICD-9-CM.**
NCHS	Maintains and updates the diagnosis portion of ICD-9-CM
HCFA	Maintains and updates the procedure portion (Volume 3)
AHA	Maintains the Central Office on ICD-9-CM to answer questions from coders and produces the *Coding Clinic for ICD-9-CM,* the official guidelines for ICD-9-CM usage
AHIMA	Provides training and certification for coding professionals

patient's encounter. In the hospital inpatient setting, this is known as the **principal diagnosis**. The principal diagnosis is the condition, after study, that brought the patient to the hospital for care. For example, if after the patient was admitted for chest pain it was found that the chest pain was caused by an acute myocardial infarction, the infarction would be the principal diagnosis.

In the outpatient or physician's office setting, the first diagnosis is known as the **primary diagnosis**. It is the main reason that caused the patient to seek treatment for that visit. This may be a symptom such as vomiting, chronic illness or acute disease, such as gastroenteritis or laceration.

HOW TO LOOK UP A TERM

ICD-9-CM consists of three volumes: Volume One includes a tabular numerical listing of diagnosis codes, Volume Two contains the alphabetic listing of diagnoses, and Volume Three includes a tabular and alphabetic listing of procedures primarily used in the hospital patient setting. The first step in coding is to locate the diagnostic term in the alphabetic index in Volume Two of ICD-9-CM. It is the Alphabetic Index to Disease and Injuries.

Step One: Locating the Main Term

The first step to looking up a term in the ICD-9-CM book is to look in the alphabetic index of Volume Two under the **main term**. The main term is printed in bold type at the left margin, and is the main "thing" (disease, injury, etc.) wrong with the patient. Examples of main terms are fracture, pneumonia, disease, injury, enlarged. Anatomic terms such as kidney, shoulder, etc., are *never* main terms in ICD-9-CM. If a coder tries to look up a code by the anatomic site, an instructional note to "See condition" will be found. This means the coder should look up the main condition that is wrong with the patient. This does not mean to look under the main term "condition". For example, if the patient comes to the physician's office for a sore throat, and the coder looked up the term "throat", there is a note that says *see* condition. (The throat is not what is wrong with the patient, the soreness is the main thing wrong, or the main condition.) The coder should look under the main term of *sore* to get a code of 462.

The **alphabetic index** is cross-referenced extremely well to allow the coder to locate the correct code using several different terms. For example, the diagnosis "Congestive Heart Failure" can be found under the main term "Failure" as well as "Congestive". By looking up this diagnosis either way, the coder is led to the correct code of 428.0.

EXERCISE 1–1

Underline the main term in each example.

1. Senile Cataract

2. Carcinoma of the Breast

3. Mitral Valve Prolapse

4. Urinary Cystitis

5. Hypertensive Cardiovascular Disease

Step 2: Identify Subterms

Below the main terms are indented subterms that further describe the condition. They may describe different sites of the illness, etiology (cause), or type of illness. Look in your ICD-9-CM book for the following main term in the alphabetic index.

> **Bronchiolitis** (acute) (infectious) (subacute) 466.19
>   with influenza, flu, or grippe 487.1
>   chemical 506.0

In the above example, Bronchiolitis was the main term. "With" and "chemical" are indented equally under the main term, so both are considered subterms. "Influenza, flu, or grippe" are subterms under the subterm "with" only. When a main term is located with many subterms, the coder may need to use a ruler to ensure correct usage.

Carryover Lines

Carryover lines are lines indented two more spaces further than subterms and are used to show the relationship between the information on both lines. They are used when there is too much information to fit on one line in the code book. For example:

> **Hypoplasia**
>   leg (*see also* Absence, limb, congenital,
>   lower) 755.30

In this case, the note in parentheses should be read as "(*see also* Absence, limb, congenital, lower)".

Nonessential Modifiers

Nonessential modifiers are terms in parentheses following main terms. These are modifiers or terms describing the main term whose presence or absence in the diagnostic statement does not change the code assignment. For example:

> **Intussusception** (colon) (enteric) (intestine)
>   (rectum) 560.0
>   appendix 543.9

Intussusception is the main term. "Colon", "enteric", "intestine", and "rectum" are nonessential modifiers. So if the coder's diagnostic statement said Intussusception only and did not mention the colon, the coder is still correct in using the 560.0 code.

TABULAR LIST

Volume One, the "Classification of Diseases and Injuries," is the **tabular listing**of diagnoses. Once a coder has identified a code in the alphabetic index, it must be verified in the tabular list. In the tabular list, codes are arranged numerically in 17 chapters and are grouped according to their cause (**etiology**), such as fractures, or body system, such as digestive system.

Chapter Title	Code Categories
1. Infectious and Parasitic Diseases	001-139
2. Neoplasms	140-239
3. Endocrine, Nutritional, and Metabolic Diseases and Immunity Disorders	240-279
4. Diseases of the Blood and Blood-Forming Organs	280-289
5. Mental Disorders	290-319
6. Diseases of the Nervous System and Sense Organs	320-389
7. Diseases of the Circulatory System	390-459
8. Diseases of the Respiratory System	460-519
9. Diseases of the Digestive System	520-579
10. Diseases of the Genitourinary System	580-629
11. Complications of Pregnancy, Childbirth and the Puerperium	630-677
12. Diseases of the Skin and Subcutaneous Tissue	680-709
13. Diseases of the Musculoskeletal System and Connective Tissue	710-739
14. Congenital Anomalies	740-759
15. Certain Conditions Originating in the Perinatal Period	760-779
16. Symptoms, Signs, and Ill-Defined Conditions	780-799
17. Injury and Poisoning	800-999

V CODES AND E CODES

Besides the numerical listing of diseases in the tabular list, three alphanumeric classifications are included in ICD-9-CM. These are V codes, E codes and M codes.

V Codes

V codes can be used to describe the main reason for the patient's visit in cases where the patient is not "sick", or used as a secondary diagnosis to provide further information about the patient's medical condition. One example would be a patient who is not sick and comes in to receive a TB skin test. There is a V code, V74.1, Screening for Pulmonary Tuberculosis, that is used if a diagnosis is not identified for the patient.

E Codes

E codes are external causes of injury and poisoning. Most of these are optional at this time, but may be required soon by many carriers. E codes are currently required by statute in many states. E codes are used as secondary diagnoses to show the cause of injury, such as a fall or automobile accident, if it is known. An example of an injury E code is E828.2, Accident involving animal being ridden, rider of animal. E codes will be covered in more detail later in this chapter.

M CODES

M (morphology) codes are found in the alphabetic index and are used primarily by cancer registries. An example of an M code is M8010/3, Carcinoma. These are used to further identify the behavior and cell type of a neoplasm and are used in conjunction with neoplasm codes from the main classification.

CATEGORIES, SUBCATEGORIES AND SUBCLASSIFICATIONS

The Tabular List of ICD-9-CM is set up in categories, subcategories, and fifth-digit subclassifications. **Categories** are groups of three-digit codes made up of similar diseases or a single disease. An example of a category is 715, Osteoarthrosis and Allied Disorders. **Subcategories** consist of four digits and provide more information such as site of the illness, cause, or other characteristics of the disease. One of the fourth-digit subcategories is 715.0, Osteoarthrosis, Generalized. Fifth-digit **subclassifications** are available in many categories to provide even greater specificity. The fifth digits for category 715 show specific sites of the osteoarthrosis, such as fifth digit 5 specifying the site of the pelvic region and thigh. Even though the coder will find both codes 715 and 715.0 in the code book, neither of these codes can be used because there is a fifth-digit subclassification that must be used. The coder must always code to the greatest level of specificity. In other words, *if there is a fifth-digit subclassification available, it must be used.*

Fifth digits may be found in various sections of the code book, so great care must be taken to make sure the correct code is being used. Many of the fifth digits are not shown in the alphabetic index, so the coder must take the time to review and verify the code in the tabular list. For example, with the diagnosis of Threatened labor, the coder would look under the main term of "threatened" and the subterm of "labor". The code given is 644.1. There is no note in the alphabetic index to indicate the need for a fifth digit, but upon verifying the code in the tabular section, it is obvious to the coder that a fifth digit is needed to show the current episode of care (delivered, antepartum, etc.) Many of the code books have been modified by the use of color coding or symbols to indicate the need to use a fifth digit. The coder should become familiar with the symbols/colors used in his or her book.

Residual Subcategories

ICD-9-CM allows for coding of all possible diagnoses and procedures. When the coder has a limited amount of information, a "residual" subcategory may be used. These include "other" and "unspecified" categories. These generally end in digits .8 for other and .9 for unspecified. For example, code 343.8 is for Other Specified

Infantile Cerebral Palsy. There is a note following this code that says to "use this code when the diagnosis is specified as a certain type of 'infantile cerebral palsy,' but is not listed above" (343.0-343.4). Code 343.9 is Infantile Cerebral Palsy, Unspecified. The note under this code reads "Use this code when the diagnosis is identified as 'infantile cerebral palsy,' but is not specified as to type." If the code found ends in a .8 or .9, this should serve as a flag for the coder. While these residual codes are used appropriately in many cases, it may mean that a more specific code can be found for the diagnosis in question. Insurance companies are reviewing payment for codes that they consider "non-specific", so the coder should be sure to check the medical record and the code book for further clarification prior to assigning a code ending with a .8 or a .9.

Trusting the Alphabetic Index

Due to space constraints, sometimes a term listed in the alphabetic index will not be repeated in the tabular list. In these cases, the coder must trust the alphabetic index and use the code listed.

For example, if the patient's diagnosis was "Horner's syndrome", the alphabetic index gives the code 337.9. When verifying this code in the tabular list, the description given for 337.9 is "Unspecified Disorder of Autonomic Nervous System" and there is no mention of Horner's Syndrome. The coder would still use code 337.9 to properly code this diagnosis.

CODING CONVENTIONS

ICD-9-CM uses several terms, abbreviations, punctuations, and symbols to lead the coder to the correct codes. These should be studied carefully and must be followed whenever present in the code book.

Braces } are used in the tabular list to reduce repetitive wording by connecting a series of terms on the left with a statement on the right.

> 461 Acute Sinusitis
>   Includes:
>   abscess
>   empyema   } acute, of sinus
>   infection

This means that if the patient has an acute abscess of the sinus or acute empyema of the sinus or acute infection of the sinus that these diagnoses are all coded properly to code 461.

Brackets [ ] are used in the tabular list to enclose synonyms, alternative wordings, and explanatory phrases such as:

> 460 Acute Nasopharyngitis [common cold]

The common cold is just another name for acute nasopharyngitis.

Slanted Square Brackets [ ] are used only in the alphabetic index to enclose a second code number that must be used with the first, and is always sequenced second. The first code (the one not in italicized brackets) represents the underlying condition. The second code represents the manifestation or what resulted from the underlying condition.

> *Official Coding Guidelines*
>
> *Codes in brackets in the Alphabetic Index can never be sequenced as principal diagnosis. Coding directives require that the codes in brackets be sequenced in the order as they appear in the Alphabetic Index.*
>
> *For example, with the diagnosis of Diabetic Retinitis, the coder is given two codes, 250.5 [362.01]. Since 362.01 is listed second and is enclosed in slanted square brackets, the coder is directed to code both the 250.5x as the principal or first diagnosis and to code 362.01 as a secondary diagnosis to fully describe the condition.*

Section Marks § indicate a footnote that normally means that a fifth digit is needed in that category. Some code books use other symbols besides the section mark to indicate the need for fifth digits.

§ 660.0 Obstruction caused by malposition of fetus

Look up code 660.0 in the tabular list. In most books, a section mark or other symbol will be located next to the code to indicate that a fifth digit must be used with this code. Some books do not use the section mark. The coder should become familiar with the symbols used in his/her individual code book to designate footnotes.

Cross-Reference Terms

There are several cross-reference terms used in the Alphabetic Index of ICD-9-CM that lead the coder to other categories or to use a second code.

See, See Also

"See" is a cross-reference that requires the coder to look up a different term. The "See also" cross-reference directs the coder to look under another main term if there is not enough information under the first term to identify the proper code. Look in the alphabetic index to locate the main term "laceration". The coder will note that there are few subterms listed under the main term laceration, and the following instruction is given:

Laceration—see also wound, open, by site

For example, if the patient had a laceration of the hand, there is not a subterm under laceration for hand. The coder would then look under the main term "wound, open" and see if there is a subterm for hand. The correct code for this diagnosis is 882.0.

Includes and Excludes Notes

Includes notes provide further examples or defines the category. For example, in the tabular list under code 785.4, Gangrene, the code book gives examples of diagnoses that can be coded using this code, such as Gangrene: Not Otherwise Specified, and Gangrenous cellulitis.

Excludes notes are easier to spot, as "Excludes" is printed in italics and in a box. If a condition is found under the excludes box, it means the condition must be coded elsewhere or needs further codes to complete the description. Under the code 382.3, Unspecified Chronic Suppurative Otitis Media, the following excludes note is found:

> *Excludes:* | *tuberculous otitis media (017.4)*

This note tells the coder that if the diagnosis is tuberculous otitis media, 382.3 is not the correct code to use. Instead, the coder should use 017.4 to correctly code the diagnosis.

There are times when the "Excludes" instruction can be confusing. When looking for the correct code for the diagnosis of Arteriosclerotic Cardiovascular Disease, the coder is led to 429.2, Cardiovascular Disease, Unspecified. A note below this code directs the coder to "use additional code, if desired, to identify presence of arteriosclerosis". A secondary code of 440.9 is needed to show both the cardiovascular disease and the arteriosclerosis. When the coder verifies the appropriateness of 440.9, there is an exclusion note that reads:

> *Excludes:* | *arteriosclerotic cardiovascular disease /ASCVD/ (429.2)*

This note is to let the coder know that both codes are necessary to fully describe the patient's condition.

Notes

Notes appear in both the tabular list and alphabetic index to provide further instructions or give definitions. For example, under the main term "Injury" in the alphabetic index, there is a note that says "*Note—for abrasion, insect bite (non-venomous), blister, or scratch, see Injury, superficial.*"

Code Also

Code also means the coder must use a second code to fully describe the condition. Sometimes the code book will instruct the coder to "use additional code, if desired". The words "if desired" should be ignored. The coder should use an additional code if the documentation supports the code assignment. Code 599.0, Urinary Tract Infection, Site Not Specified has a note that reads "Use additional code to identify organism, such as Escherichia coli, [E. coli] (041.4)." This note means that if the coder has documentation to identify the E. coli or other bacteria, a second code should be used.

Multiple Coding

Official Coding Guidelines

Multiple coding is required for certain conditions not subject to the rules for combination codes. Instructions for conditions that require multiple coding appear in the Alphabetic Index and the Tabular List:

> A. *Alphabetic Index: Codes for both etiology and manifestation of a disease appear following the subentry term, with the second code italicized and in slanted brackets. Assign both codes in the same sequence in which they appear in the Alphabetic Index.*

An example of etiology and manifestation codes is the term diabetic neuropathy. When the coder looks up the main term of neuropathy, subterm diabetic, two codes are given, 250.6 *[357.2]*. This indicates that both codes must be used to fully describe the patient's condition, with the code for diabetes (etiology), 250.6X sequenced first and 357.2 for neuropathy (manifestation) sequenced second.

> B. *Tabular List: Instructional terms, such as "Code also . . . ," "Use additional code for any . . . ," and "Note . . . ," indicate when to use more than one code.*
>
> *"Code also underlying disease"—Assign the codes for both the manifestation and the underlying cause. The codes for manifestations that are printed in italics cannot be used (designated) as principal diagnosis.*
>
> *"Use additional code, if desired, to identify manifestation as . . . ,"—Assign also the code that identifies the manifestation, such as, but not limited to, the examples listed. The codes for manifestations that appear in italicized print cannot be used (designated) as principal diagnosis.*
>
> C. *Apply multiple coding instructions throughout the classification where appropriate, whether or not multiple coding directions appear in the Alphabetic Index or the Tabular List. Avoid indiscriminate multiple coding of irrelevant information, such as symptoms or signs characteristic of the diagnosis.*

The code book does not always give hints, such as "use additional code" or "Code also" to let the coder know that more than one code is necessary. It is important that the coder use additional codes until all component parts of the diagnosis are fully described.

Abbreviations NEC (Not Elsewhere Classified) and NOS (Not Otherwise Specified)

NEC is an abbreviation that means Not Elsewhere Classified. This means that a more specific category is not available in ICD-9-CM. In the diagnosis Sudden sensorineural deafness, if the coder looks up the main term "Deafness", there is a subterm of "sudden, NEC", code 388.2. If the coder continues to search the list of subterms, sensorineural is also found, code 389.10. Since sudden is followed by NEC, it is less specific than sensorineural, so code 389.10 should be selected.

Official Coding Guidelines

Codes labeled "other specified" (NEC-not elsewhere classified) or "unspecified" (NOS-Not Otherwise Specified) are used only when neither the diagnostic

> *statement nor a thorough review of the medical record provides adequate information to permit assignment of a more specific code.*
>
> *Use the code assignment for "other" or NEC when the information at hand specifies a condition but no separate code for the condition is provided.*

NOS stands for Not Otherwise Specified. It should be interpreted as "unspecified" and is used when the coder has no further information available in the medical record to fully define the condition. Under code 780.9, Other Generalized Symptoms, one of the examples given is Chill(s), Not Otherwise Specified. If the coder had more information regarding the chills, such as cause, a more specific code could be appropriately used. If the documentation in the chart only stated "chills", then 780.9 would be the correct code assignment.

Official Coding Guidelines

Use "unspecified" (NOS) when the information at hand does not permit either a more specific or "other" code assignment.

Combination Codes

Official Coding Guidelines

A single code used to classify two diagnoses or a diagnosis with an associated secondary process (manifestation) or an associated complication is called a combination code. Combination codes are identified by referring to subterm entries in the Alphabetic Index and by reading the inclusion and exclusion notes in the Tabular List.

A. Assign only the combination code when that code fully identifies the diagnostic conditions involved or when the Alphabetic Index so directs. Multiple coding should not be used when the classification provides a combination code that clearly identifies all of the elements documented in the diagnosis. When the combination code lacks necessary specificity in describing the manifestation or complication, an additional code may be used as a secondary code.

At times, the code book provides a combination code that identifies the entire diagnostic statement. For example, in the diagnosis Pneumonia with Influenza, when the coder looks up the main term "pneumonia", there is a subterm for "with influenza". Code 487.0 is all that is needed to code both conditions.

Some coders like to use a cheat sheet that lists many of the common diagnoses and procedures used in their facility or physician practices. While this may save time in coding some diagnoses, it can also lead to many coding errors. ICD-9-CM does provide many combination codes that are to be used when two diagnoses are both present. If a coder is simply reading the code from a cheat sheet, the instructions to use combination codes will not be located. This is also true in the case of a physician simply checking off diagnoses from a fee ticket, superbill or other standardized coding form. A common mistake is that of a patient with congestive heart failure (428.0) due to hypertension (401.9). ICD-9-CM provides a combination code to describe both conditions. If the coder looks in the hypertension table at hypertension, the subterm "with, heart involvement (conditions classifiable to 425.8, 428, 429.0-429.3, 429.9 due to hypertension) (see also hypertension, heart)" is provided. When the coder then looks at hypertension, heart, subterm "with heart failure, congestive", the correct code is 402.91 (unspecified).

There is not a magic number of codes that can be used per diagnosis. Remember that coding is similar to putting a puzzle together. The coder has to solve each part of the puzzle before obtaining the entire picture.

REVIEW OF THE BASIC STEPS IN CODING

To illustrate the steps in coding, the diagnostic statement of "Cholelithiasis With Acute Cholecystitis" is coded as follows:

1. **Identify the main term(s) of the condition(s) to be coded.**

   The main term is cholelithiasis. Cholecystitis can be a main term also.

2. **Locate the main terms in the alphabetic index.**

   Using the alphabetic index, locate the main term "Cholelithiasis."

3. **Refer to any subterms indented under the main term.** This may be an extensive list, so it is important that the coder uses care in searching the listing. Also refer to any nonessential modifiers, instructional terms, or notes to select the most likely code.

   Next to the main term cholelithiasis there are two nonessential modifiers in parentheses, (impacted) (multiple). There is also a note that instructs the coder on the usage of fifth digits for this code category. The terms look as follows:

   Cholelithiasis (impacted)(multiple) 574.2
      with
        cholecystitis 574.1
         acute 574.0
         chronic 574.1

   Note   *Use the following fifth-digit subclassification with category 574:*
           0 without mention of obstruction
           1 with obstruction

   Following ICD-9-CM coding rules, the coder would use the subterms "with, cholecystitis, acute" and the note listing the fifth digits to find the most likely code of 574.00.

4. **Verify the code(s) in the tabular list.**

   The coder would go to the tabular list in numerical order to locate the code 574.00. The fourth-digit subcategory of 574.0 has a description of "Calculus of gallbladder with acute cholecystitis".

5. **Check all instructional terms in the tabular list and be sure to assign all codes to their highest degree of specificity.**

   The coder is also instructed by the symbols in the code book that code 574.0 must have a fifth digit. Since there is no mention of obstruction, the proper fifth digit is 0.

6. **Continue coding the diagnostic statement until all of the elements are identified completely.**

   All parts of the diagnostic statement are identified by using this one (combination) code.

EXERCISE 1–2

Assign ICD-9-CM codes to the following diagnoses.

1. Migraine headache _____

2. Congestive heart failure _____

3. Insulin-dependent diabetes mellitus, uncontrolled _____

4. Acute myocardial infarction, anterior wall, initial episode _____

5. Fracture of hip _____

6. Acute gastroenteritis _____

7. Esophageal ulcer _____

8. Coronary insufficiency _____

PROCEDURAL CODING WITH ICD-9-CM

ICD-9-CM classifies procedures in Volume Three, which includes the alphabetic index and tabular list for procedures. The procedures are grouped by system, and use numerical codes only. The process for coding procedures is the same as that followed in coding diagnoses, i.e., locate the main term in the alphabetic index and verify it in the tabular list. The main term for procedures is the name of the procedure itself; for example, cardiac catheterization would appear under catheterization, subterm cardiac. Volume Three of the ICD-9-CM code book is not used in the physician's office/clinic setting. Procedures in these settings are coded using another coding system called *Current Procedural Terminology (CPT)*. This is discussed in Module 2 of this text.

Subterms

Many subterms classify the procedure as to site and/or surgical technique. It is very important to search the subterms carefully to ensure use of the proper code.

Eponyms

Procedures are often named after the person who developed the procedure (an eponym), so they will often be found under that person's name. These procedures are also listed under the main term; for example, McDonald Operation is listed in the alphabetic index under both "McDonald" and "operation".

Canceled Procedure

If a procedure was canceled, the coder should code it as far as it proceeded. For example, if a laparoscopically assisted cholecystectomy was planned, and after making the laparotomy incision the patient went into cardiac arrest, the laparotomy and not the cholecystectomy would be coded. (There are V codes available to code the diagnosis of surgery canceled.)

Code Also

The instructional term "code also" is used in the tabular list for procedures to mean "code also if another procedure was performed". The note under code 36.1 states "Code also cardiopulmonary bypass [extracorporeal circulation] [heart-lung machine] (39.61). The cardiopulmonary bypass is generally a part of any heart bypass procedure (codes 36.10-36.19), as well as other heart procedures, but must be coded in addition to the bypass code.

Omit Code

Another common instructional term in coding procedures is "omit code". At times, a procedure may be done solely as an approach to be able to perform another procedure. It is at this time that the coder may see the instructional term "omit code", which means that the coder does not code this separately if it was performed as an operative approach. For example, if the patient had a laparotomy with a partial hepatectomy, the coder would only use 50.22 to code the hepatectomy.

EXERCISE 1-3

Code the following procedures using ICD-9-CM Volume Three:

1. Cholecystectomy _____

2. Esophagogastroduodenoscopy (EGD) _____

3. Suture of laceration of skin of hand _____

4. Laparotomy with herniorrhaphy, bilateral direct inguinal hernia with graft _____

5. Excision, lesion, breast _____

How to Code an Operative Report

The operative reports included here are representative of those that coders in both hospitals and clinics may have to code. To code an operative report the coder should first read through the entire report and make notes (or underline) any possible diagnoses or abnormalities noted and any procedures performed. This is an important step because sometimes the coder will find other diagnoses and procedures performed that the physician failed to list at the top of the report. The coder should then review the physician's list of diagnoses and procedures to see if these match. If the coder should locate a potential diagnosis or procedure not listed by the physician they should bring this to the physician's attention to see if it is significant enough to code. If preoperative and postoperative diagnoses are different, the coder should use the postoperative diagnosis, which was determined following the surgery.

The coder should also review the pathology report if specimens were sent to pathology, to verify the diagnosis. If there is a discrepancy between the pathologist's and surgeon's diagnoses, this matter should be discussed with the surgeon.

EXERCISE 1–4

Using all volumes of the ICD-9-CM code book, code all diagnoses and procedures in the three operative reports that follow. If more information is needed from the physician, list questions on the line provided.

---

1.   **Report of Operation**

OPERATION: 1. Total Abdominal Hysterectomy

                   2. Right Ovarian Cystectomy

PREOPERATIVE DIAGNOSIS: Symptomatic fibroids

POSTOPERATIVE DIAGNOSIS: 1. Symptomatic fibroids. 2. Endometriosis, ovary

ANESTHESIA: General endotracheal

COMPLICATIONS: None

ESTIMATED BLOOD LOSS: 200 cc

FLUIDS: 1500 lactated Ringers

FINDINGS: Diffusely enlarged uterus with normal left ovary. Right ovary had a simple cyst, 2 × 2 cm, as well as endometriosis. Specimens sent to pathology.

PROCEDURE: The risks, benefits, indications, and alternatives of the procedure were reviewed with the patient and informed consent was obtained. The patient was taken to the operating room with IV running. The patient was placed in the supine position and given general anesthesia and was prepared and draped in the usual sterile fashion. A vertical incision was made approximately at the level of the umbilicus and incised down to the symphysis pubis and extended sharply to the rectus fascia. The rectus

continues

muscles were then separated to obtain good visualization. The muscles of the anterior abdominal wall were separated in the midline by sharp and blunt dissection. The peritoneum was grasped between two pick-ups, elevated and entered sharply with the scalpel. The pelvis was examined with the findings as noted above. An O'Connor O'Sullivan retractor was placed in the incision and the bowel was packed away with moist laparotomy sponges. The uterus was clamped with a traumatic clamp for better visualization. The round ligaments on both sides were clamped, transected, and sutured with 0 Vicryl. The anterior leaf of the broad ligament was incised along the bladder reflection to the midline from both sides. The bladder was then gently dissected off the lower uterine segment of the cervix with a sponge stick. The utero-ovarian ligament, on both sides was then doubly clamped, transected, and sutured with 0 Vicryl. Hemostasis was visualized. The uterine arteries were skeletonized bilaterally, clamped with Heaney clamps, transected, and suture ligated with 0 Vicryl. Again hemostasis was assured. The cervix and uterus were amputated with a scalpel. The vaginal cuff angles were closed with figure-of-eight stitches of 0 Vicryl and were then transfixed to the ipsilateral, cardinal, and uterosacral ligaments. The remainder of the vaginal cuff was closed with a series of interrupted 0 Vicryl figure-of-eight sutures. Hemostasis was assured. Both right ovarian cysts were incised with scalpel and sacs were removed with blunt dissection. A 25 gauge needle was placed in the endometrioma to assure cystic nature. The cysts were closed with 3-0 Vicryl in a running suture. The pelvis was copiously irrigated with warm, normal saline, and all laparotomy sponges and instruments were removed from the abdomen. The fascia was closed with a running PDS and hemostasis was assured. The skin was closed with staples. Sponge, lap, needle, and instrument counts were correct times two. The patient was taken to the recovery room in stable condition. Specimens included the right ovarian cyst wall and uterus.

Diagnoses: _____

Procedures: _____

Question for Physician: _____

---

2. **Report of Operation**

PREOPERATIVE DIAGNOSIS: Ruptured disc, L-4 central

POSTOPERATIVE DIAGNOSIS: Same

PROCEDURE: Bilateral subtotal hemilaminectomy and foraminotomy with removal of the lower one-third of the fourth lumbar spinous process and exploration of L-4 right and central.

FINDINGS AT OPERATION: There was a canal stenosis secondary to hypertrophy of the facet and ligament. The disc was firm and flat. There was a small osteoarthritic spur present underneath the nerve root.

OPERATION: Under general anesthesia, after prepping and draping in the usual manner, a linear incision was made over L-4 and L-5. Removal of the lower one-third of L-4 spinous processes and bilateral subtotal hemilaminectomy and foraminotomy were performed at L-4 decompressing the canal stenosis bilaterally. The ligamental flava was removed with Kerrison rongeurs mainly on the right side and the dura was retracted medially and the above findings were present. The ball probe passed easily in the foramen after decompression. The bleeding was minimal. The incision was closed using 1 Chromic on the muscle and fascia, 2-0 Chromic on the subcutaneous tissue, and mattress 4-0 Nylon and skin clips on the skin.

The patient was taken to the recovery room in satisfactory condition.

Diagnoses: _____

Procedures: _____

Question for Physician: _____

---

3.   **Report of Operation**

ATTENDING SURGEON: Ben Davis, MD

OPERATION: Attempted Laparoscopic Cholecystectomy Followed by Open Cholecystectomy

PREOPERATIVE DIAGNOSIS: Acute Cholecystitis

POSTOPERATIVE DIAGNOSIS: Acute Cholecystitis

ANESTHESIA: General endotracheal

ESTIMATED BLOOD LOSS: Approximately 200 cc

INDICATIONS: The patient is a 25-year-old white female who notes a several day history of increasing right upper quadrant pain associated with nausea, vomiting, and fever. The patient had an ultrasound performed, which showed significant pericholecystic fluid with cholelithiasis consistent with acute cholecystitis. Risks and benefits were discussed with the patient, and she elected to proceed with the cholecystectomy.

PROCEDURE: The patient was placed in the supine position on the table. General endotracheal anesthesia was administered and the abdomen prepped and draped in the usual sterile fashion, using Betadine solution. Initially, a supraumbilical incision was made due to the patient's prior history of a laparoscopic tubal ligation as well as a cesarean section with a lower midline. The supraumbilical incision was carried down to the level of the fascia. Using sharp dissection, the fascia was incised linearly. The lateral borders of the fascia were grasped with stay sutures of heavy Vicryl. An incision was made into the posterior sheath. There were significant adhesions encountered at this level, and an inadvertent enterotomy was made, which was noted immediately. The enterotomy was closed with running 3-0 Chromic suture followed by imbricating 3-0 GI silks. Excellent closure was noted of the small intestine, which was then returned to the abdominal cavity. Adhesions were sharply taken down to allow for direct placement of a Hasson type trocar into the abdominal cavity. Capnoperitoneum was then introduced to 15 mm mercury pressure.

continues

Upon examining the abdomen, the gallbladder was incredibly distended with focal gangrenous changes. There was a significant amount of edema and adhesions of the omentum to this area with a moderate amount of free greenish fluid in the abdomen and along the right gutter. A 10 mm trocar was then placed under direct vision in the subxiphoid area and two 5 mm trocars placed in the anterior axillary line of the right upper and right lower quadrants. All this was done with direct vision. The gallbladder was then attempted to be grasped, however, due to its significant distention required decompression through percutaneous aspiration. The gallbladder was then grasped and the liver retracted superiorly, and dissection was then carried out along the gallbladder, taking down the omental adhesions inferiorly. There was a significant amount of edema and adhesions noted. As dissection proceeded more proximally, the tissue was very friable, and it was felt that with the exposure and due to the significant edema, that laparoscopic cholecystectomy would be impossible. Therefore, the laparoscopic procedure was abandoned, and other trocars all removed and capnoperitoneum released and the camera removed.

An incision was made subcostally, connecting the two superior trocar sites and carried down through to the level of the muscular fascia, using Bovie electrocautery. The muscular layers were then divided, exposing the peritoneum, which was then divided throughout the length of the incision. Retractors were placed to facilitate exposure. Dissection was then carried out from distally to proximally, initially scoring the peritoneum over the gallbladder and dissecting circumferentially around the gallbladder bed. Dissection was then carried proximally where the cystic artery was identified and a significant amount of edematous doubly ligated proximally and stapled with a surgical clip distally. The artery was then divided, and careful dissection was then carried out proximally where the cystic duct was identified and divided between heavy silk ligatures. Careful dissection was then carried out along the infundibulum, and the gallbladder was removed from the gallbladder bed and sent for permanent specimen. Again, there was a significant amount of focal necrosis noted throughout the walls of the gallbladder, and several small stones were noted within the gallbladder itself. Hemostasis was then achieved with Bovie electrocautery.

The wound was irrigated with a significant amount of sterile saline solution. The pelvis was then irrigated with saline solution and aspirated. Due to the significant edema and the fluid noted in the gallbladder bed on initial placement of the trocar, a 10 flat Jackson-Pratt drain was placed in the hole. When hemostasis was deemed adequate, the subcostal incision was closed in muscular layers, using heavy PDS suture. The wound was then irrigated, and figure-of-eight fashion was used to close the fascia at the umbilicus. A separate suture was used to secure the Jackson-Pratt drain at the skin. The patient tolerated the procedure well, and needle and sponge counts were correct at the conclusion of the case. The patient was extubated and transferred to the recovery room in stable condition.

Diagnoses: _____

Procedures: _____

Question for Physician: _____

Coding Signs and Symptoms

In many circumstances, the physician may initially not know what the patient's diagnosis is, so the coder may only be able to code the patient's signs and symptoms. It is important to understand the difference between signs and symptoms.

■ A sign is visible evidence that the physician can determine objectively (overactive bowel sounds, laceration to the skin).

■ A symptom is a subjective, descriptive term, usually in the patient's own words, e.g., "My head hurts."

Official Coding Guidelines

Conditions That Are an Integral Part of a Disease Process

Conditions that are integral to the disease process should not be assigned as additional codes.

■ Confusing Codes

Signs and symptoms must be coded with care. If a sign or symptom is a common occurrence with a particular diagnosis, then it is not coded once the diagnosis has been made. For example, chest congestion is a sign of pneumonia. Only the pneumonia would be coded.

Conditions That Are Not an Integral Part of a Disease Process

Additional conditions that may not be associated routinely with a disease process should be coded when present.

If a sign or symptom occurs that is not a part of the usual disease process, then that condition is coded. For example, if the patient had a rash on the skin (782.1) with gastroenteritis (558.9), both diagnoses would be coded.

In the emergency room setting, the physician may not be able to make an exact diagnosis, and will recommend that the patient follow up with their primary care physician. In these cases, the documentation only substantiates coding of the patient's signs and symptoms. For example, if the patient is seen in the emergency department with dizziness, the ER physician will try to determine the etiology, but may not be able to find a definitive cause. He may refer the patient to an ear, nose and throat specialist to see if there is an inner ear problem.

Uncertain Diagnosis

If the diagnosis documented at the time of discharge is qualified as "probable", "suspected", "likely," "questionable", "possible," or "rule out," code the condition as if it existed or was established.

In hospital inpatient coding, conditions listed as "suspected", "rule out", or "possible" are coded as if the condition exists. In these cases, sometimes the physician will also want the signs and symptoms coded for use in further study.

Official Coding Guidelines-Outpatient Services

Do not code outpatient diagnoses documented as "probable," "suspected," "questionable," or "rule out," or working diagnosis. Rather, code the condition(s) to the highest degree of certainty for that encounter/visit, such as symptoms, signs, abnormal test results, or other reason for visit.

Please note: This is contrary to the coding practices used by hospitals and medical record departments for coding the diagnosis of hospital inpatients.

In those instances where the physician or other health-care practitioner does not document (identify) a definite condition or problem at the conclusion of a patient care encounter/visit, the coder should select the documented chief complaint(s) as the reason for the encounter/visit.

With physician's office and outpatient/emergency room coding, the coder may only assign codes to the highest degree of certainty. In these situations, do not code suspected, ruled out or possible conditions.

To illustrate, if the patient had the diagnosis of "wheezing, rule out pneumonia," and was seen in the physician's office, the coder would only code the wheezing, 786.09. In the inpatient setting, the coder would code both the 786.09 and the 486 for the pneumonia.

Abnormal Findings

Abnormal findings (laboratory, x-ray, pathologic, and other diagnostic results) are not coded and reported unless the physician indicates their clinical significance. If the findings are outside the normal range and the physician has ordered other tests to evaluate the condition or prescribed treatment, it is appropriate to ask the physician whether the diagnosis should be added.

Lab reports usually show "normal" values, and when searching through the patient's record, the coder may find a value that is not within normal range. If the patient's potassium level was a bit high, they might possibly have Hyperkalemia (276.7). But the results may not be enough out of the normal limit range to really be significant. It is up to the physician to make this determination. The coder should ask the physician if this is truly hyperkalemia and should not code it without clarification from the physician. Abnormal findings in the chart are coded only if the physician indicates that these findings have a clinical significance.

INFECTIONS

Official Coding Guidelines

Septicemia and Septic Shock

When the diagnosis of septicemia with shock or the diagnosis of general sepsis with septic shock is documented, code and list the septicemia first and report the septic shock code as a secondary condition. The septicemia code assignment should identify the type of bacteria if it is known.

Sepsis and septic shock associated with abortion, ectopic pregnancy, and molar pregnancy are classified to category codes in Chapter 11 (630-639).

Negative or inconclusive blood cultures do not preclude a diagnosis of septicemia in patients with clinical evidence of the condition.

Septicemia/sepsis is a severe infection due to bacteria in the blood and is marked by high fever, chills, and can lead to shock and death. Usually, blood cultures (placing a sample of blood in a specially treated dish and watching the sample over a period of time to see if microorganisms grow from the specimen) are taken to determine the type of bacteria causing the severe infection.

■ Confusing Codes

Bacteremia is the presence of bacteria in the blood, and is coded to 790.7. It can lead to sepsis/septicemia, but is not necessarily the same thing.

How to Locate the Code for a Microorganism

If a specific organism causing a patient condition is identified, and the code book directs the coder to "Use additional code, if desired, to identify organism", at times the code book does not give any hints as to where to look to find the code for the organism. The coder can look under the main term "infection" to locate the code for the organism, such as 041.4, Escherichia Coli [E. coli].

For example, if the patient has the diagnosis of Urinary Tract Infection, 599.0, there is a note following the description for code 599.0 in the tabular list of the code book that says, "Use additional code to identify organism, such as Escherichia coli, [E. coli] (041.4)."

HIV INFECTIONS

Official Coding Guidelines

Code Only Confirmed Cases of HIV Infection/Illness

This is an exception to the guideline which states "If the diagnosis documented at the time of discharge is qualified as 'probable,' 'suspect,' 'likely,' 'questionable,' or 'still to be ruled out,' code the condition as if it existed or was established . . ." In this context, "confirmation" does not require documentation of positive serology or culture for HIV; the physician's diagnostic statement that the patient is HIV positive, or has an HIV-related illness, is sufficient.

■ *Highlight*

Whenever dealing with a possible diagnosis of HIV or AIDS, the coder should take extreme care to verify the accuracy of the diagnosis. The coder should always remember the patient behind the codes and must realize that a wrong code placed on a patient's chart can affect the patient's insurance coverage, employment, and life.

Selection of HIV Code

042 Human Immunodeficiency Virus [HIV] Disease

Patients with an HIV-related illness should be coded to 042, Human Immunodeficiency Virus [HIV] Disease.

V08 Asymptomatic Human Immunodeficiency Virus (HIV) Infection

Patients with physician-documented asymptomatic HIV infections who have never had an HIV-related illness should be coded to V08, Asymptomatic Human Immunodeficiency Virus [HIV] Infection.

795.71 Nonspecific Serologic Evidence of Human Immunodeficiency Virus [HIV]

Code 795.71, Nonspecific serologic evidence of human immunodeficiency virus [HIV] should be used for patients (including infants) with inconclusive HIV test results.

Previously Diagnosed HIV-Related Illness

Patients with any known prior diagnosis of an HIV-related illness should be coded to 042. Once a patient has developed an HIV-related illness, the patient should always be assigned code 042 on every subsequent admission. Patients previously diagnosed with any HIV illness (042) should never be assigned with 795.71 or V08.

Sequencing

The circumstances of admission govern the selection of principal diagnosis for patients with HIV-related illnesses. In other words, "that condition established after study to be chiefly responsible for occasioning the admission of the patient to the hospital for care."

Patients who are admitted for an HIV-related illness should be assigned a minimum of two codes: first assign code 042 to identify the HIV disease and then sequence additional codes to identify the other diagnoses.

If a patient is admitted for an HIV-related condition, the principal diagnosis should be 042, followed by additional diagnosis codes for all reported HIV-related conditions.

If a patient with HIV disease is admitted for an unrelated condition (such as a traumatic injury), the code for the unrelated condition (e.g., the nature of injury code) should be the principal diagnosis. Other diagnoses would be 042 followed by additional diagnosis codes for all reported HIV-related conditions.

Whether the patient is newly diagnosed or has had previous admissions for HIV conditions (or has expired) is irrelevant to the sequencing decision.

HIV Infections in Pregnancy, Childbirth and Puerperium

During pregnancy, childbirth or the puerperium, a patient admitted because of an HIV-related illness should receive a principal diagnosis of 647.8X, other specified infectious and parasitic disease in the mother classifiable elsewhere, but complicating the pregnancy, childbirth, or the puerperium, followed by 042 and the code(s) for the HIV-related illness(es). This is an exception to the sequencing rule above.

Patients with asymptomatic HIV infection status admitted during pregnancy, childbirth, or the puerperium should receive codes of 647.8X and V08.

Asymptomatic HIV Infection

V08 Asymptomatic human immunodeficiency virus (HIV) infection, is to be applied when the patient without any documentation of symptoms is listed as being HIV positive, known HIV, HIV test positive, or similar terminology. Do not use this code if the term AIDS is used or if the patient is treated for any HIV-related illness or is described as having any condition(s) resulting from his/her HIV positive status; use code 042 in these cases.

Inconclusive Laboratory Test for HIV

795.71 Inconclusive Serologic Test for Human Immunodeficiency Virus (HIV)

Patients with inconclusive HIV serology, but no definitive diagnosis or manifestations of the illness may be assigned code 795.71.

Testing for HIV

If the patient is asymptomatic but wishes to know his/her HIV status, use code V73.89, Screening for other specified viral disease. Use code V69.8, Other problems related to lifestyle, as a secondary code if an asymptomatic patient is in a known high-risk group for HIV. Should a patient with signs or symptoms or illness, or a confirmed HIV-related diagnosis be tested for HIV, code the signs and symptoms or the diagnosis. An additional counseling code, V65.44, may be used if counseling is provided during the encounter for the test.

When the patient returns to be informed of his/her HIV test results, use code V65.44, HIV counseling, if the results of the test are negative. If the results are positive but the patient is asymptomatic, use code V08, Asymptomatic HIV infection. If the results are positive and the patient is symptomatic, use code 042, HIV infection, with codes for the HIV-related symptoms or diagnosis. The HIV counseling code may also be used if counseling is provided for patients with positive test results.

CIRCULATORY SYSTEM CODING

Module 7 of this text covers cardiology in detail. Please refer to that module for more information on coding cardiovascular diseases and procedures.

There are many instructional notes used in the circulatory chapter of ICD-9-CM. The coder should review these notes and assign these codes with care.

Hypertension

The hypertension table, (Table 2) located under the main term "hypertension" in the alphabetic index of the code book, is very extensive concerning the coding of all conditions due to or associated with hypertension (see Table 1–2). Three columns are listed- malignant, benign, and unspecified. Benign hypertension is considered to be mild and usually under control with medication. Malignant

TABLE 1–2 ICD-9-CM Volume II: Hypertension Table (partial). *(Courtesy of St. Anthony's ICD-9-CM, 1998. Reprinted with permission of St. Anthony Publishing, Inc. 800-632-0123.)*

	Malignant	Benign	Unspecified
Hypertension, hypertensive (arterial) (arteriolar) (crisis) (degeneration) (disease) (essential) (fluctuating) (idiopathic) (intermittent) (labile) (low renin) (orthostatic) (paroxysmal) (primary) (systemic) (uncontrolled) (vascular)	401.0	401.1	401.9
with			
heart involvement (conditions classifiable to 425.8, 428, 429.0-429.3, 429.8, 429.9 due to hypertension) (*see also* Hypertension, heart)	402.00	402.10	402.90
with kidney involvement—*See* Hypertension, cardiorenal			
renal involvement (*only* conditions classifiable to 585, 586, 587) (*excludes conditions classifiable to 584*) (*see also* Hypertension, kidney)	403.00	403.10	403.90
with heart involvement—*See* Hypertension, cardiorenal			
failure (and sclerosis) (*see also* Hypertension, kidney)	403.01	403.11	403.91
sclerosis without failure (*see also* Hypertension, kidney)	403.00	403.10	403.90
accelerated (*see also* Hypertension, by type, malignant)	401.0	—	—
antepartum—*see* Hypertension, complicating pregnancy, childbirth, or the puerperium			
cardiorenal (disease)	404.00	404.10	404.90
with			
heart failure (congestive)	404.01	404.11	404.91
and renal failure	404.03	404.13	404.93
renal failure	404.02	404.12	404.92
and heart failure (congestive)	404.03	404.13	404.93

continues

Table 1–2   ICD-9-CM Volume II: Hypertension Table (partial). *(Courtesy of St. Anthony's ICD-9-CM, 1998. Reprinted with permission of St. Anthony Publishing, Inc. 800-632-0123.)* continued

	Malignant	Benign	Unspecified
cardiovascular disease (arteriosclerotic) (sclerotic)	402.00	402.10	402.90
with			
heart failure (congestive)	402.01	402.11	402.91
renal involvement (conditions classifiable to 403)			
(*see also* Hypertension, cardiorenal)	404.00	404.10	404.90
cardiovascular renal (disease) (sclerosis) (*see also* Hypertension, cardiorenal)	404.00	404.10	404.90
cerebrovascular disease NEC	437.2	437.2	437.2
complicating pregnancy, childbirth, or the puerperium	642.2	642.0	642.9
with			
albuminuria (and edema) (mild)	—	—	642.4
severe	—	—	642.5
edema (mild)	—	—	642.4
severe	—	—	642.5
heart disease	642.2	642.2	642.2
and renal disease	642.2	642.2	642.2
renal disease	642.2	642.2	642.2
and heart disease	642.2	642.2	642.2
chronic	642.2	642.0	642.0
with pre-eclampsia or eclampsia	642.7	642.7	642.7
fetus or newborn	760.0	760.0	760.0
essential	—	642.0	642.0
with pre-eclampsia or eclampsia	—	642.7	642.7
fetus or newborn	760.0	760.0	760.0
fetus or newborn	760.0	760.0	760.0
gestational	—	—	642.3
pre-existing	642.2	642.0	642.0
with pre-eclampsia or eclampsia	642.7	642.7	642.7
fetus or newborn	760.0	760.0	760.0
secondary to renal disease	642.1	642.1	642.1
with pre-eclampsia or eclampsia	642.7	642.7	642.7
fetus or newborn	760.0	760.0	760.0
transient	—	—	642.3
due to			
aldosteronism, primary	405.09	405.19	405.99
brain tumor	405.09	405.19	405.99
bulbar poliomyelitis	405.09	405.19	405.99

hypertension is a life-threatening, severe form of hypertension. The coder cannot assume that the hypertension is either malignant or benign unless specified by the physician. Otherwise, the coder must use the unspecified codes as listed.

If the patient has essential hypertension, the coder must use 401.9, unspecified.

Official Coding Guidelines

Hypertension with Heart Disease

Certain heart conditions (425.8, 428, 429.0-429.3, 429.8, 429.9) are assigned to a code from category 402 when a causal relationship is stated (due to hypertension) or implied (hypertensive). Use only the code from category 402. The same heart conditions (425.8, 428, 429.0-429.3, 429.8, 429.9) with hypertension, but without a stated causal relationship, are coded separately. Sequence according to the circumstances of the admission.

▬ Confusing Codes

ICD-9-CM makes a distinction between diagnoses "with hypertension" and "due to hypertension". Hypertensive should be interpreted as "due to hypertension" and coded appropriately.

If the patient has CHF (Congestive Heart Failure) due to hypertensive heart disease, the correct code is 402.91, Hypertensive Heart Disease with Congestive Heart Failure, since the causal relationship is specified by the words "due to". Congestive heart failure, with hypertension, on the other hand, would be coded 428.0 and 401.9 since no causal relationship is stated.

Hypertensive Renal Disease with Chronic Renal Failure

Assign codes from category 403, hypertensive renal disease, when conditions classified to categories 585-587 are present. Unlike hypertension with heart disease, ICD-9-CM presumes a cause-and-effect relationship and classifies chronic renal failure with hypertension as hypertensive renal disease. Acute renal failure is not included in this cause and effect relationship.

If the patient's diagnosis is renal sclerosis with hypertension, the coder goes to the main term "sclerosis", subterm "renal" "with hypertension (see also Hypertension, Kidney)" and assigns 403.90. No causal relationship must be stated to use this combination code.

Hypertensive Heart and Renal Disease

Assign codes from combination category 404, hypertensive heart and renal disease, when both hypertensive renal disease and hypertensive heart disease are stated in the diagnosis. Assume a relationship between the hypertension and the renal disease, whether or not the condition is so designated.

■ *Confusing Codes*

If the patient has both hypertensive heart disease and renal disease, the coder would begin under the main term "disease, heart" and will locate the subterm "with, kidney disease- see hypertension, Cardiorenal". The coder will then turn to the hypertension table and will select code 404.90, Hypertensive Heart and Renal Disease, Unspecified, Without Mention of Congestive Heart Failure or Renal Failure.

Hypertensive Retinopathy

Two codes are necessary to identify the condition. First assign code 362.11, Hypertensive retinopathy, then the appropriate code from categories 401-405 to indicate the type of hypertension.

Hypertension, Secondary

Two codes are required. One identifies the underlying condition and one from category 405 to identify the hypertension. Sequencing of codes is determined by the reason for admission to the hospital.

Secondary hypertension is different from essential hypertension. Secondary hypertension is due to a disease, such as primary renal disease (405.x1), or other (405.x9). (The x in the fourth-digit location is to indicate that the fourth digit will vary dependent on whether the hypertension is benign, malignant, or unspecified.) Therefore, both the disease causing the hypertension, as well as the secondary hypertension, must be coded.

Hypertension, Transient

Assign code 796.2, Elevated blood pressure reading without diagnosis of hypertension, unless patient has an established diagnosis of hypertension. Assign code 642.3X for transient hypertension of pregnancy.

Transient means the condition existed only temporarily. If the coder refers to the Hypertension table, the last entry is for transient, and gives the code of 796.2. Transient hypertension with a subterm "of pregnancy" is to be coded as 642.3x.

Hypertension, Controlled

Assign appropriate code from categories 401-405. This diagnostic statement usually refers to an existing state of hypertension under control by therapy.

Just because the hypertension is under control does not mean it is benign or not significant enough to be coded. If the patient is currently taking medication or receiving treatment for the hypertension, it should be coded.

> ### *Hypertension, Uncontrolled*
>
> *Uncontrolled hypertension may refer to untreated hypertension or hypertension not responding to current therapeutic regimen. In either case, assign the appropriate code from categories 401-405 to designate the state and type of hypertension. Code to the type of hypertension.*

Uncontrolled is a nonessential modifier for all diagnoses of hypertension, which means its presence or absence does not affect the code assignment. In other words, assign the code for the type of hypertension (such as hypertensive heart disease), and whether the hypertension is malignant, benign, or unspecified.

> ### *Elevated Blood Pressure*
>
> *For a statement of elevated blood pressure without further specificity, assign code 796.2, Elevated blood pressure reading without diagnosis of hypertension, rather than a code from category 401 (essential hypertension).*

Sometimes circumstances such as a trauma cause a patient's blood pressure to go up. If the patient has a high blood pressure reading without being diagnosed as having hypertension, coders should assign code 796.2, Elevated blood pressure reading without diagnosis of hypertension.

Myocardial Infarctions

Myocardial infarctions are coded according to site of the damage to the heart, with a fifth digit included to show episode of care.

0 Episode of Care Unspecified

Use this fifth digit when the source document does not contain sufficient information for the assignment of fifth digit 1 or 2.

1 Initial Episode of Care

Use fifth digit 1 to designate the first episode of care (regardless of facility site) for a newly diagnosed myocardial infarction. The fifth digit 1 is assigned regardless of the number of times a patient may be transferred during the initial episode of care.

2 Subsequent Episode of Care

Use fifth digit 2 to designate an episode of care following the initial episode when the patient is admitted for further observation, evaluation or treatment, for a myocardial infarction that has received initial treatment, but is still less than 8 weeks old.

A myocardial infarction (MI) is considered to be in the acute phase during the first eight weeks following the infarction. The fifth digits of 1 and 2 are used to distinguish the episode of care during that acute period. Fifth digit 0 should never be used on an inpatient chart, because there should be substantial documentation to specify the episode of care. If there is not sufficient documentation, the coder should ask the physician to provide the required information.

The physician should specify the site of the MI for proper code assignment. A code of "myocardial infarction, unspecified" may be rejected by the carrier as a nonspecific principal diagnosis. The coder can look at the EKG reports to see if the location is documented in the report, but the site must be verified with the physician.

Another test to look for in documenting an MI is the serum enzyme lab tests (CK, CK-MB, LD). These tests rise and fall at predictable intervals following an MI, and will be ordered and done at specific intervals according to the approximate age of the MI. They may be negative if the patient waits to seek treatment. Elevation of the cardiac enzymes may be indicative of an MI.

A previous myocardial infarction is coded to 412 when the physician states history of or old myocardial infarction presenting no symptoms during the current treatment. If the chart states "history of myocardial infarction", it is always considered relevant and should be coded to 412.

If the patient has a previous MI and presents with symptoms, the correct code is 414.8, Other Specified Forms of Chronic Ischemic Heart Disease. The included note under code 414.8 states: "Any condition classifiable to 410 specified as chronic, or presenting with symptoms after 8 weeks from date of infarction."

▬ *Highlight*

The acute myocardial infarction (410) must be specified as past the acute stage and is now chronic. Also, symptoms occurring after eight weeks must be attributable to the MI and not any new, acute condition.

Angina

Angina pectoris is chest pain with cardiac origin. All chest pains should not be coded to the angina category. Unstable angina should be coded only when documented by the physician, and is also known as "pre-infarct angina". This diagnosis should not be coded with documented evidence of myocardial infarction.

Congestive Heart Failure

Congestive Heart Failure (CHF) is the condition where the heart cannot pump the required amount of blood, causing fluid buildup in the lungs and other areas, including the lower extremities. One common medication for patients with CHF is Lasix, a diuretic that helps the body rid itself of excessive fluid.

▬ *Highlight*

When the coder is searching through the patient's chart for documentation to substantiate the CHF diagnosis, the coder can look for Lasix or other diuretics on the patient's medication sheets. Commonly, a patient presenting with severe edema of the extremities will be weighed on admission, given the diuretic, and weighed again in the morning. A patient with CHF can lose 10-15 pounds literally overnight.

Cerebrovascular Disease

Cerebrovascular disease is coded according to the type of condition, including hemorrhage, occlusion, and other cerebrovascular disease. Category 436, Acute, But Ill-Defined Cerebrovascular Disease, is used only when the diagnosis is stated as Cerebrovascular Accident (CVA) without further mention of cause.

If the physician lists the diagnosis as CVA, the coder should check the chart for further information as to the cause of the CVA (stroke). A cerebrovascular accident may be caused by many problems, including the following:

1. Subarachnoid Hemorrhage-A hemorrhage into the subarachnoid space
2. Intracerebral Hemorrhage-A hemorrhage within the brain
3. Subdural Hematoma-A localized collection of hemorrhaged blood in the subdural space
4. Occlusion-Decreased blood flow of the arteries that supply the brain tissues
5. Cerebral Thrombosis-An abnormal collection of blood causing an obstruction in the arteries supplying the brain with blood
6. Cerebral Embolism-Obstruction of the arteries that supply the brain caused by a blood clot coming from elsewhere in the body

The coder should review the chart for documentation of the cause of a CVA before using code 436. Code 436 is considered to be a non-specific diagnosis and should not be used when a more specific cause can be identified. According to the exclusion note under code 436, it is also not to be used in conjunction with codes from categories 430-435.

> | Excludes: | *any condition classifiable to categories 430-435*

▪ *Confusing Codes*

The codes in category 435 are for transient cerebral ischemia, temporary decreased blood flow to the brain. The symptoms for a TIA are the same as for a CVA, except that the symptoms disappear after about 24 hours. The codes for TIA and CVA should not be used together in a single hospital episode, unless there are two distinct episodes. (For example, the patient had a TIA with symptoms clearing, then 4 days later had a full-blown CVA.) The coder should be alerted to check with the physician prior to coding both codes.

Coding Clinic Note: Late Effect of Cerebrovascular Disease

Category 438 is used to indicate conditions classifiable to categories 430-437 as the causes of late effects (neurologic deficits). The "late effects" include neurologic deficits that persist after initial onset of conditions classifiable to 430-437. Unlike other late effects, the neurologic deficits caused by cerebrovascular disease are present from the onset rather than arising months later.

Codes from category 438 may be assigned as additional diagnoses when a patient is admitted with a current diagnosis classifiable to the 430-437 categories.

Codes in category 438 include the type of residuals (current condition) within the code. A code such as 438.41 is for Late Effects of Cerebrovascular Disease, Monoplegia of Lower Limb Affecting Dominant Side.

> *Assign code V12.59 (personal history of disease) (and not code 438) as an additional code for history of cerebrovascular disease when no neurologic deficits are present.*

Cardiovascular Procedures

Hospital coders use ICD-9-CM to code cardiovascular procedures.

Cardiac Catheterization has become a very common method of diagnosing cardiac conditions. The physician uses a catheter inserted through an artery or vein to the heart guided to the heart chambers for diagnosing lesions, blockage, and can be used in conjunction with other tools to open blocked vessels. These catheters are inserted through the femoral or antecubital vein for a right heart catheterization, and through the brachial or femoral artery for a left cardiac catheterization. ICD-9-CM provides codes for right, left and combined left and right cardiac catheterizations, so the coder should study the documentation carefully prior to coding these procedures.

CABG or Coronary Artery Bypass Graft, is where a vessel is taken from another location and anastomosed onto the blocked area to bypass the blockage. The procedure codes are based on the type of bypass and the number of vessels that are involved. For example, an aortocoronary bypass of three coronary vessels is coded to 36.13. If the mammary artery is used, it is coded to either 36.15, Single Internal Mammary-Coronary Artery Bypass, or 36.16, Double Internal Mammary-Coronary Artery Bypass.

Balloon Angioplasty, or Percutaneous Transluminal Coronary Angioplasty (PTCA) is often done in conjunction with the cardiac catheterization. In many cases, this is attempted prior to putting the patient through a CABG procedure. A catheter is placed in the blocked area and a balloon that is on the tip of the catheter is inflated to try to rid the vessel of the blocked material.

⟨EXERCISE 1–5

Using the ICD-9-CM code book, assign the correct diagnosis and procedure code(s) to the six scenarios that follow. If more information is needed from the physician, list questions on the line provided.

1. The patient was in the hospital with hemiplegia and aphasia due to acute CVA caused by subarachnoid hemorrhage as noted on CT scan of brain done on admission. On discharge, the aphasia had cleared, but the hemiplegia is present and will require home care.

   Diagnoses: _____

   Question for Physician: _____

2. The patient was admitted with a two-day history of intolerable abdominal pain. The diagnosis of acute cholecystitis with cholelithiasis was made. The patient is on medication for hypertension, chronic rheumatoid arthritis, and is a non-insulin-dependent diabetic. She also had a heart bypass procedure last April. Treatment was laparoscopically assisted cholecystectomy. Patient was discharged two days post-op to be followed by the surgeon in two weeks.

Diagnoses: _____

Question for Physician: _____

3. Mr. Jones came to the clinic today because he was feeling weak and has seen a decrease in urine output over the last two days and has not been able to keep any food down. He is HIV-positive, but has been asymptomatic until now. Lab results indicate dehydration and gastroenteritis. I am going to send him over to the hospital to be admitted for IV treatment of the dehydration.

Diagnoses: _____

Question for Physician: _____

4. Note to Home Health Nurse: Ms. Swanson is ready to be discharged from the hospital to go home. We have treated her in the hospital for pneumo-coccal pneumonia due to her AIDS and this is better but not completely resolved yet, but she insists on going home. She also has Kaposi's sarcoma of the skin due to AIDS.

Diagnoses: _____

Question for Physician: _____

5.   **Discharge Summary**

History of Present Illness:

The patient is a 54-year-old black male with a five-day history of feeling ill. When his daughter went by his house today to check on him, she found him clammy with a fever and very disoriented. Lab results in the ER showed UTI, probable sepsis, renal insufficiency. BUN, creatinine elevated. WBC was 23,000. The patient was admitted for treatment of probable urinary sepsis.

Findings While in Hospital:

WBCs fell during hospitalization to 9,000. Urine culture grew E. coli, blood cultures also grew out E. coli. No other abnormalities noted.

Hospital Course:

The patient was started on IV fluid rehydration; electrolytes improved throughout stay. He was started on IV antibiotics and was switched to oral antibiotics the day of discharge. The patient was discharged to his daughter's care at her home until he gets back on his feet again.

Diagnoses: _____

Question for Physician: _____

---

6.   **Discharge Summary**

The patient, a 53-year-old Caucasian male, was admitted through the emergency room with unstable angina pectoris, diaphoresis, and pain radiating to the left arm. The patient had a previous MI three years ago.

Hospital Course: Cardiac enzymes were done at 12, 24, and 36 hours and were elevated. Serial EKGs were performed, which confirmed the diagnosis of AMI, Inferolateral wall. A left cardiac catheterization was performed on the first day of hospitalization with findings of the LAD blocked at 95% and second artery blocked at 100%. We then scheduled the patient for bypass. On the second hospital day he had an aortocoronary bypass, two coronary arteries performed successfully. After two days in CCU, the patient was transferred to a regular hospital bed. The patient was discharged after uneventful recovery period on the sixth day of hospitalization.

Diagnoses: _____

Procedures: _____

Question for Physician: _____

DIABETES MELLITUS

Diabetes mellitus is one of the most common diseases of the endocrine system and one that coders have many problems coding.

Fifth digits are required on all diabetes mellitus codes to show if the patient is insulin dependent or non-insulin dependent, and whether the diabetes is controlled or uncontrolled.

Fifth digits are as follows:

> 0—Type II [Non-Insulin-Dependent Type][NIDDM Type] [Adult-Onset Type] or unspecified type, not stated as uncontrolled.
> 1—Type I [Insulin-Dependent Type] [IDDM Type] [Juvenile Type], not stated as uncontrolled.
> 2—Type II [Non-Insulin-Dependent Type] [NIDDM Type] [Adult-Onset Type] or unspecified type, uncontrolled.
> 3—Type I [Insulin-Dependent Type] [IDDM Type] [Juvenile Type], uncontrolled.

■ *Confusing Codes*

Fifth digits 0 and 2 are used for Type II, adult-onset diabetic patients, even if the patient requires insulin.

Insulin-dependent diabetes mellitus, or IDDM, Type I or Juvenile type, is when the patient's body does not produce insulin, thus making the patient dependent on insulin on a regular basis to survive.

Non-insulin-dependent diabetes mellitus, NIDDM, Type II or Adult-Onset diabetes is usually controlled by diet and oral medications. The NIDDM patient sometimes must be given injections of insulin, but is not dependent on the insulin to survive.

Fifth digits 2 and 3 show whether the diabetes is stated to be uncontrolled. This is not a judgment that should be made by the coder, and if the documentation in the chart does not specifically state uncontrolled, the coder must use the fifth digit (0 or 1) that shows the diabetes as "not stated to be uncontrolled".

Many diabetic patients will develop further complications caused by the diabetes. In these cases, there are usually two codes needed to fully identify the condition. The diabetes code should be listed first and the complication of the diabetes listed next, such as 250.1x followed by 362.01 for diabetic retinopathy.

If a diabetic patient develops hypoglycemia, code 250.8x should be used, diabetes with other specified complications. Code 251.2, Hypoglycemia, Unspecified, is not to be used if the patient has diabetes.

USING V CODES

V codes include factors influencing health status and contact with health services, and can be used as principal and secondary diagnoses. V codes are used when a person who is not currently sick uses health care services, such as need for a vaccination, or check-up, or when a problem affects the patient's current illness, such as a history of carcinoma, or status post coronary artery bypass graft. Sometimes it is difficult to locate a needed V code because of the main terms used in ICD-9-CM. Many common main terms to locate V codes are as follows:

> Admission for, Attention to, Examination, Follow up, History of,
> Observation for, Screening, Status post, Supervision, Testing

If the patient uses medical facilities and does not have a medical diagnosis, the V code can be used as the principal diagnosis. For example, a mother comes in for a six-week check-up following delivery and has no problems. Code V24.2, Routine postpartum follow-up is assigned.

V64.4 is used when a laparoscopic surgical procedure was converted to an open procedure. The coder can locate this code in the Alphabetic Index of Diseases by looking under the main term "Laparoscopic" or "Conversion".

To code a patient's encounter for a screening mammogram, use either code V76.12, Special Screening for malignant neoplasm, breast, Other screening mammogram, or V76.11, Screening mammogram for High-risk patient. The physician should be queried to determine which of these two codes is most appropriate for the patient. Any abnormality found on the screening mammogram, such as a lump, should be listed as a secondary diagnosis.

V codes are diagnosis codes, not procedure codes. If a patient is admitted for a service, such as the above patient's encounter for screening mammogram, the coder will also need to code a procedure code for the screening mammogram itself (87.37).

Code a patient encounter for a preoperative examination using V72.8x as the first diagnosis. The reason for the surgery should be assigned as an additional diagnosis.

If a past condition may affect the current treatment, the V code can be used as a secondary diagnosis, such as V45.81, status post CABG (heart bypass surgery).

Codes V72.5, Radiological Examination, NEC and V72.6, Laboratory Examination are not to be used if any sign, symptom, or reason for a test is documented.

Official Coding Guidelines

Codes from the V71.0-V71.9 Series, Observation and Evaluation for Suspected Conditions

Codes from the V71.0-V71.9 series are assigned as principal diagnoses for encounters or admissions to evaluate the patient's condition when there is some evidence to suggest the existence of an abnormal condition or following an accident or other incident that ordinarily results in a health problem, and where no supporting evidence for the suspected condition is found and no treatment is currently required. The fact that the patient may be scheduled for continuing observation in the office/clinic setting following discharge does not limit the use of this category.

Official Outpatient Coding Guidelines

K. For patients receiving diagnostic services only during an encounter/ visit, sequence first the diagnosis, condition, problem, or other reason for encounter/visit shown in the medical record to be chiefly responsible for the outpatient services provided during the encounter/visit. Codes for other diagnoses (e.g., chronic conditions) may be sequenced as additional diagnoses.

L. For patients receiving therapeutic services only during an encounter/ visit, sequence first the diagnosis, condition, problem, or other reason for encounter/visit shown in the medical record to be chiefly responsible for the outpatient services provided during the encounter/visit. Codes for other diagnoses (e.g., chronic conditions) may be sequenced as additional diagnoses.

The only exception to this rule is that patients receiving chemotherapy, radiation therapy, or rehabilitation, the appropriate V code for the service is listed first, and the diagnosis or problem for which the service is being performed listed second.

There are certain V codes that, according to *Coding Clinic for ICD-9-CM*, are considered to be nonspecific, used only as principal/primary diagnosis, or are only to be used secondary to other ICD-9-CM codes. In *Coding Clinic for ICD-9-CM*, Fourth Quarter, 1996, pp. 58-62, a list is provided to help the coder know appropriate usage of V codes.

Nonspecific V Codes

"Certain V codes are so nonspecific, or potentially redundant with other codes in the classification, that there can be little justification for their use in the inpatient setting. Their use in the outpatient setting should be limited to those instances when there is no further documentation to permit more precise coding. Otherwise, any sign or symptom or any other reason for the visit that is captured in another code should be used." These categories/codes are:

V11, V13.4, V13.6, V15.7, V23.2, V40, V41, V47, V48, V49

(Exceptions: V49.6 and V49.7), V51, V58.2, V58.9, V72.5, V72.6

"Codes V72.5 and V72.6 are not to be used if any sign, symptom, or reason for a test is documented. See sections K and L of the outpatient guidelines."

First Listed

The following are V codes/categories/subcategories that are only acceptable as first listed. This means they should only be listed as first (primary or principal) diagnoses; never as secondary diagnoses.

V22.0, V22.1, V58.0, V58.1 (V58.0 and V58.1 may be used together on a record with either one being sequenced first, when a patient receives both chemotherapy and radiation therapy during the same encounter.), V58.3, V58.5, V20, V24, V29, V30-39, V59, V66, (Except V66.7 Palliative care), V67, V68, V70, V71, V72 (Except V72.5 and V72.6)

Additional Only

There are certain V code categories/subcategories, that may only be used as additional codes, and never should be used as first (primary or principal) diagnoses. These are as follows:

V22.2, V66.7, V09, V10, V12, V13 (Except V13.4 and V13.6), V14, V15 (Except V15.7), V16-V19, V21, V27, V42, V43, V44, V45, V46, V49.6x, V49.7x, V60, V62, V63, V64

OBSTETRICAL CODING

Obstetric (OB) coding seems to be the section that gives coders the most trouble. See Module 8, Obstetrics and Gynecology, for more information on coding these diagnoses and procedures.

Many conditions that are normally coded in different chapters are considered complications of pregnancy, so are reclassified to the pregnancy chapter when the patient is pregnant. Conditions that complicate or are associated with pregnancy are normally listed under the main terms: Pregnancy, labor, delivery, puerperium.

Nearly all pregnancy codes require a fifth digit. The following fifth-digit subclassification is for use with categories 640-648, 651-676 to denote the current episode of care:

0 Unspecified as to Episode of Care or Not Applicable
1 Delivered, With or Without Mention of Antepartum Condition
2 Delivered, With Mention of Postpartum Complication
3 Antepartum Condition or Complication
4 Postpartum Condition or Complication

When determining the correct fifth digit to use, the coder should review the patient's medical record to determine if the patient delivered during this episode of care. If the patient did deliver during this admission, the correct fifth digit choices would be limited to either 1 or 2 only. The coder should also review the fifth digits listed in brackets below each code in the pregnancy chapter. Certain codes limit the choices of fifth digits. For example, with code 644.0, "Threatened premature Labor" the correct fifth digits can only be 0 (unspecified as to episode of care or not applicable), or 3 (antepartum condition or complication).

Official Coding Guidelines

Complication of Pregnancy

When a patient is admitted because of a condition that is either a complication of pregnancy or that is complicating the pregnancy, the code for the obstetric complication is the principal diagnosis. An additional code may be assigned as needed to provide specificity.

For example, if the patient is an insulin-dependent diabetic and is pregnant, the coder would begin under the main term "pregnancy", subterm "complicated by", "diabetes (mellitus) (conditions classifiable to 250). The principal or first diagnosis listed would be 648.0x, Other Current Conditions in the Mother Classifiable Elsewhere, But Complicating Pregnancy, Childbirth, or the Puerperium; Diabetes Mellitus. There is a note following category 648 that reminds the coder to "Use additional code(s) to identify the condition." This means that both codes are needed to fully identify the patient's condition. The coder would assign code 250.01 as a secondary diagnosis to indicate that the patient was an insulin-dependent diabetic.

Coding Non-Obstetric Conditions

If a woman is pregnant, the treatment decisions for a non-obstetrical condition may be different because of the pregnancy. To locate these conditions, the coder should look in the alphabetic section under "Pregnancy, complicated by". If the specific condition cannot be found, there is code 646.8, Other specified complications of pregnancy, that should be used in conjunction with the non-obstetrical condition. If a physician treating the non-obstetric condition uses the appropriate codes from the pregnancy chapter, and provides sufficient documentation in the patient's chart, it will indicate that the patient's condition was complicated by the pregnancy. This complication increases the amount of effort, and could increase the number of treatment options for the patient, therefore providing justification to use a higher level of office visit code in CPT.

Code 650

Code 650 is for delivery in a completely normal case, and cannot be used in conjunction with any other code in the pregnancy chapter. This code can only be used when the following criteria are met:

1. Liveborn
2. Term (37 completed weeks but less than 42)
3. Single Birth
4. No Complications
5. No instrumentation except episiotomy or artificial rupture of membranes
6. Cephalic or vertex presentation
7. No fetal manipulation (turning or version of the fetus)

If the delivery meets all of these criteria, use code 650. If not, use a code for every factor in the case that does not meet the criteria. For example, the patient delivers a single liveborn infant at 38 weeks gestation with cephalic (head) presentation. A small episiotomy was performed. Using the above list, the coder can determine that all criteria are met, so code 650 is used for the delivery. If the patient delivered liveborn twins at 36 weeks by cesarean section, this case does not meet criteria numbers 2, 3, and 5. The coder would code three diagnoses codes; one for each criteria not met (651.01, Twin Pregnancy, Delivered; 644.21, Early Onset of Delivery; 669.71, Cesarean Delivery, Without Mention of Indication).

Selection of Principal Diagnosis

When a delivery occurs, the principal diagnosis should correspond to the main circumstances or complication of the delivery. In cases of cesarean deliveries, the principal diagnosis should correspond to the reason the cesarean was performed, unless the reason for admission was unrelated to the condition resulting in the cesarean delivery.

Many hospitals use V27 codes as secondary codes to identify outcome of delivery on the mother's chart. These codes specify if the baby was liveborn, single, twin, stillborn, and so on, and are not used on the baby's chart. V27.0, for example, would be used for a single liveborn outcome of delivery.

Codes V22.0, Supervision of normal first pregnancy, and V22.1, Supervision of other normal pregnancy, are used for routine prenatal or postpartum care. These codes should not be used in conjunction with any other code from the pregnancy chapter.

Procedures having to do with labor or delivery are commonly located under the main term of "delivery". All deliveries should be coded with a procedure code. If the 650 code is used to show a totally normal delivery, then the most appropriate procedure code is 73.59, assisted spontaneous delivery.

Official Coding Guidelines

Fetal Conditions Affecting the Management of the Mother

Codes from category 655, "Known or suspected fetal abnormality affecting management of the mother," and category 656, "Other fetal and placental problems affecting the management of the mother," are assigned only when the fetal condition is actually responsible for modifying the management of the mother, i.e., by requiring diagnostic studies, additional observation, special care, or termination of pregnancy. The fact that the fetal condition exists does not justify assigning a code from this series to the mother's record.

If the fetus was known to have spina bifida, for example, this would require additional studies and additional observation and probable cesarean delivery to prevent trauma to the fetus. In this case, it would be appropriate to use code 655.03 on visits prior to the delivery, then 655.01 as one of the delivery diagnoses.

It should be noted that there are many codes to be used on the baby's chart noting problems with the mother that affected the baby. These should not be confused with pregnancy codes, and are usually codes in the 740-779 category range. For example, in the alphabetic index under the main term "pregnancy, twin", there is a subterm for "affecting fetus or newborn 761.5". This code is only to be used on the baby's chart, and only if the twin pregnancy somehow affected the newborn.

Abortion is any loss of the fetus prior to 22 completed weeks of gestation, whether it be spontaneous (miscarriage) or induced. There are several fifth digits needed in the abortion categories, and these do change according to the code, so the coder should pay careful attention to the required fifth digits. The diagnosis of abortion, spontaneous, with excessive hemorrhage, incomplete, for example, would be coded to 634.11.

Delivery of Infants and Congenital Anomalies

The V codes for newborns (which is the newborn's principal diagnosis) are included in the V30-V39 codes. These codes are not for use on the mother's chart.

Use of Codes V30-V39

When coding the birth of an infant, assign a code from categories V30-V39, according to the type of birth. A code from this series is assigned as a principal diagnosis, and assigned only once to a newborn at the time of birth.

Newborn Transfers

If the newborn is transferred to another institution, the V30 series is not used [by the receiving facility].

When coding the newborn's medical stay, the principal diagnosis is always a code from V30-V39 to show that the baby was born during this episode of care. Any complicating factors or anomalies would be coded secondarily. These codes are only used on the original chart, and are not used by a secondary hospital where the newborn was transferred.

Official Coding Guidelines

Newborn Guidelines

The newborn period is defined as beginning at birth and lasting through the 28th day following birth.

The following guidelines are provided for reporting purposes. Hospitals may record other diagnoses as needed for internal data use.

All clinically significant conditions noted on routine newborn examination should be coded. A condition is clinically significant if it requires:

- *clinical evaluation*
- *therapeutic treatment*
- *diagnostic procedures*
- *extended length of hospital stay*
- *increased nursing care and/or monitoring*
- *has implications for future health care needs*

Note: The newborn guidelines listed above are the same as the general coding guidelines for "other diagnoses," except for the final bullet regarding implications for future health care needs. Whether a condition is clinically significant can be determined only by the physician.

For example, the infant is a term liveborn, born in this hospital by vaginal delivery, in fetal distress, first noted during labor. The principal diagnosis is V30.00, with a secondary diagnosis of 768.3 for Fetal Distress, first noted during labor, in Liveborn Infant.

Use of Category V29

A. *Assign a code from V29, "Observation and evaluation of newborns and infants for suspected conditions not found," to identify those instances when a healthy newborn is evaluated for a suspected condition that is determined after study not to be present. Do not use a code from category V29 when the patient has identified signs or symptoms of a suspected problem; in such case, code the sign or symptom.*

B. *A V29 code is to be used as a secondary code after the V30, Liveborn Infants According to the Type of Birth, code. It may also be assigned as a principal code for readmissions or encounters when the V30 code no longer applies. It is for use only for healthy newborns and infants for which no condition after study is found to be present.*

The note following category V29 reads as follows: "Note: This category is to be used for newborns, within the neonatal period (the first 28 days of life), who are suspected of having an abnormal condition resulting from exposure from the mother or the birth process, but without signs or symptoms, and, which after examination and observation, is found not to exist."

For example, there is a diagnosis of term birth living child, born at another hospital and transferred here to observe for the possibility of meconium aspiration. After observation, the baby was found to be healthy. Code V29.2 would be used for this diagnosis. The coder would not assign code V30.00 because the infant was not born at this hospital.

Maternal Causes of Perinatal Morbidity

Codes from categories 760-763, Maternal causes of perinatal morbidity and mortality, are assigned only when the maternal condition has actually affected the fetus or newborn. The fact that the mother has an associated medical condition or experiences some complication of pregnancy, labor or delivery does not justify the routine assignment of codes from these categories to the newborn record.

The note following category 760 reads "Includes: The listed maternal conditions only when specified as a cause of mortality or morbidity of the fetus or newborn." If the mother is malnourished and this has affected the fetus, the coder would assign code 760.4, Fetus or Newborn Affected by Maternal Conditions Which May be Unrelated to Present Pregnancy, Maternal Nutritional Disorders, as a secondary diagnosis.

Congenital Anomalies

Assign an appropriate code from categories 740-759, Congenital Anomalies, when a specific abnormality is diagnosed for an infant. Such abnormalities may occur as a set of symptoms or multiple malformations. A code should be assigned for each presenting manifestation of the syndrome if the syndrome is not specifically indexed in ICD-9-CM.

Coding of Other (Additional) Diagnoses

A. Assign codes for conditions that require treatment or further investigation, prolong the length of stay, or require resource utilization.

B. Assign codes for conditions that have been specified by the physician as having implications for future health care needs. Note: This guideline should not be used for adult patients.

C. Assign a code for newborn conditions originating in the perinatal period (categories 760-779), as well as complications arising during the current episode of care classified in other chapters, only if the diagnoses have been documented by the responsible physician at the time of transfer or discharge as having affected the fetus or newborn.

D. Insignificant conditions or signs or symptoms that resolve without treatment are not coded.

Spina bifida, a defective closure of the vertebral column, is categorized according to the level of severity, and should be coded to the highest degree of severity that is known. It is further subdivided to show the presence/absence of hydrocephalus, abnormal accumulation of fluid in the brain. Procedures include closure of the defect (03.5x categories), and in many cases, a shunt is implanted to allow for drainage of fluid build-up.

■ *Highlight*

Congenital heart conditions can be extensive and should be coded with great care. They are divided between cyanotic and acyanotic defects. Cyanotic defects occur when the defect allows for mixing of oxygenated and deoxygenated blood within the heart. Two of the most common cardiac defects are:

Ventricular septal defect *(an opening in the ventricular septum allowing the blood to go from the left to right ventricle). The appropriate code is 745.4. The repair code should be found within the 35.xx category.*

Patent ductus arteriosus *is a condition where the fetal blood vessel connecting the aorta and pulmonary artery that allows blood to bypass the fetal lungs remains open (patent). This should close within the first few hours after birth. If it remains open, heart failure and pulmonary congestion result, and surgical repair is almost always needed. The code for the patent ductus arteriosus is 747.0; the procedure to be coded is 38.85, other surgical occlusion of vessels.*

> ***Prematurity and Fetal Growth Retardation***
>
> *Codes from categories 764 and 765 should not be assigned based on recorded birthweight or estimated gestational age, but upon the attending physician's clinical assessment of maturity of infant.*
>
> *Note: Since physicians may utilize different criteria in determining prematurity, do not code the diagnosis of prematurity unless the physician documents this condition.*

Categories 764 and 765 show slow fetal growth and low birthweight. They include fifth digits to show the weight of the newborn, and are in grams. If the baby's weight is recorded in pounds, the coder will need to use a conversion chart for appropriate coding. (500 grams is equivalent to approximately one pound, one and two-thirds ounces.)

EXERCISE 1–6

Using the ICD-9-CM code book, code the following diagnoses. If more information is needed from the physician, list questions on the line provided.

1. 33-year-old white female with history of multiple miscarriages, now at 27 weeks gestation and is put on bedrest by physician for remainder of gestation. Home care to see patient on weekly basis to monitor mother and child.

   Diagnoses: _____

   Question for Physician: _____

2. This 27-day-old infant was followed today in the clinic for jaundice. Radiology report shows congenital obstruction of the bile duct. We are going to refer the parents to the pediatric surgery clinic for surgical evaluation.

   Diagnoses: _____

   Question for Physician: _____

3. Progress Note: This baby was born prematurely this morning at 36 weeks gestation at home and is admitted for observation. Weight is 2456 grams.

   Diagnoses: _____

   Question for Physician: _____

4. Final Diagnoses: Uterine pregnancy, term. Spontaneous delivery of single liveborn infant, cephalic presentation. Postpartum hemorrhage, onset 32 hours following delivery.

Diagnoses: _____

Question for Physician: _____

NEOPLASMS

The term "neoplasm" literally means "new growth". A common error made by many people is to think that all neoplasms are malignant, or cancerous. It is important that the correct code assignment be made, especially in dealing with a disease such as cancer, and the coder must be sure of the correct diagnosis. An incorrect malignancy coded on a patient's chart can cause long-term problems, such as the loss of insurance, denial of life insurance policies, and increased rates. The final coding of a suspect mass or tumor should not be completed until after review of the pathology report.

The Neoplasm Table

ICD-9-CM has provided an extensive table that is used to code most neoplasms. Figure 1–1 shows a partial sample of this table. It is located in the alphabetic index under the main term Neoplasm. The table is divided into site, then codes to show the neoplasm's behavior.

Within the *Malignant* section there are three available choices:

Primary is the site where the neoplasm originated.

Secondary is the site to which the primary site has spread, either by metastasis (movement to another body location), direct extension to an adjacent organ, or invasion into the blood or lymph system.

In situ is where the cells are malignant, but have not spread (invaded) the basement membrane of the structure.

Benign is when the tumor is not spreading or invasive into other sites.

Uncertain Behavior diagnosis is when the pathologist is unable to determine whether the neoplasm is malignant or benign.

Unspecified Nature can be used when the documentation does not support a more specific code. This may be used when the patient is transferred to another facility or is discharged without further workup done on the neoplasm.

How to Code a Neoplasm

Step 1: The coder should first go to the alphabetic index to look for the main term of the histological type, such as carcinoma, adenoma, leiomyoma, etc. There the

Figure 1–1 ICD-9-CM Volume II: Neoplasm Table (partial). *(Courtesy of St. Anthony's ICD-9-CM, 1998. Reprinted with permission of St. Anthony Publishing, Inc. 800-632-0123.)*

	Malignant			Benign	Uncertain Behavior	Unspecified
	Primary	Secondary	Ca in situ			
Neoplasm, neoplastic	199.1	199.1	234.9	229.9	238.9	239.9

Notes—1. The list below gives the code numbers for neoplasms by anatomical site. For each site there are six possible code numbers according to whether the neoplasm in question is malignant, benign, in situ, of uncertain behavior, or of unspecified nature. The description of the neoplasm will often indicate which of the six columns is appropriate; e.g., malignant melanoma of skin, benign fibroadenoma of breast, carcinoma in situ of cervix uteri.

Where such descriptors are not present, the remainder of the Index should be consulted where guidance is given to the appropriate column for each morphological (histological) variety listed; e.g., Mesonephroma—see Neoplasm, malignant; Embryoma—see also Neoplasm, uncertain behavior; Disease, Bowen's—see Neoplasm, skin, in situ. However, the guidance in the Index can be overridden if one of the descriptors mentioned above is present; e.g., malignant adenoma of colon is coded to 153.9 and not to 211.3 as the adjective "malignant" overrides the Index entry "Adenoma—see also Neoplasm, benign."

2. Sites marked with the sign # (e.g., face NEC#) should be classified to malignant neoplasm of skin of these sites if the variety of neoplasm is a squamous cell carcinoma or an epidermoid carcinoma and to benign neoplasm of skin of these sites if the variety of neoplasm is a papilloma (any type).

	Primary	Secondary	Ca in situ	Benign	Uncertain Behavior	Unspecified
abdomen, abdominal	195.2	198.89	234.8	229.8	238.8	239.8
cavity	195.2	198.89	234.8	229.8	238.8	239.8
organ	195.2	198.89	234.8	229.8	238.8	239.8
viscera	195.2	198.89	234.8	229.8	238.8	239.8
wall	173.5	198.2	232.5	216.5	238.2	239.2
connective tissue	171.5	198.89	—	215.5	238.1	239.2
abdominopelvic	195.8	198.89	234.8	229.8	238.8	239.8
accessory sinus—*see* Neoplasm, sinus						
acoustic nerve	192.0	198.4	—	225.1	237.9	239.7
acromion (process)	170.4	198.5	—	213.4	238.0	239.2
adenoid (pharynx) (tissue)	147.1	198.89	230.0	210.7	235.1	239.0
adipose tissue (*see also* Neoplasm, connective tissue)	171.9	198.89	—	215.9	238.1	239.2
adnexa (uterine)	183.9	198.82	233.3	221.8	236.3	239.5
adrenal (cortex) (gland) (medulla)	194.0	198.7	234.8	227.0	237.2	239.7
ala nasi (external)	173.3	198.2	232.3	216.3	238.2	239.2
alimentary canal or tract NEC	159.9	197.8	230.9	211.9	235.5	239.0
alveolar	143.9	198.89	230.0	210.4	235.1	239.0
mucosa	143.9	198.89	230.0	210.4	235.1	239.0
lower	143.1	198.89	230.0	210.4	235.1	239.0
upper	143.0	198.89	230.0	210.4	235.1	239.0

continues

Figure 1–1 ICD-9-CM Volume II: Neoplasm Table (partial). *(Courtesy of St. Anthony's ICD-9-CM, 1998. Reprinted with permission of St. Anthony Publishing, Inc. 800-632-0123.) continued*

	Malignant			Benign	Uncertain Behavior	Unspecified
	Primary	Secondary	Ca in situ			
alveolar *continued*						
ridge or process	170.1	198.5	—	213.1	238.0	239.2
carcinoma	143.9	—	—	—	—	—
lower	143.1	—	—	—	—	—
upper	143.0	—	—	—	—	—
lower	170.1	198.5	—	213.1	238.0	239.2
mucosa	143.9	198.89	230.0	210.4	235.1	239.0
lower	143.1	198.89	230.0	210.4	235.1	239.0
upper	143.0	198.89	230.0	210.4	235.1	239.0
upper	170.0	198.5	—	213.0	238.0	239.2
sulcus	145.1	198.89	230.0	210.4	235.1	239.0
alveolus	143.9	198.89	230.0	210.4	235.1	239.0
lower	143.1	198.89	230.0	210.4	235.1	239.0
upper	143.0	198.89	230.0	210.4	235.1	239.0
ampulla of Vater	156.2	197.8	230.8	211.5	235.3	239.0
ankle NEC#	195.5	198.89	232.7	229.8	238.8	239.8
anorectum, anorectal (junction)	154.8	197.5	230.7	211.4	235.2	239.0
antecubital fossa or space#	195.4	198.89	232.6	229.8	238.8	239.8
antrum (Highmore) (maxillary)	160.2	197.3	231.8	212.0	235.9	239.1
pyloric	151.2	197.8	230.2	211.1	235.2	239.0
tympanicum	160.1	197.3	231.8	212.0	235.9	239.1
anus, anal	154.3	197.5	230.6	211.4	235.5	239.0
canal	154.2	197.5	230.5	211.4	235.5	239.0
contiguous sites with rectosigmoid junction or rectum	154.8	—	—	—	—	—
margin	173.5	198.2	232.5	216.5	238.2	239.2
skin	173.5	198.2	232.5	216.5	238.2	239.2
sphincter	154.2	197.5	230.5	211.4	235.5	239.0
aorta (thoracic)	171.4	198.89	—	215.4	238.1	239.2
abdominal	171.5	198.89	—	215.5	238.1	239.2
aortic body	194.6	198.89	—	227.6	237.3	239.7
aponeurosis	171.9	198.89	—	215.9	238.1	239.2
palmer	171.2	198.89	—	215.2	238.1	239.2
plantar	171.3	198.89	—	215.3	238.1	239.2
appendix	153.5	197.5	230.3	211.3	235.2	239.0

coder will find an "M" (morphology) code, which identifies the histological type, behavior and site. These M codes are used as secondary codes and are optional, used primarily by cancer registries.

Step 2: Look for a subterm that describes the site found in the diagnostic statement. If a code is located, that is as far as the coder must search to describe the condition. For example, if the patient has Leiomyoma of the uterus, the coder would look under the main term "leiomyoma", subterm "uterus" to locate the code 218.9.

Step 3: If the site is not listed, under the main term for the histological type there should be an instruction to "See also Neoplasm, by site, behavior" (such as benign, malignant, etc.).

Step 4: The coder should then turn to the neoplasm table and locate the appropriate code. The neoplasm table is located in the Alphabetic Index under the main term "Neoplasm."

For example, if the patient had a diagnosis of Liposarcoma, shoulder, the coder would begin under the main term liposarcoma. There is no subterm for shoulder, but a note located next to the main term tells the coder to "*see also* Neoplasm, connective tissue, malignant." This note directs the coder to go to the Neoplasm table to locate the correct code of 171.2.

■ *Confusing Codes*

A mistake made by many coders is to first check the table of Neoplasms and not begin by looking up the histological site. This is a common coding error, and should be avoided by the trained coder.

■ *Highlight*

Neoplasm coding tips:

- If a malignant neoplasm has been removed, but has recurred at the primary site, code the recurrence as a primary site.

- Be careful of the word "metastatic". It can be used to describe both a primary and secondary site. Metastatic from the breast means the breast is the primary site. Malignancy, breast metastatic to the liver, for example, means the breast is the primary site and the liver is the secondary site.

- If the primary or secondary site is unknown, ICD-9-CM provides 199.1 and 199.0, unknown site, to fully describe the patient's condition.

- If the patient has had a malignancy removed and is still in the initial stage of treatment, such as chemotherapy or radiation therapy, the cancer should be coded as if it was still present.

- If the patient has had a malignancy removed and is back for follow-up to look for further signs of cancer, and there is none, then a "history of malignant neoplasm" code is used from the V10 section.

- If the patient is undergoing testing because a family member has or previously had cancer, a V16 code can be used to show "family history of malignant neoplasm".

Principal Diagnosis

Neoplasms often cause problems to the coder when trying to determine the correct principal diagnosis. The following official coding guidelines provide sequencing guidance:

Official Coding Guidelines

Neoplasms

A. *If the treatment is directed at the malignancy, designate the malignancy as the principal diagnosis, except when the purpose of the encounter or hospital admission is for radiotherapy session(s), V58.0, or for chemotherapy session(s), V58.1, in which instance the malignancy is coded and sequenced second.*

B. *When a patient is admitted for the purpose of radiotherapy or chemotherapy and develops complications, such as uncontrolled nausea and vomiting or dehydration, the principal diagnosis is Encounter for radiotherapy, V58.0, or Encounter for chemotherapy, V58.1.*

C. *When an episode of inpatient care involves surgical removal of a primary site or secondary site malignancy followed by adjunct chemotherapy or radiotherapy, code the malignancy as the principal diagnosis, using codes in the 140-198 series, or, where appropriate, in the 200-203 series.*

D. *When the reason for admission is to determine the extent of the malignancy, or for a procedure such as paracentesis or thoracentesis, the primary malignancy or appropriate metastatic site is designated as the principal diagnosis, even though chemotherapy or radiotherapy is administered.*

E. *When the primary malignancy has been previously excised or eradicated from its site and there is no adjunct treatment directed to the site and no evidence of any remaining malignancy at the primary site, use the appropriate code from the V10 series to indicate the former site of primary malignancy. Any mention of extension, invasion, or metastasis to a nearby structure or organ or to a distant site is coded as a secondary malignant neoplasm to the site and may be the principal diagnosis in the absence of the primary site.*

F. *When a patient is admitted because of a primary neoplasm with metastasis and treatment is directed toward the secondary site only, the secondary neoplasm is designated as the principal diagnosis even though the primary malignancy is still present.*

G. *Symptoms, signs, and ill-defined conditions listed in Chapter 16 of the ICD-9-CM Code Book characteristic of, or associated with, an existing primary or secondary site malignancy cannot be used to replace the malignancy as principal diagnosis, regardless of the number of admissions or encounters for treatment and care of the neoplasm.*

H. *Coding and sequencing of complications associated with the malignancy neoplasm or with the therapy thereof are subject to the following guidelines:*

When admission is for management of an anemia associated with the malignancy, and the treatment is only for anemia, the anemia is designated as the principal diagnosis and is followed by the appropriate code(s) for the malignancy.

When admission is for management of an anemia associated with chemotherapy or radiotherapy and the only treatment is for the anemia, the anemia is designated as the principal diagnosis followed by the appropriate code(s) for the malignancy.

When the admission is for management of dehydration due to the malignancy of the therapy, or a combination of both, and only the dehydration is being treated (intravenous rehydration), the dehydration is designated as the principal diagnosis, followed by the code(s) for the malignancy.

When the admission is for treatment of a complication resulting from a surgical procedure such as a colon resection, performed for the treatment of a malignancy, designate the complication as the principal diagnosis if the treatment is directed at resolving the complication.

EXERCISE 1–7

Using all volumes of the ICD-9-CM code book, code the following diagnoses and procedures. If more information is needed from the physician, list questions on the line provided.

1. Malignant carcinoid of appendix with appendectomy and resection of cecum.

   Diagnoses: _____

   Procedures: _____

   Question for Physician: _____

2. Metastatic carcinoma to pelvic bone from prostate.

   Diagnoses: _____

   Procedures: _____

   Question for Physician: _____

3. Hodgkin's disease with cervical lymph node biopsy.

   Diagnoses: _____

   Procedures: _____

   Question for Physician: _____

4. Recurrence of papillary carcinoma of bladder, low-grade transitional cell.

   Diagnoses: _____

   Procedures: _____

   Question for Physician: _____

5. Carcinoma of the brain from lungs.

Diagnoses: _____

Procedures: _____

Question for Physician: _____

6. 44-year-old white male with metastatic cancer of the colon, was recently discharged from the hospital after having a permanent colostomy. Admission to home care is for instruction in care of the colostomy for patient and family.

Diagnoses: _____

Procedures: _____

Question for Physician: _____

---

7.   **Report of Operation**

PREOPERATIVE DIAGNOSIS: Carcinoma of the left breast

POSTOPERATIVE DIAGNOSIS: Carcinoma of the left breast

OPERATION: Left modified radical mastectomy

SURGEON: John Thomas, MD

PROCEDURE: The patient was adequately anesthetized. The left breast was adequately prepped and draped in a sterile fashion. With a skin marker, the portion of skin and breast tissue to be removed was delineated with the skin marker and then, at this point, incisions were made and with sharp dissection the superior and inferior flaps were fashioned. At this point, the entire breast and anterior pectoral fascia was excised en bloc into the axillary tissues and with very careful dissection a left axillary dissection was performed. The long thoracic and thoracodorsal nerves were both ligated with 3-0 silk sutures. After the breast and axillary contents had been excised en bloc, thorough antibiotic irrigation was performed. Adequate hemostasis was obtained. Two Hemovac drains were appropriately placed and sutured to the skin at their exit site with 2-0 silk suture. The wound was then closed with staples. A sterile dressing was applied. The patient tolerated the procedure well, was awakened, and taken to the recovery room in satisfactory condition.

Diagnoses: _____

Procedures: _____

Question for Physician: _____

E CODING

External causes of injury codes are used as secondary codes to show the cause of the injury whenever it is known, such as a fall or automobile accident. Most E codes are not mandatory, but it is recommended that they be used wherever possible to fully describe the patient's condition. There is a separate alphabetic E code index (in the alphabetic index section of the code book located behind the table of drugs and chemicals) to facilitate locating the appropriate E code. They include type of injury (fall, MVA), place of accident, specific person involved (pedestrian, driver of car), and E codes for late effects. Some states are now beginning to mandate the use of all E codes, or E codes for certain conditions. The use of the E codes helps to tell the whole story behind what happened to the patient. If an accident or injury code is used, such as those from codes 800-995, payment on a claim may be delayed prior to investigation of the facts surrounding the injury. By using the E code to tell the cause of the injury, the carrier then has all of the information needed to pay the claim.

There are definitions for types of accidents, such as railway accident and motor vehicle traffic accident, as well as definitions for types of vehicles and persons injured, such as off-road vehicle, pedal cyclist, and pedestrian. These definitions are located on the first page of the E code tabular list, which is located just past the V code tabular list in the ICD-9-CM book.

For example, if a patient had a closed fracture of the shaft of the femur due to crashing the snowmobile he was driving into a tree, the coder would first code the fracture, 821.01. To show the cause of the fracture, code E820.0. The coder would locate the correct E code by checking the E code alphabetic index under the main term "crash", subterm "motor vehicle". The code book gives the instruction to "*see also* Accident, motor vehicle". Under the main term Accident, motor vehicle, the subterm "nontraffic, not on public highway-*see* categories E820-E825". The coder could also look under the main term "Accident", subterm "snow vehicle, motor driven (not on public highway)" to find the code E820. When the coder verifies this code in the E code tabular list, we find that the fourth digit of 0 is needed to indicate that the injured person was the driver of the snowmobile (Driver of Motor Vehicle other Than Motorcycle).

■ *Highlight*

The coder should review the facility's policy on the use of E codes and follow it consistently. E codes are never assigned as principal diagnoses.

Official Coding Guidelines

Place of Occurrence Guideline

Use an additional code from category E849 to indicate the Place of Occurrence for injuries and poisonings. The Place of Occurrence describes the place where the event occurred and not the patient's activity at the time of the event. Do not use E849.9 if the place of occurrence is not stated.

While these E codes are not required, they do provide further information about the cause of the patient's injury. In other words, if the patient was injured on the job in a factory, the coder could use code E4849.3, Industrial Place and Premises. This would most likely be a Worker's Compensation case.

Multiple Cause E Code Coding Guidelines

If two or more events cause separate injuries, an E code should be assigned for each cause.

E codes for child and adult abuse take priority over all other E codes.

Fourth digits in the category E967, Child and Adult Battering and Other Maltreatment, show the specific person who has abused the patient, such as E967.2 By Mother or Stepmother, and E967.8 By Non-Related Caregiver.

E codes for cataclysmic events take priority over all other E codes except child and adult abuse.

Cataclysmic events are those such as hurricanes, E908.0; tornadoes, E908.1; earthquakes, E909.0; etc.

E codes for transport accidents take priority over all other E codes except cataclysmic events and child and adult abuse.

According to the ICD-9-CM book, a transport accident, E800-E848, is defined as "any accident involving a device designed primarily for, or being used at the time primarily for, conveying persons or goods from one place to another." Examples of transport accidents are those in airplanes, cars, trains, and boats. These are defined at the beginning of the E code tabular list, which can be found following the V code tabular list.

The first listed E code should correspond to the cause of the most serious diagnosis due to an assault, accident, or self-harm, following the order of hierarchy listed above.

Child and Adult Abuse Guidelines

When the cause of an injury or neglect is intentional child or adult abuse (995.50-995.59, 995.80-995.85), the first listed E code should be assigned from categories E960-E968, Homicide and injury purposely inflicted by other persons (except category E967). An E code from category E967, Child and adult battering and other maltreatment should be added as an additional E code to identify the perpetrator, if known.

For example, if a child was abused by her stepfather by attempted drowning, 994.1, Drowning and other non-fatal submersion would be listed first, then code E964, Assault by Submersion {Drowning] followed by code E967.0, Child and Adult Battering and Other Maltreatment by Father or Stepfather.

In cases of neglect when the intent is determined to be accidental, E code E904.0, Abandonment or neglect of infant and helpless person, should be the first listed E code.

Unknown or Suspected Intent Guidelines

If the intent (accident, self-harm, assault) of the cause of an injury or poisoning is unknown or unspecified, code the intent as undetermined E980-E989.

If the intent (accident, self-harm, assault) of the cause of an injury or poisoning is questionable, probable or suspected, code the intent as undetermined E980-E989.

This section of the E code tabular list is titled "Injury Undetermined Whether Accidentally or Purposely Inflicted (E980-E989)" and includes the following note: "Categories E980-E989 are for use when it is unspecified or it cannot be determined whether the injuries are accidental (unintentional), suicide (attempted), or assault."

For example, code E980.8 is for Poisoning by Solid or Liquid Substances, Undetermined Whether Accidentally or Purposely Inflicted, Arsenic and Its Compounds.

Undetermined Cause

When the intent of an injury or poisoning is known, but the cause is unknown, use codes E928.9, Unspecified accident, E958.9, Suicide and self-inflicted injury by unspecified means, and E968.9, Assault by unspecified means.

These E codes should rarely be used as the documentation in the medical record, in both the inpatient and outpatient settings, should normally provide sufficient detail to determine the cause of the injury.

INJURIES

Many injuries are classified according to the general type of injury, such as wound, injury, internal, or injury, superficial.

It is important to follow all instructional terms to "see" and "see also" to obtain the correct code.

Official Coding Guidelines

Multiple Injuries

When multiple injuries exist, the code for the most severe injury, as determined by the attending physician, is sequenced first.

Coding for Multiple Injuries

When coding multiple injuries such as fracture of tibia and fibula, assign separate codes for each injury unless a combination code is provided, in which case the combination code is assigned. Multiple injury codes are provided in ICD-9-CM, but should not be assigned unless information for a more specific code is not available.

A. The code for the most serious injury, as determined by the physician, is sequenced first.

B. Superficial injuries such as abrasions or contusions are not coded when associated with more severe injuries of the same site.

C. When a primary injury results in minor damage to peripheral nerves or blood vessels, the primary injury is sequenced first with additional code(s) from categories 950-957, Injury to nerves and spinal cord, and/or 900-904, Injury to blood vessels. When the primary injury is to the blood vessels or nerves, that injury should be sequenced first.

FRACTURES

Fractures are classified according to whether they are open or closed. A closed fracture is one where there is no open wound into the skin. An open fracture is a fracture where there is an open wound into the skin. If the diagnostic statement does not identify whether the fracture is open or closed, it is coded as closed. ICD-9-CM provides notes in the alphabetic index to indicate types of fractures and whether they are commonly considered open or closed. The coder should review these carefully. Examples of closed fractures are comminuted, greenstick, simple, and impacted. Examples of open fractures are compound, infected, puncture, and with foreign body. Refer to Module 6 of this text for more information on orthopedics.

Official Coding Guidelines

Multiple Fractures

The principle of multiple coding of injuries should be followed in coding multiple fractures. Multiple fractures of specified sites are coded individually by site in accordance with both the provisions within categories 800-829 (fractures) and the level of detail furnished by medical record content. Combination categories for multiple fractures are provided for use when there is insufficient detail in the medical record (such as trauma cases transferred to another hospital); when the reporting form limits the number of codes that can be used in reporting pertinent clinical data; or when there is insufficient specificity at the fourth-digit or fifth-digit level. More specific guidelines are as follows:

A. Multiple fractures of the same limb classifiable to the same three-digit or four-digit category are coded to that category.

B. Multiple unilateral or bilateral fractures of same bone(s) but classified to different fourth-digit subdivisions (bone part) within the same three-digit category are coded individually by site.

C. Multiple fracture categories 819 and 828 classify bilateral fractures of both upper limbs (819) and both lower limbs (828), but without any detail at the fourth-digit level other than open and closed type of fracture.

> D. Multiple fractures are sequenced in accordance with the severity of the fracture and the physician should be asked to list the fracture diagnoses in the order of severity.

Pathological fractures occur due to a disease rather than a trauma. If the fracture is stated to be "pathological", "spontaneous", or "due to disease", it is coded as a pathological fracture, with a fifth digit indicating the site of the fracture. It is necessary to also code the disease as the underlying cause of the fracture. For example, the patient has a fracture of the hip due to osteoporosis. Under the main term fracture, the coder would find the subterm "pathologic", subterm "hip" with the appropriate code assignment of 733.14, Pathologic fracture of neck of femur. The coder should also code the osteoporosis, 733.00, to show the underlying cause of the fracture.

BURNS

A burn is classified according to whether first, second or third degree. For two degrees of burn in the same location, the coder should only code to the highest degree. For example, if the patient has second- and third-degree burns of the back, the coder would only assign code 942.34, third-degree burn, back. Codes in category 948 are based on the "rule of nines" as shown in Figure 1–2. These codes indicate the extent of the body affected by the burn and the percentage of the body surface that is third degree. This category is to be used as a primary or principal diagnosis when the site of the burn is unspecified, or as a secondary diagnosis used in conjunction with the burn site code if known. The fourth digit indicates

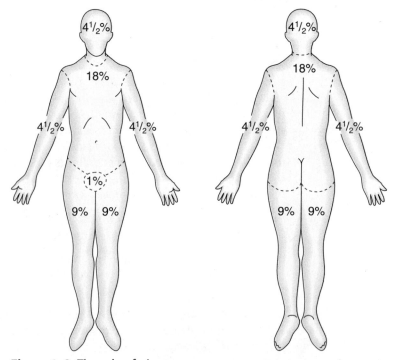

Figure 1–2 The rule-of-nines.

the percent of *body surface* burned and the fifth digit indicates the percent of body surface with *third-degree burns*. For example, if a patient had 40% of the body burned and 15% of the body surface has third-degree burns, the code used would be 948.41.

Official Coding Guidelines

Current Burns and Encounters for Late Effects of Burns

Current burns (940-948) are classified by depth, extent, and, if desired, by agent (E code). By depth burns are classified as first degree (erythema), second degree (blistering), and third degree (full-thickness involvement).

Multiple Burns

Sequence first the code that reflects the highest degree of burn when more than one burn is present.

A. *All burns are coded with the highest degree of burn sequenced first.*

B. *Classify burns of the same local site (three-digit category level, 940-947) but of different degrees to the subcategory identifying the highest degree recorded in the diagnosis.*

C. *Non-healing burns are coded as acute burns. Necrosis of burned skin should be coded as a non-healed burn.*

D. *Assign code 958.3, Posttraumatic wound infection, not elsewhere classified, as an additional code for any documented infected burn site.*

E. *When coding multiple burns, assign separate codes for each burn site. Category 946, Burns of multiple specified sites, should only be used if the location of the burns are not documented. Category 946, Burns of multiple specified sites, should only be used if the location of the burns are not documented. Category 949, "Burn," unspecified, is extremely vague and should rarely be used.*

F. *Assign codes from category 948, "Burns," classified according to extent of body surface involved, when the site of the burn is not specified or when there is a need for additional data. It is advisable to use category 948 as additional coding when needed to provide data for evaluating burn mortality, such as that needed by burn units. It is also advisable to use category 948 as an additional code for reporting purposes when there is mention of third-degree burn involving 20 percent or more of the body surface.*

In assigning a code from category 948:

- *Fourth-digit codes are used to identify the percentage of total body surface involved in a burn (all degrees).*
- *Fifth-digits are assigned to identify the percentage of body surface involved in a third-degree burn.*
- *Fifth-digit zero (0) is assigned when less than 10 percent or when no body surface is involved in a third-degree burn.*

Category 948 is based on the classic "rule of nines" in estimating body surface involved; head and neck are assigned 9 percent, each arm 9 percent, each leg 18 percent, and genitalia 1 percent. Physicians may change these percentage assignments when necessary to accommodate infants and children who have proportionately larger heads than adults and patients who have large buttocks, thighs, or abdomen that involve burns.

G. *Encounters for the treatment of the late effects of burns (i.e., scars or joint contractures) should be coded to the residual condition (sequelae) by the appropriate late effect code (906.5–906.9). A late effect E code may also be used, if desired.*

H. *When appropriate, both a sequelae with a late effect code, and current burn code may be assigned on the same record.*

Debridement of Wounds, Infection, or Burn

A. *For coding purposes, excisional debridement, 86.22 from Volume 3, is assigned only when the procedure is performed by a physician in the hospital inpatient setting.*

B. *For coding purposes, nonexcisional debridement performed by the physician or nonphysician health care professional is assigned to 86.28 from Volume 3. Any "excisional" type procedure performed by nonphysician is assigned to 86.28 in the hospital inpatient setting. Also refer to Module 5 of this text for more information on coding burns.*

POISONING VERSUS ADVERSE EFFECTS

The Table of Drugs and Chemicals is located following the alphabetic index to diseases and is used to code poisonings and adverse reactions.

Poisoning

A poisoning is a condition caused by drugs, medicines, and biological substances when taken improperly or not in accordance with the physician's orders. Examples of poisonings are:

■ Wrong dosage given in error.
■ Wrong medication given or taken by patient.
■ Overdose.
■ Prescription drugs taken in conjunction with alcohol.
■ Prescription drugs taken with over-the-counter medications not prescribed by the physician.

Official Coding Guidelines

When coding a poisoning or reaction to the improper use of a medication (e.g., wrong dose, wrong substance, wrong route of administration) the poisoning code is sequenced first, followed by a code for the manifestation. If there is also a diagnosis of drug abuse or dependence to the substance, the abuse or dependence is coded as an additional code.

For poisoning when an error was made in drug prescription or in the administration of the drug by a physician, nurse, patient or other person, use the appropriate code from the 960-979 series. If an overdose of a drug was intentionally taken or administered and resulted in drug toxicity it would be coded as a poisoning (960-979 series). If a nonprescription drug or medicinal agent was taken in combination with a correctly prescribed and properly administered drug, any drug toxicity or other reaction resulting from the interaction of the two drugs would be classified as a poisoning.

How to Code Poisonings

Poisonings are coded by looking in the Table of Drugs and Chemicals (see Figure 1–3) for the drug or causative agent. Assign the code from the poisoning column as the primary/principal diagnosis. Code the specific effect of the poisoning—such as nausea or coma. Code the external cause of the poisoning from the appropriate column of the table. Unless the medical record provides documentation otherwise, the cause should be listed as accidental. A poisoning code is never used in conjunction with an E code from the Therapeutic Use column. Many coders find it helpful to highlight the Therapeutic Use E code column to emphasize that this code can never be used with any other type of code in the Table of Drugs and Chemicals. An example of a poisoning is a child brought to the ER in a coma after ingesting his mother's Thorazine. The coder would go to the Table of Drugs and Chemicals and find the poisoning code for Thorazine, 969.1. The correct E code is E853.0, Accidental. Then the coder would select the appropriate code for the coma, 780.01.

Figure 1–3 ICD-9-CM Volume II: Table of Drugs and Chemicals (partial). *(Courtesy of St. Anthony's ICD-9-CM, 1998. Reprinted with permission of St. Anthony Publishing, Inc. 800-632-0123.)*

		External Cause (E-Code)				
Substance	Poisoning	Accident	Therapeutic Use	Suicide Attempt	Assault	Un-determined
1-propanol	980.3	E860.4	—	E950.9	E962.1	E980.9
2-propanol	980.2	E860.3	—	E950.9	E962.1	E980.9
2. 4-D (dichlorophenoxyacetic acid)	989.4	E863.5	—	E950.6	E962.1	E980.7
2. 4-toluene diisocyanate	983.0	E864.0	—	E950.7	E962.1	E980.6
2. 4, 5-T (trichlorophenoxyacetic acid)	989.2	E863.5	—	E950.6	E962.1	E980.7
14-hydroxydihydromorphinone	965.09	E850.2	E935.2	E950.0	E962.0	E980.0
A						
ABOB	961.7	E857	E931.7	E950.4	E962.0	E980.4
Abrus (seed)	988.2	E865.3	—	E950.9	E962.1	E980.9
Absinthe	980.0	E860.1	—	E950.9	E962.1	E980.9
beverage	980.0	E860.0	—	E950.9	E962.1	E980.9

continues

Figure 1–3 ICD-9-CM Volume II: Table of Drugs and Chemicals (partial). *(Courtesy of St. Anthony's ICD-9-CM, 1998. Reprinted with permission of St. Anthony Publishing, Inc. 800-632-0123.) continued*

Substance	Poisoning	External Cause (E-Code)				
		Accident	Therapeutic Use	Suicide Attempt	Assault	Un- determined
Acenocoumarin, acenocoumarol	964.2	E858.2	E934.2	E950.4	E962.0	E980.4
Acepromazine	969.1	E853.0	E939.1	E950.3	E962.0	E980.3
Acetal	982.8	E862.4	—	E950.9	E962.1	E980.9
Acetaldehyde (vapor)	987.8	E869.8	—	E952.8	E962.2	E982.8
liquid	989.89	E866.8	—	E950.9	E962.1	E980.9
Acetaminophen	965.4	E850.4	E935.4	E950.0	E962.0	E980.0
Acetaminosalol	965.1	E850.3	E935.3	E950.0	E962.0	E980.0
Acetanilid(e)	965.4	E850.4	E935.4	E950.0	E962.0	E980.0
Acetarsol, acetarsone	961.1	E857	E931.1	E950.4	E962.0	E980.4
Acetazolamide	974.2	E858.5	E944.2	E950.4	E962.0	E980.4
Acetic						
acid	983.1	E864.1	—	E950.7	E962.1	E980.6
with sodium acetate (ointment)	976.3	E858.7	E946.3	E950.4	E962.0	E980.4
irrigating solution	974.5	E858.5	E944.5	E950.4	E962.0	E980.4
lotion	976.2	E858.7	E946.2	E950.4	E962.0	E980.4
anhydride	983.1	E864.1	—	E950.7	E962.1	E980.6
ether (vapor)	982.8	E862.4	—	E950.9	E962.1	E980.9
Acetohexamide	962.3	E858.0	E932.3	E950.4	E962.0	E980.4
Acetomenaphthone	964.3	E858.2	E934.3	E950.4	E962.0	E980.4
Acetomorphine	965.01	E850.0	E935.0	E950.0	E962.0	E980.0
Acetone (oils) (vapor)	982.8	E862.4	—	E950.9	E962.1	E980.9
Acetophenazine (maleate)	969.1	E853.0	E939.1	E950.3	E962.0	E980.3
Acetophenetidin	965.4	E850.4	E935.4	E950.0	E962.0	E980.0
Acetophenone	982.0	E862.4	—	E950.9	E962.1	E980.9
Acetorphine	965.09	E850.2	E935.2	E950.0	E962.0	E980.0
Acetosulfone (sodium)	961.8	E857	E931.8	E950.4	E962.0	E980.4
Acetrizoate (sodium)	977.8	E858.8	E947.8	E950.4	E962.0	E980.4
Acetylcarbromal	967.3	E852.2	E937.3	E950.2	E962.0	E980.2
Acetylcholine (chloride)	971.0	E855.3	E941.0	E950.4	E962.0	E980.4

continues

Figure 1–3 ICD-9-CM Volume II: Table of Drugs and Chemicals (partial). *(Courtesy of St. Anthony's ICD-9-CM, 1998. Reprinted with permission of St. Anthony Publishing, Inc. 800-632-0123.) continued*

		External Cause (E-Code)				
Substance	Poisoning	Accident	Therapeutic Use	Suicide Attempt	Assault	Un-determined
Acetylcysteine	975.5	E858.6	E945.5	E950.4	E962.0	E980.4
Acetyldigitoxin	972.1	E858.3	E942.1	E950.4	E962.0	E980.4
Acetyldihydrocodeine	965.09	E850.2	E935.2	E950.0	E962.0	E980.0
Acetyldihydrocodeinone	965.09	E850.2	E935.2	E950.0	E962.0	E980.0
Acetylene (gas) (industrial)	987.1	E868.1	—	E951.8	E962.2	E981.8
incomplete combustion of—						
see Carbon monoxide, fuel, utility						
tetrachloride (vapor)	982.3	E862.4	—	E950.9	E962.1	E980.9
Acetyliodosalicylic acid	965.1	E850.3	E935.3	E950.0	E962.0	E980.0
Acetylphenylhydrazine	965.8	E850.8	E935.8	E950.0	E962.0	E980.0
Acetylsalicylic acid	965.1	E850.3	E935.3	E950.0	E962.0	E980.0
Achromycin	960.4	E856	E930.4	E950.4	E962.0	E980.4
ophthalmic preparation	976.5	E858.7	E946.5	E950.4	E962.0	E980.4
topical NEC	976.0	E858.7	E946.0	E950.4	E962.0	E980.4
Acidifying agents	963.2	E858.1	E933.2	E950.4	E962.0	E980.4
Acids (corrosive) NEC	983.1	E864.1	—	E950.7	E962.1	E980.6
Aconite (wild)	988.2	E865.4	—	E950.9	E962.1	E980.9
Aconitine (liniment)	976.8	E858.7	E946.8	E950.4	E962.0	E980.4
Aconitum ferox	988.2	E865.4	—	E950.9	E962.1	E980.9
Acridine	983.0	E864.0	—	E950.7	E962.1	E980.6
vapor	987.3	E869.3	—	E952.8	E962.2	E982.3
Acriflavine	961.9	E857	E931.9	E950.4	E962.0	E980.4
Acrisorcin	976.0	E858.7	E946.0	E950.4	E962.0	E980.4
Acrolein (gas)	987.3	E869.8	—	E952.8	E962.2	E982.3
liquid	989.89	E866.8	—	E950.9	E962.1	E980.9
Actaea spicata	988.2	E865.4	—	E950.9	E962.1	E980.9
Acterol	961.5	E857	E931.5	E950.4	E962.0	E980.4
ACTH	962.4	E858.0	E932.4	E950.4	E962.0	E980.4
Acthar	962.4	E858.0	E932.4	E950.4	E962.0	E980.4
Actinomycin (C) (D)	960.7	E856	E930.7	E950.4	E962.0	E980.4
Adalin (acetyl)	967.3	E852.2	E937.3	E950.2	E962.0	E980.2

Adverse Effects

Adverse effects of drugs are when the patient is given or takes the medication properly, but has a side effect due to the medication, such as anaphylactic shock due to Penicillin.

Official Coding Guidelines

Adverse Effect

When the drug was correctly prescribed and properly administered, code the reaction plus the appropriate code from the E930–E949 series. Adverse effects of therapeutic substances correctly prescribed and properly administered (toxicity, synergistic reaction, side effect, and idiosyncratic reaction) may be due to (1) differences among patients, such as age, sex, disease, and genetic factors, and (2) drug-related factors, such as type of drug, route of administration, duration of therapy, dosage, and bioavailability. Codes for the E930–E949 series must be used to identify the causative substance for an adverse effect of drug, medicinal, and biological substances, correctly prescribed and properly administered. The effect, such as tachycardia, delirium, gastrointestinal, hemorrhaging, vomiting, hypocalcemia, hepatitis, renal failure, or respiratory failure, is coded and followed by the appropriate code from the E930–E949 series.

How to Code Adverse Effects

To code an adverse effect, first code the effect itself, such as shock, tachycardia, etc. Then locate the drug in the Table of Drugs and Chemicals and select the E code from the Therapeutic Use column. This E code usage is mandatory. A poisoning code is never used when using a code from the Therapeutic Use column. Sequencing of these codes is very important. If a patient had vomiting and diarrhea due to prescribed Erythromycin, the coder would first code the vomiting and diarrhea, 787.03, 787.91, and then should use the E code, E930.3 to show the adverse effect caused by the medication.

▬ Highlight

The coder should always check the documentation in the record very carefully, and should not use any assault or attempted suicide codes unless the physician specifically states the cause as such.

COMPLICATIONS

Sometimes a condition will result as a complication from an implanted device or surgical procedure. ICD-9-CM distinguishes between two types of complications, medical complications, such as infection due to a procedure or device, and mechanical complications, such as failure of an implanted pacemaker. If a patient has a complication, such as rejection of an implanted device, this is not considered a mechanical complication, but a medical complication. In other words, the device did not fail, the patient's body rejected it. Code 996.0 lists examples of mechanical complications such as breakdown, displacement, leakage, perforation and protrusion. Code 996.6 is assigned for infections and inflammatory reactions due to internal prosthetic device, implant, and graft classifiable to 996.0-996.5.

Code 996.7 is used to code other complications of internal devices, such as embolism, hemorrhage, or stenosis, due to the presence of any device, implant or graft classifiable to 996.0-996.5. Category 997 codes complications affecting specified body systems, not elsewhere classified, such as nervous system, cardiac, and digestive system complications. This category also instructs the coder to "use additional code to identify complication" to provide specific information regarding the type of complication, such as heart failure or brain damage.

Official Coding Guidelines

Complications of Surgery and Other Medical Care

When the admission is for treatment of a complication resulting from surgery or other medical care, the complication code is sequenced as the principal diagnosis. If the complication is classified to the 996-999 series (complications), an additional code for the specific complication may be assigned.

How to Code Complications

To code a complication, first look under the main term for the condition and see if there is a complication code, such as colitis, due to radiation therapy. If there is not, check the main term "complication" to locate an appropriate complication code.

If the appropriate code cannot be found, ICD-9-CM has provided a few general complication codes, such as 999.9, Complication of medical care NEC, which can be used in conjunction with the code identifying the specific complication.

If the patient's reason for admission was treatment of the complication, the complication is listed first.

LATE EFFECTS

There are times when a previous illness or injury will cause a long lasting residual, or a side effect that may not show up for a period of time. The late effect is often identified in the documentation by such statements as "residual of", "sequela of", "due to previous illness", etc. There is no time limit on when a residual can occur, but is considered a residual if the initial (acute) illness or injury has resolved or healed.

Official Coding Guidelines

A late effect is the residual effect (condition produced) after the acute phase of an illness or injury has terminated. There is no time limit on when a late effect code can be used. The residual may be apparent early or it may occur months or years later, such as that due to a previous injury. Coding of late effects requires two codes:

> *The residual condition or nature of the late effect.*
> *The cause of the late effect.*
>
> *The residual condition or nature of the late effect is sequenced first, followed by the cause of the late effect, except in those few instances where the cause for late effect is followed by a manifestation code identified in the Tabular List as an italicized code and title.*
>
> *The code for the acute phase of an illness or injury that leads to the late effect is never used with a code for the cause of the late effect.*
>
> ### Residual Condition or Nature of the Late Effect
>
> *The residual condition or nature of the late effect is sequenced first, followed by the late effect code for the cause of the residual condition, except in a few instances where the Alphabetic Index directs otherwise.*

How to Code Late Effects

There are only a limited number of late effect codes for use in ICD-9-CM, and these can be located under the main term "late". This main term also directs the coder to "see also condition" because some common late effects have been included under the condition main term.

Two codes are commonly used to completely code the late effect:

1. The Residual (current condition affecting the patient).
2. The original cause, illness or injury that is no longer present in acute form.

An example of coding a late effect is scar on the face due to a previous burn. The scar, or residual, would be coded to 709.2. 906.5 would be used to code late effect, burn, face, head, and neck.

■ Confusing Codes

Late effects of a Cerebrovascular Accident are coded differently. The 438 category is expanded to include different residuals. For example, if the patient has the diagnosis of hemiplegia affecting the dominant side due to previous Cerebrovascular Accident, Code 438.21 would be used. A note following code 438 reads:

Note This category is to be used to indicate conditions in 430-437 as the cause of late effects, themselves classifiable elsewhere. The "late effects" include conditions specified as such, or as sequelae, which may occur at any time after the onset of the causal condition.

EXERCISE 1-8

Using all volumes of the ICD-9-CM code book, code the following diagnoses and procedures. If more information is needed from the physician, list questions on the line provided.

1. The patient was seen in the ER following an MVA; patient was passenger in car. Examination revealed fracture of the shaft of the radius and ulna, right arm, laceration of the forehead. Fracture was set and cast was applied and laceration was sutured in the ER.

   Diagnoses: _____

   Procedures: _____

   Question for Physician: _____

2. The patient's chief complaint was itching and redness around the site of the pacemaker implanted two months ago. After examination, diagnosis was made of inflammation of the pacemaker site. The patient was started on antibiotics and is to be rechecked in one week.

   Diagnoses: _____

   Procedures: _____

   Question for Physician: _____

3. The patient came to the ER complaining of dizziness; the patient recently started a prescription of Sinequan and this evening had three vodka tonics. The patient took the prescribed amount of his medication; the patient was cautioned against drinking while taking this medication.

   Diagnoses: _____

   Procedures: _____

   Question for Physician: _____

4. The patient is seen in the ER after two days of diarrhea and abdominal cramping. She has been undergoing radiation therapy for carcinoma of the colon, and the diagnosis was made of colitis due to radiation therapy.

   Diagnoses: _____

   Procedures: _____

   Question for Physician: _____

5. The patient was seen to evaluate his scar on right forearm received from burns nine months ago.

Diagnoses: _____

Procedures: _____

Question for Physician: _____

6. Patient was seen due to severe vomiting due to Cytoxan, which is being administered for bone metastasis. After giving IV fluids, the patient could again hold down her food.

Diagnoses: _____

Procedures: _____

Question for Physician: _____

7. The patient was burned by hot liquid grease from a fry basket at the Crowne Drive-Inn Restaurant where she works. Exam revealed second and third degree burns of the trunk involving 30% of the body. 10% of the body was burned with third degree burns.

Diagnoses: _____

Procedures: _____

Question for Physician: _____

---

8.   **Report of Operation**

PREOPERATIVE DIAGNOSIS: Minimally displaced right intertrochanteric fracture of femur

POSTOPERATIVE DIAGNOSIS: Same

TITLE OF PROCEDURE: Open reduction, internal fixation with Richard's classic dynamic hip compression screw

ATTENDING SURGEON: John Ingalls, MD

ANESTHESIA: General

ESTIMATED BLOOD LOSS: 300 cc

SPECIMENS: Femoral neck reamings sent to Pathology

FLUIDS: Normal saline

INDICATIONS: The patient is a 75-year-old black male who suffered a same height fall with the above mentioned fracture requiring surgical stabilization.

DESCRIPTION OF PROCEDURE: The patient was positioned for adequate visualization of his right intertrochanteric femur fracture. The fracture site was confirmed using image and adequate reduction was obtained with a minimal amount of traction and internal rotation of the lower extremity. The patient's right upper leg was then prepped and draped in the usual sterile fashion.

An approximately 10 cm incision was made over the lateral thigh starting at the greater trochanter and proceeding distally. Dissection was carried down sharply to the level of the tensor fascia lata, which was split sharply in line with its fibers. The vastus lateralis was then also split sharply in line with its fibers. Blunt dissection was carried down posteriorly, separating the fascia from the muscular layer to the level of the bone. The muscle was then retracted anteriorly and the lateral aspect of the proximal femur was cleaned off using the elevator. Image intensification was then used to identify adequate positioning for initial drill hole. The lateral cortex was then drilled. A guide pin was placed through the hole under vision with image intensification. Adequate positioning of the pin was confirmed using AP and lateral images. The guide pin was then advanced to subchondral bone. Reaming was then done over the guide pin to the level of 100 mm. The hole was then tapped over the guide pin as well. A 100 mm Richard's lag compression screw was then passed and fitted into the hole with a three-hole 135 degree sideplate placed over the screw. The sideplate was then seated using a candlestick. Next, the distal screw was placed in the barrel. The distal 38 mm screw and the remaining two screws both being 40 mm, were placed into the sideplate. After release of traction, using image intensification the compression screw was tightened with adequate reduction of the fracture site visualized on image.

The wound was then copiously irrigated and a Hemovac drain was placed deep to the muscular layer. The vastus lateralis fascia was then closed using a running #0 Vicryl suture. A subcutaneous layer of interrupted #2-0 Vicryl sutures was then placed and the skin was closed using skin staples. After the skin was closed the wound was dressed using Adaptic and 4 × 4 dressing sponges with Selofix tape on top. The patient was then transferred to the recovery room in stable condition.

All counts were reported as correct. The patient tolerated the procedure without any complications.

Diagnoses: _____

Procedures: _____

Question for Physician: _____

OFFICIAL CODING GUIDELINES

Many official guidelines from the AHA's *Coding Clinic* have been cited throughout this module. The following are general guidelines that pertain to all sections of the ICD-9-CM code book.

All diagnoses that affect the current encounter must be coded. In the hospital inpatient setting, the Principal Diagnosis, which by definition is the condition established after study to be chiefly responsible for occasioning the admission of the patient to the hospital for care," must be listed first. The circumstances of the admission to the facility always determine the order of diagnoses.

In the outpatient, physician's office or clinic setting, the primary, or first diagnosis should be the main reason for the visit that day. For example, if the patient has hypertension and was seen in the clinic today for shortness of breath, the shortness of breath would be the primary, or first, listed diagnosis. The hypertension would also be coded if it was still being treated.

Official Inpatient Coding Guidelines

Two or More Interrelated Conditions, Each Potentially Meeting the Definition for Principal Diagnosis:

When there are two or more interrelated conditions (such as disease in the same ICD-9-CM chapter or manifestation characteristically associated with a certain disease) potentially meeting the definition of principal diagnosis, either condition may be sequenced first, unless the circumstances of the admission, the therapy provided, the Tabular List, or the Alphabetic Index indicate otherwise.

Two or More Diagnoses That Equally Meet the Definition for Principal Diagnosis:

In the unusual instance when two or more diagnoses equally meet the criteria for principal diagnosis as determined by the circumstances of admission, diagnostic workup and/or therapy provided, and the Alphabetic Index, Tabular List, or another coding guideline does not provide sequencing direction, any one of the diagnoses may be sequenced first.

Two or More Comparative or Contrasting Conditions

In those rare instances when two or more contrasting or comparative diagnoses are documented as "either/or" (or similar terminology), they are coded as if the diagnoses were confirmed and the diagnoses are sequenced according to the circumstances of the admission. If no further determination can be made as to which diagnosis should be principal, either diagnosis may be sequenced first.

A Symptom Followed by Contrasting/Comparative Diagnoses

When a symptom(s) is followed by contrasting/comparative diagnoses, the symptom code is sequenced first. All the contrasting/comparative diagnoses should be coded as suspected conditions.

Original Treatment Plan Not Carried Out

Sequence as the principal diagnosis the condition, which, after study, occasioned the admission to the hospital, even though treatment may not have been carried out due to unforeseen circumstances.

Official Coding Guidelines

If the same condition is described as both acute (subacute) and chronic and separate subentries exist in the Alphabetic Index at the same indentation level, code both and sequence the acute (subacute) condition first.

Previous or history of illnesses or injuries should not be coded unless they affect the patient's current treatment.

Official Coding Guidelines

Impending or Threatened Conditions

Code any condition described at the time of discharge as "impending" or "threatened" as follows:

If it did occur, code as confirmed diagnosis.

If it did not occur, reference the Alphabetic Index to determine if the condition has a subentry term for "impending" or "threatened" and also reference main term entries for Impending and for Threatened.

If the subterms are listed, assign the given code.

If the subterms are not listed, code the existing forerunner condition(s) and not the condition described as impending or threatened.

Reporting Additional Diagnoses

"Other diagnoses" are defined as "all conditions that coexist at the time of admission, that develop subsequently, or that affect the treatment received and/or the length of stay. Diagnoses that relate to an earlier episode which have no bearing on the current hospital stay are to be excluded."

Previous Conditions

If the physician has included a diagnosis in the final diagnostic statement, such as the discharge summary or the face sheet, it should ordinarily be coded. Some physicians include in the diagnostic statement resolved conditions or diagnoses and status-post procedures from a previous admission that have no bearing on the current stay. Such conditions are not to be reported and are coded only if required by hospital policy.

However, history codes V10-V19 may be used as secondary codes if the historical condition or family history has an impact on current care or influences treatment.

Diagnoses Not Listed in the Final Diagnostic Statement

When the physician has documented what appears to be a current diagnosis in the body of the record, but has not included the diagnosis in the final diagnostic statement, the physician should be asked whether the diagnosis should be added.

Diagnostic Coding and Reporting Guidelines for Outpatient Services (Hospital-Based and Physician Office)

Revised October 1, 1995

The terms "encounter" and "visit" are often used interchangeably in describing outpatient service contacts and, therefore, appear together in these guidelines without distinguishing one from the other.

Coding guidelines for outpatient and physician reporting of diagnoses will vary in a number of instances from those for inpatient diagnoses, recognizing that:

> *The Uniform Hospital Discharge Data Set (UHDDS) Definition of principal diagnosis applies only to inpatients in acute, short-term, general hospitals.*

> *Coding guidelines for inconclusive diagnoses (probable, suspected, rule out, etc.) were developed for inpatient reporting and do not apply to outpatients.*

> *Diagnoses often are not established at the time of the initial encounter/visit. It may take two or more visits before the diagnosis is confirmed.*

> *The most critical rule involves beginning the search for the correct code assignment through the Alphabetic Index. Never begin searching initially in the Tabular List as this will lead to coding errors.*

BASIC CODING GUIDELINES FOR OUTPATIENT SERVICES

A. *The appropriate code or codes from 001.0 through V82.9 must be used to identify diagnoses, symptoms, conditions, problems, complaints, or other reason(s) for the encounter/visit.*

B. *For accurate reporting of ICD-9-CM diagnosis codes, the documentation should describe the patient's condition, using terminology which includes specific diagnoses as well as symptoms, problems, or reasons for the encounter. There are ICD-9-CM codes to describe all of these.*

C. *The selection of codes 001.0 through 999.9 will frequently be used to describe the reason for the encounter. These codes are from the section of ICD-9-CM for the classification of diseases and injuries (e.g. infectious and parasitic diseases; neoplasms; symptoms, signs, and ill-defined conditions, etc.).*

D. *Codes that describe symptoms and signs, as opposed to diagnoses, are acceptable for reporting purposes when an established diagnosis has not been diagnosed (confirmed) by the physician. Chapter 16 of ICD-9-CM, Symptoms, Signs, and Ill-defined conditions (codes 780.0 – 799.9) contain many, but not all codes for symptoms.*

E. *ICD-9-CM provides codes to deal with encounters for circumstances other than a disease or injury. The Supplementary Classification of factors influencing Health Status and Contact with Health Services (V01.0 – V82.9) is provided to deal with occasions when circumstances other than a disease or injury are recorded as diagnosis or problems.*

F. *ICD-9-CM is composed of codes with either 3, 4, or 5 digits. Codes with 3 digits are included in ICD-9-CM as the heading of a category of codes that may be further subdivided by the use of fourth and /or fifth digits which provide greater specificity.*

A three-digit code is to be used only if it is not further subdivided. Where fourth-digit subcategories and/or fifth-digit subclassifications are provided, they must be assigned. A code is invalid if it has not been coded to the full number of digits required for that code.

G. *List first the ICD-9-CM code for the diagnosis, condition, problem or other reason for encounter/visit shown in the medical record to be chiefly responsible for the services provided. List additional codes that describe any coexisting conditions.*

H. *Do not code diagnoses documented as "probable," "suspected," "questionable," "rule out," or working diagnosis. Rather, code the condition(s) to the highest degree of certainty for that encounter/visit, such as symptoms, signs, abnormal test results, or other reason for visit.*

Please note: This is contrary to the coding practices used by hospitals and medical record departments for coding the diagnosis of hospital inpatients.

I. *Chronic diseases treated on an ongoing basis may be coded and reported as many times as the patient is receiving treatment and care for the condition(s).*

J. *Code all documented conditions that coexist at the time of the encounter/visit, and that require or affect patient care treatment or management. Do not code conditions previously treated that no longer exist. However, history codes (V10-V19) may be used as secondary codes if the historical condition or family history has an impact on current care or influences treatment.*

K. *For patients receiving diagnostic services only during an encounter/visit, sequence first the diagnosis, condition, problem, or other reason for encounter/visit shown in the medical record to be chiefly responsible for the outpatient services provided during the encounter/visit. Codes for other diagnoses (e.g., chronic conditions) may be sequenced as additional diagnoses.*

L. *For patients receiving therapeutic services only during an encounter/visit, sequence first the diagnosis, condition, problem, or other reason for encounter/visit shown in the medical record to be chiefly responsible for the outpatient services provided during the encounter/visit. Codes for other diagnoses (e.g., chronic conditions) may be sequenced as additional diagnoses.*

The only exception to this rule is that patients receiving chemotherapy, radiation therapy, or rehabilitation, the appropriate V code for the service is listed first, and the diagnosis or problem for which the service is being performed listed second.

N. *For patients receiving preoperative evaluations only, sequence a code from category V72.8, Other specified examinations, to describe the pre-op consultations. Assign a code for the condition to describe the reason for the surgery as an additional diagnosis. Code also any findings related to the pre-op evaluation.*

O. *For ambulatory surgery, code the diagnosis for which the surgery was performed. If the postoperative diagnosis is known to be different from the preoperative diagnosis, select the postoperative diagnosis for coding, since it is the most definitive.*

ICD-10-CM

ICD-9-CM is scheduled to be replaced in 2001 by **ICD-10-CM**, a completely new version of the International Coding System. The World Health Organization (WHO) published the *International Statistical Classification of Diseases and Related Health Problems, Tenth Revision,* known as ICD-10, in 1992. Work on this 10th revision started in 1983 and is a significant revision of ICD-9-CM. The traditional ICD structure remains, but is now an alphanumeric coding scheme. The former supplementary classification information ("V" and "E" codes) were incorporated into the main classification system with different letters preceding the numerical portions of the codes. ICD-10-CM contains new chapters, and several of the categories have been restructured and new features have been added to maintain consistency with modern medicine. A technical advisory panel was established in the United States to study ICD-10-CM to see if it was a significant improvement over ICD-9-CM to warrant its implementation in the United States. The panel, made up of members of the health care and coding communities including federal and non-federal members, came to the conclusion that ICD-10-CM was not significantly better, but a clinical modification would be suitable for implementation in the United States. WHO retained the copyright on ICD-10-CM, but authorized the adaptation for use in the United States, as long as all modifications conform to WHO conventions for the ICD. ICD-10-CM diagnostic codes have been developed by the National Center for Health Statistics, the federal agency responsible for updating the diagnosis portion of ICD-9-CM, by consulting with physician groups, clinical coders, a technical advisory panel, and others "to assure clinical accuracy and utility." (NCHS, 98) ICD-10-CM includes an increase in the number of codes seen in ICD-10-CM, as well as improvements in the content and format such as expanded injury codes, combination diagnosis/symptoms codes; the addition of a sixth character/digit; incorporation of common fourth and fifth digit subclassifications; and greater specificity in code assignment. The format of ICD-10-CM will allow for major expansion in the future. A draft of ICD-10-CM was available in early 1998 to allow for public comments.

ICD-10-CM contains 21 chapters, which are divided similarly to those found in ICD-9-CM. The following is information from chapter XV, entitled "Pregnancy, childbirth, and the puerperium," which includes codes from O00-O99. Note that these codes begin with the letter O, not the number zero.

> O09.0 Encounter for supervision of pregnancy with history of infertility
>
> O09.00 Encounter for supervision of pregnancy with history of infertility, unspecified trimester
>
> O09.01 Encounter for supervision of pregnancy with history of infertility, first trimester
>
> O09.02 Encounter for supervision of pregnancy with history of infertility, second trimester
>
> O09.03 Encounter for supervision of pregnancy with history of infertility, third trimester
>
> **Note** Trimesters are counted from the first day of the last menstrual period. They are defined as follows:
>
> 1st trimester-less than 14 weeks 0 days
>
> 2nd trimester-14 weeks 0 days to less than 28 weeks 0 days
>
> 3rd trimester- 28 weeks 0 days until delivery

The former "V" codes, Factors influencing health status and contact with health services are located in Chapter 21 and range from Z00-Z99 in ICD-10-CM. For example, codes Z00-Z13 are used for Persons encountering health services for examination and investigation.

Procedures in ICD-10-CM

Since ICD-10-CM does not contain a procedure index, in 1992 the Health Care Financing Administration (HCFA) awarded a contract to 3M Health Information Systems to develop one. The revision is developed as a replacement for Volume 3 of ICD-9-CM, and is known as *The International Classification of Diseases, 10th Revision Procedure Classification System, or ICD-10-PCS.* According to 3M, ICD-10-PCS has a multiaxal seven character alphanumeric code structure. Each character has up to 34 different values. The ten digits 0-9 and the 24 letters A-H, J-N and P-Z comprise each character. Procedures are divided into sections that relate to the general type of procedure (e.g., medical and surgical, imaging, etc.). The first character of the procedure code always specifies the section. The second through seventh characters have a standard meaning within each section but may have different meanings across sections. In most sections, one of the characters specifies the precise type of procedure being performed (e.g., excision, resection, etc.), while the other characters specify additional information such as the body part on which the procedure is being performed. Codes can be located in an alphabetic index based on the type of procedure being performed. In medical and surgical procedures, the seven characters mean as follows:

    1=Section
    2=Body System
    3=Root Operation
    4=Body Part
    5=Approach
    6=Device
    7=Qualifier

For example, code 095HBYZ is the code for Dilation Eustachian Tube, Right with Device NEC, Transorifice Intraluminal. Following the meanings listed above, the seven digits show:

    0 means the code falls in the Surgical Section
    9 refers to the Body System of Ear, nose, sinus
    5 shows this procedure is a Dilation
    H is the Eustachian tube, right
    B Transorifice Intraluminal Approach
    Y means this is a Device NEC
    Z means there is no Qualifier

A technical advisory panel including representatives from the American Health Information Management Association, American Hospital Association and the American Medical Association have extensively reviewed the development of **ICD-10-PCS**. Several tests have been held, including one in 1996 where seventy medical records professionals were trained in ICD-10-PCS and then asked to code a sample of records from their own institutions. They then reported on their findings and provided feedback. Other testing occurred before the final version was published in 1998. (3M Working Paper, 11-97)

It is estimated that both the ICD-10-CM and ICD-10-PCS will be implemented on October 1, 2001. Coders should stay current with the latest developments on these revisions. Extensive training sessions will be provided across the country prior to the implementation date.

SUMMARY

- ICD-9-CM is the *International Classification of Diseases, 9th Revision, Clinical Modification*, and is used to uniformly classify diagnoses and procedures.

- HCFA (Medicare) requires the usage of ICD-9-CM diagnoses for billing of patients in the inpatient, outpatient, clinic, and physician office setting. The procedure section of ICD-9-CM is not used in the clinic/physician office setting at this time.

- Official coding guidelines for all users of ICD-9-CM are published in *The Coding Clinic for ICD-9-CM* by the American Hospital Association.

- The basic steps in coding are:
    a. Identify the main term(s) of the condition to be coded.
    b. Locate the main term in the alphabetic index.
    c. Refer to any subterms indented under the main term. Refer to any nonessential modifiers, instructional terms, or notes to select the most likely code.
    d. Verify the code(s) in the tabular list. Never code directly from the alphabetic index.
    e. Check all instructional terms in the tabular list and be sure to assign all codes to their highest degree of specificity.
    f. Continue coding the diagnostic statement until all of the elements are identified completely.

- In the inpatient setting, diagnoses referred to as "probable," "suspected," "questionable," "possible," or "rule out" are coded as if the condition existed or was established. In all other settings, the coder should only code to the highest degree of specificity known, even if that is a sign or symptom.

- V codes can be used as primary or principal diagnoses to indicate the reason for visit if no sign or symptom is present, or as secondary diagnoses to provide further information regarding the patient's visit or health.

- Coders should be familiar with tools available, such as books and publications, organizations, the Internet, etc., that can help to increase knowledge and awareness of coding rules, guidelines, new medical techniques and changes to the coding systems.

- ICD-10-CM (diagnoses) and ICD-10-PCS (procedures) are the replacements for ICD-9-CM and are designed as a complete alphanumeric coding system. It is projected that the new system will be implemented in the year 2001 in the United States.

REFERENCES

Bowman, Elizabeth. "Coding and Classification Systems" *Health Information: Management of a Strategic Resource.* Philadelphia: W.B. Saunders, 1996.

Brown, Faye. *ICD-9-CM Coding Handbook, With Answers, 1997 Revised Edition.* Chicago, Illinois: American Hospital Association, 1997.

Graham, Launa L. *Advanced Clinical Topics for ICD-9-CM.* Chicago, Illinois: American Health Information Management Association, 1996.

Nicholas, Toula. *Basic ICD-9-CM Coding.* Chicago, Illinois: American Health Information Management Association, 1998.

Prophet, Sue. "OIG Releases Compliance Program Guidance for Hospitals," *Journal of the American Health Information Management Association.* April, 1998 69/4.

Puckett, Craig D. *The 1998 Annual Hospital Version The Educational Annotation of ICD-9-CM, 5th Edition.* Reno, Nevada: Channel Publishing, Ltd., 1997.

Steigerwald, Jo Ann. *Advanced ICD-9-CM Coding.* Birmingham, AL: Southern Medical Association, 1994.

Module 2
CPT Coding: Evaluation & Management

Lois M. Smith, RN, CMA

KEY TERMS

Chief Complaint
Comprehensive
Concurrent Care
Consultation
Coordination of Care
Counseling
Detailed
Established Patient
Examination
Expanded Problem Focused
Face-to-Face Time
History
Level of Service
Medical Decision Making
Modifier
New Patient
Problem Focused
Unit/Floor Time

LEARNING OBJECTIVES

Upon successful completion of this module, you should be able to:

1. List the components of an Evaluation and Management code assignment.
2. Distinguish the levels of service included in Evaluation and Management codes.
3. Relate the appropriate code to documented patient encounter.
4. Identify the specific categories and subcategories of Evaluation and Management services.
5. Apply modifiers to Evaluation and Management codes.

INTRODUCTION

Current Procedural Terminology, referred to as CPT, is a publication of the American Medical Association. It is a listing for physicians and other medical service providers of specific codes to be used in describing and reporting the medical services and procedures performed. The verbal description of specific medical, surgical and diagnostic services translates into a numeric code. These are used to provide a reliable nationwide form of communication among providers, patients and involved third parties such as insurance agencies and health maintenance organizations. It also serves to identify procedures for statistical information used in research and healthcare management. The codes are intended to be reflective of current services provided in our healthcare delivery systems. They are revised annually to include new procedures and indicate changes or deletions to previous codes. The *current* edition is always the one to be used when coding for billing or other purposes. It is available prior to each calendar year, generally by November, to allow time for necessary changes and review updates for the current year. Physicians' Current Procedural Terminology has been available since 1966, with a major change in 1992, introducing the new codes for evaluation and management that will be discussed in detail in this module.

The key to understanding Current Procedural Terminology is to keep in mind that this process is used to communicate *what* a practitioner is doing when performing medical services. The goal is to be as descriptive and inclusive as possible while using a five-digit code! There are times when multiple codes may be used to accomplish this goal and there are instances when the use of an additional 2-digit **modifier** will complete the explanation of services provided. Details are an important factor in determining an appropriate code. These are available in documented accounts of care provided in the patient record as well as recorded protocol in diagnostic testing facilities. Certain components must be present to justify the use of a particular code. They help explain the actual medical procedure performed.

The Health Care Financing Administration (HCFA) and the American Medical Association (AMA) continue to work on revision of Evaluation/Management documentation guidelines. These guidelines are based on the multi-system exam and the individual single-system exam to outline specific requirements for each of the four exam levels: problem-focused, expanded problem-focused, detailed, and comprehensive. The content and documentation requirements are as follows:

Level of Exam	Perform and Document
Problem-focused	One to five elements identified by a bullet.
Expanded problem-focused	At least six elements identified by a bullet.
Detailed	At least two elements identified by a bullet from each of six areas/systems OR at least twelve elements identified by a bullet in two or more areas/systems.
Comprehensive	At least two elements identified by a bullet from each of nine areas/systems.

General guidelines are outlined as follows:

Multi-System Exam	
	Problem-focused—1 to 5 bullets
	Expanded problem-focused—6 or more bullets
	Detailed—6 areas, 2 bullets each OR 2 or more areas, 12 bullets total
	Comprehensive—9 areas, 2 bullets each

Constitutional
- any 3 of 7 vital sign measurement: Sitting or standing blood pressure, supine blood pressure, pulse rate and regularity, respiration, temperature, height, weight
- general appearance of patient (e.g., development, nutrition, grooming, deformities)

Eyes
- conjunctivae, lids
- pupils, irises
- ophthalmoscopic exam of optic discs, posterior segments for appearance, hemorrhages, exudates

Ears, nose, mouth, throat
- ears, nose (external)
- otoscopic exam of auditory canals, tympanic membranes
- hearing
- nasal mucosa, septum, turbinates
- lips, teeth, gums
- oropharynx: oral mucosa, salivary glands, hard and soft palates, tongue, tonsils, posterior pharynx

Neck

- neck (overall appearance, masses, symmetry)
- thyroid (enlargement, tenderness, mass)

Respiratory

- respiratory effort
- percussion of chest
- palpation of chest
- auscultation of lungs

Cardiovascular

- palpation of heart
- auscultation of heart (abnormal sounds, murmurs)
- carotid arteries
- abdominal aorta
- femoral arteries
- pedal pulses
- extremities (edema, varicosities)

Chest (breasts)

- inspection of breasts
- palpation of breasts and axillae (masses, lumps, tenderness)

Gastrointestinal (abdomen)

- abdomen (masses, tenderness)
- liver and spleen
- hernia (presence/absence)
- anus, perineum, rectum (sphincter tone, hemorrhoids, masses)
- stool sample (occult blood, if indicated)

Genitourinary (male)

- scrotal contents
- penis
- digital rectal exam of prostate

Genitourinary (female)

- external genitalia, vagina
- urethra
- bladder
- cervix
- uterus
- adnexa/parametria

Lymphatic

Palpation of lymph nodes in two or more:
- neck
- axillae
- groin
- other

Musculoskeletal

- gait and station
- digits and nails

Exam of joints, bones and muscles of one or more of the following: head and neck/spine, ribs, pelvis, right upper extremity, left upper extremity, right lower extremity, left lower extremity. Each must include:

- inspection or palpation (misalignment, asymmetry, crepitation, defects, tenderness, masses, effusions)
- range of motion (pain, crepitation, contracture)
- stability (dislocation, subluxation, laxity)
- muscle strength and tone (atrophy, abnormal movements)

Skin

- inspection of skin and subcutaneous tissue
- palpation of skin and subcutaneous tissue

Neurologic

- test cranial nerves (deficits)
- deep tendon reflexes (pathological reflexes)
- sensation

Psychiatric

- judgment, insight
- time, place, person orientation
- recent and remote memory
- mood and affect (depression, anxiety, agitation)

Module 3 also will address documentation requirements and give detailed instruction of the exam requirements. The complete guidelines can be located on the Internet at the website of the Health Care Financing Administration at http://www.hcfa.gov/medicare/mcarpti.htm.

The sections of Current Procedural Terminology include Evaluation and Management, Anesthesia, Surgery, Radiology (including Nuclear Medicine and Diagnostic Ultrasound), Pathology & Laboratory and Medicine. This broad scope covers all of the possible medical services and procedures performed by all specialties. A certain degree of exclusivity exists in sections like Anesthesia, Radiology and Pathology & Laboratory. There is minimal overlap in these specialty areas to primary care providers who may *request* a particular procedure described in those sections, but the actual procedure would be performed by the specialist in that area. The Surgery section would apply primarily to general and specialty surgeons with some overlap to primary care providers performing minor, outpatient surgical procedures. The Medicine section includes procedures specific to various medical specialties, such as Cardiology, Pulmonary, Allergy, Neurology etc. This helps define the placement and assists in the search of appropriate codes. The Evaluation and Management section is applicable to all areas of specialty and general medical care. This is where we will find the codes for the primary encounter with patients, which can lead to subsequent medical services. The broad categories of office visits, hospital visits and consultations are performed by a wide array of providers. These categories are well defined and expanded to include all possibilities of medical services. A systematic approach to successful evaluation and management coding will be provided to include the detailed information required to assign the specific code. This is how we will say *what* we are doing when we provide medical services, using a five-digit code!

EVALUATION AND MANAGEMENT

Evaluation and management services (E/M) can be recognized and understood by reviewing the basic meaning of the two terms. Evaluation is the process of looking at information in a detailed fashion in order to come to a specific conclusion. In the healthcare setting this is primarily the process of obtaining a medical history and examination. Management is the process of working within an organized framework to achieve a goal. In the healthcare setting this is the diagnosis and treatment of medical problems. In 1992, when CPT coding was revised, the components of *time, skill, knowledge,* and *risk* were used to re-evaluate the entire procedural system. The element of time is easily recognized as appointments are scheduled in specific time allotments and procedures have recognized time limits. It is easily understood that to do more takes more time. However, in the coding process, the range of time spent in a patient visit will vary with the particular clinical circumstance. Studies conducted to determine total time spent in the process of "work", which can be difficult to quantify in the clinical setting, correlates to intraservice times (face to face) in the office and other outpatient visits and unit/floor time for hospital and other inpatient visits. There are some E/M code categories that list specific time parameters such as critical care, case management and counseling, while other categories recognize time as an integrated factor in the clinical service performed. The elements of skill and knowledge are generally recognized as a "given" in the healthcare setting. It is standard to expect established education and training requirements of all personnel involved in patient care activities. License to practice and other credentials are in place to verify this process. It is the level of skill and knowledge necessary for a specific procedure that is taken into consideration in the CPT coding system. Certainly all physician practitioners have the basic requirement of medical school education and internship. Various residency or continuing education training programs advance that basic knowledge and are recognized as providing the necessary skills for specialty procedures. Other clinical practitioners such as physical therapists, laboratory technicians and radiology technicians will also be performing specific procedures and must have the accepted qualifications. The level of skill and knowledge required for each procedure listed has been evaluated and is reflected in the description of the particular code. The range includes everything from routine office visits to complex brain surgery. Risk easily comes to mind at the mention of surgical procedures, but it too is a consideration in all procedures. The risk of potential complications associated with a clinical condition and the risk of omission of pertinent patient history data can both impact patient care. It is the degree of risk that is evaluated in determining a specific code. Certainly surgical procedures do carry more of a risk factor than most medical procedures. The evaluation and management section is a grouping of medical procedures, all of which will have the components of time, skill, knowledge and risk, the basic elements of all procedural codes.

LEVELS OF EVALUATION AND MANAGEMENT SERVICES

The degree to which the elements of time, skill, knowledge and risk will be used in each individual procedure is established by recognizing specific components that must be present to qualify the particular code. The levels of service in evaluation and management will include examinations, evaluations, treatments, conferences, preventive pediatric and adult health supervision and other similar medical services. This encompasses a wide variation in skill, effort, time, responsibility and the medical knowledge necessary to provide for diagnostic evaluation and treatment of illness and injury as well as to promote optimal health. To develop the appropriate code for services, certain descriptive components must be present. These are:

- history
- physical examination
- medical decision making
- counseling
- coordination of care
- nature of presenting problem
- time

The first three components (history, examination and medical decision making) are key components and the remainder are contributory factors. Each of these components will be discussed.

History

In most instances, patients seek medical care because of a problem. This can be a symptom, illness, injury or disease. For healthy individuals, this can be for advice, support and confirmation of preventive health measures. In both the outpatient and inpatient healthcare setting, a **history** of the problem(s) is the first step to providing care. The information gathered is subjective in nature, relayed by the patient with pertinent questions from the healthcare provider for clarification. A patient history can be a minimal statement that describes the reason for seeking healthcare—such as "I have a sore throat." This is referred to as the **chief complaint**. More detail can be structured around that information by asking: "when did it start, what have you done for relief, how often does this problem occur, has this occurred before, are there any other symptoms present such as .... and other relevant who, what, when, where, why directed questions. As more detail is obtained, a clearer picture develops as to the extent of a presenting problem. A chief complaint is always going to be present in any patient encounter, even if it is not really a "complaint." An example would be the patient being seen for a routine physical exam without having any current problems or symptoms. What this initial history does is direct the provider to the problem source and subsequent appropriate service. As we continue the process, history can become more involved. Add to the above "I have a sore throat" . . . "cough, fever, difficulty breathing and chest pain," and we are extending the problem area from the throat to the lungs and possible systemic involvement due to fever. History of the upper respiratory system, past and present would be obtained. The complaint of chest pain could expand the history to include the cardiovascular system. We can take history from chief complaint to a single system review to total or complete body system review. The complete history consists of obtaining information on all body systems, referred to as ROS (Review of Systems) (see Figure 2–1). This is a typical format used to outline the body systems and related structures and characteristics. Pertinent questions are asked that refer to particular system function. It is done in an organized fashion so as not to miss any area. Additional information in this process includes past medical history, surgery, injury or hospitalization; current medical conditions and treatment; family medical history including siblings, parents and grandparents; social and work history including marital status, alcohol/tobacco/drug use, environmental exposure, travel and safety; immunizations and allergies. The degree of history obtained is going to be relevant to the level of service required for the presenting problem. The CPT code descriptor will include:

- **Problem Focused**—chief complaint; brief history of present illness or problem.
- **Expanded Problem Focused**—chief complaint; brief history of present illness; problem pertinent system review.

FORM 8184

MEDICAL RECORD

NAME			AGE	SEX	S M D W
ADDRESS		PHONE		DATE	
SPONSOR		ADDRESS			
OCCUPATION		REF BY		ACKN	

CHIEF COMPLAINT

PRESENT ILLNESS

FAMILY HISTORY			URINARY TRACT		
MOTHER	FATHER		NOCTURIA		FREQUENCY
BROTHERS			PAIN		BURNING
SISTERS			BLEEDING		INFECTION
TB	DIAB	MALIG	INCONTINENCE		
HT DIS	NEPH	EPILIP	GENITAL TRACT		
PSYCH			AGE AT MENST		TYPE PERIOD
PAST HISTORY—GENL HEALTH			INTERMEN BLEEDING		
			AMENORRHEA		DYSMENORRHEA
CHILDHOOD DISEASES			VAG DISCH		IRRITATION
SC FEV	RHEUM FEV	ALLERGY	PAINFUL PERIOD		
OTHER			L M P		
USUAL WEIGHT			CHILDREN—L	D	S B
ACCIDENTS			MARRIED YRS.	YOUNGEST CHILD	

HABITS COFFEE	TOBACCO	ALCOHOL	NEURO—MUSCULAR		
REVIEW OF SYSTEMS			STRENGTH		NERVOUSNESS
E E N T—EYES			SLEEP		WORRY
EARS			MUSCULAR PAIN		
NOSE			JOINT PAIN		
THROAT			ABNORMAL SENSATIONS		
NECK			DEFORMITIES		
BREASTS					
HEART—LUNGS			OPERATIONS		
PAIN	COUGH				
BLEEDING	DYSPNEA				
IRREG	EDEMA				
GASTRO—INTESTINAL			TREATMENTS		
APPETITE	DIET				
INDIGESTION	PAIN				
NAUSEA	VOMITING				
JAUNDICE	BLEEDING		COMMENT		
BOWEL HABITS					
HEMORRHOIDS					
PAIN WITH STOOL	ITCHING				
OTHER					

FORM 8184 COLWELL CO   CHAMPAIGN ILL

Figure 2–1 Example of a form used for Review of System (ROS) in the Medical Record. *(Courtesy Stephen B. Goodman, MD, 191 E. Orchard Road, Littleton, CO 80121.)*

- **Detailed**—chief complaint; extended history of present illness; extended system review; pertinent past, family, and/or social history.
- **Comprehensive**—chief complaint; extended history of present illness; complete system review; complete past, family, and social history.

Examination

Examination is the process used to obtain objective data relevant to a presenting problem. Examination begins where history leads us. The history example of "I have a sore throat" is followed by the provider looking at or examining the throat and confirming conditions, such as redness or edema, to validate the problem. The examination technique includes inspection (visual observation), palpation (feeling), auscultation (listening), percussion (tapping), and mensuration (measuring). As body function is both internal and external, the examination technique has to be expanded in order to evaluate what is happening within a particular body system. For example, the cardiovascular system can be evaluated by history of symptoms relating to function, listening to the heart with a stethoscope, feeling pulses both near and distal to the heart and observing body fluid distribution (edema). While this will provide a great deal of medical data, additional testing can give even greater detail to cardiovascular function. An electrocardiogram can be performed to validate the electrical activity of the heart muscle, both at rest and as a stress test during activity. A cardiac catheterization will give detailed information about the heart vessels and pressure within the chambers of the heart. Radiologic—X-ray and ultrasound techniques have been developed to show heart activity and blood flow. In addition, laboratory testing of blood and urine samples can provide information to support the examination process. The objective data required for complete examination correlates to the complete history with the established review of systems (ROS) as the basis for examination techniques employed. The complete physical exam (CPX) indicates this very thorough history and examination process (see Figure 2–2). The additional technological support available through diagnostic testing moves the process along to a medical decision regarding the presenting problem(s). The degree of examination required will be dependent on the actual clinical situation. The CPT code descriptor will include:

- Problem Focused—an examination that is limited to the affected body area of organ system.
- Expanded Problem Focused—an examination of the affected body area or organ system and other symptomatic or related organ systems.
- Detailed—an extended examination of the affected body area(s) and other symptomatic or related organ system(s).
- Comprehensive—a complete single system specialty examination or a complete multi-system examination.

Medical Decision Making

After establishing history and examination information, the next step in the medical process is to arrive at a conclusion, specifically, a medical diagnosis. In some instances, an actual diagnosis may not be present. For instance, a complete history and physical examination of a normal, healthy individual may conclude or confirm a normal, healthy individual. In essence, "normal, healthy individual" is the diagnosis, loosely translated. Recommendations may be made including advice on continuing a healthy lifestyle, cancer or other disease screening and time

PHYSICAL EXAMINATION

WT	HT	TEMP	BLOOD PRESSURE	PULSE	RESP

GENERAL APPEARANCE

SKIN—SCALP

BLOOD VESSELS

EYES			EARS		NOSE

MOUTH—TEETH

THROAT

NECK

BREASTS

HEART

LUNGS

RIBS

SPINE

ABDOMEN

HERNIA

EXTREMITIES

REFLEXES

LYMPH NODES

GENITALIA

PERINEUM			CYSTOCELE
VULVA			RECTOCELE
VAGINAL VAULT			PROLAPSE

CERVIX

FUNDUS

ADNEXAE

MALE

RECTAL

SPECIAL EXAMINATION

IMPRESSION

TREATMENT	LABORATORY	
	URINE	BLOOD
	COLOR	HBG
	SP GR	RBC
	ALB	WBC
	SUGAR	C P
	MICRO	SED

Figure 2–2 Example of a form used for physical examination in the medical record.

frame for follow-up exams. These recommendations would be considered management options. In the presence of a diagnosis or a problem, specific treatment with follow-up would be given. There are also instances where the diagnosis is not fully established and further diagnostic testing or referral to a specialist may be required. Patients can present with a chronic health problem in which case a diagnosis is already established, but they may require additional treatment, develop complications or need counseling/advice to adequately cope with their health problem. Once again, the degree of complexity within the history and examination process will determine the degree of complexity involved in medical decision making. Establishing a diagnosis on the basis of previous health records, history and physical exam, diagnostic testing and consultant input is a very involved process. Providing the appropriate care can include prescribing medications and treatments, counseling, specialty referral and follow-up evaluations. While considerable skill and knowledge are required to come up with a diagnosis, the risk element plays a heavy role in **medical decision making** as the process deals with the degree of complexity for a particular diagnosis, the presence of multiple diagnoses and the determination of appropriate treatment and follow-up. To determine the complexity of medical decision making, the CPT guideline is:

- The number of possible diagnoses and/or the number of management options that must be considered.
- The amount and/or complexity of medical records, diagnostic tests, and/or other information that must be obtained, reviewed and analyzed.
- The risk of significant complications, morbidity and/or mortality, as well as comorbidities, associated with the patient's presenting problem(s), the diagnostic procedure(s) and/or the possible management options.

The above criteria are used in CPT to indicate four types of medical decision making.

These are: **Straightforward**—indicating a minimal level of diagnosis, management and risk, basically an uncomplicated presenting problem.

Low Complexity—indicating a limited level of diagnosis and management with low risk. This can be a controlled chronic disease situation.

Moderate Complexity—indicating multiple diagnoses with moderate management and risk. Key is multiple or greater depth to system review.

High Complexity—indicating extensive diagnoses and management with high risk. This is for complicated, multi-system problems.

The diagnosis, whether established or unknown, will indicate to the physician a level of complexity. The range is from minimal diagnosis with minimal data review and risk on to extensive or multiple diagnoses with complex data review and high risk. Elements of history and examination relative to one or multiple body systems must be indicated. Determination of the complexity of medical decision making is the responsibility of the provider of services who is most aware of the extent of the presenting problem. Recorded data in the medical record confirms the extent of required services. In the coding and billing process, we have to be able to recognize the parameters of specific codes and be able to justify them from information we have in the medical record, including reports of diagnostic testing and consultations. We are reminded of this process with the cliché, if it isn't documented, it isn't done!

Counseling and Coordination of Care

In a patient encounter there is continuous discussion of the problem, from history to exam to diagnosis and management. In the process we are explaining what is going on in the disease process, recommending specific treatment, reviewing diagnostic tests and instructing the patient on their role in achieving effective results. The role of the provider is also to ascertain how well the patient understands what is happening so that they can indeed participate in the effective management of their healthcare. This **counseling** or advice is an integral component in providing medical services. As we are dealing with issues ranging from simple to complex, what we need to cover from a counseling standpoint can develop into a separate entity or service that is purely counseling. If that is the case, the counseling becomes a subcategory under Preventive Medicine Services and would require a separate code.

Coordination of care is a similar circumstance. The physician relates necessary treatments to his medical assistant who can either perform the treatment or arrange for the appropriate healthcare professional to provide the service. A prescription can be written or called in to the pharmacy by the physician or his assistant. The pharmacist will assist in counseling the patient about the prescribed medication. A specialist may be consulted for their expertise in managing the patient's problem. All of this activity and more can be directed or coordinated by the physician. This is inclusive activity in a typical office visit. However, taking the simple to complex route, a medical condition can require enough additional services that specific conference time needs to be spent with all of the personnel involved. This is typical in rehabilitation services where the primary care physician, physical therapist, occupational therapist, speech therapist, nutritionist and home health nurse would all be providing services. A team conference would be necessary to correlate treatments and update care while also monitoring the patient's general physical condition. Coding for this type of service would be found under Case Management Services.

Nature of Presenting Problem

We have discussed the presenting problem as chief complaint, with further development through history and examination to become the diagnosis, noting the various degrees of "problem" possibilities. The AMA in CPT describes presenting problem as a disease, condition, illness, injury, symptom, sign, finding, complaint or other reason for encounter, with or without a diagnosis being established at the time of the encounter. Because a diagnosis or related symptoms are why we seek medical services and because this is necessary information for claims processing, it is a valid consideration in procedural coding. It is important to recognize the five types of presenting problems as defined in Evaluation & Management:

■ **Minimal**—A problem that may not require the presence of the physician, but service is provided under the physician's supervision. (The patient has a blood pressure check following a medication change.)

■ **Self-limited or Minor**—A problem that runs a definite and prescribed course, is transient in nature and is not likely to permanently alter health status OR has a good prognosis with management/compliance. (The patient has a mild upper respiratory infection.)

■ **Low severity**—A problem where the risk of morbidity without treatment is low; there is little to no risk of mortality without treatment; full recovery without functional impairment is expected. (The patient has mild viral gastroenteritis.)

■ **Moderate severity**—A problem where the risk of morbidity without treatment is moderate; there is moderate risk of mortality without treatment; uncertain prognosis OR increased probability of prolonged functional impairment. (The patient has chronic obstructive pulmonary pisease and pneumonia.)

■ **High severity**—A problem where the risk of morbidity without treatment is high to extreme; there is a moderate to high risk of mortality without treatment OR high probability of severe, prolonged functional impairment. (The patient has Hypertension and has suffered a cerebral vascular accident – stroke.)

As you can see the level of risk increases with each presenting problem, which will change the level of service reflected in an evaluation and management code. Note the similarity to criteria for medical decision making: Straightforward, Low, Moderate and High Complexity.

Time

Looking at the key components of an evaluation and management encounter which are history, examination and medical decision making, time is certainly a relevant factor. We can readily acknowledge the additional time spent as we gather and act upon increasing amounts of medical information. Typically with office visits, consultations and some other outpatient services, there is certainly **face-to-face time** spent with the patient. This is the actual direct contact with the patient or family, usually involving history, examination and treatment. However, there is also time spent in preparation for the visit and details to take of afterward. Consequently the timing consideration, while not listed as actual minutes/hours, is called face-to-face time as it is the only time measurable for coding purposes. Time is a factor in determining an office visit E/M code when counseling involves more than 50% of the visit. This timing pattern of looking at total work time includes inpatient services as well, when the physician spends a portion of time at the bedside examining the patient and a considerable amount of time reviewing diagnostic studies in other parts of the hospital as well as reviewing the patient record. Communication with other healthcare professionals as well as family members is included. This is referred to as **unit/floor time**. In areas of concentrated time, such as critical care, counseling and coordination of care, you will see time listed as a key factor for that particular level of evaluation and management services.

New and Established Patient

When a patient is being seen for the first time, a more detailed history will have to be obtained. CPT defines a **new patient** as one who has not received any professional services from the physician or another physician of the same specialty who belongs to the same group practice, within the past three years. This reiterates that the importance of history warrants a full review if the patient has not been seen by a physician for three years. In group practice, patients may be new to a particular physician in the group, but the recorded information would be kept current, giving the patient an **established patient** status. The established patient has been receiving medical services from the same physician (or physician group member) with recorded progressive health data on file. The major component affected here is time. A physician will have to spend more time with a new patient to obtain health history and establish adequate medical information for effective treatment. Depending on the presenting problem, the level of service could still vary. For that same reason, you will see that in some E/M categories, the level of service is the same for new and established patients. Emergency department services and hospital services are examples of how the presenting problem requires the same amount of detail whether the patient is new or established.

E&M CATEGORIES AND SUBCATEGORIES

Within the evaluation and management section of CPT, there are established broad categories such as office visits, hospital visits and consultations. These categories can be further divided into subcategories. The basic format is the same in each category. First, a brief descriptive account of the section with noted reference to changes and other pertinent data. The code number is listed, followed by specified place and/or type of service along with a description of service content. Examples of patient encounters along with presenting problem indicators and typical time spent are included. This is very helpful information. Each category and subcategory will be addressed in detail with patient encounter scenario and rationale for code selection.

HIGHLIGHTS OF E&M STRUCTURE

Basis: Time, skill, knowledge and risk

Structure: Levels of service determined by the extent to which the following components are utilized in a medical encounter

Key components: History, examination, medical decision making

Contributory components: Counseling, coordination of care, presenting problem and time

Extent of history and exam: Problem focused, expanded problem focused, detailed and comprehensive

Medical decision making: Straightforward, low complexity, moderate complexity and high complexity

Patient status: New and established

EXERCISE 2–1

1. Name the three key components of an evaluation and management code.
   _____

2. Name and describe the contributory components. _____
   _____
   _____
   _____

3. Describe the method used for a comprehensive history and examination.
   _____
   _____

4. What is the significance of determining whether the patient status is new or established? _____
   _____
   _____

5. What activities are included in unit/floor time? _____
   _____
   _____

OFFICE AND OTHER OUTPATIENT SERVICES   99201–99215

All providers use this category across the board. Specialty practitioners will use consultation codes when appropriate, but revert back to office visit codes for patients they see on a regular basis. As you see the components come together, along with brief counseling and presenting problem information, a pattern is developed. The example situations listed after each level of service in the CPT text typically include history and diagnosis. The examination and diagnostic elements are not listed. This is done to keep focus on the presenting problem. Also it separates diagnostic testing and treatments from the office visit. If a treatment *is* given it will have its own CPT code. For example: a 65-year-old woman, established patient, is seen for hypertension management and is also advised to have a PneumoVax injection. The office visit code would be 99213 and the immunization would be 90732. If that same patient were sent to a laboratory for blood tests, the laboratory would code and bill for the requested tests. If the venipuncture to obtain the blood sample was performed in the office with the blood being sent to a laboratory, the office would code 36415 for the venipuncture procedure and the laboratory would code for performing the requested tests. The office visit codes are inclusive of presenting problem verification, which includes the degree of history, exam and medical decision making required. This can include review of relevant medical reports and tests. They also recognize advice and counseling as part of treatment along with detailed coordination of care. Remember, if treatment or management of care requires additional procedures, specific codes for those procedures would be necessary. We have to know when to separate an item in the encounter into its own code and what activities are inclusive. The key to code verification is adequate documentation in the medical record of all that transpired in the course of a patient encounter. A complete, accurate record makes for easy access to patient information in any clinical setting as well as supportive information for the billing process. While the physician will generally indicate the level of E&M service he provided, follow-up questions from involved third party payers will be directed to his staff who relies on the documented information.

The following scenarios will take a New Patient through the levels of Office Visit codes. Example 1: Mrs. Johnson, a 55-year-old woman, is being seen for the first time by Dr. Hanson. She has been exposed to a grandchild with Beta-hemolytic strep and requests a throat culture. On examination her throat is normal and a culture is obtained. A rapid strep test is negative. She is advised to return if symptoms should develop.

- Problem focused history—exposure to strep infection
- Problem focused examination—normal throat
- Straightforward medical decision—throat culture negative for strep

Visit included counseling—return if symptoms should develop.	CODE.........99201
Additional service/procedure—rapid strep culture	CODE.........87082

Example 2: Mrs. Johnson, a 55-year-old woman, is being seen for the first time by Dr. Hanson. She has been exposed to a grandchild with Beta-hemolytic strep, complains of a severe burning sensation in her throat with some difficulty swallowing. On exam, her throat is inflamed. There is no glandular enlargement. A rapid strep test is obtained and it is negative. She is advised that her sore throat is likely due to a virus and to gargle with warm salt water every 3–4 hours, increase fluid intake and observe voice rest. Aspirin or Tylenol may be used every 3–4 hours for the discomfort. She is advised to call or return if symptoms do not improve.

■ Expanded problem focused history—exposed to a grandchild with Beta-hemolytic strep, complains of a severe burning sensation in her throat with some difficulty swallowing.

■ Expanded problem focused examination—On exam, her throat is red and inflamed. There is no glandular enlargement.

■ Straightforward medical decision making—sore throat.

As you can see, we have an uncomplicated diagnosis, a more involved history and examination that included a diagnostic test, with management in the form of specific counseling.   CODE.........99202

    Additional service/procedure—rapid strep culture   CODE.........87082

Example 3: Mrs. Johnson, a 55-year-old woman, is being seen for the first time by Dr. Hanson. She has been exposed to a grandchild with Beta-hemolytic strep and complains of a severe burning sensation in her throat with some difficulty swallowing. In addition, she has a persistent cough, tightness in her chest, and a fever. On exam, her throat is inflamed and her glands are swollen. She has a temperature of 103.4° F. Breath sounds are decreased with wheezing present in both lower lobes of the lungs. A chest X-ray confirms acute bronchitis with no pneumonia present. A rapid strep test is obtained and it is negative. Mrs. Johnson is given a prescription for Ampicillin 500 mg every 6 hours, advised to take Robitussin DM for her cough and gargle with warm salt water for her sore throat. She is to return in two weeks or sooner if not improved.

■ A detailed history—She has been exposed to a grandchild with Beta-hemolytic strep and complains of a severe burning sensation in her throat with some difficulty swallowing. In addition, she has a persistent cough, tightness in her chest and a fever.

■ A detailed examination—On exam, her throat is inflamed and her glands are swollen. She has a temperature of 103.4° F. Breath sounds are decreased with wheezing present in both lower lobes of the lungs. A chest X-ray confirms bronchitis with no pneumonia present. A rapid strep test is obtained and it is negative.

■ Medical decision making of low complexity—acute bronchitis, sore throat.

In this situation, Mrs. Johnson has a more involved history and exam of the throat and lungs along with diagnostic testing that leads to a diagnosis that should respond to the prescribed treatment and counseling, hence the low complexity to the medical decision making.   CODE.........99203

    Additional service/procedure—rapid strep culture   CODE.........87082
    (Chest X-ray billed by radiology department)

Example 4: Mrs. Johnson, a 55-year-old woman, is being seen for the first time by Dr. Hanson for a complete physical examination. She has developed shortness of breath on exertion, following treatment for acute bronchitis three months ago while on vacation. A blood chemistry panel, CBC, EKG, pulmonary function test and chest X-ray have been obtained prior to this visit. A complete history is obtained including her past and present medical history, family and social history and review of systems. This is followed by a complete physical exam and review of the diagnostic data obtained. Concluding diagnoses are allergies with desensitization 5 years ago and early emphysema. Further pulmonary function studies will be done to determine prognosis.

- A comprehensive history—per form outline (Figure 2–1)
- A comprehensive examination—per form outline (Figure 2–2)
- Medical decision making of moderate complexity—Allergies, Emphysema

A comprehensive history and exam is a lengthy, time consuming process, even for a normal, healthy individual. In our scenario, the patient has a diagnosis of moderate complexity with counseling for additional testing as well as lifestyle accommodations.   CODE..........99204

In the absence of a medical diagnosis at the conclusion, the status of "normal, healthy individual" can be coded using ICD-9-CM V-codes and the CPT code would be the 99204.

Example 5: Mrs. Johnson, a 55-year-old woman, is being seen for the first time by Dr. Hanson for a complete physical examination. She has had allergies and asthma since the age of 15, controlled by desensitization and the use of inhalant bronchodilating medication when needed. Over the past year, she has been experiencing more frequent asthma attacks and increased shortness of breath. She also has hypertension, controlled with 10mg. Ziac daily. A blood chemistry panel, CBC, EKG, pulmonary function test and chest X-ray have been obtained prior to this visit. A complete history is obtained including her past and present medical history, family and social history and review of systems. This is followed by a complete physical exam and review of the diagnostic data obtained. Concluding diagnoses are COPD (Chronic Obstructive Pulmonary Disease), allergies and hypertension. Prognosis is only fair due to the sharp decline in pulmonary function studies as well as lung changes on X-ray.

- A comprehensive history—per form outline (refer to Figure 2–1)
- A comprehensive examination—per form outline (refer to Figure 2–2)
- Medical decision making of high complexity—COPD, Allergies, Hypertension

While the history and examination processes are essentially unchanged from the previous code format, the complexity of the diagnoses increases the depth of information required (particularly past occurrences of disease, treatments, etc.). The severity of illness indicated adds to the risk associated with this comprehensive visit as well as the management of potential complications. In this scenario, we have a comprehensive visit of *high complexity.*   CODE..........99205

This group of scenarios will take an Established Patient through the levels of Office Visit codes. Example 1: The first code listed in this category allows for a brief visit that may not require the presence of a physician. Mr. Brown, a 48-year-old male, is seen for an interim blood pressure check after having a change in his medication.   CODE..........99211

Other instances can include a dressing change, medication instruction reinforcement, return to work or other medical validation form, wound healing status and observation of skin tests. The key here is minimal healthcare service provided to maximize benefit and/or reassure the patient.

Example 2: Mr. Brown, a 48-year-old male with a history of hypertension is being seen to evaluate the effect of a change in his medication. Two weeks ago, his blood pressure was elevated at 170/100 with a report from the patient of readings of 160/90 to 160/100 at home. His Zestril 10mg. was increased to 20mg. daily. Today his blood pressure is normal at 130/80, along with normal interim readings. His pulse rate is 68 and regular. He is not experiencing any other symptoms. Mr. Brown was advised to continue with 20mg. of Zestril daily for his hypertension, take and record his blood pressure at home 2–3 times a week and to return in 6 months.

- A problem focused history—his blood pressure was elevated at 170/100

- A problem focused examination—his blood pressure is normal at 130/80, along with normal interim readings. His pulse rate is 68 and regular. He is not experiencing any other symptoms.
- Straightforward decision making—hypertension

This visit also included counseling—continue with 20mg. of Zestril daily for his hypertension, take and record his blood pressure at home 2–3 times a week and to return in 6 months. CODE..........99212

Example 3: Mr. Brown, a 48-year-old male with hypertension has been experiencing some mild ankle edema for two weeks. On examination he has mild edema present, both ankles, extending about 2 inches above the ankle bone. Pedal pulses are present. Heart and lungs are clear to auscultation. He is not experiencing any shortness of breath and his blood pressure is 130/84. This is thought to be some mild dependent edema and he was advised to keep his feet elevated when sitting and to observe a "no-added salt" diet. Instruction on the salt limitation and a dietary brochure was given to him. He is to continue his Zestril 20mg. daily and return in 3 months.

- An expanded problem focused history—a 48-year-old male with hypertension has been experiencing some mild ankle edema for two weeks.
- An expanded problem focused examination—On examination he has mild edema present, both ankles, extending about 2 inches above the ankle bone. Pedal pulses are present. Heart and lungs are clear to auscultation. He is not experiencing any shortness of breath and his blood pressure is 130/84.
- Medical decision making of low complexity—hypertension with mild dependent edema

Both the history and examination contain more detail with regard to this patient's office visit for his hypertension. The examination considered his blood pressure, pedal pulses and listening to his heart and lungs. Counseling in regard to foot elevation and diet change were also part of this office visit. CODE..........99213

Example 4: Mr. Brown, a 48-year-old male with hypertension complains of shortness of breath when lying down and after moderate exercise. He can only walk about one block before experiencing the shortness of breath and feeling his heart "race." He has also noted increased swelling in his legs. On examination, his blood pressure is 140/94, his pulse is 88 and regular and his weight has increased 6 lbs. He has 1+ pitting edema of both ankles, extending to about 3 inches above the ankle. Soft crackles are heard at the base of both lungs. Heart sounds are normal. A chest X-ray was obtained, which indicated pulmonary changes consistent with mild failure. Mr. Brown was given 20mg. of Lasix, IV in the office and a prescription for 10mg. of Lasix, daily along with his Zestril, 20mg. The diuretic action of Lasix was explained to Mr. Brown, particularly the intravenous dose, with the expected outcome of decreasing the fluid retention he is experiencing. The degree of congestive heart failure he is experiencing should be adequately controlled with the addition of the Lasix. His diet was changed to "Low Salt" and he was advised on this further limitation of salt intake. He is to return in one week or sooner if symptoms do not improve.

- A detailed history—shortness of breath when lying down and after moderate exercise. He can only walk about one block before experiencing the shortness of breath and feeling his heart "race." He has also noted increased swelling in his legs.
- A detailed examination—On examination, his blood pressure is 140/94, his pulse is 88 and regular and his weight has increased 6 lbs. He has 1+ pitting

edema of both ankles, extending to about 3 inches above the ankle. Soft crackles are heard at the base of both lungs. Heart sounds are normal. A chest X-ray was obtained which indicated pulmonary changes consistent with mild failure.

- Medical decision making of moderate complexity—hypertension, mild congestive heart failure

The presence of mild congestive heart failure adds to the complexity of the medical decision making with additional testing required to confirm the diagnosis, additional treatment and increase in the risk factor for complications of his existing hypertension. The patient was counseled on the addition of medication, diet change and expected outcome. CODE..........99214

Example 5: Mr. Brown, a 48-year-old man with a history of hypertension and an episode of mild congestive heart failure is being seen for a complete physical examination. He has been experiencing periodic episodes of chest pain, particularly at bedtime, which he has attributed to "heartburn." This has been occurring for the past 2–3 weeks. His hypertension is controlled with 20 mg. Zestril and 10 mg. Lasix daily. A blood chemistry panel, CBC, EKG, pulmonary function test and chest X-ray have been obtained prior to this visit. A complete history is obtained including his past and present medical history, family and social history and review of systems. This is followed by a complete physical exam and review of the diagnostic data obtained. Concluding diagnoses are: hypertension, controlled, with no evidence of congestive heart failure and a differential diagnosis of coronary artery disease vs. gastro-esophageal reflux syndrome. Further testing will be scheduled to determine the basis for the chest pain and subsequent treatment. In the meantime, the patient will continue with his current medications and diet therapy. Prognosis is deferred pending outcome of diagnostic testing.

- A comprehensive history—per form outline (refer to Figure 2–1)
- A comprehensive examination—per form outline (refer to Figure 2–2)
- Medical decision making of high complexity—hypertension, controlled, with no evidence of congestive heart failure and a differential diagnosis of coronary artery disease vs. gastro-esophageal reflux syndrome

A comprehensive history and physical examination always includes the establishment of chief complaint, history of present illness, past, family and social history and review of systems. This is followed by general multi-system examination. Subsequent counseling, treatment and diagnostic evaluation will also be included, specific to related diagnoses. CODE..........99215

■ Highlights

- *New patient is one who has* not *received services for three years—from one physician or another physician in the same specialty group.*

- *Documentation of medical service provided must match descriptors in selected code.*

EXERCISE 2–2

1. When the patient is seen by office staff for services such as a blood pressure check, dressing change or skin test evaluation, what level of office visit code would be used? _____

Code the following scenarios:

2. Mr. Johnson, a 48-year-old male, an established patient, is being seen for management of hypertension, which is well controlled, and weight management. _____

3. Mrs. Deeds, a new patient, is seen for a complete physical examination. She has osteoarthritis, hypertension and diabetes. _____

4. James Jenkins, a 12-year-old boy, is seen for an injury to his right shoulder during football practice. He is a new patient. _____

5. Mr. Griffith, a 62-year-old established patient, is seen for fever of 102 degrees, shortness of breath and chest pain. He has chronic asthma. _____

HOSPITAL OBSERVATION SERVICES   99217–99220

This category is used to indicate medical services for patients requiring additional testing and monitoring of their condition before a decision can be made for full admission to the hospital or possible discharge to home. Hence, the term "observation" services rather than hospital inpatient services even though the patient will be occupying a hospital bed. Some facilities have specified areas for observation care but this is not essential. Care must be given to ascertain the length of stay in regard to "same day" status. Patients admitted and discharged on the same day will be shifted to the coding section Observation or Inpatient Services. Hospital Observation Services codes 99217, 99218, 99219 and 99220 are to be used when a patient is admitted under observation status on one date and discharged from observation status on a subsequent date. These observation services begin with the first encounter with the patient. For example: a patient seen in the office for chest pain with a determination to be transferred to hospital observation services will not be charged for that office visit. Instead, a code selected for Initial Observation Care in Hospital Observation Services will be used to describe the services. This would also apply if the patient were first evaluated in a hospital emergency room or nursing facility. Bottom line is one service for one day. Regardless of where the first services were provided, a patient admitted on observation status will qualify for the Initial Observation Care codes on the day of admission, and if discharged from observation status on the *next* day their service will qualify for the Observation Care Discharge code. Until patient status is determined, usually within a 12–30 hour period of time, you should defer coding and billing for the services. As of now, there is not a specific time allotment for the observation status, just the determination of appropriate code category for all services included in the initiation of observation care.

Example: Mrs. Johnson is a 68-year-old woman with history of a cerebral vascular accident five years ago. Her recovery was excellent and her residual effect is limited to weakness in her left leg, requiring the use of a walker. Her daughter calls to relate an episode of a brief lapse of consciousness this morning, about a minute or so, followed by incoherent speech. This too has improved but the patient feels very weak and dizzy. Mrs. Johnson's daughter is advised to bring her mother to the emergency room for evaluation. The doctor examines the patient and finds her to be quite coherent, with no additional limb weakness present, but her blood pressure is elevated at 180/110. She is admitted under observation status to treat and monitor her blood pressure and perform diagnostic tests to evaluate CVA (stroke) potential. Her previous hospital record is obtained and reviewed, and the physician completes a full history and examination, prepares hospital orders for her care plan and discusses this with Mrs. Johnson and her daughter.

■ A comprehensive history—Mrs. Johnson is a 68-year-old woman with history of a cerebral vascular accident five years ago. Her recovery was excellent and her residual effect is limited to weakness in her left leg, requiring the use of a walker. Her daughter calls to relate an episode of a brief lapse of consciousness this morning, about a minute or so, followed by incoherent speech. This too has improved but the patient feels very weak and dizzy.

■ A comprehensive examination—The doctor examines the patient and finds her to be quite coherent, with no additional limb weakness present, but her blood pressure is elevated at 180/110. She is admitted under observation status to treat and monitor her blood pressure and perform diagnostic tests to evaluate CVA (stroke) potential. Her previous hospital record is obtained and reviewed, and the physician completes a complete history and examination.

■ Medical decision making of moderate complexity—Hypertension, post CVA, TIA

Actual admission to observation status was on a Wednesday at 12 noon.

CODE..........99219

The physician was contacted by nursing personnel as tests were completed and to keep him apprised of her blood pressure and level of consciousness. The physician saw the patient again that evening and reviewed her progress. One more test was scheduled for the next morning. At 11 AM on Thursday, with all tests completed and the patient's condition stable, the physician was able to review the results with Mrs. Johnson and her daughter. It was determined that she had suffered a TIA (transient ischemic attack) that was of no further danger to her at this time. She was given a discharge plan that included her medication list and recommendations for follow-up.

CODE.........99217

In this CPT category the discharge care code precedes the initial care codes. There are also two other levels to initial care: detailed history and examination with medical decision making of low complexity and comprehensive history and examination with medical decision making of high complexity. You will note that certainly observation status does indicate some degree of complexity to the medical situation while the actual history and examination can be less than comprehensive.

■ *Highlights*

■ *This category is to be used when observation services are provided over at least two dates.*

■ *The codes are inclusive of all services provided on each date.*

■ *Codes apply to both new and established patients.*

HOSPITAL INPATIENT SERVICES   99221–99239

With this category we code medical services for patients admitted to a hospital facility. Upon admission, considering that in general the medical condition of the patient is going to require more extensive management, the physician will do a comprehensive history and physical examination of the patient. This will be followed by establishing a medical care plan and re-evaluation of the patient's condition on a regular basis. If the admission followed a same day office visit or observation service, the initial hospital care code would be the only code used for the service on that day. As with observation care, the one service code for one day rule applies. Hospital admissions are generally decided on the basis that more than one day will be required to stabilize the medical condition, so we have a subcategory for subsequent care and discharge services in addition to the initial hospital care. Very often more than one physician is involved with patient care in the hospital setting. In this instance, similar services may be provided by each physician to the same patient on the same day. This is referred to as **concurrent care**. When concurrent care is provided, no special reporting is required. Within this category is also a subcategory dealing with admission and discharge on the same date. This is termed observation or inpatient care services (including admission and discharge services).

Initial Hospital Care

Our first scenario will be a hospital admission for Mr. Jacobsen, a 60-year-old man with a wound infection at the site of his laparoscopic gallbladder removal one month ago. The infection developed about 10 days ago and has not responded to systemic antibiotic therapy. His hospital record is reviewed; the patient is examined with particular attention to the surgical site. Treatment will consist of an incision and drainage of the wound, followed by intravenous antibiotics. Wound and blood cultures will be obtained prior to the initiation of therapy.

■ A detailed history—The infection developed about 10 days ago and has not responded to systemic antibiotic therapy. His hospital record is reviewed.

■ A detailed examination—the patient is examined with particular attention to the surgical site.

■ Medical decision making of low complexity—treatment will consist of incision and drainage of the wound followed by intravenous antibiotics. Wound and blood cultures will be obtained.

History and examination are centered on the wound infection problem and with good prognosis expected as a result of the treatment; the medical decision is of low complexity. This code can also be used in the instance of re-admission when the comprehensive history and examination are current and the need is to address the particular changes that have caused a relapse in the patient's condition.

CODE..........99221

The initial hospital care for most admissions will involve a full comprehensive history and examination. This is an appropriate level of service needed for complex medical services performed in the hospital setting. It is also recognized as the standard of care required by hospital staff rules. What will effect a difference in the code selected for initial hospital services will be the degree of severity in the presenting problem or diagnosis. If we take the above scenario and add the presence of high fever and delirium, we would need to advance the level of coding to 99222, indicating the need for a comprehensive history and examination with medical decision making of moderate complexity. Add to the initial scenario, unconsciousness, fever and cardiac arrhythmia and we have the basis for the code 99223, once again the comprehensive history and examination but this time with medical decision making of high complexity. All of the above situations required inpatient hospital services but at different levels of severity of illness.

Subsequent Hospital Care

Once full hospital admission status has been initiated, the patient will have to be reassessed at intervals that will be determined by the underlying medical problem and any other changes that may occur. Generally, this is done on a daily basis and referred to as the physician making "rounds." As the patient condition changes, so do the amount of medical services required. There is always going to be the overall review of the patient record and diagnostic test results, with confirmation and changing of orders. This can involve management of the problem with the addition of consultants to assist with or take over care of the patient. A second physician seeing the patient will use specific consultation codes, however, the admitting physician, when continuing to evaluate the progress of the patient's condition, will code using the subsequent hospital care category.

Looking at the admission of Mr. Jacobsen, the following day the physician reviewed his laboratory tests, checked the wound and confirmed tolerance of the intravenous antibiotics.

■ A problem focused interval history
■ A problem focused interval examination
■ Medical decision making that is of low complexity

CODE..........99231

On day three, Mr. Jacobsen develops a fever of 103 degrees and a generalized rash. After examination of the patient and review of the record and laboratory data, the medications are changed. Allergic reaction is occurring. Additional treatments are added to the care of the wound.

■ An expanded problem focused interval history
■ An expanded problem focused interval exam
■ Medical decision making of moderate complexity

CODE..........99232

On day four, Mr. Jacobsen continues to maintain a fever of 103 to 104 degrees. He is becoming delirious. On further examination and review of the records, his physician concludes to consult with an infectious disease specialist.

■ A detailed interval history
■ A detailed interval examination
■ Medical decision making of high complexity

CODE..........99233

Individual inpatient subsequent services can vary. They are in place to accommodate the changes that do occur during the process of hospitalization. As more medical services are required, the coding level increases. If services intensify, requiring more constant physician attendance than general follow-up, we would advance to the critical care services category. Remember that the purpose of CPT codes is to identify the actual extent of medical services. There can be more than one physician using the same code for like services during a hospitalization as the severity of illness increases. Often, the physicians may be addressing different medical problems. For instance, in our scenario with Mr. Jacobsen, the infectious disease consultant may be requested to resume full care of the patient and code follow-up visits using 99232 while the admitting physician may be continuing to see the patient for follow-up of the wound care, coding the same 99232.

Observation or Inpatient Care Services (Including Admission and Discharge Services)

This subcategory is specifically for those patients who are admitted and discharged on the same day! The admission can begin as an observation status that progresses to discharge, but within the same day. Then, this would be the appropriate CPT code category as it includes both the admission and discharge process. It is always advisable to postpone coding for services that begin at the observational level since they have the potential to change code category. When it has been determined that the service is a **same day** admission and discharge, these codes are the ones used: The variable is the extent of medical evaluation based on severity of the medical problem. The levels are:

- A detailed history
- A detailed examination
- Medical decision making of low complexity

CODE..........99234

- A comprehensive history
- A comprehensive examination
- Medical decision making of moderate complexity

CODE..........99235

- A comprehensive history
- A comprehensive examination
- Medical decision making of high complexity

CODE..........99236

Hospital Discharge Services

Given that the patient has had full admission to the hospital, received care on at least one subsequent date, the next step is for discharge management. This is based on the assumption that full hospital admission is generally for a longer period of time and because of more serious medical problems. The discharge process will include final examination, discussion of hospital stay, instructions for continuing care, medication prescriptions, and referrals if necessary and preparation of discharge records. Relative to the complexity of the patient's medical condition, discharge planning can be a very integral part of the hospital stay. As for the appropriate CPT codes, they are determined by the amount of time spent on the discharge day.

| 30 minutes or less | CODE..........99238 |
| more than 30 minutes | CODE..........99239 |

■ *Highlights*

- *Inpatient hospital services for full admission will include initial, subsequent and discharge services codes.*

- *With observation services you will use different codes depending on whether the admission and discharge are on the same date or different dates.*

EXERCISE 2–3

Code the following scenario:

> A 57-year-old man was admitted to the coronary care unit for an acute myocardial infarction. The admission included comprehensive history and physical examination of high complexity medical decision making. He was seen in the CCU 3 subsequent days, first day expanded problem-focused, following 2 days problem-focused. He was then transferred to the medical floor where he was followed 3 additional days on a problem-focused level as his condition improved. The following day he was discharged home, requiring 40 minutes to perform the final examination of the patient and preparation of discharge records and prescriptions.

CONSULTATIONS   99241–99275

The term **consultation** indicates that advice or an opinion is requested from one physician to another in order to pursue with appropriate evaluation and management of the patient's care. Typically we see this in the scenario of medical specialty care. The family practitioner has a patient with hypertension, chest pain and a family history of cardiac problems. He requests a consultation by a cardiologist who evaluates the patient with full history, examination and possible diagnostic studies, and a diagnostic and therapeutic recommendation. This information is then reported back to the family practitioner. Clearly this is a consultation and the specialist would code the service from this category. However, this does not mean that every medical service provided by a specialist is coded under the consultation category. While the medical specialist is always going to be the consultant, he will not always be using consultation codes. For instance, if after the initial consultation, the specialist then assumes management of all or a portion of the patient's medical care, coding for these follow-up services would revert back to the office-visit or subsequent hospital care section (whichever is appropriate) for all practitioners. The subcategories of office, initial inpatient and follow-up consultations will have the services of the consultant requested by another physician. A fourth subcategory is available for confirmatory consultation to be used when the request comes from another appropriate source such as the patient or third party second opinion, usually an insurer.

Office or Other Outpatient Consultations

This subcategory is appropriately used in coding consultations that occur in the traditional outpatient setting, the physician's office or clinic, as well as other ambulatory facilities such as the patient's home, domiciliary, rest home, custodial care, hospital observation services or emergency. These codes should be viewed as initial consultation. Services such as follow-up, initiated by the physician consultant, would be coded using office visit codes for established patients. With documentation of a new problem or a request for additional information, the office consultation codes may be used again. Patient status can be new or established when using this subcategory.

The code choices begin with the "problem focused" situation: Mrs. White, a 60-year-old female is referred to Dr. Watson, a dermatologist, for evaluation of a facial keratosis. The lesion has been present for two years but in the past month it has become inflamed. On examination there is minimal evidence of inflammation. The lesion is about the size of a dime. It is recommended that the lesion be removed and arrangements are made for this to be done in two weeks.

■ A problem focused history—The lesion has been present for two years but in the past month it has become inflamed.

■ A problem focused examination—On examination there is minimal evidence of inflammation. The lesion is about the size of a dime.

■ Straightforward decision making—keratosis

Advising the patient of the need for removal and scheduling the procedure are also part of the services being coded. The physician initiating the referral will receive a report, in this case following the surgical removal.   CODE..........99241

Mrs. White, a 60-year-old female, is referred to Dr. Watson, a dermatologist, for evaluation of a facial keratosis. The lesion has been present for two years but in the past month it has become inflamed and is very itchy. On examination there is marked redness about 3mm. around a lesion that is about the size of a dime. Mrs. White is advised to apply warm soaks to the area, 4–6 times daily, followed by the application of Neosporin ointment. It is recommended that the lesion be removed and arrangements are made for this to be done in two weeks.

■ An expanded problem focused history—The lesion has been present for two years but in the past month it has become inflamed and is very itchy.

■ An expanded problem focused examination—On examination there is marked redness about 3mm. around a lesion that is about the size of a dime.

■ Straightforward medical decision making—keratosis

The presence of actual inflammation in this scenario adds to the length of examination and counseling of the patient in regard to treatment required before the surgical removal can be accomplished.   CODE..........99242

Mr. Taylor, a 58-year-old male is referred to Dr. Hill, a urologist, for treatment of kidney stones—urolithiasis. He has had three recurrences in the last six months, being able to pass the urinary calculi. He continues to strain his urine, which has been clear of any debris for the past month. Intravenous pyelogram indicates the presence of multiple small stones in the pelvis of the right kidney. Dr. Hill discusses the option of lithotripsy to dissolve the existing stones, preventing the recurrence of trying to pass a stone as well as eliminating those stones too large to pass through the urinary tract. The dietary control of calcium was also discussed.

■ A detailed history—He has had three recurrences in the last six months, being able to pass the stones. He continues to strain his urine, which has been clear of any debris for the past month.

■ A detailed examination—Intravenous pyelogram indicates the presence of multiple small stones in the pelvis of the right kidney

■ Medical decision making of low complexity—nephrolithiasis

While a current problem with the kidney stones is not evident, the recurrences warrant further evaluation by the specialist. Counseling in regard to the recommended treatment with the potential side effects as well as other alternatives is the major thrust of this consultation.   CODE..........99243

Mr. Smith, a 48-year-old male, is referred to Dr. Kenny, a cardiologist, for recurrent chest pain, a history of hyperlipidemia and hypertension and a recent positive treadmill. Dr. Kenny proceeds with the complete history and physical examination per review of systems. His findings conclude that further diagnostics should be obtained, mainly a Thallium treadmill. Recommendation is made to add a lipid-lowering agent to his treatment along with the low-fat, low-carbohydrate, low-calorie diet. Blood pressure is well controlled on his current medication.

- A comprehensive history—per form outline (refer to Figure 2–1)
- A comprehensive examination—per form outline (refer to Figure 2–2)
- Medical decision making of moderate complexity—recurrent chest pain, a history of hyperlipidemia and hypertension

CODE..........99244

Mr. Smith, a 48-year-old male, is referred to Dr. Kenny, a cardiologist, for recurrent chest pain, a history of hyperlipidemia and hypertension, and angioplasty of two coronary arteries 8 months ago. Dr. Kenny proceeds with the complete history and physical examination per review of systems. His findings indicate that in addition to chest pain, the patient also has been experiencing shortness of breath on exertion along with episodes of tachycardia. Further evaluation will be done with cardiac catheterization. Adjustment of medications may be required. Prognosis is guarded.

- A comprehensive history—per form outline (refer to Figure 2–1)
- A comprehensive examination—per form outline (refer to Figure 2–2)
- Medical decision making of high complexity—recurrent chest pain, a history of hyperlipidemia and hypertension, post angioplasty for CAD

CODE..........99245

Typically, consultations tend to be comprehensive in nature. This is particularly true on the initial consultation and of course, dependent on the complexity of the medical problem. The distinction has to be made with regard to the follow-up process: subsequent care by the physician consultant is coded using office visit codes, while a *new* problem or request by the referring physician for additional information would qualify for the office consultations code.

Initial Inpatient Consultations

This subcategory deals with consultations performed when the patient is in a hospital or nursing care facility. Only one *initial* consultation should be reported by a consultant per admission. Subsequent services will be coded in the *follow-up* inpatient consultation category. Patient status can be new or established.

Mr. Kingsley, a 68-year-old man, was admitted for hip replacement surgery. During his post-operative exam, Dr. Simpson, his orthopedic surgeon, observed his left eye to be inflamed. There was also considerable watery drainage. Dr. Simpson requests that Dr. Brown, an ophthalmologist examine and treat Mr. Kingsley. Dr. Brown indicates that the drainage has been present since that morning according to the patient. On examination he finds the left eye to be quite pink with moderate mucous drainage. The right eye is clear. His diagnosis is conjunctivitis and he prescribes Neosporin ophthalmic drops every four hours.

- A problem focused history—drainage has been present since that morning
- A problem focused examination—On examination he finds the left eye to be quite pink with moderate mucous drainage. The right eye is clear.
- Straightforward medical decision making—conjunctivitis

This self-limiting type of problem would not likely require any follow-up and that is the type of service we are coding. CODE..........99251

Mrs. Hanover, a 64-year-old female, is recovering from reconstructive hand surgery to relieve contractures that are a result of her rheumatoid arthritis. She develops moderate abdominal pain. Her surgeon requests that Dr. Benson, a gastroenterologist, be consulted to evaluate her condition. Dr. Benson confirms that the pain has been present for one day in the epigastric region. Mrs. Hanover is taking Naprosyn. On examination the abdomen is tender but not distended, bowel sounds are present, there is no nausea, vomiting or diarrhea. Diagnosis is gastritis, probably due to the Naprosyn. Tagamet is prescribed to offset the effects of the Naprosyn.

■ An expanded problem focused history—Dr. Benson confirms that the pain has been present for one day in the epigastric region. Mrs. Hanover is taking Naprosyn.

■ An expanded problem focused examination—On examination the abdomen is tender but not distended, bowel sounds are present, there is no nausea, vomiting or diarrhea.

■ Straightforward medical decision making—Diagnosis is gastritis, probably due to the Naprosyn

The diagnosis is once again rather uncomplicated but required more detail in the history and examination.   CODE..........99252

Mr. Jacobs, a 59-year-old male who has insulin-dependent diabetes, is admitted to the hospital for hip replacement. Dr. Simpson, his surgeon, requests that Dr. Weiss, an endocrinologist, evaluate Mr. Jacobs' insulin needs for the operative day. Dr. Weiss reviews with the patient his usual insulin requirements and any other past incidents that would refer to insulin/glucose imbalance. Dr. Weiss reviews admission lab tests, determines expected fluid intake and prescribes insulin coverage.

■ A detailed history—Dr. Weiss reviews with the patient his usual insulin requirements and any other past incidents that would refer to insulin/glucose imbalance.

■ A detailed examination—Dr. Weiss reviews admission lab tests, determines expected fluid intake and prescribes insulin coverage.

■ Medical decision making of low complexity—insulin-dependent diabetes

This diagnosis has the potential for some degree of complexity. Additional history and examination are required to obtain the data necessary for optimum control during a surgical procedure.   CODE..........99253

Mr. Smith, a 45-year-old male is admitted for pneumonia. He is on IV antibiotic therapy but is not responding well to treatment. Dr. James, his internist, requests a consult from Dr. Evans, infectious disease, for evaluation and treatment. Dr. Evans does a complete history and physical examination per review of systems and evaluation of his current hospital data. Additional cultures and skin tests are performed. His drug therapy is adjusted accordingly.

■ A comprehensive history—per form outline (refer to Figure 2–1)

■ A comprehensive examination—per form outline (refer to Figure 2–2)

■ Medical decision making of moderate complexity—pneumonia, unresponsive to current therapy

This condition being resistant to conventional therapy requires in-depth evaluation and management because of the potential risk of complications.

CODE.........99254

Mr. Smith, during the above hospitalization, develops severe shortness of breath and wheezing. There is danger of respiratory arrest. Dr. James requests a consult of Dr. Berger, a pulmonary specialist. Dr. Berger does a complete history and physical examination per review of systems, evaluation of his current hospitalization data and orders additional diagnostic testing to evaluate his respiratory system. It is determined that he is experiencing an asthma attack along with his pneumonia. Appropriate drug therapy and respiratory protocol are advised.

- A comprehensive history—per form outline (refer to Figure 2–1)
- A comprehensive examination—per form outline (refer to Figure 2–2)
- Medical decision making of high complexity—pneumonia and asthma

The patient has developed a high-risk situation, with the pneumonia process decreasing lung capacity and the complication of asthma adding to the risk of respiratory arrest.   CODE..........99255

Follow-Up Inpatient Consultations

This subcategory is used to code for continued monitoring of the patient's progress and advising on care plan changes at the request of the attending physician. The provision here is that these are requested services. If the consultant physician assumes follow-up care after initiating treatment, the situation would call for subsequent hospital care codes. Patient status is established.

Dr. Simpson requests Dr. Weiss, the endocrinologist, to re-evaluate Mr. Jacobs who has insulin-dependent diabetes following his surgery because of elevated glucose levels. Dr. Weiss confers with the patient and staff, reviews his glucose and insulin levels and readjusts the insulin scale.

- A problem focused interval history—Dr. Weiss confers with the patient and staff.
- A problem focused examination—Dr. Weiss reviews his glucose and insulin levels and readjusts the insulin scale.
- Medical decision making that is straightforward or of low complexity—insulin-dependent diabetes

The medical service is requested and the consultant is not participating on a regular basis in the management of care.   CODE..........99261

Dr. James, attending physician for Mr. Smith, who is being treated for pneumonia, requests that Dr. Evans re-evaluate the patient because of laboratory findings that indicate a resistance to one of his prescribed antibiotics. Dr. Evans reviews the medical record and discusses progress of treatment with the patient. He examines the patient, reviews laboratory data and recommends changes in the antibiotic therapy.

- An expanded problem focused interval history—Dr. Evans reviews the medical record and discusses progress of treatment with the patient.
- An expanded problem focused examination—He examines the patient, reviews laboratory data and recommends changes in the antibiotic therapy.
- Medical decision making of moderate complexity—pneumonia

Once again, the medical services are requested due to changes in the presenting problem.   CODE..........99262

Mr. Smith develops an acute asthmatic attack during his hospitalization. Dr. James requests that Dr. Berger, the pulmonary specialist, evaluate the patient. Dr.

Berger obtains history information from Dr. James and hospital staff, examines the patient, reviews laboratory data and recommends placing the patient on ventilation assist.

- A detailed interval history—Dr. Berger obtains history information from Dr. James and hospital staff.

- A detailed examination—Dr. James examines the patient, reviews laboratory data and recommends placing the patient on ventilation assist.

- Medical decision making of high complexity—Acute asthma with pneumonia

The patient has developed a significant complication and the consultant is requested by the attending physician to re-evaluate the situation.

CODE..........99263

Confirmatory Consultations

This subcategory is used when the medical service requested is for establishing a second or third opinion and not treatment of an established medical problem. The request can come from the patient, patient's family or third party involvement (insurance/employer). The codes are used when the consultant is aware that the diagnosis is established and that opinion rather than treatment is requested. Certainly there can be confirmed or recommended alternative treatment as a result of this medical service. If the service is required as in a request from a third party payer, the modifier "32" should be added to indicate mandated services. Patient status can be new or established.

The coding levels, from 99271 to 99275, follow the problem focused history and exam with straightforward medical decision making to comprehensive history and exam with medical decision making of high complexity. The components as described in office and inpatient consultations would be the same, only the origin of the request would change. The medical service would include counseling and recommendation or confirmation of treatment.

▬ Highlights

- *Consultation services are provided by a physician at the request of another physician for advice/opinion regarding medical care.*

- *If the consultant continues to attend the patient for medical services rendered as the result of initial consultation, use office visit or subsequent care codes (99211–99215/99231–99233).*

- *If the request is from a patient or third party for opinion, use confirmatory consultation codes.*

EXERCISE 2–4

Code the following scenarios:

1. Office consultation for a 64-year-old female with recurrent chest pain and cardiac arrhythmia, unresponsive to medical treatment. _____

2. Initial inpatient consultation for a 39-year-old male with incisional abscess requiring management of antibiotic therapy by Infectious Disease specialist. _____

3. Follow-up inpatient consultation for patient with acute renal failure.

   _____

4. When a third party requires a consultation, what modifier is used?

   _____

EMERGENCY DEPARTMENT SERVICES   99281–99288

In this category, the place of service is given prime consideration. Commonly we think of medical services performed in the emergency room as being those requiring immediate attention. To qualify for the Emergency Department service codes, the facility must be hospital based and equipped for the evaluation and management of unscheduled episodic services required for those immediate problems. Patient status can be new or established. It is important to note that if the patient requires admission by the same physician seeing the patient in the Emergency Department, only one service code, that of initial hospital inpatient services would be used. It is possible for a patient to receive services from an emergency department physician and then have admission services provided by another physician. Each physician would code from his or her respective category (Emergency Department Services 99281–99285 and Initial Hospital Care 99221–99223).

Josh Powers, a 10-year-old, is seen for a bee sting on his right forearm. On examination the area is only slightly inflamed. Cool compresses and Cort-Aid ointment is prescribed.

- A problem focused history—Josh Powers, a 10-year-old, is seen for a bee sting on his right forearm
- A problem focused examination—On examination the area is only slightly inflamed
- Straightforward medical decision making—bee sting

While uncomplicated problems may be seen in the emergency department, the situation surrounding the actual event may dictate this place of service. This can include time of day, concern for complications or lack of information regarding traditional medical services.   CODE..........99281

Jean Smith, a 24-year-old woman, splashed some window cleaner into her right eye. She immediately flushed the eye with cool water. On examination there is moderate inflammation of the conjunctiva but no abrasion to the cornea or visual disturbance. Additional irrigation of the eye with saline is done and the patient is advised to apply cool compresses and follow-up with her personal physician if there is any continuing problem.

- An expanded problem focused history—Jean Smith, a 24-year-old woman, splashed some window cleaner into her right eye. She immediately flushed the eye with cool water
- An expanded problem focused examination—On examination there is moderate inflammation of the conjunctiva but no abrasion to the cornea or visual disturbance
- Medical decision making of low complexity—inflammation of the eye

CODE..........99282

Mrs. Patterson, an 80-year-old woman, is seen for vomiting and diarrhea for the past 10 hours. On examination she has mild abdominal discomfort and no evidence of bloody stool. She has a history of diverticulitis. Her last episode of vomiting and diarrhea was 2 hours ago. She does not show signs of dehydration. Mrs. Patterson was advised not to eat anything for the next 4–8 hours and then resume a clear liquid diet. An antiemetic was prescribed and she was advised to follow-up with her personal physician if her symptoms persisted. Her diagnosis is gastroenteritis.

- An expanded problem focused history—Mrs. Patterson, an 80-year-old woman, is seen for vomiting and diarrhea for the past 10 hours. She has a history of diverticulitis. Her last episode of vomiting and diarrhea was 2 hours ago.
- An expanded problem focused examination—On examination she has mild abdominal discomfort and no evidence of bloody stool. She does not show signs of dehydration.
- Medical decision of moderate complexity—Her diagnosis is gastroenteritis and diverticulosis.

While the gastroenteritis may be self-limiting, we have the situation of a patient who is elderly and prone to dehydration, plus the problem of diverticulosis, while not currently a problem, did require additional consideration.

CODE..........99283

John Wilson, a 32-year-old man, fell on icy pavement, landing on his right shoulder. The area is painful and motion is limited. He is in good general health. On examination the patient can only extend his arm about 10 degrees. The skin area is bruised. An X-ray is obtained which shows no fracture. The patient's arm is placed in a sling for immobilization. Non-steroidal anti-inflammatory medication is prescribed for the shoulder pain. The patient is advised to follow-up with his personal physician to monitor the effect of the medication and immobilization.

- A detailed history—John Wilson, a 32-year-old man, fell on icy pavement, landing on his right shoulder. The area is painful and motion is limited. He is in good general health.
- A detailed examination—On examination the patient can only extend his arm about 10 degrees. The skin area is bruised. An X-ray is obtained which shows no fracture.
- Medical decision making of moderate complexity—*shoulder pain*

CODE..........99284

Michelle Crawford, a 48-year-old woman, is seen for a fainting episode. She was observed to demonstrate seizure-like activity during the period of unconsciousness. She is experiencing a severe headache presently. She also has hypertension, controlled with 20mg. Inderal daily. A complete history and physical examination per review of systems is obtained. Except for the current headache, there are no other significant problems. A MRI is ordered because of this and the report of seizure activity. A consult by a neurologist is obtained. Diagnosis is deferred pending additional evaluation.

- A comprehensive history—per form outline (refer to Figure 2–1)
- A comprehensive examination—per form outline (refer to Figure 2–2)
- Medical decision making of high complexity—syncope/seizure activity

CODE..........99285

Other Emergency Services

In addition to on-site emergency department services, the physician may be required to direct emergency care via two-way communication (phone/video link) with ambulance and rescue teams outside the hospital. Currently there is only one code to identify this service. It can represent direction of telemetry, cardio-pulmonary resuscitation, airway intubation, drug administration and any other appropriate emergency medical support.   CODE..........99288

■ *Highlights*

- *This is a place of service indicator code—facility must be Emergency Department.*

- *For immediate medical attention services that are performed in the physician's office, use office visit codes.*

CRITICAL CARE SERVICES   99291–99292

This category will address the medical services provided when the patient's condition requires concentrated, continuous medical direction. This can involve failure of one or more body systems, acute post-operative complications, severe injuries and overwhelming infections. It is the maximum severity of illness and intensity of services scenario. Critical care begins when a patient's condition deteriorates and management of care to understand and direct necessary treatment and procedures requires the physician's constant presence. Often the level of care is such that it takes place in a critical care or coronary care unit. However, place of service is not a deciding factor here. What is appropriate in the coding of these services is to differentiate critical care **time** from other procedures that may be performed during patient management. Some procedures are inclusive in the critical care codes. These are: diagnostic interpretation, gastric intubation, temporary transcutaneous pacing, ventilator management and vascular access procedures. Other procedures that may be performed would be coded separately. These could be items like tracheostomy, intubation, angioplasty and various other surgical or medical procedures. The key is that critical care codes are used to identify the time spent in a one to one situation with the patient to manage a complex and unstable medical situation. A code is selected according to the amount of time spent.

Critical care, evaluation and management, first hour	CODE..........99291
Critical care, each additional 30 minutes	CODE..........99292

The next time frame is considered after 15 minute intervals. For example: care that takes one hour and 10 minutes would still be 99291, while care that takes one hour and 15 minutes up to one hour and 44 minutes would be 99291, plus 99292 x1. As the half-hour increments increase, the code 99292 is indicated with the addition of x1, x2, x3, depending on the number of additional units. For time spent in critical care that is *less than a half-hour*, an appropriate hospital subsequent hospital care code would be used. Typically this would be 99232 or 99233.

Once the patient's condition has become more stable, even though the place of service may still be the intensive or critical care unit, the codes used will be subsequent hospital care.

■ *Highlights*

- *Critical care codes depend on the severity of illness and constant medical attention required, not the location where the service was provided.*

- *Critical care codes are based on time spent for management of unstable medical conditions.*

- *To report follow-up care of patients with stable conditions, even though they are in a critical care area, the subsequent hospital care codes are used.*

NEONATAL INTENSIVE CARE   99295–99297

This category addresses the critical care issue for the neonate or infant. As the CPT description implies, it is inclusive of monitoring and treatment of the patient including enteral and parenteral nutritional maintenance, metabolic and hematological maintenance; pharmacological control of the circulatory system; parent counseling; case management services and personal, direct supervision of the health care team in the performance of cognitive and procedural activities. There is also "global" inclusion of other procedures listed in the CPT book. Many of these procedures are typical of what becomes part of the management for the critically ill neonate or infant. It is the intense, continuous direction and responsibility for maintenance of all body systems in a fragile environment. If the physician responsible for the patient in the intensive care setting also assisted in the delivery and newborn resuscitation, those services would be coded separately.

On admission to a neonatal intensive care unit, the medical services include full monitoring and preparation for possible surgery per description in the CPT text. This code applies to the first day of admission and is termed:

Initial neonatal intensive care   CODE..........99295

For the next 24 hours and for subsequent 24-hour periods, the next two codes will be chosen based on the degree of healthcare direction.

For the critically ill and *unstable* neonate or infant with frequent monitoring and regulation of ventilators, IV fluid alteration, unstable post-operative situations and other variables:

Subsequent neonatal intensive care   CODE..........99296

For the critically ill though *stable* neonate or infant with less frequent changes and adjustments to respiratory, cardiovascular and nutritional needs but still requiring frequent physician monitoring and re-evaluation:

Subsequent neonatal intensive care   CODE..........99297

With the degree of variables and global or inclusive procedures listed in this category, it is advisable to read the parameters closely in the CPT book when determining the appropriate code.

■ *Highlights*

- *Very specific codes for Neonatal Intensive Care.*

- *Pre-admission services (delivery and newborn resuscitation) are coded separately.*

EXERCISE 2–5

1. A patient comes to the physician's office with severe chest pain, shortness of breath and marked perspiration. After examination and EKG, it is determined that he is having a myocardial infarction. 911 is called and the patient is taken to the hospital for admission to the coronary care unit. The physician who provided the emergency office services will be his attending physician on admission. Which category below would be used to code his services? _____

 A. Office or other outpatient services

 B. Emergency department services

 C. Critical care services

 D. Hospital inpatient services

 E. Prolonged services

2. What is the difference between Newborn Care and Neonatal Intensive Care categories? _____

NURSING FACILITY SERVICES   99301–99316

A patient requiring supervised medical care for chronic health problems that cannot be managed in their home environment will be admitted to a "nursing home." These facilities can be distinguished by the extent of services they provide. Some facilities provide varying levels of service within one physical location. It is also possible for hospitals to have designated areas for intermediate care. These can be referred to as transitional care units (TCU). Most nursing homes are now referred to as long term care facilities (LTCF) and they typically include skilled nursing, intermediate and long term care units. When these facilities provide convalescent, rehabilitative or long term care they are required to conduct comprehensive, accurate, standardized and reproducible assessments of each resident's functional capacity using a Resident Assessment Instrument (RAI). This means maintaining a medical record on each resident (patient) so that problems are identified and follow-up is pursued. All residents are under the supervision of a physician. It can be their personal physician or an assigned facility physician. Their role is to ensure physical assessment of the patient and development of a medical care plan with periodic evaluations of patient status. They are available for any medical or psychosocial intervention required during the resident's stay in the facility. There are two subcategories involved in coding for nursing facility services, comprehensive and subsequent.

Comprehensive Nursing Facility Assessments

The following codes will cover the admission evaluation and management services provided in a nursing facility. If the patient is seen in an emergency room, hospital or physician's office on the same date as nursing facility admission, the nursing facility codes will be used to cover all services performed on that date. If a patient is admitted following hospitalization, the physician may code for the hospital discharge and the admission to the nursing facility on the same date. Patient status of new or established does not affect the code.

Mrs. Henry is an 86-year-old resident at Mountain View Nursing Center. She has been in the facility for two years. Her health problems include osteoarthritis, hypertension and hearing loss. She takes four aspirin and one Dyazide daily. On examination, her blood pressure is normal and complete review of systems does not indicate any change in her physical status. Dr. Zimmer, an otolaryngologist, will be consulted regarding her hearing loss. She uses the support of a walker for ambulation, has a good appetite and participates in activities.

■ A detailed interval history—Her health problems include osteoarthritis, hypertension and hearing loss. She takes four aspirin and one Dyazide daily

■ A comprehensive examination—On examination, her blood pressure is normal and complete review of systems does not indicate any change in her physical status. Dr. Zimmer, an otolaryngologist, will be consulted regarding her hearing loss. She uses the support of a walker for ambulation, has a good appetite and participates in activities.

■ Medical decision making of low complexity—osteoarthritis, hypertension and hearing loss

This would be a routine annual evaluation.   CODE..........99301

Mr. Burton is an 88-year-old resident at Mountain View Nursing Center. He has been at the facility for one year following a CVA (stroke). Three weeks ago, he fell and fractured his left hip. He has been readmitted following hospitalization. His medications for hypertension and ASHD (arteriosclerotic heart disease) are unchanged. A complete physical examination is done, revealing normal vital signs and good general condition except for residual gait instability. He will be continuing with physical therapy to improve ambulation. Revision of care plan will include new therapy.

■ A detailed interval history—He has been at the facility for one year following a CVA (stroke). Three weeks ago, he fell and fractured his left hip. He has been readmitted following hospitalization. His medications for hypertension and ASHD (arteriosclerotic heart disease) are unchanged.

■ A comprehensive examination—A complete physical examination is done, revealing normal vital signs and good general condition except for residual gait instability. He will be continuing with physical therapy to improve ambulation.

■ Medical decision making of moderate complexity—Fracture, left hip, CVA, ASHD

Annual exam incorporating new problem.   CODE..........99302

Mrs. Rogers, a 68-year-old woman, is admitted to Mountain View Nursing Center. She has been diagnosed with multiple sclerosis for 8 years. Her condition has deteriorated to the point where she has very limited movement. She can only sit in a wheelchair for short periods of time, requires assistance for eating and dressing. A complete history and physical examination is obtained using the review of systems. An evaluation is made for establishing a care plan to indicate proper assistance in personal care and daily functions along with parameters to monitor her medical condition.

■ A comprehensive history—per form outline (refer to Figure 2–1)

■ A comprehensive examination—per form outline (refer to Figure 2–2)

■ Medical decision making of high complexity—multiple sclerosis

CODE..........99303

While there may be additional forms required by nursing facility administration, the general history and physical guidelines apply for this admission process. It is the development of the care plan to cover all of the patient needs with recognition of family input that constitutes a major role in providing nursing facility services. Because of the nature of long term care, the coding covers annual evaluation and the admission/readmission process.

Subsequent Nursing Facility Care

Following the admission and in between major changes that may occur in the patient's condition, medical services may be required. The physician responsible for the patient's care will be evaluating their status periodically for management of the resident's chronic conditions. Patient status for this subcategory is new or established.

Mrs. Andrews, a 75-year-old at Mountain View Nursing Center, is seen by her physician for follow-up on a decubitus ulcer on her right ankle. On examination the area is properly supported to relieve pressure and there is evidence of new tissue growth. Current treatment protocol will be continued.

- A problem focused interval history—Follow-up on a decubitus ulcer on her right ankle.

- A problem focused examination—On examination the area is properly supported to relieve pressure and there is evidence of new tissue growth.

- Straightforward medical decision making—decubitus ulcer, right ankle

CODE..........99311

Mr. Hollingsworth, an 87-year-old resident of Mountain View Nursing Center, has developed nausea, vomiting and diarrhea for 24 hours. He is seen by his physician who finds his abdomen to be a little distended. Bowel sounds are active and other than the cramping with diarrhea, there is no abdominal pain or tenderness. His temperature is 99.6. The patient is placed on clear liquids only and prescribed an antiemetic. He will also have his temperature monitored every four hours for the next 24 hours. The nursing staff will report on the patient's progress on the following day.

- An expanded problem focused interval history—Mr. Hollingsworth, an 87-year-old resident of Mountain View Nursing Center, has developed nausea, vomiting and diarrhea for 24 hours.

- An expanded problem focused examination—He is seen by his physician who finds his abdomen to be a little distended. Bowel sounds are active and other than the cramping with diarrhea, there is no abdominal pain or tenderness. His temperature is 99.6.

- Medical decision making of moderate complexity—nausea, vomiting, diarrhea

CODE..........99312

Mrs. Jones, an 84-year-old resident at Mountain View Nursing Center, has developed a fever of 102 degrees, along with a productive cough. She also suffers from chronic obstructive pulmonary disease (COPD). She is seen by her physician who thoroughly evaluates her respiratory system, listening to her lungs and obtaining pulse oximetry. There is no evidence of pneumonia but with her comprised lung capacity, the patient is placed on antibiotic therapy and respiratory protocol. The nursing staff will report on her condition the following day.

■ A detailed interval history—Mrs. Jones, an 84-year-old resident at Mountain View Nursing Center, has developed a fever of 102 degrees, along with a productive cough.

■ A detailed examination—She is seen by her physician who thoroughly evaluates her respiratory system, listening to her lungs and obtaining pulse oximetry.

■ Medical decision making of moderate to high complexity—Upper respiratory infection/COPD

CODE..........99313

The patient's illness can be managed in the nursing facility but there is added risk when the patient has an upper respiratory infection along with the COPD. Close monitoring will be required.

Nursing Facility Discharge Services

When the patient's medical condition has advanced to the point where services at the nursing facility are no longer needed, the patient is discharged. As with hospital discharge services, a similar protocol exists here. There is a final examination of the patient to verify discharge and discuss facility stay. Instructions are given to the patient and family for continuing care, medication use and prescriptions. Discharge records are prepared as well as any other paperwork issues. The code is chosen dependent on the amount of time involved.

Nursing facility discharge day management
30 minutes or less   CODE..........99315
more than 30 minutes   CODE..........99316

■ *Highlights*

■ *Nursing facility services are provided in established centers for resident care.*

■ *This can be long term, intermediate or transitional, skilled and psychiatric care.*

■ *Physician supervision of care is required.*

DOMICILIARY, REST HOME (E.G., BOARDING HOME), OR CUSTODIAL CARE SERVICES   99321–99350

This category is used in the instance when the patient needs to have supervised care, generally from the standpoint of personal care issues. The patient can be in a facility that provides this service to others as in a boarding home or domiciliary, or they can be receiving the care in their home by an assigned custodian. There is no medical supervision provided as would be found in a nursing care facility. Facility services provided are personal care, meal preparation and general supervision of activities. When particular health care issues need to be addressed in some instances the patient can be taken to a medical office or clinic for services. In this instance, office visit codes would be used. If the healthcare provider comes to the facility, then this category of codes would be applicable. This category actually indicates "place of service." The procedural codes are identified as new and established, the same as in the office visit category. The necessary components are history, examination and medical decision making.

CODE range for New Patient   99321–99323
CODE range for Established Patient   99331–99333

■ *Highlights*

- *Note that the level of service only goes to <u>Detailed</u> history and examination.*
- *Remember to indicate "New" or "Established" patient.*

HOME SERVICES

This category is used to code "house calls." When evaluation and management services are provided in the patient's private residence these codes will reflect the "place of service." Once again, the components of history, examination and medical decision making are present at varying levels of service, including comprehensive services. The provider of services can be a physician or home health services personnel. A distinction is made between a new or an established patient as in office visit codes.

CODE range for New Patient   99341–99345
CODE range for Established Patient   99347–99350

PROLONGED SERVICES   99354–99360

When medical services extend beyond the usual and customary parameters as stated in the procedural code description, this category can be used to adequately describe the services rendered. This area should not be confused with Critical Care codes. If the patient's condition is *unstable*, critical care codes are used. The patient in this situation has not deteriorated to unstable but requires more intense management generally to prevent more serious consequences. The following subcategories will give the details necessary to choose the appropriate code.

Prolonged Physician Service with Direct (Face to Face) Patient Contact

This subcategory describes medical services when the physician is personally seeing the patient in either outpatient or inpatient settings. The appropriate evaluation and management code for these respective areas may indicate the type of service being provided but the situation may require additional monitoring, more in-depth history or diagnostic testing review. This would extend the actual time spent beyond that indicated in the code. In essence, we have an extension of time spent with the patient for valid reasons. If the patient is in the office, the appropriate office visit evaluation and management code could be used for the first half hour and the prolonged services code(s) would be used to indicate additional time spent. Both inpatient and outpatient services have a code indicating the first hour of prolonged service and then another code for each additional 30 minutes. The actual time spent on a given date does not have to be continuous. Any period of time less than 30 minutes would be included in the original evaluation and management code.

Outpatient Prolonged Service, first hour	99354
Each additional 30 minutes	99355
Inpatient Prolonged Service, first hour	99356
Each additional 30 minutes	99357

Prolonged Physician Service Without Direct (Face to Face) Patient Contact

When the prolonged service includes review of extensive records or tests and communication with other professionals or family members in regard to the patient's current condition, this subcategory is used. The actual time spent on a given date does not have to be continuous. While some of the time spent may be on the telephone, prolonged service codes are not used to report telephone calls. These will be discussed later. There are two codes used to indicate the time spent for prolonged service without face to face patient contact:

Prolonged Evaluation and Management, first hour	99358
Each additional 30 minutes	99359

Remember that in this category, 15 minutes must elapse before assigning another additional 30 minute code. For example: 1 hr. 15 min.—1 hr. 44 min. would be 99354 (99356 or 99358) x1 AND 99355 (99357 or 99359) x1. 1 hr. 45 min.—2 hr. 14 min. would be 99354 (99356 or 99358) x1 AND 99355 (99357 or 99359) x2. Always refer to the tables listed in CPT for qualifying time limits.

Physician Standby Services

This subcategory is used when the medical situation requires the *potential* need of the physician services. One physician will request the presence of another physician to be available for a high-risk delivery, cesarean section or other surgical or medical service. There is no direct patient contact nor should the physician be providing any other medical services at the time. In surgical situations, if the standby physician actually participates in the procedure, his services would be included in the surgical procedure code, thereby eliminating the standby service. One code is used to identify this service for each 30 minutes.   CODE..........99360

CASE MANAGEMENT SERVICES   99361–99373

The physician is the one responsible for the overall management of patient care. In the procedural coding system, we are identifying specific activities that provide for medical care. Various members of the healthcare team can be involved in the provision of services. Patients and their families, neighbors and employers need to be included in the communication loop. There are times when it is necessary for the physician to organize a group conference to effectively manage patient care, particularly when therapists, social workers and nursing staff are all needed. The telephone is a critical tool in relaying medical management information. Therapists, home health providers, pharmacists, nutritionists, laboratory and diagnostic facilities are all reporting to the physician on behalf of the patient. The physician is calling the patient to update on diagnostics, make changes in the care plans or to allay anxieties of both the patient and family members. This does represent a good deal of time spent and these services are coded by time and extent of service.

Team Conference

Medical Conference—physician with healthcare team

Approximately 30 minutes	99361
Approximately 60 minutes	99362

Telephone Calls

Telephone call by a physician to the patient or other healthcare team members for coordination of care, to report on diagnostic tests or integrate new treatment plan.   CODE..........99371

Intermediate telephone call to provide advice on a new problem, initiate therapy when appropriate, discuss diagnostic results in detail and coordinate medical management.   CODE..........99372

Complex or lengthy telephone call for counseling of patient, prolonged discussion with family of seriously ill patient or coordination of complex services.
                                                                      CODE..........99373

CARE PLAN OVERSIGHT SERVICES   99374–99380

In previous categories we have discussed the physician role in developing a medical care plan. In the outpatient setting (office visits) this generally includes the treatment and counseling given to the patient and documented in the medical record. In various facilities such as hospitals, nursing home, domiciliary and home services, a care plan is developed to outline specific treatments, medications, dietary and activity needs. It is used to track medical care information, adding and deleting procedures as necessary. This documentation is in addition to medical record entries that would include physician orders and progress notes relating to the medical care plan. When patients have multiple medical problems, requiring various therapies or complications and/or changes in their medical status, regardless of where the patient is located, there is physician supervision and responsibility for care. What differentiates this category is the fact that there is increased activity in medical care and consequences. For example: a patient with diabetes is reporting high glucose levels to the home health nurse, but no adverse symptoms. She reviews testing technique, insulin administration and diet with the patient and finds that he cannot read the label and syringe accurately. The patient also has a prosthesis for his left leg that he is not using because it feels too tight. The physician is notified; he requests a Hgb. A1C test, talks with the patient about his diabetes and calls the prosthetic technician to adjust the prosthesis. He also refers the patient to an ophthalmologist for an eye exam. The home health agency will visit three times a day for the next several days to review glucose levels and administer insulin per physician's order. This will be reported to the physician. Arrangements will be made for the patient to have larger print supplies and a magnifying glass. Over the next few days, the laboratory tests are reviewed, the dosage of insulin is changed and progress is made with the home health personnel, prosthetic technician and patient to ensure more accurate medical management. The recurrent nature of the medical care in this category differentiates it from coding for the telephone calls involved. It is the management of interim problems occurring in a medical situation that is ongoing. The following codes identify the facility and time involved within a calendar month.

Physician supervision of a patient under care of home health agency, requiring complex and multidisciplinary care. . .

15–29 minutes	CODE..........99374
30 minutes or more	CODE..........99375

Physician supervision of a hospice patient requiring complex and multidisciplinary care. . .

15–29 minutes	CODE..........99377
30 minutes or more	CODE..........99378

Physician supervision of a nursing facility patient requiring complex and multidisciplinary care. . .

15–29 minutes	CODE..........99379
30 minutes or more	CODE..........99380

PREVENTIVE MEDICINE SERVICES 99381–99440

This category is used to report services that are exclusively for the purpose of preventive medicine as opposed to a medical problem situation. It is used when a "healthy individual" is seeking a medical evaluation to maintain the healthy status, detect a problem early or be counseled further on preventive measures specific to their health experience (i.e., annual physical examination). As a result, there can be instances where actual medical problems are identified and the procedure would revert back to basic office visit evaluation and management codes. The modifier "-25" would be added to indicate both preventive medicine and office visit services were provided. The major thrust of preventive medicine services is a comprehensive history and physical examination with counseling for anticipated guidance and risk factor intervention. This could require additional counseling and that factor is also included as a subcategory of preventive medicine services. Patient status is both new *and* established.

New Patient

Initial preventive medicine evaluation and management of an individual including a comprehensive history and physical examination, counseling, anticipatory guidance and risk factor reduction:

Infant (age under one year)	CODE..........99381
Early Childhood (age 1–4 years)	CODE..........99382
Late Childhood (age 5–11 years)	CODE..........99383
Adolescent (age 12–17 years)	CODE..........99384
18–39 years	CODE..........99385
40–64 years	CODE..........99386
65 years and over	CODE..........99387

Established Patient

Periodic preventive medicine, re-evaluation and management of an individual including comprehensive history and physical examination, counseling, anticipatory guidance and risk factor reduction:

Infant (age under one year)	CODE..........99391
Early Childhood (age 1–4 years)	CODE..........99392
Late Childhood (age 5–11 years)	CODE..........99393
Adolescent (age 12–17 years)	CODE..........99394
18–39 years	CODE..........99395
40–64 years	CODE..........99396
65 years and over	CODE..........99397

Counseling and/or Risk Factor Reduction Intervention

In order to adequately promote health and prevent illness, additional counseling can be necessary. The initial preventive service would identify the individuals with a specific need and subsequent counseling could be arranged for the individual or for a group of persons with the same need. Typical issues could be diet, exercise, substance abuse, dental health, injury prevention, family problems and a variety of potential health problems identified as risk potential via medical history. Remember that this subcategory is for individuals who *do not* have the established symptoms or illness. Codes are differentiated by individual and group and represent time spent.

Individual Counseling

Preventive medicine counseling,	15 minutes	CODE..........99401
	30 minutes	CODE..........99402
	45 minutes	CODE..........99403
	60 minutes	CODE..........99405

Group Counseling

Preventive medicine counseling,	30 minutes	CODE..........99411
	60 minutes	CODE..........99412

Other Preventive Medicine Services

Administration and interpretation of health risk assessment instrument	CODE..........99420
Unlisted preventive	CODE..........99429

NEWBORN CARE

This category is used to report services to the newborn. They can be provided in a hospital, birthing center or other location and include initial examination, subsequent care, attendance at delivery and resuscitation. This is, in essence, an admission to the hospital or birthing center and the same-day rule applies. The infant seen for initial examination and discharged on the same day will use code 99435. Extended stays would have newborn care codes for initial examination, subsequent care and discharge services using code 99238 (hospital discharge services).

History and examination, initiation of treatment, preparation
  of hospital records, including birthing centers   CODE..........99431
Normal newborn care in *other* setting   CODE..........99432
Subsequent hospital care, per day   CODE..........99433
History and examination for *same day* assessment
  and discharge   CODE..........99435
Attendance at delivery and initial stabilization   CODE..........99436
  (used when services are requested by another physician)
Newborn resuscitation   CODE..........99440

SPECIAL EVALUATION AND
MANAGEMENT SERVICES   99450–99456

Under this category codes are used to report baseline information gained on evaluation and management for the purpose of life or disability application. Most of the insurance companies requesting the medical information have a specific form and format to be followed. Their goal is to match an applicant's health status against the norms for their age and gender. A fairly detailed history and examination is completed but there is no treatment or management of established medical problems included in the procedure. This service is for reporting purposes only.

Basic Life and/or Disability Evaluation Services

In this subcategory there is one code to include the services provided to establish the content of a basic life and/or disability examination. The components include vital sign measurement, medical history per form, collection of laboratory specimens and completion of necessary examination/documentation as required by the insurance company.

Basic life and/or disability examination   CODE..........99450

Work Related or Medical Disability Evaluation Services

In the process of completing the necessary information required by the insurer or agency involved in a Workers' Compensation or Disability Determination evaluation, reports are obtained from the treating physician as well as other physicians requested to examine and evaluate the condition for comparison and/or confirmation purposes. The services performed include medical history, examination, and diagnosis with assessment of capabilities, projected medical plan and completion of required forms or report. There are two codes used to differentiate between the *treating* and *other* physician.

Work related or medical disability examination
  by treating physician   CODE..........99455
Work related or medical disability examination
  by other than the treating physician   CODE..........99456

OTHER EVALUATION AND MANAGEMENT SERVICES 99499

This is the miscellaneous category, used to report an evaluation and management service that does not match a description listed in this section. It is advisable to include a detailed description of the service when using this code and copy any relevant information to clarify the content and purpose of the service.

Unlisted evaluation and management service   CODE..........99499

EXERCISE 2–6

1. A physician's office arranges group counseling for diet and exercise strategies to reduce the incidence of heart disease. The 60-minute session is available to patients in the 35–45-year-old range who do not have any current risk of heart disease. What would be the appropriate E&M code? _____

2. When courtesy calls are made to patients regarding their progress, is it appropriate to code and bill for them under the category of Case Management Services? _____

MODIFIERS USED IN EVALUATION AND MANAGEMENT

The listed services in Evaluation and Management as discussed in this chapter provide a specific category or subcategory to distinguish the type and extent to which medical services are provided. There can be circumstances where additional information, not included in the code description, needs to be added. The use of a **modifier** may be appropriate. The modifier is a two-digit number placed after the usual procedure number, separated by a hyphen. This number represents a particular explanation to further describe the procedure or circumstances involved with the procedure. The guidelines at the beginning of the Evaluation and Management section of CPT list the current, applicable, modifiers for this section. They include:

-21 *Prolonged E/M Services*—to be used when services exceed those described in the highest level E/M code within a given category for the basic service. Be sure to refer to the Prolonged Services category to differentiate code choice. Often a separate report may be needed to describe the actual circumstances. The five-digit modifier code for this service is 09921.

-24 *Unrelated E/M Service by the Same Physician during a Postoperative Period*—to be used when the patient, while recovering from a surgical procedure, is seen for another problem (or diagnosis) unrelated to the original procedure. The five-digit modifier for this service is 09924.

-25 *Significant, Separately Identifiable E/M Service by the Same Physician on the Same Day of a Procedure or Other Service*—to be used to clarify "same day" services as there is generally an appropriate E/M code to encompass all services provided for a given condition on a given day. A situation could occur where a patient is seen in the morning for follow-up related to asthma and then develop acute abdominal pain in the late afternoon. The five-digit modifier for this service is 09925.

-32 *Mandated Services*—to be used when a third party requests the service. If the service is a confirmatory consultation, this modifier is used in addition to that code. The five-digit modifier for this service is 09932.

-52 *Reduced Services*—to be used when the physician elects to reduce part of the service provided but not to the extent of changing the basic components of the service. The five-digit modifier for this service is 09952.

-57 *Decision for Surgery*—to be used when the medical service provided resulted in the initial decision to perform surgery. The five-digit modifier for this service is 09957.

While the use of a modifier can substantially support the information required to justify the use of a specific E/M code, keep in mind that if the circumstances are complex, a written report can provide the necessary clarification.

SUMMARY

- Codes for medical services that describe the cognitive skills involved in providing medical care are included within the Evaluation and Management section of *CPT*.

- The E&M codes are determined by identifying three key components: history, examination and medical decision making.

- The E&M codes are supported by contributory components: counseling, coordination of care, presenting problem and time and the *extent or degree* to which these components are combined in a given service is referred to as level of service.

- The time that it takes to accomplish a medical service is also factored into the coding process.

- Another identifying element is the place where the service occurred; the various categories and subcategories lead coders to particular places where services are rendered with descriptive information to help coders decide when there is an overlap of services into one or more categories.

- The actuality of what occurred is documented in the medical record when medical services are provided, to verify that the code(s) chosen represent the medical service.

- Evaluation and management services relate *what* is done in a medical encounter into a 5-digit code.

REFERENCES

American Medical Association: Physicians' Current Procedural Terminology, CPT 98, Chicago, IL: American Medical Association, 1997.

Warden-Tamparo C., Lewis, M. *Diseases of the Human Body*, 2nd edition. Philadelphia: F.A. Davis, 1995.

Bates, B. *A Guide to Physical Examination*, 3rd edition. Philadelphia: Lippincott.

Module 3
Primary Care

Marie A. Moisio, MA, RRA

LEARNING OBJECTIVES

Upon successful completion of this module, you should be able to:

1. Describe the meaning of primary care.
2. Differentiate between a primary care physician and a specialist.
3. Discuss the relevance of Evaluation and Management Codes to primary care.
4. Explain the significance of the terms and phrases presented in the Medicine section guidelines.
5. Correctly assign Evaluation and Management and Medicine codes to services provided by the primary care physician.
6. Compare the criteria between a Consultation and a Referral.

INTRODUCTION

The term **primary care** has been part of the health care industry for a very long time. It has been applied to hospital services, nursing services, and physician services. No matter where the term is used, primary care is defined as the initial care rendered to an individual who exhibits a health problem. This initial care usually leads to decisions regarding the best way to resolve the health problem. Module 3 focuses on primary care as applied to physician services and related coding systems and conventions.

Other modules in this series have included specific references to ICD-9-CM diagnostic and procedure codes associated with physician specialties. Since primary care physicians provide initial services and treatments to patients who exhibit a variety of diagnoses, there is no one specific ICD-9-CM section associated with this type of practice. Coding conventions and guidelines described in previous and future modules or chapters apply to Module 3 as well.

Current Procedural Terminology (CPT) Evaluation and Management (E/M) and Medicine codes are the mainstay of primary care. However, keep in mind that every service provided by a primary care physician must be coded using the appropriate CPT code from the appropriate CPT section. The patient's diagnosis or problem that triggers the service must be coded using the appropriate ICD-9-CM code. This module will describe the term **primary care physician**, discuss

CPT service or procedure codes associated with primary care, and identify Medicare considerations.

Primary Care Physician

A primary care physician is often described as the first health practitioner to assess or examine an individual or patient. The primary care physician is usually responsible for identifying the patient's health problems, developing a treatment course, and providing recommendations for referrals or consultations as necessary. Historically, general practitioners were identified as primary care physicians who managed all patient problems, often from birth to death. As medicine became more specialized, general practitioners decreased in number. The recent explosion of health care costs provided the impetus for the re-emergence of general practitioners, now known as primary care physicians.

In today's health care environment, family practice physicians, internal medicine physicians, pediatricians, and the traditional general practitioner represent the majority of primary care physicians. It is conceivable that other physician specialties could assume the role of primary care physician. However, as the name implies, most physician specialists focus their expertise on specific body systems or disease processes.

Managed Care

Increasing health care costs have also given rise to the concept of **managed care**. Managed care, simply put, is a method of delivering quality health care in a manner that places a priority on cost savings. There are any number of managed care programs available, and many programs are put in place by employers who provide health benefits for their employees. The central figure in the vast majority of managed care programs is the patient's primary care physician (PCP). Under a managed care contract, the individual selects a PCP from a list of physicians who participate in the managed care program. Since the PCP is responsible for monitoring referrals to other specialists, the primary care physician is often called the **gatekeeper**.

The primary care physician is the patient's first contact for any health problem. If the PCP cannot resolve the problem, he/she will "open the gate" to other physicians or specialists. As the patient's gatekeeper, the primary care physician must provide written justification for any referrals. If the patient chooses to seek treatment without the PCP referral, the patient could be held entirely responsible for paying the specialist's fee.

Whether the primary care physician is part of a managed care program or not, the CPT coding issues remain the same. All physicians must ensure that the documentation of patient care supports the selected CPT code. Coding specialists and, in some practices, billing specialists must take responsibility for coding accuracy. Accurate coding affects the financial health of the practice as well as the legal and ethical considerations surrounding physician reimbursement. Primary care physicians and primary care practices rely heavily on CPT evaluation and management and medicine codes.

EVALUATION AND MANAGEMENT (E/M) CODES

As previously stated, **Evaluation and Management (E/M)** and Medicine codes are the mainstay of primary care. The E/M codes are assigned to services provided in the office, hospital, nursing home, or other appropriate location. The general public may refer to these services as "visits." Evaluation and Management codes, numbered 99201–99499, are listed in the first section of the CPT manual. There are several key words and/or phrases associated with the E/M section. Module #1, CPT Coding: Evaluation and Management, provides a detailed discussion of E/M terms; a complete explanation of the factors that influence E/M levels of service; and a description of applicable two-digit modifiers. Individuals who are employed in a primary care setting are strongly encouraged to acquire a working knowledge of Evaluation and Management codes and guidelines, especially those subsections that are most applicable to the primary care setting. Table 3–1 identifies the E/M subsections that are often used to code primary care services and procedures. Cod-

TABLE 3–1   Evaluation and Management Subsections Related to Primary Care.

Subsection	Range of Codes	Primary Care
Office/Outpatient Services	99201–99215	highly related
Hospital Observation Services	99217–99220	highly related
Hospital Inpatient Services	99221–99239	highly related
Consultations	99241–99275	related
Emergency Department Services	99281–99288	related
Critical Care Services	99291, 99292	related
Neonatal Intensive Care	99295–99297	related
Nursing Facility Services	99301–99316	highly related
Domiciliary, Rest Home (e.g., Boarding Home), or Custodial Care Services	99321–99333	highly related
Home Services	99341–99350	highly related
Prolonged Services	99354–99360	highly related
Case Management Services	99361–99373	highly related
Care Plan Oversight Services	99374–99380	highly related
Preventive Medicine Services	99381–99429	highly related
Newborn Care	99431–99432	highly related
Special E/M Services*	99450–99456	highly related

*Special E/M Services include basic Life and/or Disability Evaluation Services *and* Work Related or Medical Disability Evaluation Services.

ing Exercise 3–1, which follows Table 3–1, provides an opportunity to apply E/M subsection codes to primary care physician services. In order to accurately utilize E/M subsections, the coder must be able to identify where the service was provided and whether the individual qualifies as a new or established patient.

EXERCISE 3–1

Assign the ICD-9-CM diagnostic codes and the CPT service and procedure codes to the following statements.

1. Hospital admission, 71-year-old female, long-standing insulin-dependent diabetes mellitus, poorly controlled, severe hypertension. _____

2. Initial nursing facility assessment for an 82-year-old malnourished, hypokalemic, hypotensive, edematous male in end-stage-renal disease (diabetic nephropathy) requiring hemodialysis 3x per week. Medical care plan developed and discussed with family and nursing facility staff. _____

3. Normal newborn history and physical examination. _____

4. Insurance history and physical examination. _____

5. Routine well-baby care for 6-month-old infant. Infant was previously seen at 6-week check-up. _____

6. Hospital visit for a 65-year-old female, complaining of nausea, chest pain, and difficulty swallowing, admitted four days ago with acute myocardial infarction. _____

7. Prolonged care of a 65-year-old hospitalized patient with CPR, 1 hour 30 min., for cardiac arrest _____

8. Allergy injection, single injection allergenic extract not provided, given to an established patient at home. _____

9. Initial office visit for a 71-year-old female with severe chronic obstructive pulmonary disease, congestive heart failure, renal hypertension, and a history of deep vein thrombosis. _____

Since primary care physicians are involved in consultations with and referrals to specialists, the criteria for consultations and referrals are discussed in this Module.

Consultation and Referral

While the CPT manual clearly delineates the difference between a consultation and a referral, many physicians use these terms interchangeably. Individuals who work in primary care must recognize and use the CPT definition for consultation and referral regardless of how the physician(s) may use the terms.

According to CPT, a **consultation** is "a type of service provided by a physician whose opinion or advice regarding evaluation and/or management of a specific problem is requested by another physician or other appropriate source." In other words, the primary physician may ask another physician, often a specialist, for treatment advice. Documentation of the consultation must include the name of the person who requested the consultation, name and results of any diagnostic tests, specific diagnoses if appropriate, and any recommended treatment. In a purely consultative relationship, the primary care physician retains responsibility for the management of patient care.

In the event that the primary care physician, after discussion with the patient, determines that patient care can be more appropriately managed by another physician, usually a specialist, the patient is then referred to the other physician. **Referral**, then, is defined as the transfer of the management of patient care from one physician to another. In this situation, the primary care physician relinquishes responsibility for the patient's care for that particular problem. As with a consultation, the referral process must be documented. The majority of managed care programs provide specific referral guidelines and forms that must be completed by the primary care physician. For coding and reimbursement purposes, most insurance companies use the terms consultation and referral as defined in this module.

Although consultations and referrals are often associated with requests and transfers between primary care physicians and specialists, there are circumstances under which the primary care physician may provide consultation services. Second opinions are an excellent example of consultation services between primary care physicians. A second opinion consultation, which CPT describes as a **confirmatory consultation**, can be initiated by the patient, the insurance carrier, the insurance company, or the physician. The purpose of a confirmatory consultation is to secure the opinion and/or advice of another physician. Primary care coders should be familiar with the guidelines governing the Consultation subsection of the Evaluation and Management codes.

Referrals between primary care physicians may occur when the patient changes location, insurance coverage, or simply desires to be treated by another physician. The circumstances surrounding the referral do not change the way in which a referral should be accomplished. Appropriate and timely documentation must be forwarded to the new physician and insurance forms should be completed promptly. Quality patient care is the primary goal of all health care practitioners.

Documentation Guidelines for Evaluation and Management Services

Documentation guidelines for E/M services are developed by the American Medical Association (AMA) and the Health Care Financing Administration (HCFA). The guidelines are intended to maintain consistency with information contained in CPT; minimize any changes in record-keeping practices; and facilitate uniform interpretation of E/M codes across the country. Accurate medical record documentation provides an excellent tool for evaluating patient care and monitoring that care over time; contributes to communication and continuity of patient care among physicians and other health care professionals; facilitates accurate and timely claims processing and payment; supports collection of data for education and research; and provides written testament that the physician met both professional and legal obligations as related to patient care.

Payers, individuals or insurance companies, have a financial stake in monitoring documentation of patient care. Medical insurance fraud and abuse seem rampant. Large health care systems and small private practices are under intense scrutiny to justify any and all claims. Never before has the maxim "if it isn't documented, it hasn't been done" been more relevant in all sectors of the health care industry.

The current E/M documentation guidelines are a direct result of the fact that all payers focus on controlling health care costs and exhibit an increased concern over ethical physician billing and insurance claim practices. It is not surprising that the federal Medicare program, which represents a substantial percentage of insurance coverage, takes an active role in developing documentation guidelines. The evaluation and management documentation guidelines address the three key components of E/M service levels and for visits which consist predominately of counseling or coordination of care.

Most evaluation and management subsections have three or four codes that are used to describe what the physician does during his/her interaction with the patient. These codes are known as E/M service levels. Terms like problem focused, expanded problem focused, detailed, and comprehensive are used to differentiate the levels of E/M services. There are seven components that are associated with each E/M service: history, physical examination, medical decision making, counseling, coordination of care, nature of presenting problem, and time. Module 2, CPT Coding: Evaluation and Management, presents detailed coverage of the seven components, six of which are used in defining the levels of E/M services.

Not all components are present in all E/M service codes. However, CPT does identify three **key components** associated with E/M service codes. Key components used to select the appropriate level of E/M service are history, physical examination, and medical decision making. Some service codes require all three "key" components and others require two of the three key components. As a general rule, all three components are required in order to select "new patient" or "initial inpatient" E/M codes. When a visit or service consists predominantly (50% or more) of counseling or coordination of care, time is the key or controlling factor used to select the appropriate E/M service level. As previously stated, a complete discussion of the CPT Evaluation and Management Section is presented in Module 2.

Since primary care practices rely heavily on E/M codes, this module focuses on the documentation guidelines for the three key components mentioned previously, as well as the guidelines for services that are influenced by time. Each component, including time, is discussed individually.

History

The patient's history is one of three key components for evaluation and management service levels. There are four types of history: problem focused; expanded problem focused; detailed; and comprehensive. The general elements of a patient history include a chief complaint (CC), history of present illness (HPI), review of systems (ROS), and past, family, and/or social history (PFSH). Each of these general elements contributes to the overall type of history, depending on how much of the patient history is documented by the physician. The general elements are categorized as brief, problem pertinent, extended, pertinent, and complete. Documentation guidelines developed by AMA and HCFA describe the type of information that differentiates each category of each history element. Table 3–2 lists the general element, specific topics related to each general element, and the documentation requirements for each general element category.

After reviewing Table 3–2 the difference between the terms "brief," "problem pertinent," "extended," "pertinent," and "complete" as applied to each element of a history is readily apparent. For example: An extended history of present illness describes at least four of the topics associated with the present illness, or the status of at least three chronic or inactive conditions.

TABLE 3–2   Categories and Documentation Requirements for History Elements.

Element/Topics	*Category/Documentation Requirements*
History of Present Illness ■ location ■ quality ■ severity ■ duration ■ timing ■ context ■ modifying factors ■ associated signs and symptoms	<u>BRIEF</u> History or Present Illness: The medical record describes one to three topics of the history of present illness. <u>EXTENDED</u> History of Present Illness: The medical record describes at least four topics of the history of present illness, or the status of at least three chronic or inactive conditions.
Review of Systems ■ constitutional symptoms (fever, weight loss, etc.) ■ eyes ■ ears, nose, mouth, throat ■ cardiovascular ■ respiratory ■ gastrointestinal ■ genitourinary ■ musculoskeletal ■ integumentary (skin and/or breast) ■ neurological ■ psychiatric ■ endocrine ■ hematologic/lymphatic ■ allergic/immunologic	<u>PROBLEM PERTINENT</u> Documentation of the patient's positive responses and pertinent negatives for the system related to the problem <u>EXTENDED</u> Documentation of the patient's positive responses and pertinent negatives for *two* to *nine* systems <u>COMPLETE</u> Documentation that at least *ten* organ systems were reviewed. Systems with positive or pertinent negative responses are individually documented. For the remaining systems, a notation indicating all other systems are negative is adequate. In the absence of such a notation, at least *ten* systems are individually recorded.
Past, Family and/or Social History ■ *past history:* past illnesses, injuries, and treatments ■ *family history:* a review of medical events in the patient's family, including diseases that may be hereditary or place the patient at risk ■ *social history:* an age appropriate review of past and current activities	<u>PERTINENT</u> Documentation of at least one specific item from any of the three history areas <u>COMPLETE</u> For **established patient** services in the office or other outpatient setting, domiciliary care, home care, or in the emergency department, at least one specific item from *two* of the three history areas must be documented. For **new patient** services in the office or other outpatient setting, domiciliary care, and home care; hospital observation services; hospital inpatient services, initial care; consultations; and comprehensive nursing facility assessments, at least one specific item from each of the *three* history areas must be documented.

Each history element contributes to the identification of the type of history generated by the physician/patient interaction. As previously stated, there are four types of history: problem focused, expanded problem focused, detailed, and comprehensive. Table 3–3 organizes the categories of each history general element in relation to a specific type of history. Note that *all* types of history require a chief complaint.

TABLE 3–3 General Elements Required for Each Type of History.*

History of Present Illness	Review of Systems	Past, Family, and/or Social History	Type of History
brief	n/a	n/a	**problem focused**
brief	problem pertinent	n/a	**expanded problem focused**
extended	extended	pertinent	**detailed**
extended	complete	complete	**comprehensive**

*A Chief Complaint required for ALL history types.

In order for the patient history to qualify as a specific type of history all four elements listed for the specific type of history must be met. Therefore, a comprehensive history must include a chief complaint, an extended HPI, a complete ROS, and a complete PSFH.

Examination

The physical examination of the patient is another of the three key components for evaluation and management service levels. As with history, there are four types of examination: problem focused, expanded problem focused, detailed, and comprehensive. The four types of examinations can be applied to a general multi-system exam or a single organ system exam. Table 3–4 compares the systems/body

TABLE 3–4 Systems/Body Areas Associated with General Multi-Systems Examinations and Single Organ System Examinations.

Systems/Body Areas: General Multi-System Exams	Systems/Body Areas: Single Organ System Exams
Constitutional	Cardiovascular
Eyes	Ears, Nose, Mouth, Throat
Ears, Nose, Mouth, Throat	Eyes
Neck	Genitourinary (Female)
Respiratory	Genitourinary (Male)
Cardiovascular	Hematologic/Lymphatic/Immunologic
Chest (Breasts)	Musculoskeletal
Gastrointestinal (Abdomen)	Neurological
Genitourinary (Male/Female)	Psychiatric
Lymphatic	Respiratory
Musculoskeletal	Skin
Skin	
Neurologic	
Psychiatric	

areas associated with a general multi-system and the systems/body areas associated with a single organ system.

The content and documentation requirements for a general multi-system examination and a single organ system examination are discussed individually.

General Multi-System Examination The content of **general multi-system examinations** is clearly delineated in the AMA/HCFA joint documentation guidelines. In order to qualify for a given type of multi-system examination, a specific number of examination topics must be included in the performance and documentation of the exam. Topics included in a general multi-system exam are summarized in Table 3–5. Note that the topics are preceded by a bullet.

TABLE 3–5 Topics Included in a General Multi-System Exam.

System/Body Area	Topics
Constitutional	■ any *three* of *seven* vital signs ▪ blood pressure, sitting or standing ▪ blood pressure, lying down ▪ pulse rate and regularity ▪ respiration ▪ temperature ▪ height ▪ weight ■ general appearance of the patient
Eyes	■ conjunctivae and lids ■ pupils and irises, reaction to light and accommodation, size and symmetry ■ ophthalmoscopic exam of optic discs and posterior segments
Ears, Nose, Mouth and Throat	■ external inspection of ears and nose ■ otoscopic examination of ears ■ hearing assessment ■ inspection of nasal mucosa, septum and turbinates ■ inspection of teeth and gums ■ examination of oral mucosa, salivary glands, hard and soft palates, tongue, tonsils, and posterior pharynx
Neck	■ examination of neck ■ examination of thyroid
Respiratory	■ assessment of respiratory effort ■ percussion of chest ■ palpation of chest ■ auscultation of lungs
Cardiovascular	■ palpation of heart ■ auscultation of heart with notation of abnormal sounds and murmurs Examination of: ■ carotid arteries ■ abdominal aorta ■ femoral arteries ■ pedal pulses ■ extremities for edema and/or varicosities

continues

Table 3–5 Topics Included in a General Multi-System Exam *continued*

System/Body Area	Topics
Chest (Breasts)	■ inspection of breasts ■ palpation of breasts and axillae
Gastrointestinal (Abdomen)	■ examination of abdomen, note presence of masses or tenderness ■ examination of liver and spleen ■ examination for presence/absence of hernia ■ examination, when necessary, of anus, perineum, and rectum ■ when indicated, obtain stool samples for occult blood tests
Genitourinary	**MALE** ■ examination of scrotal contents ■ examination of the penis ■ examination of the prostate, digital rectal **FEMALE:** Pelvic exam, with or without specimen collection, including: ■ external genitalia ■ urethra ■ cervix ■ uterus ■ adnexa/parametria
Lymphatic	Palpation of lymph nodes in **two or more** areas: ■ neck ■ axillae ■ groin ■ other
Musculoskeletal	■ examination of gait and station ■ inspection and/or palpation of digits and nails Examination of muscles, bones, and joints of **one or more** of the following areas: ■ head and neck ■ spine, ribs, pelvis ■ right upper extremity ■ left upper extremity ■ right lower extremity ■ left lower extremity The examination of any one of the listed areas includes: ■ inspection and/or palpation with notation of any problems ■ assessment of range of motion with notation of pain, crepitation, or contracture ■ assessment of stability with notation of any dislocation, subluxation, or laxity ■ assessment of muscle strength and tone, with notation of any atrophy or abnormal movements
Skin	■ inspection of skin and subcutaneous tissue ■ palpation of skin and subcutaneous tissue
Neurologic	■ test cranial nerves with notation of any deficits ■ examination of deep tendon reflexes with notation of pathological reflexes ■ examination of sensation

continues

Table 3–5 **Topics Included in a General Multi-System Exam** *continued*

System/Body Area	Topics
Psychiatric	■ description of adjustment and insight Brief assessment of mental status including: ■ orientation to time, place, and person ■ recent and remote memory ■ mood and affect

Each type of examination, problem focused, expanded problem focused, detailed, and comprehensive, requires that a specific number of systems must be reviewed and documented. Additionally, a specific number of each system's bulleted topics must also be reviewed and documented. Table 3–6 identifies the content and documentation requirements for each type of examination as they relate to a general multi-system exam.

After reviewing Tables 3–5 and 3–6, it is apparent that the types of examinations are dependent on the number of systems reviewed or affected, and the amount of documented information related to those systems. Examination documentation should clearly describe any abnormal findings. A notation of "abnormal" is not sufficient. Relevant negative findings associated with the affected or symptomatic organ systems and body areas should also be documented. Statements like "neg-

TABLE 3–6 **General Multi-System Examinations Content and Documentation Requirements for Each Type of Examination.**

Type of Examination	Content/Documentation Requirements
Problem Focused Examination	one or more organ system(s) or body area(s) with one or more bulleted topics
Expanded Problem Focused	one or more organ system(s) or body area(s) with a total of at least six bulleted topics
Detailed Examination	at least six organ systems or body areas with at least two bulleted topics for each system or body area system/area
	OR
	two or more organ systems or body areas with at least twelve bulleted topics
Comprehensive Examination	at least nine organ systems or body areas with all bulleted topics, unless specific conditions limit the content
	under all conditions at least two bulleted topics for each system must be included

ative" and "normal" are sufficient to document normal findings related to unaffected or asymptomatic systems and areas.

Single Organ System Examinations The eleven systems and body areas related to **single organ system examinations** are: cardiovascular; ears, nose, mouth, throat; eyes; genitourinary, male and female; hematologic/lymphatic/immunologic; musculoskeletal; neurological; psychiatric; respiratory; and skin. Each of these single organ systems is recognized by CPT. The content of single organ system examinations is clearly delineated in the AMA/HCFA joint documentation guidelines. Each single organ system exam has a unique set of emphasized or required topics. Beginning with Table 3–7 and continuing through Table 3–16, content and documentation requirements for each single organ system exam are presented. Note that the topics are preceded by a bullet.

Since each single organ system exam is associated with specific types of CPT examinations, each system is discussed individually. Following the appropriate single organ system content and documentation table, each examination type is defined. It is important to note that although the guidelines state a comprehensive examination should include performance of all bulleted topics, the expected documentation requirements are limited to specific bulleted topics.

Cardiovascular Examinations System/body areas and topics included in a cardiovascular examination are listed in Table 3–7.

Each level or type of cardiovascular examination requires that a specific number of bulleted topics be reviewed and documented. A problem focused examination must have one to five bulleted topics; an expanded problem focused examination must have at least six bulleted topics; and a detailed examination calls for at least twelve bulleted topics. In order to meet the comprehensive examination criteria, the physician should address all bulleted topics; document all bulleted topics listed under constitutional, respiratory, cardiovascular, gastrointestinal, and neurological/psychiatric systems or body areas; and document at least one bulleted topic listed under eyes; ears, nose, mouth, and throat; neck; musculoskeletal; extremities; and skin.

Ear, Nose, and Throat Examinations System/body areas and topics included in an ear, nose, and throat examination are listed in Table 3–8.

Each level or type of ear, nose, and throat examination requires that a specific number of bulleted topics be reviewed and documented. A problem focused examination must have one to five bulleted topics; an expanded problem focused examination must have at least six bulleted topics; and a detailed examination calls for at least twelve bulleted topics. In order to meet the comprehensive examination criteria, the physician should address all bulleted topics; document all bulleted topics listed under the following systems/body areas: constitutional; head and face; ears, nose, mouth, and throat; and neck; and document at least one bulleted topic listed under eyes, respiratory, cardiovascular, lymphatic, and neurological/psychiatric systems/body areas.

Eye Examinations System/body areas and topics included in eye examinations are listed in Table 3–9.

Each level or type of eye examination requires that a specific number of bulleted topics be reviewed and documented. A problem focused examination must have one to five bulleted topics; an expanded problem focused examination must have at least six bulleted topics; and a detailed examination calls for at least nine bulleted topics. In order to meet the comprehensive examination criteria, the physician should address all bulleted topics; document all bulleted topics related to the eyes; and document at least one bulleted topic from the neurological/psychiatric system.

TABLE 3–7   Topics Included in a Cardiovascular Examination.

System/Body Area	Topics

Constitutional	■ any *three* of *seven* vital signs
	  ▪ blood pressure, sitting or standing
	  ▪ blood pressure, lying down
	  ▪ pulse rate and regularity
	  ▪ respiration
	  ▪ temperature
	  ▪ height
	  ▪ weight
	■ general appearance of the patient

Eyes	■ inspection of conjunctivae and lids
Ears, Nose, Mouth and Throat	■ inspection of teeth, gums, palate ■ inspection of oral mucosa, with notation of presence of pallor or cyanosis
Neck	■ examination of jugular veins ■ examination of thyroid
Respiratory	■ assessment of respiratory effort ■ auscultation of lungs
Cardiovascular	■ palpation of heart ■ auscultation of heart including sounds, abnormal sounds, and murmurs ■ measurement of blood pressure in two or more extremities when indicated Examination of: ■ carotid arteries ■ abdominal aorta ■ femoral arteries ■ pedal pulses ■ extremities for peripheral edema and/or varicosities
Gastrointestinal (abdomen)	■ examination of abdomen, with notation of presence of masses or tenderness ■ examination of liver and spleen ■ obtain stool samples for occult blood tests from patients being considered for thrombolytic or anticoagulant therapy
Musculoskeletal	■ examination of back with notation of kyphosis or scoliosis ■ examination of gait with notation of ability to undergo exercise testing and/or participate in exercise programs ■ assessment of muscle strength and tone, with notation of any atrophy or abnormal movements
Extremities	■ inspection and palpation of digits and nails
Skin	■ inspection and palpation of skin and subcutaneous tissue
Neurological/Psychiatric	Brief assessment of mental status including: ■ orientation to time, place, and person ■ mood and affect

TABLE 3–8   Topics Included in an Ear, Nose, and Throat Examination.

System/Body Area	Topics

Constitutional	▪ any *three* of *seven* vital signs
	  ▫ blood pressure, sitting or standing
	  ▫ blood pressure, lying down
	  ▫ pulse rate and regularity
	  ▫ respiration
	  ▫ temperature
	  ▫ height
	  ▫ weight
	▪ general appearance of the patient
	▪ assessment of ability to communicate

Head and Face	▪ inspection of head and face ▪ palpation and/or percussion of face with notation of presence or absence of sinus tenderness ▪ examination of salivary glands ▪ assessment of facial strength
Eyes	▪ test ocular motility including primary gaze alignment
Ears, Nose, Mouth	▪ otoscopic examination of external auditory canals and tympanic membranes including pneumo-otoscopy with notation of mobility of membranes ▪ hearing assessment with tuning forks and clinical speech reception thresholds ▪ external inspection of ears and nose ▪ inspection of nasal mucosa, septum, and turbinates ▪ inspection of lips, teeth, and gums ▪ examination of oropharynx: oral mucosa, hard and soft palates, tongue, tonsils, and posterior pharynx ▪ inspection of pharyngeal walls and pyriform sinuses ▪ examination by mirror of larynx including the condition of the epiglottis, false vocal cords, true vocal cords, and mobility of larynx (mirror not required for children) ▪ examination by mirror of nasopharynx including appearance of the mucosa, adenoids, posterior choanae and eustachian tubes (mirror not required for children)
Neck	▪ examination of neck ▪ examination of thyroid
Respiratory	▪ inspection of chest including symmetry, expansion, and/or assessment of respiratory effort ▪ auscultation of lungs
Cardiovascular	▪ auscultation of heart with notation of abnormal sounds and murmurs ▪ examination of peripheral vascular system by observation and palpation
Lymphatic	▪ palpation of lymph nodes in neck, axillae, groin, and/or other location
Neurological/Psychiatric	▪ testing of cranial nerves with notation of any deficits Brief assessment of mental status including: ▪ orientation to time, place, and person ▪ mood and affect

TABLE 3–9   Topics Included in an Eye Examination.

System/Body Area	Topics
Eyes	■ test visual acuity ■ gross visual field testing ■ test ocular motility including primary gaze alignment ■ inspection of bulbar and palpebra conjunctivae ■ examination of ocular adnexa including lids, lacrimal glands, lacrimal drainage, orbits, and preauricular lymph nodes ■ examination of pupils and irises, including shape, direct and consensual reaction and morphology ■ slit lamp examination of corneas including epithelium, stroma, endothelium, and tear fill reaction to light and accommodation, size and symmetry ■ slit lamp examination of the anterior chambers including depth, cells, and fire ■ slit lamp examination of the lenses including clarity, anterior and posterior capsule, cortex, and nucleus ■ ophthalmoscopic examination through dilated pupils ■ optic discs including size, C/D ratio, appearance, and nerve fiber layer ■ posterior segments including retina and vessels
Neurological/Psychiatric	Brief assessment of mental status including: ■ orientation to time, place, and person ■ mood and affect

Genitourinary Examinations   System/body areas and topics included in genitourinary examinations are listed in Table 3–10. Note that there are differences in the topics associated with male and female patients.

Each level or type of genitourinary examination requires that a specific number of bulleted topics be reviewed and documented. A problem focused examination must have one to five bulleted topics; an expanded problem focused examination must have at least six bulleted topics; and a detailed examination calls for at least twelve bulleted topics. In order to meet the comprehensive examination criteria, the physician should address all bulleted topics; document all bulleted topics listed under constitutional, gastrointestinal, and either the male or female genitourinary system topics; and document at least one bulleted topic listed under neck; respi-

TABLE 3–10   Topics Included in a Genitourinary Examination.

System/Body Area	Topics
Constitutional	■ any *three* of *seven* vital signs ▪ blood pressure, sitting or standing ▪ blood pressure, lying down ▪ pulse rate and regularity ▪ respiration ▪ temperature ▪ height ▪ weight ■ general appearance of the patient

continues

Table 3–10   **Topics Included in a Genitourinary Examination** *continued*

System/Body Area	Topics
Neck	■ examination of neck ■ examination of thyroid
Respiratory	■ assessment of respiratory effort ■ auscultation of lungs
Cardiovascular	■ auscultation of heart with notation of abnormal sounds and murmurs ■ examination of peripheral vascular system by observation and palpation
Gastrointestinal (Abdomen)	■ examination of abdomen, with notation of presence of masses or tenderness ■ examination of liver and spleen ■ examination for presence/absence of hernia ■ when indicated, obtain stool samples for occult blood tests
Genitourinary	**MALE** ■ inspection of anus and perineum Examination, with or without collection for smears and cultures, of genitalia including: ■ scrotum ■ epididymides ■ testes ■ urethral meatus ■ penis Digital rectal examination including: ■ prostate gland ■ seminal vesicles ■ sphincter tone, presence of hemorrhoids, rectal masses
Genitourinary	**FEMALE:** Includes at least **seven of the eleven** listed items: ■ inspection and palpation of breasts ■ digital rectal examination including sphincter tone, presence of hemorrhoids, rectal masses Pelvic examination, with or without specimen collection for smears and cultures, including: ■ external genitalia ■ urethral meatus ■ urethra ■ bladder ■ vagina ■ cervix ■ uterus ■ adnexa/parametria ■ anus and perineum
Lymphatic	Palpation of lymph nodes in neck, axillae, groin, and/or other location
Skin	■ inspection and palpation of skin and subcutaneous tissue
Neurological/Psychiatric	Brief assessment of mental status including: ■ orientation to time, place, and person ■ mood and affect

ratory; cardiovascular; lymphatic; skin; and neurological/psychiatric systems/body areas.

Hematologic/Lymphatic/Immunologic Examinations System/body areas and topics included in hematologic/lymphatic/immunologic examination are listed in Table 3–11.

Each level or type of hematologic/lymphatic/immunologic examination requires that a specific number of bulleted topics be reviewed and documented. A problem focused examination must have one to five bulleted topics; an expanded problem focused examination must have at least six bulleted topics;

TABLE 3–11 Topics Included in a Hematologic/Lymphatic/Immunologic Examination.

System/Body Area	Topics
Constitutional	■ any *three* of *seven* vital signs 　▩ blood pressure, sitting or standing 　▩ blood pressure, lying down 　▩ pulse rate and regularity 　▩ respiration 　▩ temperature 　▩ height 　▩ weight ■ general appearance of the patient
Head and Face	■ palpation and/or percussion of face with notation of presence or absence of sinus tenderness
Eyes	■ inspection of conjunctivae and lids
Ears, Nose, Mouth and Throat	■ otoscopic examination of external auditory canals and tympanic membranes ■ inspection of nasal mucosa, septum and turbinates ■ inspection of teeth and gums ■ examination of oropharynx
Neck	■ examination of neck ■ examination of thyroid
Respiratory	■ assessment of respiratory effort ■ auscultation of lungs
Cardiovascular	■ auscultation of heart with notation of abnormal sounds and murmurs ■ examination of peripheral vascular system by observation and palpation
Gastrointestinal (Abdomen)	■ examination of abdomen, with notation of presence of masses or tenderness ■ examination of liver and spleen
Lymphatic	■ palpation of lymph nodes in neck, axillae, groin, and/or other locations
Extremities	■ inspection and palpation of digits and nails
Skin	■ inspection and palpation of skin and subcutaneous tissue
Neurological/Psychiatric	Brief assessment of mental status including: ■ orientation to time, place, and person ■ mood and affect

and a detailed examination calls for at least twelve bulleted topics. In order to meet the comprehensive examination criteria, the physician should address all bulleted topics; document all bulleted topics listed under constitutional; ears, nose, mouth, and throat; respiratory; cardiovascular; and gastrointestinal; systems or body areas; and document at least one bulleted topic listed under head and face; eyes; neck; lymphatic; extremities; skin; and neurological/psychiatric systems/body areas.

Musculoskeletal Examinations System/body areas and topics included in musculoskeletal examinations are identified in Table 3–12.

Each level or type of musculoskeletal examination requires that a specific number of bulleted topics be reviewed and documented. A problem focused examination must have one to five bulleted topics; an expanded problem focused examination must have at least six bulleted topics; and a detailed examination calls for at least twelve bulleted topics. In order to meet the comprehensive examination criteria, the physician should address all bulleted topics; document all bulleted topics listed under constitutional; musculoskeletal; skin; and neurological/psychiatric systems or body areas; and document at least one bulleted topic listed under cardiovascular; and lymphatic systems/body areas.

Neurological Examinations System/body areas and topics included in neurological examinations are listed in Table 3–13.

Each level or type of neurological examination requires that a specific number of bulleted topics be reviewed and documented. A problem focused examination must have one to five bulleted topics; an expanded problem focused examination must have at least six bulleted topics; and a detailed examination calls for at least twelve bulleted topics. In order to meet the comprehensive examination criteria, the physician should address all bulleted topics; document all bulleted topics listed under constitutional; eyes; musculoskeletal; and neurological systems/body areas; and document at least one bulleted topic listed under the cardiovascular system.

Psychiatric Examinations System/body areas and topics included in a psychiatric examination are listed in Table 3–14.

Each level or type of psychiatric examination requires that a specific number of bulleted topics be reviewed and documented. A problem focused examination must have one to five bulleted topics; an expanded problem focused examination must have at least six bulleted topics; and a detailed examination calls for at least nine bulleted topics. In order to meet the comprehensive examination criteria, the physician should address all bulleted topics; document all bulleted topics listed under constitutional and psychiatric system/body areas; and document at least one bulleted topic listed under the musculoskeletal system.

Respiratory Examinations System/body areas and topics included in a respiratory examination are listed in Table 3–15.

Each level or type of respiratory examination requires that a specific number of bulleted topics be reviewed and documented. A problem focused examination must have one to five bulleted topics; an expanded problem focused examination must have at least six bulleted topics; and a detailed examination calls for at least twelve bulleted topics. In order to meet the comprehensive examination criteria, the physician should address all bulleted topics; document all bulleted topics listed under constitutional; ears, nose, mouth, and throat; respiratory; cardiovascular; and gastrointestinal system/body areas; and document at least one bulleted topic listed under lymphatic, musculoskeletal, extremities, skin, and neurological/psychiatric system/body areas.

TABLE 3–12   **Topics Included in a Musculoskeletal Examination.**

System/Body Area	Topics
Constitutional	<ul><li>any *three* of *seven* vital signs<ul><li>blood pressure, sitting or standing</li><li>blood pressure, lying down</li><li>pulse rate and regularity</li><li>respiration</li><li>temperature</li><li>height</li><li>weight</li></ul></li><li>general appearance of the patient</li></ul>
Cardiovascular	<ul><li>examination of peripheral vascular system by observation and palpation</li></ul>
Lymphatic	<ul><li>palpation of lymph nodes in neck, axillae, groin, and/or other locations</li></ul>
Musculoskeletal	<ul><li>examination of gait and station</li></ul> Examination of joint(s), bone(s), and muscle(s)/tendon(s) of **four** of the following **six** areas:<ul><li>head and neck</li><li>spine, ribs, and pelvis</li><li>right upper extremity</li><li>left upper extremity</li><li>right lower extremity</li><li>left lower extremity</li></ul><ul><li>inspection, percussion, and/or palpation with notation of any misalignment, asymmetry, crepitation, defects, tenderness, masses or effusions</li><li>assessment of range of motion with notation of pain, crepitation, or contracture</li><li>assessment of stability with notation of any dislocation, subluxation, or laxity</li><li>assessment of muscle strength and tone, with notation of any atrophy or abnormal movements</li></ul>NOTE: For the comprehensive level of examination, all four bulleted topics must be performed and documented for each of four anatomic areas. For the three remaining levels of examination, each element is counted separately for each body area. For example, assessing range of motion in two extremities constitutes two topics.
Skin	<ul><li>inspection and/or palpation of skin and subcutaneous tissue in **four** of the following **six** areas:<ul><li>head and neck</li><li>spine, ribs, and pelvis</li><li>right upper extremity</li><li>left upper extremity</li><li>right lower extremity</li><li>left lower extremity</li></ul></li></ul>NOTE: For the comprehensive level of examination, the examination of all four **anatomic areas** must be performed and documented. For the three remaining levels of examination, each body area is counted separately. For example, inspection and/or palpation of the skin and subcutaneous tissue of two extremities constitutes two topics.
Neurological/Psychiatric	<ul><li>test coordination</li><li>examination of deep tendon reflexes with notation of pathological reflexes</li><li>examination of sensation</li></ul>Brief assessment of mental status including:<ul><li>orientation to time, place, and person</li><li>mood and affect</li></ul>

TABLE 3–13   Topics Included in a Neurological Examination.

System/Body Area	Topics
Constitutional	■ any *three* of *seven* vital signs ▪ blood pressure, sitting or standing ▪ blood pressure, lying down ▪ pulse rate and regularity ▪ respiration ▪ temperature ▪ height ▪ weight ■ general appearance of the patient
Eyes	■ ophthalmoscopic exam of optic discs and posterior segments
Cardiovascular	■ auscultation of heart with notation of abnormal sounds and murmurs ■ examination of carotid arteries ■ examination of peripheral vascular system by observation and palpation
Musculoskeletal	■ examination of gait and station Assessment of motor function including: ■ muscle strength in upper and lower extremities ■ muscle tone in upper and lower extremities with notation of any atrophy or abnormal movements
Neurological	Evaluation of higher integrative functions including: ■ orientation to time, place, and person ■ recent and remote memory ■ attention span and concentration ■ language ■ fund of knowledge Testing of the following cranial nerves: ■ 2nd cranial nerve, visual acuity, visual fields, fundi ■ 3rd, 4th, and 6th cranial nerves, pupils, eye movements ■ 5th cranial nerve, facial sensation, corneal reflexes ■ 7th cranial nerve, facial symmetry, strength ■ 8th cranial nerve, hearing with tuning fork, whispered voice and/or finger rub ■ 9th cranial nerve, spontaneous or reflex palate movement ■ 11th cranial nerve, shoulder shrug strength ■ 12th cranial nerve, tongue protrusion ■ examination of sensation ■ examination of deep tendon reflexes in upper and lower extremities with notation of pathological reflexes ■ test coordination

TABLE 3–14   **Topics Included in a Psychiatric Examination.**

System/Body Area	Topics

Constitutional	■ any *three* of *seven* vital signs
	  ▪ blood pressure, sitting or standing
	  ▪ blood pressure, lying down
	  ▪ pulse rate and regularity
	  ▪ respiration
	  ▪ temperature
	  ▪ height
	  ▪ weight
	■ general appearance of the patient

Musculoskeletal	■ examination of gait and station ■ assessment of muscle strength and tone, with notation of any atrophy or abnormal movements
Psychiatric	■ description of speech including: rate, volume, articulation, coherence, and spontaneity with notation of abnormalities ■ description of thought processes including: rate of thoughts; content of thoughts; abstract reasoning; and computation ■ description of associations ■ description of abnormal or psychotic thoughts including: hallucinations, delusions, preoccupation with violence, homicidal or suicidal ideation; and obsessions ■ description of the patient's judgment and insight Complete mental status examination including: ■ orientation to time, place, and person ■ recent and remote memory ■ attention span and concentration ■ language ■ fund of knowledge ■ mood and affect

Skin Examinations   System/body areas and topics included in a skin examination are listed in Table 3–16.

Each level or type of skin examination requires that a specific number of bulleted topics be reviewed and documented. A problem focused examination must have one to five bulleted topics; an expanded problem focused examination must have at least six bulleted topics; and a detailed examination calls for at least twelve bulleted topics. In order to meet the comprehensive examination criteria, the physician should address all bulleted topics; document all bulleted topics listed under constitutional, ears, nose, mouth, and throat, and skin; and document at least one bulleted topic listed under eyes, neck, cardiovascular, gastrointestinal, lymphatic, extremities, and neurological/psychiatric system/body areas.

After reviewing Tables 3–7 through 3–16 it is apparent that, as with the general multi-system examinations, the higher levels or types of examinations associated with single organ systems must be supported by increased documentation. The AMA/HCFA guidelines should be viewed as minimum requirements. Physicians are encouraged to include other information as necessary.

TABLE 3–15   **Topics Included in a Respiratory Examination.**

System/Body Area	Topics
Constitutional	▪ any *three* of *seven* vital signs 　▪ blood pressure, sitting or standing 　▪ blood pressure, lying down 　▪ pulse rate and regularity 　▪ respiration 　▪ temperature 　▪ height 　▪ weight ▪ general appearance of the patient
Ears, Nose, Mouth and Throat	▪ inspection of nasal mucosa, septum and turbinates ▪ inspection of teeth and gums ▪ examination of oral mucosa, salivary glands, hard and soft palates, tongue, tonsils, and posterior pharynx
Neck	▪ examination of neck ▪ examination of thyroid ▪ examination of jugular veins
Respiratory	▪ inspection of chest with notation of symmetry and expansion ▪ assessment of respiratory effort ▪ percussion of chest ▪ palpation of chest ▪ auscultation of lungs
Cardiovascular	▪ auscultation of heart including sounds, abnormal sounds, and murmurs ▪ examination of peripheral vascular system by observation and palpation
Gastrointestinal (Abdomen)	▪ examination of abdomen, with notation of presence of masses or tenderness ▪ examination of liver and spleen
Lymphatic	▪ palpation of lymph nodes in neck, axillae, groin, and/or other locations
Musculoskeletal	▪ examination of gait and station ▪ assessment of muscle strength and tone, with notation of any atrophy or abnormal movements
Extremities	▪ inspection and palpation of digits and nails
Skin	▪ inspection and/or palpation of skin and subcutaneous tissue
Neurologic/Psychiatric	Brief assessment of mental status including: ▪ orientation to time, place, and person ▪ mood and affect

TABLE 3–16 Topics Included in a Skin Examination.

System/Body Area	Topics
Constitutional	■ any *three* of *seven* vital signs 　▪ blood pressure, sitting or standing 　▪ blood pressure, lying down 　▪ pulse rate and regularity 　▪ respiration 　▪ temperature 　▪ height 　▪ weight ■ general appearance of the patient
Eyes	■ inspection of conjunctivae and lids
Ears, Nose, Mouth and Throat	■ inspection of teeth and gums ■ examination of oropharynx
Neck	■ examination of thyroid
Cardiovascular	■ examination of peripheral vascular system by observation and palpation
Gastrointestinal (Abdomen)	■ examination of liver and spleen ■ examination of anus for condyloma and other lesions
Lymphatic	■ palpation of lymph nodes in neck, axillae, groin, and/or other locations
Extremities	■ inspection and palpation of digits and nails
Skin	■ palpation of scalp and inspection of hair of scalp, eyebrows, face, chest, pubic area (when indicated), and extremities ■ inspection and/or palpation of skin and subcutaneous tissue in **eight** of the following **ten** areas: 　▪ head, including the face 　▪ neck 　▪ chest, including breast and axillae 　▪ abdomen 　▪ genitalia, groin, buttocks 　▪ back 　▪ right upper extremity 　▪ left upper extremity 　▪ right lower extremity 　▪ left lower extremity NOTE: For the comprehensive level, the examination of at least eight anatomic areas must be performed and documented. For the remaining three levels, each body area is counted separately. For example: inspection and/or palpation of the skin and subcutaneous tissue of the right upper extremity and the left upper extremity constitutes two elements. ■ inspection of eccrine and apocrine glands of the skin and subcutaneous tissue with identification and location of any hyperhidrosis, chromhidroses, or bromhidrosis
Neurological/Psychiatric	Brief assessment of mental status including: ■ orientation to time, place, and person ■ mood and affect

Medical Decision Making

The third key element associated with E/M levels of service is **medical decision making**. The phrase medical decision making refers to the complexity of establishing a diagnosis and/or selecting a management or treatment option. There are four types of medical decision making: straightforward; low complexity; moderate complexity; and high complexity. Each type of medical decision making is dependent on three elements: number of diagnoses or management options; the amount and/or complexity of data to be reviewed; and the risk of complications and/or morbidity or mortality. Each element is further categorized as minimal, limited, low, multiple, moderate, extensive, or high. Table 3–17 lists the types of medical decision making, the elements, and the category of each element.

In order to qualify for a given type of decision, two of the three elements listed in the table must be met or exceeded. For example, high complexity decision making must be supported by two of the following: an extensive number of diagnoses or management options, an extensive amount/complexity of data to be reviewed, and a high risk of complications and/or morbidity or mortality.

The AMA/HCFA documentation guidelines associated with medical decision making are not as clear-cut as the guidelines for history and examination. However, for each medical decision-making element, the guidelines provide some direction to the physician.

Number of Diagnoses or Management Options   The number of diagnoses or management options is dependent on whether or not the problem can be diagnosed; the number and type of diagnostic tests needed to establish the diagnosis; the need for consultations; and whether or not the problems or diagnoses are improving, worsening, or failing to change as expected. Documentation guidelines for this element require the following: problem identification; statement of diagnosis, if possible; status of problem(s) or diagnoses; initiation of, or changes in treatment options; and identification of all referrals and consultations.

Amount and/or Complexity of Data to be Reviewed   The amount and/or complexity of data to be reviewed is dependent on the types of diagnostic tests ordered or reviewed. Reviewing previous medical records increases the amount and complexity of data to be reviewed. Documentation guidelines for this element require the following: identification of the type of service that is planned, ordered, performed, or scheduled during the E/M visit; notation of the review of any diagnostic tests or previous medical records; documentation of the results of discussions with the physician who performed or interpreted a specific diagnostic test; and

TABLE 3–17   **Medical Decision-Making Elements and Categories.**

Type of decision making	Number of diagnoses or management options	Amount and/or complexity of data to be reviewed	Risk of complications and/or morbidity or mortality
Straightforward	Minimal	Minimal or None	Minimal
Low Complexity	Limited	Limited	Low
Moderate Complexity	Multiple	Moderate	Moderate
High Complexity	Extensive	Extensive	High

documentation of direct visualization and independent interpretation of an image, tracing, or specimen that may be interpreted by another physician.

Risk of Complications, Morbidity, and/or Mortality The risk of significant complications, morbidity, and/or mortality is based on the risks associated with the present problem(s), the diagnostic procedure(s), and possible management options. Documentation guidelines for this element require the following: identification of comorbidities or underlying diseases; surgical or invasive diagnostic procedures ordered, planned, or scheduled at the time of the E/M visit; documentation of the name of any procedure performed during the E/M visit; and an indication if the referral for or decision to perform a surgical or invasive diagnostic procedure was done on an urgent basis.

Accurate documentation of the three key elements associated with E/M service levels provides the primary care physician with a complete record of patient care; a valuable source document for coding and billing; and a solid defense against any challenges related to reimbursement for services rendered. Coding and billing specialists must take an active role in reviewing documentation requirements and practices so that any contested claims can be readily resolved.

Time

The three key elements discussed on previous pages are the usual controlling factors used to select the appropriate E/M service level. Primary care physicians often engage in services related to counseling and coordination of care. Coordination of care is particularly applicable when the physician is working with nursing home patients. Due to the fact that the primary care physician is in the unique position of spending more time with his/her patients, the time element takes on greater importance. In fact, according to AMA/HCFA guidelines, when a visit or service consists predominantly (more than 50%) of counseling or coordination of care, time is the key or controlling factor used to select the appropriate level of E/M.

In the Evaluation and Management section, time is defined as face-to-face and unit/floor time. Face-to-face time is the time the physician spends with the patient and/or family. Unit/floor time is time the physician spends in the patient's care setting. Unit/floor time includes physician activities such as reviewing medical records, reviewing or ordering tests, documenting information in the patient's medical record, communicating with other members of the patient's health care team, and counseling the patient and/or the patient's family.

For coding purposes, when more than 50% of the physician's face-to-face and/or unit/floor time is spent on counseling or coordination of care, then time only becomes the deciding factor in selecting the correct E/M code. The following scenario illustrates this point.

Barbara visits her primary care physician for a follow-up visit related to her diabetes. Barbara's blood sugar has been under good control because she has followed the diabetic diet to the letter. During the first 5 minutes of the office visit, Barbara confesses to her physician that she doesn't know how much longer she can take the work involved in following so many dietary restrictions. Dr. Worrell takes the time to discuss the implications of "falling off" the program. She describes the pros and cons of insulin and makes a call to the hospital dietitian to find out when the next diabetic cooking class will be held. By the time Barbara and Dr. Worrell finish, the office visit has expanded from a 15 minute follow-up appointment, to a 35 minute diabetic counseling session.

Barbara's established-patient office visit for routine follow-up of non-insulin-dependent diabetes could easily fall into E/M code 99213, based on the history, examination, and decision-making key factors. Since Barbara's visit consumed 35 minutes of the physician's time, and more than 50% of the time was spent counseling Barbara and arranging for dietetic services, the physician or coder would be justified in selecting the E/M service code that accounts for this extended time. In this case, code 99214 would be the code of choice.

Physicians and coders must apply the time-only factor with great care. Delays or interruptions not associated with patient counseling or coordination of care that may prolong the expected encounter time cannot be used to justify selecting a higher level E/M code. Also, the physician must clearly document the nature of the counseling and/or coordination of care.

The Nursing Facility Services subsection of Evaluation and Management codes is another potential time-only group of encounters. Physicians must keep accurate time records and document all patient related activities that have influenced the amount of counseling and coordination of care time spent during the nursing facility visit. Once again, delays related to unavailability of staff, equipment, or supplies cannot be used to justify implementing the time-only criteria.

This section of Module 3 provides a brief overview of the documentation issues associated with Evaluation and Management levels of service. Since the E/M codes are a large part of a primary care practice, coding and billing specialists should keep up with current information about this important CPT section. Primary care physicians have a tremendous responsibility as gatekeepers, and as such deserve to receive full reimbursement for their services. However, in order to justify any reimbursement level, the patient's medical record must support the selected E/M code.

EXERCISE 3-2

Review the following exercise case studies and assign the ICD-9-CM diagnostic procedure codes and the CPT service and procedure codes to the following statements. Note that exercise number 2 is based on actual physician documentation. For confidentiality reasons, all names have been changed.

1. During a follow-up appointment for a 15-year-old insulin-dependent diabetic patient with stable blood sugars, both the patient and his parents expressed concern about the teasing episodes at school that focus on "needle users get AIDS." The physician spends an additional 20 minutes counseling the patient and family about HIV infection, and strategies for diminishing the teasing episodes.

   ICD-9-CM code(s) _____

   CPT code(s) _____

2. Minerva Most is a 47-year-old woman presenting to the Emergency Department after a motor vehicle accident with an apparent left ankle injury. Dr. Leaflet, her primary care physician, was on call, and came in to assess the patient.

   ICD-9-CM code(s) _____

   CPT code(s) _____

   > EMERGENCY DEPARTMENT REPORT: The patient was driving down Main Street and was struck on the driver's side by a car that ran a stop sign. The patient's car slid into a snowbank and then hit another car. Minerva

   continues

is the only one injured. She denies head, chest, back, neck, or other extremity injury. She was seatbelted at the time of the accident. The airbag did not inflate. The patient denies any change in mental status including confusion, unconsciousness, dizziness, headache, vision changes, blurriness or diplopia. The patient has been anticoagulated with Coumadin 5 mg orally, and two days ago had an INR of 4.0. She was instructed not to take her Coumadin yesterday and she did not. Her current medications include Coumadin, Synthroid, Keflex, and Prozac. She states she has no allergies.

PAST MEDICAL HISTORY: Ulcerative colitis, resolved with a total procto-colectomy last year; clotting abnormality; pyoderma gangrenosum; arterial emboli; psoriasis; and steroid induced obesity.

REVIEW OF SYSTEMS: Head and neck: The patient denies any neck pain, head pain, changes in mental status or vision changes. General: The patient denies any fever, weight loss, chills or night sweats. Respiratory: The patient denies any shortness of breath, cough, hemoptysis, asthma or chronic obstructive pulmonary disease. She denies ever smoking. Cardiovascular: The patient denies any heart disease, murmurs, arrhythmia, orthopnea, failure or heart attacks. Genitourinary: Denies dysuria, polyuria or hematuria. Musculoskeletal: Denies any other extremity damage, pain or swelling.

PHYSICAL EXAMINATION: General: The patient remains in no apparent distress, ice over her left ankle. Vital Signs: Blood pressure 122/80; pulse 72; respirations 18; temperature 96.8. HEENT: Pupils are round, equal, and reactive to light. Extraocular movements intact. Fundi visible without pathology. Mouth without evidence of lesion or blood. Ears: Tympanic membranes are intact, ear canals clear of discharge. Nose: No evidence of hematoma, open lesion or other clear discharge. Lungs: Clear on auscultation. Heart: Regular without murmurs. Abdomen: No tenderness or masses on palpation. Bowel sounds are present. Back: There is no cervical, thoracic, lumbar or sacral tenderness. No costovertebral angle tenderness. Extremities: Femoral pulses palpable bilaterally. All four extremities have strength and full range of motion. Her left foot is swollen at the medial and lateral malleolus. There is ecchymosis on the dorsal surface of the foot. There is a large ecchymosis on the medial side of the thigh just above the knee. There is tenderness at both malleoli inferior anteriorly on the dorsal part of the foot. There is tenderness on the heel portion of the foot. The patient is able to wiggle her toes, and pulses are intact but weak. This is symmetric. No evidence of shin contusion. The extensor tendon sheaths appear swollen.

EMERGENCY DEPARTMENT COURSE: The patient remained in no apparent distress. She received Toradol 10 mg orally for pain. She received an ankle and a foot x-ray, and a left thigh x-ray which showed a lateral malleolus avulsion and a lateral calcaneus comminuted fracture. She received two units of fresh frozen plasma because of anticoagulation. Dr. Orthopodic was called in for surgical consultation.

ASSESSMENT AND PLAN: Left lateral malleolus avulsion and left calcaneus comminuted fracture. The patient was admitted to the operating room for an open reduction, pin fixation of the fracture.

MEDICINE

The CPT Medicine section is another important source of primary care service codes. **Medicine codes**, numbered 90700–99199, are listed in the last section of the CPT manual. The Medicine Guidelines describe how general CPT terms and phrases like multiple procedures, add-on codes, separate procedures, special report, modifiers, materials supplied by the physician, unlisted services or procedures, and subsection information apply to the Medicine section. The unique application of each term or phrase is discussed individually.

Multiple Procedures

The concept of **multiple procedures** allows the physician to report several procedures or services, rendered on the same day, by the appropriate CPT code. For example, an office visit that includes a hepatitis B vaccination would generate two codes: an E/M code to describe the office visit *and* a Medicine code for the hepatitis B vaccination.

Add-on Codes

The description for Add-on Codes in the Medicine section is the same as the description in the Surgery section. Basically, add-on codes are exempt from the multiple procedure concept and from Modifier -51. Add-on codes are readily identified throughout the CPT manual by phrases such as "each additional" or "List separately in addition to primary procedure." The destruction of common warts provides an example of Add-on Codes. According to the 1998 CPT code book, destruction of common warts falls under codes 17000, 17003, and 17004. If a patient presents with 14 common warts, the coder would assign 17000 to indicate the destruction of the first wart, and code 17003 to indicate the destruction of the second through fourteenth warts. Code 17003 is to be listed separately in addition to the code for the first wart.

Separate Procedures

In 1998 the CPT Medicine Guidelines included a discussion concerning separate procedures. The Medicine section guidelines state that "when a procedure or service that is designated as a 'separate procedure' is carried out independently or considered to be unrelated or distinct from other procedures/services provided at that time, it may be reported by itself, . . . or by appending the modifier '-59'." (CPT 98). For example, phlebotomy for therapeutic purposes (CPT 98 code 99195) is identified as a separate procedure. Therefore, if a primary care physician performs a phlebotomy that is not related to other procedures/services provided at the same time, the phlebotomy may be coded separately.

On the other hand, when a procedure that is identified as a separate procedure is also an integral part of another service or procedure, the separate procedure may not be reported or coded separately. For example: A primary care physician may perform a "proctosigmoidoscopy, rigid, diagnostic, with or without collection of specimen(s) by brushing or washing." This procedure is designated as a separate procedure and can be coded as such. However, if during the proctosigmoidoscopy, the physician performs additional procedures, such as biopsy; removal of tumor, polyp, or foreign object; or other surgical or treatment activity, the proctosigmoidoscopy cannot be reported as a separate procedure. The procedure must be coded as a proctosigmoidoscopy . . . with biopsy; with removal; or other appropriate designation and code.

Special Report

The description for Special Report services in the Medicine section is the same as the description in the Surgery section. Basically, a rarely provided service, or one that is new, unusual or varies from the norm, may require additional medical information to support or justify the service. The **special report** should include documentation of all factors involved in the decision to perform the service or procedure.

Modifiers

As with all CPT sections, modifiers in the Medicine section are used to explain different or special circumstances that affect the provision of a service or performance of a procedure. Table 3–18 summarizes the modifiers associated with CPT's Medicine section.

Materials Supplied by the Physician

Supplies and materials provided by the physician that exceed the expected amount for a particular service or procedure may be listed separately. The Medicine section provides a specific CPT code, 99070 in CPT 98, to cover this contingency.

Unlisted Service or Procedure

As with other CPT sections, the Medicine section includes a number of **unlisted service or procedure** codes. These codes are used when the service provided to the patient is not found elsewhere in the current CPT edition. Table 3–19 displays the Medicine Section Unlisted Service or Procedure Codes based on the 1998 CPT manual. Coders are advised to check the current CPT manual for updated codes.

The unlisted service or procedure codes presented in Table 3–19 are categorized based on Medicine subsections, which are discussed later in this module.

Medicine Subsections

The Medicine section contains several subsections or subheadings ranging from Immunization Injections to Special Services and Reports. Table 3–20 summarizes these subsections.

Several of the Medicine subsections are more appropriately related to specialists than to primary care. Subsections often associated with primary care physicians are summarized in Table 3–21. A description of each subsection in Table 3–21 follows the table.

TABLE 3–18   Two Digit CPT Modifiers: Medicine Section.

Modifiers	Title	Brief Description
-22	Unusual Procedural Service	greater than usual service; special report may be needed
-26	Professional Component	physician component of a procedure
-32	Mandated Service	service is required by regulatory or legislative entity
-51	Multiple Procedures	indicates additional procedures performed on the same day or at the same time
-52	Reduced Services	service is partially reduced or deleted by the physician
-53	Discontinued Procedure	physician elects to terminate a surgical or diagnostic procedure
-55	Postoperative Management Only	physician provides postoperative care; another physician has performed the surgery
-56	Preoperative Management Only	physician provides preoperative care; another physician has performed the surgery
-57	Decision for Surgery	an E/M service that results in the initial decision to perform surgery
-58	Staged or Related Procedure by the Same Physician During the Postoperative Period	procedures or services performed by the physician that are pre-planned; more extensive than the original procedure; or for therapy following a diagnostic surgical procedure
-59	Distinct Procedural Service	describes a procedure or service that is independent from other services
-76	Repeat Procedure by Same Physician	procedure or service was repeated
-77	Repeat Procedure by Another Physician	procedure or service was repeated by a different physician
-78	Return to the Operating for a Related Procedure During the Postoperative Period	a related procedure was necessary during a postoperative time
-79	Unrelated Procedure by the Same Physician During the Postoperative	procedure was not related to initial procedure
-90	Reference (Outside) Lab	lab procedures are performed by someone other than the treating physician
-99	Multiple Modifiers	more than one modifier is needed to adequately describe the service

TABLE 3–19   Unlisted Service or Procedure Codes: Medicine Section.

Code Number	Description	Primary Care
90749	unlisted immunization procedure	yes
90799	unlisted therapeutic or diagnostic injection	yes
90899	unlisted psychiatric service or procedure	possible
90915	unlisted biofeedback procedure	possible
90999	unlisted dialysis procedure inpatient or outpatient	possible
91299	unlisted diagnostic gastroenterology procedure	unlikely
92499	unlisted ophthalmological service or procedure	unlikely
92599	unlisted otorhinolaryngological service or procedure	unlikely
93799	unlisted cardiovascular service or procedure	unlikely
94799	unlisted pulmonary service or procedure	unlikely
95199	unlisted allergy/clinical immunologic service or procedure	possible
95999	unlisted neurological or neuromuscular diagnostic procedure	unlikely
96549	unlisted chemotherapy procedure	possible
96999	unlisted special dermatological service or procedure	unlikely
97039	unlisted physical medicine modality	unlikely
97139	unlisted physical medicine therapeutic procedure	unlikely
97799	unlisted physical medicine	unlikely
99199	unlisted special service or report	yes

Immunization Injections

The **immunization injections** subsection of the CPT Medicine section applies to a wide variety of primary care physicians. Pediatricians who function as PCPs will, due to the age of the patients, have many opportunities to provide immunization services. The coder should keep in mind that the office visit must be coded using the appropriate E/M code, and the immunization injection must be coded as well. If the immunization is the only service performed, a minimal service E/M code should be listed.

Hepatitis B immunizations are coded according to the age of the patient. Therefore, primary care physicians who treat adult patients will use the age-appropriate code. As with the pediatric patient, the office visit, minimal or otherwise, should be coded as well.

TABLE 3–20 Medicine Subsections.

Title	Codes	Brief Description
Immunization Injections	90700–90749	aka vaccinations
Therapeutic or Diagnostic Infusions	90780–90781	prolonged IV injections
Psychiatry	90801–90899	psychiatric diagnostic or evaluative interview procedures; other therapeutic procedures
Biofeedback	90901–90911	biofeedback training
Dialysis	90918–90999	all services related to end-stage renal and dialysis
Gastroenterology	91000–91299	analysis of gastric motility, washings, intubations, and other tests
Ophthalmology	92002–92499	services related to contact lens, exams, prosthetics; surgery services excluded
Otorhinolaryngology	92502–92599	special services not usually included in a comprehensive otorhinolaryngologic evaluation
Cardiovascular Therapeutic	92950–93278	includes CPR, balloon procedures, catheter placement, and cardioversion
Cardiography and Echocardiography	93000–93350	EKG services, cardiac ultrasound services
Cardiac Catheterization	93501–93562	services related to introducing catheters into the heart
Intracardiac Electrophysiological Procedures	93600–93660	recording of electrical activity of the heart
Other Vascular Studies	93720–93790	pacemaker analysis, venous pressure monitoring
Non–Invasive Vascular Diagnostic Studies	93875–93900	arterial and venous studies of the head, extremities, viscera, and penis
Pulmonary	94010–94799	laboratory studies and interpretation of test results
Allergy and Clinical Immunology	95004–95199	allergy testing; injection and/or provision of allergenic extracts
Neurology and Neuromuscular	95805–95999	sleep testing, EEG, muscle testing, electromyography
Central Nervous System Assessment/Tests	96100–96117	testing of cognitive processes, visual motor responses, and abstractive ability
Chemotherapy Administration	96400–96549	various chemotherapy infusion techniques
Dermatological Procedures	96900–96999	ultraviolet light therapy, microscopic examinations, photochemotherapy
Physical Medicine/Rehabilitation Modalities	97001–97028	application of physical agents
Constant Attendance	97032–97039	direct patient contact
Therapeutic Procedures	97110–97546	various physical therapy treatments
Osteopathic Manipulative Treatment	98925–98929	applied to one or more body regions
Chiropractic Manipulative Treatment	98940–98943	applied to the spine
Special Services and Reports	99000–99199	specimen handling, medical testimony; unusual travel

TABLE 3–21   Medicine Subsections Associated with Primary Care.

Subsection	Codes	Brief Description
Immunization Injections	90700–90749	vaccinations ranging from hepatitis B to DPT
Therapeutic/Diagnostic Infusions	90780–90781	prolonged IV injections
Therapeutic/Diagnostic Injections	90782–90799	subcutaneous, intramuscular, intra-arterial, intravenous
Cardiovascular Services Therapeutic Services	92950, 92953 92960	transcutaneous pacing, CPR, cardioversion
Cardiography	93000–93278	EKG and related services
Allergy and Clinical Immunology	95004–95199	allergy testing; injection and/or provision of allergenic extracts
Special Services/Reports	99000–99199	specimen handling; medical testimony; unusual travel

Therapeutic or Diagnostic Infusions (Excluding Chemotherapy)

Prolonged intravenous injections should be coded to this Medicine subsection. In order to use these codes, the intravenous infusion must be completed by a physician or accomplished under the *direct* supervision of the physician. The infusion codes are given in hourly increments with 90780 covering the first hour, and 90781 covering each additional hour, up to eight hours.

Therapeutic or Diagnostic Injections

Therapeutic or diagnostic injections include subcutaneous or intramuscular routes of administration. The specific substance being injected must be documented and coded in addition to the injection code. In order to code the specific substance being injected, the coder must refer to section **J** of the HCPCS (**HCFA** **C**ommon **P**rocedural **C**oding **S**ystem) National Coding Manual. This manual is updated annually by the Medicare program.

Cardiovascular Services and Cardiography

Cardiovascular services and procedures are most often provided and performed by cardiac specialists. However, there are some diagnostic interventions that may be accomplished by the primary care physician. Table 3–22 summarizes the cardiovascular subsection codes that may apply to primary care physicians.

Allergen and Clinical Immunology

Although allergists are often associated with large practices or urban settings, primary care physicians in other settings may provide allergy testing and allergen immunotherapy. Allergy testing ranges from the well known scratch and patch tests to specialized tests involving the eyes, nose, or bronchial tree. Allergen

TABLE 3–22 **Primary Care Physicians and Cardiovascular Service Codes.**

Code	Description
92950	Cardiopulmonary resuscitation (e.g., in cardiac arrest)
92953	Temporary transcutaneous pacing
92960	Cardioversion, elective, electrical conversion of arrhythmia, external
93000	Electrocardiogram, routine ECG with at least 12 leads; with interpretation and report
93005	tracing only, without interpretation and report
93010	interpretation and report only
93012	Telephonic transmission of post-symptom electrocardiogram rhythm strip(s), per 30 day period of time; tracing only
93014	physician review with interpretation and report only
93015	Cardiovascular stress test using maximal or submaximal treadmill or bicycle exercise, continuous electrocardiographic monitoring, and/or pharmacological stress; with physician supervision, with interpretation and report
93016	physician supervision only, without interpretation and report
93017	tracing only, without interpretation and report
93018	interpretation and report only
93024	Ergonovine provocation test
93040	Rhythm ECG, one to three leads; with interpretation and report
93041	tracing only without interpretation and report
93042	interpretation and report only
93224	Electrocardiographic monitoring for 24 hours by continuous original ECG waveform recording and storage, with visual superimposition scanning; includes recording, scanning analysis with report, physician review and interpretation
93225	recording (includes hook-up, recording, and disconnection)
93226	scanning analysis with report
93227	physician review and interpretation
93230	Electrocardiographic monitoring for 24 hours by continuous original ECG waveform recording and storage, without superimposition scanning utilizing a device capable of producing a full miniaturized printout; includes recording, microprocessor-based analysis with report, physician review and interpretation

continues

Table 3-22   **Primary Care Physicians and Cardiovascular Service Codes** *continued*

Code	Description
93231	recording (includes hook-up, recording, and disconnection)
93232	microprocessor-based analysis with report
93233	physician review and interpretation
93235	Electrocardiographic monitoring for 24 hours by continuous computerized monitoring and non-continuous recording, and real-time data analysis utilizing a device capable of producing intermittent full-sized waveform tracings, possibly patient activated; includes monitoring and real-time data analysis with report, physician review and interpretation
93236	monitoring and real-time data analysis with report
93237	physician review and interpretation
93268	Patient demand single or multiple event recording with presymptom memory loop, per 30 day period of time; includes transmission, physician review and interpretation
93270	recording (includes hook-up, recording, and disconnection)
93271	monitoring, receipt of transmissions, and analysis
93272	physician review and interpretation only

immunotherapy involves injecting the patient with allergenic extracts or a specific number of insect venoms. Coders must carefully screen the use of office visit codes in conjunction with allergen immunotherapy codes. Office visit codes can be used in addition to allergen immunotherapy codes **only** if other identifiable services have been provided at the same time. The patient's record must clearly document the other identifiable services.

Special Services/Reports

The special services and reports subsection covers physician and physician directed activities that range from handling and/or conveying lab specimens to providing medical testimony. Some of the more interesting, and possibly little known, codes are as follows: services requested after office hours in addition to basic service; office services provided on an emergency basis; educational supplies, such as books, tapes, and pamphlets, provided by the physician for the patient's education at cost to physician; physician educational services rendered to patients in a group setting (e.g., prenatal, obesity, or diabetic instructions) code; and analysis of data stored in computers (e.g., ECGs, blood pressures, hematologic data). It is important to know that while there are codes for these special circumstances, third party payers do not always reimburse the provider.

Even though selected Medicine subsections have been highlighted, coders should keep in mind that any and all documented services or procedures provided or performed by the primary care physician can and should be coded. While "up-coding" creates serious legal and ethical problems, "under-coding" is detrimental to the practice as well. Insurance companies and regulatory agencies closely monitor physician billing and coding patterns. In order to generate the most accurate data, all appropriate CPT and ICD-9-CM codes are needed. As long as the patients' records support the selected codes, and coders and reimbursement specialists follow coding and insurance provider guidelines, the practice should have no trouble securing appropriate reimbursement for services rendered.

EXERCISE 3–3

Assign the ICD-9-CM diagnostic codes and the CPT service and procedure codes to the following statements.

1. Initial office visit for a 6-month-old female. Third DTP dose given.

   ICD-9-CM code(s) _____

   CPT code(s) _____

2. Physician supervised cardiovascular stress test on a 52-year-old white male with recent ECG changes.

   ICD-9-CM code(s) _____

   CPT code(s) _____

3. Hepatitis B vaccination provided in the dorm for a 22-year-old second year nursing student who recently broke her foot and cannot come to the office.

   ICD-9-CM code(s) _____

   CPT code(s) _____

4. Intravenous injection of ACTH (adrenocorticotropic hormone) to stimulate adrenal gland function of a 49-year-old established patient.

   ICD-9-CM code(s) _____

   CPT code(s) _____

5. Physician supervised intravenous infusion of iron over a 2-hour period.

   ICD-9-CM code(s) _____

   CPT code(s) _____

MEDICARE

Primary care physicians often have a substantial population of patients who qualify for **Medicare**, the federal health insurance program that covers both hospital care and physician services. Since Medicare funnels a substantial amount of taxpayer money into the health care industry, agencies that oversee this program have an interest in controlling health care costs. Medicare's influence on physician billing is most notable in the recently published AMA/HCFA documentation guidelines. Although the guidelines were heralded as a "joint" venture, the impetus for the guidelines was the government's attempt to provide physicians and claims reviewers with direction in the selection and validation of E/M service codes.

Insurance carriers associated with the Medicare program keep very close track of the type of codes an office uses most often. Coding patterns and profiles are monitored in order to identify potential misuse of codes. Physicians' offices that are guilty of violating coding practices may be required to repay any and all Medicare payments and may be dropped from the Medicare program altogether.

Coding and billing specialists who work in offices that receive Medicare payments should have access to updated Medicare regulations that affect physician service reimbursement. Updates are usually available from Medicare fiscal intermediaries, the insurance companies that are responsible for paying Medicare claims. There are situations when CPT definitions are different from Medicare definitions, as in the case of follow-up care for therapeutic surgical procedures. Medicare defines a number of days to be included in the surgical package, and CPT guidelines do not.

In addition to CPT, the American Medical Association also publishes *AMA's Medicare RBRVS: The Physician's Guide.* This valuable text describes how the Resource Based Relative Value Scale (RBRVS) works; explains payment for nonphysician services; and provides a wealth of information related to surgical teams, co-surgeon, and surgical assistant restrictions. This guide is an important reference tool for Medicare claims coding.

SUMMARY

- A primary care physician provides services and treatments to patients who exhibit a variety of health problems.
- Family practice physicians, internal medicine physicians, pediatricians, and the traditional general practitioner represent the majority of primary care physicians.
- Evaluation and Management (E/M) codes are the mainstay of primary care practices.
- The Health Care Finance Administration and the American Medical Association have published E/M documentation guidelines that delineate the type of information that must be in the patient's medical record in order to justify a specific E/M service level.
- There are four types of E/M service levels: problem focused, expanded problem focused, detailed, and comprehensive.
- Three key elements for determining E/M service levels are history, examination, and medical decision making.
- When a physician visit or service consists predominantly of counseling or coordination of care, *time* is the controlling factor used to select the E/M service level.
- The patient's history consists of a chief complaint, history of present illness, review of systems, and past, family, and/or social history.
- The physical examination of the patient may be categorized as a general multi-system exam or a single organ system exam.

- Medical decision making is based on the number of diagnoses or management options, the amount and/or complexity of data to be reviewed, and the risk of complications and/or morbidity or mortality.
- Medicine CPT codes are associated with primary care practices.
- Medicine subsections associated with primary care are: immunization injections, therapeutic/diagnostic infusions, therapeutic/diagnostic injections, cardiovascular services and cardiography, allergy and clinical immunology, and special services reports.
- Primary care practices often have a substantial Medicare patient population.
- Physicians, coders, and insurance specialists have a professional, legal, and financial interest in keeping up with Medicare regulations as they affect physician services.

REFERENCES

American Medical Association: CPT 98, Chicago, 1997.

Documentation Guidelines for Evaluation and Management Services. Washington, D.C.: American Medical Association and Health Care Financing Administration, 1997.

Morin-Spatz, P. *CP "Teach."* Richardson, Texas: MedBooks, 1998.

Rowell, Joanne. *Understanding Health Insurance.* Albany, N.Y.: Delmar Publishers, 1998.

Module 4
Anesthesia/General Surgery

Nancy Heldt, CCS

LEARNING OBJECTIVES

Upon successful completion of this module, you should be able to:

1. Identify how and when anesthesia codes are used.
2. Identify the physical status modifiers and know how they apply.
3. Identify the organs upon which general surgery is performed.
4. Identify the major procedures performed within general surgery.

INTRODUCTION

This module reviews the codes used by physicians performing **anesthesia** for surgeries performed by another physician, and the codes used by surgeons describing general surgical procedures.

ANESTHESIA

Anesthesia is defined as pharmacological suppression of nerve function that can be administered by general, regional, or local method. The CPT codes for anesthesia are used to report the administration of anesthesia by or under the responsible supervision of a physician. They are reported only by the physician who is administering the anesthesia, and only if that physician is not performing the surgery. If a physician provided anesthesia for a surgery that he performed, the appropriate codes from the surgery section would be applied with a modifier of -47, anesthesia by surgeon, except in the case of conscious sedation (see Sedation With or Without Analgesia [Conscious Sedation] section of the Medicine chapter). **General, regional, local anesthesia** and other supportive services are included in the anesthesia codes. Preoperative and postoperative visits by the anesthesiologist, care during the procedure, monitoring of vital signs, and any fluid administration are also included in the anesthesia codes. There are unusual forms of monitoring that may be required from the anesthesiologist (such as central venous monitoring or Swan-Ganz), which should be reported separately as they are not normally part of the anesthesia services. The anesthesia codes may be accessed in the index under the key word anesthesia, and then by body site upon which the surgery is performed.

Anesthesia codes are applied based upon the body site being operated on, and are not based on the type of anesthesia administered. In the Anesthesia chapter of CPT the subheadings are the different body sites that could be operated upon. Select the appropriate code under the subheading that represents the surgery being performed on that body site. Keep in mind that codes from this chapter are applied only for the anesthesia that is being performed for surgery in that area. The surgeon would assign codes from the surgery chapter to represent his or her work.

All anesthesia services require the use of the five-digit CPT code plus an additional two-digit modifier to indicate the physical status of the patient. The **physical status modifiers** are consistent with the American Society of Anesthesiologists (ASA) ranking of a patient's physical status. The anesthesiologist provides the ASA ranking, or physical status of the patient. This can usually be found on the anesthesia graph. These modifiers consist of the letter "P" followed by a single digit from 1 to 6 as outlined in Figure 4–1.

For example, an anesthesiologist who provides general anesthesia for a patient who is undergoing a corneal transplant would select the 5-digit code 00144, Anesthesia for procedures on eye: corneal transplant. Included in that code is a preoperative evaluation during which the anesthesiologist discovers that the patient has a severe systemic disease. The 5-digit code of 00144 should be appended with the modifier P3 to indicate the physical status of the patient.

■ Highlight

Sometimes anesthesia may be provided under particularly difficult circumstances. These circumstances may be the condition of the patient, notable operative conditions, or unusual risk factors. It would be appropriate to add a code from 99100 to 99140 to indicate these qualifying circumstances. These codes are never to be used alone, but in association with the code for the anesthesia procedure or service. Patients of extreme age (under one year or over seventy), and emergency conditions, are examples of unusual risk factors.

P1—A normal healthy patient

P2—A patient with mild systemic disease

P3—A patient with severe systemic disease

P4—A patient with severe systemic disease that is a constant threat to life

P5—A moribund patient who is not expected to survive without the operation

P6—A declared brain-dead patient whose organs are being removed for donation

---

Figure 4–1 Physical status modifiers.

EXERCISE 4–1

Assign the CPT code that an anesthesiologist would report for the following:

General anesthesia provided for a patient with mild systemic disease who is undergoing a ventral hernia repair. _____

GENERAL SURGERY

General surgery refers to operations performed on the following body systems: respiratory, cardiovascular, hemic and lymphatic, mediastinum and diaphragm, digestive, urinary, male genital, female reproductive, endocrine, nervous, eye and ocular adnexa, and auditory. The female reproductive system will be covered separately in Module 8 of this text. Subsections within each system list the specific organ followed by the procedure performed on each of these organs.

Modifiers are used extensively in the surgical section. A modifier describes a specific circumstance or an unusual event that alters the definition of the procedure. Unilateral surgery performed upon organs that have a definite right and left side are reported with either the -LT (left side) or -RT (right side) modifier. Surgery performed on eyelids, fingers and toes should be modified from the list shown in Table 4–1 to prevent erroneous denials when duplicate HCPCS codes are billed reporting separate procedures performed on different anatomical sites or different sides of the body.

THE RESPIRATORY SYSTEM

The respiratory system is divided into upper and lower tracts. The organs of the upper tract include the nose, nasal cavity, nasopharynx, oropharynx, laryngopharynx and larynx. The lower tract (see Figure 4–2) includes the trachea, the bronchi, bronchioles, and alveoli that comprise the lungs. The respiratory section in the CPT code book is subdivided into the following categories: nose, accessory sinuses, larynx, trachea and bronchi, and lungs and pleura.

TABLE 4–1 **HCPCS Level II Modifiers.**

-E1 Upper left, eyelid	-TA Left foot, great toe
-E2 Lower left, eyelid	-T1 Left foot, second digit
-E3 Upper right, eyelid	-T2 Left foot, third digit
-E4 Lower right, eyelid	-T3 Left foot, fourth digit
-FA Left hand, thumb	-T4 Left foot, fifth digit
-F1 Left hand, second digit	-T5 Right foot, great toe
-F2 Left hand, third digit	-T6 Right foot, second digit
-F3 Left hand, fourth digit	-T7 Right foot, third digit
-F4 Left hand, fifth digit	-T8 Right foot, fourth digit
-F5 Right hand, thumb	-T9 Right foot, fifth digit
-F6 Right hand, second digit	
-F7 Right hand, third digit	
-F8 Right hand, fourth digit	
-F9 Right hand, fifth digit	

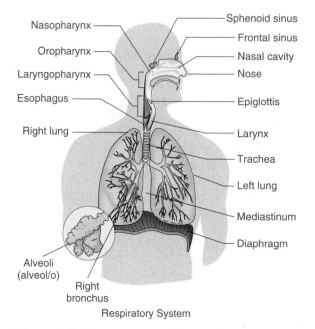

Nasopharynx — Sphenoid sinus
— Frontal sinus
Oropharynx — — Nasal cavity
Laryngopharynx — — Nose
Esophagus — — Epiglottis
Right lung — — Larynx
— Trachea
— Left lung
— Mediastinum
— Diaphragm
Alveoli (alveol/o) —
Right bronchus —
Respiratory System

Figure 4–2 The structures of the respiratory system.

Nasal Polyps

An excision of nasal polyps, simple, means that there was just one polyp on one side of the nasal cavity. An extensive procedure involves the excision of multiple nasal polyps on one side. Use the bilateral modifier (-50) to report the excision of nasal polyps from both sides of the nasal cavity only if the same degree of excision is performed on both sides.

General Sinus Surgery

For repair codes on the nasal sinus (30400–30630), primary repair refers to the first repair of any structure. Secondary repair is a repair performed subsequent to a primary repair. Minor revision rhinoplasty, or plastic surgery of the nose, involves only nasal cartilage. Intermediate revision rhinoplasty involves an osteotomy or the cutting of bone. Major revision rhinoplasty includes both cartilage (work on the nasal tip) and an osteotomy.

Code 30520 is reported for a septoplasty or submucous resection, with or without cartilage scoring, contouring, or replacement with graft. This is the only code assigned if the cartilage used for the graft is obtained from the immediate surgical area. If, however, the physician must go outside of the septum to obtain enough cartilage for the graft, it would be appropriate to add the code 20912, cartilage graft, nasal septum.

In order to correctly code the control of nasal hemorrhage, the following questions must be answered:

1. Was the hemorrhage anterior (the forward or front part of the body or body part) or posterior (the back part of the body or body part)?
2. If it was anterior, was the hemorrhage simple or complex?
3. If it was posterior, was the control an initial or a subsequent procedure?

The physician should document in the medical record if the procedure was simple or complex.

The simple control of an anterior nasal hemorrhage (epistaxis) is coded to 30901. If the repair of the anterior nasal hemorrhage is complex, apply code 30903. The first time a posterior nasal hemorrhage is controlled (by any method), assign code 30905. For every subsequent time that the posterior nasal hemorrhage is controlled, assign code 30906. If, however, the control of the hemorrhage is done by nasal endoscopy, the appropriate code would be 31238, nasal/sinus endoscopy, surgical; with control of epistaxis.

Paranasal sinuses are spaces that contain air and are lined with mucous membranes. The four sinus cavities on each side of the face are:

1. frontal, on each side of the forehead, above each eye medially
2. maxillary (also called antrum), located in the cheekbones below each eye
3. sphenoid, located behind the nasal cavity
4. ethmoid, located between the nose and the eye

Laryngoscopy

Laryngoscopy codes are subdivided into diagnostic and surgical. Diagnostic involves viewing only, while surgical involves any excision, destruction, repair, or biopsy. A surgical laryngoscopy always includes a diagnostic laryngoscopy, so the two codes would not be assigned together. A direct laryngoscopy involves passing a rigid or fiberoptic endoscope through the mouth and pharynx to allow for direct visualization of the larynx. An indirect laryngoscopy uses a light source and two mirrors, one positioned at the back of the throat, and the other held in front of the mouth. The tongue is grasped and held out as far as possible and the larynx is observed.

Bronchoscopy

A surgical bronchoscopy includes a diagnostic bronchoscopy. If a biopsy is taken, a foreign body removed, or a tumor or blockage is destroyed, it is considered a surgical bronchoscopy and the appropriate code applied. It would be inappropriate to assign 31622, bronchoscopy, diagnostic, in addition to the surgical bronchoscopy.

EXERCISE 4–2

Assign the appropriate ICD-9-CM and CPT code(s) for the following surgery:

Postoperative Diagnosis: Bronchomalacia, Bronchitis

Procedure Performed: Bronchoscopy

Procedure: While the patient was receiving supplemental oxygenation, a heparin lock was placed in for administration of medication. The fiberoptic bronchoscope was introduced through the nostril and upper airways were observed to be within normal limits. The vocal cords appeared normal and no growth or bleeding was observed on them. The bronchoscope was then introduced in the trachea, which was noted to be within normal limits. The main carnia appeared sharp and well-demarcated. The right- and left-sided bronchial trees were subsequently visualized. The right upper lobe and its subsegments, the right middle lobe and its subsegments, and the right lower lobe and its subsegments showed bronchitis without any evidence of endobronchial lesions or gross active bleeding. Plenty of mucus plugging was noted on the right side. On the left side of the left upper lobe lingula and subsegment and the left lower lobe and its subsegments, changes suggestive of bronchitis were shown with plenty of mucus plugging and significant amount of inflammation and friability especially in the left lower lobe. No endobronchial lesion was seen. Bronchomalacia was noted in the left lower lobe. Brushings, washings, and biopsy were done from the left lower lobe.

ICD-9-CM code(s) _____

CPT code(s) _____

THE CARDIOVASCULAR SYSTEM

The cardiovascular system involves the heart and blood vessels. Some heart surgery requires the use of cardiopulmonary bypass (heart lung machine). A pericardiectomy without the use of cardiopulmonary bypass would be coded 33030, whereas the use of cardiopulmonary bypass during a pericardiectomy would be coded 33031 because the use of cardiopulmonary bypass is stated within the code. The same holds true with the repair of wounds of the heart and great vessels (33300–33335).

■ *Highlight*

Assign the code that fully describes all procedures performed.

Pacemakers

A pacemaker system includes a pulse generator and one or more electrodes (leads) inserted through a vein (transvenous) or on the surface of the heart (epicardial). A single chamber device includes the generator and one electrode inserted into either the atrium or ventricle of the heart. A dual chamber device includes the generator and electrodes inserted into *both* the atrium and the ventricle of the heart. The changing of a battery is actually the replacement of a generator. This procedure requires the code for the removal of the old generator and a second code for the insertion of the new generator. Any repositioning or replacement within the first 14 days after initial insertion of the pacemaker is included in the code assignment. Insertion of a temporary pacemaker (33211) is a separate procedure and therefore would not be assigned if the reason for the temporary pacer was for the performance of other heart surgery. Often the temporary pacemaker is inserted to ensure the steady rhythm of the heart while other surgery is being performed. In this case, the temporary pacemaker is inherent in the major procedure and would not be coded separately. There is a specific code for the upgrade of a single chamber system to a dual chamber system (33214). This code includes the removal of the previously placed generator, the testing of the existing lead, the insertion of a new lead, and the insertion of a new pulse generator.

Coronary Artery Bypass Graft

Veins and/or arteries can be used for the performance of coronary artery bypass graft (CABG) surgery (see Figure 4–3). There are separate code ranges for the use of veins, arteries, or a combination of veins and arteries for the graft. If only the veins are used, a code from 33510–33516 must be applied. If only arteries are used, a code from 33533–33545 is applied. When a combination of both veins and arteries are used, it is necessary to report two codes: 1) the appropriate combined arterial-venous graft code (33517–33523); and 2) the appropriate arterial graft code (33533–33536). The procurement of the saphenous vein for grafting is included in the description of the code for the venous grafting.

Catheters

The insertion of catheters into the venous system can be especially difficult to code because there are many types and uses of catheters. Catheters are placed into a vein with a needle and syringe (see Figure 4–4). The catheter is left in place and blood can be withdrawn for analysis, or substances can be added directly to the blood through the catheter, which acts as access to the vein. The most common types of central venous catheters (36488–36491) are:

> Broviac
> Hickman
> Hydrocath
> Groshong
> dual lumen
> triple lumen

■ Confusing Codes

There is no CPT code used to report the removal of a catheter when it requires only the removal of the skin suture holding it in place. To report a simple removal of a catheter, refer to the appropriate Evaluation and Management code. If a catheter becomes embedded and must be removed, assign code 37799 (unlisted vascular procedure) and provide supporting documentation.

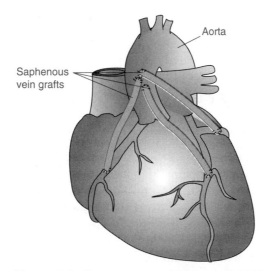

Figure 4–3 Coronary artery bypass graft (CABG) with a saphenous vein.

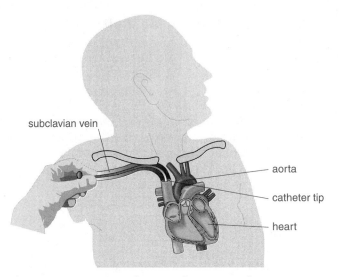

Figure 4–4 Insertion of a central venous catheter.

Vascular Access Devices

Vascular access devices (VADs) are devices that provide prolonged vascular access for chemotherapy, IV fluids, medications and the withdrawal of blood for sampling. VADs are surgically implanted creating a subcutaneous pocket to house the portal. A simple venous catheter does not contain a portal, therefore a subcutaneous pocket is not created. There is one CPT code that describes the insertion of an implantable venous access port (36533). Some of the common types are:

> Infuse-a-Port
> Micro Port
> Dual Port
> Groshong
> Port-a-cath
> Q-Port
> Medtronic CAP

The removal of a vascular access device is code 36535. The removal of an old vascular access device and the insertion of a new device is considered a revision and is coded to 36534.

THE HEMIC AND LYMPHATIC SYSTEMS

The hemic system consists of the spleen and the bone marrow. The harvesting of bone marrow or peripheral stem cells is reported using 38230 or 38231. The transplantation of these cells is reported using 38240 or 38241, depending on if the bone marrow or stem cells are allogenic (donated) or autologous (from the patient). Bone marrow aspiration for biopsy purposes would be coded using 85095.

The lymphatic system contains the lymph nodes and the lymphatic channels. The biopsy or excision of a single or random lymph nodes is coded to 38500–38555. A radical lymphadenectomy (38700–38780) is the removal of all or most of the lymph nodes in a certain area. The code for the excision of internal mammary nodes (38530) is a separate procedure, meaning it is not to be assigned if it is commonly carried out as an integral component of another procedure. For example, it is common to excise some internal mammary nodes during a breast biopsy or mastectomy. In this case, the code 38530 would not be applied separately. This code may be applied if it is carried out independently or is considered to be unrelated or distinct from other procedures provided at that time.

THE MEDIASTINUM AND DIAPHRAGM

Procedures on the mediastinum and diaphragm are reported using codes 39000–39599. Diaphragmatic hernias are repaired by transthoracic approach or by abdominal approach. Code selection depends upon the approach used to repair the hernia. In the event that a physician repairs the hernia by some other method (endoscopic repair), the unlisted code for procedures on the diaphragm (39599) would be assigned.

THE DIGESTIVE SYSTEM

The digestive system is composed of the following organs and structures: the mouth, pharynx, esophagus, stomach, large intestine and small intestine. Accessory organs of the digestive system include the teeth, salivary glands, liver, gallbladder and pancreas (see Figure 4–5). The main functions of the digestive system

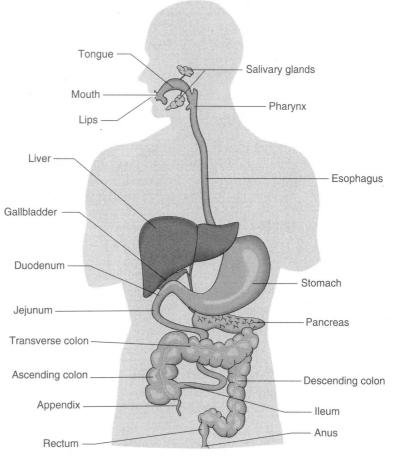

Figure 4–5 The structures of the digestive system.

are the digestion, absorption and elimination of food. Physicians who specialize in the diagnosis and treatment of disorders of this body system are called gastroenterologists. Gastro is the root word meaning stomach.

Similar to the other body system areas of CPT, the digestive system subsection is organized by body site and includes codes for the abdomen, peritoneum, and the omentum (a double fold of the peritoneum that hangs down over the small intestine and lies between the liver and the lesser curvature of the stomach). Codes for hernias and **endoscopy** are also included in this subsection.

For procedures done on the lips (40490–40761), the vermillion refers to the part of the lip between the outer skin and the moist oral mucosa of the mouth. It is sometimes referred to as the "lipstick area". The vestibule of the mouth (codes 40800–40845) refers to the oral cavity, not including the dentoalveolar structures.

A uvulopalatopharyngoplasty (UPPP) is the removal of mucosa and muscle from the pharyngeal walls, uvula, and soft palate. What is left is a permanent, noncollapsing, oropharyngeal airway that attempts to correct sleep apnea of the obstructive type. The correct code assignment for UPPP is 42145. The same procedure done by laser or thermal, cryotherapy, or chemicals is coded to 42160. This procedure is often completed in the physician office since it is minimally invasive and has been referred to as the snore-cure.

Tonsillectomy

A tonsillectomy is coded in conjunction with an adenoidectomy when appropriate.

■ *Confusing Codes*

It is essential to know the age of the patient receiving the tonsillectomy and/or adenoidectomy. The surgery performed on children under the age of 12 is assigned one set of codes, while the procedure performed on a patient age 12 and over is coded with a different set of codes.

Endoscopy

A surgical endoscopy always includes a diagnostic endoscopy. Diagnostic refers to viewing only. Once surgery is performed during an endoscopy procedure, it would not be appropriate to the diagnostic code, as viewing is part of the surgery. Code the diagnostic endoscopy only if a surgical procedure was not performed.

An upper endoscopy is a scope passed through the mouth into the esophagus and in some cases into the stomach and even into the duodenum.

An esophagoscopy is limited to the study of the esophagus. An esophagogastroscopy is when the endoscope passes the diaphragm. An esophagogastroduodenoscopy (EGD) is when the endoscope traverses the pyloric channel. An ileoscopy passes the third part of the duodenum. It is essential to read the operative report to determine how far the scope was passed in order to assign the correct code.

When coding a surgical endoscopy, the following rules must be considered:

1. If a single lesion is biopsied but not excised, use only the biopsy code.
2. If a biopsy of a lesion is obtained and the remaining portion of the same lesion is then excised, code only the excision.
3. If multiple biopsies are obtained (from the same or different lesions) and none of the lesions are excised, use only the biopsy code once.

4. If a biopsy of a lesion is performed and a different lesion is excised during the same procedure, code both the Excision and Biopsy, if the code for the excision does not include the statement "With or Without Biopsy". If this statement is included, use a separate biopsy code.

There are several methods for the removal of lesions by endoscopy. An understanding of these will help you in the code assignment. Hot biopsy is when the forceps uses an electrical current that excises and fulgurates the polyp simultaneously. Forceps may be passed through a scope to remove tissue for biopsy. Ablation involves the elimination or control of a hemorrhage of a tumor or mucosal lesion. Electrocautery destroys the remaining tissue after a specimen is obtained. Snare is when a loop is slipped out of a long plastic tube and is closed down around the lesion, removing it. Bipolar cautery is electrosurgery using a pair of electrodes. The tissue that lies between the electrodes is coagulated using a flow of current from one electrode to another. Cold biopsy is used for smaller specimens and is the same as hot biopsy that is not hooked up to the fulgurator. Bleeding can be controlled using several different methods but all are reported using a single code.

Strictures and achalasia of the esophagus, or the inability of muscles to relax, can be treated using esophageal dilation. Using an instrument, the orifice is expanded or enlarged to relieve the obstruction.

▬ *Highlight*

There are several factors that need to be considered for proper coding of esophageal dilation. These factors involve the type of endoscopy involved, the method of dilation, and direct or indirect visualization. Direct visualization implies an endoscopic procedure. It is important to read the operative report to determine if the esophagus alone was examined, or if the scope was inserted all the way to the duodenum. Types of dilators that can be used include balloon, guide wires, bougie, or retrograde dilators.

Patients that cannot get enough nutrition by mouth can have a percutaneous endoscopic gastrostomy (PEG) tube placed. This is a procedure in which the endoscope is passed into the stomach, and a gastrostomy tube is placed percutaneously through the wall of the stomach as the endoscopist visualizes the insertion from inside. The code assignment for a PEG is 43246.

Endoscopic Retrograde Cholangiopancreatography

Endoscopic retrograde cholangiopancreatography (ERCP) is the injection of contrast medium into the papilla to visualize the pancreatic and common bile ducts by radiographic examination. As implied by the name, this is an endoscopic procedure, meaning that a scope is passed through the patient's mouth and into the duodenum where dye is instilled and then x-rays are taken. Before the endoscope is removed, many other procedures can be performed. A diagnostic ERCP includes the taking of specimens by brushing or washing. If a biopsy is obtained by other methods, the correct code would be 43261. If the ERCP is done and a sphincterotomy (incision of the sphincter) is performed, use code 43262. Pressure measurements can be made of the sphincter of Oddi and would be coded to 46263. Stones are often removed with such devices as a basket or balloon and code 43264 should be applied. If the stones are too large for simple removal, a device known as a lithotriptor can be passed through the endoscope and into the bile duct to crush the stones. The use of the lithotriptor necessitates the use of 43265. A drainage tube may be left in place to allow these crushed stones to pass and code 43267 should be applied. If indicated, a stent may be placed. A stent is an indwelling device that is left in position for long-term drainage. Stents are coded to 43268. A replacement of a stent is code 43269. When it is necessary to do a dilation of the bile or pancreatic duct, code 43271 would be applied (see Table 4–2).

It is considered unbundling to assign the code for ERCP, diagnostic when any of the above procedures are done at the same operative episode.

Lower endoscopy procedures include: anoscopy, the examination of the anus only; proctoscopy, the examination of the rectum; sigmoidoscopy, the examination of the rectum and sigmoid colon and may include a portion of the descending colon; and colonoscopy, examination of the entire colon from the rectum to the cecum.

Hemorrhoidectomy

A hemorrhoid is a mass of dilated vascular tissue in the anorectum. A hemorrhoid could be either internal, proximal to the anorectal line, or external, distal to the anorectal line. A hemorrhoidectomy is considered simple unless a plastic procedure is needed in association with the hemorrhoidectomy, in which case it is a complex or extensive hemorrhoidectomy. If a **fistula** or **fissure** is present, and treated at the same time as a hemorrhoidectomy, the use of the combination code (hemorrhoidectomy with fistulectomy or fissurectomy) is necessary. Use the code for subcutaneous fistulectomy if the procedure does not involve the muscle. A submuscular fistulectomy involves the division of muscle. A fistulectomy is considered complex if multiple fistulas are excised.

TABLE 4–2   **Procedures That Can Be Performed in Conjunction with ERCP, Using One CPT Code.**

ERCP	43260
ERCP with biopsy	43261
ERCP with sphincterotomy/papillotomy	43262
ERCP with pressure measurement	43263
ERCP with removal of stones	43264
ERCP with lithotripsy	43265
ERCP with insertion of drainage tube	43267
ERCP with stent insertion	43268
ERCP with removal of foreign body	43269
ERCP with balloon dilation	43271
ERCP with ablation of lesion	43272

Liver Biopsy

A percutaneous or needle biopsy of the liver is a closed procedure done percutaneously through the skin. A liver biopsy is considered to be open if it is an excisional biopsy or a wedge biopsy. A closed liver biopsy can be accomplished, even during an open abdominal procedure. If, during another procedure in which the abdomen is open, the operative report indicates that a needle or trochar is used to obtain liver tissue, it is considered to be a closed liver biopsy. If the operative report indicates that a wedge of liver tissue was excised, it is considered an open biopsy. Normally, an open biopsy of the liver requires the use of a suture after the removal of the tissue. A fine needle aspiration of the liver is coded from the Laboratory and Pathology chapter of the CPT book (see codes 88170 and 88171).

Cholecystectomy

A cholecystectomy is the surgical removal of the gallbladder. Use codes 47600–47620 if the procedure is open. For laparoscopic procedures, see codes 56340–56342.

EXERCISE 4–3

Assign the appropriate ICD-9-CM and CPT code(s) for the following surgery:

Preoperative Diagnosis: Cholecystitis with Cholelithiasis

Postoperative Diagnosis: Cholecystitis with Cholelithiasis

Operation Performed: Laparoscopic Cholecystectomy

Operative Findings: Chronic cholecystitis with cholelithiasis, otherwise negative exploration of the abdominal and pelvic cavity.

Procedure: With the patient under adequate general endotracheal anesthesia in the supine position, the operative area was prepped and draped in the usual fashion. A small incision was made above the umbilicus. With a needle, a pneumoperitoneum was obtained. This was followed by introduction of the trocar and a video camera. Once exploration was completed and with the patient in the reverse Trendelenburg and left lateral decubitus position, the epigastric and the 2 lateral ports were placed in. The gallbladder was grasped and retracted cephalad and lateral. The porta hepatis was dissected away. The cystic and common bile ducts were identified. The cystic duct was isolated, clipped and transected. The cystic artery was handled in the same fashion. Following this, the gallbladder was elevated from the undersurface of the liver with the spatula and electrocautery until it was completely free. The area was irrigated and suctioned out. There was no active bleeding. Therefore, the gallbladder was brought up through the umbilical port. It was opened, bile suctioned out, and some of the stones removed to allow easy removal of the organ, which was carried out and sent to pathology for further studies. The operative area was again explored. There was no bleeding, therefore all of the trocars were removed. After the pneumoperitoneum was allowed to dissipate, the deep incisions were closed with 2-0 Vicryl and all of the skin incisions with subcuticular 5-0 undyed Vicryl.

ICD-9-CM code(s) _____

CPT code(s) _____

Hernia Repair

A hernia is the projection or protrusion of an organ through the wall of the cavity that normally contains it. Reducible hernias can be corrected by manipulation. Nonreducible hernias cannot be reduced by manipulation, but are fixed in the hernial sac, allowing for no mobility of the hernia. An incarcerated hernia is one that is constricted, confined, or imprisoned in the hernia sac, and thus is nonreducible. Strangulation is the most serious complication of a hernia. When the hernia strangulates (or cuts off the blood supply to the herniated part, the result is tissue ischemia or death. A recurrent hernia is one that has been surgically treated prior to the current treatment.

Hernias are classified based on the location (see Figure 4–6). An inguinal hernia is the most common form of hernia, and is a protrusion of the abdominal contents through the inguinal canal, or groin area. A lipoma of the spermatic cord is frequently excised during a hernia. A separate code for the lipoma excision is not applied when an inguinal hernia is repaired, as it is considered a normal part of the procedure.

A femoral hernia is the protrusion of intestine through the femoral canal, next to the femoral vessels. An umbilical hernia is a protrusion of part of the intestine at the umbilicus. An epigastric hernia is the protrusion of fat or peritoneal sac between the umbilicus and the bottom of the sternum. The sac may be empty or contain an incarcerated viscus.

An incisional hernia occurs at the incision site from previous surgery. A hernia may develop at the site of an incision when the wound is new, recent, or even if it is an old wound. Ventral hernias are coded as incisional.

Often the repair of the hernia includes the implantation of mesh or other prosthetic material to hold the surrounding tissue in place. The only time that an additional code is used to indicate the use of mesh (49568) is when an incisional or ventral hernia is repaired. The other types of hernia repairs do not require an additional code to indicate the use of mesh or other prostheses.

If repair or excision is completed to the strangulated organs or structures from a hernia, an appropriate code for the excision or repair should be applied in addi-

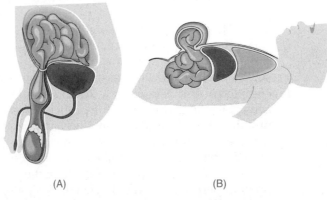

(A)   (B)

Figure 4–6 (A) Inguinal hernia. (B) Umbilical hernia.

tion to the hernia repair. For example, if a portion of the sigmoid colon needs to be removed because it is strangulated into the hernia sac, the code for the sigmoid resection would be applied in addition to the hernia repair.

■ *Highlight*

The key elements in the coding of hernia repair are as follows:

The age of the patient

The kind of hernia being repaired

The stage of the hernia (initial or recurrent)

The clinical presentation (reducible or incarcerated/strangulated)

The method of repair (open or laparoscopic)

Codes for bilateral hernia repairs do not exist, so the use of the modifier -50 "bilateral procedure" is imperative when a hernia is repaired on both sides.

EXERCISE 4–4

Assign the appropriate ICD-9-CM and CPT code(s) for the following surgery:

Preoperative Diagnosis: Right Inguinal Hernia

Postoperative Diagnosis: Right Inguinal Hernia

Operation Performed: Right inguinal hernia repair with Marlex mesh

Operative Findings:

1. 56-year-old male with right indirect inguinal hernia sac

2. Lipoma of the cord

3. Weakness of the floor of the inguinal canal

Procedure: With the patient under adequate general endotracheal anesthesia in the supine position, the operative area was shaved, prepped and draped in the usual fashion. An incision was made following the lower crease of the abdomen on top of the right inguinal canal and deepened through layers. The external oblique fascia was incised. The nerves were identified and protected. A Penrose drain was passed around the cord. The indirect hernia sac was separated from the vessels of the cord and it was opened and found to be empty. Therefore, it was suture ligated with 2-0 silk, excised out and the stump was allowed to retract. The lateral lipoma was handled in the same fashion. The weakness of the floor was repaired following the Liechtenstein technique with 2-0 Prolene and Marlex mesh, including a wraparound. Once the repair was completed, the Penrose drain was removed. The cord and the nerves returned to their anatomical position. The external oblique fascia was closed with running 3-0 Vicryl; 40 cc of 0.5% Marcaine with adrenaline were infiltrated to the operative field. The Scarpa fascia was closed with 3-0 Vicryl and the skin with staples.

ICD-9-CM code(s) _____

CPT code(s) _____

EXERCISE 4–5

Assign the appropriate ICD-9-CM and CPT code(s) for the following surgery:

Preoperative Diagnosis: Right-sided abdominal pain, possible appendicitis

Postoperative Diagnosis: Appendicitis, pending path report

Operation Performed: 1. Exploratory Laparotomy
                           2. Appendectomy

Anesthesia: General Endotracheal

Indications for the Operation: This 33-year-old white female with right-sided abdominal pain was admitted to the service of gastroenterology. Surgical consultation was requested for the purposes of consideration of exploratory laparotomy for her right-sided abdominal pain. The risks, benefits and options were discussed with the patient concerning the same. Having understood, she strongly desired to proceed to surgical intervention.

Operative Findings: The appendix has mild serosal injection at its distal aspect, possibly consistent with early appendicitis. No enlarged mesenteric lymph nodes were noted. The omentum was without obvious lesion and there were no obvious twisted appendices epiploica. The distal small bowel was without evidence of Crohn's disease, nor was there any evidence of a Meckel diverticulum. The cecum and ascending colon were normal. The gallbladder was without palpable stone. The left and right lobe of the liver along the anterior/inferior edge were smooth and without palpable lesions. The left colon was without adhesive disease and there was no evidence of diverticulitis. The pelvis was surgically empty without uterus, tubes or ovaries palpable.

Operative Technique: The patient was placed in the supine position, after induction of general anesthesia. The abdomen prepped and draped in the usual sterile fashion. With Claforan 1 g and Flagyl 500 mg having been administered intravenously, a short transverse incision was made in the right lower quadrant. Subcutaneous tissue was divided. The abdominal wall was incised and the peritoneal cavity was entered with findings as noted above. After an exploratory laparotomy with the aforementioned findings was noted, the cecum was delivered into the surgical incision. The appendix was ligated with a double 2-0 silk suture at the base of the cecum. Distal the appendix was ligated with a 2-0 silk suture. The appendix was then transected. The appendiceal stump on the base of the cecum was then cauterized. The mesoappendix was clamped, divided and ligated with 2-0 silk suture. The right lower quadrant was then inspected for hemostasis and no bleeding was appreciated. A continuous 2-0 Vicryl suture was used to close the peritoneum and the posterior rectus layer as well as transversus abdominis layer. On the anterior rectus sheath and on the external oblique fascia, a continuous 2-0 Vicryl suture was placed. The skin was closed with wide stainless steel clips and dry dressing applied.

ICD-9-CM code(s) _____

CPT code(s) _____

THE URINARY SYSTEM

Urinary system coding includes procedures performed on the kidney, ureter, bladder and urethra. Included in this section are also procedures on the prostate that are performed by the transurethral method. Open procedures on the prostate are in the male genital system section. Identify the parts of the urinary system shown in Figure 4–7.

A nephrostomy is the creation of an artificial fistula into the renal pelvis. If the nephrostomy is completed with a nephrotomy (incision into the kidney), assign code 50040. If the procedure is a percutaneous nephrostomy, use code 50395. A nephrolithotomy (50060–50075) is the surgical removal of stones from the kidney through an incision in the body of the kidney. A nephrostolithotomy is a percutaneous procedure used to establish a passageway from the kidney through which stones can be extracted. The code assignment is based on the size of the stone. If a stone that is two centimeters or less is extracted through a nephrostolithotomy, assign code 50080. If the stone extracted through the nephrostolithotomy is over two centimeters, assign code 50081. Sometimes the passageway for removing stones already exists from a previous procedure (nephrostomy or pyelostomy) and a physician will remove a stone through it (see Figure 4–8). In this case assign code 50561 because a new nephrostomy has not been created in this operative episode.

There are many codes in this section that state "exclusive of radiological service". Several procedures on the urinary system are done in conjunction with a radiological procedure to further visualize the organs being examined. The codes in this section do not include the taking of the radiological images. An additional

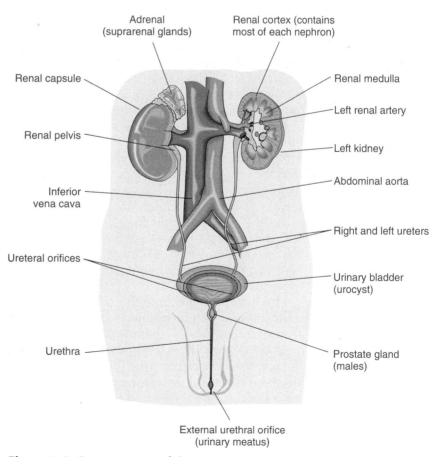

Figure 4–7 Gross anatomy of the urinary system.

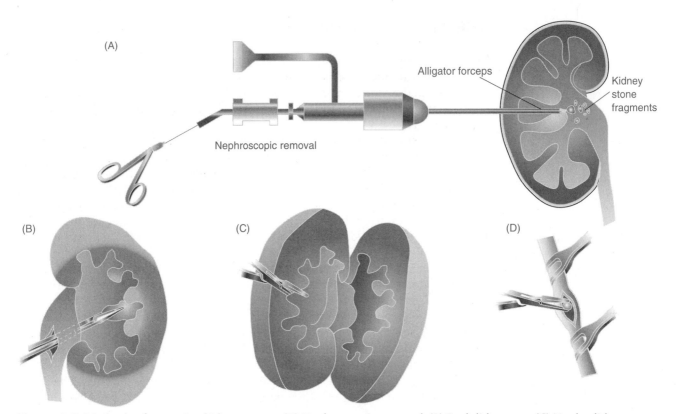

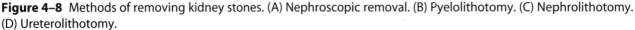

Figure 4–8 Methods of removing kidney stones. (A) Nephroscopic removal. (B) Pyelolithotomy. (C) Nephrolithotomy. (D) Ureterolithotomy.

code from the radiology section of the CPT code book must be assigned in order to classify the radiological service performed.

For the surgical removal of stones from the ureter through a direct incision into the ureter, use codes 50610–50630, depending upon what portion of the ureter was incised, the upper one-third, the middle one-third, or the lower one-third.

Indwelling ureteral catheters are inserted into the renal pelvis through the ureter to allow drainage from the renal pelvis when something is impinging the ureters. The most common types of ureteral stents are Gibbons and double-J stents. The approach for the insertion of the catheters determines the code assignment. Insertion of indwelling ureteral catheters through established nephrostomy is code 50553 while those through established ureterostomy is code 50953.

An ileal conduit is a method of diverting the urinary flow by making a conduit with the ureter through a segment of the ileum and out the abdominal wall. A special receptacle collects the urine. This procedure is usually performed when a bladder carcinoma or pelvic tumor is obstructing the ureter making the patient unable to pass urine.

The insertion of temporary stents during diagnostic or therapeutic cysto-urethroscopic interventions is included in 52320–52339 and should not be reported separately. Use code 52332 in addition to the primary procedure and add modifier -51 multiple procedures when the stents are self-retained and indwelling, not just temporary during the time of the procedure. Because code 52332 is considered a unilateral procedure, assign the modifier -50 bilateral procedure if the procedure was performed on both ureters. The removal of indwelling ureteral stents is coded to 52310 (simple procedure) or 52315 (complicated procedure) with the modifier -58 staged or related procedure or service by the same physician during the postoperative period. The operative report should substantiate the use of the complicated removal of ureteral stents.

All minor procedures done concurrently with endoscopic or transurethral surgeries are included in the main procedure and are not to be coded separately (see instructional notes under Endoscopy-Cystoscopy, Urethroscopy, Cysto-urethroscopy in the CPT book).

THE MALE GENITAL SYSTEM

The male genital system contains the penis, testes, epididymis, tunica vaginalis, vas deferens, scrotum, spermatic cord, seminal vesicles, and prostate.

Codes 54050–54065 are used for the destruction for condylomas, papillomas, molluscum contagiosums, and herpetic vesicle lesions. All other lesions of the penis are coded in the integumentary system of CPT. Simple destruction of the lesion of the penis is coded based on the method of the destruction (electrodesiccation, cryosurgery, laser surgery or surgical excision). If the physician states that the procedure was extensive, assign code 54065, regardless of the method used.

The excision of a hydrocele from the tunical vaginalis is code 55040 and the excision of a hydrocele from the spermatic cord is code 55500. For a hydrocelectomy that is performed with an inguinal hernia repair, see code 49515.

Vasectomies are reported using code 55250. The code description states unilateral or bilateral, therefore the modifier -50, bilateral procedure, would be inappropriate for use with this code. Note that included in this code is any postoperative semen examination(s), no matter how many are performed.

Prostate biopsies are codes 55700–55705. The code assignment is based on the type of biopsy performed (needle or punch, or incisional). The description of the code indicates that any approach used is included in the code assignment. For fine needle aspiration of the prostate, refer to code 88170.

EXERCISE 4–6

Assign the appropriate ICD-9-CM and CPT code(s) for the following surgery:

Preoperative Diagnosis: Elevated Prostate-Specific Antigen
Urinary Retention

Postoperative Diagnosis: Elevated Prostate-Specific Antigen
Urinary Retention

Operation Performed: Cystoscopy
Transperineal needle biopsy of the prostate

Procedure: The patient was taken to the operating room and given general anesthesia. He was placed in the dorsal lithotomy position, prepared and draped in the usual sterile fashion. A cystoscopy was performed with a flexible cystoscope using saline and light source. The above-noted findings were made. Following this Tru-Cut needle biopsies were obtained using a Tru-Cut needle in the perineal area without difficulty. Perineal pressure was applied. The procedure was terminated.

ICD-9-CM code(s) _____

CPT code(s) _____

LAPAROSCOPY/HYSTEROSCOPY

More and more procedures are being performed by laparoscopy upon a variety of organ systems in the abdominal and peritoneal region. This less-invasive method greatly reduces the risk to the patient and less recovery time is needed than with open procedures. Procedures that are performed by laparoscopy or hysteroscopy, the inspection of the uterus with a special endoscope, must be reported using codes 56300–56399 (see Figure 4–9).

THE NERVOUS SYSTEM

The central nervous system (CNS) includes the brain and spinal cord. The peripheral nervous system (PNS) includes the cranial nerves, the spinal nerves and the autonomic nervous system. The autonomic nervous system is the portion of the nervous system concerned with regulation of the activity of cardiac muscle, smooth muscle, and glands. Twist drill, Burr Holes and Trephine all refer to the making of small openings into the bone of the skull.

Surgery on the Base of the Skull

Several surgeons are often required for the surgical management of lesions involving the base of the skull (base of anterior, middle, and posterior cranial fossae). These physicians from different specialties work together or in tandem (one after the other) during the operative session. These operations are usually not staged

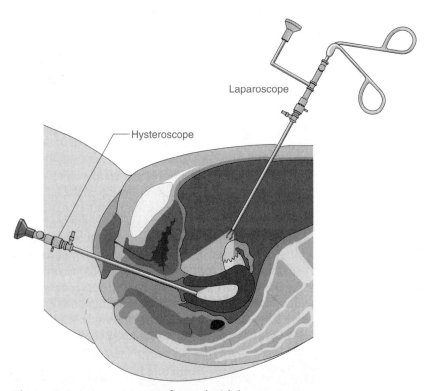

Figure 4–9 Laparoscopy performed with hysteroscopy.

because it is necessary to close the dura, subcutaneous tissues, and skin in a definitive way in order to avoid serious infections. These procedures are categorized according to:

1) the approach or anatomical area involved
2) the definitive procedure, biopsy, excision, resection, or treatment of lesions
3) repair/reconstruction of defect—reported separately if extensive dural grafting, cranioplasty, pedicle flaps, extensive skin grafts

The 1998 *Physicians' Current Procedural Terminology* book states that "When a surgeon performs the approach procedure, another surgeon performs the definitive procedure, and another surgeon performs the repair/reconstruction procedure, each surgeon reports only the code for the specific procedure performed."

Use of Operative Microscope

Code 61712 is for the use of the operative microscope for dissection of the anatomic structure or pathology that are too small for adequate visualization otherwise. Note the code ranges for which this procedure can be applied. Do not use the modifier -20 "microsurgery" when CPT code 61712 is used to report the microdissection.

Lumbar Puncture

In a lumbar puncture, an anesthetic is first injected, then a spinal needle is inserted between the spinous processes of the vertebrae (usually between the third and fourth lumbar vertebrae). The stylet is removed from the needle, and cerebral spinal fluid (CSF) drips from the needle. The CSF pressure is measured and recorded. The physician also evaluates the appearance of the CSF. After the specimen has been collected, a final pressure reading is taken, and the needle is removed.

A blood patch is performed if the spinal fluid continues to leak after the patient has had a spinal puncture or **epidural** anesthesia. The leakage causes the patient to suffer from headaches. The blood patch involves injecting the patient's blood into the site where the spinal puncture catheter originally was inserted. This injection of blood forms a patch, and as a result, stops the leakage of the spinal fluid.

Catheter Implantations

Codes 62350, 62351, and 62355 are not percutaneous procedures. Percutaneous procedures are coded to 62274–62284, 62288, 62289, 62298. Report two codes when a spinal reservoir or pump is implanted or replaced. Assign a code for the catheter implantation and a code for the reservoir or pump. The refilling of implantable pumps is reported with code 96530 in the Medicine chapter of CPT.

Laminotomy/Laminectomy/Decompression

These codes are determined based on the surgical approach, the exact anatomic location within the spine and the actual procedure performed. For a laminotomy (hemilaminectomy), note that the codes are based on one interspace in a specific area of the spine. If the procedure is performed on more than one interspace, then additional codes should be applied.

EXERCISE 4–7

Assign the appropriate ICD-9-CM and CPT code(s) for the following surgery:

Preoperative Diagnosis: Spinal stenosis lumbar spine

Postoperative Diagnosis: Spinal stenosis lumbar spine

Operation Performed: Lumbar laminectomy L5 level with diskectomy at the L5 level right and foraminotomy bilaterally at the L5 level.

With the patient under satisfactory general anesthesia, the patient was transferred onto the Wilson frame in the prone position. He was then appropriately positioned with the frame flexed to allow the abdomen to hang freely. The back was then prepared and draped in the usual sterile fashion. The skin incision was an 8 cm midline incision from L4 to the sacrum. Dissection was carried down through the subcutaneous tissues down through the deep fascia. The fascia was dissected off the L5 lamina bilaterally. X-ray was then obtained and the spinous process and lamina were removed. The dura was exposed all the way from L4 to the sacrum. There was a whitish discoloration suggestive of epidural steroid injections on the dura. After the dura was exposed, using a Penfield and a nerve root retractor, the L5 nerve root was identified bilaterally. The lateral gutters were opened by fully removing the overlying bone. The L5 nerve root was identified and followed out to the foramina. Foraminotomy was performed both on the left and right sides. At the end of the procedure a fat graft was taken from the subcutaneous tissues and placed over the exposed dura. Hemostasis was obtained with bipolar electrocautery, cottonoid and Gelfoam soaked in thrombin.

ICD-9-CM code(s) _____

CPT code(s) _____

THE EYE AND OCULAR ADNEXA

The Eyeball

Evisceration refers to a partial enucleation wherein the white of the eye, the scleral shell is left intact but the intraocular contents are removed. Exenteration is a radical procedure that is performed for malignant, invasive orbital tumors. The procedure involves the removal of the eye, the orbital contents, the extraocular muscles, the orbital fat and lids.

Secondary Implants

Secondary implants into the eye are inserted subsequent to initial surgery of eyeball removal. If the implant is put in at the same time as the initial removal, it is reported with a combination code (65093, 65103, or 65105). Ocular implants are placed inside the muscular cone. Orbital implants are placed outside the muscular cone. Note that these are not intraocular lens implants for cataracts and refer to codes 66983–66986.

Removal of Foreign Body

It is important to determine if the slit lamp (an operative lamp used in the operative field) is used on patients with removal of foreign body from the cornea, as it affects the code assignment (see codes 65220 and 65222). Equally important is to determine if a magnet is used to remove a foreign body from the posterior segment of the eye as the codes specifically state "magnetic extraction", or "nonmagnetic extraction"(see codes 65260 and 65265).

Anterior Segment of the Eye

The anterior segment of the eye involves the cornea, the anterior chamber, the anterior sclera, the iris, and the lens itself. Keratoplasty is a corneal transplant. If the transplant is involving the outer layer of the cornea only, it is coded as lamellar, code 65710. It the transplant includes all layers of the cornea, it is considered penetrating. If the keratoplasty is penetrating, be sure to identify if aphakia or pseudophakia are present, as it affects the code assignment (see codes 65730–65755). The operative report should state if aphakia or pseudophakia was encountered. If no mention is made, assume that neither is present.

Glaucoma is a condition in which the aqueous humor is unable to drain correctly through the trabecular meshwork. The fluid stays in the eyeball and causes pressure within the eye. In goniotomy the surgeon uses a gonioknife to release the pressure from glaucoma. In trabeculotomy ab externo the surgeon uses a trabeculotome to release the aqueous from outside the eye (ab externo). A trabeculoplasty by laser surgery does not use an incision technique. This procedure is done in a series of single treatment sessions and evaluation is done in between sessions to determine the effect of the treatment. This code is applied only once for the treatment series. Each session would not be coded separately. See the instructional note in the CPT book about the establishment of a new treatment series and the use of a modifier.

Codes 66150–66172 are used for glaucoma filtering surgery. Sometimes medication and laser treatment fail to adequately control the glaucoma. In these cases, a tiny opening can be made into the sclera, which establishes a new pathway for the fluids in the eye. Use code 66170 for a trabeculectomy upon an eye that has not had previous surgery. Use code 66172 when a trabeculectomy is performed on an eye that has scarring from previous surgery or injury. Examples of previous surgery are history of failed trabeculectomy, history of cataract surgery, history of strabismus surgery, history of penetrating trauma to the eyeball, and conjunctival lacerations.

Iris and Ciliary Body

An iridectomy is the penetrating of the iris, usually for excision of lesions beyond the iris. A cyclectomy goes deeper, going through the iris into the ciliary body.

Lens

A cataract is the opacity of the lens of the eye. To correct this abnormality, the lens of the eye is removed and an artificial one is implanted. This is known as intraocular lens or IOL. When a lens is removed, the patient is said to have **aphakia**, the absence of the lens. When a new lens is inserted, the patient is said to have pseudophakia, an artificial lens. There are two basic types of cataract extractions, intracapsular cataract extraction (ICCE), and extracapsular cataract extraction (ECCE). An ICCE is the surgical removal of the entire lens along with the front and back of the lens capsule. An ECCE is the surgical removal of the front portion and the nucleus of the lens, leaving the posterior capsule in place (see Figure 4–10). This is sometimes called an endocapsular cataract extraction. If the physician does not clearly state if an ICCE or an ECCE procedure was performed, carefully review the operative report to determine if the posterior capsule was excised.

Phacofragmentation and phacoemulsification are the two methods used to destroy the lens for removal.

When an intraocular lens is inserted within the same operative episode as a cataract extraction, one code is used to describe both procedures. However, if the insertion of the IOL was subsequent to the initial removal of the cataract, the code assignment would be 66985. Make sure that aphakia is present if you assign the code 66985.

For a list of procedures that are considered part of the cataract surgery, refer to the CPT code book under the cataract subsection.

When the hospital provides the IOL, they receive the ASC payment, plus a designated amount for the lens. If a physician provides the lens, the appropriate HCPCS code should be reported for proper reimbursement (see codes V2630–V2632).

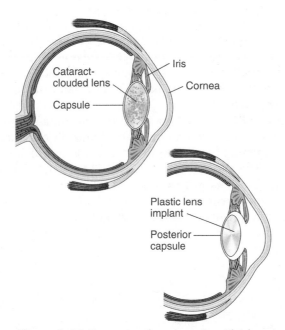

Figure 4–10 Extracapsular extraction. The lens is removed, the posterior lens capsule is left intact and the intraocular lens (IOL) is placed.

Posterior Segment

A vitrectomy is the removal of the vitreous humor from the eye. An anterior vitrectomy is performed through the front of the eye. A posterior vitrectomy is performed through the core of the vitreous. Sometimes, during other surgery on the eye, a partial vitrectomy is necessary because the vitreous is in the surgical field, or impedes the operation. When a code exists to describe the primary surgery and the vitrectomy, use only that code. A cataract removal is a good example because it states "with or without vitrectomy". An additional code for the vitrectomy would be inappropriate.

Retinal detachments usually start as a break, hole, or tear in the retina which is easily repaired by laser or cryoretinopexy. A more extensive procedure is required for retinal detachments in which fluid has accumulated under the retina. The severity of the detachment determines which procedure is used.

A scleral buckling procedure is the suturing of an elastic sponge to the sclera at the site of the detachment. A band can also be placed around the circumference of the eye, depending on the severity of the detachment.

Cryotherapy is the freezing of tissue to destroy abnormal tissue and cause the retina to adhere back to the eye. Diathermy causes the same result, but uses heat to burn through the back of the eye.

Ocular Adnexa

Strabismus surgery is used to correct a misalignment of the eyes. These codes are divided into initial surgery and repeat surgery. The reoperation on strabismus requires more physician effort and skill.

Recession is the lengthening of the muscle and resection is the shortening of the muscle. Strabismus surgery is coded based on the operation being performed on the horizontal muscles or the vertical muscles of the eye. The following chart defines which eye muscles are horizontal and which are vertical:

> inferior oblique—vertical
> inferior rectus—vertical
> lateral rectus—horizontal
> medial recuts—horizontal
> superior oblique—vertical
> superior rectus—vertical

Codes 67320, 67331, 67332, 67335, and 67340 are "add on" codes that are added to the strabismus surgery currently being performed. The add on codes clarify the specific circumstances and show additional physician work.

Strabismus surgery is considered to be unilateral, so be certain to add the modifier -50 "bilateral procedure".

EXERCISE 4–8

Assign the appropriate ICD-9-CM and CPT code(s) for the following surgery:

Preoperative Diagnosis: Cataract, right eye

Postoperative Diagnosis: Cataract, right eye

Operation Performed: Extracapsular Cataract Extraction, posterior chamber lens implantation, right eye.

After local anesthesia was obtained, a wire speculum was introduced, and a 4-0 silk suture was passed underneath the superior rectus muscle so as to act as a stay suture. A stab incision was done at approximately 2 o'clock with a super sharp # 11 blade. This wound was made beveled so that it would be self-sealing. A conjunctival periotomy was cut from approximately 11 to 12 o'clock superiorly. Hemostasis of the sclera was obtained with bipolar cautery. A partial depth groove was cut using a guarded crystal blade 2 mm posterior to the limbus and measuring 3.5 mm in length. A cresenctic blade was then used to sharply dissect a scleral tunnel into clear cornea. A 3.1 super sharp angle blade was then passed through the partial-depth groove, through the scleral tunnel and was used to enter the anterior chamber. The chamber was filled with Occucoat. A can opener style anterior capsulectomy was performed using a bent 25 gauge needle. The nucleus was gently rocked and loosened with the bent needle. The nucleus was fragmented and removed using a phacoemulsification device. The posterior capsule was cleaned with the irrigation-aspiration device. Additional cleaning was done using an olive-tipped cannula as a polish. The capsular bag was filled with Occucoat, and a 20.5 diopter posterior chamber intraocular lens was implanted in the capsular bag and centered horizontally. Miochol was instilled to make sure the pupil would come down on top of the optic of the intraocular lens. Occucoat was removed with the irrigation-aspiration device. The wound was tested and found to be watertight, so no sutures were placed.

ICD-9-CM code(s) _____

CPT code(s) _____

THE AUDITORY SYSTEM

The auditory system consists of the external, middle and inner ear (see Figure 4–11).

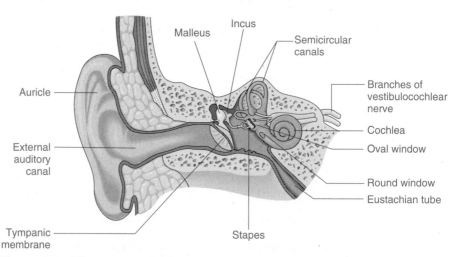

Figure 4–11 The structures of the ear.

The External Ear

For surgeries performed on the external ear be certain that the procedure is being done on the external auditory canal and not the skin of the outer ear. Procedures on the skin of the outer ear would be coded from the Integumentary System section.

Code 69220, debridement, mastoidectomy cavity, simple, is for routine cleaning in patients who have had a mastoidectomy. This type of cleaning usually needs to happen every 3–6 months. For patients who require extensive cleaning, or cleaning that is more than just routine cleaning, code 69222 would be applied.

The Middle Ear

Code 69400 is the inflation of the eustachian tube by placing a catheter through the nose to force the air into the eustachian tube. Code 69401 is the forcing of air into the eustachian tube through the nose without a catheter. Code 69405 is the catheterization of the eustachian tube through and incision and raising of the eardrum.

A myringotomy is also called a tympanotomy. It is an incision into the eardrum. Notice that code 69424 indicates that it is assigned for the removal of the ventilating tube when they were originally inserted by another physician. The removal of the tubes by the same physician is considered part of the surgical package and would be paid as such. Therefore, when the tubes are removed by the physician who inserted them, a code from this section is not applied.

A tympanostomy is the creation of an artificial opening into the eardrum by the insertion of tubes. Use care in selecting a code for the tympanostomy because the selection of the code is based upon the type of anesthesia used (local or general). This is often done as a bilateral procedure, so be certain to add the modifier -50 "bilateral procedure".

The Inner Ear

Fenestration (69820) creates a new window and sound pathway, bypassing the fixed stapes and oval window.

EXERCISE 4–9

Assign the appropriate ICD-9-CM and CPT code(s) for the following surgery:

Preoperative Diagnosis: Serous Otitis Media, both ears
Chronic Adenotonsillitis

Postoperative Diagnosis: Serous Otitis Media, both ears
Chronic Adenotonsillitis

Operation Performed: 1. Myringotomy with tubes, both ears with the insertion of the micro-gel paparella tubes
2. Tonsillectomy and adenoidectomy

Indications for the operation: This is a little, almost 2-year-old child, with a history of recurrent episodes of otitis media, now with serous otitis media refractory to medical therapy. Patient also has markedly hypertrophic cryptic tonsils with an adenoid fascia and history of chronic mucopurulent rhinorrhea.

Findings and Procedure: With the patient under adequate general endoctracheal anesthesia utilizing the Zeiss operating microscopy, the right ear was cleansed of cerumen and a myringotomy was accomplished in the posterior-inferior quadrant of the tympanic membrane. Serous fluid was aspirated from the middle ear space and a micro-gel Paparella tube was inserted. In likewise fashion, myringotomy with tube was accomplished in the left ear. Findings on the left side were also consistent with purulent middle ear secretions. Attention was turned to the tonsils and adenoids. The patient was placed in the rose position. A self-retaining mouthpiece was inserted. A large central mass of adenoid tissue was removed with adenoid curette. A temporary adenoid pack was inserted. Attention was turned to the tonsils. A right tonsil was grasped with a tonsil tenaculum and the mucous membrane was stripped with a #12 blade. The tonsil was dissected to the inferior pole and snared. In likewise fashion, the left tonsil was removed. All bleeding was controlled with Bovie coagulation. The patient was well suctioned, extubated without difficulty and returned to the recovery room with stable vital signs.

ICD-9-CM code(s) _____

CPT code(s) _____

SUMMARY

- Anesthesia codes are used to report the administration of anesthesia by or under the responsible supervision of a physician.
- Anesthesia codes are always followed by a physical status modifier that must come from the physician.
- When general surgery is performed, the operative report will identify the organ upon which surgery is performed, and the procedure performed. Experience at reading and interpreting Operative Reports will assist the coder in the correct code assignment.
- Modifiers are used extensively in the surgery section of CPT to describe a special circumstance or unusual event that alters the definition of the procedure.

REFERENCES

ASC Payment Groups. Alexandria, Virginia: St. Anthony, 1997.
Dorland's Illustrated Medical Dictionary. Philadelphia: W.B. Saunders, 1981.
The Merck Manual. Rahway, N.J.: Merck & Co., 1987.
CPT Assistant. Chicago, Illinois: American Medical Association, 1998.

Module 5
Integumentary System

Katie Cianciolo, MA, RRA, CCS, CCS-P

KEY TERMS

Abscess
Benign Lesion
Burns
Cellulitis
Debridement
Dermatitis
Destruction
Fasciocutaneous Flap
Malignant Lesion
Muscle Flap
Myocutaneous Flap
Pedicle
Pedicle Flap
Removal
Repair
Skin Graft
Skin Tag
Split Thickness
Ulcer
Wheal

LEARNING OBJECTIVES

Upon successful completion of this module, you should be able to:

1. Assign ICD-9-CM diagnosis codes to various diseases involving the integumentary system.
2. Assign CPT procedure codes to describe procedures performed on the skin and subcutaneous structures, nails, and breast.
3. Identify common terminology related to disorders of the skin and dermatology procedures.
4. Apply official coding guidelines in the assignment of all codes.

INTRODUCTION

The integumentary system includes the skin or integument, and its specialized structures including the nails, hair and sebaceous and sweat glands. The skin is composed of three layers: the epidermis or outer layer, the dermis or middle layer, and the subcutaneous or the inner layer (see Figure 5–1). The epidermis is a layer of squamous epithelial cells. Through keratinization, specialized epithelial or keratinocytes, produce a tough, fibrous protein called keratin. Keratin serves as a barrier repelling bacteria and other substances. The epidermal cells on the palms of the hands or the soles of the feet, for example, contain large concentrations of keratin. The epidermis also contains cells called melanocytes that produce melanin, or the pigment giving skin its color. The dermis is connective tissue made up of collagen and elastic fibers, blood, lymph vessels, nerves, sweat and sebaceous glands, and hair roots. The subcutaneous layer consists of connective and adipose tissue and is where the skin attaches to the muscles and bones.

The skin performs many functions, including protecting internal body organs, regulating body temperature, helping maintain fluid and electrolyte balance, excreting certain body waste, and producing vitamin D.

This module discusses codes used for the procedures performed on the integumentary system, with a focus on CPT. Codes for ICD-9-CM

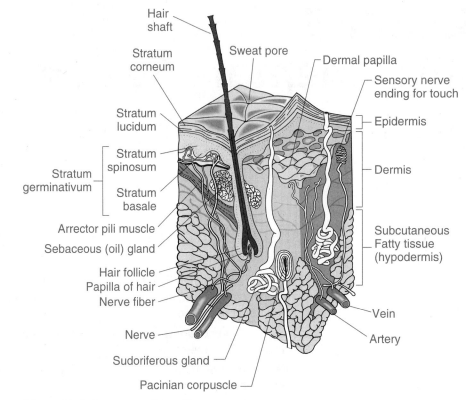

Hair shaft

Sweat pore

Dermal papilla

Stratum corneum

Sensory nerve ending for touch

Stratum lucidum

Epidermis

Stratum spinosum

Stratum germinativum

Dermis

Stratum basale

Arrector pili muscle

Subcutaneous Fatty tissue (hypodermis)

Sebaceous (oil) gland

Hair follicle
Papilla of hair
Nerve fiber

Vein

Nerve

Artery

Sudoriferous gland

Pacinian corpuscle

Figure 5–1 Anatomy of the skin.

are introduced where appropriate and the exercises incorporate both types of codes.

ICD-9-CM

Diseases of the skin and subcutaneous tissue are found in Chapter 12 of ICD-9-CM. This chapter also includes diseases of the hair and nails. The range of three-digit categories and sections are as follows:

680–686 Infections of Skin and Subcutaneous Tissues (i.e. **cellulitis**, abscess)

690–698 Other Inflammatory Conditions of Skin and Subcutaneous Tissue (i.e., rash, eczema, **dermatitis**, psoriasis)

700–709 Other Diseases of Skin and Subcutaneous Tissue (i.e., corn, keratosis, acne, ingrown nail, sebaceous cyst, **ulcer**, scar)

Other conditions affecting the skin or subcutaneous system on which integumentary procedures may be performed can also be found in other chapters of ICD-9-CM. For example, lacerations or burns would be located in Chapter 17, Injury and Poisoning (800–999); benign or malignant neoplasms would be found in Chapter 2, Neoplasms (140–239); and fibrocystic disease of breast is located under the section Disorders of Breast (610–611) within Chapter 10, Diseases of the Genitourinary System.

CPT

Integumentary System procedures in CPT are a subsection of the Surgery section and fall in the code range 10040–19499. This range includes procedures on the skin and subcutaneous tissue such as incision and drainage, debridement, paring, biopsy, removal of skin tags, shaving, excision and destruction of lesions, repair of lacerations, Moh's surgery, and **skin grafts**. Other plastic procedures involve skin grafts, liposuction, cosmetic procedures, treatment of burns, and excision of pressure ulcers. The term plastic surgery refers to procedures that involve tissue transplantation and repositioning. Nail procedures include debridement, excision, and reconstruction of the nail bed. Procedures on the breast include biopsy, mastectomy and reconstruction.

INCISION AND DRAINAGE

Incision and drainage procedure codes (range 10040–10180) are further specified by the terms "simple" and "complicated". The CPT book does not include defined criteria for the use of these terms, and their use is subjective by the physician. However, "complicated" can be substantiated by the difficulty in performing a procedure that may include the presence of infection with an unusual length of time and/or depth.

DEBRIDEMENT

Debridement is a procedure where foreign material and contaminated or devitalized tissue is removed from a traumatic or infected lesion or wound until the surrounding healthy tissue is exposed. The notes in CPT instruct the coder to another subcategory if the debridement is of the nails or for burn treatment. Some of the codes in this subcategory refer to debridement not only of the skin and subcutaneous tissue, but also the fascia, muscle, and bone (i.e., open fractures).

PARING OR CUTTING

Paring or curettement involves a superficial removal of a lesion using a curette. CPT codes ranges 11055–11057 refer only to hyperkeratotic lesions, such as a corn or callus. Also, these codes reference the number of lesions, rather than the site. A cross-reference note directs the coder to CPT (17000–17004) if hyperkeratotic lesions are destroyed rather than pared.

BIOPSY

A biopsy refers to taking a piece of a lesion rather than excising the entire lesion. This is usually done to determine whether the lesion is benign or malignant. The coder should be aware of the term "excisional biopsy" when assigning CPT codes. Physicians tend to use this term to mean "excision of an entire lesion," instead of simply a piece of it.

REMOVAL OF SKIN TAGS

A **skin tag**, or acrochordon, is a small, flesh-colored, benign outgrowth of epidermal and dermal tissue that generally appears on the eyelids, neck and armpits. A physician may remove a skin tag through a variety of methods, including scissoring, ligature strangulation, electrosurgical destruction, or a combination of these. The coder should read the patient's medical record carefully to see the number of skin tags removed, since choosing the correct code is based on the number removed.

Shaving of Epidermal/Dermal Lesions

Shaving is a sharp removal by horizontal slicing to remove epidermal or dermal lesions without a full-thickness excision and no incision made. The size of the lesion is used to make the correct code assignment.

Proper Coding for Lesion Removal

There are several steps that should be followed when coding removal of lesions. These include:

1. Determine the location of the lesion. Codes in the lesion removal categories group specific body sites together as follows:
   a. trunk, arms and/or legs.
   b. scalp, neck, hands, feet, and/or genitalia.
   c. face, ears, eyes, eyelids, nose, lips, and/or mucous membranes.
2. Determine the size of the lesion. This information should be taken from the operative report. Specimen size noted on the pathology report may not represent the exact size due to shrinkage of the lesion from the preservative agent. Also, many times, the physician removes more tissue (skin margins) than the actual lesion size. Only the actual lesion size is used to determine the correct code assignment.
   a. Lesion diameter is the length of a straight line segment that passes through the center of a circle or sphere.
   b. An asymmetrical or irregular shaped lesion is measured by the largest width.
   c. Many lesions are measured in three dimensions. Select the longest dimension.
3. Assign a CPT code for each lesion removed. Assign an ICD-9-CM code for each lesion, unless of the same site in which case the code is the same.

▥ *Highlight*

For insurance carriers requiring modifiers (Medicare Part B), -51 multiple procedures would be appended to the CPT code for any lesions removed, after the first one. Table 5–1 can assist the coder in converting the measurement when stated in inches or millimeters (mm.) to centimeters (cm.).

TABLE 5–1   **Metric Conversions.**

1 mm. = 0.1 cm.	.3937 inch = 1 cm.
10 mm. = 1 cm.	3/16 inch = 0.5 cm.
1 inch = 2.54 cm.	

Example: A 1-inch ellipse of skin is removed. The skin margins are marked and specimen reveals an ulcerated lesion of 13/16 inch. The actual lesion size is 13/16, inch which converts to 2.0 cm.

LESION REMOVAL OR DESTRUCTION

Skin lesions are growths that can be either benign or malignant. Lesions may be primary or secondary. Examples of primary lesions include macules, papules, nodules, **wheals** and tumors (see Figure 5–2). Secondary lesions generally develop from primary lesions and include ulcers, excoriations, fissures, and scars.

Excision-Benign Lesions (11400–11471)

Excision of **benign lesions** falls within code range 11400–11471. Excision is the full-thickness removal of a lesion, which includes a simple closure. Benign lesions are harmless and nonrecurring. A closure other than simple (i.e., layered) would be coded in addition to the lesion removal. Types of wound closure are discussed later in this module. A plastic repair (i.e., skin graft) includes the lesion removal. If lesion excision is performed by other methods (i.e., electrosurgical destruction, laser, cautery), the CPT notes refer the coder to the destruction codes (17000–17999).

The correct code cannot be assigned without verification from the pathology report. This is the only definitive way to determine if a lesion is benign or malignant.

■ *Highlights*

In most circumstances, excision of a cyst is coded to a benign lesion. However, the CPT book will refer the coder elsewhere for certain sites, such as cyst of breast (19120), ganglion cyst of wrist (25111 or 25112), or mucous cyst of finger (26160).

Excision-Malignant Lesions (11600–11646)

A **malignant lesion** grows worse over time and resists normal treatment. Often malignant lesions are cancerous. The same guidelines are followed for coding malignant lesions as for coding benign lesions. When a lesion is removed, the physician may not know if it is benign or malignant. If the lesion is malignant, usually further wide excision or resection is done to determine if the lesion has spread to its margins. However, if the resection proves to be negative for malignancy, the ICD-9-CM code is still coded to the neoplasm, skin, malignant site, and the CPT code the excision of malignant lesion (11600–11646).

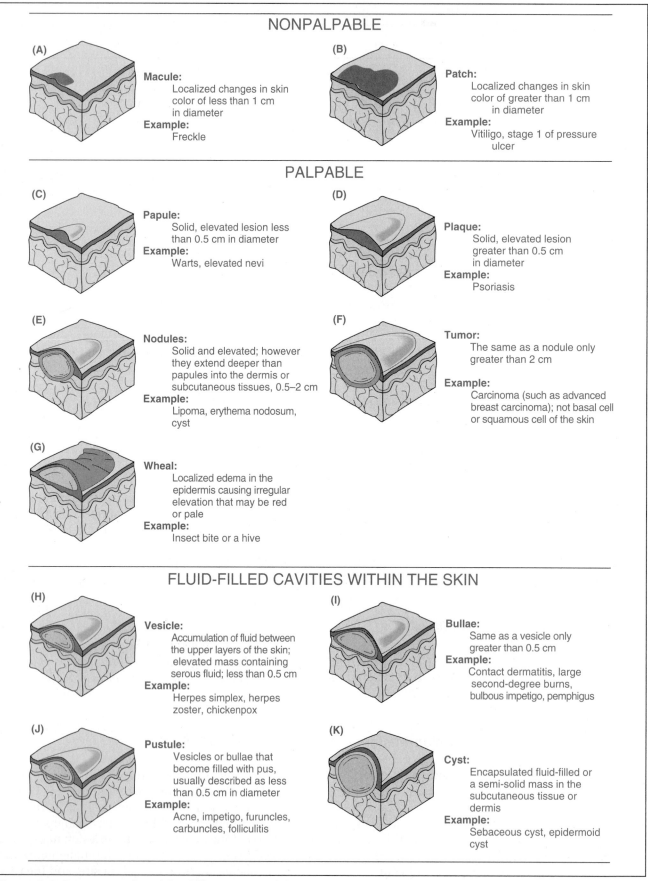

NONPALPABLE

(A) Macule:
Localized changes in skin color of less than 1 cm in diameter
Example:
Freckle

(B) Patch:
Localized changes in skin color of greater than 1 cm in diameter
Example:
Vitiligo, stage 1 of pressure ulcer

PALPABLE

(C) Papule:
Solid, elevated lesion less than 0.5 cm in diameter
Example:
Warts, elevated nevi

(D) Plaque:
Solid, elevated lesion greater than 0.5 cm in diameter
Example:
Psoriasis

(E) Nodules:
Solid and elevated; however they extend deeper than papules into the dermis or subcutaneous tissues, 0.5–2 cm
Example:
Lipoma, erythema nodosum, cyst

(F) Tumor:
The same as a nodule only greater than 2 cm
Example:
Carcinoma (such as advanced breast carcinoma); not basal cell or squamous cell of the skin

(G) Wheal:
Localized edema in the epidermis causing irregular elevation that may be red or pale
Example:
Insect bite or a hive

FLUID-FILLED CAVITIES WITHIN THE SKIN

(H) Vesicle:
Accumulation of fluid between the upper layers of the skin; elevated mass containing serous fluid; less than 0.5 cm
Example:
Herpes simplex, herpes zoster, chickenpox

(I) Bullae:
Same as a vesicle only greater than 0.5 cm
Example:
Contact dermatitis, large second-degree burns, bulbous impetigo, pemphigus

(J) Pustule:
Vesicles or bullae that become filled with pus, usually described as less than 0.5 cm in diameter
Example:
Acne, impetigo, furuncles, carbuncles, folliculitis

(K) Cyst:
Encapsulated fluid-filled or a semi-solid mass in the subcutaneous tissue or dermis
Example:
Sebaceous cyst, epidermoid cyst

Figure 5–2 Some examples of the different types of skin lesions.

continues

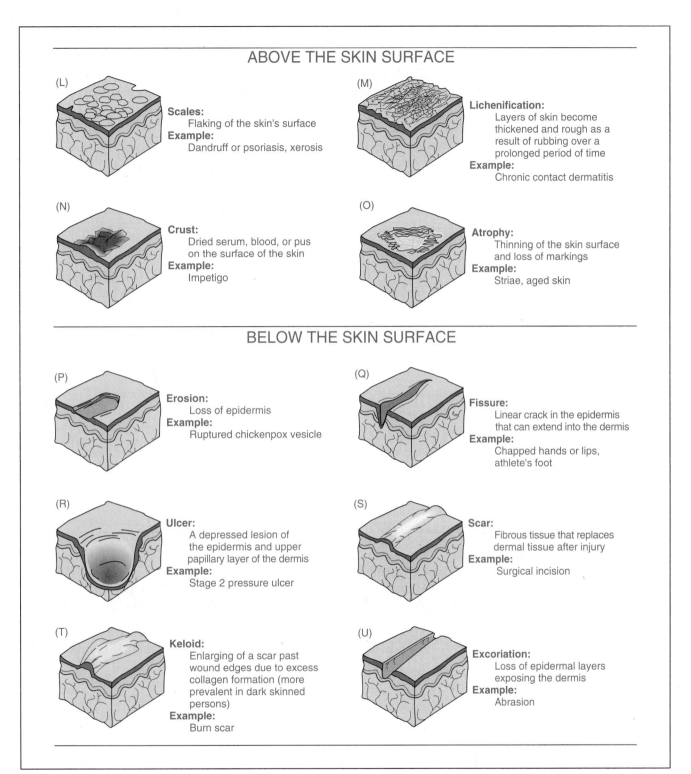

Figure 5-2 Some examples of the different types of skin lesions. *continued*

EXERCISE 5–1

Using your CPT and ICD-9-CM coding books, assign the ICD-9-CM code, ICD-9-CM Procedure Code and CPT Procedure Code to the following:

Diagnosis: Pigmented, ulcerated lesion, left forehead.

Operation: Excisional biopsy.

Procedure: A 6 mm pigmented, centrally ulcerated lesion on the forehead was anesthetized with 1% Lidocaine and then elliptically excised. The wound was closed with interrupted 5-0 nylon and a sterile dressing applied.

Pathology: Specimen-forehead lesion. Specimen consists of an ellipse of skin measuring 0.9 × 0.6 cm. The epidermal surface shows a 5 mm granular lesion. Diagnosis-Actinic keratosis.

ICD-9-CM code(s) _____

CPT code(s) _____

EXERCISE 5–2

Using your CPT and ICD-9-CM coding books, assign the ICD-9-CM code, ICD-9-CM Procedure Code and CPT Procedure Code to the following:

Diagnosis: Mass on back.

Operation: Excision of mass.

Procedure: The mid back area was prepped and a scalpel was used to make a transverse incision after anesthetic infiltration. Incision was carried down until the lesion was encountered and excised from surrounding subcutaneous tissue. The lesion measured 2.5 × 1.5 cm and was sent to pathology.

Pathology: Specimen-back lesion. Specimen consists of adipose tissue measuring 2.5 × 1.5 cm. No evidence of malignancy noted. Diagnosis-lipoma.

ICD-9-CM code(s) _____

CPT code(s) _____

EXERCISE 5–3

Using your CPT and ICD-9-CM coding books, assign the ICD-9-CM code, ICD-9-CM Procedure Code and CPT Procedure Code to the following:

Diagnosis: Probable hydradenitis of the right axilla.

Procedure: The cystic structure in the axilla was excised and skin was sutured.

Pathology: Specimen-skin, right axilla. The specimen shows chronic inflammatory changes consistent with chronic hydradenitis.

ICD-9-CM code(s) _____

CPT code(s) _____

NAILS

Code ranges 11719–11765 include procedures on the nail(s) and nailbed.

■ *Highlights*
- *Biopsy of a nail unit (11755) is only reported once, regardless of the number of biopsies done on a single nail.*
- *If procedures are performed on different nails, these can be identified by HCPCS Level II modifiers and/or the number of different nails listed in the units column on the bill. Check with your carrier for specific guidelines.*

■ *Confusing Codes*
Note that excision of pilonidal cysts (11770–11772) is included within the nail section. A pilonidal cyst is located in the sacral area and usually contains a sinus or opening at the postanal dimple.

References to "extensive" or "complicated" are subjective to physician interpretation, since CPT has no defined criteria. These terms usually imply that either an infection occurred, treatment was delayed, or the procedure took longer to perform than usual. For example, when referring to excision of a pilonidal cyst, "simple" would indicate sutured closure; "extensive" may refer to a sinus greater than 2 cm or excision of a recurrent cyst; and complicated would require plastic surgery. The medical record documentation must support the complicated code assignment.

INTRODUCTION

Codes in ranges 11900–11977 refer to the injection of lesions, tattooing, collagen injection, insertion/replacement/removal of tissue expanders or of contraceptive capsules.

Code 11900 or 11901 is reported for the number of lesions, regardless of the number of injections performed.

Tissue expansion involves creating extra soft tissue and skin for use in reconstruction procedures. In this procedure, a fluid-filled bag is inserted under the skin to which saline is added at intervals to slowly expand the skin. This creates extra skin that may be used for a subsequent skin grafting procedure or a reconstruction. The codes referenced here are for tissue expansion of skin other than the breast.

WOUND REPAIR (CLOSURES)

The *Physician's Current Procedural Terminology* has detailed notes before the Repair (Closure) category (codes 12001–13300). In order for the coder to accurately code repairs, the following must be documented in the medical record:

a. Type of repair.

b. Body site involved.

c. Length of repair in centimeters.

Types of Wound Repair

Types of repairs are classified as simple, intermediate and complex.

1. Simple Repair is a one-layer closure and is used to close superficial wounds, or wounds involving the epidermis, dermis, or subcutaneous tissues, without involvement of deeper structures. Wounds closed with steri-strips, or strips used to hold lacerated skin together for healing instead of sutures or staples, are included in the physician's evaluation and management services. No procedure code is assigned.

2. Intermediate Repair requires the layered closure of one or more of the deeper layers of subcutaneous tissue and superficial fascia. Heavily contaminated wounds that have required extensive cleaning or removal of particulate matter would also be classified as an intermediate repair.

Figure 5–3 shows some examples of different types of wound closure.

■ *Highlights*

The use of two different suture types, where one is absorbable (Vicryl, chromic, gut, or Dexon) is an indication that the repair is intermediate. However, the coder should verify with the physician that the closure is intermediate when using two different suture types. Sometimes, two sutures are used to repair an elliptical or irregularly shaped wound, and

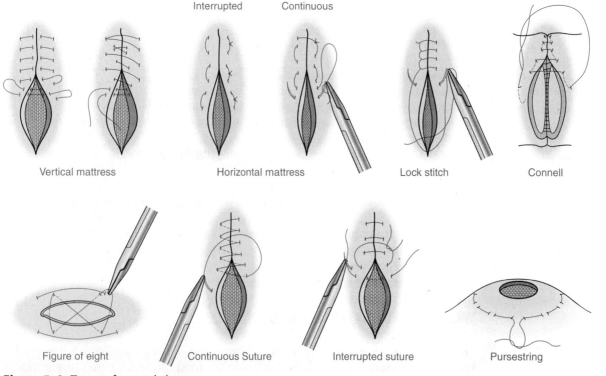

Figure 5–3 Types of wound closure.

the closure is a simple repair, not an intermediate. The coder should not assume that the term "plastic closure" refers to a layered closure, as this term is used in different contexts by physicians.

3. Complex Repair includes wound repair requiring more than a layered closure, such as scar revision, debridement, extensive undermining, stents, or retention sutures.

■ *Highlight*

When coding multiple wound repairs within the same indented specific body site categories, the lengths of the repairs are added together and reported as a single code.

Codes in the simple and intermediate repair (closure) categories group like body sites as follows:

a. scalp, neck, axillae, external genitalia, trunk and/or extremities (including hands and feet)
b. face, ears, eyelids, nose, lips, and/or mucous membranes

Codes in the complex repair (closure) category group like body sites as follows:

a. trunk
b. scalp, arms, and/or legs
c. forehead, cheeks, chin, mouth, neck, axillae, genitalia, hands, and/or feet
d. eyelids, nose, ears, and/or lips

■ When coding multiple wound repairs, the most complicated repair is listed first.
■ In coding a lesion excision from a prior mastectomy site, the site is coded to "trunk" not "breast", since the breast has been previously removed.

For insurance carriers requiring modifiers (Medicare Part B), -51 multiple procedures is appended to the CPT code for repairs, after the first one.

Example: 2.5 cm scalp wound-simple repair and 2.5 cm arm wound-simple repair. Since both wounds are of the same body group, the wound sizes are added together, (2.5 cm + 2.5 cm = 5.0 cm). The correct code is 12002 simple repair, 2.6 cm to 7.5 cm.

Example: 2.5 cm scalp wound-simple repair and 2.5 cm arm wound-intermediate repair. Since the arm wound is a more complicated type repair than simple, the two wound repair types would be reported separately with the intermediate repair listed first. The correct codes are: 12031 intermediate repair, 2.5 cm or less; 12001 simple repair, 2.5 cm or less.

The modifier (if applicable) would be appended to 12001-51.

■ *Confusing Codes*

Any debridements should be coded separately (11040–11044) when prolonged cleansing or removal of devitalized tissue occurs. This code assignment is subjective to the physician's interpretation, as the CPT book does not provide a definition of what prolonged means. Facilities should develop internal guidelines with their medical staffs in order to provide consistent data.

Repair of blood vessels, nerves, and tendons are coded separately under each of the appropriate anatomical sections.

Wound dehiscence is a separation of the suture site either after a surgical incision or a laceration repair. It is listed in ICD-9-CM under Complication, Surgical and Medical Care. The CPT codes for this dehiscence repair are listed within simple repair (12020–12021) or complex repair (13160).

EXERCISE 5–4

Using your CPT and ICD-9-CM coding books, assign the ICD-9-CM code, ICD-9-CM Procedure Code and CPT Procedure Code to the following:

Simple repair of multiple lacerations after falling against a window, which broke. The repairs consist of the leg, 8.5 cm; forearm, 5.5 cm; and hand, 2.5 cm. There was also a superficial abrasion of the left hand which was cleansed and steri-stripped.

ICD-9-CM code(s) _____

CPT code(s) _____

EXERCISE 5–5

Using your CPT and ICD-9-CM coding books, assign the ICD-9-CM code, ICD-9-CM Procedure Code and CPT Procedure Code to the following:

Patient presents to Urgent Care with a 3 cm laceration on the top of the mid thigh. Patient cut it on the tailgate of a truck. The wound extends down to the subcutaneous level, but does not appear to be a deep penetrating laceration. Wound was cleansed with saline and closed with 5-0 Vicryl in the subcutaneous twice and 4-0 Prolene horizontal mattress skin sutures.

ICD-9-CM code(s) _____

CPT code(s) _____

GRAFTS

Adjacent Tissue Transfer or Rearrangement

Codes for Adjacent Tissue Transfer or Rearrangement are in range 14000–14350. This procedure involves moving sections of skin, or flaps, from one location to an adjacent location. At least one side of the flap remains intact. There are many different methods of performing this procedure. For example, for a rotation flap the surgeon rotates a semicircular flap of skin to position it over the wound. Table 5–2 describes the many methods used in these procedures.

▪ *Highlights*

Prior to code assignment for adjacent tissue transfer or rearrangement, the following documentation is needed:

a. site
b. size of defect in square centimeters

Excision of a lesion prior to the tissue transfer or rearrangement is included in this series of codes.

A skin graft used in addition to the tissue transfer or rearrangement requires an additional code assignment from that series of codes.

TABLE 5–2 Examples of tissue transfer/rearrangement. (Courtesy of *St. Anthony's Complete Coding Tutor: ICD-9-CM, CPT, HCPCS Level II*, 1998. Reprinted with permission of St. Anthony Publishing, Inc. 800-632-0123.)

Adjacent Tissue Transfer/Rearrangement

Type of Tissue Transfer/ Rearrangement	Brief Description of Procedure	Comments (if applicable)
Z-plasty	A scar is lengthened, straightened or realigned to help reduce tension on the wound and, thus, produce a better cosmetic effect.	
W-plasty	This procedure is similar to a Z-plasty, but is used for less linear scar/wound repair.	
Advancement flap	This is the simplest of all flaps—the surgeon simply "stretched" nearby skin over a wound.	
V-Y plasty	In the V-Y procedure, an incision is made in the shape of V and sutured in the shape of Y to lengthen an area of tissue; conversely, a Y-V plasty begins with a Y-shaped incision that is sutured in the shape of a V to shorten an area of tissue.	Considered a type of advancement flap.
Rotation flap	A semicircular flap of skin is rotated into position over the wound site.	Also called transpositional or interpolation flap.
Pedicle or double-pedicle flaps	Flaps consisting of the full thickness of the skin and the subcutaneous tissue are transferred to a clean tissue bed.	Ideal for covering exposed bone and tendon.
Sliding flap	A flap is transferred to its new position using a sliding technique.	Similar to advancement flap.
Melolabial flap	A flap from the medial cheek is used as a transposition flap to repair a defect on the side of the nose. It is used for deep nasal defects, providing thick sebaceous skin and subcutaneous fat for rebuilding tissue lost in surgery. Folded on itself, it can recreate an alar rim.	This flap is often erroneously referred to as "nasolabial flap" in the medical record.
Kutler procedure	Two flaps are developed, one on each side of the finger, which are then mobilized toward the tip of the finger and sutured to conform to the normal shape of the end of the finger. This is an example of a V-Y plasty.	

Free Skin Grafts

Type of graft	Description	Comments
Split graft	A graft that contains both epidermis and dermis layer, portions of the graft contain only part of the dermal layer.	For a site that requires a full epidermal layer with some areas of the site requiring dermal layer.
Full thickness graft	A graft that contains an equal and continuous portion of both epidermis and dermis.	For sites requiring full epidermal and dermal layer.
Autograft	Both the donor and recipient site are of the same individual.	For the purpose of replacing damaged tissue.
Allograft	The donor is a different individual than the recipient.	For the purpose of temporary coverage until appropriate autograft material is available.
Xenograft	The graft material is of nonhuman origin, for example a porcine graft from a pig.	For the purpose of temporary coverage until appropriate autograft material is available.
Pinch graft	A small autograft.	

■ *Confusing Codes*

The codes for tissue transfer or rearrangement do not apply when direct closure or rearrangement of traumatic wounds incidentally result in these configurations. The procedure must be developed by the physician to perform the repair. Always query the physician when in doubt.

Example: Advancement flap, forehead (3 cm × 3 cm), with removal of a 2 cm lesion would be coded with one code, 14040.

EXERCISE 5–6

Using your CPT and ICD-9-CM coding books, assign the ICD-9-CM code, ICD-9-CM Procedure Code and CPT Procedure Code to the following:

Diagnosis: Probable basal cell carcinoma, right auricle, helical rim.

Operation: Excision of tumor, right auricle.

Procedure: Under local anesthetic, an incision was made around this 1.3 cm ulcerated lesion on the helix of the right auricle. A 3 mm margin was allowed entirely around it and incision was carried down to the perichondrium. The superior end of the specimen for margins was tagged with a suture. An advancement flap was elevated on both medial and lateral surfaces of the auricle over the cartilage. A portion of the helical rim of the cartilage was resected to facilitate closure.

Pathology: Specimen-Right ear lesion. Specimen consists of a skin ellipse measuring 2.0 × 1.7 × 0.3 cm. The suture is noted in the margins. There is an ulcerated area which measures 0.8 × 0.5 cm. Diagnosis—Invasive, differentiated squamous cell carcinoma. Tumor extends into all the margins.

ICD-9-CM code(s) _____

CPT code(s) _____

Free Skin Grafts

A skin graft consists of the epidermis and dermis and is done for burns and wound repairs. Depending on how much of the dermis is used for the graft determines whether it is a full thickness skin graft (FTSG) or split thickness skin graft (STSG) type. The *donor site* is the body part that donates skin, muscle, etc. This is the wound created by the surgeon. The *recipient site* is the body part that has the defect or wound that is covered by the harvested tissue. Examples of skin grafts include:

Autograft: (Autogenous) Skin graft is transferred from a donor site to a recipient site in the same individual.

Allograft: (Homograft) Skin graft is transplanted between two different individuals. These are temporary and may be used to cover large burn areas as new skin grows beneath it.

Xenograft: (Heterograft) Skin graft transplanted between an animal and human. These are also temporary grafts used to cover large areas.

■ **Confusing Codes**

When a skin graft is cut, it turns pale due to being separated from its blood supply. The graft slowly regains its pink color as the circulation returns. This usually occurs within 5 to 7 days. If the graft does not become revascularized, partial or complete necrosis develops. If the graft is thick, the upper portion of the graft may slough, but the deeper portions may remain.

A graft may fail for a variety of reasons. The ICD-9-CM classifies skin graft failure to complications due to graft of other tissue, 996.52. Sloughing of the temporary allografts would not have an ICD-9-CM assigned.

EXERCISE 5–7

Using your CPT and ICD-9-CM coding books, assign the ICD-9-CM code, ICD-9-CM Procedure Code and CPT Procedure Code to the following:

Diagnosis: Nonhealing wound, tip of nose measuring 3 × 2 cm.

Operation: **Split thickness** skin graft, nose.

Procedure: Borders of granulation tissue are debrided and skin edges freshened. Due to the defect, skin approximation cannot be accomplished. Using a dermatome, a split thickness skin graft is harvested from the right thigh. The graft is placed onto the nose defect and secured with interrupted 5-0 Prolene sutures. The donor site is examined and reveals good hemostasis.

ICD-9-CM code(s) _____

CPT code(s) _____

Flaps (Skin and/or Deep Tissues)

Codes for flaps (skin and/or deep tissues) are in range 15570–15738. When a flap is being attached in transfer or to the final site, the body regions listed in this section refer to the recipient areas, instead of to the donor sites. An exception is for codes 15732–15738 that are described by the donor site of the muscle, myocutaneous, or fasciocutaneous flaps as listed below.

Pedicle Flap:	A flap of skin is lifted from a healthy site and a portion is immediately grafted to the new site. Part of the graft, or the **pedicle**, remains temporarily attached to the original site and blood supply.
Muscle Flap:	A layer of muscle is dissected and is moved to a new site.
Myocutaneous Flap:	A muscle flap which contains overlying skin.
Fasciocutaneous Flap:	A muscle flap which contains overlying skin and connective tissue.

Other Flaps and Grafts

Other flaps and grafts (code range 15740–15776) include composite grafts, derma-fascia-fat grafts, and punch grafts. A composite graft (15760) includes more than one type of tissue, such as cartilage located in the ear or nostrils. These grafts are used to fill in a defect to provide skin and structural support to the recipient site.

Derma-fascia-fat grafts (15770) are similar to composite grafts and are used to blend in defects.

Punch grafts (15775 and 15776) are used for the scalp or hairline areas. The code selection is based on the number of punches.

For revisions on coding grafts, refer to the *CPT Assistant*, Nov. 1998, Vol. 8, Issue 11. This is the official source for CPT coding provided by the American Medical Association (AMA).

OTHER PROCEDURES

Many of the procedures in this section (code range 15780–15879) refer to cosmetic procedures that may not be covered by the patient's insurance payer. Dermabrasion (15780–15783) involves scraping unwanted scars, wrinkles, or other defects using an abrasive type device. Laser devices are not included in these codes. Suction assisted mastectomy should be reported with code 15877 since this is the code for the trunk.

PRESSURE ULCERS (DECUBITUS ULCERS)

A pressure ulcer is a sore caused by extended pressure on an area of the body that interferes with circulation. Pressure from an appliance, such as a splint, may also cause a pressure ulcer to develop. They may also be called pressure sores, dermal ulcers, decubitus ulcers or bedsores. Pressure ulcers commonly occur in areas of the body where the bones come close to the surface of the skin, such as the elbows, hips, heels, shoulders, ankles, sacrum, and knees (see Figure 5–4)

Use code range (15920–15999) to code excision of pressure ulcers. Excision of pressure ulcer sites other than of the coccyx, sacrum, ischium, or trochanter are reported with an appropriate code such as debridement, closure or flap, based on the documentation of the procedure performed.

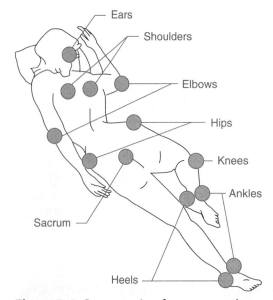

Figure 5–4 Common sites for pressure ulcers.

BURNS, LOCAL TREATMENT

Burns are classified into four categories: first degree, second degree, third degree, and fourth degree. Categorization depends on the depth of the burn and the extent of the surface area involved. First- and second-degree burns are partial-thickness burns, involving only the epidermis (first degree) or the dermis and epidermis (second degree). Third- and fourth-degree burns are full-thickness burns, meaning the epidermis and dermis have been completely destroyed.

The excision of burn wound codes 16040–16042 will no longer exist and will be replaced by codes 15000 and 15001. The surgical preparation of burn wounds is known as tangential excision and is included in code 15000. CPT code 15000 has been revised from an add-on code which could only be used with a skin graft code to a stand-alone procedure code which can be used when a skin graft is not recommended or may be delayed for a subsequent session. Code 15000 should also be used as a stand-alone code when alloplastic dressings are applied.

The new burn preparation/excision codes also indicate the body surface area. The anatomic sites of hands, feet, and scalp listed in codes 15100, 15101, 15120, 15121 have been recategorized. The measurement of 100 sq cm is applicable to adults and children age 10 and over. Percentages apply to infants and children under the age of 10. Code 15400 refers to xenograft or more commonly known as pigskin.

■ *Highlight*

Note should be made under CPT code 15000 that excision of lesions (benign or malignant) will be coded in addition to the graft preparation.

Escharotomy (16035) refers to removal of the scab or slough produced by a thermal burn.

The rule of nines is used to estimate the percentage of body burned. The patient's age is also a determining factor. ICD-9-CM classifies burns in this fashion, with the most severe burn taking priority. Refer to Module 1, ICD-9-CM, for more information on the rule of nines and ICD-9-CM coding for burns.

DESTRUCTION

Destruction is the ablation or **removal** of a lesion by any method that includes local anesthesia and does not usually require closure. Destruction methods may include electrocautery, electrodesiccation, cryosurgery, laser, and chemical treatment. The types of lesions removed may include condylomata, papillomata, molluscum contagiosum, herpetic lesions, flat warts, milia, and/or other benign, pre-malignant, or malignant lesions. Refer back to Figure 5–2 on pages 196 and 197 to see illustrations of various types of lesions. The Destruction section is further subdivided into Benign or Premalignant Lesions (code ranges 17000–17250) and Destruction, Malignant Lesions, Any Method (code ranges 17260–17286).

■ *Highlights*

Codes (17000–17004, 17110–17111) are assigned for the destruction based on the number of lesions. Code 17000 must be used in addition to any other codes indented underneath it. For example, if twenty benign lesions are destroyed, the following codes would be reported on the HCFA-1500:

In the units column, 1 unit would correspond to code 17000 and 19 units would correspond to code 17004.

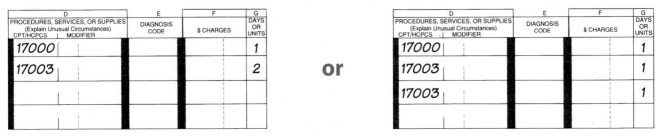

If three benign lesions are destroyed, the following codes would be reported:

D PROCEDURES, SERVICES, OR SUPPLIES (Explain Unusual Circumstances) CPT/HCPCS | MODIFIER		E DIAGNOSIS CODE	F $ CHARGES	G DAYS OR UNITS
17000				1
17003				2

or

D PROCEDURES, SERVICES, OR SUPPLIES (Explain Unusual Circumstances) CPT/HCPCS | MODIFIER		E DIAGNOSIS CODE	F $ CHARGES	G DAYS OR UNITS
17000				1
17003				1
17003				1

Codes 17106–17108 refer to the sq cm destroyed usually by laser technique.

Destruction of common or plantar warts are coded to 17000–17004.

▪ Confusing Codes

Destruction of malignant lesions (17260–17286) are determined by the site and size of the lesion and are reported separately. Lesions in this section of CPT are never added together by site or size.

MOHS' MICROGRAPHIC SURGERY

Mohs' micrographic surgery (code range 17304–17310) is used for the treatment of complex or ill-defined skin cancer where the physician acts in two integrated, but separate capacities, as the surgeon and pathologist.

If a repair is performed, a separate code is assigned for the repair, flap, or graft codes. These codes are reported by stages and the number of specimens taken. Documentation must be present to support the code assignment.

Other Procedures

Codes in range 17340–17999 refer to acne procedures and electrolysis.

Breast Procedures

Breast procedures include incision, excision, **repair**and/or reconstruction and are within code range 19000–19499.

Breast biopsies are done by three different techniques:

- 19100 needle biopsy.
- 19101 incision biopsy, a specimen of the lesion is biopsied, leaving the mass. However, depending on the type of needle used with a stereotactic technique, this code may now be used.
- 19120 excisional biopsy, the entire lesion is removed.

Needle localization is a technique where the breast lesion is identified by placement of a preoperative wire. Codes 19290 and 19291 are used as additional codes. These codes link with a code from the radiology section which identifies the actual placement. Both must be present for proper component billing.

A lesion can also be identified by preoperative placement of a radiological marker before excision and is assigned with codes 19125 and 19126.

Codes 19291 and 19126 are used for each additional lesion identified only.

If excisions are performed on different sites of the breast through different incisions, code 19120 would be reported for each incision made. Modifier -59 would be used on the second, third, etc. codes.

Code 19000 is intended to describe an aspiration of a cyst only. A hematoma or an abscess would be reported using code 10160. Code 19020 is intended to describe incision and drainage of an **abscess** in the breast only. Any Incision and Drainage (I&D) of a hematoma or seroma would be reported with code 10140.

If a breast implant is removed and a new one reinserted, then two codes would be required, 19328 and 19340.

Mastectomy

The operative report must be read carefully to determine the extent of a mastectomy, which may be partial, simple, subcutaneous, radical, or modified radical.

Partial (19160):	Only partial tissue is removed, while leaving the breast intact.
Simple, complete (19180):	All breast tissue is removed, but not the lymph nodes or muscle.
Subcutaneous (19182):	Breast tissue removed, but skin and nipple are intact.
Radical (19200 or 19220):	Excision of all breast tissue, including pectoral muscles and axillary lymph nodes. Refer to the codes in CPT for further description.
Modified radical (19240):	Same as radical, however the muscles may or may not be removed.

Insertion of a breast prosthesis is reported with the appropriate code when done at the same time as the mastectomy or at a later episode.

EXERCISE 5-8

Using your CPT and ICD-9-CM coding books, assign the diagnosis code, ICD-9-CM Procedure Code and CPT Procedure Code to the following:

Diagnosis: Intraductal carcinoma, left breast.

Operation: Needle-localized left breast biopsy.

Procedure: The patient had a stereotactic biopsy of the left breast the week prior, which confirmed the carcinoma. Patient is having biopsy to remove any remaining calcifications. The patient was first taken to the Radiology Department for the left breast needle localization. Utilizing mammographic guidance, a Kopan's type needle was inserted into the left breast.

After confirmation that the needle was within the calcifications, the patient was transported to the surgical suite. An elliptical incision was made and carried down through the skin and subcutaneous tissue to the breast tissue. A block of breast tissue was removed to include the needle and sent for specimen mammogram. Specimen was then sent to pathology.

Pathology: Breast tissue with no recurrence of the carcinoma.

ICD-9-CM code(s) _____

CPT code(s) _____

EXERCISE 5–9

Using your CPT and ICD-9-CM coding books, assign the diagnosis code, ICD-9-CM Procedure Code and CPT Procedure Code to the following:

Diagnosis: Right breast asymmetry, status post mastopexy and augmentation mammoplasty. Postop Diagnosis: Capsule formation and breast asymmetry.

Operation: Release of capsule and replacement of a prosthetic.

Procedure: Through the previous incision, this was carried down through the subcutaneous tissue, through the breast tissue and through the muscle. An attempt was made to place a fill tube into the prosthetic; however, the prosthetic ruptured at that point and was removed. The pocket was then examined and there was a capsule contracture inferiorly and laterally. This was released with removal of a portion of the capsule. A 250 cc implant was placed and inflated to 300 cc. Patient examined in a sitting position and wounds were sutured closed.

ICD-9-CM code(s) _____

CPT code(s) _____

SUMMARY

Tips to remember when coding in the integumentary system are:

- Determine location and size of lesion and code separately.
- Determine pathology of a lesion to code correctly.
- Determine repairs types as simple, intermediate, or complex.
- Add repair lengths together of grouped body sites.
- Determine size, anesthesia, percentage of burns.
- Follow rules for adding codes that are not integral to the procedures listed.
- Learn the different types of skin graft techniques.

REFERENCES

Berkow, Robert et al. *The Merck Manual of Medical Information, Home Edition.* West Point, PA: Merck & Co., Inc., 1997.

Coding for Ambulatory Surgery Procedures, An Instructional Guide to Coding & Reimbursement for Hospital-Based Ambulatory Surgical Procedures. Minneapolis, MN: MedLearn, 1997.

CPT Assistant. Chicago, IL: American Medical Association.

Medicare Part B publications and communiqué.

Nicholas, Toula. *Basic ICD-9-CM Coding.* Chicago, IL: American Health Information Management Association, 1998.

St. Anthony's Guide to Ambulatory Surgery Center Payment Groups, A Clinical Coding and Reimbursement Reference for Hospitals and ASC's. Reston, VA: St. Anthony's Publishing.

Module 6
Orthopedics

Eugene Richard, RRA, CCS, CCS-P

KEY TERMS

Arthropathy
Closed Fracture
Dislocation
Internal Derangement
Myelopathy
Open Fracture
Orthopedics
Osteomyelitis
Radiculopathy

LEARNING OBJECTIVES

Upon successful completion of this module, you should be able to:

1. Explain the proper application of coding rules and conventions in the ICD-9-CM and CPT classification systems as they apply to orthopedics and use them to solve any coding problem.

2. Demonstrate your clinical knowledge of the normal structure and function of the musculoskeletal tissues by always referencing the proper body system in CPT and ICD-9-CM.

3. Explain the most common diseases, disorders, and injuries of the musculoskeletal system and be able to differentiate between similar conditions with different codes.

4. Accurately and completely classify diagnoses and procedures applicable to orthopedics without overcoding or undercoding the case.

INTRODUCTION

Orthopedics (orthopaedics) is a medical specialty concerned with the prevention, investigation, diagnosis and treatment of diseases, disorders, and injuries of the musculoskeletal system. Figure 6–1 presents an overview of the musculoskeletal system. The specialty may employ medical, surgical, physiological, pathological, and other related sciences in the scope of diagnosis and treatment.

This module covers the broader concepts and most common themes seen in the field of orthopedics. It is designed to give learners a better understanding of the most common diagnoses and procedures and help them understand classification rules in ICD-9-CM and CPT. Learners will also have the opportunity to see and use some code designations that may be new or unfamiliar to them, learn more about the details of the many diagnoses and procedures available in the classification systems, and gain practical knowledge of how to handle some difficult orthopedic classification issues.

Most orthopedic diagnoses will fall into the ICD-9-CM chapters on Diseases of the Musculoskeletal System and Connective Tissue code

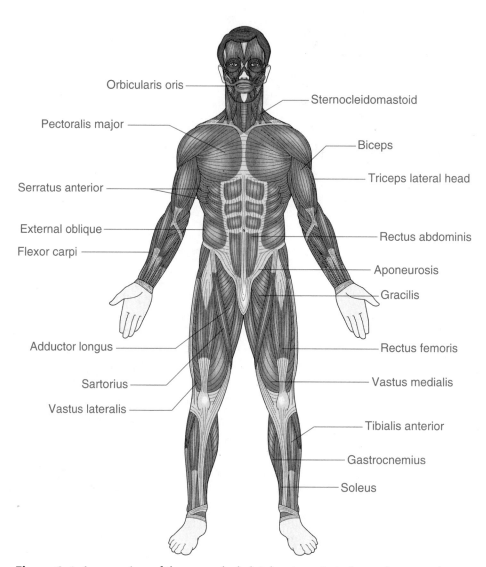

Orbicularis oris

Pectoralis major

Serratus anterior

External oblique

Flexor carpi

Adductor longus

Sartorius

Vastus lateralis

Sternocleidomastoid

Biceps

Triceps lateral head

Rectus abdominis

Aponeurosis

Gracilis

Rectus femoris

Vastus medialis

Tibialis anterior

Gastrocnemius

Soleus

Figure 6–1 An overview of the musculoskeletal system. Anterior surface muscles.

range 710–739, and Injuries and Poisonings code range 800–999. Some other conditions which are amenable to orthopedic treatment can be found in other chapters, such as malignant neoplasms of bone in the Neoplasms chapter, and musculoskeletal anomalies found in the Congenital Anomalies chapter. Orthopedic procedures are mostly classified between code categories 76–84 in ICD-9-CM Volume Three. CPT classifies most orthopedic procedure within the Musculoskeletal System chapter, code range 20000–29909.

In the next section of this module, we will examine the most common conditions and procedures encountered in orthopedics, and review the proper coding and reporting of these in ICD-9-CM and CPT.

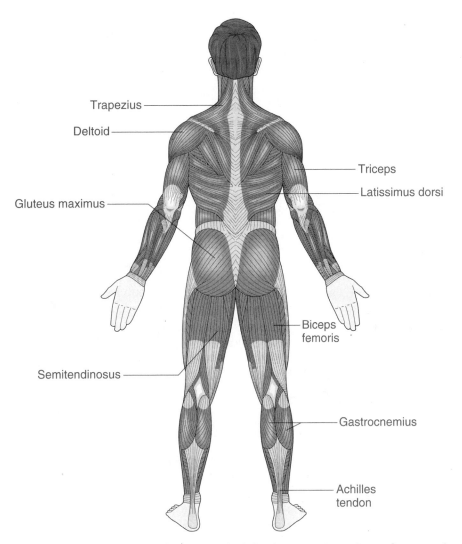

Figure 6–1 An overview of the musculoskeletal system. Posterior surface muscles.

FRACTURES AND DISLOCATIONS

Fractures

A fracture is a break or disruption in an organ or tissue (see Figure 6–2). In orthopedics, fractures of the bone are classified in the ICD-9-CM code category range 800–829 (a few other specific bone fractures are classified elsewhere). They refer to a structural break in the continuity of bone as a result of physical forces exerted beyond its ability to accommodate by resistance, elasticity, or bending. Fractures can occur as a result of direct injury such as being hit in the upper arm with a heavy object, or by indirect injury such as a fracture of the clavicle as a result of falling upon an outstretched hand, where the initial force is transmitted indirectly through one or more joints. Muscular contractures, stress, and pathology can also result in fractures (Richard, 1996).

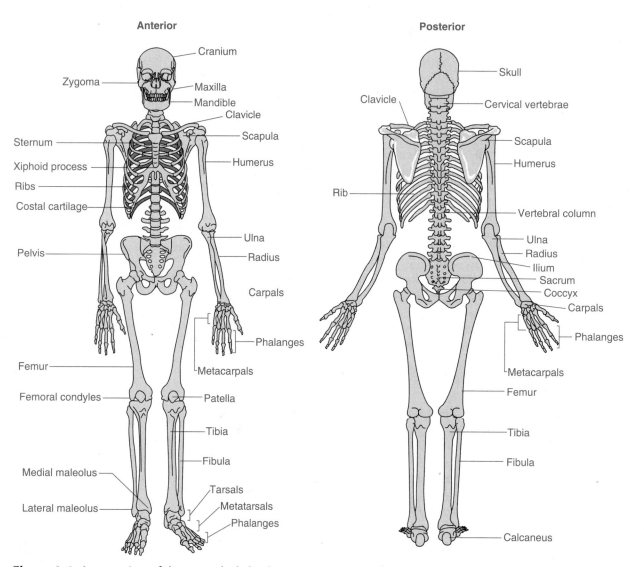

Anterior

Cranium
Zygoma
Maxilla
Mandible
Clavicle
Sternum
Scapula
Xiphoid process
Humerus
Ribs
Costal cartilage
Pelvis
Ulna
Radius
Carpals
Phalanges
Femur
Metacarpals
Femoral condyles
Patella
Tibia
Fibula
Medial maleolus
Tarsals
Metatarsals
Lateral maleolus
Phalanges

Posterior

Skull
Clavicle
Cervical vertebrae
Scapula
Humerus
Rib
Vertebral column
Ulna
Radius
Ilium
Sacrum
Coccyx
Carpals
Phalanges
Metacarpals
Femur
Tibia
Fibula
Calcaneus

Figure 6–1 An overview of the musculoskeletal system. Anterior and posterior views of the human skeleton.

To properly classify fractures in ICD-9-CM, there are two important pieces of information the coder must have. The first is the site of the fracture and the second is determining whether or not the fracture is open or closed. The site of the fracture is first classified by the name of the fractured bone, and then by the anatomical subclassification of the region, section, or part of the bone where the fracture occurred. At the beginning of the ICD-9-CM tabular list for fractures code, category range 800–829, the coder will find a list of descriptive terms associated with **open** and **closed fractures** (see Table 6–1).

It is important to remember that some of the terms for closed can sometimes indicate either a closed or an open fracture, depending upon the circumstances and the terms in the table do not take precedence over the clinical presentation. An open fracture is defined as one in which the fracture site communicates with the outside environment. Thus, it is possible for example, to have a depressed skull fracture which is classified as an open fracture, if the fracture site has a wound over it which is deep and communicates the fracture site with the outside environment. Open fractures are sometimes graded according to the Gustilo classification in Table 6–2 (Mallon, et al., 1990).

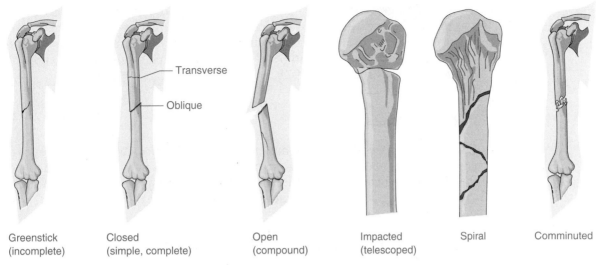

Greenstick (incomplete)

Closed (simple, complete)

Open (compound)

Impacted (telescoped)

Spiral

Comminuted

— Transverse

— Oblique

Figure 6–2 Types of bone fractures.

TABLE 6–1   Open and Closed Fracture Terms.

Closed Fracture Terms		*Open Fracture Terms*
comminuted	impacted	compound
depressed	linear	infected
elevated	march	missile
fissured	simple	puncture
fracture, unspecified	slipped epiphysis	with foreign body
greenstick	spiral	

TABLE 6–2   Gustilo Classification of Open Fractures.

Type	*Description*
Grade I	An open fracture with a wound less than one centimeter in diameter
Grade II	An open fracture with a wound greater than one centimeter and less than 10 centimeters in diameter, but without extensive soft tissue loss or devitalization, and no vascular injury.
Grade III	An open fracture with a high-energy wound with extensive soft tissue loss or devitalization, or one in which there has been a major vascular injury.
Grade IIIa	A type III injury, but one without extensive periosteal stripping or a vascular injury requiring repair.
Grade IIIb	A type III injury accompanied by extensive periosteal stripping or gross contamination.
Grade IIIc	A type III injury accompanied by a major vascular injury requiring repair.

Note that a grade IIIc open fracture will require additional codes to classify the vascular injury and any subsequent repair. Grade III fractures with extensive soft tissue damage and/or devitalized tissue may require a wound debridement procedure classified to subcategory 79.6, in addition to fracture reduction and fixation in Volume Three of ICD-9-CM.

Pediatric Fractures

Children's fractures differ from those seen in the adult because of the presence of a growth plate called the physis or cartilago epiphysialis in long bones. Whenever the fracture involves this growth plate, a classification system is used to describe the extent and severity of the fracture, as shown in Table 6–3.

Skull and Facial Fractures

Skull fractures are classified to categories 800–802, 804 and facial fractures are classified to category 802 in ICD-9-CM. Skull fractures require the coder to determine the level of consciousness at the fifth-digit level. Consciousness is a general state of wakefulness and the ability to perceive oneself, one's acts, and one's environment. There are different levels of altered consciousness ranging from slight drowsiness to obtundation to light coma to deep coma. Conditions seen in the awake (conscious) patient that are sometimes confused with a loss of consciousness include inattention, confusion, delirium, hallucinations, and delusions (Weiderholt, 1988).

Another clinical feature which the coder needs to determine is whether or not the skull fracture is accompanied by an intracranial injury. Contusion, laceration, bleeding and any other term indicating trauma to the meninges, the brain, or the brain stem affect code selection at the fourth-digit level. Fractures of specified

TABLE 6–3   Salter-Harris Classification.

Type	Description
Type I	The fracture line goes directly through the physis.
Type II	The fracture line is mostly through the physis, but it exits one cortex such that a small fragment of metaphysis is included with the fracture fragment containing the physis and epiphysis.
Type III	The fracture line is mostly through the physis, but it exits one cortex such that a small fragment of epiphysis is included with the fracture fragment containing the metaphysis and diaphysis.
Type IV	The fracture line crossed the physis such that both the fragments contain portions of the metaphysis, physis, and epiphysis.
Type V	In this injury there is no definite fracture line. Like the Type I fracture, it cannot be easily diagnosed radiographically. The injury involves a crush injury to the physis in which the metaphysis and epiphysis are acutely impacted upon one another.

facial bones are classified simply to category 802 by site. Interestingly, ICD-9-CM does not provide a code for facial bone(s) unspecified, so coders must seek additional information when confronted with this unqualified diagnosis.

Fractures of the Neck and Trunk

Code categories 805–806 classify fractures of the vertebral column, with code category 807 covering the rib(s), sternum, larynx, and trachea. The pelvis is classified under category 808 and category 809 is reserved for ill-defined fractures of the trunk. Category 805 classifies vertebral fractures not associated with spinal cord injuries. Only subcategories 805.0 and 805.1 for cervical fractures require a fifth digit for specificity. Category 806 classifies fractures of the vertebral column and requires much more detailed information before assigning the proper code. This category is much more specific regarding the site of the fracture, and requires further delineation of the spinal cord injury at the fifth-digit level. Spinal cord injuries generally result in paralytic symptoms and syndromes and are classified at the fifth-digit level.

Category 807 classifies fractures of the ribs, sternum, larynx and trachea. The number of ribs is indicated in subcategory 807.0 and 807.1 at the fifth-digit level. A flail chest is a condition where there is instability of the chest wall, often accompanied by respiratory distress due to massive trauma, and involves a fractured sternum and/or ribs. Note that code 807.4 for flail chest is not assigned with any code from 807.0 or 807.1. Fractures of the larynx and trachea, which include the hyoid and thyroid cartilage, are often accompanied by other significant conditions such as respiratory distress or failure.

Fractures of the Upper and Lower Extremities

Code categories 810–819 classify fractures of the upper extremities, and categories 820–829 classify fractures of the lower extremities. There are two categories that provide codes for certain bone combinations. They are:

813 Fracture of the radius and ulna
823 Fracture of the tibia and fibula

Fifth digits are provided to classify each bone either separately or in combination when the fracture occurs at the same fourth-digit level of specificity. Whenever a fracture occurs to both bones at different fourth-digit levels, it is necessary to assign the codes separately. For example, a closed fracture of the head of the radius and the distal end of the ulna requires two codes, 813.05 and 813.43, because each bone's fracture occurred at a different fourth-digit level site.

Traumatic hip fractures classified to category 820 are very common in the elderly population, and may also involve an impaction type fracture of the acetabulum, codes 808.0 and 808.1. Because of the stresses placed upon this joint and the weakness of the bones in the elderly population, the most common method of treating these fractures is by partial or complete joint replacement. A total hip replacement involves the replacement of both the femoral head and the acetabulum, and a partial hip replacement involves either the acetabulum or the femoral head, although the femoral head is most common. When referencing procedures in ICD-9-CM for total or partial hip replacement, look under index terms such as arthroplasty, reconstruction, and replacement. The elderly are also subject to pathological hip fractures and the classification of these fractures will be discussed later in the chapter.

Multiple Fractures—General Guidelines

The principle of multiple coding of injuries should be followed in coding multiple fractures. Combination categories 819 and 829 should only be used when there is insufficient detail to code each fracture more specifically. Other purposes for categories 819 and 829 are for primary tabulation of data when only one code can be used, and, when there is a need for multiple fracture data that has an impact on patient functional status during an episode of care. Use of code categories 819 and 829 is discouraged in the acute care hospital setting.

As illustrated previously, multiple fractures of the same bone(s) classified to different fourth-digit levels require separate codes. ICD-9-CM does not distinguish between unilateral and bilateral fractures in diagnosis classification. Thus, bilateral closed fractures of the ulna shaft, code 813.22, would only require this code to be reported once. However, if the patient sustains two fractures of the ulna classifiable with two distinct ICD-9-CM codes, such as a closed fracture of the ulna shaft left arm and a closed fracture of the ulna olecranon process right arm, the two codes assigned would be 813.22 and 813.01. Procedure coding in ICD-9-CM does allow for multiple reporting of the same procedure code. Two categories allow for coding multiple fractures of the same bone. They are:

> 815 Fracture of metacarpal bone
> 816 Fracture of one or more phalanges of hand

A multiple sites fifth digit is available for both categories (Converse, 1986).

Reporting and sequencing of multiple fractures in acute care hospitals are based upon the Uniform Hospital Discharge Data Set (UHDDS) definitions and generally take into account the severity of the fractures. In the outpatient setting, the UHDDS definitions do not apply and the reason for the outpatient encounter should be based upon the condition chiefly responsible for the outpatient encounter.

Pathological Fractures

Code subcategory 733.1 classifies pathological fractures with fifth digits added in 1993 to further delineate the site of the fracture. Strictly speaking, a pathological fracture is any fracture through diseased bone, but for classification purposes it has been further defined as "without any identifiable trauma or following only minor trauma" (Pickett, 1993). To classify a fracture as pathologic, the qualifying terms of "pathologic" or "spontaneous" should be documented, or the chart should document a cause and effect relationship between the fracture and some underlying pathology. In the latter instance, there should always be a code reported for bone pathology with the pathological fracture code to complete the coding profile.

Fractures not specified as pathologic, spontaneous, or due to an underlying bone disease are classified to the code category range 800–829 as if they were due to injury or trauma. For this reason, when a pathological fracture is implied but not clearly stated in the chart documentation, the responsible physician should be queried as to whether or not this represents a pathological fracture. Situations which imply a pathological fracture include those where the fracture seems out of proportion to the degree of injury or trauma and when there is a disease present which is often associated with pathological fractures, but no cause and effect is documented. Etiologies for pathologic fractures include:

> metastatic bone disease
> osteoporosis

osteopenia
disuse atrophy
hyperparathyroidism
osteitis deformans
avascular necrosis of bone
osteomyelitis
osteogenesis imperfecta
osteopetrosis
neuromuscular disorders with disuse osteoporosis

Note that multiple myeloma also causes pathological fractures, but as it is an integral part of the disease process, only the code for multiple myeloma code subcategory 203.0 (with the appropriate fifth digit indicating remission status) is assigned (Richard, 1996). Although virtually all pathologic fractures involve some degree of precipitating trauma or injury, a code from code category range 800–829 is never assigned with a code from subcategory 733.1 for the same fracture.

Fracture Procedures

ICD-9-CM Classification There are many different ways to treat a fracture. It depends upon the fracture's clinical presentation, which includes its severity, the bones involved, the type and number of fractures, and even related factors such as the age of the patient and underlying bone pathology. ICD-9-CM classifies most orthopedic procedures within the code category range of 76–84 in Volume Three, with a few related miscellaneous procedures found in code category range 87–99.

Reduction and fixation are the two most common procedures associated with fractures. A reduction of a fracture is a procedure where the physician aligns fractured bones and bone fragments back into their normal anatomical alignment. Except in very rare instances, a reduction will be performed whenever there is a displaced fracture. Non-displaced fractures, and fractures where the displacement is minimal and judged to be insignificant, do not require reduction. Fixation is a procedure where the fractured bones or bone fragments are secured in their normal anatomical alignment. Fixation may or may not occur following a reduction. Sometimes the fixation is done to stabilize a non-displaced fracture.

The terms "open" and "closed" as they apply to fracture procedures have specific meanings which are unrelated to whether or not the fracture itself is open or closed. Coders must be careful when reviewing chart documentation not to confuse statements relating to the diagnosis with statements relating to the procedure. The fact that a fracture is open or closed has no bearing upon whether or not the procedures to treat the fracture will be open or closed.

A closed reduction is one by which the physician manually or through the use of traction devices, realigns the bone ends or fragments, without surgically exposing the fracture site. In an open reduction, the fracture site is exposed during the reduction procedure, and it is normally performed in an operating room. If the fracture was an open fracture, the operative report may describe the procedure with terms such as "reopening" "debriding" or "exploring" the wound down to the fracture site prior to reduction. In some cases, a closed reduction is followed by an open reduction. In the case of a failed closed reduction, no code is assigned for closed reduction. If the closed reduction was accomplished and later judged to be suboptimal, or if the bones or bone fragments fell out of alignment at a later time, then codes for both the initial closed and the subsequent reduction, (which may be open or closed), may be assigned.

Open reduction is indicated when one or more of the following conditions are met:

1. Fractures irreducible by manipulation or closed means.

2. Displaced intra-articular fracture, where the fragments are sufficiently large to allow internal fixation.

3. Certain displaced physeal injuries such as displaced Salter III and IV injuries.

4. Major avulsion fractures with significant disruption of an important muscle or ligament. These include fractures of the greater tuberosity of the humerus, the greater trochanter, the olecranon, the patella, the intercondylar eminence of the tibia, and the tibial tubercle.

5. Nonunion of a fracture which has received adequate treatment by a closed method.

6. Replantations of extremities or digits. In this case, rigid fixation is necessary to protect the repair of the neurovascular structures (Crenshaw, 1987).

Internal fixation is the process of directly securing bone ends or fragments together by means of surgical hardware, such as with nails, screws, plates and rods. In directly securing the bone ends or fragments, some part of the hardware will come in contact with the fracture site, in the same way that a carpenter's nail driven through two wooden boards will come in contact with both boards to directly connect them together. Although Steinmann pins and Kirschner wires are normally associated with external fixation, they can also be used for internal fixation. For this reason, the coder should be careful to review the chart documentation to determine exactly which type of fixation is being performed and not make assumptions based upon a piece of hardware's typical usage. Orthopedic surgeons can be very creative in their use of hardware. For example, intra-articular phalangeal fractures involve the joint surface. If displaced, they are often treated with open reduction and internal fixation using fine Kirschner wire as the fixation hardware (Salter, 1984).

Internal fixation can be performed without the need for a fracture reduction and is classified to subcategory 78.5. This occurs in two instances. First, the fracture may be in good anatomical alignment so no reduction is necessary. In this case, the internal fixation is performed to stabilize the fracture site. The internal fixation subcategory code 78.5 can also be used to revise or replace a previous internal fixation, such as in the case where the original internal hardware has become displaced or broken. Note that subcategory code 78.5 is assigned only when there has been no reduction of the fracture performed during this episode of care. If a reduction is performed prior to an incision for the internal fixation, this is classified to subcategory 79.1 as a closed reduction with internal fixation.

External fixation is any method of securing the bone ends or fragments in their proper anatomical alignment without directly connecting them with hardware. Simply put, in external fixation the bone ends or fragments are held together without nailing, screwing rodding, plating or wiring the bone ends or fragments together at the point of fracture. Casts, wraps, splints and similar immobilization devices are some external fixation devices classified to subcategory 93.5, and should not be confused with the more complex external fixation devices classified to subcategory 78.1. Pins, wires and screws are used in these external fixation devices (sometimes called minifixators). The key difference is that these pins, wires and screws are used solely to hold the bone ends or fragments in their normal anatomical position. They do not connect bone (fragment) to bone (fragment) and the fracture site is not touched. Small incisions are normally made near the fracture site to secure them to the adjacent bone. Care must be exercised not to confuse these minor procedures with the surgical procedure of internal fixation. In external fixation, the hardware does not come in contact with or cross the fracture site. When a reduction is performed in addition to an external fixation not classifiable to subcategory 93.5, two codes will be assigned. One is from category 79 to describe the reduction, and one is from subcategory 78.1 for the external fixation. Internal and external fixation should not be coded concurrently for the same fracture during the same operative episode as surgeons will not incorporate both methods of fixation at the same time.

Fourth digits are used to classify the site of fracture reduction in category 79. It is important to note the Excludes note here. The fourth digit of "9" for other specified bone does not include fractures of the following:

facial bones (76.70–76.79)
nasal bones (21.71–21.72)
orbit (76–78–76–79)
skull (02.02)
vertebra (03.53)

The fourth digit of "3" for the carpals and metacarpals covers thirteen different bones. They are shown in Table 6–4 and Figure 6–3.

TABLE 6–4   Carpal and Metacarpal Bones.

Carpals	*Metacarpals*
Scaphoid (navicular)	First metacarpal
Lunate (semilunar)	Second metacarpal
Triquetral	Third metacarpal
Pisiform	Fourth metacarpal
Trapezoid (lesser multangular)	Fifth metacarpal
Capitate	
Trapezium (greater multangular)	
Hamate	

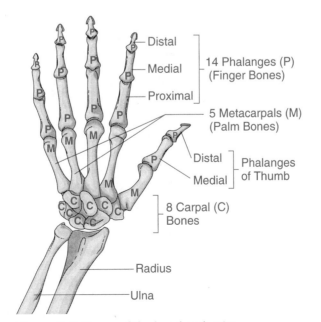

Figure 6–3 Bones of the hand and wrist.

The tarsals and metatarsals are made up of twelve bones as shown in Table 6–5 and Figure 6–4.

The information in Tables 6–3 and 6–4 is also useful for assigning codes in category 78 even though the order and content of the fourth-digit classification is different. Also, be wary of preoperative anesthesia notes, nursing notes, and consent forms when doing chart reviews. Often these forms will routinely refer to any fracture surgery as "ORIF" (open reduction with internal fixation), when in fact the operative report will describe a different classifiable procedure.

Non-surgical treatment of fractures include casting, taping, splinting, bandaging, immobilization and traction. These codes can be found in subcategories 93.4 and 93.5.

CPT

Codes for reporting fracture procedures can be found throughout the CPT chapter on the Musculoskeletal System, code range 20000–20005. As in ICD-9-CM, the codes differentiate between closed or open treatment, but add "percutaneous skeletal fixation" as a third alternative. Closed treatment is used to describe pro-

TABLE 6–5   **Tarsals and Metatarsals.**

Tarsals	Metatarsals
Talus (astragalus)	First metatarsal
Calcaneus	Second metatarsal
Navicular	Third metatarsal
Cuboid	Fourth metatarsal
Medial cuneiform	Fifth metatarsal
Intermediate cuneiform	
Lateral cuneiform	

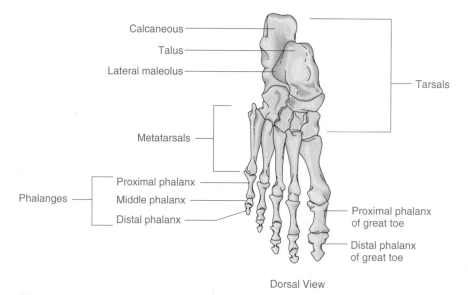

Dorsal View

Figure 6–4 Bones of the ankle and foot.

cedures where the fracture site is not surgically opened. It may be used in conjunction with the following methods of treating the fracture: with manipulation, without manipulation, or with or without traction. Open treatment is used when the fracture site is surgically opened; the fracture site is visualized and internal fixation may be used. Percutaneous skeletal fixation describes fracture treatment in cases where the fracture is not exposed, but fixation is placed across the fracture site, usually under x-ray imaging (AMA, 1997).

The term manipulation is used synonymously for reduction in CPT. It is the actual or attempted restoration of a fracture or joint dislocation to its normal anatomical alignment. Note that codes indicating manipulation can be assigned in CPT, even if a fracture reduction is not accomplished. When a closed treatment is done without manipulation, it usually means that no attempt to reduce the fracture has been made, and a cast, splint, bandage or other traction or immobilization device has been applied. CPT does not classify reductions with open procedures, and the use of internal or external fixation is normally found within the code narrative for the open procedure. When an external fixation is done and it is not listed in the code narrative for the basic fracture or dislocation procedure, select either code 20690 or 20692 as an additional code assignment. If a revision of the external fixation device is performed, code 20693 is assigned.

Some CPT procedure codes for fractures and dislocations use anesthesia as a decision point in determining the correct code. Anesthesia is the pharmacological suppression of nerve function and can be general, regional, or local. It should not be confused with sedation (calming), analgesia (pain reduction), or topical anesthetics (ointments, salves), which are not included in CPT as anesthesia.

Multiple codes can be assigned in CPT for fixation devices and fracture procedures depending upon the number of fractures and the clinical circumstances involved just as in ICD-9-CM. Some important differences do exist however, such as the global services concept for most surgical procedures. If a surgical procedure does not have an asterisk after the code number, the procedure includes variable preoperative and postoperative services. For fracture procedures such as subsequent suture removal and casting, strapping or other immobilization revision or removal, the surgeon performing the service should not bill for these minor procedures at a later date. Certain fracture procedures encourage multiple reporting of the same code by using the terms "each," "single," or "one" in the code narrative. Code 26600 for "Closed treatment of metacarpal fracture, single: without manipulation, each bone," requires the coder to assign this code as many times as necessary to report each metacarpal bone treated in this manner. The bones may be on one or both hands.

Dislocations

A **dislocation** is a disarrangement of two or more bones from their articular processes. It is synonymous with the term luxation. In a true dislocation, there is a complete loss of congruity between the articular surfaces of a joint. An incomplete dislocation is called a subluxation, but the two terms are sometimes used interchangeably (and incorrectly). ICD-9-CM classifies both dislocations and subluxations with the same codes. When a dislocation is associated with a fracture, only the fracture code is assigned. In a fracture/dislocation, the fracture is located near the joint where the disarticulation took place. It is possible to have a fracture and a dislocation of the same bone, without it being classified as a fracture/dislocation. For example, a patient may have a dislocation of the proximal femur (at the hip joint) and a fracture at the distal femur (at the knee joint). In this case, the fracture and the dislocation have occurred at different sites and two codes can be assigned.

The terminology and coding rules for dislocations are virtually the same as they are for fractures. Dislocations and subluxations are classified to category range 830–839 and the terms open and closed as discussed in the section on fractures have basically the same meaning. Three types of dislocations not classified to this area are:

1. Congenital dislocations (754.0–755.8). These are dislocations which were existing at birth.

2. Pathological dislocations (718.2). Dislocations which may be due to an underlying disease or disorder, and include spontaneous dislocations.

3. Recurrent dislocations (718.3). Dislocations frequently occurring in a major joint such as the shoulder or hip, due to a lack of integrity of the soft tissues of the joint capsule.

Dislocation Procedures

ICD-9-CM Classification Reduction and fixation terminology applies to dislocations as it does to fractures. Closed reductions are classified to subcategory 79.7 and open reductions to subcategory 79.8. The major difference is that subcategory 79.7 includes the application of an external traction device, and subcategory 79.8 includes any internal or external fixation device. A repair of a recurrent dislocation involving soft tissue repair (i.e. arthroplasty) is classified elsewhere, such as code 81.82, Repair of recurrent dislocation of shoulder.

CPT Classification The terms for open treatment, closed treatment, and percutaneous skeletal fixation have the same meaning for dislocations as they do for fractures. The code ranges classifying different parts of the skeletal system in the Musculoskeletal System chapter of CPT are inconsistent with regard to how dislocations are coded. The terminology of the code ranges may appear in the following five ways:

1. Bones which are part of fixed cartilaginous joint and thus not typically described as a dislocation may be listed with the subtitle "Fracture and/or Dislocation" even though the term dislocation is not present in any of the code descriptions. For example, Fractures of the ribs are classified within the code range 21800–21810. The subtitle of this code range is "Fracture and/or Dislocation" but none of these codes mention the term dislocation, only the fracture.

2. Combination fracture and/or dislocation codes. These codes will describe fractures alone, dislocations alone, or fracture/dislocations. Example: 27217 "Open treatment of anterior ring fracture and/or dislocation with internal fixation (includes pubic symphysis and/or rami)."

3. Fracture/dislocation codes. These codes specifically classify fractures associated with dislocations. Example: 26665 "Open treatment of carpometacarpal fracture dislocation, thumb (Bennett Fracture), with or without internal or external fixation."

4. Dislocation only codes. These codes specifically classify treatment of dislocations alone. Example: 27250 "Closed treatment of hip dislocation, traumatic; without anesthesia."

5. Specified clinical types of dislocations. Example: 27265 "Closed treatment of post hip arthroplasty dislocation: without anesthesia."

From these varied code narratives, it is easy to see why it is so important to thoroughly read and understand the code narrative before assigning a code.

EXERCISE 6–1

Assign ICD-9-CM diagnosis and procedure codes, as well as CPT procedure codes, to the following statements. Do not assign E-codes.

1. Fracture dislocation of the surgical neck of the humerus, with closed reduction and internal fixation of same.

   ICD-9-CM code(s) _____

   CPT code(s) _____

2. Open reduction without internal fixation of closed navicular and cuboid bone ankle fractures.

   ICD-9-CM code(s) _____

   CPT code(s) _____

3. Closed fracture of the forearm (Colles type) with percutaneous reduction and mini-fixation.

   ICD-9-CM code(s) _____

   CPT code(s) _____

4. Dislocated patella. Dislocation reduced under intravenous sedation.

   ICD-9-CM code(s) _____

   CPT code(s) _____

5. Fracture of the pelvic ring with slight degree of subluxation, due to advanced osteoporosis. Closed reduction under regional nerve block.

   ICD-9-CM code(s) _____

   CPT code(s) _____

6. Intertrochanteric hip fracture, closed, with femoral head replacement using a Medicon alloy femoral head and Geigger nonmetallic screws with methomethacrylate cement.

   ICD-9-CM code(s) _____

   CPT code(s) _____

ARTHROPATHY

Arthropathy is a vague, general term meaning pathology affecting a joint. There are many different descriptive types, which overlap each other, including infective, rheumatoid, degenerative, and internal derangements. This next section will examine the most common types seen by orthopedic physicians.

Infective Arthropathy

Infective arthropathy is any arthritis, arthropathy, polyarthritis, or polyarthropathy associated with an infective agent and is classified to category 711. The agent is most often bacterial, but can also be viral, fungal (mycotic), mycobacterial, parasitic (micro and macroparasites), or helminthic (worms). It should not be confused with infective osteomyelitis, which is an infection of the bone and/or bone marrow classified to category 730. But both infective arthropathy and infective osteomyelitis can occur concurrently.

All of the subcategory codes in category 711 are italicized manifestation subcategories with the exception of 711.0, Pyogenic arthritis, and 711.9, Unspecified infective arthritis. To assign a code from subcategories 711.1–711.8 you must be able to identify the infectious organism by name or type as indicated in the ICD-9-CM index. This will be the first listed diagnosis code, followed by the manifestation code for the arthropathy.

Pyogenic arthritis is arthropathy due to a specific bacterial organism known to produce suppuration. It is important to reference the ICD-9-CM index carefully when coding bacterial arthropathy because certain non-pyogenic bacteria will fall into subcategory 711.4 for "Arthropathy associated with other bacterial disease." Coders should make the effort to first determine from the chart documentation the name of the specific bacteria caused arthropathy, and then read and be guided by the index entries under the main term "Arthritis." When the code assignment is directed to subcategory 711.0, it will always be listed first following by the code for the bacterial organism classifiable to subcategories 041.0–041.8. Infective bacterial arthropathy classifiable to subcategory 711.4 will always list the underlying pathogen first as indicated by the index entries. Subcategory 711.9 will classify conditions specified as infective arthropathy, without mention of the type or name of the infectious agent, and thus will not be accompanied by a second code.

Rheumatoid Arthropathy

A distinction needs to be made between arthropathy which falls into the general category of rheumatoid arthritis, and arthropathy associated with acute rheumatic fever. Rheumatic fever is an acute inflammatory disease which attacks the connective tissue in the heart, blood vessels, and joints of children. It is due to infection by group A hemolytic streptococci. Due to the transient nature of the joint lesions and effectiveness of antibiotics, arthropathy associated with rheumatic fever is considered symptomatic and rarely leads to permanent joint pathology (Salter, 1984). When arthropathy is due to or associated with acute rheumatic fever, only code 390 for Acute rheumatic fever is assigned.

Rheumatoid arthritis as classified to subcategory 714.0 is a chronic, systemic, inflammatory connective tissue disease. It primarily attacks the peripheral joints and surrounding muscles, tendons, ligaments, and blood vessels (see Figure 6–5).

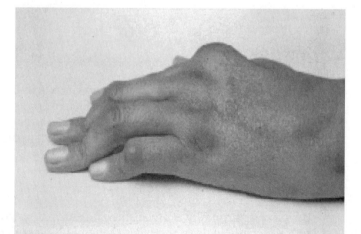

Figure 6–5 Arthritic hands. (Courtesy of the Arthritis Foundation.)

The severity and frequency of exacerbations can vary greatly from patient to patient. The etiology of rheumatoid arthritis is unknown. The disease also goes by the names of primary progressive arthritis and proliferative arthritis.

Subcategory code 714.1, Felty's syndrome, is rheumatoid arthritis associated with splenomegaly and leukopenia. Mild anemia and thrombocytopenia may accompany the severe neutropenia, and skin and pulmonary infections are frequent complications. Subcategory code 714.2 classifies rheumatoid arthritis with extra-articular lesions of connective tissue disease in the cardiovascular, reticuloendothelial, digestive, and respiratory systems. Subcategory code 714.3 classifies a number of juvenile chronic polyarthritis diseases, which are rheumatoid-like disorders affecting children, but have a much better prognosis than the adult onset diseases. Subcategory code 714.4 Chronic postrheumatic arthropathy is a form of arthropathy affecting the hands and feet caused by repeated attacks of rheumatic arthritis. Rheumatoid lung code 714.81 is a disease of the lung associated with rheumatoid arthritis. It is sometimes seen in Caplan's Syndrome, a disease which features rheumatoid pneumoconiosis (Richard, 1994).

As evidenced by the information in the preceding paragraph, rheumatoid arthritis can be associated with a wide variety of concomitant clinical conditions. It can be quite difficult for the coder to determine what concomitant conditions need to be classified separately, and what is integral to the disease processes classifiable to subcategories and subclassifications under category 714. When in doubt, the responsible physician should be consulted before breaking out the variables of rheumatoid arthritis into individual codes.

Degenerative Arthritis

Code category 715 classifies degenerative arthritis, also known as degenerative joint disease, osteoarthritis, senescent arthritis and hypertrophic arthritis. The term arthritis may also be further specified as polyarthritis when more than one joint is involved. Category 721 classifies degenerative arthritis when it involves the bones of the spinal column. This condition is sometimes referred to as spondylosis or spondylarthritis. Categories 715 and 721 should not be considered mutually exclusive for classification purposes. Arthritis of the spine will be discussed later in this chapter under vertebral disorders. Degenerative arthritis is a condition marked by a deterioration of articular cartilage, hypertrophy and remodeling of the subchondral bone, and secondary inflammation of the synovial membrane.

Within category 715 there are qualifying terms which must be understood to properly assign codes to the fourth-digit level. These terms are:

Generalized: a form of arthritis involving multiple joints that is almost always characterized as a primary osteoarthritis.

Localized: arthritis restricted or limited to a specific joint. It is possible for arthritis to affect more than one joint and not be classified as generalized. For example, a patient may have a localized arthritis in the right wrist and left elbow, but no indications of arthritis in any other joint. This condition would not be considered generalized.

Primary: degeneration of the joints without any known preexisting abnormality. It is sometimes referred to as idiopathic.

Secondary: degeneration of the joints due to an identifiable initiating factor. The factors can include obesity, trauma, congenital malformations, foreign bodies, malalignments of joints, fibrosis and scarring from previous inflammatory disease or infection, metabolic or circulatory bone diseases, and iatrogenic factors such as continuous pressure put on joint surfaces during orthopedic treatment of congenital anomalies (Richard, 1994).

Internal Derangements

Category code 717 classifies internal derangements of the knee, and category 718 classifies other types of internal derangements involving other joints. It is important to note that conditions of the knee not classified under category 717 may be classified under category 718. For example, a pathological dislocation of the knee is classified 718.26. The square brackets underneath each subcategory code in category 718 will tell you whether or not the code may be used for the knee. Note that some subcategory codes exclude the fifth digit of "6" for lower leg (knee). The term internal derangement refers to a range of injuries of the joint involving the soft tissues such as the synovium, cartilage, and ligaments. It is important to differentiate between pathology classified to 717 and 718, and acute injuries classified to sprains, strains and other acute injuries in the Injury and Poisoning chapter, Chapter 17, of ICD-9-CM. Acute injuries of the joints are always classified to Chapter 17 even if the physician uses the term internal derangement. The acute phase of the injury is variable depending upon the joint involved and the severity of injury, but typically lasts between two and six weeks. Conditions classifiable to categories 717 and 718 refer to lasting or old internal derangements, and most often with degenerative changes.

Arthropathy Procedures

ICD-9-CM Classification

A wide variety of procedures are used to treat arthropathy and many of them are found in categories 80 and 81 in ICD-9-CM Volume Three. The following is a discussion to the most common joint procedures indexed in ICD-9-CM.

Arthrotomy: incision into a joint, This procedure may be performed to drain a joint of blood, synovial fluid, or purulence. When documented as the approach to further surgery, it should not be coded.

Arthroscopy: the viewing of a joint by means of an endoscope (arthroscope). As with arthrotomy, when the arthroscopy is used to gain entrance to a joint in order to perform further surgery, it is considered an operative approach and not coded.

Biopsy: the removal of a tissue sample for examination. When the entire lesion or tissue is removed, an excision code is used rather than a biopsy code.

Arthrodesis: the process of making a joint immobile by binding it together, usually by grafting bone or bone chips to the joint. The term is used synonymously with fusion.

Arthroplasty: an operation to restore the integrity and function of a joint. An arthroplasty may or may not involve the use of prosthetics and artificial materials.

Replacement: the removal of diseased or deranged joint tissue or bone and replacement with artificial materials, allograft or autograft tissue.

Revision: surgery on a joint which has already undergone a primary repair procedure. A revision may make minor repairs to the existing joint, or repeat steps of the primary repair procedure right up to a complete redo of the primary repair procedure.

CPT Classification

CPT organizes all of its procedures in the chapter of the Musculoskeletal System according to the anatomical part, and then by the type of procedure involved. The way that the procedures are listed are fairly consistent throughout the chapter. For example, under the subheading of Forearm and Wrist, the following order of procedures is found:

■ Incision

■ Excision

■ Introduction or Removal

■ Repair, Revision, and/or Reconstruction

■ Fracture and/or Dislocation

■ Arthrodesis

■ Amputation

■ Other Procedures

Other types of procedures such as Grafts or Replantations may be added to certain anatomical sites whereas some procedure types may be eliminated from others.

It is important to note that Endoscopy/Arthroscopy is found at the end of the chapter in code range 29800–29909. CPT does not follow the same coding rules for arthroscopic procedures as for ICD-9-CM. All CPT arthroscopic procedures will be found at the end of the chapter when the operative approach is documented as arthroscopic (endoscopic). The code assigned will be chosen from this list. When a procedure is converted from endoscopic to an open procedure, the code for the endoscopic procedure may be assigned according to what was done under arthroscopy, and a separate code may be assigned for the open procedure. Some payers will require adding modifier "-51" to the arthroscopy procedure to identify it as a multiple procedure performed on the same day.

A common error is that some of the arthroscopic procedures in this chapter, particularly those of the knee, are easy to unbundle (separate). The Correct Coding Initiative (CCI), developed and used by the Health Care Financing Administration (HCFA) for Medicare and Medicaid, has many edits to prevent unbundling these codes. To begin with, all surgical endoscopies include a diagnostic endoscopy. When assigning more than one knee procedure code for a particular surgery, be sure that the additional codes are not integral parts of the main procedure. For example, code 29880 is for "Arthroscopy, knee, surgical; with meniscectomy (medial and lateral) including any meniscal shaving." In reading through the operative report, you may notice mention of any or all of the following:

■ Minor synovectomy

■ Fat pad resection

■ Articular shaving

■ Removal of loose bodies

■ Evacuation of debris

■ Shaving of meniscus or cruciate stump

■ Splinting or Casting

All of these procedures are integral parts of an arthroscopic knee meniscectomy and should not be coded and reported separately (AAOS, 1996). They are all found in the CCI billing editing software as well.

EXERCISE 6–2

Assign ICD-9-CM diagnosis and procedure codes, as well as CPT procedure codes, to the following statements. Do not assign E-codes.

1. Acute Pseudomonas infection of the left shoulder and wrist. Incision and drainage of both joints.

   ICD-9-CM code(s) _____

   CPT code(s) _____

2. Bucket handle tear of lateral meniscus, status post bicycle accident two months ago. Lateral meniscectomy with partial synovectomy and debridement of the patella under endoscopic control.

   ICD-9-CM code(s) _____

   CPT code(s) _____

3. Arthritis of the left proximal humerus due to multiple myeloma, not currently in remission. Debulking of tumor, proximal humerus.

   ICD-9-CM code(s) _____

   CPT code(s) _____

4. Degenerative joint disease localized in both knees and hips due to morbid obesity. Bilateral total knee replacement of both knee joints.

   ICD-9-CM code(s) _____

   CPT code(s) _____

5. Internal derangement of the knee, status post bicycle accident this morning. Incision and drainage of bloody effusion of the left knee.

   ICD-9-CM code(s) _____

   CPT code(s) _____

VERTEBRAL DISORDERS

ICD-9-CM code categories 720–724 classify disorders of the vertebral column along with some other related pathology of the spinal musculature and the spinal cord and spinal roots. Acute injuries of the vertebral column are not classified here, and should be classified to Chapter 17 through the specific type of injury as referenced in the ICD-9-CM index. The terms spondylosis and spondylitis refer respectively to degeneration and inflammation of the vertebrae. Spondylarthritis is an inflammation of the vertebral articulations.

Important qualifying terms used in the subcategories for spinal arthritis include:

> **Myelopathy:** pathology of the spinal cord due to the arthritic changes of the vertebrae. Paresthesia, loss of sensation, and loss of sphincter control are the most common forms of myelopathy.

Cervical: referring to the seven cervical vertebrae. The first and second cervical vertebrae are also known as the atlas and axis respectively.

Thoracic: referring to the twelve thoracic vertebrae.

Lumbar: referring to the five lumbar vertebrae.

Sacral: referring to a single fused bone made up of five segments.

Coccyx: referring to a single fused bone at the end of the spinal column made up of three to five segments.

Lumbosacral: referring to one or more lumbar vertebrae in conjunction with the sacrum.

Enthesopathy: pathology occurring at the site where muscle tendons and ligaments attach to bones or joint capsules.

Category 721 classifies degenerative spondylosis and spondylarthritis excluding those inflammatory spondylopathies of the vertebral column classified to category 720. Category 722 classifies intervertebral disk disorders. Both categories 721 and 722 have subcategories that differentiate between conditions "with myelopathy" and "without myelopathy." For coding purposes, myelopathy includes any symptomatic impingement, compression, disruption, or disturbance to the spinal cord or blood supply to the spinal cord, due to spondylosis in category 721 or intervertebral disk disorder in category 722. It is possible for a patient to have concurrently conditions classifiable to both categories 721 and 722.

Sometimes the term radiculitis or radiculopathy is confused with myelopathy in category 722. **Radiculopathy** and radiculitis are diseases and/or inflammation of the spinal nerve roots. The spinal nerves emerge from the spinal cord and can become entrapped, compressed, or irritated by diseased vertebral bodies, or more commonly, displaced intervertebral disks. Radiculopathy manifests itself almost exclusively as sensory symptoms (radicular pain or paresthesia) and/or motor symptoms (painless weakness). Radiculopathy can occur at any level, although involvement of the thoracic vertebrae and coccyx is very rare (Weiderholt, 1988). In all there are 31 pairs of spinal nerves; eight cervical, twelve thoracic, five lumbar, five sacral, and one coccygeal.

Categories 723 and 724 contain a lot of symptomatic conditions which are excluded when used in conjunction with codes from categories 721 and 722. For example, spinal stenosis, codes 723.0 and 724.0X, are often mistakenly assigned as additional codes when the stenosis was caused by spondylosis or by narrowing of the spinal canal due to intervertebral disk displacement. Neuralgia, radiculitis, panniculitis, ankylosis, and compression of the spinal nerve roots are also symptomatic terms found here, that with a more complete review of the chart or better documentation by the physician, will almost always refer back to a condition classifiable to categories 721 and 722.

Curvatures and related deformities of the spine can either be congenital (present at birth) or acquired, and ICD-9-CM classifies each type to different chapters. The congenital deformities are found classified to subcategory 756.1 with fifth digits describing the specific type of anomaly. Acquired deformities are classified to all of category 737, and codes 738.4 and 738.5. Acquired deformities may be due to a variety of etiologies including:

■ Trauma

■ Pathologic weakness of bone

■ Degenerative joint disease

■ Surgical intervention

■ Congenital conditions (e.g., congenital shortness of limb, with acquired compensatory defect)

- Paralytic syndromes
- Poor posture
- Muscle spasms

The subterm "traumatic" listed in the ICD-9-CM index under the main term "Spondylolisthesis" is sometimes misinterpreted by coders. Traumatic spondylolisthesis is a congenital defect due to birth or intrauterine trauma and is classified to code 756.12. Spondylolisthesis due to acute trauma at any time after birth is classified as a current injury in Chapter 17. Spondylolisthesis as a late effect of trauma, such as due to a prior fracture of the vertebrae, is classified as acquired and should also carry the appropriate ICD-9-CM code for late effect—e.g., 905.1 as a secondary code (Richard, 1996).

Vertebral Procedures

ICD-9-CM Classification

In ICD-9-CM Volume Three, the three most common procedures for disorders of the vertebra are decompression of the spinal nerve root, vertebral disk excision, and spinal fusion. A decompression of the spinal nerve root is a procedure designed to relieve pressure and irritation of the root which causes radiculopathy. Code 03.09 classifies nerve root decompression without concurrent intervertebral disc excision. The procedure can be a laminotomy or an incision into one or more vertebral laminae; or a laminectomy, which is an excision of vertebral laminae, usually the posterior arch. These procedures can be modified with the prefix "foramen", meaning at the site of the aperture into the vertebral canal bounded by the pedicles of adjacent vertebrae above and below the vertebral bodies anteriorly, and the articular processes posteriorly. In procedures classifiable to 03.09, only a small amount of cartilaginous tissue is removed from around the nerve root—the disc is left essentially intact.

When the spinal root is decompressed by excision of the intervertebral disk, either in part (e.g. hemilaminectomy) or in total, code 80.51 is assigned. Code 03.09 is not assigned with code 80.51 unless a separate nerve root decompression classifiable to 03.09 is performed at a different vertebral level than an excision of intervertebral disk classifiable to 80.51. It is advisable to have the dictated operative report available when coding these procedures, as it can be difficult to differentiate between the two, and preoperative notes and pathology reports can be misleading. Chemical or enzymatic nerve root decompression is classified to code 80.52 and is rarely, if ever, performed in conjunction with procedures classified to codes 03.09 or 80.51. Also note that any facetectomy associated with a laminectomy or hemilaminectomy is not coded as it is considered an incidental part of the main surgical procedure.

Spinal fusion is the process of immobilizing two or more vertebrae by fixation or stiffening. Bones grafts and/or orthopedic hardware may be used to accomplish this task classifiable to subcategory 80.1. Fourth digits are used to identify the region of the vertebra being fused, and the technique used. If hardware is used to do the fusion or bone from a bone bank, no secondary code is necessary, but if an autograft of the patient's bone is used, a secondary code from subcategory 77.7 will be assigned to classify the harvesting of the bone for grafting.

CPT Classification

CPT has many codes to classify spinal nerve decompression and intervertebral disc excision, and they can be found in the code range 63001–63290. There are many decision points the coder must be aware of including:

1. Was the main procedure a laminectomy, laminotomy, or diskectomy?

2. What region (lumbar, thoracic, cervical, sacral) was involved?

3. Was the main procedure accompanied by a facetectomy, foraminotomy, diskectomy, decompression or spinal cord, cauda equina and/or nerve root, myelotomy, cordotomy, or nerve section?

4. Was the procedure a primary or reexploration?

5. How many interspace levels were involved?

6. Was a concurrent arthrodesis performed?

With so many decision points and precise language used in the code narratives, it is imperative to read the descriptions and choose only the one which matches precisely what was done.

Arthrodesis is classified to the code range 22548–22812. These codes classify only the arthrodesis; additional codes are needed if a bone graft was obtained (20930–20938) or if hardware was used (22840–22855). Modifier "-51" for multiple procedures are not reported with these codes as they are considered add-on procedure codes. As with ICD-9-CM, CPT classifies arthrodesis by vertebral level and by technique. If a hemidiskectomy was performed with arthrodesis by instrumentation and bone graft, four codes would need to be assigned: one for the hemidiskectomy, one for the arthrodesis, one for the bone graft, and one for the instrumentation. Arthrodesis is also considered a primary procedure if it is performed for a spinal deformity, and these codes are located in the code range 22800–22812. Note that bone grafts and instrumentation are reported in addition to these codes also.

EXERCISE 6–3

Assign ICD-9-CM diagnosis and procedure codes, as well as CPT procedure codes, to the following statements. Do not assign E-codes.

1. Cervical spondylosis with severe spinal cord compression. Anterior diskectomy at C1-2 with decompression of spinal cord.

   ICD-9-CM code(s) _____

   CPT code(s) _____

2. Spinal stenosis due to herniated nucleus pulposus, L1-2, with radiculitis. Foraminotomy, laminectomy, decompression of spinal nerve root L1-2 with partial resection of bony facet.

   ICD-9-CM code(s) _____

   CPT code(s) _____

3. Degenerative spondylolisthesis. Insertion of Harrington rod, anterolateral technique, dorsolumbar spine spanning four segments.

   ICD-9-CM code(s) _____

   CPT code(s) _____

4. Thoracic and lumbosacral spondylosis with displacement of T10-12. Laminectomy and excision of disk at T10-11, foraminotomy and freeing of spinal nerve root at T11-12. Morcellated bone graft from left hip to posterior T10-11 and T11-12 interspaces for arthrodesis.

ICD-9-CM code(s) _____

CPT code(s) _____

SPRAINS AND STRAINS

Sprains and strains of joints and adjacent muscles are classified to code category range 840–848 in ICD-9-CM. A sprain is defined as a severe stretching of a ligament with minor tears and hemorrhage, without subluxation, dislocation or fracture. A severe sprain can result in occult joint instability. A strain is a less precise term that applies to any soft tissue injury (joint capsule, ligament, muscle, tendon) that occurs from overexertion. Strains and sprains that occur secondarily to any condition classifiable as a fracture, subluxation or dislocation are incidental and not coded. Sprains and strains usually require only non-operative procedures such as casting, strapping, splinting, etc., and only when there is joint instability and chronic pain will surgery be indicated.

OTHER CONDITIONS AND PROCEDURES

A few of the other more common orthopedic conditions and procedures are discussed in this section. These include malunion and nonunion of fractures, and bone infections.

Malunion and Nonunion of Fractures

These conditions classifiable to codes 733.81 and 733.82 respectively occur when fractured bones do not heal properly. A distinction needs to be made between malunion and nonunion following a traumatic or pathological fracture, and malunion and nonunion of bone following surgery. When a malunion or nonunion occurs following a fracture, codes 733.81 or 733.82 are assigned. This includes instances where there has been an open or closed reduction and an internal or external fixation. In cases where bone has been grafted for either arthrodesis or to further stabilize and strengthen a fracture site, if the grafted bone does not properly join to the graft site, this is considered a postoperative complication, and a code from the category range 996–999 should be selected such as 996.4 "Mechanical complication of internal orthopedic device, implant, or graft."

When a malunion of a fracture is surgically repaired, the most common method is to perform osteoclasis, code subcategory 78.7, along with an internal fixation with fracture reduction, code subcategories 79.1 (closed reduction) or 79.3 (open reduction) in ICD-9-CM. A small amount of debridement or excision of the bone ends may also be done. A nonunion is more likely to be repaired with an arthrodesis classifiable to subcategory range 81.0–81.2 in ICD-9-CM. As with other arthrodesis procedures, harvesting of bone for grafting should also be reported. In

CPT, codes for malunion and nonunion repair are found in each anatomical subsection in the musculoskeletal system chapter under the heading "Repair, Revision, and/or Reconstruction." For example, a repair of a malunion of the tibia without a graft would be coded 27720.

Bone Infections

Acute osteomyelitis, ICD-9-CM subcategory code 730.0, is any acute or subacute infection of the bone or bone marrow. It is usually due to bacteria but can be caused by other infective agents, and is more common among children where the pathogen settles into the metaphyseal bed of the developing long bones. Chronic osteomyelitis code subcategory 730.1 is a persistent or recurring infection of the bone, and is extremely difficult to eradicate completely in the chronic stage. Periostitis is the inflammation of the periosteum, the thick fibrous membrane covering the bone surfaces except at the articular cartilage.

Common ICD-9-CM procedures for these conditions include bone biopsy subcategory code 77.4, local excision of tissue or lesion of bone subcategory code 77.6, sequestrectomy subcategory code 77.0, and bone grafts subcategory codes 78.0 and 77.7. In CPT, most procedures for bone infection will be found in each anatomical subsection in the musculoskeletal chapter under the heading "Excision". Here you will find sequestrectomy codes, as well as various types of excisions with or without grafts. There are two other CPT codes that coders should be aware of. Code 20000 and 20005 classify excisions of superficial or deep soft tissue abscesses which sometimes accompany osteomyelitis. These codes are at the beginning of the chapter and apply to all sections in the musculoskeletal chapter.

EXERCISE 6–4

Assign ICD-9-CM diagnosis and procedure codes, as well as CPT procedure codes, to the following statements. Do not assign E-codes.

1. Nonunion of a bone graft to the lumbosacral fusion performed eight weeks prior to admission. Regrafting of bone fragment from the left iliac crest to the L1-S1 unstable site using posterior interbody technique.

    ICD-9-CM code(s) _____

    CPT code(s) _____

2. Acute osteomyelitis of the radial head due to E. coli. Sequestrectomy of radial head and debridement of surrounding muscle and fascia of the radius.

    ICD-9-CM code(s) _____

    CPT code(s) _____

SUMMARY

■ Sections of the ICD-9-CM and CPT code books that deal primarily with orthopedics are: ICD-9-CM Chapter 13: Diseases of the Musculoskeletal System and Connective Tissue, ICD-9-CM Chapter 17: Injury and Poisoning, CPT Code range 20000–29999: the Musculoskeletal System.

■ It is important to remember that both the index and the tabular list in each classification system must be referenced for accuracy. In some cases, the correct code may be classified in a different section of the code book, as in the case of congenital deformities in ICD-9-CM.

REFERENCES

American Academy of Orthopaedic Surgeons. *Complete Global Services Data for Orthopaedic Surgery.* Park Ridge, IL: American Academy of Orthopaedic Surgeons, 1996.

Converse, M. *Coding Clinic for ICD-9-CM.* Chicago, Illinois: American Hospital Association, 1986.

Crenshaw, A.H. *Campbell's Operative Orthopedics.* St. Louis, MO: Mosby Year Book, 1987.

Mallon, W.J. *Orthopedics for the House Officer.* Baltimore, MD: Williams & Wilkins, 1990.

Pickett, D. *Coding Clinic for ICD-9-CM.* Chicago, Illinois: American Hospital Association, 1993.

Richard, E. "Fractures: Now's the Time to bone Up on Coding Them". *St. Anthony's Clinic Coding and Reimbursement Newsletter,* March 1996, pp. 3–4.

Salter, R.B. *Textbook of Disorders and Injuries of the Musculoskeletal System.* Baltimore, MD: Williams & Wilkins, 1984.

Weiderholt, W.C. *Neurology For Non-Neurologists.* Philadelphia, PA: W.B. Saunders, 1988.

Module 7
Cardiology

Gay Boughton-Barnes, CPC, MPC

LEARNING OBJECTIVES

Upon successful completion of this module, you should be able to:

1. Recognize cardiac anatomy, physiology and terminology.
2. Identify common cardiac diagnostic services.
3. Differentiate a standard cardiac therapeutic service from an interventional service.
4. Recognize nuclear cardiology procedures.
5. Distinguish electrophysiology procedures and services.

INTRODUCTION

This module introduces the many facets of the modern cardiology practice. Electrophysiology procedures and services, medical or non-invasive cardiology, invasive, therapeutic or interventional cardiology, and nuclear diagnostic cardiology are all incorporated into the average practice.

Procedures performed within this subspecialty of internal medicine are percutaneous and intravascular, rather than open cutting procedures as seen in the surgical side of cardiovascular healthcare delivery. Many procedures routinely provided are similar, and thus pose an enormous coding challenge for the novice or for the coder unfamiliar with either the wide array of cardiology services or the actual cardiovascular anatomy.

This module explores the various routine services, procedures and encounters likely to be billed from this subspecialty. Special attention will be paid, not only to the financial and legal aspects of billing, but also to the physiological and anatomical demands of accurate code selection when billing for cardiology services.

Table 7–1 presents some common acronyms used in cardiology and their meanings.

TABLE 7–1   Common Cardiology Acronyms.

ACVD	arteriosclerotic cardiovascular disease	**LV**	left ventricle
AICD	automatic implantable cardio-verter-defibrillator device	**LVH**	left ventricular hypertrophy
		MVP	mitral valve prolapse
AMI	acute myocardial infarction	**MUGA**	nuclear and multigated ventriculogram
ASHD	atherosclerotic heart disease	**NTG**	nitroglycerin
BP	blood pressure	**PVD**	peripheral vascular disease
CABG	coronary artery bypass graft	**PT**	prothrombin time
CAD	coronary artery disease	**PTCA**	percutaneous transluminal coronary angioplasty
CHF	congestive heart failure		
CPR	cardiopulmonary resuscitation	**RA**	right atrium
DOE	dyspnea on exertion	**RBBB**	right bundle branch block
DVT	deep vein thrombosis	**RCA**	right coronary artery
EST/ETT	exercise stress test or exercise tolerance test	**RV**	right ventricle
		SOA	shortness of air
HDL	high density lipoprotein	**SOB**	shortness of breath
HR	heart rate	**SBE**	subacute bacterial endocarditis
HTN/HPN	hypertension	**VAD**	ventricular access devices
LAD	left anterior descending	**VSD**	ventricular septal defect
BLBBB	left bundle branch block	**WPW**	Wolff-Parkinson-White Syndrome

CARDIAC AND VASCULAR ANATOMY AND PHYSIOLOGY

Function and Structure

The heart is a fist-sized organ that weighs approximately 250 to 350 grams. Pumping in excess of 6,800 liters of blood daily, each heartbeat results in an average expulsion of 145 ml. Its primary purpose is to supply blood to all organs and tissues as well as to furnish a pathway for nutrients, oxygen, hormones and immunologic substances. An organ that not only delivers, it also furnishes its own clean-up function by removing tissue waste and by-products through venous blood return. The venous blood, depleted of oxygen and full of waste products, is routed through the lungs for fresh oxygenation and the clearing away of waste products.

Muscle Layers

The heart is a muscle that is extremely rich in nerves and vessels and is made up of three major layers. The outermost layer of muscle is called the **epicardium**. The middle layer, or **myocardium**, performs the contractile function. The **endocardium** is the innermost layer. It lines the heart's inner chambers.

The Heart Sac

The outside of the heart has a thick and fibrous covering or sac called the **pericardium**. Also in multiple layers, the outer, fibrous pericardium is loose and elastic. The inner layer or serous pericardial layer is also made up of more than one layer of tissue. These are the parietal and the visceral layers. The parietal layer lines the fibrous pericardium while the visceral layers or epicardium adheres to the outside of the heart itself. The pericardial space is located between the visceral and parietal layers. It is filled with a clear fluid that lubricates the heart's surface and prevents friction or rubbing from the sac. Though normal fluid retention in this space is 10–30 ml, up to 300 ml of fluid may accumulate before the heart's contractile function is impaired. Figure 7–1 shows all the major cardiac landmarks as well as the multiple muscle layers discussed previously in this module.

Heart Chambers

Four major chambers are found in the heart. The upper two chambers, or the right and left **atrium**, and the lower chambers, called right and left **ventricles**, represent the four major chambers. Each is designed with a specific task and process. Figure 7–1 also displays the four distinct heart chambers. The right atrium receives systemic or deoxygenated blood from the extremities through the inferior and superior vena cavae (inferior drains the lower body, and the superior drains the upper regions). The right ventricle is divided into inflow and outflow tracts to account for the progress of the blood through this chamber. In the left atrium, oxygenated blood is returned fresh from the lungs. From here, the blood is expelled into the left ventricle. The left ventricle possesses the thickest and most muscular walls in order to propel fresh blood out into the blood's circulatory pathway throughout the body.

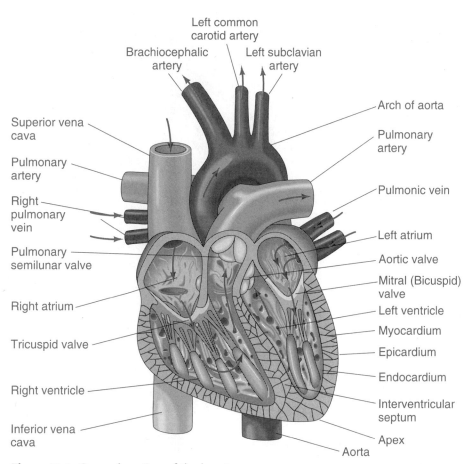

Figure 7–1 Coronal section of the heart.

Heart Valves

Two atrioventricular valves and two semilunar valves are found inside the heart's vessels and chambers. The atrioventricular (AV) valves are the **tricuspid**, or three-leafed valve, and the bicuspid (**mitral**) or two-leafed valve. The **semilunar valves** are the **pulmonic** valves. These valves are called semilunar due to their resemblance to the shape of the moon (see Figure 7–2).

The Cardiac Cycle

During a cardiac cycle, two phases occur. They are systole and diastole. In diastole, there are two phases. Phase one of diastole occurs when the atria contract and force the AV valves to open. About 70% of the blood is expelled from the atria into the relaxed ventricles. Phase two of diastole involves a slowing of blood flow until accelerated atrial contraction forces any remaining blood into the ventricles. In systole, ejection of the blood occurs. Phase one forces the AV valves to snap shut and ventricles begin the contractile phase of the ventricles. When pressure in the ventricles is greater than that in the aorta, the semilunar valves open and blood is expelled into the pulmonary artery and the aorta. As the contraction phase subsides, the muscles of the ventricles relax and intraventricular pressure decreases.

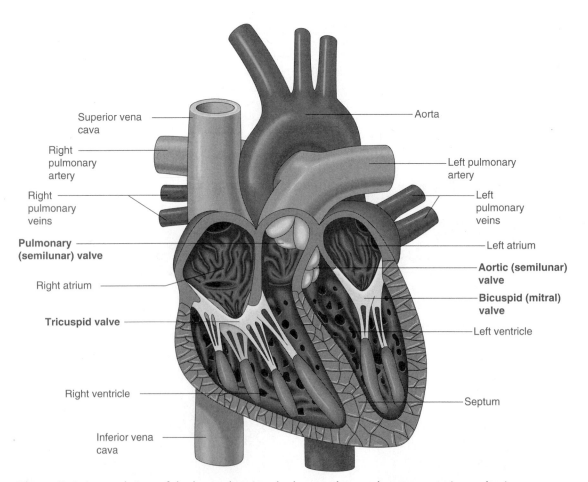

Figure 7–2 Internal view of the heart showing the heart valves, pulmonary arteries and veins.

Major Cardiac Vessels

The heart receives its blood supply from the coronary arteries. Major coronary vessels include the right coronary artery, and two major left coronaries: the left anterior descending (LAD) and the **circumflex**. **Occlusion** or obstruction of blood flow to any of these vessels due to thrombus or **plaque** deposits can result in a myocardial infarction, or heart attack. Blood circulates throughout the coronary vasculature all during the cardiac cycle but is decreased with systole and increased during diastole. Figure 7–3 shows the position and location of the major vessels previously discussed in this module. Major vessels branching off the aortic arch at the top of the heart are the left common carotid, the left subclavian, and the brachiocephalic.

Electrical Conduction Pathway

The heart is a rich electrical conduction relay mechanism. Specialized tissue is scattered strategically throughout the cardiac anatomy designed to relay impulses that provoke the contractile action of the pump. The sinoatrial (SA) node is known as the heart's natural pacemaker. From here, impulses travel over the conduction paths to the atrioventricular (AV) node. The impulse is then transmitted to the **Bundle of His** and terminate at the Purkinje fibers. Figure 7–4 illustrates the conduction pathway.

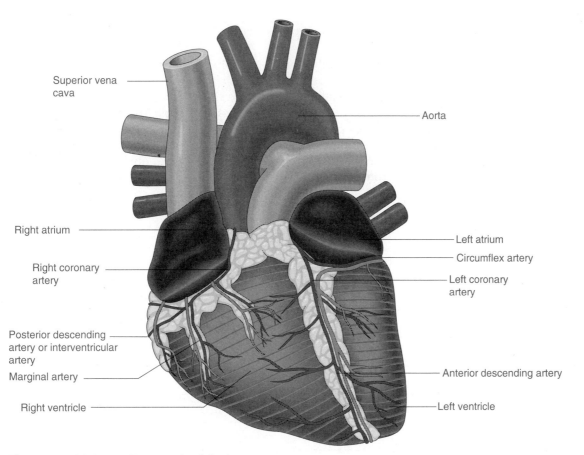

Figure 7–3 Major cardiac vessels of the heart.

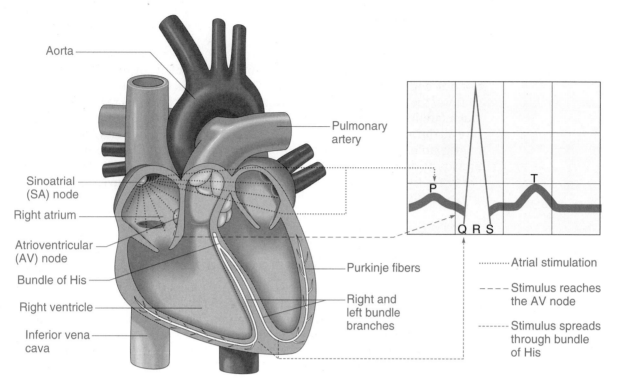

Figure 7–4 Electrical conduction system of the heart.

Subspecialties of Cardiology

Because the heart is not only a pump and pipe organ but an electrical unit, three (or in large practices, invasive and noninvasive cardiologists further divide the specialty into four) subspecialties exist within the general cardiovascular medicine specialty. Table 7–2 depicts the work division in a large, single-specialty clinic; it is easy to see how only certain physicians do specialized procedures or therapeutic interventions. Though smaller cardiology offices may not divide the work exactly as illustrated in this table, electrophysiology and nuclear work is still usually segregated from routine cardiology functions in most practices.

TABLE 7–2   Cardiology Services by Subspecialties.

Encounter/Services or Procedure	EP	Invasive	Noninvasive	Nuclear
Office Visits	X	X	X	X
Pacer/AICD Interrogations	X	X	X	
MUGAs				X
Treadmills		X	X	X
Exercise Echo			X	X

continues

Table 7–2 **Cardiology Services by Subspecialties** *continued*

Encounter/Services or Procedure	EP	Invasive	Noninvasive	Nuclear
Echocardiography/Doppler/Color-Flow			X	
Left Ventriculogram		X		
Heart Catheterization	X	X		
Atherectomy		X		
Intravascular Ultrasound		X		
Stent		X		
PTCA		X		
Peripheral Angioplasty		X		
Temporary Pacemakers	X	X	X	
Swan-Ganz Placement	X	X	X	
Holter Monitor/Event Recorder Analysis	X		X	
EP Studies	X			
Pacemaker/AICD Implantation	X	X		
Tilt-Table Evaluations	X			
Cardioversion	X	X	X	
Central Line Placement	X	X	X	
Arterial Physiologics			X	
Duplex Scans			X	
Outpatient Consultations	X	X	X	X
Inpatient Consultations	X	X	X	X
Pericardiocentesis	X	X	X	
Observation Services	X	X	X	
Discharge Day Management	X	X	X	
Skilled Nursing Encounters	X	X	X	
Hospital Consultations	X	X	X	
Emergency Services	X	X	X	
Critical Care Services	X	X	X	
Prolonged Services	X	X	X	
Other Cardiac Interventions	X	X	X	
Intra-aortic Balloon Insertion	X	X	X	

Electrophysiology (EP) is the study of the heart's conduction pathway as well as the evaluation, intervention, and treatment of aberrant and life-threatening rhythms.

Nuclear cardiology is designed for diagnostic and assessment purposes. Non-invasive diagnostics are performed through Doppler, spectral analysis, **echo** or echocardiography, duplex scanning and physiologic evaluation.

Invasive cardiology concentrates on percutaneous vascular exploration and intervention in cases of occlusion or obstruction. Deployment of **stents**, removal of clots, and insertion of intra-arterial balloons may be part of this interventional process. In each of these procedures, the cardiologist does not perform an open surgical procedure, but rather performs the intervention through the vessel itself. Stents are deployed or delivered by means of a catheter threaded through the appropriate vessels where they are used to assist in shoring up the intima or lining of the vessel to prevent collapse. Intra-arterial balloons press soft plaque against the vessel wall, thus opening the lumen or inside diameter of the vessel to permit a greater volume of blood flow. Clots or thrombi can be removed by means of a specialized catheter.

Noninvasive cardiology deals with the monitoring of blood pressure, measurement of cholesterol and other lipids, control of weight, cessation of smoking, institution of behavior modification with gradually increased exercise as well as education for coping with stress. Medication and life-style alteration is often key to the medical management of the cardiac patient.

■ *Highlight*

The most important thing for the new coder or biller to remember is that cardiologists do many surgery-like procedures, but these are not considered surgical as they are not done through an open surgical site. Therefore, with the exception of some of the electrophysiologic procedures, cardiology providers will find the majority of their billing codes in the CPT Medicine section, rather than in the Surgery section.

EXERCISE 7–1

1. Cardiologists are trained in Medicine or Surgery? _____

2. Name the subspecialty areas cardiologists may choose. _____

3. Name the two phases of the cardiac cycle. _____

4. Name the three layers of heart muscle. _____

5. Semilunar valves are so-named because they resemble the shape of the _____.

UNDERSTANDING E&M SERVICES IN THE CARDIOLOGY SETTING

Cardiology Office or Hospital Scenarios

Because cardiology is a subspecialty of internal medicine, most patients are referred to the office setting at the initial visit. This visit may originate with the patient's primary care physician, as a result of an insurance mandate, or as a second opinion sought by an outside entity (or the patient). See CPT Module 2 of this text for more information on consultations and other Evaluation and Management encounters for the cardiology provider. Office, ER, CCU as well as admitted and/or observation unit patients who are not critical are discussed in detail in this module.

STANDARD NONINVASIVE CARDIAC DIAGNOSTICS

In the cardiology practice, many diagnostic tools are used to evaluate and assess various vessels, valves, electrical pathways, and the heart muscle. Furthermore, some diagnostic procedures naturally terminate with a therapeutic intervention; this is explored later in this module.

CPT

CPT is the action coding system for the cardiology practice. Codes to describe and report the work performed in cardiology will be found primarily in the Medicine, Radiology and Surgery sections of CPT. Additionally, many laboratory panels are ordered by cardiologists. Therefore, billing staff should develop an awareness of commonly ordered metabolic and/or electrolyte panels required for diagnosis and treatment of cardiac patients.

Cardiography

Electrocardiograms (EKGs/ECGs) are a staple in the cardiology practice and are performed routinely to assess the heart's electrical activity patterns. Used for monitoring and evaluating many cardiovascular diseases, EKGs are especially helpful with congenital heart disease, congestive heart failure, arrhythmias, MIs and valvular problems. In addition to performing 12-lead EKGs in the office and hospital setting, telephonic transmission of rhythm strips (short, EKG strips that define and isolate specific arrhythmias or indicate a developing trend that requires further investigation) is sometimes ordered and performed for patients unable to travel to the physician office or hospital for a reading.

EKGs are an inherent component of another diagnostic tool commonly used in the cardiology office, which is known as a treadmill or stress test. Various components of this EST/ETT test (known as the exercise stress or exercise tolerance test) use maximal or submaximal exercise via a bicycle or treadmill to stimulate and "stress" the heart. Maximal exercise involves an all-out effort on the patient's part. The provider pushes the patient to the maximum degree of performance. Submaximal levels indicate that the physician is keeping the level of endeavor just under the patient's potential maximum output or performance zone.

Drugs and/or radionuclides may also be administered during this test to provide additional assessment tools for the cardiologist or provided to patients unable to exercise physically. The most commonly used radionuclide is thallium. However, Technetium can be used depending upon the cardiologist and which type of test is being performed. A continuous EKG is produced and closely monitored and evaluated during the period in which the heart is stressed.

Recently, cardiologists have increasingly ordered a stress echocardiogram in which the treadmill or bicycle is used to stress the heart. As with previously mentioned stress testing, drugs may be administered to produce additional diagnostic effects or used in the place of actual physician exercise in patients unable to perform strenuously. Dobutamine is often the pharmacologic agent used in this test scenario as it appropriately challenges the heart as if the patient was performing strenuous exercise. To properly code echocardiograms, multiple CPT codes are needed. Table 7–3 describes the combination options. To properly code a stress echocardiogram, each component of the test must be itemized as well as codes included for any pharmacologic agent used. Additionally, the biller needs to dif-

TABLE 7–3   **Echocardiography Diagnostics.**

Type of Echocardiogram	Description
Echocardiogram for congenital anomalies	Echocardiogram, complete, for congenital anomalies
	Echocardiogram, limited, for congenital anomalies
Echocardiogram for normal structures	Echocardiogram, complete, real-time with image documentation (2D) with or without M-Mode recording
	Echocardiogram, limited, real-time with image documentation (2D) with or without M-Mode recording
TEE for normal cardiac structures	Echocardiography, transesophageal, complete, real-time with image documentation (2D) (with or without M-Mode recording); including probe placement, image acquisition, interpretation and report
	Placement of transesophageal probe only
	Image acquisition, interpretation and report only
TEE for congenital anomalies	Echocardiography, transesophageal, for congenital cardiac anomalies; including probe placement, image acquisition, interpretation and report
	Placement of transesophageal probe only
	Image acquisition, interpretation and report only
Doppler echo	Doppler echocardiography, pulsed and/or continuous wave with spectral display, complete
	Doppler echocardiography, pulsed and/or continuous wave with spectral display, limited
Color-flow mapping	Doppler color-flow velocity mapping
Stress echocardiography	Echocardiography, real-time with image documentation (2D) with or without M-Mode recording, during rest and cardiovascular stress test using treadmill, bicycle exercise and/or pharmacologically induced stress, with interpretation and report

ferentiate between normal cardiac structures and **congenital anomalies** when choosing both the CPT and ICD-9-CM codes.

When physicians need a quick diagnostic tool, they may elect to order a rhythm strip, which involves a short strip of tracings fed from one to three electrodes attached to the patient as previously discussed.

Holter monitors are often used to monitor a patient's cardiac and rhythm status for at least 24 hours. Event or patient demand single and multiple event recorders are worn for 30 days to trend activities, abnormalities and fluctuations. In addition to capturing abnormalities automatically, patient's can trip or depress a button on the monitor to immediately record the heart's activity when they experience unusual or painful symptoms. Multiple event monitors can record multiple abnormalities or episodes, which the physician can then evaluate when the monitor is turned in for assessment.

Signal-averaged EKGs are performed over 9 10–20 minute periods. Events, abnormalities, and so on are then calculated and averaged in a computerized format to trend electrical activity fluctuations. As with a 12-lead EKG, multiple electrodes are placed on the patient's chest and extremities.

Echocardiography

By using echocardiography, physicians can assess the heart's structure, blood flow and direction and valvular function. By bouncing ultrasonic signals off various cardiac structures, this noninvasive diagnostic procedure provides a two-dimensional image of the heart. Just as there are multiple approaches to cardiography, echocardiography has multiple mechanisms for diagnostic purposes.

A complete transthoracic (across the chest) 2D/M Mode echo study can be performed. This is a two-dimensional study which can be performed either as an initial or follow-up study.

With a transesophageal echo (TEE) , the equipment permits the physician to pass a probe into the patient's esophagus just as a gastroenterologist would pass an endoscope into the esophagus. The tip of the transducer (a transmitting or camera-like device) is manipulated for viewing the patient's heart valves, chambers and larger vessels. As with other codes, echocardiography codes exist for normal anatomy as well as for patients with congenital anomalies. As previously noted, both the CPT and ICD-9-CM codes must indicate the presence of congenital anomalies to use codes from this range.

Doppler echocardiography by pulsed wave or continuous wave with spectral display can also be reported as an initial or follow-up study.

Doppler color-flow mapping is used to determine valvular diameters, flow volumes and pressure gradients within the heart. It is critical to the cardiologist to know how large the valve opening is, whether any vegetation (bacterial or plaque-like deposits) exists, whether or not the valves seal and open properly, and how great the intracardiac pressure is when exerted against or in conjunction with the opening or closing of the valves. Each phase of the blood's progress through the heart and its structures can be monitored through this diagnostic tool.

Table 7–3 presents the many components and types of echocardiography employed by the cardiology practice to determine and measure heart and valve function.

Vascular Studies

Additional vascular studies can be reported in the CPT Medicine section. Although pacemakers and AICDs are discussed in the electrophysiology procedure portion of this module, those codes are also found within this range in the Medicine section of CPT. Noninvasive vascular diagnostics include Doppler evaluation, duplex scanning (two-window scanning of a cardiac structure), spectral analysis (variegated color patterns indicating the degree or force of the blood flow through the cardiac structures) and/or color-flow velocity mapping or imaging similar to that found in the echocardiography section. Venous and arterial studies are reported from this area of CPT with coding emphasis on the type and anatomical location of the vessel scanned as well as the method of scanning. Additional attention is required to ensure separate consideration of unilateral and bilateral studies in this subsection.

EXERCISE 7–2

1. TEE is the acronym for a _____ _____.

2. What is the most common pharmacologic agent used in a "stress" echo? _____

3. Holter monitors are worn for at least _____ hours.

4. When coding for congenital cardiac anomalies, billers should take care that the _____ code matches and links to the appropriate CPT code category.

5. CPT is the _____ coding system for the cardiology practice.

6. Read the following medical report for an echocardiography study, then assign the correct ICD-9-CM and CPT codes.

Patient: Adrian Babb
DOB: 06/11/33
Hospital #:   32116897
Physician: Jason Finkle, DO
Date: July 15, 1999

CLINICAL INDICATION: This is a 66-year-old female recently presenting to Memorial Hospital with congestive heart failure and new onset atrial fibrillation. She is here for assessment of mitral regurgitation after treatment with Sotalol and reversion to sinus rhythm. However, the patient is now back in atrial fibrillation with moderate to fast response and is still taking Sotalol and Coumadin.

STUDIES PERFORMED: Evaluation includes 2-D echocardiography, color-flow imaging, and Doppler exam, and is technically adequate.

IMPRESSION:

1. Technically adequate study.

2. Overall left ventricular size is mildly dilated with normal wall thickness with diastolic function to assess because of atrial fibrillation. Overall systolic function appears to be at the lower limit of normal with an ejec-

continues

---

tion fraction of 50% though evaluation is somewhat difficult because of the fast irregular rhythm. Segmental evaluation reveals no gross abnormality though the septum is difficult to assess in terms of its function and the posterior wall is not seen. However, other walls appear to contract normally.

3. Right ventricular size is normal with normal wall thickness and normal overall right ventricular function.

4. There is mild right atrial enlargement and moderate left atrial enlargement.

5. Valvular structures: The aortic valve is a normal structure without stenosis or regurgitation. The mitral valve is a normal structure without stenosis or prolapse and there is a 1+, mild mitral regurgitation. The tricuspid valve is a normal structure with stenosis with trace to 1+, trace to mild tricuspid regurgitation.

6. There is no pericardial effusion. No gross intracardiac mass or thrombus is appreciated; however, left atrial appendage is never completely visualized.

7. Inferior vena cava collapsibility is normal, indicating normal right atrial pressure. Pulmonary artery pressure is normal.

CONCLUSION: Echocardiography reveals the patient to be back in atrial fibrillation with overall fairly well-preserved right and left ventricular systolic function though left ventricular function is somewhat difficult to assess and mild decrease in ejection fraction cannot be excluded. Diastolic function could not be assessed. There is only mild mitral regurgitation at this time. Right-sided pressures are normal.

Jason Finkle, DO

ICD-9-CM code(s) _____

CPT code(s) _____

COMMON INVASIVE AND/OR INTERVENTIONAL PROCEDURES

Cardiovascular Therapeutic Services

Invasive cardiologists perform a number of procedures located in the Medicine section of CPT. Any cardiologist is trained to perform CPR in case of cardiac arrest. When performed outside the critical care setting, this procedure may be reported independently for this intervention. Additionally, in many instances, patients may require regulation of the heart's rhythm for a brief period of time. A temporary **pacemaker** for transcutaneous pacing may be reported in such cases.

Cardioversion is performed to shock the heart rhythm into a normal pattern. Elective cardioversion, commonly an electrophysiologist's therapeutic tool, is reported when such cases occur.

Thrombolysis is the process of blood clot destruction. This can be carried out directly in the coronary vessels by means of selective coronary angiography or through intravenous infusion. Many different drug therapies can be used as clot busters. Sometimes known as TPA (tissue plasminogen activator) therapy this procedure is being tested in ambulances and infused by paramedics in some cities allowing patients an increased opportunity to survive fatal thromboses in certain circumstances.

Recently, intravascular ultrasound has been used during therapeutic interventions. The reporting of the initial and subsequent vessels viewed is permitted by individual CPT codes. The services included with these codes are transducer manipulation and repositioning as well as the before and after look common to therapeutic procedures. In using the camera-like transducer, the physician or technician moves the device to zero in on the affected structures. The transducer is used to assist in locating the trouble spot. The physician/technician looks both before and after the intervention to ensure that improvement has been achieved.

Stents are deployed to reinforce vessel walls and prevent the re-formation of plaque deposits or snared blood clots that collect and obstruct blood flow on jagged vessel walls. Single vessel intracoronary stent placement is reported separately from placement in additional vessels, which is reported individually for each vessel involved.

PTCAs (percutaneous transluminal coronary angioplasties) are also reported as (1) the initial vessel intervention and (2) subsequent vessel procedures. If multiple lesions are treated within the same vessel, billers should look to the Modifier section of CPT for guidance as to the reporting of this unusual but not uncommon occurrence. Figure 7–5 provides a better look at how a PTCA is performed through the patient's vessel.

Some invasive cardiologists repair valvular structures non-surgically. Codes exist within the Medicine section for the reporting of such procedures.

An atherectomy is the removal of an atheromatous deposit blocking blood flow within a major vessel. Such a procedure commonly occurs in a coronary vessel, although fatty or plaque deposits may also occur in other vessels throughout the body, thus impeding blood flow and prohibiting adequate circulation to a specific body area or organ. Codes exist for the treatment of single vessel lesions as well as for each additional vessel intervention. A directional atherectomy such as an AtheroCath (shown in Figure 7–6) is used when the cardiologist directs the instrument to the plaque deposit and shears the plaque or cholesterol plug away from the vessel wall. In a **rotablator** (commonly referred to a "roto-rooter"), the instrument has a rotating burr that reams out the vessel by rotating and cutting through the plaque or cholesterol deposits. In an extraction atherectomy, the cardiologist guides an extraction instrument (such as a transluminal extraction catheter [TEC]) toward the cholesterol or plaque deposit and attempts to remove the entire plug as a unit. In some cases, however, the fatty plug breaks up, and the cardiologist removes all the pieces thereby extracting the barrier to blood flow.

■ *Confusing Codes*

Do note that these codes state "with or without balloon angioplasty" in the description. Therefore, separate listing of this procedure would be considered "unbundling" and not acceptable.

Payor policies vary for payment of multiple interventional procedures. Even though atherectomies, PTCAs and stents usually include a diagnostic **heart catheterization**, most carriers refuse to pay full price for both. HFCA (Medicare) allows 100% of the allowed charge for the interventional procedure and 50% of the allowed charge for the diagnostic heart catheterization. If deemed integral to the interventional procedure, the catheterization is considered inherent, and therefore, not payable separately.

For percutaneous pulmonary artery angioplasty, CPT has added two codes for such unique circumstances: 92997 for a single vessel and 92998 for each additional vessel.

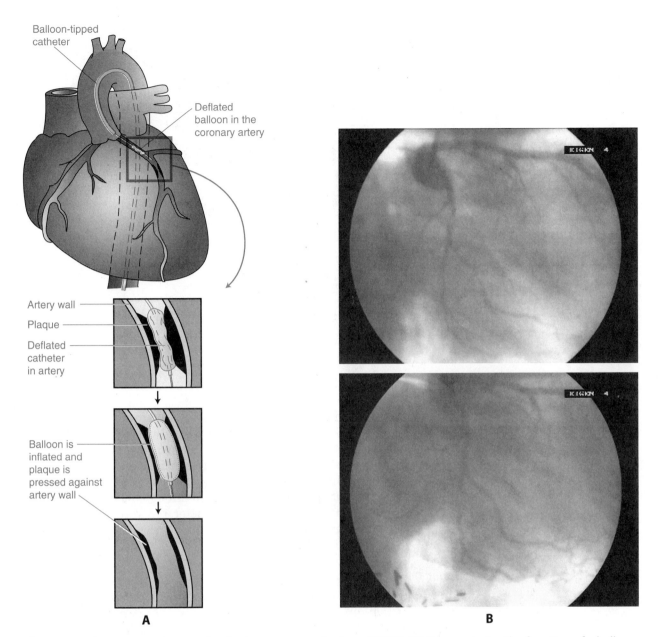

Figure 7–5 A percutaneous transluminal coronary angioplasty (PTCA). (A) Demonstrates the function of a balloon-tipped catheter during PTCA. (B) An x-ray showing a blocked artery and revascularization of the vessel after the angioplasty *(Photo courtesy of Ken Hicks, Fort Wayne, IN)*.

Cardiac Catheterization

When invasive cardiologists evaluate patients, often a heart catheterization or angiogram is performed. This medical diagnostic tool involves introduction and manipulation of a specialized catheter, recording of intravascular and intracardiac pressure gradients (various internal pressures near and away from the valves, the septal wall and the center of the heart's chambers), obtaining of blood samples for measurement of blood gases and cardiac output and/or vascular injection if appropriate. Heart catheterizations are often the precursor to more in-depth therapeutic or interventional procedures such as PTCA, stent, atherectomy, etc.

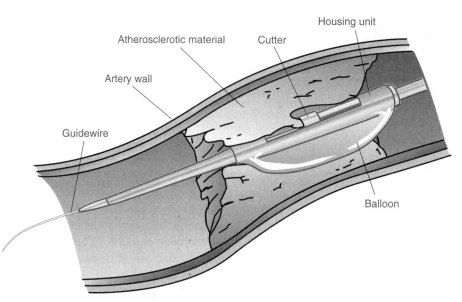

Figure 7–6 The Simpson Coronary AtheroCath cuts the atherosclerotic plaque away from the artery wall.

A simple right heart catheterization reports a procedure done on normal cardiac structures. This code would be required for patients with congenital cardiac defects. Most right heart catheters are inserted percutaneously into a large vessel such as the femoral, internal jugular, brachial or subclavian veins. The catheter is threaded over a guide wire and directed into the right atrium, ventricle, pulmonary artery and pulmonary capillary wedge. Access to and through the vessel, sedation, monitoring, insertion and manipulation of the catheter, pressure measurements, cardiac output, oxygen saturation and catheter removal are all included in this code and not separately reportable.

■ Confusing Codes

Swan-Ganz catheters are often inserted for patients in order to carefully monitor their hemodynamic (blood-flow) status. Table 7–4 presents a detailed explanation of when to use a Swan-Ganz catheter code and when a right heart catheterization code is the proper choice. A code is provided in CPT to report an endomyocardial biopsy. This code is used when myxomas (cardiac tumors) are discovered and removed for biopsy.

In some cases, placement of a coronary artery catheter without a subsequent left heart catheterization for coronary angiography might be required. A CPT code does exist for this situation.

When cardiologists access the left side of the heart from the back, the correct code will indicate an antegrade or rear access. Percutaneous access routes include the brachial, femoral or axillary artery with this code selection. In cases of peripheral vascular collapse, a code for a venous cutdown would be required for accurate reporting.

■ Highlights

■ *In very rare instances, the invasive cardiologist might access the left heart via a left ventricular puncture. A very specific code exists in the CPT medicine section for reporting this rare occasion.*

TABLE 7–4   Right Heart Catheterization vs. Swan-Ganz Catheter Placement.

Right heart catheterization
Placement of a Swan-Ganz catheter

According to the *American College Of Cardiology's Practical Reporting of Cardiovascular Services and Procedures,* RHC is distinguished from Swan-Ganz placement by the following grid:

Context	Swan-Ganz	RHC
Typically performed in the cath lab and/or in conjunction with other cardiac catheterization procedures		X
The catheter is removed after the procedure		X
The catheter may be *left in place for further monitoring/ measurement purposes*	X	
Typically placed in ICU	X	
Typically used for diagnostics		X
Can be placed preoperatively to monitor hemodynamic status	X	

- *When a combination approach across the heart's septum and to the back for visualization of the left heart is performed, a code is provided in CPT to report this unique approach.*

- *Combination right and left heart cath procedures are commonly performed on normal cardiac structures. Combination right and left heart cath procedures for congenitally defective hearts are also found in the Medicine section.*

- *Intra-aortic balloon catheter can also be introduced via the percutaneous method by cardiologists. Specific codes are available to report this method of IAB introduction.*

- *A variety of injection procedures are performed by the cardiologist. Depending upon what structures the physician plans to visualize, code selection is specific to cardiac regions and vessels. Additionally, supervision and interpretation for the injection procedures are separately reported.*

- *Indicator dilution studies done with dye or thermal dilution are not reported with catheterization procedures. Unless performed separately, these are included in the actual catheterization and should not be itemized.*

- *For correctly coding a left and right heart catheterization with ventriculogram and selective coronary angiography, the coder would choose the following combination:*

  Left & right heart catheterization

  Ventriculogram

  Selective coronary arteries

  Ventriculogram reading and interpretation

  Selective coronaries, reading and interpretation

EXERCISE 7–3

Read the following medical reports and assign the correct ICD-9-CM and CPT codes.

1.

Patient:	Rudy, Carlton
DOB:	11/28/46
Hospital #:	5790873
Physician:	Walter Hill, MD
Date:	March 16, 199–

CLINICAL INDICATIONS: The patient was found to have a severe blockage of the LAD involving a large diagonal.

METHOD: After 10,000 units of heparin were given, a 10 French system was placed. A 1 French #4 Judkins left guide was advanced to the left coronary artery. A 0.014 extra support exchange wire was advanced down the diagonal. Then, a 6 French atherocath was advanced over the wire to the diagonal. There were four cuts made in this area. We then pulled the cutter back and noted insufficient relief of the blockage; therefore, the atherocath was readvanced and three more cuts were made. Then the same wire was advanced down the LAD. A 7 French atherocath was advanced to the LAD lesion, and a series of cuts were made. At this point, the patient was having pain and it seemed to be getting worse. A 0.014 Traverse wire was advanced down the diagonal with the support wire remaining in the LAD. A 2-mm Rally balloon was advanced to the diagonal lesion, and this was inflated up to 6 atmospheres. The pain felt much better after this balloon was deflated. Then a 3.5-mm Rally balloon was advanced down into the LAD lesion. We inflated in both areas separately and then simultaneously. At this point, angiography showed successful resolution of both lesions. The procedure was then completed. The patient was returned to his room in good condition. Surgery was on standby.

SUMMARY: Successful atherectomy and angioplasty of the left anterior descending and diagonal.

Walter Hill, MD

ICD-9-CM code(s) _____

CPT code(s) _____

2.

Patient: Shelton, Kevin

DOB:	09/23/55
Hospital #:	5438558709
Physician:	Phyllis Kitts, MD
Date:	August 24, 199–

CLINICAL INDICATIONS: Angina, congestive heart failure, non-sustained ventricular tachycardia, atrial fibrillation and multiple familial cardiac risk factors.

continues

HEMODYNAMICS: The right ventricular end diastolic pressure is elevated. The pulmonary capillary wedge pressure, pulmonary artery pressure, and left ventricular end diastolic pressure are severely elevated. Severe systemic hypertension is present. There are no valvular gradients detected. The resting cardiac index is preserved.

LEFT VENTRICULOGRAPHY: Left ventriculography was performed with the patient in the right anterior oblique projection. The left ventricle is normal in size and demonstrates severe inferobasal hypokinesis. The remainder of the left ventricle contracts normally. The overall extent of contraction is mildly to moderately reduced. There is trace mitral insufficiency without prolapse.

CORONARY ARTERIOGRAPHY: Selective coronary arteriography was performed with the patient in various right and left anterior and sagittal oblique projections.

The left main coronary artery is mildly irregular but free of significant disease. The left main provides a ramus intermedius branch. The ramus intermedius bifurcates shortly after its origin. The more lateral branch is narrowed 90% at the junction between the proximal and middle thirds of the vessel.

The left anterior descending coronary artery is large in caliber and extends over the apex. The anterior descending is moderately irregular throughout its course. The anterior descending is narrowed 80% in its mid portion.

The left circumflex is non-dominant. The left circumflex is narrowed 80% proximally. There are two small distal obtuse marginals that are mildly irregular.

The right coronary artery is dominant. The right coronary artery is totally occluded at the junction between the proximal and middle thirds of the vessel. The distal vessel fills extensively via left to right collateral circulation.

The native left internal mammary artery was non-selectively visualized and appears to be suitable for use as a graft.

Aortography of the distal abdominal aorta reveals severe, diffuse extasia of the distal aorta below the renal arteries. The right common iliac is occluded at its origin. The left iliac and femoral arteries are heavily calcified and with diffuse moderate disease. There are two renal arteries supplying the left kidney. The inferior artery is narrowed 80–90% proximally. The right renal artery is narrowed at least 80%.

CONCLUSIONS:

1. CAD, severe, triple vessel

2. Left ventricular dysfunction

3. Severe elevation of the left heart-filling pressure

4. Severe pulmonary hypertension

5. Elevated right heart-filling pressure

6. Mitral insufficiency, trace

continues

ICD-9-CM code(s)_____

CPT code(s)_____

7. Bilateral renal artery stenosis

8. Peripheral vascular disease with total occlusion of the right common iliac artery at its origin

COMMENTS: This patient is with symptomatic triple vessel coronary artery disease with left ventricular dysfunction. He would benefit by CABG surgery although such surgery would be at increased risk for complications. The patient has significant bilateral renal artery stenosis and should undergo evaluation by Wilson Nesmith, DO, for possible renal arterial intervention by way of stent or balloon placement.

Phyllis Kitts, MD

Other Vascular Injection Procedures

When invasive cardiologists examine peripheral vessels, the coder must access the cardiovascular subsection of the Surgery section in CPT. In doing so, codes may be selected for upper and lower arterial and venous placement. Depending upon where the catheter is introduced, the catheter may be selectively manipulated to the physician's preference. Vessels in selective placement are visualized as branches of a tree. The aorta would be the initial trunk or first order placement, followed by subsequent limbs (second order) and branches (third order), etc. Careful reading of the CPT instructional notes will assist greatly with code selection. Companion codes from the Radiology section are required for accurate and specific reporting and billing of these procedures.

Specific codes report insertion, revision and removal of implanted intra-arterial infusion pumps. Another common cardiology procedure is percutaneous central venous catheter placement in adult patients. This placement is reported for subclavian, jugular, vessels, etc. Codes are distinct for reporting in adults when venous cutdown is required to place the central line. If repositioning of a previously placed line is required, usually fluoroscopic guidance is required for proper placement, and therefore, should be reported.

Other therapeutic services performed by cardiologists may include a **pericardiocentesis**, which can be initial or subsequent in nature. In this procedure, the cardiologist withdraws fluid from the pericardium or heart sac to allow proper constriction or pumping of the heart. Occasionally a tube pericardiostomy or the creation of a pericardial window will be needed in order to drain excess pericardial fluid or infection.

EXERCISE 7–4

1. Define thrombolysis. _____

2. Pericardiocentesis withdraws fluid from what cardiac structure? _____

3. Cardiac tumors are known as _____.

4. Name the three types of atherectomy. _____

5. PTCA is an acronym for _____ _____

   _____ _____.

6. Read the following medical report for angioplasty and stent implantation, then assign the correct ICD-9-CM and CPT codes.

ICD-9-CM code(s) _____

CPT code(s) _____

Patient: Yandell, Vernon
DOB: 2/14/39
Hospital #:   9674538
Physician: Barton Sellers, MD
Date: June 19, 199–

CLINICAL INDICATIONS: Status post PTCA of the right coronary artery now with recurrent angina. Patient underwent cardiac cath earlier today that revealed a tight proximal mid-RCA at the site of previous angioplasty.

METHOD: Patient was brought to the cardiac cath laboratory and was prepped and draped in the usual sterile fashion. The patient had been premedicated with dextran for possible stent placement. The previously placed 5 French sheath was exchanged for an 8 French sheath over a guide wire. An 8 French right 4 hockey stick was then advanced over the guide wire and positioned in the right coronary ostium. A #1 guide wire was then advanced down to the right coronary artery across the proximal mid-RCA stenosis. A 1.5 mm Rally balloon was then advanced over the guide wire and positioned across the mid-RCA. Balloon angioplasty was performed to a peak atmospheric pressure of 6 atmospheres at one minute. The balloon was withdrawn and repeat angioplasty was performed. This time the balloon was readvanced and positioned in the proximal mid-RCA and angioplasty was performed to a peak atmospheric pressure of 12 atmospheres for 2 minutes. The balloon was withdrawn and a repeat angiogram was performed. The balloon was then exchanged for a 3 mm. Cook stent balloon. This was advanced into the vasculature and positioned in the proximal mid-RCA. Balloon was inflated over 2 minutes to a peak atmospheric pressure of 6 atmospheres. The balloon was withdrawn and repeat angiogram was performed.

RESULTS: The proximal mid-RCA was successfully angioplastied from a 70% stenosis to a 0% residual with intracoronary stent placement.

RECOMMEND: Persantine, aspirin, Coumadin, and heparin.

Barton Sellers, MD

NUCLEAR CARDIOLOGY PROCEDURES

The nuclear cardiologist often splits his/her domain between an office in the hospital nuclear lab and the office setting. Some physicians only remain in the hospital, and do not see routine patients outside the nuclear facility. Whatever the scenario, multiple tests can be performed by this highly specialized physician. Stress testing, aside from that conducted during echocardiography, can be carried out with a fair number of tacked-on diagnostic assessment tools.

Myocardial perfusion imaging evaluates the viability of the heart, how well the blood is circulating through major vessels, and what risk may exist for future or subsequent cardiac problems. Thallium chloride is injected for radioactive uptake in the bloodstream. When the radionuclide tags the red blood cells or serum albumin, the cardiologist can visualize through planar or spectral analysis the pertinent cardiac structures. Two doses are administered. One dose is administered at rest and one during stress.

Additionally, dipyridamole (Persantine) or adenosine (Adenocard) may be infused intravenously as pharmacologics, which produce a stress effect on the heart in place of physical exercise. Stress test codes must be added when coding for myocardial perfusion imaging, as the descriptors do not include that information. If Dobutamine is selected as the stressor, it may be selected rather than dipyridamole or adenosine.

Myocardial infarct (MI) avid imaging may be performed in conjunction with other diagnostics to diagnose MIs.

Cardiac blood pool imaging is used to assess right and left ventricular function. These procedures are commonly referred to as MUGAs (multiple-gated acquisition studies) by cardiologists. In these tests, blood flow is assessed during specific phases of contraction and relaxation of the heart muscle.

Gated exercise study includes wall motion study and measurement of the blood's ejection fraction or the assessment of the force that expels the blood from the ventricle. A gated dipyridamole thallium study would require reporting multiple codes as well as the code for thallium and dipyridamole.

▦ Highlight

Resting radionuclide angiography can also be reported along with the code for the infusion of technetium. Coders and billers should remember that drug codes will only be reported if the physician office is providing and paying for the drugs used on the patients. If the nuclear physician is hospital-based, the hospital will charge for and recoup the cost of the drug from the insurer.

When the ejection fraction of the heart (the rate of blood expulsion) is the only consideration, the nuclear cardiologist may elect to use a single code for reporting, which permits reporting of cardiac blood pool imaging with gated equilibrium and wall motion study plus ejection fraction.

PET (positron emission tomography) scanning is a popular diagnostic tool with nuclear cardiologists. With the new technology, cardiologists can report the viability of the heart from a metabolic standpoint. CPT has added codes for reporting single or multiple PET scans either at rest or stress. Medicare has approved payment for its beneficiaries who have demonstrated coronary artery disease (CAD).

Before leaving the topic of noninvasive diagnostics, coders should become familiar with Radiology subsections entitled Heart, Aorta and Arteries. Under the subsection Heart, the cardiac magnetic resonance imaging (MRI) codes are found. A code can be used for reporting cardiac morphology (internal defects or anomalies) found on MRI without the infusion of contrast dye. By the same token, a code exists for the same diagnostic test with the infusion of dye. When the cardiologist is assessing ventricular function along with any morphology, specific codes can be found for this scenario either with or without dye infusion. A code also exists for the physician to report when using MRI technology for velocity flow mapping. If this test is done as well as morphologic and/or function studies, two codes will be required to explain the circumstances and method used.

The subsection Aorta and Arteries in the Radiology section includes aortography and angiography codes for reporting peripheral angiography and/or aortography. Careful attention must be directed toward the instructional notes in this portion of CPT. Additional codes are needed to accurately and specifically report these procedures. As previously seen with invasive procedures, selective placement requires attention to the detail of the catheterization report to locate the correct codes for these complex procedures. Module 9 of this text provides additional information on the radiology section of CPT.

ELECTROPHYSIOLOGIC THERAPEUTICS AND DIAGNOSTICS

Electrophysiology is defined as the evaluation and study of the heart's electrical conduction system. It encompasses the study of arrhythmias as well. Electrophysiologists are commonly called the electrical engineers of cardiology because their subspecialty is centered around electrical impulses and the resulting heart rhythms.

In the cardiology context, electrophysiology is coded from the two distinct CPT sections Medicine and Surgery. For the most part, the diagnostic studies and assessment services will be located in the Medicine section, while the implantation, repositioning, extraction, procedures will be found in the Surgery section.

Intracardiac Electrophysiology Procedures

From the Medicine section of CPT, electrophysiology (EP) is organized according to the procedure, the device, and the body site. Codes can be found for recording and pacing from various sites within the heart.

Atrial electrogram pacing and/or recording with or without a ventricular electrogram from an esophageal site can be coded from the Medicine section. Additionally, various components of a comprehensive EP evaluation can be reported with selected Medicine codes.

Codes are available to describe therapeutic interventions, EP follow-up studies, cardioverter-defibrillator (AICD) assessment and intracardiac ablation of arrhythmias. Instructional notes found beneath the codes in parentheses provide valuable direction as to what additional coding is required for accuracy in reporting.

Tilt-table testing or evaluation (with or without drug therapy challenge) may be reported and is often used as a diagnostic tool by electrophysiologists. In this test, the patient is evaluated in different positions to assess whether hypotension, syncope or rhythm disturbances occur when the patient is in different positions.

Monitoring and analysis of pacemaker and/or AICD (automatic implantable cardioverter-defibrillator) function can be reported with specific CPT codes. See Figure 7–7 for a better look at the parts and the placement of the AICD in the patient's body.

▬ *Confusing Codes*

Careful reading of the full description of each code will provide the data needed for code selection. Care should be taken to select accurate codes because the language is specific for reprogramming vs. no programming of single chamber devices and dual chamber devices and for AICDs vs. pacemakers. Telephonic analysis-only codes also can be found for reporting assessments done by telephone.

▬ *Confusing Codes*

Moving into the Surgery series, coders should read descriptors very carefully. It is extremely important, when coding for EP procedures, that coders/billers understand the terms and the way they are interchanged by physicians. For example, a pacemaker device and a defibrillator have multiple parts: a pulse

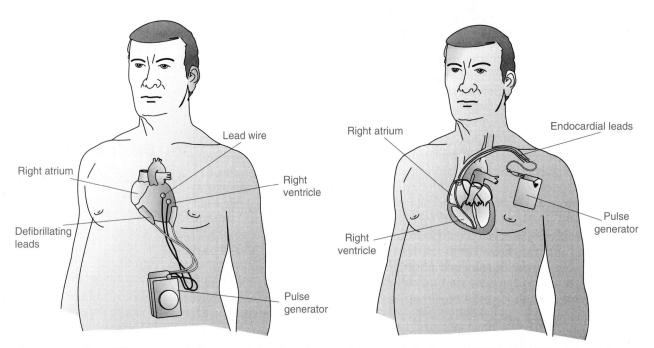

Figure 7–7 Two different types of automatic implantable cardioverter-defibrillators (AICD). (A) AICD with a pulse generator implanted in the subcutaneous tissue of the abdomen with lead wires and a defibrillating lead going to the heart. (B) AICD with pulse generator implanted below the collarbone with endocardial leads positioned in the heart through a vein.

generator which includes a battery and electronics and one or more electrodes or leads. A skin pocket is created either under the collarbone or inside the abdominal cavity for the device prior to implantation. The electrodes or leads may be threaded through a vein (transvenous insertion) or placed directly on the surface of the heart (epicardial placement).

■ When the cardiologist changes the battery in one of these devices, they actually change out the pulse generator. Battery or pulse generator replacement requires the selection of a code for the removal of the generator and an additional code for insertion of a new pulse generator.

■ In a single-chamber pacer, one electrode is inserted in either the ventricle or the atrium and connected to a pulse generator. Dual chamber devices include a pulse generator and an electrode in the ventricle and one in the atrium.

■ Code selection is tricky, unless the coder approaches the options presented in CPT systematically and without preconceived assumptions. A checklist is provided to assist in ensuring that the components found in the code description accurately convey the physician's actions or interventions.

■ Many items must be considered prior to code selection:
  ■ Is it a pacemaker or a defibrillator?
  ■ Is it a single or dual chamber unit?
  ■ Is it a primary insertion (implantation) or a replacement?
  ■ Is it a temporary or permanent device?
  ■ Is it a removal or a revision?
  ■ Where is the electrode placed?
  ■ Is the procedure for the device or the skin pocket?

■ Since these implantation/removal/revision/system upgrade codes are located in the Surgical section of CPT, many have a 90-day surgical follow-up period. This means that for 90 days after the procedure, any visits relative to the implantation (excluding treatment of complications) or testing of the device, will not be covered. This is considered the global postoperative period. Insurers surmise that the cost of the initial procedure also covers up to three months of follow-up care.

When postoperative complications occur, whether they be mechanical, medical or surgical, diagnosis is key to matching procedures and justifying medical necessity for unplanned treatment or interventions. Utilization of correct codes is essential for truthful reporting and accurate reimbursement consideration.

EXERCISE 7–5

1. The acronym AICD describes what device? _____.

2. "EP" signifies which subspecialty of cardiology? _____

3. What two main categories do pacemakers fall into? _____

4. A pacemaker "battery" is also known as a _____.

5. Electrophysiologists are known as the electrical _____ of cardiology.

Read the following medical reports, then assign the correct ICD-9-CM and CPT codes.

6.

Patient: Murphy, Bonnie
DOB: 02/17/50
Hospital #: 2789670
Physician: James Reesor, MD
Date: May 21, 199–

CLINICAL INDICATIONS: History of ventricular fibrillation requiring DC cardioversion. This episode occurred while patient was having an episode of ischemia with STT wave changes. However, the patient did not rule in for a myocardial infarction.

METHOD: The patient was brought to the EP laboratory. He was prepped and draped in the usual sterile fashion. After local anesthesia was obtained, the right femoral vein was entered percutaneously at two separate sites. Two 6 French sheaths were advanced over guide wires and positioned into the right femoral vein. A 6 French quad Foley catheter was then advanced into the vasculature and positioned at the high right atrium. In addition, 6 French quadripolar Foley catheter with a deflec-

---

continues

table tip was advanced into the vasculature and positioned in the most proximal His-Purkinje area. Programmed electrical stimulation was performed in the high right atrium. The atrial catheter was then repositioned in the right ventricular apex, and again programmed electrical stimulation was performed. Finally, the ventricular catheter was positioned in the right ventricular outflow track, and again programmed electrical stimulation was performed. Following completion of the procedure, the sheaths were removed and hemostatis obtained with hand pressure.

ICD-9-CM code(s) _____

CPT code(s) _____

PROTOCOLS:

1. Baseline intervals were measured.

2. Programmed atrial extra stimulation was performed using a drive train of 600 msec with the introduction of two extra stimuli in order to determine the refractories.

3. Rapid atrial pacing was performed in order to assess the point of AV node of Wenckebach.

4. Sinus node recovery times were measured using drive trains of 600, 500, and drive trains of 600, 500 and 400 msec.

5. Ventricular extra stimulation was performed using sensed and paced ventricular extra stimulation according to a Wellens Protocol. This stimulation protocol was again repeated at the right ventricular outflow track.

RESULTS:

1. Baseline intervals—the AH interval is 75 msec. The HV interval was 47 msec. The RS duration was 106 msec.

2. Sinus node: The patient has normal sinus node function. The longest corrected sinus node recovery time was 303 msec. This occurred using paced trial drive train of 500 msec.

3. AV node: The patient maintained 1:1 AV conduction to a cycle length of 350 msec. The patient developed AV node on Wenckebach at 340 msec. The AV node FRP was 410 msec. Ventricular dysrhythmias—no ventricular dysrhythmias could be induced.

CONCLUSIONS:

1. Normal sinus node function

2. Normal AV node function

3. No ventricular dysrhythmias could be induced

RECOMMENDATIONS: Would recommend continuing the patient on his anti-ischemic medication. I do not feel that anti-arrhythmic therapy or an implantable defibrillator is justified at this point since the patient's symptoms did occur with ischemia.

James Reesor, MD

ICD-9-CM code(s) _____

CPT code(s) _____

7.

Patient:	Williams, Betty
DOB:	01/20/35
Hospital #:	4507789
Physician:	Alene Walker, MD
Date:	May, 17 199–

CLINICAL INDICATIONS: Syncope

METHOD: The patient was brought to the Head-Up Tilt lab and was placed supine for 5 minutes and was then tilted to 30 degrees for 5 minutes and finally to 60 degrees for 30 minutes.

Next, the patient again was laid supine. I.V. Isuprel was administered at 0.04 mcg/kg/min. The patient was then tilted to 60 degrees for 22 minutes, again with continuous ergodynamic monitoring.

RESULTS: The baseline head-up tilt test revealed normal heart rate and blood pressure response following the administration of I.V. Isuprel. The patient's heart rate fell from 127 to 71/min and blood pressure fell from 123 to 105 mmHg. The patient felt nauseated, but no syncope was elicited.

CONCLUSIONS: The patient probably does have a vasodepressor component to her syncope; however, the specificity of this test is impaired because the patient did not actually have a syncopal episode while on the table.

RECOMMENDATIONS: It would be reasonable to try a trial of low-dose beta blockade.

Alene Walker, MD

ICD-9-CM code(s) _____

CPT code(s) _____

8.

Patient:	Foster, Martin
DOB:	10/24/45
Hospital #:	6398254
Physician:	Davis Abercrombie, MD
Date:	April 21, ——

CLINICAL INDICATIONS: Easily inducible sustained monomorphic ventricular tachycardia in a patient with an LV aneurysm.

METHOD: The patient was brought to the EP lab and was prepped and draped in the usual sterile fashion. The left subclavian vein was entered percutaneously, and a guide wire was inserted under fluoroscopic guidance by Dr. Judson Danielson. A pacemaker pocket was then fashioned down into the area underlying the pectoralis fascia. An 11 French peel-away introducer sheath was then advanced over a guide wire. The 10 French Endotek lead was then advanced through the sheath and posi-

continues

tioned in the right ventricular apex. Bradycardia pacing was performed followed by defibrillation threshold testing. The defibrillation testing was performed via the AICD. The AICD was programmed, positioned in the generator pocket, and the pocket was closed using three layers including a subcuticular stitch by Dr. Danielson.

AICD DATA: The AICD is a Ventak mini II, model #1763, serial #800132. The Endotek lead is a CPI, model #0125, serial #0125211359, and this is a 70 cm. length. The bradycardia pacing-the R wave is 12 millivolts. The threshold was 0.5 volts. The resistance at threshold was 460 ohms using a pulse width of 0.5 msec. During the defibrillation threshold testing in test #1 the patient received a one joule shock with an impedance of 30 ohms.

Defibrillation threshold testing #1: The patient was induced into ventricular fibrillation using overdrive pacing via the device. A 15-joule shock was then delivered that was unsuccessful in bringing the patient back to normal sinus rhythm. A 270-joule rescue shock was administered via the device and successfully converted the patient back to a normal sinus rhythm.

Test #2—The patient was induced into ventricular fibrillation with overdrive pacing. A 20-joule shock was then administered via the device. It also was unsuccessful in converting the patient back to a normal sinus rhythm. A 28-joule rescue shock was administered via the device and successfully converted the patient back to a normal sinus rhythm.

Test #3—The proximal cord was pulled back further into the IVC. The patient was induced into ventricular fibrillation using the overdrive pacing. A 20-joule shock was administered via the device and successfully converted the patient back to normal sinus rhythm. This was also with reverse polarity.

Test #4—The patient was induced into ventricular fibrillation with overdrive pacing. A 20-joule shock was administered, which successfully converted the patient back to a normal sinus rhythm. The energy was delivered via the device. This was also performed by the reverse polarity.

CONCLUSIONS: Successful AICD implantation with a defibrillation threshold of less than or equal to 20 joules using reverse polarity.

David Abercrombie, MD

ICD-9-CM code(s) _____

CPT code(s) _____

9.

Patient: Crow, Bill
DOB: 03/22/29
Hospital #:   778414968
Physician: Michael DuBonnet, MD
Date: November 12, 199–

CLINICAL INDICATION: Arrhythmia due to a pacemaker lead fracture and malfunction

continues

METHOD: After informed consent was obtained, the patient was brought to the operative suite in a fasting state. Conscious sedation was administered by anesthesia throughout this case. The patient's chest was prepped and draped in a sterile fashion. Sensorcaine 0.5% was infiltrated in the left pre-pectoral area over the chronic packing pocket for local anesthesia. A 4 cm incision was made over the chronic pulse generator. The old pulse generator was removed. The atrial and ventricular leads were disconnected from the pulse generator. Atrial sensing and pacing thresholds were measured and found to be excellent. Ventricular lead showed evidence for fracture, which was intermittent. A new Active fixation ventricular lead was placed via a 10 French peel-away sheath into the left subclavian venous system under fluoroscopic guidance with only modest difficulty in passing the HRA-SVC juncture. Excellent pacing system thresholds were obtained. Ten-volt output showed no extra cardiac capture. Chronaxie and rheobase measurements were obtained. The lead was affixed to underlying fascia using 0 strength Ethibond in the prescribed manner and using the provided anchoring sleeves. The pocket was then washed with antimicrobic solution. The chronic ventricular lead was capped. The new leads were attached to the chronic pulse generator and the system was placed in the left pre-pectoral pocket after revision to accommodate the new hardware. The wound was then closed in three layers using 2-0 and 3-0 Vicryl. The patient tolerated the procedure well and without apparent complication.

FINDINGS: The chronic ventricular lead was a CPI4262060500. It showed evidence for intermittent fracture and was capped. The chronic atrial lead was a CPI4269254320. The atrial sensing was 2.0 millivolts. The impedance was 440 ohms. The capture threshold was 1.1 volts at 0.5 millisecond pulse width. The new ventricular led was a CPI426952 cm lead, serial number 288198. The sensing was unmeasurable due to lack of underlying rhythm. The impedance was 740 ohms. The capture threshold was 0.7 volts at 0.5 milliseconds pulse width. The rheobase was a 0.4 volts and the chronaxie was 0.3 milliseconds. The generator was a chronic pulse generator, serial number CPI230405627.

CONCLUSIONS: Successful new ventricular lead placement, successful ventricular capping, successful pocket revision.

PLAN: Return to the patient's room, check PA and lateral chest x-ray in the morning. Continue IV antibiotics. Check rhythm without magnet EKG in the morning. Discharge tomorrow if no complications are apparent.

Michael DuBonnet, MD

USING MODIFIERS EFFECTIVELY

Modifiers allow the coder and biller to alter the circumstances found in a CPT code descriptor. Not all codes describe real-life scenarios as they are presented in the procedural coding manual. By appending a five-digit code with a two-digit modifier, special circumstances can be explained to the insurer.

With E&M codes, only six modifiers can be legally used. These modifiers are found and thoroughly discussed in the Evaluation and Management Module of this text. Within the Medicine, Radiology and Surgery sections of CPT, specific modifiers are found in the guidelines which apply to specific circumstances. Because modifiers clarify operative or medical situations, billers and coders should be very familiar with the correct application of these critical two-digit appendages.

ILLUSTRATING MEDICAL NECESSITY THROUGH ICD-9-CM

Ensuring medical necessity for procedures and services rendered by the cardiologist can be very challenging. Because cardiology procedures can be very expensive and because large volumes of services originate in the subspecialty, heavy scrutiny is often focused on these providers. If CPT is the action coding system, ICD-9-CM is the validation or justification coding system.

Appropriate and accurate ICD-9-CM diagnosis coding is required as well as scrupulous linking of diagnosis to procedure. Payment decisions often hinge entirely on these two billing and coding functions.

1. Cardiac Risk Factors

In cardiac medicine, risk factors are extremely important in the clinical area. Family or personal history of cardiovascular compromise is always an important piece of a patient's puzzle. Additionally, lifestyle differences may be contributory if smoking, drinking, drug abuse, high blood pressure, diabetes, high salt or lipid intake, a sedentary lifestyle or a history of rheumatic or scarlet fever exists. All of these problems have ICD-9-CM codes and may be helpful in reporting when submitting claims.

2. Chronic Disease Processes

Patients with compromised cardiovascular systems do not recover. Medical treatment, surgical or therapeutic intervention or open-heart surgery may lessen the symptoms or offer a band-aid for the current problem, but unless radical changes occur, this disease process marches forward and worsens with time. As long as the physician is addressing a chronic process or is adjusting treatment or medication for the problem, the disease may be reported as justification for an encounter. These are sequenced after acute problems on the HCFA-1500 claim form (unless ICD-9-CM directs otherwise).

3. Acute Problems

Acute problems are frequently the precursor to the patient's presentation for care. Since the new and present problem is what prompts the patient to seek medical care, these should be sequenced in a primary or top-of-the-list location on the claim form. Signs and symptoms will suffice if no hard diagnosis is known at the time of the encounter. The common physician terminology rule out, suspected, or probable is not a basis for code selection. These terms represent the physician's logic pathway but are incorrect for code selection. Diagnosis codes should reflect only what is known at the time of the encounter or service. Therefore, guessing what the patient might have is a disastrous practice with long-reaching adverse effects for the practice and the patient.

4. Trauma

Though rarely seen by cardiologists, occasionally closed chest trauma is treated by this specialty. When reporting services for these problems, coders should access not only the actual outcome of the trauma (e.g., chest contusion), but also the E or External Cause code describing the context and circumstances of the trauma.

5. Complications: Medical, Surgical or Mechanical

As with any surgery, pacers and AICDs are common sources for complications. Three categories exist in ICD-9-CM for reporting complications. Medical complications occur as a result of a medical problem. For example, a CHF patient develops bacterial pneumonia while hospitalized for management of the heart failure. This is considered a medical complication and should be coded thus from the diagnosis coding system.

Surgical complications usually involve infections, inflammations, hemorrhages, emboli, thrombi, seromas or hematomas. All of these problems are reportable in the ICD-9-CM system. Because cardiologists enter major vessels when performing percutaneous procedures, hematomas may form at the puncture site. Additionally, skin pockets may be traumatized and infected prior to pacer or AICD insertion, removal or repositioning.

Mechanical complications occur due to perforation, leakage, or malfunction of an implanted device, graft or prosthetic. Such complications may include (but are not limited to) bypass grafts, ventricular access devices, worn-out pulse generators, broken electrodes or leads, implanted AICDs, balloon pumps, stents or pacers.

Complications should be sequenced first on the HCFA-1500 form. (*See the Modifier section for information on which modifiers may be appropriately added.*) Linking the complication diagnosis with the correct CPT code (and modifier, if applicable) will assist the claim in appropriate payment consideration.

6. Justifying Lab Testing

As with all diagnoses, accurate diagnoses and corresponding ICD-9-CM codes must be submitted to justify lab procedures. No longer cost-effective is the 1950's approach to excessive screening and diagnostic lab testing. Now insurers require that offices draw lab for specific monitoring of established disease processes. For this reason, Medicare and AMA worked feverishly on revamping the Laboratory section of CPT to eliminate large, nonspecific lab panels. Generalized automated, multichannel tests have been deleted. Specific new organ panel codes are found for reporting purposes.

■ *Highlight*

Screening lab tests that produce no abnormal findings may be disallowed for payment and denied as medically unnecessary by payors. Good diagnosis coding will assist reimbursement potential greatly in justifying these diagnostic services.

MORE CONFUSING CARDIOLOGY CODES

In cardiology, as in any other specialty, coders/billers and medical professionals alike struggle with "whens," "wheres," "hows" and "whys."

Cardiac Output

Table 7–5 illustrates the coding ramifications of reporting cardiac output.

CPR

According to the American College of Cardiology, CPR should not be billed if Critical Care is reported/billed for the same time period. Additionally, cardioversion would not be separately reported in the context of critical care delivery.

Fluoroscopic Lead Placement

ACC recommends that cardiologists/electrophysiologists select the code for evaluation of pacer/AICD lead placement and/or integrity. Though a code can be found which states insertion pacemaker, fluoroscopy and radiography, radiological supervision and interpretation only, ACC states this code is primarily used by radiologists. One last word of caution, separate procedure is included in the description. This means that this code is usually a part of a greater procedure and should not be reported unless performed separately.

Congenital Anomalies

Coders should take special care when selecting echocardiography and angiography codes if the patient has a congenital cardiac or vascular defect. Specific CPT codes must be used in such cases. Additionally, for patients with this diagnosis, it is *always* important to sequence this code as one of the justifiers for medical, therapeutic or diagnostic services.

TABLE 7–5   Cardiac Output Measurement.

Indicator dilution studies such as days or thermal dilution, including arterial and/or venous catheterization; with cardiac output measurement (separate procedure)

Indicator dilution studies such as dye or thermal dilution, including arterial and/or venous catheterization; subsequent measurement of cardiac output

According to the *American College of Cardiology's Practical Reporting of Cardiovascular Services and Procedures,* cardiac output measurement is not reportable when:

- Cardiac catheterization is performed (dye dilution curves, the Fick method [or any other method] is included in the cath procedure)
- Measurement is obtained at the bedside in the ICU/CCU.
- The only time cardiac output measurement is reportable is when performed as a separate procedure in the cardiac cath lab (but not at the time of a cardiac catheterization!)

EXERCISE 7–6

1. ICD-9-CM is the _____ or _____ coding system.

2. If congenital anomalies exist should they or should they not be indicated in the choice of the diagnosis (ICD-9-CM) code(s)? _____

3. If CPR is performed during a critical care encounter, should this procedure be billed/reported separately? _____

4. Are lab screening tests paid for by most insurers? _____

5. Name the three categories of complications found in ICD-9-CM. _____

SUMMARY

▪ The practice of cardiology incorporates distinctive services and procedures within the specialty: electrophysiology, medical or noninvasive; invasive, therapeutic or interventional; and nuclear diagnostic.

▪ Due to the great variety of cardiac services rendered, comprehension of the anatomy of the heart and its functions is essential.

▪ Cardiology is ever-changing and technologically on the cutting-edge of development requiring coders and billers to stay abreast of regulatory changes, payment and bundling rules, and new and deleted diagnosis and procedure codes each year.

REFERENCES

Code It Right, 2nd edition. Salt Lake City, UT: Medicode 1998.

Coder's Desk Reference. Salt Lake City, UT: Medicode 1998.

CPT Billing Guide. Salt Lake City, UT: Medicode 1998.

Heger, Joel W. *Cardiology for the House Officer, 2nd Edition.* Baltimore: Williams & Wilkins, 1987.

1998 Coding Illustrated—Cardiovascular & Respiratory. Salt Lake City, UT: Medicode 1998.

Physicians' Common Procedural Terminology. Chicago: American Medical Association, 1999.

Rich, Michael W., ed. *Coronary Care for the House Officer.* Baltimore: Williams & Wilkins, 1989.

Sacks, Edmond J. *Pediatric Cardiology for the House Officer.* Baltimore: Williams & Wilkins 1989.

St. Anthony's Cardiovascular Coding Newsletter. Alexandria, VA: St. Anthony Publishing, Inc., 1998.

St. Anthony's ICD-9-CM Code Book for Physician Payment. Alexandria, VA: St. Anthony Publishing, Inc., 1999.

Module 8
OB/GYN

Linda L. French, CMA-C
Amy C. Morgan, RRA

LEARNING OBJECTIVES

Upon successful completion of this module, you should be able to:

1. Recognize and define female reproductive anatomy and physiology.
2. Name the primary organs of the reproductive system.
3. Define and illustrate proper usage of OB/GYN terminology.
4. Accurately assign ICD-9-CM and CPT codes for exercises.
5. Sequence a series of codes with the most appropriate principal or primary diagnosis and procedure.
6. Explain the significance of global service in the practice of obstetrics and gynecology.
7. State the differences between obstetric and gynecologic services.
8. Name diagnostics used in obstetrics and gynecology.

INTRODUCTION

Overview of Obstetrics and Gynecology (OB/GYN)

This module introduces the many facets of obstetrics and gynecology. Physicians working within this specialty care for the healthy obstetrical patient and treat diseases of the female reproductive organs such as benign or malignant tumors, hormonal disorders, infections, and disorders related to pregnancy. Basic terms, office and hospital procedures, and diseases related to this specialty are identified and described.

This module discusses how to accurately assign diagnoses codes using the *International Classification of Diseases, 9th Revision, Clinical Modification, Volumes 1 and 2* (ICD-9-CM). Diagnoses are used to identify the reason for the service. Do not assign diagnostic codes for outpatient services where "suspected," "rule-out," "possible," or "probable" phrases precede the physician's impression. Instead, code the sign or symptom that prompted the visit.

This module also explores how to assign procedure codes relating to the specialty of obstetrics and gynecology using the *Current Procedural Terminology* (CPT) manual. Procedure codes are used to identify the service that was rendered. Great care should be taken when assigning a code, and the medical record or any other available pertinent documentation should be reviewed to identify the most appropriate and inclusive code. Only by using the most complete and detailed codes can the coder be certain that the resulting collection of data will be of use to a health care facility or other group needing information and that the assignment of codes results in the provider's maximum allowable reimbursement.

Unique Aspects of Coding OB/GYN

A woman's reproductive organs are a very private part of her body and many female patients discuss a variety of sensitive issues with their OB/GYN physician. Tactfulness in obtaining coding information and patient confidentiality must be observed by the coder. Female patients often feel close to their OB/GYN physicians and not only divulge delicate information, but want the physician to act as their primary care physician (PCP). This is sometimes allowed by insurance companies and managed care plans and occasionally the physician is listed as both a PCP and a specialist in the insurance directory. The coder needs to be aware if the patient is seeking treatment from a PCP or a specialist because this impacts the coding of evaluation and management services. Other physicians involved in the delivery of gynecologic and obstetric services would include family practice physicians, general practitioners, doctors of osteopathic medicine, general surgeons, and internal medicine physicians.

Often the physician's evaluation and management service turns into a counseling session and appropriate documentation and coding must be used for these situations. Because of the close proximity of the urogenital system, many OB/GYN physicians also diagnose and treat urinary problems. An understanding of urinary system CPT codes 50010 to 53899 is necessary. Other unique aspects of coding OB/GYN are mentioned throughout this module.

Subspecialties of OB/GYN

Because of the complexities of the female reproductive system, several subspecialties exist to help deliver the best medical care. Some would include fetal diagnostics, gynecologic endoscopy, gynecologic oncology, clinical geneticist, perinatologist, premenstrual syndrome medicine, reproductive endocrinology, and urogynecology. See Table 8–1 for a complete description of these subspecialties.

Other Health Care Providers in OB/GYN

Several types of physician extenders are utilized in the practice of obstetrics and gynecology and perform routine services and encounters that are "incident to" the physician. These services are billed using the physician's provider number as if the physician performed the service. Physician extenders include nurse practitioners, nurse midwives, physician assistants, and certified lactation consultants.

To assist the physician with the education and treatment of the OB/GYN patient are registered nurses, vocational nurses, medical assistants, and childbirth educators. A Certified Childbirth Educator (CCE) receives certification through the International Childbirth Educator's Association (ICEA). Other childbirth educator certifications include Lamaze and Bradley. A Doula is a labor assistant who helps the mother during the labor process. A Monitrice is a registered nurse or licensed vocational nurse who assists the mother during labor and monitors the baby. If educational supplies, such as books, pamphlets, or tapes are provided at the physician's expense, CPT code 99071 may be used. When physician educational services are rendered to a patient in a group setting (e.g., prenatal or labor and delivery instructions), code 99078 may be assigned. Various surgical assistants might be uti-

TABLE 8–1   Subspecialties of OB/GYN.

Subspecialty	Definition
Fetal Diagnostics	Provides antepartum diagnostic and therapeutic services including antepartum fetal heart rate testing, high resolution obstetrical ultrasound, fetal echocardiography, biophysical profile, fetal Doppler flow studies, chorion villus sampling, amniocentesis, fetal umbilical vein blood sampling, and fetal surgery.
Gynecologic Endoscopy	Specializes in the use of hysteroscopy, laparoscopy, and pelviscopy to diagnose and manage gynecologic conditions. Provides the service of laser therapy.
Gynecologic Oncology	Provides comprehensive care for women with gynecologic neoplasms, including the surgical management of patients with cancer and preinvasive disease of the female genital tract. Provides the administration of chemotherapy, immunotherapy, and the coordination of radiation treatments.
Geneticist (Clinical)	Specializes in the study of the causes and inheritance of genetic disorders including chromosomal aberrations and the transmission of genetic factors from generation to generation.
Perinatologist	Specializes in maternal-fetal medicine and provides consultation on patients with complications of pregnancy. Services include genetic counseling, prematurity prevention, fetal echocardiography, and antenatal testing using the most current diagnostic and treatment modalities.
Premenstrual Syndrome Medicine	Provides patients with accurate diagnosis and individualized treatment for premenstrual syndrome.
Reproductive Endocrinology	Provides medical care for women suffering from problems with menstruation, symptoms of masculinization, abnormal milk production of the breast, menopause, hormone replacement, and endometriosis. Specializes in the diagnosis and treatment of infertility including diagnostic laparoscopy, ovulation induction, intrauterine insemination, in vitro insemination, intrafallopian transfer, microsurgery, and donor oocyte transfer.
Urogynecology	Provides diagnosis and treatment for women with functional disorders of the lower urinary tract such as urinary stress incontinence and problems of anatomical support of the female pelvis.

lized in a surgical setting when an insurance carrier, such as Medicare, does not allow for a physician assistant surgeon. Such assistants are usually employees of the hospital or surgical center and bill for their services through their employer. Table 8–2 lists some abbreviations used for various health care professionals.

ANATOMY AND PHYSIOLOGY OF THE FEMALE REPRODUCTIVE SYSTEM

Primary Functions

In this module basic anatomy of the female reproductive system is discussed as well as basic functions of each organ. The primary function of the female repro-

TABLE 8–2 Abbreviations Relating to OB/GYN Health Care Professionals.

Abbreviation	Position
CCE	Certified Childbirth Educator
CCS	Certified Coding Specialist
CFA	Certified First Assistant (surgical)
CMA	Certified Medical Assistant
CNM	Certified Nurse Midwife
CPC	Certified Procedure Coder
CST	Certified Surgical Technician (2nd surgical assistant)
FACOG	Fellow of the American College of Obstetricians and Gynecologists
HIM	Health Information Management
IBCLC	International Board Certified Lactation Consultant
LPN	Licensed Practical Nurse
LVN	Licensed Vocational Nurse
MD	Doctor of Medicine
PA–C	Physician's Assistant–Certified
RMA	Registered Medical Assistant
RNFA	Registered Nurse First Assistant (surgical)
RNP	Registered Nurse Practitioner

ductive system is to produce offspring. The ovaries are the sex organs that produce eggs to be fertilized by the male sperm. The ovaries also produce hormones that control the menstrual cycle and help maintain pregnancy. The sex hormones, estrogen and progesterone, play a vital role in the development and function of the reproductive organs and in sexual behavior and drive. They are also responsible for the development of secondary sex characteristics. Follicle-stimulating hormone (FSH) and lutenizing hormone (LH) are referred to as gonadotropinsi, which stimulate the production of other hormones and help produce the ovum (egg). The uterus houses the developing fetus and the vagina provides a route for delivery. The female breasts produce milk to feed the infant after birth.

Reproductive Organs

The female reproductive system consists of external and internal organs. The external organs are called the external genitalia and the internal organs consist of the vagina, the uterus, fallopian tubes, and ovaries.

External Structures

External Genitalia The external genitalia, also called the vulva, can be seen on physical examination and include the labia majora, labia minora, clitoris, urethral orifice, and mons pubis (see Figure 8–1). The labia majora (large vaginal lips) are the outer folds of the vagina and the labia minora (small vaginal lips) are the inner folds on either side of the orifice, the opening to the vagina. These serve as protective barriers. The Bartholin's glands, located on either side of the vaginal orifice and the Skene's glands, located near the meatus, which is the external opening to the urethra, secrete lubricating fluids. Occasionally these glands get blocked and a cystic formation or abscess develops, which may become large and painful needing incision and drainage. The clitoris, a very sensitive organ of erectile tissue, plays a role in sexual arousal and is the structure that corresponds to the male penis. The mons pubis is the hairy skin that surrounds the vulva. The perineum is the area located between the vaginal opening and the anus. This area is often cut during childbirth in a procedure called an episiotomy to prevent tissue from being torn.

Breasts The breasts are two mammary glands that are considered accessory organs of the female reproductive system (see Figure 8–2). Their primary function is to produce milk for the nourishment of the infant. After giving birth, which is referred to as **parturition**, hormones stimulate **lactation**, which is the production of milk. These glands are divided into a number of lobes that are further subdivided and produce secretions that are channeled through ducts that culminate in the opening of the nipple. The pigmented area that surrounds each nipple is referred to as the areola.

Internal Structures

Vagina The vagina is a muscular tube that extends from the uterus to the exterior of the body (see Figures 8–3 and 8–4). This thin, elastic canal provides an entrance from the outside to the internal organs. It receives the penis (and semen) during sexual intercourse, which is referred to as **copulation**, and serves as the birth canal when it dilates, thus enlarging to provide a passageway for the delivery of the infant.

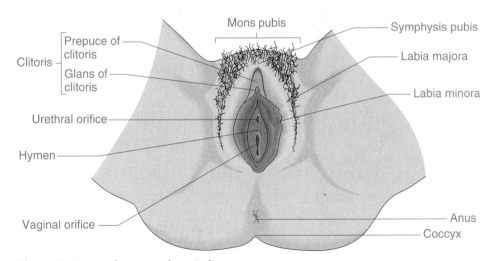

Figure 8–1 Female external genitalia.

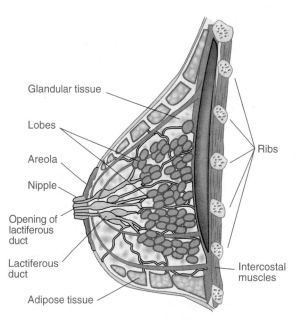

Glandular tissue

Lobes

Areola

Nipple

Opening of lactiferous duct

Lactiferous duct

Adipose tissue

Ribs

Intercostal muscles

Figure 8–2 Female mammary glands (sagittal view).

Ovaries The ovaries are the primary organs of the female reproductive system. They are two small almond-shaped organs that are suspended by ligaments above and on either side of the uterus (see Figure 8–4). They produce ova (eggs) every twenty-eight days during the reproductive years from **menarche** to **menopause**. The ovaries also provide hormones, which serve the needs of the reproductive cell

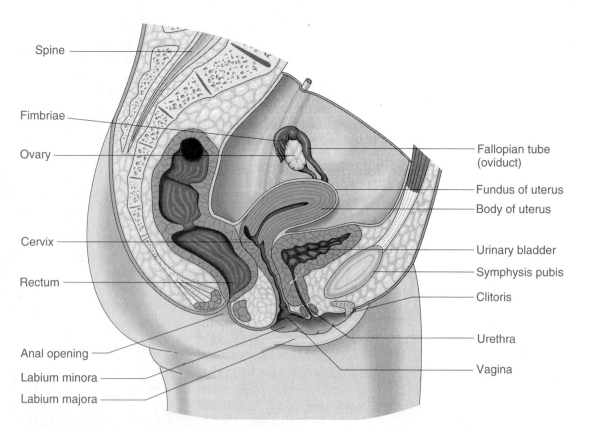

Spine

Fimbriae

Ovary

Cervix

Rectum

Anal opening

Labium minora

Labium majora

Fallopian tube (oviduct)

Fundus of uterus

Body of uterus

Urinary bladder

Symphysis pubis

Clitoris

Urethra

Vagina

Figure 8–3 Female reproductive organs (sagittal view).

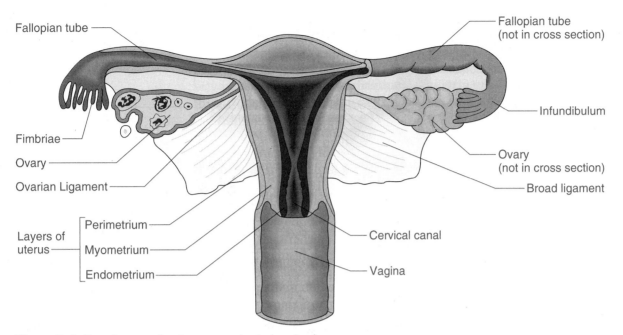

Figure 8–4 Female reproductive organs (anterior view).

and/or developing fetus. These hormones, estrogen and progesterone, are referred to as sex hormones and are responsible for the maturation of secondary sex characteristics such as axillary and pubic hair, onset of menses, widening of the pelvis, increased fat deposits, enlargement of accessory organs, and the development of breasts. The ovum grow and develop within a small sac in the ovary, referred to as a follicle. The ovum matures under the influence of hormones and the follicle grows and finally bursts open to release the egg. This is referred to as **ovulation**.

Fallopian Tubes The fallopian tubes, sometimes called oviducts or uterine tubes, originate just below the fundus of the uterus (see Figure 8–4). The outer end of each tube curves over the top of each ovary and opens into the abdominal cavity. Although they are not connected to the ovary, the flared ends of the oviducts have finger-like projections called fimbriae that sweep the ovum into the oviduct where fertilization occurs. The fertilized egg then travels down the tube toward the uterus.

Uterus The uterus is a pear-shaped structure situated between the urinary bladder and the rectum (see Figure 8–3). It is a muscular organ that receives the fertilized ovum and provides an appropriate environment for the developing offspring (see Figure 8–4). The wall of the uterus consists of three layers. The endometrium is the innermost glandular layer that is ever-changing with the menstrual cycle. The superficial portion of this mucous membrane pulls loose and sloughs with menstruation each month. The myometrium is the bulky middle layer which consists of smooth muscle. This muscle plays an important role during labor as it contracts and forces the fetus out of the womb. The perimetrium is the outer, membranous tissue layer, which is continuous with the broad ligaments that suspend the uterus.

The top rounded portion of the uterus is called the fundus. As the uterus grows during pregnancy, the fundus is palpated by the obstetrician and a measurement is taken from the top of the fundus to the pubic bone to determine the size of the developing fetus (see Figure 8–5). The major portion of the uterus is referred to as the corpus or body. The lower portion, a narrow outlet which extends into the vagina, is called the cervix. The cervix is the neck of the uterus and the area from

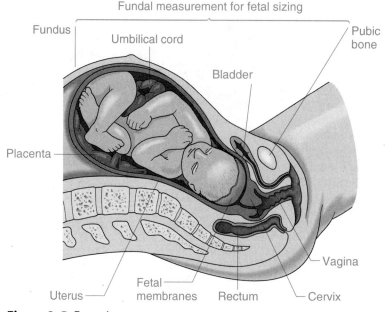

Fundal measurement for fetal sizing

Fundus

Umbilical cord

Pubic bone

Bladder

Placenta

Vagina

Uterus

Fetal membranes

Rectum

Cervix

Figure 8–5 Fetus in utero at term.

which a Papanicolaou smear (Pap test) is taken. The opening in the cervix, referred to as the endocervical canal, dilates during labor to allow passage of the fetus. Four sets of ligaments hold the uterus in place and permit it to grow and move during pregnancy.

After the ovum implants in the rich blood supply offered by the endometrium, the placenta forms to serve as a transport system for blood and nutrients. The hormone, human chorionic gonadotropin (hCG) begins to secrete and is essential for the maturation and maintenance of pregnancy. This hormone can be measured in serum blood and urine and is detected in various forms of pregnancy testing.

OBSTETRICS AND GYNECOLOGY (OB/GYN)

As the name implies, obstetrics and gynecology (OB/GYN) are two specialties in one. Unlike other specialties, OB/GYN deals with women only. For details concerning specific coding challenges, the OB/GYN specialty is divided into separate areas dealing with the pregnant and the non-pregnant patient.

Coding Obstetrics (OB)

Obstetrics is the branch of medical science that has to do with the pregnancy process from conception to childbirth and through the puerperium. The puerperium is the recovery time, after delivery, that it takes for the uterus to return to normal size; usually three to six weeks. The obstetrician provides maternity care, including the delivery of the child, and postpartum care for the healthy obstetrical patient as well as the patient experiencing complications brought on by the pregnancy and conditions that complicate the pregnancy such as anatomical defects or disease. Maternity CPT codes 59000 to 59899 are used for obstetrical care including abortion. This area of medicine is especially difficult to code because of the many intricacies, which may stem from a complication, generating complex details that can affect a diagnosis. If the patient were not pregnant, these conditions would be found in various chapters of ICD-9-CM; however, since the patient is pregnant, these conditions have been reclassified to the pregnancy chapter. The following main terms are used to locate various pregnancy complications in the Alphabetic Index of ICD-9-CM:

1. Childbirth
2. Delivery
3. Labor
4. Pregnancy
5. Puerperium

The obstetrician often administers anesthesia to the obstetrical patient. However, according to HCFA Global Surgery Policy, when anesthesia is provided by the physician performing the primary service, the anesthesia services are included in the primary procedure. If the obstetrician performs ultrasound, also called **echography**, for fetal and maternal evaluation, CPT codes 76805 to 76830 are used.

Newborn services are coded separately from the mother's services. Use V27.0–V27.9 to identify the outcome of delivery on the mother's chart. See Module 1, ICD-9-CM for information regarding newborn guidelines and the coding of newborn services.

Terms Common to OB

Gravidity and **parity** are terms used to describe a woman's history of pregnancy and childbirth. Gravidity refers to the number of pregnancies and parity refers to the number of pregnancies in which the fetus has reached viability; approximately twenty-two weeks of gestation. See Table 8–3 for a complete description of terms relating to reproductive history.

The time a woman is pregnant and fetal development takes place is referred to as **gestation**. The pregnancy is divided into three **trimesters**. The total gestation, from fertilization of the ovum to delivery of the baby, is approximately 266 days. However, the figure 280 days is used most often to calculate the estimated date of delivery (EDD) starting from the first day of the last menstrual period (LMP). The time from the LMP to the end of the twelfth week make up the first trimester. The fertilized ovum is referred to as an embryo during the first eight weeks of life. Starting from the thirteenth week of gestation to the end of the twenty-seventh week make up the second trimester. The third trimester starts at the twenty-eighth week of gestation and extends to the estimated date of confinement (EDC). When coding, it is important to understand what trimester a patient is in. The severity of a condition accompanying pregnancy can often be substantiated by the number of weeks gestation in which it occurs.

Rhythmic contractions, dilation of the cervix, and a discharge of bloody mucus from the cervix and vagina, referred to as "show," mark the start of true labor. Labor is divided into three stages. Stage 1, the dilation stage, is the time from the onset of true labor to the complete dilation of the cervix; usually reaching 10 cm in diameter. This may last from six to twenty-four hours and is the longest stage. Stage 2, the expulsion stage, is the period from full dilation to delivery of the infant. This stage usually takes about an hour for the first birth and approximately twenty minutes for subsequent births, but may take as long as two hours. Stage 3, the placental stage, is the final phase when the placenta, also called afterbirth, is delivered. This stage is usually accomplished in fifteen minutes. Failure to progress in any of the above stages of labor may constitute a complication and the possible

TABLE 8–3   Terms Relating to Reproductive History.

Term	Meaning
para	A term used with numerals to designate the number of pregnancies that have resulted in the birth of a viable offspring
nullipara (O)	No live offspring
unipara (I)	One live offspring
bipara (II)	Two live offspring
tripara (III)	Three live offspring
quadripara (IV)	Four live offspring
multipara	Two or more live offspring (also called pluripara)
para 0-2-3-2	Series of numbers used to indicate the complete reproductive history. When a series of numbers are used:
para <u>0</u>	the first number represents full term infants
para 0-<u>2</u>	the second number represents preterm infants
para 0-2-<u>3</u>	the third number represents abortions
para 0-2-3-<u>2</u>	the fourth number represents living children
gravida (G)	Pregnant woman
primigravida	First pregnancy (also called unigravida)
primipara	Delivery of one offspring regardless of whether it is alive or dead
secundigravida	Second pregnancy
multigravida	Many pregnancies (also called plurigravida)
G-2 para-1	Combination of gravidity and parity; two pregnancies with one live birth

need of a cesarean section to secure safe delivery of the fetus. Complications may include obstructed labor, abnormality of forces of labor, and long labor. These and other complications occurring during the course of labor are coded using ICD-9-CM codes 660–669.

Evaluation and Management Codes Used with OB

One of the unusual aspects of OB is the global fee that encompasses the **antepartum**, delivery, and **postpartum** period of a normal pregnancy. The initial and subsequent history, all physical examinations, recording of blood pressure, weight, fetal heart tones, routine urinalysis, and monthly visits up to twenty-eight weeks gestation are included in antepartum care. After twenty-eight weeks, biweekly visits up to thirty-six weeks gestation, and weekly visits until delivery are also covered in antepartum care. All other visits or services should be coded separately.

Delivery services include the hospital admission with history and physical, the management of uncomplicated labor, and the vaginal or cesarean delivery. Episiotomy and use of forceps are also included. Any medical problems complicating the labor and delivery management should be coded separately utilizing codes in the Evaluation and Management Section and Medicine Section of the CPT manual.

Hospital and office visits for six weeks following vaginal or cesarean section (C/S) delivery are included in postpartum care.

Because of the extended length of care of the OB patient, it is not unusual for more than one physician to provide complete obstetrical care. If a physician provides part or all of the antepartum and/or postpartum care, but does not perform delivery due to referral to another physician or termination of pregnancy by abortion, the antepartum and postpartum care CPT codes 59409–59410 and 59414–59430 should be used.

Other E/M services used in OB include a new or established patient office visit to determine pregnancy (CPT codes 99201–99215), hospital observation services (CPT codes 99217–99220), office and hospital consultations and confirmatory consultations (CPT codes 99241–99275), emergency department services (CPT codes 99281–99285), possible critical care services (CPT codes 99291–99292), and newborn care (CPT codes 99238 and 99431–99440).

EXERCISE 8-1

Use the ICD-9-CM and CPT manuals to code the following exercises.

1. The obstetrician performs an ultrasound on a pregnant patient, 16 weeks gestation, for complete fetal and maternal evaluation. What CPT code would be used to bill for this service? _____

2. An obstetrical patient has just delivered twins. One is liveborn and one is stillborn. What ICD-9-CM code(s) would be used to show the outcome of delivery? _____

3. A 38-year-old nulligravida patient sees her family practitioner due to persistent vomiting. Her doctor does a pregnancy test, which is positive. The patient is then referred to an obstetrician for consultation. The patient is a smoker and her husband has a family history of Down's syndrome. What E/M code would the OB/GYN specialist use to bill for this visit? _____

4. A woman was seeing her OB/GYN physician for the first and part of the second trimesters of her pregnancy until the doctor moved to another city. What evaluation and management code would this physician use to bill for the first five prenatal visits? _____

Maternity Care and Delivery of Normal Pregnancy

The vast majority of OB care is provided without complication and can be coded using CPT code 59400, routine obstetric care including antepartum care, vaginal delivery (with or without episiotomy, and/or forceps) and postpartum care. ICD-9-CM code 650, normal delivery requiring no assistance, and V27.0, indicating the outcome of delivery as a single liveborn infant, would be appropriate. For a cesarean delivery with routine obstetric care including antepartum and postpartum care CPT code 59510 is used. Occasionally patients who have had a previous C/S have the expectation of a vaginal delivery and CPT codes 59610–59622 may be used. If a vaginal birth after cesarean section (VBAC) is successful, CPT codes 59610–59614 are used.

If Pitocin is administered to induce labor, it is considered an inclusive component of the complete obstetrical package and no additional code should be reported. Fetal monitoring during labor by the attending physician is also considered a part of the obstetrical package. If a consulting obstetrician or perinatologist performs fetal monitoring during labor, CPT codes 59050 or 59051 may be reported. Fetal non-stress tests and fetal contraction stress tests may be reported separately.

Complications in and of Pregnancy

When a patient is admitted because of a condition that is complicating the pregnancy or is a complication of pregnancy, the code for the obstetric complication should be the principal diagnosis. Additional codes to add detail and specificity may be used where appropriate.

Some of the more common complications of pregnancy include anemia, gestational diabetes, and hydramnios. Anemia is a reduction, below normal in the number of erythrocytes (RBCs) in the concentration of hemoglobin, or in the volume of packed red blood cells (RBCs). These all affect the oxygen-carrying capacity of the blood and can be diagnosed by an abnormal complete blood count (CBC) or hematocrit (HCT), which are included in a routine prenatal laboratory test or obstetric panel. Gestational diabetes occurs when there is a glucose intolerance with the onset of pregnancy. This can be determined from a fasting blood sugar (FBS) test to screen for diabetes. The patient may also have to undergo a postprandial (PP) blood test or glucose tolerance test (GTT) to better determine the level of intolerance. Hydramnios refers to an excess amount of amniotic fluid that is seen on ultrasound.

Toxemia is a rarer complication that may arise in pregnancy, as is toxoplasmosis. Toxemia, a potentially life-threatening condition for the patient and fetus, occurs most frequently in primiparas (see Table 8–4) who are twelve to eighteen years old and women thirty-five years of age and older. It is rarely apparent before the twenty-fourth week of pregnancy. The toxemic patient presents with pregnancy-induced hypertension, proteinuria, and edema. This condition is also known as preeclampsia and if the patient's condition is not successfully treated, it may progress to eclampsia. As symptoms worsen, the patient may experience sudden weight gain, headaches, dizziness, spots before the eyes, nausea, vomiting, and ultimately have a seizure. If convulsions occur, they may result in abruptio placentae, which is a separation of the placenta from the uterus.

Toxoplasmosis is an acute or chronic widespread disease of animals and humans caused by the parasite Toxoplasma gondii. It is acquired by eating uncooked lamb, pork, or goat meat, and exposure to infected cat litter. It can infect a fetus transplacentally as a result of maternal infection. If the mother acquires toxoplasmosis, lesions may occur in the brain, heart, liver, lungs, and muscles. If the fetus contracts the congenital form, central nervous system lesions may occur, causing blindness, brain defects, and death.

The appropriate diagnosis code should be applied as the principal diagnosis if a pregnant patient experiences septicemia, a condition of bacteria in the blood-

TABLE 8–4   Types of Abortion.

Type	Definition
accidental	abortion that occurs spontaneously
ampullar	tubal abortion
artificial	abortion surgically induced
complete abortion	abortion in which the complete products of conception are expelled
criminal abortion	illegal abortion
early abortion	abortion within the first 12 weeks of pregnancy
elective abortion	induced abortion done at the request of the mother for other than therapeutic reasons
habitual abortion	three or more consecutive spontaneous abortions occurring within the 20th week of gestation
imminent abortion	impending abortion
incomplete abortion	abortion in which parts of the products of conception are retained in the uterus
inevitable abortion	abortion that cannot be stopped
infected abortion	abortion associated with infection from retained material in the uterus
missed abortion	abortion in which the embryo or fetus has died prior to the 20th week of gestation and the products of conception have been retained for at least 8 weeks
septic abortion	abortion in which there is an infection of the products of conception and in the endometrial lining of the uterus
spontaneous abortion (SAB)	abortion occurring before the 20th week of gestation without apparent cause
therapeutic abortion (TAB)	abortion induced for the safeguard of the mother's mental or physical health; term also used for any legal abortion
threatened abortion	signs and symptoms of uterine bleeding and cramping before the 20th week of gestation that appear to threaten the continuation of pregnancy
tubal abortion	abortion where the embryo or fetus has been expelled through the distal portion of the fallopian tube

stream, or septic shock. A pregnancy complication code should also be used to add emphasis to the patient's condition.

Example

038.2   Pneumococcal septicemia

647.9   Infectious and parasitic conditions in the mother classifiable elsewhere, but complicating pregnancy, childbirth, or the puerperium; other specified infections and parasitic diseases

Sepsis and septic shock associated with abortion, ectopic pregnancy, and molar pregnancy are classified to codes 630 to 639 (Complications of Pregnancy, Childbirth, and the Puerperium) of ICD-9-CM, Chapter 11. See Complications Mainly Related to Pregnancy in Chapter 11, categories 640–648 for problems such as hemorrhage in pregnancy, hypertension complicating pregnancy, excessive vomiting, threatened labor, infections in the mother, and so forth.

Various medications may be used to rid complications of pregnancy, such as Braxton-Hicks contractions or premature **dilation**. Braxton-Hicks contractions are light, usually painless, irregular uterine contractions that gradually increase in intensity and frequency and become more rhythmic during the third trimester. They are often referred to as "false labor." Although usually harmless, if they occur with great frequency during the first or second trimester, they occasionally cause premature **effacement** and/or dilation of the cervix. Effacement is the obliteration of the cervix as it shortens from 1 or 2 centimeters in length to paper thin, leaving only the external os. Dilation is the stretching and opening of the cervix during labor to facilitate the baby's passage through the pelvis. The stages of effacement and dilation can usually let the health care staff determine how close a mother is to delivery. An oral or injectable medication, such as terbutaline sulfate, may be administered to "calm down" the Braxton-Hicks contractions and delay delivery of a premature infant. Appropriate injection codes from the Medicine section of the CPT and possible Level II HCPCS codes (**H**ealth **C**are **F**inance Administration **C**ommon **P**rocedure **C**oding **S**ystem) should be assigned to such situations. These are national codes developed for and updated by the Medicare system.

EXERCISE 8–2

Use the ICD-9-CM manual to code the following exercises.

1. hyperemesis gravidarum (mild), 1st trimester _____

2. threatened labor (38 weeks gestation) _____

3. An expectant woman is on her way to a friend's house for lunch. While driving there she becomes very weak and takes herself to a nearby health care clinic. Her blood sugar is checked, and it is elevated. A diagnosis of gestational diabetes is made. _____

4. A 24-week pregnant woman with current edema of the joint areas and a history of high blood pressure suddenly began to have seizure-like convulsions. Her husband called 911 and explained what was happening. An ambulance rushed her to the nearest hospital due to severe eclampsia. _____

5. At her scheduled doctor's appointment, a 32-week primigravida mentions that she has been experiencing some bleeding on occasions. She states that it has not been painful; therefore, she only thought it to be normal for this stage of pregnancy. There is usually enough blood to cause her to wear undergarment protection. She also says this has been happening for the past three days. The physician sends her to the hospital for an ultrasound and a diagnosis of antepartum hemorrhage is made. _____

Multiple Births More than one fetus may or may not present a complication depending on the number, position, and week of gestation in which delivery occurs. With the use of fertility drugs, the number of multiple births has increased significantly. When coding deliveries, always include a code for the status of the infant. These include codes V27.0–V27.9 and are found under "outcome of delivery" in Volume 2 of the ICD-9-CM. If a multiple pregnancy affects the fetus or newborn, use code 761.5.

Ectopic Pregnancy Ectopic pregnancy is a term used to indicate all forms of pregnancy in which implantation occurs outside the uterus. It is also called tubal pregnancy because 95 percent of ectopic pregnancies occur in the fallopian tube. If the embryo does not spontaneously abort, its growth may cause the tube to rupture. This becomes a life-threatening condition as hemorrhage occurs and may lead to peritonitis, an inflammation of the lining in the abdominal cavity, causing future infertility. Surgical intervention is needed and CPT codes 59120–59151 may be used in conjunction with ICD-9-CM codes from category 633.

Placental Anomalies Abnormalities in the size, shape, or function of the placenta, placental membranes and cord, and the amniotic fluid make up placental anomalies. The most common occurrences are placenta accreta, in which the placenta grows deep into the muscle tissue of the uterus. The placenta does not release at the time of birth and bleeding may occur. Placenta previa occurs with implantation anywhere in the lower segment of the uterus. It may present a partial blockage of the cervix, called partial placenta previa, or full blockage, called full placenta previa. In either case, the patient is prone to bleeding and normally delivers by cesarean section to prevent hemorrhage and interruption of the fetal oxygen supply. Placenta abruptio, as mentioned earlier, is the premature separation of the placenta from the wall of the uterus. This usually happens after the twentieth week of gestation in women over thirty-five years of age who are multigravidas. This, also, can be a life-threatening condition as hemorrhage may occur and interrupt the fetal blood supply. ICD-9-CM codes from category 641 are used for the above conditions.

Postpartum Disorders Puerperal infections are those related to childbirth and occur during the postpartum period. Cleanliness and sterile techniques have improved the chances of avoiding such infections, and antibiotics have improved the chances of recovery. The treatment of most puerperal infections would fall under the global obstetrical package and not be coded separately. However, in the case of severe infection needing extended treatment, additional codes would be used.

Example

99254	Initial inpatient consultation
99183	Hyperbaric oxygen therapy
11000	Debridement of infected skin
670.04	Puerperal cellulitis (postpartum)

Administration of Medication for OB Complications To a coder, understanding which medications an obstetric patient received may allow for more defined and accurate coding. For instance, a patient enters the hospital for Braxton-Hicks contractions and her insurance provider is a diagnostic-related group (DRG) payor. Researching her Medication Administration Record (MAR) and determining that she received an antibiotic could prompt the coder to further query the physician and learn that she was also treated for a pregnancy-induced kidney infection, although such was poorly documented. Since resources were used for this complication during the same episode of care, it may be coded to incorporate a complication or comorbidity (cc) into the DRG. The original reason for the patient seeking care, the premature contractions, must still be used as the principal diagnosis; however, depending upon the DRG used (cc-dependent vs. non cc-dependent), adding such a code could bring the facility greater monetary intake to help pay for that patient's stay, strengthen the case mix index, and ultimately increase overall profits.

EXERCISE 8-3

Use the ICD-9-CM and CPT manuals to code the following exercises as if billing for the obstetrician.

1. abruptio placenta, antepartum _____

2. Echography of a 24-week pregnant female shows a multiple gestation. The physician informs her she is carrying triplets. _____

3. surgical treatment of a tubal ectopic pregnancy requiring salpingectomy _____

Diagnostics in OB There are diagnostic procedures that are used in the detection of pregnancy complications. Included is amniocentesis, a percutaneous transabdominal puncture of the uterus to obtain amniotic fluid. The fluid is examined in a laboratory to determine abnormalities in the fetus. An ultrasound, also called sonogram, may be used to visualize deep structures, such as the uterus, ovaries, and a baby in utero. The use of ultrasound can determine location, position, size, and some defects of the fetus, as well as placental localization and amount of amniotic fluid.

Chorionic villus sampling, a procedure usually performed during the end of the first trimester, can be used to diagnose certain genetic disorders. Fetal tissue is aspirated by catheter through the cervical canal from the villi area of the chorion under ultrasonic guidance. The chorionic villi are branching projections on the outer layer of the developing embryo which provide exchange of oxygen and nutrients with carbon dioxide and waste products.

Abortion The term **abortion** refers to the termination of a pregnancy before the fetus is viable. A spontaneous abortion (SAB) occurs naturally and is often referred to as a miscarriage. A therapeutic abortion (TAB) is an induced abortion, which is a deliberate interruption of the pregnancy. The term TAB originally referred to an abortion done for the physical and mental well-being of the mother; however, today it is applied to all elective abortions. Although the term abortion is used to refer to both the SAB and the TAB, care should be exercised when speaking to a patient who has experienced a miscarriage. Various terms are used to better describe specific situations when an abortion occurs. Table 8-4 offers a complete listing of these terms with definitions. CPT codes 59812 to 59870, found under Maternity Care and Delivery in the Surgery section, are used for various types of abortion. Medical treatment of spontaneous complete abortion should be coded using Evaluation and Management codes 99201-99233. Occasionally, a patient will be placed under observation in a hospital due to a spontaneous abortion. Evaluation and Management codes 99217 to 99220 should be assigned.

Anatomic Problems The manner in which the fetus appears to the examiner during delivery is referred to as the fetal **presentation**. The correct fetal position is for the head to present first in a vertex presentation. Occasionally, housed within the uterus the fetus may be stationed in an inappropriate and incorrect position for birthing. It may become necessary for the health care provider to turn the baby to the correct delivery position. This is considered to be a type of pregnancy complication. Examples of such include breech presentation, brow presentation, face presentation, shoulder presentation, and transverse presentation. See Table 8–5 for a complete listing of presentations with definitions. ICD-9-CM codes in category 652 are used for malposition and malpresentation of the fetus.

When there is a disproportionate relationship of the fetal head to the maternal pelvis, it is called cephalopelvic disproportion. Disproportions can be due to an unusually large fetus, an abnormally formed fetus, or an abnormality of the bony pelvis. ICD-9-CM codes found in category 653 are used for various disproportion problems.

Fetal Problems When a fetal condition affects the management of the mother (i.e., extra observation, in-depth diagnostic studies, or termination of pregnancy), ICD-9-CM codes from categories 655, *Known or suspected fetal abnormality affect-*

TABLE 8–5   **Birthing Presentations.**

Presentation	Description
breech presentation:	feet or buttocks present first
complete breech	thighs of the fetus are flexed on the abdomen and the legs are flexed upon the thighs
frank breech	legs of the fetus are extended over the anterior surface of the body
footling breech	foot or feet present first
brow presentation	baby's head is slightly bent forward so that the forehead (brow) presents first
cephalic presentation	head of fetus presents in any position
compound presentation	limb presents alongside the presenting part
face presentation	head is sharply extended so that the face presents first
funic presentation	umbilical cord appears during labor
longitudinal presentation	long axis of fetus is parallel to long axis of mother
oblique presentation	long axis of fetus is oblique (neither perpendicular nor parallel) to that of the mother
placental presentation	placenta presents first
shoulder presentation	shoulder presents first
transverse presentation	side presents first; fetus is lying crosswise
vertex presentation	upper and back parts of fetal head present first

ing management of mother, and 656, *Other fetal and placental problems affecting the management of the mother,* are assigned.

Disease Gestational trophoblastic disease (GTD) is a term used for abnormalities of the placenta that lead to tumor-like changes. Two of the more common types are hydatidiform mole and choriocarcinoma. Hydatidiform mole, also called molar pregnancy, appears as a mass of cysts resembling a bunch of grapes growing in the uterus and results from abnormal fertilization. The uterus enlarges and there are abnormally high levels of hCG, but there is no sign of fetal movement. Some moles are aborted spontaneously in mid-pregnancy; however, if the diagnosis is made early, abortion is usually performed to ensure complete removal of the abnormal cells which could give rise to malignant tumors. Choriocarcinoma is a malignant tumor made up of placental tissue which often arises from a preexisting complete mole. The tumor cells are highly invasive and secrete abnormally high levels of hCG. This type of cancer metastasizes rapidly, but fortunately it responds to chemotherapy if found early. A hydatidiform mole is classified using ICD-9-CM 630 unless it presents a malignancy, then it is classified using code 236.1. If a previous molar pregnancy affects the management of a current pregnancy, code V23.1 is used.

Rh incompatibility occurs when a mother is Rh-negative, the father is Rh-positive, and the baby is Rh-positive. The mother and baby's blood are incompatible, and, if mixed during delivery, can cause an immune response that results in a condition called erythroblastosis fetalis. In this condition, hemolysis occurs, which is the destruction of the fetal red blood cells. The medication RhoGAM, an Rh immune globulin, is given to the mother to suppress the immune reaction. This is usually administered half-way through the pregnancy and again within seventy-two hours of delivery. ABO blood typing can alert health care personnel to the possibility of this condition and amniocentesis can aid both in the detection of erythroblastosis fetalis and in the intrauterine or fetal transfusion. RhoGAM is also recommended to Rh-negative patients who have had abortion, miscarriage, and ectopic pregnancy, to protect future Rh-negative infants. HCPCS code J2790 is used to bill for RhoGAM injections.

Lactation

Obstetricians are responsible for evaluating the female breast and diagnosing breast diseases and complications due to pregnancy. Disturbances in lactation may be due to a variety of reasons including abnormalities of parts of the mammary glands, anemia, emotional disturbances, malnutrition, and inflammation of the breast, referred to as mastitis. Most procedure codes relating to the breast would be found within the integumentary system of the Surgery section in the CPT manual.

Lactation consultants are persons trained in the art of breastfeeding. If certified, they hold the title International Board Certified Lactation Consultant (IBCLC). They may be independent or employed by an obstetrician, a clinic or lactation institute.

EXERCISE 8–4

Use the ICD-9-CM, Volumes 1 and 2 and CPT manuals to code the following exercise.

1. chorionic villus sampling, any method _____

2. breech presentation of fetus in womb _____

3. amniocentesis with ultrasonic guidance _____

4. A woman 20 weeks pregnant is seen with complaints of severe abdominal cramping and no fetal movement for the past 24 hours. The physician suspects early fetal death, and, after tests, confirms a missed abortion. Surgical completion is performed. _____

Assign ICD-9-CM diagnosis and procedure codes to the following as if billing in a hospital setting. *Sequence* codes as appropriate with *principal* diagnosis and procedure listed first.

5. A 35-week pregnant female comes into the hospital complaining of bleeding. An ultrasound and urinalysis are done. Placenta previa is seen and the urinalysis indicates the patient has a urinary tract infection. The physician decides that an emergency cesarean section is necessary to enable the baby to live. A low cervical C/S is performed that night, and both mother and baby do fine. _____

6. An expectant mother of 27 weeks gestation begins experiencing small contractions that are approximately five minutes apart. As the contractions become closer and stronger, she decides they are not Braxton-Hicks contractions and that she must go to the emergency room. The ER physician wants to place her on a monitor to look at the frequency and duration of the contractions. While being wheeled to an OB observation bed, she accidentally scrapes her elbow on an IV cart. The doctor applies an antibiotic ointment to the injury and gives her Brethine to stop the premature contractions. You are billing for the ER physician. _____

Coding Gynecology (GYN)

The gynecologist treats females experiencing infertility, structural abnormalities of female organs, sexually transmitted diseases, sexual dysfunction, menstrual abnormalities, and other diseases. Female Genital System CPT codes 56405 to 58999 and Laparoscopy/Hysteroscopy CPT codes 56300 to 56399 are used for most gynecological procedures including in vitro fertilization.

Evaluation and Management Services

As mentioned earlier, the OB/GYN physician can serve as a primary care physician and a specialist. The insurance coder must be aware of the capacity in which the physician is serving the patient in order to code correctly. An established patient consultation could be coded as an established patient office visit if the physician were acting as a PCP and not a specialist.

When the physician's evaluation and management service turns into a counseling session, appropriate documentation and coding must be used. When counseling and/or coordination of care dominates more than 50 percent of the physician/patient face-to-face time spent in the office or other outpatient setting (or floor/unit time in a hospital or nursing facility), then time is considered the key factor to qualify for a particular level of E/M services.

Example

An established GYN patient is seen for leukorrhea (white vaginal discharge). The physician performs a problem-focused history and examination with a straightforward medical decision, diagnosis Trichomonas vaginalis. When the physician prescribes medication and instructs the patient to give one-half of the prescription to her sexual partner, the patient reveals she has multiple sexual partners. A conversation evolves in which the patient asks several questions regarding other sexually transmitted diseases, contraceptive methods, and the effects of all of this on a possible future pregnancy. The face-to-face time the physician spends in counseling the patient ends up being thirty minutes.

With this type of visit the physician typically spends ten minutes face-to-face with the patient; however, because of the patient's questions the extended time the physician spent was more than 50 percent and becomes the controlling factor to qualify for a higher level of E/M service. This office visit typically would be coded 99212; however, because of the extra time spent face-to-face with the patient (30 minutes instead of 10 minutes), the E/M service can be upgraded to 99214. The physician must carefully document the nature of counseling in this case. The time-only factor cannot include any delays or interruptions not associated with patient counseling or coordination of care.

Preventive medicine counseling provided as a separate encounter, such as sexual practices or family problems, should be coded using individual counseling Evaluation and Management CPT codes 99401 to 99404. These codes cannot be used if the patient seeking counseling has symptoms or an established illness.

Special Service and Report Codes Special service codes commonly used in the OB/GYN practice, found in the Medicine section of the CPT manual, are as follows:

1. 99000   Handling of specimens for transfer from the physician's office to a laboratory
2. 99204   Postoperative follow-up visit, included in global service
3. 99025   Initial visit, when starred surgical procedure constitutes major service at that visit
4. 99058   Office services provided on an emergency basis
5. 99070   Supplies and materials provided by the physician over and above those usually included with the office visit or other services rendered
6. 99071   Educational supplies
7. 99078   Physician educational services rendered to patients in a group setting

EXERCISE 8–5

Use the ICD-9-CM and CPT manuals to code the following exercises.

1. A 25-year-old established patient comes to the gynecologist for a routine periodic comprehensive reevaluation. _____

2. Office consultation for a 30-year-old with dysfunctional uterine bleeding; blood is drawn and sent to an outside laboratory for testing. _____

3. A 36-year-old patient calls in a panic because she has just found a large lump in her breast. She states "the skin looks funny around it and it hurts". The physician asks the staff to work her in on an emergency basis.

_____

Contraception

One of the main reasons women see their gynecologists is for recommendations and prescriptions regarding contraception. Most methods of contraception are prescribed during an evaluation and management service. Birth control pills are the most used contraceptive product in the United States. The patient requires a prescription from a physician and periodic monitoring of blood pressure and other risk factors. Other physician services regarding contraception that are not included in E/M services are injections of birth control medications, implantation of birth control capsules, insertion of birth control devices, and surgery. See Table 8–6 for a complete listing of birth control methods. The procedure code for the insertion of implantable contraceptive capsules is found in the Surgery/Integumentary section of the CPT manual. Induced abortion is usually performed using the surgical procedure dilation and curettage. CPT codes 59840–59857 would apply to such services and are found in the Surgery/Maternity section.

Tubal ligation is a permanent method of birth control typically performed with a laparoscope. An incision is made in the abdomen, often in the umbilicus, and a small tube is inserted through which the ligation instrument is introduced. A cut, referred to as a transection, is made across the oviducts, and the uterine tubes are blocked so that a fertilized egg cannot pass into the uterus for implantation. Methods for blocking the tubes include fulguration (burning the ends of the tubes) or securing devices such as bands, clips, or Falope rings (which are put in place on the ends of the tubes). Various ligation procedure codes are found in the Laparoscopy/Hysteroscopy section of the CPT manual. If tubal ligation is performed at the same time as a cesarean section, code 58611 would apply.

Office Procedures

A variety of office procedures are performed in a gynecologist's practice. During a routine gynecologic examination, a Pap smear is taken to evaluate cervical tissue for cancer. If the laboratory reports an abnormal Pap smear, a colposcopy may be performed. The colposcope is an instrument used to look into the vagina, opened with the use of a speculum, and to observe the cervix. The physician can see, under magnification provided by the colposcope, what areas of the cervix have abnormal cells. Often a sampling of cells is taken from the cervix and scrapings from the inner canal, referred to as a cervical biopsy with endocervical curettage. Procedure codes for colposcopy are found under Endoscopy in the Surgery/Female Genital System.

A common procedure performed to evaluate the endometrial lining of the uterus is an endometrial biopsy. This may be performed if the patient is experiencing dysfunctional uterine bleeding (DUB) or postmenopausal bleeding. A plastic tube is passed through the cervix into the uterine cavity and a sample of tissue is aspirated into the tube. A biopsy, using a metal instrument to collect a sample, may also be performed.

A more invasive procedure is dilation and curettage (D & C). The small cervical canal is opened or dilated to allow passage for a curette, an instrument used to

TABLE 8–6   Female Contraceptive Methods.

Method	Description
abortion	removal of embryo after implantation in the uterus
abstinence	voluntarily refraining from sexual intercourse
birth control pill (BCP)	synthetic hormones taken orally that interrupt normal hormone secretion and prevent ovulation
cervical cap	a small cap-like device placed over the cervix prior to intercourse
chemical barriers	spermicidal creams, foams, and jellies placed deep in the vagina that create an unfavorable environment for sperm to survive
coitus interruptus	withdrawing the penis from the vagina before ejaculation
diaphragm	a rubber or plastic dome-shaped mechanical barrier placed in the vagina near the cervix that prevents sperm from entering the uterus
intrauterine device (IUD)	a small plastic or metal object placed in the uterus by the physician to prevent implantation of the fertilized egg
morning-after pill (MAP)	drug taken orally that contains estrogen and progesterone. When taken within 72 hours of unprotected intercourse it interrupts the fertilization and/or implantation of the egg
progesterone implant	a synthetic implant, called Norplant, placed under the skin that releases progestin over a 5-year period to prevent ovulation
progesterone injection	synthetic progesterone, called Depo-Provera, administered every three months to prevent ovulation
rhythm method	abstaining from intercourse at the time of ovulation
tubal ligation	surgical procedure in which the uterine tubes are cut and ligated (tied) or cauterized (burned) or closed off with a small ring

scrape the lining of the endometrium. Both endometrial sampling and D & C allow for microscopic visualization of malignant cells for diagnostic purposes and are coded using CPT codes 58100–58120. When a D & C is performed with any other pelvic surgery, it may be viewed by some third-party payers as an integral part of the pelvic surgery and therefore not reimbursed.

Other office procedures include laser treatment for the destruction of vaginal warts and cryosurgery, performed on the cervix to freeze abnormal dysplastic tissue and allow normal tissue to grow in its place. These procedure codes would be found in the Surgical/Integumentary section. Incision, destruction, and excision of lesions and areas of the external genitalia are listed in the Surgery/Female Genital System section under codes 56405 to 56810. Important definitions describing a simple procedure, radical procedure, partial procedure, and complete procedure are found preceding this section.

When performing office surgeries and procedures it is important to understand the meaning of the starred procedure. Explanations of starred procedures are found in the Surgery Guidelines at the beginning of the surgery section. Procedure codes followed by a star (*) are considered "stand-alone" codes. The use of these codes typically allows other codes to be added on a service-by-service basis. Procedures without the star follow the surgical package or global package rules and include routine services.

Example

57100* Biopsy of vaginal mucosa; simple (separate procedure)

This procedure typically *does not* include an office visit, which may be billed separately

57105 Biopsy of vaginal mucosa: extensive, requiring suture (including cysts)

This procedure typically *does* include an office visit, which may not be billed separately

▬ Confusing Codes

CPT codes 88141–88158 are pathology codes used to describe the screening method of Pap smear reported. These codes are not used by physician offices in the procedure of obtaining the Pap smear specimen. It is part of the E/M code in performing the examination.

EXERCISE 8–6

Use the ICD-9-CM and CPT manuals to code the following exercises.

1. Removal of Norplant on an established patient and insertion of new capsule. _____

2. Laparoscopic tubal ligation using Falope ring. _____

3. Colposcopy with cervical biopsy and endocervical curettage for cervical dysplasia performed during a comprehensive initial consultation involving high complexity of medical decision making. _____

4. Endometrial biopsy for postmenopausal bleeding on a new patient. _____

5. Laser treatment for the destruction of ten vaginal warts (molluscum contagiosum) on an established patient. _____

Hospital Procedures

The gynecologist is a specialized surgeon in the area of female reproductive organs. The CPT code 57410, pelvic examination under anesthesia, is included in routine evaluation of the surgical field in all major and many minor gynecological procedures and is not to be reported separately.

The most common surgery a gynecologist performs is a hysterectomy; however, there are many forms of this procedure. The uterus may be removed through an abdominal incision or through a vaginal approach. One or both ovaries and/or fallopian tubes may also be removed, depending on the diagnosis. The word "total" in the procedure total abdominal hysterectomy can be confusing. When hysterectomies were performed in the early years, the surgeon took only the top portion (fundus and corpus) of the uterus and it was referred to as a supracervical hysterectomy. The cervix was left because it was thought to play a role in sexual pleasure. Later, that finding was dismissed along with a newfound fact that the cervix, if left, could pose additional health risks. Surgeons began removing the entire uterus and this procedure was called a total hysterectomy. The uterine tubes and ovaries are not removed during this procedure; thus, many patients and even health care workers are confused by this term. See Table 8–7 for a complete listing of various hysterectomies.

Other common surgeries are a uterine suspension performed to position a prolapsed uterus back in its normal place, and lysis of adhesions to rid scar tissue in the abdominopelvic cavity.

All surgical procedures include generic activities that are assumed to be included as routine surgical practice and should not be considered separate even though they could be performed as separate procedures. Such pre-procedure and post-procedure work is considered bundled into the comprehensive procedure code. As an example, all surgical procedures require a routine exploration. This careful examination allows the surgeon to evaluate the surgical field to determine its anatomic nature and discover any irregularities. The CPT code 49000, exploratory laparotomy, is typically bundled in with other services, e.g., exploratory laboratory with lysis of adhesions, code 58740. It is usually not reported separately

TABLE 8–7   **Types of Hysterectomies.**

Procedure	Definition
hysterectomy	surgical removal of the uterus
supracervical hysterectomy	surgical removal of the fundus and corpus portions of the uterus (leaving the cervix)
total abdominal hysterectomy (TAH)	complete surgical removal of the entire uterus using an abdominal approach
vaginal hysterectomy (Vag Hyst)	surgical removal of the uterus using a vaginal approach
oophorectomy	surgical removal of the ovary
salpingectomy	surgical removal of the fallopian tube
salpingo-oophorectomy	surgical removal of both the fallopian tube and the ovary (unilateral/one—bilateral/two)
hysterosalpingo-oophorectomy	surgical removal of the uterus, fallopian tube, and ovary
total abdominal hysterectomy with bilateral salpingo-oophorectomy (TAHBSO)	surgical removal of the uterus, both fallopian tubes, and both ovaries

unless it is performed for a biopsy only, or is followed by another procedure unrelated to the primary procedure. There are two types of unbundling. One results from a misunderstanding of coding and is unintentional. The second is intentional and occurs when providers manipulate coding in order to maximize payment. The following are examples of unbundling:

Example

1. Breaking out bilateral procedures when one code is appropriate.
2. Downcoding a service to use an additional code when one comprehensive code is appropriate.
3. Fragmenting one service into component parts and coding each part as if it were a separate service.
4. Reporting separate codes for related services when one comprehensive code includes all related services.
5. Separating a surgical approach from a major surgical service.

When an endoscopic procedure is attempted and fails and another surgical procedure becomes necessary, only the successful service may be reported.

Example:

A female patient is undergoing an infertility workup. Several factors have been ruled out and the physician suspects tubal blockage because the patient has a history of PID. A laparoscopic lysis of peritoneal adhesions is attempted and fails. An open laparotomy with lysis of adhesions is performed.

58740	Lysis of adhesions (salpingolysis, ovariolysis)
614.6	Pelvic peritoneal adhesions, female
628.2	Infertility, female; of tubal origin

Only the laparotomy lysis of adhesions can be reported. The laparoscopic lysis of adhesions (CPT code 56304) is bundled in with the larger procedure. These procedures are considered "sequential procedures," and generally only the more invasive service should be reported.

Tubal ligation was covered in the previous section entitled Contraception; however, if a patient has a tubal ligation and later wants her tubes reconnected, the procedure of anastomosis is performed. A tubotubal anastomosis, also referred to as reanastomosis, is a delicate surgery that repairs the fallopian tubes so the patient can attempt conception.

Many types of surgery are done on the ovaries to treat an abnormal cyst, abscess, or malignancy. CPT codes 58800–58960 apply to these services.

Modifiers The use of modifiers expands the information provided by five-digit CPT codes. These two-digit modifiers, made up of either numbers or letters, are intended to convey specific information regarding the CPT code to which they are added. For instance, if a patient has more than one genital lesion that needs biopsy and which are completely separate lesions not described by a single CPT code, the modifier -59 (distinct procedural service) can be used to indicate this to the third party payer. This modifier is not frequently used and should be used only if no more descriptive modifier is available. Some modifiers that are used more commonly in the OB/GYN practice are as follows:

1. -20 (Microsurgery)–For surgical services performed using the techniques of microsurgery and requiring the use of an operating microscope, such as anastomosis of the fallopian tubes.

2. -51 (Multiple Procedure)–For multiple procedures performed at the same operative session by the same surgeon, the additional or lesser procedure(s) should be identified by adding modifier -51.

3. -57 (Decision for Surgery)–Used to identify an E/M service which resulted in the initial decision for surgery.

4. -80 (Assistant Surgeon)–Used to report surgical assistant services when the assistant surgeon aids the primary surgeon and is present for the entire, or a substantial portion of, the operation.

5. -81 (Minimum Assistant Surgeon)–Used to report minimum surgical assistant services when the assistant surgeon's services are required for only a short period of time and not for the entire operation.

6. -99 (Multiple Modifiers)–Used when two or more modifiers may be necessary to completely describe services, such as an assistant surgeon's services (80) on multiple procedures (51) during the same operative session.

Infertility

When a woman comes to the gynecologist for infertility, often the husband is included in the initial workup. Since most couples do not know where the problem lies, a simple semen analysis can rule out most male-related problems. Female problems are more plentiful and complicated to explore. Some common problems include incompatible vaginal secretions or cervical mucus, anovulation, implantation problems, and blockage of the fallopian tubes. Following are a few of the tests and procedures performed on infertility patients with a brief description of each. A postcoital test (PCT) is an inspection of the mucus from the vagina after intercourse to detect the motility and viability of the sperm as it appears in the cervical mucus. Semen washing, using a chemical, is performed to produce better sperm motility. Hormone blood levels may be drawn at a specific time of the menstrual cycle to determine if the patient is ovulating. Hysteroscopy may be performed to visualize the lining of the uterus. Laparoscopy is used to visualize the outside of the uterus, the ovaries, and fallopian tubes. In a procedure called hysterosalpingogram, frequently done with laparoscopy, dye is inserted via the cervix and forced up through the uterus and fallopian tubes. If it easily spills into the abdominal cavity it is an indication that the uterine tubes are free from blockage. If it does not spill, or requires much force to spill, it is an indication that there is a blockage. A catheter may also be inserted into the fallopian tube for diagnostic purposes or to help free the tube from obstruction.

Various forms of artificial insemination, intracervical or intrauterine, may be performed on the infertile woman. CPT codes 58321 and 58322 are used for such procedures. CPT codes 58970, 58974, and 58976 are used for in vitro fertilization procedures.

EXERCISE 8–7

Use the ICD-9-CM and CPT manuals to code the following exercises.

1. sperm washing for artificial insemination _____

2. A woman has tried to conceive for over a year. After a thorough physical examination and other diagnostic tests, she learns that her cervix is considered incompetent. _____

3. repair of enterocele (vaginal approach) and rectocele with posterior colporrhaphy _____

4. hysterosalpingogram done on an infertility patient for tubal occlusion _____

5. surgical assist for abdominal hysterectomy with bilateral salpingectomy, removal of right ovary, and lysis of adhesions _____

Structural Abnormalities of the Female Organs

The normal position of the uterus is tipped slightly forward and referred to as **anteverted**. A **retroverted** uterus is tipped backward. With aging, trauma, or excessive stretching from the act of childbirth, the supporting ligaments of the uterus and bladder may become weakened and **pelvic relaxation** occurs. The displacement of the uterus, bladder, vagina, and rectum may cause significant discomfort and a variety of symptoms that may necessitate surgical correction.

Uterine **prolapse** occurs as pelvic muscles and ligaments become overstretched or weakened and allow the uterus to fall downward into the vaginal canal. A cystocele is the prolapse of the urinary bladder into the vagina causing pressure, urinary frequency, urgency, and incontinence with coughing, sneezing, laughing, or activity, referred to as urinary stress incontinence. A uterine suspension and anterior vaginal colporrhaphy may need to be performed to bring the bladder to its normal position and repair the stretched vagina. A vaginocele, also known as a colpocele, is a prolapse or falling of the vagina, or hernia protruding into the vagina. A rectocele is the prolapse of the rectum into the vagina. This causes constipation, a bearing down feeling, and possibly incontinence of gas and feces.

Sexually Transmitted Diseases (STD)

Sexually transmitted diseases (STD), also called venereal diseases, are among the most common contagious diseases in the United States. Transmission occurs through body fluids such as blood, semen, and vaginal secretions during vaginal, anal, or oral sex. Occasionally they are spread by contact with infected skin. The physician is often able to make a diagnosis from visual examination. Serum blood tests and vaginal cultures are used to confirm the disease. Most treatment includes medication; often it is the administration of oral or injectable antibiotics. Lesions are removed using chemical or surgical methods. Patient education and counseling are often involved to ensure patients do not spread the disease. See Table 8–8 for a listing and description of sexually transmitted diseases.

Cancer of the Female Reproductive Tract

Tumors of the reproductive tract are found in women of reproductive age and are most common in postmenopausal women. Various forms of benign and malignant neoplasms occur in all areas of the female reproductive tract. Malignant lesions account for ten percent of all cancer deaths in women. See Table 8–9 for a listing and description of the most common forms of female cancer.

Other Diseases of the Female Reproductive Tract

Endometriosis is a condition that occurs when endometrial tissue migrates outside of the uterus into the pelvic or abdominal cavity. This tissue implants on other

TABLE 8–8   Sexually Transmitted Diseases.

Name	Definition
AIDS	acquired immunodeficiency syndrome is caused by human immunodeficiency virus (HIV). The virus attacks and destroys the immune system leaving the body vulnerable to invasion by other microorganisms.
chancroid	a bacterial infection, also called soft chancre, that causes ulceration and enlargement of the lymph glands (lymphadenopathy). It is usually contacted through sexual intercourse and can spread to other areas of the body.
chlamydia	an infection that is caused by the bacteria *Chlamydia trachomatis,* which invades the vagina and cervix. It is the leading cause of infertility and pelvic inflammatory disease.
condylomata acuminata	an infection that causes genital warts which may itch or burn. It is spread by direct skin-to-skin contact during sexual intercourse.
gonorrhea	a contagious inflammation of the genital mucous membrane transmitted chiefly by sexual intercourse and caused by the bacteria Neisseria gonorrhoeae. It often spreads unknowingly and can cause infertility, eye and throat infections, and pelvic inflammatory disease.
hepatitis B	an inflammation of the liver, also called serum hepatitis, that results in liver cell destruction. As it travels throughout the body the patient feels ill and may have fever, weight loss, jaundice, fatigue, abdominal pain, and digestive disturbances.
herpes genitalis	herpes simplex virus (HSV), type 2 is spread by direct skin-to-skin contact and causes a local infection that produces ulcerations on the skin and mucosa of the genitals.
syphilis	the spirochete bacterium causes a chronic infection which sometimes appears as a chancre sore in the primary stage. In the second stage, as the organism spreads, it may involve any organ or tissue. During this time numerous symptoms can be present as it becomes systemic. A latent period usually follows which may last from one to forty years when the patient is asymptomatic. Later, widespread invasion may take place resulting in disabling or life-threatening conditions.
trichomoniasis	infection of the genitourinary tract caused by Protozoa trichomonas. It can cause urethritis (inflammation of the urethra) with dysuria (painful urination) and itching.

organs and responds to hormonal signals as if it were within the uterus. The misplaced tissue fills with blood and sloughs causing severe pain. Although benign and self-limiting, it is a cause of infertility. Laparoscopy may confirm the diagnosis of endometriosis and is used to remove the endometrial implants.

Uterine fibroid tumors are the most common tumors of the female reproductive tract. They occur in fifty percent of all women who reach age fifty. They are nonmalignant tumors, also called leiomyomas, which are made up of smooth muscle that grows within the myometrium of the uterus. The patient may be asymptomatic, or experience pelvic pain, constipation, urinary frequency, and heavy or prolonged periods. Leiomyomas are treated surgically with myomectomy, a shelling out of the myometrium with preservation of the rest of the uterus. In younger women of child-bearing age, myomectomy would be the recommended surgical treatment. In cases where there are multiple tumors or tumors large in size, or the woman is not concerned with childbearing, a hysterectomy may be performed.

TABLE 8–9   Female Reproductive Cancer.

Type	Description
cervical	one of the most common forms of gynecologic cancer. An ulceration of the cervix occurs causing vaginal discharge and spotting. A Pap smear usually detects this slow growing cancer in early stages. Cryotherapy, laser ablation, electrocautery, surgical resection (referred to as conization), and hysterectomy are all treatment options.
endometrial	the most common cancer of the female reproductive tract where ulcerations of the endometrium develop causing vaginal bleeding accompanied by a white or yellow vaginal discharge (leukorrhea). Most commonly occurs in postmenopausal women who have never had children. Diagnosis is made by endometrial biopsy or dilation and curettage. Complete hysterectomy with bilateral salpingo-oophorectomy is usually performed.
ovarian	the leading cause of female reproductive cancer deaths in women. Abnormal tissue development occurs leading to ovarian cancer which is the most difficult of all female cancers to detect. A pelvic mass may be palpated on physical examination, however this is usually at a later stage. The patient may experience lower abdominal pain, weight loss, and general poor health. A total abdominal hysterectomy with bilateral salpingo-oophorectomy is usually performed as well as excision of nearby lymph glands. If found in later stages, a complete exenteration of the abdomen and pelvic organs may be necessary.
uterine	several types of endometrial carcinoma arise from the endometrial lining and may invade the uterine wall. Found most commonly in nullipara women between the ages of 50 and 60 years old, this form of cancer may metastasize to the ovaries, fallopian tubes, and other organs. Symptoms include menorrhagia, metrorrhagia, watery or thick, foul-smelling discharge, and postmenopausal bleeding. Depending on the stage and age of the woman, a hysterectomy and bilateral salpingo-oophorectomy may need to be performed.
Vaginal	a rare form of cancer exhibiting symptoms of leukorrhea and bloody vaginal discharge. Treatment usually involves surgical excision of the tumor.
Vulvar	squamous cell carcinoma of the vulva accounts for 3 percent of all gynecologic cancers. It occurs mainly in postmenopausal women. A small hard lump develops and grows into an ulcer. It may weep and bleed and if not treated, will metastasize to other areas.

A collection of different types of cysts may occur on the ovaries. Occasionally they become large and cause discomfort or menstrual irregularities. If they rupture and bleed into the pelvic cavity they may require surgical intervention. Mittelschmerz is abdominal pain that occurs at the time of ovulation, midway between menstrual periods.

As instructed in Module 1, locate the main term(s) in the Alphabetic Index, Volume 2 first. Review any subterms under the main term and follow any cross reference instructions. Always verify the code which has been selected from the Index in the Tabular List, Volume 1. Refer to any instructional notations and assign the code to the highest level of specificity. Code the diagnosis until all elements are completely identified.

Example

A patient has a hysterectomy for intramural leiomyoma of uterus.

ICD-9-CM code 218.1

Although the diagnosis uterine leiomyoma is listed under code 218, this three-digit code cannot be used because there are four selections below it which are described further, all having four digits. You must choose from one of the four-digit codes, 218.0, 218.1, 218.2, or 218.9. In this case, code 218.1 describes the diagnosis exactly. There are no five-digit codes listed under this category, so the highest level of specificity is a four-digit code. Always sequence the primary diagnosis first. The primary diagnosis is listed by the use of the ICD-9-CM code that represents the diagnosis, condition, problem, or other reason for the encounter/visit shown in the medical record to be chiefly responsible for the outpatient services provided during the encounter/visit. Second, list all additional codes that describe any coexisting conditions that affect patient care or management.

Menstrual Abnormalities

The beginning of menstruation is called menarche. As mentioned earlier, this occurs at puberty with the secretion the female sex hormones estrogen and progesterone. Menstrual disorders are often triggered by hormonal abnormalities which control the menstrual cycle. The normal menstrual cycle is twenty-eight days with an average length of blood flow lasting five days. The first day of any blood loss is considered the first day of the menstrual cycle whether it is spotting or a regular flow. This day is important in the calculation and determination of what may be happening to cause an abnormal cycle. A woman typically menstruates throughout her reproductive years until the onset of menopause, which is the cessation of menses. If a patient does not have a menstrual flow it is called amenorrhea. Painful or difficult menstruation is referred to as dysmenorrhea. Excessive menstrual flow or too frequent menstruation is called abnormal uterine bleeding. See Table 8–10 for a list of common terms relating to the menstrual cycle.

Inflammatory Conditions

Inflammatory conditions of the female genital tract may be localized or involve other genital organs and adjacent structures. The suffix -itis on the end of a word indicates an inflammation. The beginning of the term indicates the organ involved. Some conditions are cervicitis (cervix), endometritis (endometrium), oophoritis (ovaries), salpingitis (uterine tubes), vaginitis (vagina), vulvitis (vulva), and vulvovaginitis (vulva and vagina). There are many reasons for female genital inflammation. A spermicide, tampon, or the act of intercourse could cause a local inflammation. The fungal infection *Candida albicans,* also known as Monilia or yeast infection, can cause vulvovaginitis. Bacterial and viral infections, such as those found in venereal disease, are common causes of inflammation, genital tract infections, and pelvic inflammatory disease (PID). PID is an inflammation of the entire female reproductive tract the most common cause of which is STD. As these organisms travel up the fallopian tubes into the abdominal cavity the body fights to rid them. PID symptoms include fever, chills, backache, a foul-smelling vaginal discharge, and a painful, tender abdomen. During this process adhesions may form attaching organs to other organs and blocking the lumen (opening) of the fallopian tube. This is the most common cause of infertility. In severe cases, the peritoneum, a membrane that covers the abdominal wall, becomes inflamed and a condition called peritonitis may result. If the infection gets into the bloodstream, septicemia and even death may occur.

The Female Breast

Gynecologists are responsible for evaluating the female breast and diagnosing breast disease. Most procedure codes for these services would be found within the

TABLE 8–10 Terms Relating to Menstruation.

Term	Definition
amenorrhea	without menses
dysmenorrhea	painful menstruation
menarche	beginning of menstrual function at time of puberty
menometrorrhagia	excessive uterine bleeding at and between menstrual periods
menopause	cessation of hormone production and menstruation
menorrhalgia	painful menses
menorrhagia	excessive uterine bleeding at time of menstruation
menorrhea	discharge at time of menses
menostaxis	prolonged menstrual period
menses	the regular recurring uterine bleeding from the shedding of the endometrium
metrorrhagia	uterine bleeding occurring at irregular intervals
oligomenorrhea	scanty or infrequent menstruation
postmenopause	the period of life after menopause
premenstrual	occurring before regular menstruation

integumentary system of the surgery section in the CPT manual. A common benign condition of the breast in which small sacs of tissue and fluid develop is fibrocystic breast disease. In this disease cystic lumps or nodules are noticed in the breast and may be accompanied by premenstrual tenderness. A mammogram confirms this diagnosis.

A fibroadenoma is a common benign neoplasm of the breast derived from glandular tissue. Following the coding instructions of a neoplasm in Module 1, first research the main term fibroadenoma in the alphabetic index. The subclassifications are referenced to "M" codes which are used primarily in cancer registries. Refer to the Neoplasm table, breast, benign, to assign the code 217.

The American Cancer Society statistics shows breast cancer to be the most commonly occurring malignant disease in women and is the second leading cause of cancer death in American women (lung cancer is the first). A majority of breast lumps are discovered by women on self-examination. Others are found by the gynecologist who performs a breast examination as part of the routine gynecologic examination, or by mammography, a radiographic examination of the breasts for the detection of cancer. Some signals include skin changes, puckering, or leakage from the nipple. Most women needing lumpectomy or mastectomy for the removal of malignant tumors and breast tissue are referred to general surgeons. See Module 4, Anesthesia/General Surgery, for more information on coding these operations.

While breast cancer occurs mostly in women, it does occur in men. ICD-9-CM does contain specific codes for male breast as well as female breast.

EXERCISE 8–8

Use the ICD-9-CM manual to code the following exercises.

1. endometriosis of the broad ligament _____

2. chlamydial vulvovaginitis _____

3. fibrocystic breast disease _____

4. Mittelschmerz _____

5. carcinoma in situ of the cervical canal _____

Use the ICD-9-CM and CPT manuals to code the following exercises.

6. uterine suspension with anterior colporrhaphy for uterine prolapse with cystocele _____

7. I & D of Bartholin's gland abscess complicating pregnancy _____

8. resection of ovarian malignancy with bilateral salpingo-oophorectomy and omentectomy _____

9. A new patient, gravida 5 para 0-0-5-0 appears in the gynecologist's office with acute urethritis, leukorrhea, and severe pelvic pain. The patient is a habitual aborter with a history of irregular menses. She confides in the doctor about her drug use and sexual promiscuity. The physician performs a comprehensive examination and takes a vaginal culture to rule out gonorrhea. The culture is sent to an outside laboratory along with a blood sample for a CBC and sed rate. A urine pregnancy test and urinalysis (automated with microscopy) are performed in the office. The pregnancy test is negative and the UA indicates a mild nonspecific UTI. The physician orders an intramuscular injection of antibiotic and the patient is advised to schedule a follow-up appointment in three days. _____

Use the ICD-9-CM and CPT manuals to code the following exercise sequencing the principal diagnosis with the appropriate procedure.

10. A 19-year-old sexually active teenager is seen as a new patient complaining of pain with intercourse. She states that there has been no hemorrhaging other than her normal monthly menses and that she does not have any nausea, dizziness, or vomiting. As part of the routine exam, the physician performs a quantitative hCG serum pregnancy test, which is negative. A pelvic examination is done with Pap smear and the physician palpates several abnormal masses along the patient's abdominal wall. The patient flinches in pain when this area is touched. The physician performs a complete pelvic ultrasound to rule out leiomyoma and malignant neoplasm. The results are

essentially negative, so a vaginal hysteroscopy is recommended. The patient wants to proceed immediately. Endometrial polyps are seen covering the lower one-third of the woman's endometrium. The physician then removes the polyps by ablation at the same episode of care. _____

SUMMARY

- The practice of obstetrics and gynecology are two specialties in one serving the needs of pregnant and non-pregnant women.
- The reproductive organs consist of the external genitalia, the vagina, uterus, fallopian tubes, and ovaries.
- The primary purpose of the reproductive organs are to produce offspring.
- Obstetrics is the branch of medical science that has to do with the pregnancy process from conception to childbirth and through the puerperium.
- A global package concept is used to code and bill for obstetrical services, which includes antepartum, delivery, and postpartum care.
- A pregnancy is divided into three trimesters and labor is divided into three stages.
- Complications in and of pregnancy are numerous and include abortion, anatomic problems, anemia, ectopic pregnancy, fetal problems, gestational diabetes, hydramnios, placental anomalies, malpresentations, multiple births, postpartum disorders, and Rh incompatibility.
- A gynecologist is a physician and surgeon who treats females experiencing infertility, structural abnormalities of female organs, sexually transmitted diseases, sexual dysfunction, menstrual abnormalities, inflammatory conditions, breast disease, female cancer, and other diseases.
- Gynecologists perform preventative services including contraceptive counseling, screening Pap smears, breast examinations, and complete physical examinations.
- Unique aspects of coding OB/GYN include the dual role of the physician serving the pregnant and non-pregnant patient, and acting as primary care physician and specialist. Many sensitive issues surrounding OB/GYN services and the complexities of the complications of and in pregnancy add to the difficulty in coding this specialty.

REFERENCES

Chabner, Davi-Ellen. *The Language of Medicine, 5th Edition*. Philadelphia: W.B. Saunders Company, 1996.

Davis, F.A. *Taber's Cyclopedic Medical Dictionary, 17th edition*. Philadelphia: F.A. Davis Company, 1993.

Dorland's Illustrated Medical Dictionary. Philadelphia: W.B. Saunders, 1998.

Fordney, Marilyn Takahashi. *Insurance Handbook for the Medical Office, 5th Edition*. Philadelphia: W.B. Saunders Company, 1997.

Huffman, Edna K. *Health Information Management, 10th Edition*. Berwyn, IL: Physicians' Record Company, 1994.

Miller-Keane, *Encyclopedia & Dictionary of Medicine, Nursing, & Allied Health, 6th Edition.* Philadelphia: W.B. Saunders Company,

Mosby's Medical and Nursing Dictionary. St. Louis, MO: Mosby-Yearbook Inc., 1983.

St. Anthony Publishing, Inc. *St. Anthony's Medicare Unbundling Guidebook.* Reston, VA: St. Anthony Publishing, Inc., 1998.

UCLA Medical Center/Medical Group. *Physician's Handbook for Patient Referral.* UCLA Medical Center, Los Angeles, CA, 1996–1997.

Module 9
Radiology, Pathology, & Laboratory

Julie Orloff, RMA, CMA, CPT

KEY TERMS

Automated
Brachytherapy
Computerized Axial
  Tomography (CAT)
Hyperthermia
Intracavitary
Magnetic Resonance
  Imaging (MRI)
Manual
Qualitative
Quantitative
Radiation Absorbed Dose
  (RAD)
Ribbons
Sources

LEARNING OBJECTIVES

Upon successful completion of this module, you should be able to:
1. Identify subsections of the radiological section.
2. Code the various types of radiological procedures.
3. Identify the different types of laboratory procedures.
4. Explain the difference between qualitative and quantitative.
5. Code the different procedures related to the radiology and laboratory sections.

INTRODUCTION

This module introduces learners to specialty coding in the areas of radiology and laboratory and pathology. The module focuses mainly on CPT coding, with relevant examples from ICD-9-CM integrated where appropriate. The first half of this module covers the specialty of radiology and includes nuclear medicine and diagnostic ultrasound. The second half of this module discusses pathology and laboratory guidelines. Learners should have a copy of the CPT code book nearby as they begin studying this module.

RADIOLOGY

Radiology is a medical specialty that involves the use of radioactive substances such as x-rays and radioactive isotopes, in the prevention, detection, diagnosis and treatment of disease. The field of radiology includes many specialty areas, including radiation therapy, nuclear medicine, ultrasound, computed tomography, magnetic resonance imaging, and special procedures such as angiography. A radiographer is a specialist who produces images (or radiographs) of parts of the human body. Depending on their level of training and experience, radiographers may also perform more complicated tests such as preparing contrast media for patients to drink and operating special equipment used for computerized tomography, magnetic resonance imaging, and ultrasound. Radiation therapists prepare cancer patients for treatment, and administer prescribed radiation doses to parts of the body. A radiologist is a physician who interprets the images prepared by the radiographer and makes patient treatment recommendations.

CPT-RADIOLOGY

The radiology section of the CPT code book includes four subsections:

> Diagnostic Radiology (Diagnostic Imaging)
> Diagnostic Ultrasound
> Radiation Oncology
> Nuclear Medicine

The coder should become familiar with the differences between these subsections and not code based on the area of the body being treated because each subsection covers details of the area of the anatomy being treated. For example, diagnostic procedures on the spine and pelvis such as a radiologic examination of the spine, are included within the Diagnostic Radiology subsection. Ultrasound procedures such as echography of the spinal canal, are included within the Diagnostic Ultrasound subsection. "Notes" are provided at the beginning of, as well as, within other parts of the subsections that explain terminology, such as A-mode, M-mode, or B scan ultrasound.

Physician Billing

Most physician offices do not have radiologic equipment in their offices and, therefore, refer patients to hospitals or radiologic outpatient facilities. In these cases, the coders for these physicians would not be assigning radiology codes unless the physician provides radiological supervision and interpretation.

Radiological Supervision and Interpretation

Many codes in the Radiology section of CPT include the following phrase in the description—"radiological supervision and interpretation." These codes are used to describe the radiological portion of a procedure that two physicians perform. In situations where the physician provides the supervision, interpretation and the performance of the procedure, two codes are reported: a radiological code and a code from the surgery section. This is often referred to as a "complete procedure."

> *Example: Percutaneous placement of ivc filter-complete procedure. The physician submits the following codes: 75940 and 37620. Code 75940 identifies the radiologic procedure—including interpretation of the results—and Code 37620 identifies the procedure.*

▬ **Highlight**

> *The radiological supervision and interpretation codes do not apply to the radiation oncology subsection.*

RADIOLOGY MODIFIERS

It is often necessary to modify procedures or services codes. This section introduces the common radiology modifiers and provides examples of how each might be used.

■ -22 (09922) Unusual Procedural Services

This modifier is intended for use when the service provided is greater than that usually required for the listed procedure. Modifier -22 may be used with **computerized tomography (CAT scan)** codes when additional slices are required or more detailed examination is necessary.

■ -26 (09926) Professional Component

The professional component includes supervision of the procedure, reading and interpreting the results and documenting the interpretation in a report. This service can be done by the physician who ordered the radiologic procedure or by the radiologist on staff at the hospital or outpatient center. The technical component includes performing the actual procedures and expenses of the supplies and equipment. This service is usually provided by the technician at a hospital or an outpatient facility. The physician would report a professional component by attaching the modifier -26 to the appropriate radiologic procedure. The outpatient facility would report the technical component modifier -tc (technical component) to the same procedure. Modifier -tc is a Level II HCPCS modifier.

> *Example: 73550—Radiological examination of femur. The physician should report the following: 73550-26. The clinic should report the following: 73550-tc.*

■ *Confusing Codes*

> *When reporting a code describing "radiological supervision and interpretation," do not report modifier -26 along with the procedure. The "radiologic supervision and interpretation" code already describes the professional component.*

> *Example: Peritoneogram with the physician providing only the supervision and interpretation of this procedure. The physician should report the following: 74190-peritoneogram, radiologic supervision and interpretation.*

In this example, modifier -26 would not be appropriate because the descriptor code 74190 already indicated that the physician provided only the supervision and interpretation for the procedure. Reporting that would cause the claim to be denied.

> *Example: 74329—Endoscopic catheterization of the pancreatic ductal system, radiological supervision and interpretation.*

■ -51 (09951) Multiple Modifiers

Modifier 51 may be reported to identify that multiple radiologic procedures were performed on the same day or during the same episode. Adding 09951 on the HCFA 1500 claim form justifies a multiple procedure.

■ -52 (09952) Reduced Services

Modifier -52 may be reported to identify that a radiologic procedure is partially reduced or eliminated at the discretion of the physician.

■ -53 (09953) Discontinued Procedure

Modifier -53 is used when the physician elected to discontinue or terminate a diagnostic procedure usually because of risk to the patient.

■ -59 (09959) Distinct Procedural Service

Modifier -59 may be used to identify that procedure or service was distinct or independent from other services provided on the same day.

■ -RT and -LT Modifiers

Modifiers -RT and -LT are level II HCPCS modifiers that should be used when bilateral procedures are performed. To report these modifiers to reflect a bilateral radiological procedure, code the procedure twice and attach -rt to one of the codes and -lt to the other.

Example: 73520-RT and 73520-LT-radiologic examination, hips, minimum two views each hip, bilateral.

■ **Highlight**

These two modifiers apply to Medicare claims, and their use varies according to reporting requirements of medical programs and other third party payers.

EXERCISE 9–1

Assign the appropriate CPT codes for the following procedure(s); include modifiers and Level II modifiers when applicable.

1. Radiologic examination, temporomandibular joint, open and closed mouth; unilateral _____

2. Radiologic examination, chest, two views, frontal and lateral; professional component only _____

3. Radiologic examination, knee, arthrography, radiological supervision and interpretation _____

4. Barium enema with KUB _____

5. Hysterosalpingography, radiological supervision and interpretation _____

DIAGNOSTIC RADIOLOGY (DIAGNOSTIC IMAGING)

The production of a picture, image, or shadow that represents the object being investigated is diagnostic radiology. The classic technique for imaging is the x-ray.

Codes 70010–76499 describe diagnostic radiology services. They are further subdivided by anatomic site and then by specific type of procedure performed: CAT scan, MRI, x-ray, and MRA scan. These radiology procedures may be found in the alphabetic index of the CPT manual by referring to the main term "x-ray", "cat scan", **"magnetic resonance imaging"**, and "magnetic resonance angiography".

CPT provides separate codes for radiologic procedures using contrast media. Contrast media is a term used to describe chemical substances that are introduced into the body to enable the soft tissue vessels and organs (for example, the liver) to be seen with x-rays. The contrast medium is administered either orally or intravenously. Examples of some contrast media are barium, iohexol, and renografin. Common x-ray procedures using contrast material include barium enema, endoscopic retrograde cholangiopancreatogram, fistulogram, intravenous pyelogram and hysterosalpingogram.

CAT scans may also be performed with or without contrast material (see Figure 9–1). This radiological procedure is helpful in evaluating the brain, lung, mediastinum, retroperitoneum, and the liver.

In most instances, MRI scans are almost equal to CAT scans, but MRIs are superior in evaluating the brain, spinal cord, soft tissues, adrenal and renal masses (see Figure 9–2). For patients who have metallic objects, such as pacemakers, metallic fragments, and vascular clips in the central nervous system, this procedure is contraindicated. Contrast material may also be used when performing MRI scans, the most common is gadolinium (gadipentetate dimeglumine).

DIAGNOSTIC ULTRASOUND

Diagnostic ultrasound is considered a subsection that lists codes 76506–76999. Similar to Diagnostic Radiology, it is also further subdivided by anatomical sites. These codes may be found in the index by referring to "ultrasound" or "echography". Diagnostic ultrasound involves the use of high frequency waves to visualize internal structures of the body. Ultrasounds are commonly performed for evaluation of the abdomen, pelvis and ear, and for gynecologic and obstetrical diagnoses. Figure 9–3 shows some examples of diagnostic ultrasound procedures.

Four types of diagnostic ultrasound are recognized:

A-Mode   A one-dimensional ultrasonic measurement procedure.

M-Mode   A one-dimensional ultrasonic measurement procedure with movement of the trace (delayed time for the sound to hit the specimen being scanned and then back to screen) to record amplitude and velocity of moving echo-producing structures. This mode is used for the heart and vessels using color flow.

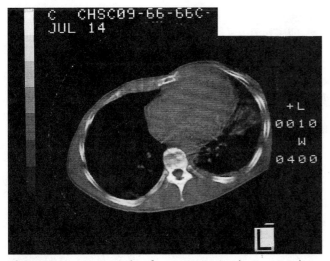

Figure 9–1 An example of a computerized tomography: a CT scan of a chest showing pleural effusion.

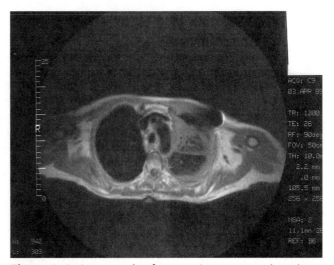

Figure 9–2 An example of magnetic resonance imaging: an MRI of a chest.

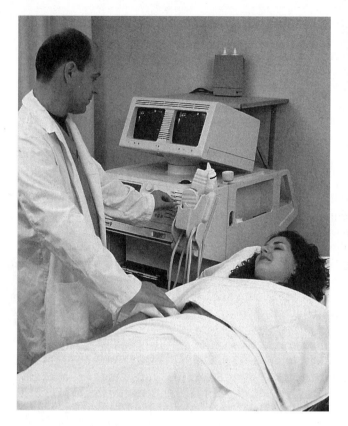

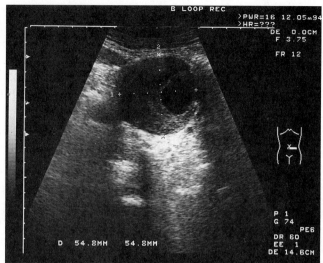

Figure 9–3 Modern ultrasonic equipment.

B-scan	A two-dimensional ultrasonic scanning procedure with a two-dimensional display. This scan is the same as A-mode, except with two display dimensional.
Real-Time Scan	A two-dimensional ultrasonic scanning procedure with display of both two-dimensional structure and motion with time. "Real time" means that the image can be visualized as it is being produced.

■ *Highlight*

The medicine chapter in the CPT manual also includes ultrasound involving the following areas:

Arterial Studies of the Extremities (93922–93931)
Venous Studies of the Extremities (93965–93971)
Cerebrovascular Arterial Studies (93875–93888)
Visceral and Penile Vascular Studies (93975–93981)
Ultrasound of the Heart—Echocardiography (93303–93350)

EXERCISE 9–2

Assign the appropriate CPT codes for the following procedure(s); include CPT modifiers and Level II modifiers, when applicable.

1. Echography, pregnant uterus, B-scan and/or real time with image documentation; complete _____

2. Echography, transvaginal _____

3. Ultrasonic guidance for pericardiocentesis, radiological supervision and interpretation _____

4. Ultrasonic guidance for interstitial radioelement application _____

5. Gastrointestinal endoscopic ultrasound, radiological supervision and interpretation _____

RADIATION ONCOLOGY

The radiation oncology codes (77261–77999) describe therapeutic use of radiation to treat diseases, especially neoplastic tumors. Radiation therapy is used as a primary therapy to treat certain types of malignancies, such as leukemia. The most common type of radiation used in treatment is electromagnetic radiation with x-rays and gamma rays.

X-rays are photons generated inside a machine, while gamma rays are photons emitted from a radioactive source. Radiation is measured in units known as the rad (radiation absorbed doses) or the gray, which is equal to 100 rad.

The delivery of radiation may be external or internal. External radiation therapy involves the delivery of a beam of ionizing radiation from an external source through the patient's skin toward the tumor region. Internal radiation therapy, also known as brachytherapy, involves applying a radioactive material inside the patient or in close proximity. This material may be contained in various types of devices such as tubes, needles, wires, seeds, and other small containers (see Figure 9–4). Common radioactive materials used in brachytherapy include radium-226, cobalt-60, cesium-137 and iodine-125. The three types of brachytherapy are interstitial (into the tissues), intracavitary (implanted into body cavities), and surface applications. Interstitial brachytherapy involves the use of radiation sources placed in special devices and then implanted in body cavities. Surface application brachytherapy uses radioactive material that is contained on the surface of a plaque or mold and applied directly or close to the surface of the patient.

Radiation Treatment Delivery

The following series of codes (77401–77417) describes the technical component of delivering the radiation treatment, as well as the various energy levels administered. To assign these codes, the appropriate information is needed:

1. The number of treatment areas involved.
2. The number of ports, or parts or devices that are surgically implanted for easy removal of blood, for example, involved.
3. The number of shielding blocks, or shields used to protect parts of the body from radiation.
4. The total million electron volts (MEV) administered.

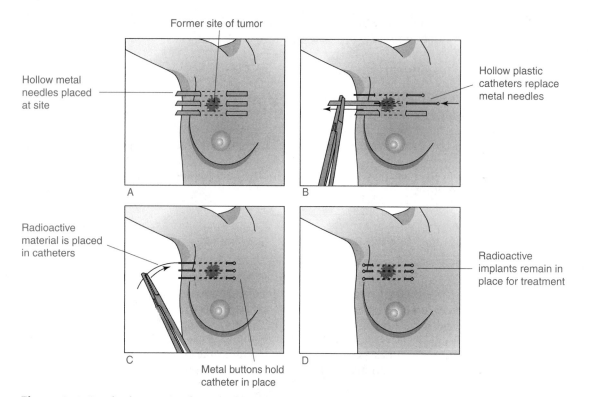

Former site of tumor

Hollow metal needles placed at site

Hollow plastic catheters replace metal needles

Radioactive material is placed in catheters

Radioactive implants remain in place for treatment

Metal buttons hold catheter in place

Figure 9–4 Brachytherapy is often used in the treatment of breast cancer.

Hyperthermia

Hyperthermia involves using heat to raise the temperature of a specific area of the body to try to increase cell metabolism and, consequently, increase the destruction of cancer cells. Hyperthermia is usually performed as an adjunct to radiation therapy or chemotherapy. The hyperthermia codes (77600–77615) in the CPT book include external, interstitial, and **intracavitary** treatment. If administered at the same time, radiation therapy should be reported separately.

Clinical Brachytherapy

Clinical **brachytherapy** uses natural or man-made radioactive elements that are applied in or around a particular treatment field. A therapeutic radiologist provides supervision of radioactive elements and interpretation of appropriate dosages. When the services of a surgeon are needed, a modifier -66 (surgical team) or -62 (two surgeons) may be reported to ensure that both physicians are reimbursed. Codes 77750–77799 include the admission to the hospital and daily visits provided by the physician. The codes differentiate between interstitial and intracavitary brachytherapy and are further subdivided to identify the number of **sources/ ribbons** applied: simple (1–4 source ribbons), intermediate (5–10 source ribbons), or complex (>10 ribbons). CPT defines sources as intracavity placement or permanent interstitial placement. Ribbons refer to temporary interstitial placement.

▪ Highlight

Surgeons are required for this type of therapy because this procedure is done internally on a patient. If any type of complication occurs invasively, a surgeon might need to assist the radiologist.

EXERCISE 9-3

Assign the appropriate CPT codes for the following procedure(s); include modifiers and level II modifiers when applicable.

1. Teletherapy isodose plan (hand); simple (one or two) parallel opposed unmodified ports directed to a single area of interest _____

2. Radiation treatment delivery, two separate treatment areas three or more ports on a single treatment area, use of multiple blocks, 15 MEV _____

3. Hyperthermia, externally generated; superficial heating degree is 8 cm _____

4. Intracavitary radioelement application; complex _____

5. Supervision, handling, loading of radioelement _____

NUCLEAR MEDICINE

Nuclear medicine involves the administration of radioisotopes (radioactive elements that assist in the diagnosis of disease). The radioactive isotope deteriorates spontaneously and emits gamma rays from inside the body that enable the physician to view internal abnormalities. Some radioisotopes are selectively absorbed by tumors or by specific organs in the body and thus make them visible on the scan. This subsection (78000–79999) includes nuclear medicine procedures according to body systems, such as cardiovascular. Some of the more common diagnostic nuclear medicine scans include bone, cardiac, lung, renal, and thyroid scans, as well as thallium 201, technetium 99m pyrophosphate, the technetium 99m ventriculogram, and the multigated acquisition scans.

Bone Scans

Bone scans are performed as part of metastatic workups, to identify infections such as osteomyelitis; to evaluate the hip with a prosthetic device; to distinguish pathologic fractures from traumatic fractures; and to evaluate delayed union of fractures.

Cardiac Scans

Cardiac scans are performed for diagnosis of myocardial infarction, stress testing, measurement of cardiac output, and diagnosis of ventricular aneurysms.

Thallium 201 Scan

The thallium 201 scan examines myocardial perfusion, with normal myocardium appearing as "hot", and ischemic or infarcted areas appearing as "cold".

Technetium 99m Pyrophosphate Scan

The technetium 99m pyrophosphate scan identifies recently damaged myocardial tissue, and it is most sensitive 24 to 72 hours after an acute myocardial infarction.

Technetium 99m Ventriculogram Scan

The technetium 99m ventriculogram scan identifies abnormal wall motion, cardiac shunts, size and function of heart chambers, cardiac output, and ejection fraction.

Multigated Acquisition Scan

The multigated acquisition scan is another form of this type of study.

■ *Confusing Codes*

When these tests are performed during exercise and or pharmacologic stress, the appropriate stress testing code from the 93015–93018 range should be reported in addition to the appropriate code from the nuclear medicine subsection.

Lung Scans

Lung scans ventilation-perfusion [V/Q] can reveal pulmonary disease, chronic obstructive pulmonary disease, and emphysema. When performed along with chest x-rays, these scans are important tools in evaluating pulmonary emboli.

Renal and Thyroid Scans

Renal scans are performed to evaluate the overall functions of the kidneys. Thyroid scans are most commonly performed with technetium 99m pertechnetate, and they are useful in detecting nodules.

EXERCISE 9–4

Assign the appropriate CPT code for the following procedure(s). Include modifiers and Level II modifiers when applicable.

1. Thyroid imaging, with uptake; single determination _____

2. Liver and spleen imaging; static only _____

3. Cardiac shunt detection _____

4. Whole body scan _____

5. Renal scan with vascular flow and function study _____

Read the following report, then assign the correct ICD-9-CM and CPT codes for physician billing.

RADIOLOGY REPORT

Patient Name: Jan Clure   **Admitting Physician:** Ken Shallow, M.D.
Hospital No.: 11049   **Procedure:** Intraoperative cholangiogram.
X-ray No.: 98-1504   **Date:** 03/12/----

FINDINGS: Intraoperative cholangiogram was performed. Contrast was injected through the cystic duct remnant. There was mild dilatation of the common duct with free flow of contrast into the duodenum. However, there was a 6-mm filling defect in the proximal common duct that probably represents a stone.

IMPRESSION: Evidence of a common duct stone. Mild dilatation of the common bile duct.

_____
Ann Jones, M.D.

AJ:xx
D:03/13/----
T:03/13/----

C: Bernard Kester, M.D.

ICD-9-CM code(s) _____   CPT code(s) _____

Read the following report, then assign the correct ICD-9-CM and CPT codes for physician billing.

RADIOLOGY REPORT

Patient Name: Sam Chandler   **Admitting Physician:** Lisa Andrews, M.D.
Hospital No.: 11503   **Procedure:** Chest, PA only.
X-ray No.: 98-29050   **Date:** 12/13/----

When films are compared to previous radiographs, there is interval increase of the right subcutaneous emphysema. There is interval demonstration of very small pneumothorax along the right lower chest. There is some interval change in the position of the right lower chest catheter, the tip of which is seen at a lower level than in the previous exam. There is no interval change in the position of the second catheter. Heart and lungs appear unremarkable without any active process; unchanged since previous exam.

IMPRESSION: 1. Increase in right subcutaneous emphysema.
               2. Recurrent right pneumothorax, small.

_____
Larry Erwin, M.D.

LE:xx
D:12/13/----
T:12/13/----

ICD-9-CM code(s) _____   CPT code(s) _____

Read the following report, then assign the correct ICD-9-CM and CPT codes for physician billing.

RADIOLOGY REPORT

Patient Name: Ellen Parker
Hospital No.: 11259
X-ray No.: 98-2823

Admitting Physician: Sara Loyola, M.D.
Procedure: Right hip and pelvis.
Date: 09/25/----

RIGHT HIP

There is a fracture through the right femoral neck. There is also evidence of intertrochanteric fracture of the right hip. No other joint or soft tissue abnormalities.

IMPRESSION: Intertrochanteric fracture of the right hip. There also appears to be a fracture of the right femoral neck.

PELVIS

A bipolar left hip prosthesis is noted in place. There is an intertrochanteric fracture of the right hip. There also appears to be a nondisplaced fracture through the right femoral neck. No other joint or soft tissue abnormalities.

IMPRESSION: Intertrochanteric fracture of the right hip. There is also evidence of a nondisplaced fracture through the right femoral neck.

_____
Paula Robins, M.D.

PR:xx
D:09/25/----
T:09/25/----

ICD-9-CM code(s) _____   CPT code(s) _____

Read the following chart notes and radiology report and assign the correct ICD-9-CM and CPT codes for physician billing.

Grahm, Craig   6/28/----

This is a new patient in the office today complaining of an injury to the right foot. This morning he accidentally smashed his RT foot into a kitchen cabinet and has noticed pain, swelling and ache on ambulation since then.

EXAMINATION: V.S.: W-191.5, BP-110/80 (sitting), P-64 & reg, R-16, T-96. His LT FOOT is quiescent. His RT FOOT has an enlarging hematoma on the dorsum with warmth and flexion deformities of the PIP's as before with tenderness over the entire FOREFOOT region.

IMPRESSION: Trauma RT foot

PLAN: We will check an x-ray of the RT foot to R/O fracture. If there is none, he will treat with rest, ice, mild compression from a sock and elevation and after a day or 2 if he feels well may then proceed to prn heat.

ADDENDUM: Because of the results of the x-ray the 2nd and 3rd toe were taped with paper tape to help in immobilization.

_____
Lowery Johnson, M.D.

ICD-9-CM code(s) _____   CPT code(s) _____

RADIOLOGY REPORT

Patient Name: Craig Grahm   **Physician:** Lowery Johnson, M.D.

Hospital No.: 11259989-998   **Procedure:** AP & lateral of RT foot

X-Ray No.: 88-7784511   **Date:** 06/28/----

Views of the **RT FOOT** reveal a faint line of translucency in the proximal shaft in the 2nd toe about 1/3 proximal to PIP. There is also soft tissue swelling.

IMPRESSION: 1. A small non-displaced fracture of the shaft of the 2nd proximal phalanx.

_____
Carole Kincaid, M.D.
Radiologist

ICD-9-CM code(s) _____   CPT code(s) _____

Read the following chart notes and radiology report and assign the correct ICD-9-CM and CPT codes for physician billing.

Highgrove, Lynn   10/18/----

She is again about the same as on her last visit. She has had no stomatitis, dermatitis, pruritis, GI upset or increase in bruisability.

EXAMINATION: V.S.: W-178.5, BP-130/80 (sitting), P-64 & reg, R-16, T-96.4 SKIN, MOUTH & NOSE are clear (she has a rather chronic malar flush). I believe that there is more synovial thickening of PIP 5 and especially 4 on the RT which is becoming more cystic. Thickening of MCP's 2 & 3, RT greater than LT, remains a problem. Her WRISTS, ELBOWS, & SHOULDERS are unremarkable. HIPS & TROCHANTERS are essentially normal. KNEES show cool soft tissue hypertrophy with crepitation. Her ANKLES are puffy. Her FEET are quintessence with bony hypertrophy.

IMPRESSION: RA

PLAN: Call in Rx for MTX 2.5 mg #16 with no refills. Continue 10 mg q week. Continue Prednisone 7.5 mg q.o.d., calcium and vitamin D and the folic acid. I will monitor her CBC and because of the meds a liver profile and SMA. We will now evaluate x-rays of her hands to compare with those taken in 1995 to see the extent of joint damage and/or progression. We will also arrange for a DEXA bone density over the next month or two because of the chronic Prednisone dosage. She will RTO in 4 weeks but call sooner if needed.

_____
Lowery Johnson, M.D.

ICD-9-CM code(s) _____   CPT code(s) _____

RADIOLOGY REPORT

Patient Name: Lynn Highgrove   **Physician:** Lowery Johnson, M.D.
Hospital No.: 225987   **Procedure:** Bilateral Hands, AP and lateral
X-Ray No.: 99-55894778   **Date:** 10/18/----

Multiple views of the **HANDS** reveal juxta-articular osteoporosis. There is some degenerative change at each 2nd and 3rd DIP and each 1st IP joint in the LT 1st MCP. There is significant erosive and cystic change in the 3rd LT PIP with joint space narrowing, soft tissue swelling and ulnar deviation of the middle phalange. There is loss of cartilage space in the 2nd LT, 2nd 3rd RT MCP's with erosive change at MCP 2 on the RT and possibly 3. These films were compared to taken on June 5th, 1998. They show definite progression of erosive change and cartilage loss at the 3rd LT PIP and some increase in cartilage loss at the 2nd LT MCP. On the RT there is no significant change and degenerative change with spur formation is also noted from both sets of films at the 2nd RT PIP.

IMPRESSION: 1. Rheumatoid arthritis of the hands with erosions and some progression particularly in the LT 3rd PIP since 1998.

_____
Carole Kincaid, M.D.
Radiologist

ICD-9-CM code(s) _____   CPT code(s) _____

Read the following chart notes and radiology report and assign the correct ICD-9-CM and CPT codes for physician billing.

Thomas, Daniel   11/12/----

He was doing well until 4 to 5 weeks ago when he noted the onset of pain again in his LT shoulder and upper arm. It is often worse after bed and definitely worse on motion of the LT shoulder. This happened after he began gardening but he does not particularly remember traumatizing it. He also had pain and swelling in his RT 2nd PIP which is starting to feel slightly better. He has had no stomatitis, dermatitis, GI upset, chest pain or increase in fatigue.

EXAMINATION: V.S.: W-170, BP-166/76 (sitting), P-68 & reg, R-16, T-96.4 He is in some distress from LT SHOULDER pain on motion. His HANDS show bony hypertrophy but there is definite thickening, slight erythema, warmth, tenderness and pain on flexion of the RT 2nd PIP. In addition the PIP's again show some restriction of flexion due to a rather chronic tenosynovitis. His MPC's & DIP's are otherwise unremarkable. There is decrease in extension of the LT ELBOW, which is not tender or inflamed. The RT ELBOW and each WRIST are normal. There is significant limitation of abduction of the LT SHOULDER by almost 60 degrees with pain on abduction, external and internal rotation; rotation is also limited. His RT SHOULDER shows restriction of abduction by about 30 degrees with some stiffness on rotation. There is limitation of rotation and lateral tilt of the CERVICAL SPINE. THORACIC SPINE is unremarkable. He has straightening of the LUMBOSACRAL SPINE with decrease in extension and flexion but denies pain or tenderness. There is decrease in external rotation of each HIP by 40 degrees on the RT, 60 on the LT with some ache in the LT. His KNEES & ANKLES are unremarkable. His FEET show some bony hypertrophy.

IMPRESSION: Arthritis, SLE vs. RA. He also has LT shoulder capsulitis.

PLAN: I will continue to monitor his UA, SMA-7 and liver profile because of the NSAID and also check a sed rate again to R/O traumatic arthropathy. We will check an x-ray of his LT shoulder today. In addition he will receive 80 mg of DepoMedrol IM and begin the use of Darvocet-N-100 q 6 h prn pain. Given Rx for #60 with 3 refills. He may increase the Naprolan to 500 mg t.i.d., p.c. for 10 days. He was then reminded again about ROM exercises for his LT shoulder including wall, crawl, pendulum exercises and isometric rotator cuff strengthening. If he is not better over the next 10 days he will call and injection may be warranted. Otherwise RTO in about 6 months but call sooner if needed.

_____
Lowery Johnson, M.D.

ICD-9-CM code(s) _____   CPT code(s) _____

RADIOLOGY REPORT

Patient Name: Daniel Thomas **Physician:** Lowery Johnson, M.D.
Hospital No.: 11503 **Procedure:** Left Shoulder, AP and Lateral
X-ray No.: 98-2922560 **Date:** 11/12/----

Views of the **LT SHOULDER** reveal large cystic areas in the humeral head. There is a considerable amount of calcification around the bicipital groove and in the subacromial space with corticated erosions on the superior surface of the humeral head near the bicipital groove and another erosive lesion on the inferomedial aspect of the humerus. A small spur is also seen near the superior border of the glenoid fossa and at the medial inferior border of the head of humerus at the medial aspect of the erosion. The acromioclavicular joint is well maintained. The glenohumeral articulation appears normal.

IMPRESSION: 1. Erosive arthropathy of the LT humeral head with degenerative osteoarthritis.
　　　　　　　　2. Calcific subacromial bursitis.

　　　　　　　　　　　　　　　　　　　Carole Kincaid, M.D.
　　　　　　　　　　　　　　　　　　　Radiologist

ICD-9-CM code(s) _____　　CPT code(s) _____

CPT-PATHOLOGY AND LABORATORY

Similar to radiology, clinical laboratory testing is critical to the detection, diagnosis, and treatment of disease. Under physicians' orders, medical technologists, technicians, or other qualified laboratory personnel perform a range of specialized tests by examining body fluids, such as urine or blood, tissues, and cells. Laboratory personnel prepare patient specimens for examination and interpret tests, looking for microorganisms, such as parasites, analyzing the chemical contents of body fluids, and matching blood types. All test results are then reported to the physician who initially ordered the test.

The pathology and laboratory section of CPT includes services by a physician or by technologists under the responsible supervision of a physician. This section includes codes for such services and procedures as organ or disease panel tests, urinalysis, hematologic and immunologic studies and surgical and anatomic pathologic examinations.

These are the specific subsections in this chapter:

Organ or Disease Oriented Panels	80049–80092
Drug Testing	80100–80103
Therapeutic Drug Assays	80150–80299
Evocative/suppression Testing	80400–80440
Consultations (clinical Pathology)	80500–80502
Urinalysis	81000–81099
Chemistry	82000–84999
Hematology and Coagulation	85002–85999
Immunology	86000–86849
Transfusion Medicine	86850–86999
Microbiology	87001–87999
Anatomic Pathology	88000–88099
Cytopathology	88104–88199
Cytogenetic Studies	88230–88299
Surgical Pathology	88300–88399
Other Procedures	89050–89399

Physician Billing

When reporting laboratory services provided by the physician, the coder must determine whether the physician performed the complete procedure or only a component of it. Some physician offices maintain sophisticated laboratory equipment on their premises so they are able to provide complete lab testing. A complete test would include obtaining the sample/specimen (blood or urine), handling the specimen, performing the actual procedure/test, and analyzing and interpreting the results. Most physicians will send their blood to an outside lab or a hospital lab for testing. In these cases the physician may only report the collection and handling of the specimen.

> *Example: Biopsy of the ovary performed by Dr. Smith and the specimen was sent to a pathologist for review and interpretation. Dr. Smith uses the code 58900 for the actual biopsy of the ovary. The pathologist reports 88305 for the review and interpretation of the specimen.*

CLIA '88

The Clinical Laboratory Improvement Amendments (CLIA 1988) was passed by Congress in 1988 and enacted in 1992 to improve the quality of laboratory tests performed on specimens taken from the human body and used in diagnosis, prevention and treatment of disease. All laboratories must register with CLIA '88 and comply with its requirements to be certified by the United States Department of Health and Human Services (DHHS). A few laboratories, such as those that perform only forensic tests, those certified by the National Institute on Drug Abuse to perform urine testing, those that perform research unrelated to patient treatment, and those that are with licensure are exempt (such as Rhode Island) from CLIA '88 regulations.

CLIA '88 designated four levels of testing based on complexity: waived tests, physician-performed microscopy tests (also waived tests), moderate complexity tests, and high complexity tests. Waived tests and physician-performed microscopy tests are of low complexity (see Table 9–1). To perform these tests a laboratory must obtain a certificate of waiver. Approximately 75% of all tests performed in the United States are of moderate complexity and include tests such as throat cultures, white blood counts, Gram staining, and urine cultures. High complexity tests involve specialized procedures in cytogenetics, histocompatability, histopathology and cytology. Laboratories performing moderate- and high-complexity tests go through a series of HCFA certifications and are inspected by the DHHS every two years.

Quantitative and Qualitative Studies

The laboratory and pathology section includes codes that will state whether the procedure is **quantitative** or **qualitative** in nature. Qualitative screening refers to tests that detect the presence of a particular analyte (substance), constituent or condition. Typically, qualitative studies are performed first to determine if a particular substance is present in the sample being evaluated. In contrast, quantitative studies provide results expressing specific numerical amounts of an analyte in a sample. These tests are usually performed after a qualitative study and identify the specific amount of a particular substance in the sample.

> *Example: Gonadotropin Chorionic (hcg) quantitative code 84702 represents a pregnancy test. When this test comes back from the lab it will have a titer or number that*

TABLE 9–1   Waived Tests.

Dipstick or tablet reagent urinalysis for the following:

- Bilirubin
- Glucose
- Hemoglobin
- Ketone
- Leukocytes
- Nitrite
- pH
- Protein
- Specific gravity
- Urobilinogen

Fecal occult blood

Spun microhematocrit

Microscopic examination of the following:

- Urine sediment
- Pinworm preparation
- Vaginal wet mount preparation

Ovulation tests: visual color tests for human luteinizing hormone

Whole blood clotting time

Urine pregnancy tests

Slide card agglutination tests to screen for the following:

- Antistreptolysin O (ASO)
- C reactive protein (CRP)
- Rheumatoid factor
- Infectious mononucleosis

Gram stain (on discharges and exudates)

Potassium hydroxide (KOH) preparation on cutaneous scrapings

Erythrocyte sedimentation rate

Sickle cell screening: methods other than electrophoresis

Glucose screen whole blood dipstick method: visual color comparison determination

Semen analysis

Automated hemoglobin by single analyte instruments

represents how many weeks the patient is pregnant. Gonadotropin Chorionic (hcg) qualitative code 84703 represents a pregnancy test with a negative or positive reading.

Pathology and Laboratory Modifiers

These are some of the most commonly used modifiers in the pathology and laboratory section.

- **-22 (09922)   Unusual Procedural Services**

  This modifier is intended for use when the service provided is greater than the one usually required for the listed procedure.

- **-26 (09926)   Professional Component**

  In circumstances where a laboratory or pathologic procedure includes both a physician (professional) component and a technical component, modifier -26 can be reported to identify the physician (professional) component.

- **-32 (09932)   Mandated Services**

  Modifier -32 may be reported when groups such as a third party payer or peer review organization mandates a service.

- **-52 (09952)   Reduced Services**

  Modifier -52 may be reported to indicate that a laboratory or pathologic procedure is partially reduced or eliminated at the discretion of the physician.

- **-53 (09953)   Discontinued Procedure**

  Modifier -53 may be reported to indicate that the physician elected to terminate a procedure due to circumstances that puts the patient at risk.

- **-59 (09959)   Distinct Procedural Service**

  Modifier -59 may be used to identify that a procedure or service was distinct or independent from other services provided on the same day. This modifier may be used when procedures are performed together because of a specific circumstance, though they usually are not.

- **-90 (09990)   Reference (Outside) Laboratory**

  Modifier -90 may be reported to indicate that another party besides the reporting physician performed the actual laboratory procedure.

  > *Example: Dr. Smith performed a venipuncture to obtain a blood sample for an obstetrical panel. He prepared the sample for transport and it was sent to an outside lab for testing. Dr. Smith should report 80055-90 or 80055 and 09990 to describe the laboratory test with the interpretation and analysis being performed at an offsite lab, along with a code for the venipuncture, 36415.*

ORGAN OR DISEASE ORIENTED PANELS

The series of codes 80049–80092 describe laboratory procedures known as panels or profiles in which more than one procedure is typically performed from one blood sample. Some of the panels in this series include the basic metabolic panel, the general health panel, and the electrolyte panel. For example, the basic metabolic panel includes all of the following:

Carbon Dioxide
Chloride
Creatinine
Glucose
Potassium
Sodium
Urea Nitrogen (Bun)

Previously, CPT listed automated multichannel testing, which included a series of chemistries from one to nineteen tests. CPT has eliminated these multichannel tests and has developed a new series of tests that are located in the organ or disease oriented panels. These panel components are not intended to limit the performance of other tests. If one performs tests specifically indicated for a particular panel, those tests should be reported separately in addition to the panel. (CPT-98)

EVOCATIVE/SUPPRESSION TESTING

These tests (code range 80400–80440) allow the physician to determine a baseline of the chemical and the effects on the body after evocative (materials that a patient must take because the body does not produce them naturally) or suppressive agents are administered. In reviewing the codes in this series, note that the description for each panel identifies the type of test included in that panel, as well as the number of times a specific test must be performed.

> *Example: 80422 Glucagon tolerance panel, for insulinoma. This panel must include the following:*
> *Glucose (82947 x 3)*
> *Insulin (83525 x 3)*

Note Attendance and monitoring by the physician during the test should be reported with the appropriate code as well as the prolonged physician care codes if they apply.

CHEMISTRY

This series of codes (82000–84999) is used to report individual chemistry tests. Examination of these specimens is quantitative unless specified. Clinical information derived from the results of laboratory data that is mathematically calculated (final calculations after all specimens have been analyzed through a machine) is considered part of the test procedure and therefore is not a separately reportable service. (CPT-1998)

> *Example: Free Thyroxine Index (T7)*

HEMATOLOGY AND COAGULATION

This series of codes in range 85002–85999 is used to report such procedures as complete blood counts (CBC) and bone marrow aspiration and biopsy, and coagulation procedures such as a partial thromboplastin time (PTT). A complete blood count includes:

White Blood Cell Count (WBC)	Mean Corpuscular Volume (MCV)
Red Blood Cell Count (RBC)	Differential Screen (WBC)
Hemoglobin (HGB)	Platelet Count
Hematocrit (HCT)	Mean Corpuscular Hemoglobin (MCH)
Mean Corpuscular Hemoglobin Concentration (MCHC)	

▬ *Confusing Codes*

When coding the different types of procedures in the hematology and coagulation section, the coder should understand the difference between automated and manual testing. **Automated** *testing is the use of clinical laboratory instruments that assay large numbers of samples (blood, urine, etc.) mechanically, and* **manual** *testing is performed by or with hands.*

IMMUNOLOGY

This series of codes (86000–86849) is used to report components of the immune system and their functions. Different procedures that are done in this section are HIV testing and testing for infectious agents/antigens.

> *Example: 86592 Syphilis test Qualitative*
> *86803 Hepatitis C Antibody*

TRANSFUSION MEDICINE

This series of codes (86850–86999) is used to report blood typing, transfusion, and antibody identification.

MICROBIOLOGY

This series of codes (87001–87999) is used to report identification and classification of different types of bacteria identification methods. For example, separate codes exist for different types of cultures, such as stool, throat or urine. This section also covers mycology, parasitology, and virology.

ANATOMIC PATHOLOGY

This series of codes (88000–88099) is used to report autopsies. These codes represent physician services only. Use modifier -90 or 09990 for outside laboratory services.

CYTOPATHOLOGY

This series of codes (88104–88299) is used to report Pap smears, needle aspirations, and chromosomal testing.

SURGICAL PATHOLOGY

This series of codes (88300–88399) is used to report specimens removed during surgical procedures known as a unit of service. CPT defines a specimen as "tissue or tissues that is/are submitted for individual and separate attention, requiring examination and pathologic diagnosis."

Services 88300–88309 include accession, examination and reporting of the specimen. Service codes 88304–88309 describe all other specimens requiring gross and microscopic examination, and represent additional ascending levels of physician work.

Level I	88300	Surgical pathology diagnosed by gross examination only, without microscopic examination Example: Gross examination of renal calculi
Level II	88302	Gross and microscopic to confirm identification and the absence of disease. Example: Foreskin, newborn
Levels III–VI	88304–88309	All other specimens requiring gross and microscopic examination, and represent additional ascending levels of physician work.

Examples:
Level III 88304 Tonsil and/or adenoids
Level IV 88305 Kidney biopsy; colorectal biopsy
Level V 88307 Non-traumatic extremity amputation
Level VI 88309 Total resection of colon

When submitting two or more specimens, separate codes should be used to identify the appropriate level for each.

Example: Gross and microscopic examination of two separate fallopian tube biopsies. The pathologist reports the codes 88305 and 88305 to identify the examination of two separate specimens.

■ Highlight

Codes 88300–88309 include the accession, examination, and reporting of a specimen. When performed by the pathologist, services identified in codes 88311–88365 and 88399 may be reported.

EXERCISE 9–5

Code the pathology and laboratory procedures; use two-digit modifiers when applicable.

1. Sedimentation rate _____

2. Urine pregnancy test, by visual color comparisons _____

3. General health panel _____

4. Cytopathology smears up to three with definitive hormonal evaluation _____

5. Vitamin K _____

6. Confirmatory test for HIV-1 antibody _____

7. Folic acid; serum _____

8. Chlamydia, IGM _____

9. Ova and parasites, direct smears concentration and identification _____

10. Hemogram and platelet count automated and manual differential count _____

11. Urinalysis non-automated without the microscope _____

12. Histamine _____

13. Basic metabolic panel _____

14. Prothrombin time _____

15. Syphilis test qualitative _____

SUMMARY

As doctors and scientists learn about the causes of various types of diseases, we as coders will continue to learn each and every year more and more codes with higher levels of specificity. Each year as the American Medical Association looks at the changes in the health field, we will continue to see new and better technology.

In dealing with Radiology and Pathology/Laboratory, technology will always be advancing and will give you an opportunity for more coding of very exciting procedures.

REFERENCES

Cowling, Cynthia (1998). *Delmar's Radiographic Positioning and Procedures, Volume II Advanced Imaging Procedures.* Albany, NY: Delmar Publishers.

Lindh, W.Q., et al, (1998). *Delmar's Comprehensive Medical Assisting: Administrative and Clinical Competencies.* Albany, NY: Delmar Publishers.

Pfeiffer, MaryLou, BA, RT, (R)(M). *Basic Radiography* (Self Manual). (1997).

Stepp, C. and Woods, M.A. (1998) *Laboratory Procedures for Medical Office Personnel.* Philadelphia, PA: W.B. Saunders.

Module 10
Billing and Collections

Sandra L. Johnson, CMA

LEARNING OBJECTIVES

Upon successful completion of this module, you should be able to:

1. Explain the importance of billing and collection practices in the outpatient setting.
2. Demonstrate the patient registration process.
3. Prepare a ledger card showing charges, payments, and adjustments, indicating new patient balance.
4. Compare the advantages and disadvantages between cycle billing and monthly billing.
5. List the advantages and disadvantages of a computerized billing system.
6. Explain the accounts receivable process.
7. Explain account aging and the purpose of an age analysis.

INTRODUCTION

Previous modules have discussed coding rules including specialty area guidelines. This module gives instruction in proper billing techniques and the collection of payment in the ambulatory care setting.

It is estimated that 94% of patients have some type of insurance coverage or third party payer involvement. This requires the following responsibilities of front office personnel:

- new patient registration and established patient recheck
- interpretation of insurance contracts
- preparation of the encounter form
- posting financial transactions to the patient account or ledger card

A major objective of accurately coding diagnoses and procedures and submitting claims with correct information is to receive reimbursement for services rendered. This leads to another vital function in any facility—the billing and collections process. Obtaining information for billing occurs the first time the patient comes into the office, clinic or hospital and completes the registration form. This information is then checked with the patient on each return to the facility in order to maintain updated patient records, both medical and financial.

Lowery B. Johnson, M.D.
Hwy 311 Suite A31
Sellersburg, IN 47172
812-246-1234

Please complete this form.

NAME: _____

STREET ADDRESS: _____ APT: _____

CITY: _____ STATE: _____ ZIP: _____

HOME PHONE (& area code) _____

WORK PHONE: (& area code) _____

SOCIAL SECURITY NUMBER: _____

SEX: Male _____ Female _____ Age _____ Date of Birth _____

MARITAL STATUS: Married _____ Single _____ Separated _____ Divorced _____ Widowed _____

PERSON TO CONTACT IN EMERGENCY: _____ PHONE: _____

EMPLOYED: Full Time _____ Part Time _____ Retired _____ Not Employed _____

EMPLOYER: Company Name: _____ Phone: _____

       Address: _____

       Location/Department Where You Work: _____

STUDENT STATUS: Full-time Student _____ School _____

                Part-time Student _____ School _____

INSURANCE COMPANY: _____

    Policy Number: _____ Group Number: _____

    Name of Insured: _____ Relationship to You: _____

    Address: _____

    Deductible: _____ Percent of Coverage: _____

OTHER INSURANCE COMPANY: _____

    Policy Number: _____ Group Number: _____

    Name of Insured: _____ Relationship to You: _____

    Address: _____

    Deductible: _____ Percent of Coverage: _____

WHAT BRINGS YOU TO SEE THE DOCTOR? _____

_____

IS YOUR CONDITION RELATED TO:

      AUTO ACCIDENT: _____ DATE: _____ STATE WHERE OCCURRED: _____

      OTHER ACCIDENT: _____ DATE: _____ STATE WHERE OCCURRED: _____

      YOUR EMPLOYMENT: _____

ARE YOU ALLERGIC TO ANY MEDICATIONS: _____

REFERRED TO US BY: _____

CHECK HERE IF REFERRED BY PHYSICIAN: _____

Figure 10–1 Patient Registration Form.

PATIENT REGISTRATION

Patient registration forms vary from practice to practice but all should contain the following information (as exhibited in Figure 10–1):

- patient name, address, birth date, social security number, marital status
- telephone numbers where patient can be reached, both home and work
- insurance information—carrier's name, name of insured, plan name/identification number, group and/or policy numbers
- name of responsible party (spouse, parent, guardian)
- address, phone number, social security number of responsible party and the relationship to the patient
- a photocopy of the patient's driver's license

▪ *Highlight*

It is important to always request the insurance card(s) and photocopy both the front and back sides to keep in the patient file as indicated in Figure 10–2.

Fee Schedules

Before the process of billing and the collection of payment is discussed, it is essential to understand that patient fees are based on three commodities the physician provides: time, judgment, and services.

Individual medical practices determine fees that will be charged for those services and procedures performed in the office. This fee schedule may be based upon several factors:

- The economic level of the community
- The physician's experience
- The medical specialty of the practice
- Charges of other physicians in the area
- The cost of the service or supply

Anthem

THIS CARD REQUIRES PRIOR AUTHORIZATION
Refer to back of card.

An independent licensee of the Blue Cross and Blue Shield Association. Anthem Blue Cross and Blue Shield is the trade name of the Anthem Insurance Companies, Inc. ®Registered marks Blue Cross and Blue Shield Association.

Member Name
Hannah Marks
Identification Number
XPN330-11-6723

CUSTOMER SERVICE
LOCAL 317-889-8779
TOLL FREE 1-800-553-2084

Account Number	BS Plan Code	BC Plan Code
24995	630	130

PPN INCENTIVE/COST GUARD
Benefit Code
89999   Community R$_X$

Effective Date
07-01-97

NOTICE: Precertification or Preauthorization does NOT guarantee coverage for or the payment of the service or procedure reviewed.

You must call COST GUARD before hospitalization except in these cases:
Emergency – call within 48 hours
Maternity – call within 24 hours
LOCAL (317) 298-6600
TOLL FREE 1(800) 367-4207

HOSPITALS/PHYSICIANS OUTSIDE OF INDIANA: file Medical claims with your local BCBS plan.

Submit ALL OTHER claims to:
ACORDIA OF CENTRAL INDIANA, INC.
P.O. Box 567
Greenwood, Indiana 46142

Transplant Benefits: 1-800-443-2269

Figure 10–2 Insurance card (front and back).

EXERCISE 10–1

1. List the three commodities a physician has to sell when setting fees for the medical office.

   a. _____

   b. _____

   c. _____

2. What is the purpose of copying the patient's insurance card and retaining it in the patient's medical chart?

The maximum amount the insurance carrier or government program will cover for specified services is called the allowable charge. The difference between the physician charge and the allowable charge is called a non-allowed charge. Allowable charges are often based on **Usual, Customary and Reasonable fees (UCR)**.

USUAL—The physician's average fee for a service or procedure.

CUSTOMARY—The average fee for that service or procedure within an area, based on national trends rather than regional or local customs.

REASONABLE—A fee that is generally accepted for a service or procedure that is extraordinarily difficult or complicated, requiring more time or effort for the physician to perform.

EXAMPLE—Dr. Johnson charges $150 for a new patient office visit including a complete history and physical examination. The usual fee charged for this same service of other physicians in the same community with similar training and experience ranges from $125 to $200. Dr. Johnson's fee of $150 is within the customary range and would be paid under an insurance plan's usual and customary basis.

EXERCISE 10–2

1. Dr. Dogood, a gastroenterologist, performs flexible diagnostic sigmoidoscopies in the office. His charge for this procedure is $195. The usual fee charged for this procedure by other gastroenterologists in this city is from $190 to $210.

   Is Dr. Dogood's fee within the usual and customary range for insurance payment?

Physicians who participate in federally funded medical insurance programs, such as Medicaid, CHAMPUS/TRICARE, and CHAMPVA, must accept the UCR fee as payment in full. The patient cannot be billed the difference between their fee and the UCR fee. The amount would be adjusted on the patient's account. Most private insurance carriers utilize UCR fees but are not regulated under federal law. Therefore, the patient with a private insurance company can be billed the difference.

Before 1989, Medicare Part B used customary, prevailing and reasonable charges in a fee-for-service payment system. In 1989, the **Resource-Based Relative Value System (RBRVS)** was passed to reform Medicare payments to physicians. In January 1992, implementation of the RBRVS took place with the new payment system of **Medicare Fee Schedule (MFS)**. All physicians' services are listed on the MFS with reimbursement made at 80% of the fee schedule amount. The Medicare Fee Schedule is the method of payment for physicians' services, outpatient physical and occupational therapy services, radiology services, and diagnostic tests. This fee schedule is updated annually on April 15.

RBRVS assigns a CPT code, which has an associated relative value unit (RVU). Therefore, each medical service reflects the physician's skill and time required to perform the service, professional liability expenses related to that service, and overhead costs associated with the service.

The relative value units are converted to dollar amounts based on the code assignments, which form the basis of the RBRVS fee schedule. This schedule, in turn, creates uniform payments with adjustments made for geographic differences. Thus, the growth rate of spending for physicians' services, procedures, and supplies has been significantly reduced for Medicare Part B patients since the 1992 implementation of RBRVS.

A **limiting charge** is percentage limitation on fees that **nonparticipating physicians(nonPARs)** are allowed to bill Medicare patients above the fee schedule amount. The limiting charge applies to every service listed in the Medicare Physician's Fee Schedule that is performed by a nonparticipating (nonPAR) physician, including global, professional, and technical services. Different prices are listed for each CPT code. The fee schedule amount is determined by multiplying the relative value unit (RVU) weight by the geographic index and the conversion factor. The **participating physician (PAR)** receives the fee schedule amount. For the nonparticipating physician, the fee schedule amount of the allowable payment is slightly less than the participating physician's payment. Module 11 further explains nonPAR versus PAR requirements.

The limiting amount is a percentage over the allowable 115 percent times the allowable amount. The limiting charge is important because that is the maximum amount a Medicare patient can be billed for a service. Medicare usually pays 80 percent of the allowable amount for covered services. The patient can then be billed the difference between the Medicare payment and the limiting charge. The patient is notified of the limiting charge for each service on the Medicare Remittance Advice.

AMBULATORY PATIENT GROUPS

Another proposed change in the billing of outpatient services and procedures for Medicare patients will be implemented in the near future. **Ambulatory Patient Groups (APGs)** or Ambulatory Patient Classification (APC) are outpatient classification system for Medicare patients where payment is based on procedure rather than on the diagnosis. The Diagnosis-Related Groups (DRGs) classification, used for payment of inpatient services, has proven to be a cost-effective payment system. APGs are expected to do the same for outpatient services.

APG services will be classified as either medical visits or procedure visits. The assignment of the procedure APG is based on the CPT and ICD-9-CM codes, the patient's age and sex, and other information submitted on the Medicare claim form. Each procedure will be assigned to one of the twelve body systems and then subdivided based on the method of the procedure.

The medical APG is based on the diagnosis coded as the reason for the patient's visit. The etiology of the diagnosis is used to subdivide the APG such as well care, pregnancy, or trauma. Further division will be based on body system.

DRGs is a classification system that groups inpatients in relation to diagnosis and treatment of the hospitalization. This results in a fixed-fee payment to the hospital based on the diagnosis rather than fee for service.

DRG classifications were derived from more than 10,000 ICD-9-CM codes divided into 25 major diagnostic categories (MDGs). These diagnoses were assigned a DRG number and a specific value in relation to geographic area, type of hospital, teaching status of the hospital, and other specifications. DRG classifications are based on:

- principal diagnosis
- secondary diagnosis
- surgical procedures
- age and sex of the patient
- comorbidity and complications
- discharge status

APGs will differ in that this patient classification system explains the amount and type of resources used in an outpatient visit.

PAYMENT & BILLING PROCESSES

Payment at Time of Service

Communication lines must be open between the patient and the medical office to maintain effective collection practices. Patients should know upfront the provider's billing policies and collection procedures. Use the patient's initial contact with the office as the first point of control for collections. When making the appointment for the new patient, take a few minutes to discuss payment policies. Get insurance information at this time to check provider participation agreement. This saves both the staff and the patient valuable time. When appointments are scheduled for established patients, they can be reminded of an outstanding balance and asked to make a payment when they come in.

A patient brochure is an effective method to explain the office's payment and collection policies established by the physician employers and managers of the practice as indicated in Figure 10–3. The brochure can be mailed to the new patient prior to the first appointment. Patients appreciate knowing their payment responsibilities. If the patient anticipates a problem in meeting the outlined payment policy, a payment schedule can be worked out that is agreeable to both the patient and the office.

Displaying a notice in the office stating that payment at time of service is required has the following advantages:

- It ensures prompt collection of fees.
- It eliminates further bookkeeping work.
- It reduces the cost of preparing and mailing a statement to the patient.
- It increases cash flow for the practice.

Many offices encourage payment at time of service by accepting cash, personal checks and major credit cards.

When a patient pays in cash, carefully count the cash before placing it in the cash drawer. Always prepare a receipt to give to the patient as a record of cash payment as shown in Figure 10–4.

Figure 10–3 Billing and insurance excerpts from a patient brochure.

When a patient pays by check, review the check to see that it is properly written:

- The date is current.
- The amount of the check is the correct amount.
- The name of the physician or practice is spelled properly.
- The person whose name is imprinted on the check signs the check.
- Never accept a check for more than the amount due.
- If a patient is new or unfamiliar, identification can be requested.

An example is shown in Figure 10–5.

Immediately endorse the check and place in the cash drawer for the bank deposit to be made that day.

Credit cards are now becoming an accepted method of payment in the medical office. Patients find credit cards convenient especially when the bill is large. When a patient pays by credit card, follow these steps for proper processing of the charge:

Figure 10–4 Receipt for payment given to a patient, especially cash payments.

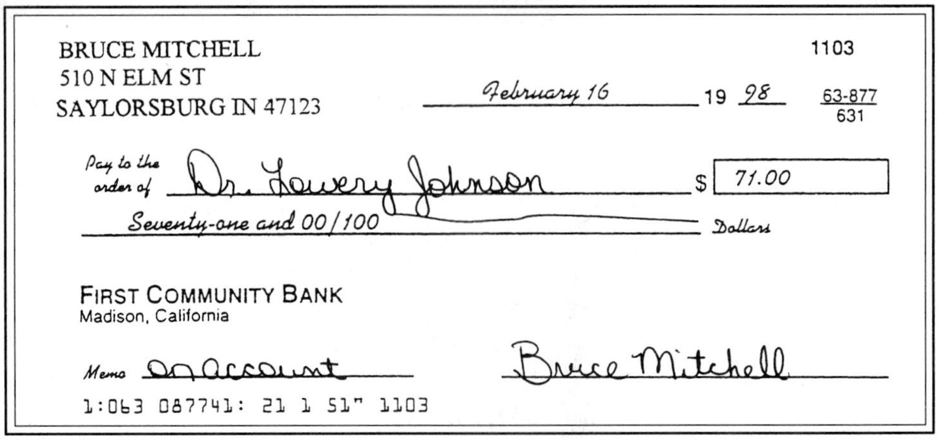
BRUCE MITCHELL
510 N ELM ST
SAYLORSBURG IN 47123
1103
February 16 19 98
63-877
631
Pay to the order of Dr. Lowery Johnson $ 71.00
Seventy-one and 00/100 Dollars
FIRST COMMUNITY BANK
Madison, California
Memo on account
Bruce Mitchell
1:063 087741: 21 1 51" 1103

Figure 10–5 Payment by check.

1. Check the expiration date.
2. Place the credit card and voucher in the credit card imprinter.
3. Write in the date.
4. Circle the type of credit card used.
5. Obtain the authorization code. This is done by calling the credit card company, or automatically transmitting the credit card information by a telephone transmission device. The credit card is swiped through the device. The amount to be charged is entered on the keypad, and the authorization code is displayed on the screen. This number is then written on the voucher.
6. Enter services provided and the amount of charges including total charge.
7. The patient signs the voucher. Verify the signature on the voucher with the one on the credit card.
8. Keep one copy of the voucher for the office.
9. Return the card and the other copy of the voucher to the patient.

To accept credit cards in the medical office, the credit card company must be contacted to establish the account. There is a service charge to accept credit cards that is deducted from payment issued to the office. For example, if a patient charges services totaling $50 on a credit card, the office will receive between $45 and $49.

The American Medical Association (AMA) condones the acceptance of credit cards in the medical office but advises not to use this as an advertising lure for the practice. Also, patients paying by credit card should not be charged higher fees to recover the service charge by the credit card company to the practice.

Credit and Payment Policy

Payment at time of service is not always possible for all patients and for many practices. Therefore, it is important to have a formal credit and collection policy established. Following are some questions to address in setting up this policy:

- When will payment be due from the patient?
- What kind of payment arrangements can be made?
- How and when will patients be reminded of overdue accounts?
- When is the bill considered delinquent?

- When exceptions are made to the policy, who makes them?
- Will a collection agency be utilized?

A written, straightforward credit and collection policy will eliminate confusion and serve as a guide to both the patient and the billing personnel.

In some situations, a payment schedule is arranged with determination of a down payment, whether interest is to be charged, and scheduling of installment payments scheduled. When there is a bilateral agreement between the physician and the patient to pay for a procedure in more than four installments, the physician must disclose finance charges in writing. The **Truth-In-Lending Act** (also known as Regulation Z of the Consumer Protection Act of 1969) requires providers of installment credit to clearly state the charge in writing and express the interest as an annual rate. Even if no finance charges are made, the form must be completed and must contain the following conditions:

- fees for services
- amount of any down payment
- the date each payment is due
- the date of the final payment
- the amount of each payment
- any interest charges to be made

The AMA rules that it is appropriate to assess finance or late charges on past due accounts, if the patient is given advance notice. This can be done by:

- displaying a notice at the reception desk.
- publishing the notice in the patient brochure.
- including the notice on the patient statement.

Figure 10–6 gives an example of notice of late charges on the patient registration form.

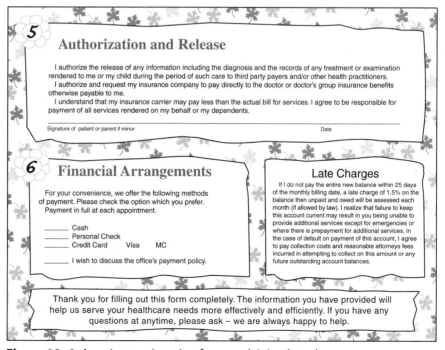

5 Authorization and Release

I authorize the release of any information including the diagnosis and the records of any treatment or examination rendered to me or my child during the period of such care to third party payers and/or other health practitioners.
I authorize and request my insurance company to pay directly to the doctor or doctor's group insurance benefits otherwise payable to me.
I understand that my insurance carrier may pay less than the actual bill for services. I agree to be responsible for payment of all services rendered on my behalf or my dependents.

_____
Signature of patient or parent if minor   Date

6 Financial Arrangements

For your convenience, we offer the following methods of payment. Please check the option which you prefer. Payment in full at each appointment.

_____ Cash
_____ Personal Check
_____ Credit Card   Visa   MC

_____ I wish to discuss the office's payment policy.

Late Charges

If I do not pay the entire new balance within 25 days of the monthly billing date, a late charge of 1.5% on the balance then unpaid and owed will be assessed each month (if allowed by law). I realize that failure to keep this account current may result in you being unable to provide additional services except for emergencies or where there is prepayment for additional services. In the case of default on payment of this account, I agree to pay collection costs and reasonable attorneys fees incurred in attempting to collect on this amount or any future outstanding account balances.

Thank you for filling out this form completely. The information you have provided will help us serve your healthcare needs more effectively and efficiently. If you have any questions at anytime, please ask – we are always happy to help.

Figure 10–6 A patient registration form explaining late charges.

The patient signs the agreement and is given a copy. A copy is retained with the patient's record. If a patient decides to pay a certain amount on a bill monthly, with the office billing monthly for the full amount, and there are no interest charges applied, the Truth-In-Lending Act does not apply. Figure 10–7 gives an example of this agreement.

Lowery B. Johnson, M.D.
Hwy 311 Suite A31
Sellersburg, IN 47172
812-241-1234

TRUTH-IN-LENDING PAYMENT AGREEMENT

Patient ___Autumn Leaf___

Address ___10586 Payment Place #2 E___

___Sellersburg, IN 47178___

I agree to pay $ 200.00 per ~~week~~/month on my account balance of $ 1000.00 .

Payments are due by the ___5th___ of each Month and will begin ___May 5, 19XX___
                                        (week/month)   (date)

Interest will/will not be charged on the outstanding balance (see Truth-In-Lending form below for rate of interest).

I agree that if payments are not made in the full amount stated above or if payments are not received on time, the entire account balance will be considered delinquent and will be due and payable immediately.

I agree to be responsible for any reasonable collection costs or attorney fees incurred in collecting a delinquent account.

_____   _____
Date   Signature

This disclosure is in compliance with the Truth-In-Lending Act.

_____   _____
Responsible Party if other than patient   City, State Zip Code

1. Cash Price (Medical and/or Surgical Fee)	$	1200.00
Less cash down payment (Advance)	$	200.00
2. Unpaid Balance of Cash Price	$	1000.00
3. Amount Financed	$	1000.00
4. FINANCE CHARGE	$	– 0 –
5. Total of Payments (3+4)	$	1000.00
6. Deferred Payment Price (1+4)	$	1200.00
7. ANNUAL PERCENTAGE RATE		– 0 –

The "Total of Payments" shown above is payable to Lowery B. Johnson, M.D., at the address shown above in ___5___ monthly installments of $ 200.00 , the first installment being payable ___May 5th___ , 19XX, and all subsequent installments are due on the same day of each consecutive month until paid in full.

_____   _____
Date   Signature

Figure 10–7 Truth-In-Lending Agreement.

BILLING

Patient billing can range from a simple process to a more complicated procedure. It must be done efficiently and accurately and in an organized manner. Receiving payment for services rendered is the income of the practice and necessary for it to succeed. Billing can be handled internally by the medical office staff, or, for a fee, by an outside billing agency. The type of billing done within the medical facility depends on the size of the practice, the patient load and financial goals.

Payment at the time of service is becoming increasingly common and is the best opportunity to collect fees. The superbill or charge slip, as indicated in Figure 10–8, is given to the patient at the end of the visit, serving as the first statement.

The Complete Statement

Statements to patients must be professional looking, legible, accurate, and include all services and charges. They should contain not only the information for the patient but information needed to process medical insurance claims:

- Patient's name and address
- Patient's insurance identification number
- Insurance carrier
- Date of service
- Description of service
- Accurate procedure (CPT) and diagnosis (ICD-9-CM) codes for insurance processing

DUPLEX PRODUCTS INC.

PLEASE RETURN THIS FORM TO THE RECEPTIONIST

PREVIOUS BALANCE | NAME JANE HENSON

ATTENDING PHYSICIAN'S STATEMENT AMA Current Procedural Terminology (1996)

CODE*	PROCEDURE	FEE
99202	Office visit, new patient (20 min.)	$
99203	Office visit, new patient (30 min.)	55.00
99212	Office visit, established patient (10 min.)	
99214	Office visit, established patient (25 min.)	
99242	Consultation, outpatient	
99252	Consultation, inpatient	
99221	Hospital visits, initial	
99231	Hospital visits, subsequent	
85013	Hematocrit	
82948	Glucose	
45310	Sigmoidoscopy	
93000	Electrocardiogram	
99000	Blood Handling	
81000	URINALYSIS	18.00

*Copyright 1996, American Medical Association

DIAGNOSIS: CYSTITIS 595.9

RB40BC-5-96

RETURN: ____ Days ____ Weeks ____ Months NEXT APPT. ____ Day ____ Month ____ Date ____ Time AM PM

Date of Service 5/6/9X

PATIENT JANE HENSON

PLACE OF SERVICE: (If Other Than Office)

☐ Hospital ________ ☐ Other ________

I hereby authorize payment directly to the physician whose name appears on this form.

Signature ________________ __/__/__

TOTAL CHARGE $ 73.00

260

I.D. # 23 7485319 Provider # 19368

Lowery B. Johnson, M.D.
Hwy 311 Suite A31
Sellersburg, IN 47172
812-246-1234

Figure 10–8 Superbill, encounter form, charge slip.

- Itemization of fees for services performed with changes totalled
- Provider's name, address, and telephone number

Figure 10–9A & B are examples of a complete statement.

Not all patients are able to pay at time of service and not all practices can accommodate this type of payment method. Sending a statement in the mail can be accomplished by:

- mailing a copy of the ledger card as a statement.
- mailing a special statement form, which can be typed or printed.
- mailing a computer-generated statement resulting in a more professional looking statement.

In mailing any statement, always enclose a self-addressed return envelope to make payment convenient for the patient.

DATE	TRANSACTION TYPE	AMOUNT	TRANSACTION DESCRIPTION	RESPONSIBLE PARTY	ITEM BALANCE
03/11/98	Charg	80.00	OFFICE VISIT, NEW PATIENT - LEVEL 3 Insur Filed on 03/30/98 to Payer-A	Patient	46.95
04/03/98	Charg	1157.79	FISTULECTOMY SUBMUSCULAR Insur Filed on 04/21/98 to Payer-A	Payer-A	1157.79
04/13/98	Paymt	−26.55	From Payer-A, for 03/11/98		
04/13/98	Adjmt	−6.50	From Payer-A, for 03/11/98 PER EOB PT RESP DEDUCT/COPAY 4-13-9		

ACCOUNT NO.	0–30 DAYS	31–60 DAYS	61–90 DAYS	91–120 DAYS	OVER 120 DAYS	PATIENT DUE
17665	46.95	0.00	0.00	0.00	0.00	$46.95

ACORDIA OF CENTRAL IND (461)   ID: XPN406761759   PRI   <-- Payer-A

INS. PENDING
$1157.79

4723

Figure 10–9A Two examples of patient statements showing procedure, charge, payment, adjustment. Figure 10–9A gives an aging of the bill, the amount currently due and the amount pending insurance.

ANESTHESIOLOGY ASSOCIATES OF CLARK COUNTY, INC.

PLEASE INDICATE CHANGES IN THIS INFORMATION ON THE REVERSE SIDE

ACCOUNT NO.

129438-00   406761759

BALANCE DUE

$40.00

AMOUNT PAID

TO INSURE PROPER CREDIT PLEASE REMOVE AND RETURN THIS PORTION WITH YOUR PAYMENT

DATE OF SERVICE	DESCRIPTION OF SERVICE	AMOUNT
4/03/98	FOR ANESTHETIC CARE DIAGNOSIS CODE 565.0 PROCEDURE CODE 46270 TIME 8:30 TO 9:15	$400.00
6/15/98	BLUE SHIELD PAYMENT	$360.00-
	***CURRENT BALANCE	$40.00
	YOUR INSURANCE HAS PAID ITS PORTION. THE BALANCE IS YOUR RESPONSIBILITY.	

TAX ID# - 35-1273296

DATE	PATIENT NAME	ACCOUNT NO.	PLEASE PAY THIS AMOUNT	
6/17/98		129438-00		$40.00

▲ PAYMENTS RECEIVED AFTER THIS DATE WILL APPEAR ON NEXT STATEMENT

IMPORTANT MESSAGE REGARDING YOUR ACCOUNT

PLEASE MAKE CHECK PAYABLE TO: ANESTHESIOLOGY ASSOCIATES OF CLARK COUNTY, INC.

Figure 10–9B

Ledger Card

A **ledger card** is a financial record of the patient's account showing the date and description of service, charge, payment and balance within the billing cycle as demonstrated in Figure 10–10.

If the ledger card is used as a statement, a photocopy is made. It is then placed in a window envelope and mailed to the person responsible for the account. This type of billing is faster and simpler, but a disadvantage is that the ledger card is handwritten, using the pegboard method of bookkeeping. When photocopied, it can be difficult to read. This is discussed later in this module.

STATEMENT

Practon Medical Group, Inc.
4567 Broad Avenue
Woodland Hills, XY 12345-4700
Tel. 013/486-9002

JANE HENSON
PO BOX 205
JONESVILLE IN 47155

| DATE | REFERENCE | DESCRIPTION | CHARGES | CREDITS | | BALANCE |
				PYMNTS.	ADJ.	
			BALANCE FORWARD ⟶			
5/6/9x		OS-UA 99203 81000	73 —	20 —		53 —

RB40BC-2-96   PLEASE PAY LAST AMOUNT IN BALANCE COLUMN ⟶

THIS IS A COPY OF YOUR ACCOUNT AS IT APPEARS ON OUR RECORDS

Figure 10–10 Ledger card as a statement in the pegboard system.

Special Statement Form

A special statement form is another way to bill the patient. It is typed or printed and also mailed in a window envelope. The statement lists the date of service, description of service, charges, payments and balance since the last statement mailed.

Computerized Statement

Many offices now have computerized billing systems. When a medical office decides to convert to a computerized billing system, consideration must be given to changes in the way administrative procedures are performed.

Computerizing the medical office has disadvantages as well as advantages. It is important to recognize these and to make adequate preparation for any disruption to the efficiency of office functions during the transition to computerization. Training in basic computer functions and terminology is essential.

The advantages of a computerized medical office include:

- *Efficiency.* Repetitive tasks can be performed in a variety of formats. Once initial patient data is entered into the computer, it can be used in different formats without re-entering the same information, such as insurance forms, patient statements, superbills and mailing labels.
- *Accessibility.* Information entered into the computer is much easier to retrieve when needed. Patient information, once entered, can be retrieved and displayed on the monitor (screen) with a few simple functions, without having to search manually through filing systems to locate information needed.
- *Updates and Corrections.* Updating and/or correcting patient files can be performed much more quickly and easily than in a manual system where changes/updates would need to be made in several different areas. Changing a patient's address can be performed in the patient information menu and once changes are made they are automatically transferred to other data fields existing in the program.
- *Production.* Computers can process a large amount of information much faster than using manual methods. Compiling information for statistical or research purposes can be performed with very few keystrokes using a computerized system. Patient files can be searched to generate reports requesting information such as past due accounts.
- *Reduced Costs.* After the initial cost of purchasing the computer system and software, operating costs are decreased due to the reduction of time required in performing administrative procedures.

Many offices will attest that the advantages of a computerized billing system outweigh the disadvantages. Some of the disadvantages are:

- *Initial cost.* There is an initial investment for the purchase of the computer and peripherals such as a printer and the programs (software) the office has selected for setting up a computer system. Medical management software costs will vary from vendor to vendor. Hardware expense will depend on the number of computer terminals and the type and number of printers required for the practice. Determining the computer requirements that meet the needs of the medical office is important before purchasing the computer system. It is also financially beneficial to shop around and negotiate the best deal that meets the specific needs of the practice.
- *Initial investment of time.* It takes considerable time to learn how to operate a computer and the billing program. Many software vendors will provide staff

training as well as technical support when problems are encountered. Converting from a manual to a computerized system can take six months to a year and frustration can occur in the conversion process. Once the conversion process is completed, the outcome is positive. Proper training of all personnel will help overcome some of the frustration that may occur.

■ *Transition Process.* There is data that must be entered before complete conversion to computerization can occur. For example, patient registration records must be set up by entering demographic information on each patient. Diagnosis and procedure codes most frequently used in the medical office will also need to be entered. There are software programs available with codes already included so that only a few codes may need to be entered. Coding software is also available for purchase. While this data is being entered, front office procedures are still being performed manually. Once all information is entered, and the computer system is operational, additional information can be entered without being a time-consuming task.

■ *Malfunctions.* Even the best computer system and software can and will occasionally fail due to operator error, malfunction of the hardware or a "bug" in the system.

It is important when purchasing a medical management program to look closely at the administrative needs of the office and what type of features or options will allow the office to perform tasks easily and efficiently. These programs are available through software vendors. Systems of specialization in a medical management computer program are:

1. File maintenance
2. Appointment scheduling
3. Patient registration
4. Posting transactions
5. Insurance billing
6. Reports

File Maintenance. Before the office can perform administrative procedures, there are a number of tasks that must be performed in the file maintenance system so that the program will operate properly. These tasks include entering the practice and provider information, diagnosis and procedure codes, insurance carriers and referring physicians into the database and assigning passwords.

Scheduling Appointments. Computerized appointment scheduling allows front office staff to schedule, cancel, reschedule, and locate an appointment rapidly. In addition, a daily appointment list can be printed, as well as a cancellation log and patient reminder card.

Patient Registration. Once the patient has completed the patient registration form, an account can be established. This is done by entering the demographic and insurance data into the database. The patient's chart can also be prepared at this time.

Posting Transactions. Charges for procedures and services performed by the provider can be entered as well as payments made by the patient or third party payer to generate a current balance. A hard copy can be printed for the patient as a superbill, patient statement or insurance claim.

Patient Billing. When charges and payments are posted to the patient's account, the information is stored in the database and is available for patient billing. The management program can search the database to retrieve information necessary to generate statements for patients with outstanding balances. After the statements are printed, they are folded and mailed in window envelopes, or a self-mailer can be used.

Insurance Billing. When posting charges to a patient account, procedure and diagnosis codes are also entered. This information is stored in the database and is later used to complete the insurance claim form.

Reports. This system can generate a variety of reports to allow the physician to review practice and business activities. For example, information can be obtained to track volume and type of procedures performed in the office.

Generating the Computerized Statement

The Patient Billing Routine

To generate statements, the correct software application will need to be selected. All financial accounts in the practice database with a balance due will be processed. In preparing the bills, the computer will select the accounts that meet the criteria that have been selected for processing, such as accounts that are 30 days past due with a finance charge applied. Another example for this process is to omit statement preparation for Medicaid patients. When this preparation process is complete, the statement will be printed. The order in which statements are printed can also be selected to meet the needs of the office and/or postal regulations for presort rates. This could be alphabetical order for office needs or by zip code for lower presort rates.

Medical office management software can be purchased with options that include messages to be placed on the statement such as overdue payment reminders and status of insurance filing or even the patient's next appointment date. Other options include mailing labels for statements generated and a summary report listing patients billed that include account numbers and the total amount of the statement. In addition, a grand total of all statements can also be printed.

Patient statements are now ready to be mailed and there are options for this process. Standard envelopes may be used with the printed labels attached to the envelopes. Window envelopes can be used with statements inserted along with a return envelope for payment. A time-saving method is the mailer statement, which prints the patient statement and a return envelope in continuous form with perforation for separation, also called a self-mailer, as seen in Figure 10–11.

THE PEGBOARD ACCOUNTING SYSTEM

When discussing the use of a ledger card as a statement, it is necessary to explain the most common manual accounting system used in the medical office, the **pegboard system**.

Also called the "Write-It-Once" system, the pegboard gets its name from the lightweight masonite board with a row of pegs down one side used in preparing the statement. The forms used in the posting (transferring of information from one record to another) of daily patient financial transactions align on the pegs. These forms can be purchased using NCR paper (no carbon required) to allow posting of a single entry for multiple forms. These forms are:

- **Daysheet**, or day journal, is a record of each day's charges, payments, credits and adjustments.

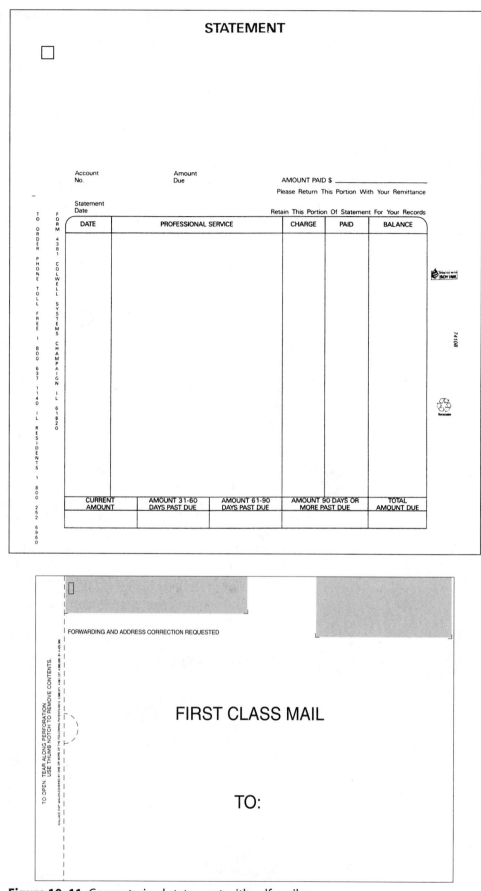

Figure 10–11 Computerized statement with self-mailer.

- **Ledger Card** is the patient's account or financial record of date, description, services provided and charges and payments, and any balance due.
- **Charge Slip**, **Superbill** or **Encounter Form** is a 3-part form that provides the patient with a record of account information for that day's services and charges. It can also serve as an insurance reporting form.

Figure 10–12 shows the pegboard accounting system and these forms.

The pegboard accounting system including these forms can be purchased from medical office supply companies. The forms can be customized to incorporate the most common procedures and services including CPT codes as well as a list of diagnoses and ICD-9-CM codes usual to a particular practice.

There are several advantages in using the pegboard accounting system:

- The "Write-It-Once" method of bookkeeping is less complicated than single or double entry recordkeeping.
- Instruction is provided by most programs, including training in medical office procedures.
- It provides a daily record of every patient financial transaction with the accounts receivable totals readily available. (Transaction is defined as the occurrence of a financial event to be recorded.)

Each day a new daysheet is placed on the pegboard. The supply of receipts and charge slips or superbills are usually numbered so it is important to retain and use them in correct numerical order. The ledger cards for patients scheduled to be seen that day are pulled in preparation of the financial activity expected that day.

The following steps are then performed in posting the financial transactions:

1. The charge slip is attached to the patient's chart.
2. The physician enters the service performed and the diagnosis.
3. The patient "checks out," either making a payment or a charge to the account.

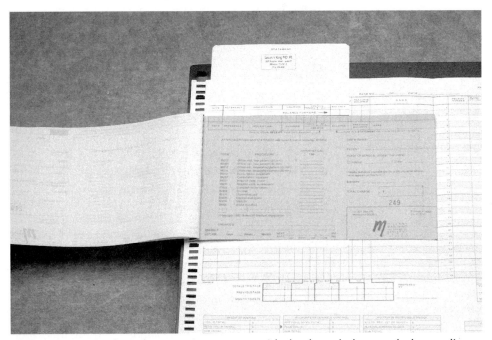

Figure 10–12 Pegboard accounting systems with daysheet, ledger card, charge slip.

4. The ledger card is inserted under the charge slip or superbill next to the daysheet.
5. The date of service, description of service and/or CPT code is recorded.
6. The charge is posted from the office fee schedule.
7. Any payment received is recorded.
8. The current balance is calculated and recorded. If there is none, a zero or line can be used to denote there is no balance remaining.

With this one entry, the daysheet and ledger card have been posted, and a receipt has been made for any payment received, and a copy given to the patient. The ledger card is refiled, and the charge slip retained in numerical order for office records.

Many payments are received daily in the mail, particularly insurance payments. These payments are posted on the daysheet and ledger card in the same manner. No receipt is required unless specifically requested by the patient. Physician charges for visits, surgeries and other services performed in a hospital, nursing home or other facility are also posted on the ledger card and daysheet.

In addition to charges added to an account and payments credited to an account, adjustments can also be applied to an account.

Adjustments, also known as "write-offs," are changes made in a patient's account not related to charges incurred or payments received. An adjustment occurs when corrections indicate changes in a previously submitted statement, such as adding a late charge or a participating provider's deduction per contract agreement, as shown in the ledger in Figure 10–13.

Figure 10–14 shows a Blue Shield discount on a hospital charge.

Adjusting the account keeps the account current and the accounts receivable figure up to date.

At the end of the day, all columns on the daysheet are totaled and balanced. One disadvantage of the pegboard accounting system is when an error is discovered on the daysheet, the ledger card must be retrieved to make the correction. Drawing a single line through the error, make a new corrected entry on the next open line available on the daysheet. If the patient has been given a receipt or superbill, a corrected one must be made and sent to the patient. A completed daysheet is demonstrated in Figure 10–15.

Bookkeeping Tips

Bookkeeping is the recording of daily business transactions. The physician's office is a business, and complete, correct, and current financial records are important for:

■ Prompt billing and collection procedures.
■ Accurate reporting of income to federal and state agencies.
■ Financial planning of the practice.

Bookkeeping errors such as duplicate billing and incorrect charge totals can result in lost income as well as patients for the practice.

Some suggestions for bookkeeping accuracy are:

1. Pay attention to detail.
2. Write clearly and legibly, using the same type of pen, preferably black ink.
3. Do not erase, write-over, or mark out a figure. Do not use correction fluid. A single line can be drawn through the incorrect figure with the correct figure written above it.

STATEMENT

Practon Medical Group, Inc.
4567 Broad Avenue
Woodland Hills, XY 12345-4700
Tel. 013/486-9002

DONNA LACEY M.D.
5450 MILAN ST
SELLERSBURG IN 47172

DATE	REFERENCE	DESCRIPTION	CHARGES	CREDITS PYMNTS.	CREDITS ADJ.	BALANCE
		BALANCE FORWARD →				
5/6/9x		OS – EKG	130 00			130 00
6/8/9x		ROA – AETNA		73 50		56 50
6/8/9x		ADJ – P.C.			56 50	——

RB40BC-2-96   PLEASE PAY LAST AMOUNT IN BALANCE COLUMN ↑

THIS IS A COPY OF YOUR ACCOUNT AS IT APPEARS ON OUR RECORDS

Figure 10–13 Adjustment or write-off on ledger card.

4. Keep columns of figures aligned.
5. Double check columns of figures by adding twice. Financial records cannot be *almost* correct. Bookkeeping is either right or wrong—there is no in-between.

External Billing

An outside or external billing service can be contracted to manage patient accounts. The service maintains the ledger cards and posts charges and payments from copies of superbills provided by the medical office. The service prepares monthly

STATEMENT

Clark Memorial Hospital
Jewish Hospital Health Network Partner

P.O. Box CS10
Jeffersonville, IN 47131-7010
812-283-2389

STATEMENT DATE	PAY THIS AMOUNT	ACCOUNT NUMBER
5/16/98	243.27	1025411

DATE OF SERVICE 4/03/98 SHOW AMOUNT PAID HERE $

PATIENT NAME

PLEASE DETACH AND RETURN TOP PORTION WITH YOUR PAYMENT

DATE	DESCRIPTION	PAYMENTS	BALANCE
4/23/98	FINAL BILL AMOUNT		4,025.75
05/11/98	BLUE CROSS OF IN DISCOUNT	1,520.52CR	
05/11/98	PAYMENT-BLUE CROSS 13	2,261.96CR	

TOTAL AMOUNT DUE**** 243.27

PLEASE NOTE

YOUR INSURANCE COMPANY HAS PAID ITS SHARE OF YOUR BILL.
THE ABOVE BALANCE IS NOW DUE FROM YOU.
**QUESTIONS CONCERNING YOUR ACCOUNT CALL

Your Insurance has been billed. This copy of your bill is for your records.

Figure 10–14 Insurance payment and adjustment of a hospital statement.

statements with instructions that payments be returned to them. It deposits payments directly to the medical office's bank account and submits a report of all transactions.

This billing method works well in practices with limited clerical staff or those with a large patient load. There should be one employee responsible for coordinating activities between the office and the billing service.

THE BILLING PROCESS

When to mail out statements to patients is often determined by the size of the medical practice and the economic status of the community. Smaller offices may

RECORD OF DEPOSITS

Office visits | Hosp. visits | Labor-atory | Diag-nostic

DAY SHEET (RECORD OF CHARGES AND RECEIPTS) PAGE NO______ OF______ DATE 5-1-98

DATE	REFERENCE	DESCRIPTION	CHARGES	CREDITS PYMNTS.	CREDITS ADJ.	BALANCE	PREVIOUS BALANCE	NAME		RECEIPT NUMBER	DATE	CASH	CHECKS	BUSINESS ANALYSIS SUMMARIES (OPTIONAL)
5/1/98		OS – 99203	55 —	10 –		45 —	——	JACK HILL	1	3234		10 –		
5/1/98		OS-PAP – 99214	78 —			78 —	——	PAM SMITH	2	3235				
5/1/98		EKG – 93000	125 —			125 —	——	RITA STALL	3	3236				
5/1/98		OS – 99213	46 —	32 –		46 —	32 —	TOM WINGFIELD	4	3237			32 –	
5/1/98		INJ – 90782	18 —	18 –		——	——	HANNAH MARKS	5	3238			18 –	
5/1/98		OS-UA 99203 81100	73 —	20 –		53 —	——	JANE HENSON	6	3239		20 –		
5/1/98		CONS – 99242	150 —			150 —	——	FLOYD SIMMONS	7	3240				
5/1/98		HCG – PREG.	45 —	45 –		——	——	JENNA HAINES	8	3241			45 –	
5/1/98		OS-VP 99213 36415	56 —	10 –		58 —	12 —	DONNA TINES	9	3242		10 –		
5/1/98		HV – 99231	87 —			287 —	200 —	TIM DAY	10	3243				
5/1/98		OBSV – 99235	130 —			130 —	——	SALLY HECK	11	3244				
5/1/98		OS-EKG – 99214 93000	183 —	58 –		125 —	——	DANIEL DANIELS	12	3245			58 –	
5/1/98		OS-CBC 99203 85031	76 —			76 —	——	KIM DOWNS	13	3246				
5/1/98		HS – 99352	85 —			170 —	85 —	GEORGE BARNES	14	3247				
5/1/98		OS-STREP 99213 86403	61 —	61 –		——	——	HECTOR BALL	15	3248			61 –	
5/1/98		ROA – CK		55 60		——	55 60	BRUCE MITCHELL	16				55 60	
5/1/98		ROA – BS		249 20		275 80	525 —	ROBERT SMITH	17				249 20	
5/1/98		ROA – BS		26 55	6 50	46 95	80 —	JOAN JOHNSON	18				26 55	
									19					
									20					
									21					
									22					
									23					
									24					
									25					
									26					
									27					
									28					

	COL. A	COL. B-1	COL. B-2	COL. C	COL. D
TOTALS THIS PAGE	1268 —	585 35	6 50	1665 75	989 60
PREVIOUS PAGE	——	——	——	——	——
MONTH-TO-DATE	1268 —	585 35	6 50	1665 75	989 60

PREPARED BY ______

TOTAL CASH	40. —
TOTAL CHECKS	545.35
TOTAL DEPOSIT	585.35

PROOF OF POSTING	
COL. D TOTAL	$ 989.60
PLUS COL. A TOTAL	$ 1268.00
SUBTOTAL	$ 2257.60
LESS COLS. B-1 & B-2	$ 591.85
MUST EQUAL COL. C	$ 1665.75

ACCOUNTS RECEIVABLE CONTROL	
PREVIOUS DAY'S TOTAL	$ ——
PLUS COL. A	$ 1268.00
SUBTOTAL	$ 1268.00
LES COLS. B-1 & B-2	$ 591.85
TOTAL ACCTS. REC.	$ 676.15

ACCOUNTS RECEIVABLE PROOF	
ACCTS. REC. 1ST OF MONTH	$ –0–
PLUS COL. A MO TO DATE	$ 1268.00
SUBTOTAL	$ 1268.00
LESS COLS. B-1 & B-2 MO. TO DATE	$ 591.85
TOTAL ACCTS. REC.	$ 676.15

CASH PAID OUT	
	$
	$
	$

CASH CONTROL	
Beginning Cash On Hand	$
Receipts Today (Col. B-1)	$
Total	$
Less Paid Outs	$
Less Bank Deposit	$
Closing Cash On Hand	$

Figure 10–15 A complete, balanced daysheet.

find the monthly billing cycle to be the most efficient. Large practices may prefer cycle billing as it allows flexibility in the billing schedule.

Monthly Billing

Monthly billing is just what the name states: billing all patients at a designated time of the month. Typically, statements should leave the office on the 25th of the month to be received by the first day of the following month. A major disadvantage of monthly billing is other duties may be neglected during this time-consuming period.

Cycle Billing

In cycle billing, all accounts are divided alphabetically into groups with each group billed at a different time. Statements are prepared in the same schedule each month. In a large practice with numerous statements to process monthly, this is a more efficient method of billing. The statements can be mailed as they are completed or mailed at one time. A typical cycle billing schedule is shown in Table 10–1. This can be varied to accommodate the needs of the individual practice. The major advantage of cycle billing is that it provides a steady flow of funds throughout the month.

Past Due Accounts

No matter how efficient and effective the billing process may be, there will still be collections on some accounts. The most common reasons for a past due account are:

- Inability to pay—simply not having the money to pay the bill. Medical bills have last priority.
- Negligence or forgetfulness, or misplacing the statement.

TABLE 10–1   Typical Schedule for Cycle Billing System.

To Cycle Bill Patient Accounts:

1. Divide the alphabet into four sections: A–F, G–L, M–R, S–Z.

2. Prepare statements for patients whose last names begin with A through F on Wednesday and mail them on Thursday of the first week of the month. (Week 1)

3. Prepare statements for patients whose last names begin with G through L on Wednesday and mail them on Thursday of Week 2.

4. Prepare statements for patients whose last names begin with M through R on Wednesday and mail them on Thursday of Week 3.

5. Prepare statements for patients whose last names begin with S through Z on Wednesday and mail them on Thursday of Week 4.

■ Unwillingness to pay. When a patient complains about a charge or refuses to pay, it may have nothing to do with finances. There could be dissatisfaction with the care or treatment received. The physician or office manager should be made aware of those situations for immediate attention.

EXERCISE 10–3

1. Name the three most common reasons an account may become past due.

a. _____

b. _____

c. _____

2. Name the two types of billing

THE COLLECTIONS PROCESS

Collection of delinquent accounts begins with determining how much has been owed for what length of time.

Accounts receivable (A/R) is the amount of money owed to the medical practice by its patients. **Account aging** is a method of identifying how long an account is overdue by the length of time it has been unpaid. The accounts are aged into the following categories:

> Current—0 to 30 Days
> 31 to 60 Days
> 61 to 90 Days
> 91 to 120 Days
> 120 Days and over

Aging begins the date the statement is sent to a patient indicating current charges. If these charges have not been paid by the next billing date, the account is classified 30 days old because the patient has had 30 days in which to pay the bill. The unpaid amount ages by a 30-day time period each time statements are sent and the bill is unpaid.

Medical office management computer systems can automatically calculate and age the balance due on individual overdue accounts to indicate the length of time the account has been overdue.

The classification of past due accounts and the account aging process is necessary to review and determine which accounts need follow-up. An age analysis is a summary that lists all patient account balances, when the charges were made, the most recent payment received, and any special notes concerning the account, as shown in Figure 10–16.

Management consultants recommend fees to be collected at the time of service, and a collection ratio of at least 90 percent should be maintained. A collection ratio is a method used to gauge the effectiveness of the ambulatory care setting's billing practices. This is calculated by dividing the total collections by the net charges (gross charges minus adjustments). This yields a percentage, which is the collection ratio, as explained in Table 10–2.

04/04/2000									Page 1
SUMMARY AGING REPORT BY ACCOUNT BASED ON DATE PATIENT BILLED (Pat. Only)									
All Accounts									
Aging Category: 1–5 DOL Pay <= 04/04/2000									
Acc #	*Name*	*Phone No.*	*DOL Pay*	*Unapplied*	*Current*	*31–60*	*61–90*	*120+*	*Total*
114	Rawles, Deb	812-246-1256	03/20/2000		102.50				102.50
25	Leaf, Autumn	812-246-7789	12/02/1999					250.00	250.00
110	Martin, Kathy	502-585-1134	02/14/2000			115.00			115.00
214	Burton, Craig	502-585-1459	03/15/2000		53.75				53.75
REPORT TOTALS					156.25	115.00		250.00	521.25

Figure 10–16 Summary of account aging.

TABLE 10–2

Total Receipts		=	$40,000
Managed Care Adjustments		+	$ 3,000
Medicare Adjustments		+	$ 2,000
TOTAL			$45,000
Total Charges			$52,000
Total Receipts	($45,000)		= 86.5% Collection Ratio
Total Charges	($52,000)		After Adjustments

Another important factor is the accounts receivable ratio, which measures the speed with which outstanding accounts are paid, which is generally two months. The accounts receivable ratio is figured by dividing the current A/R balance by the average monthly gross charges. The A/R ratio provides a picture of the state of collections and probable loss within the practice. The longer an account is past due, the less the likelihood of successfully collecting the account.

COLLECTION TECHNIQUES

An effective approach to the collection of past due accounts in the medical office is a combination of letters and telephone calls. It is preferable to first call the patient concerning the delinquent account. The patient may have misplaced or forgotten the bill, and a telephone call can often resolve the situation quickly and inexpensively. When making telephone collection calls, there are ethical issues to remember:

- Be tactful, courteous and diplomatic.
- Treat patients respectfully.
- Do not threaten or antagonize.

The **Fair Debt Collection Practices Act** is designed to protect consumers against abusive practices by debt collectors. This Act mandates that when making collection calls, personnel cannot:

- Call before 8 a.m. or after 9 p.m. or make excessive calls.
- Use abusive language or make threats to coerce a consumer into making a payment.
- Publish a list of consumers who allegedly refuse to pay debts, except to report to a credit-reporting agency.
- Threaten to notify an employer that a consumer has not paid bills.
- Advertise or publicize the debt to embarrass a consumer into paying.
- Send misleading letters that appear to be from a government agency or court.
- Try to collect more than is owed.

In addition to the Fair Debt Collection Practices Act and the Truth-In-Lending Act discussed earlier, other laws governing collection practices that health care employees must be familiar with are:

- *Fair Credit Reporting Act of 1971.* Provides guidelines for the reporting and collecting of credit background information to businesses to use in evaluation of an individual's application for credit, insurance, or employment. It allows consumers to learn the nature and substance of information collected about them by credit-reporting agencies, and to correct and update information.
- *Guide Against Debt Collection Deception (Federal Trade Commission).* Provides guidelines for creditors in their collection efforts, and provides the consumer with protection from fraudulent and deceptive tactics.
- *Notice On Use of Telephone for Debt Collecting (Federal Communications Commission).* Outlines specific times calls can be made, and prohibits threatening phone calls and other harassment. States and localities may also have additional statutes concerning the use of the telephone for debt collection.
- *Equal Credit Opportunity Act of 1975.* Prohibits discrimination in the granting of credit on the basis of sex, race, age, marital status, religion or nationality.

▨ *Highlight*

Keep accurate records in telephone collections. Document what was said, any amount of a promised payment, and date of the promised payment. If nothing is received at that time, follow-up will be necessary.

Collection Letters

The most effective approach to collections combines telephone calls and letters on past due accounts. Collection letters are sent to encourage patients to pay past due balances after regular statements have been mailed. Lack of payment is usually not considered serious until after 60 days. When there has been no response to telephone calls and statements, a series of collection letters begins. Collection experts recommend the steps shown in Table 10–3:

TABLE 10–3   Steps in Collection

---

60 DAYS PAST DUE

Telephone call to discuss account.

Send letter #1 to follow up telephone conversation (see Figure 10–17).

90 DAYS PAST DUE

Friendly reminder letter #2.

(see Figure 10–18).

120 DAYS PAST DUE

120 Day Final Notice (see Figure 10–19).

Notice of Termination to patient (see Figure 10–20).

Lowery B. Johnson, M.D.
Hwy 311 Suite A31
Sellersburg, IN 47172
812-246-1234

May 3, 19--

Autumn Leaf
10586 Payment Place #2E
Sellersburg, IN 47178

Dear Ms Leaf:

As we discussed in our telephone conversation today, we will expect a payment from you in the amount of $125.00 on May 15 and the balance of $125 on June 15, 19xx.

Please notify our billing office immediately if any problem should occur to prevent payment of this past due account.

Sincerely,

Susan B. Dunn
Office Manager

Figure 10–17 Telephone follow-up letter.

Lowery B. Johnson, M.D.
Hwy 311 Suite A31
Sellersburg, IN 47172
812-246-1234

July 5, 19--

Autumn Leaf
10586 Payment Place #2E
Sellersburg, IN 47178

Dear Ms Leaf:

We have not received payments from you as promised in the telephone call with you on May 3, 19xx.

Your account remains unpaid with a balance of $250.00, which is 90 days past due.

Please call me at 555-2244 if you have a question about your account. Otherwise we expect your payment immediately.

Sincerely,

Susan B. Dunn
Office Manager

Figure 10–18 Collection letter 90 days.

The final-notice letter should be exactly that: a final demand for payment. If you continue to send letters after the final notice, the patient will doubt your attempts at collecting the account. The final-notice letter should be sent certified mail, return receipt requested. This provides documentation the letter was mailed and received by the patient. If the letter is undeliverable, it will be returned to the billing office marked accordingly.

When all collection attempts by the medical office have been unsuccessful, many practices seek the assistance of an outside collection agency. At this point, many practices will terminate medical services to the patient. An example of this Notice of Termination of Medical Services Letter is seen in Figure 10–20. This letter is also mailed to the patient by certified mail, return receipt requested for legal purposes for documentation of delivery and receipt. If undeliverable, it will be returned to the billing office, marked accordingly.

▪ ***Never*** *place a past due notice on the mailing envelope of the statement, or use a postcard to communicate financial or collection information. This is an invasion of privacy.*

Lowery B. Johnson, M.D.
Hwy 311 Suite A31
Sellersburg, IN 47172
812-246-1234

August 9, 19--

Autumn Leaf
10586 Payment Place #2E
Sellersburg, IN 47178

Dear Ms Leaf:

Your account with our office remains unpaid after several telephone calls and letters. Your account is seriously past due at 120 days.

Unless we receive your payment within the next ten (10) days, we will have no alternative but to turn this account over to a collection agency.

Please send us our payment or call this office before August 19, 19xx. This is our final attempt to collect this past due account.

Sincerely,

Susan B. Dunn
Office Manager

Figure 10–19 Collection letter 120 days—final notice requesting payment.

Collection Agencies

When choosing a collection agency, ask for referrals from other physicians, ambulatory care centers and hospitals. Many agencies deal specifically with health care facilities and will work compatibly with the medical office's philosophy of ethics in patient care. Ask what the agency's approach is for collection methods and request sample letters and notices.

When a collection agency has been selected, the following patient information must be supplied:

- Full name and last known address
- Name of employer and business address
- Name of spouse, if applicable
- Total debt
- Date of last payment or charge on the account
- Method taken by the office to collect the debt
- Any response to collection attempts

Lowery B. Johnson, M.D.
Hwy 311 Suite A31
Sellersburg, IN 47172
812-246-1234

August 19, 19--

Autumn Leaf
10586 Payment Place #2E
Sellersburg, IN 47178

Dear Ms Leaf:

Since we have received no response from you regarding your past due account, this has now been turned over to the Goody Medical Collections Bureau. Further attempts at collecting this debt using whatever legal action necessary will come from this agency.

Because of the unsatisfactory manner in which you have handled your financial obligations to Dr. Johnson, we find it necessary to terminate further medical care from this office.

We will remain available for your medical care for the next 30 days from the date you receive this letter. This will give you sufficient time to choose a physician for your continued medical care. With your signed consent, your medical records will be made available to the physician you designate.

In the event you require medical services from this office in the next 30 days, payment, in full will be required at the time of service.

Sincerely,

Susan B. Dunn
Office Manager

Figure 10–20 Notice of termination letter.

Once the account has been turned over to the collection agency, the medical office should follow these guidelines:

1. Note on the patient's ledger that the account has been given to the collection agency.
2. Discontinue sending statements.
3. Refer the patient to the collection agency if he or she contacts the office about the account.
4. Promptly report any payments received by the office to the agency, as a percentage of this payment is due them.
5. Contact the agency if new information is obtained that could help in collecting the debt.

The collection agency will retain a portion of payment recovered, usually 40–60 percent.

Small Claims Court

In certain circumstances, consideration may be given to bringing a delinquent case to small claims court. Small claims courts typically:

- Handle cases that involve only a limited amount of debt (which varies from state to state)
- Do not permit representation by an attorney or collection agency
- Are efficient in their proceedings and less expensive to utilize

A key factor when using small claims court: the court only determines if the charge or account is valid. If the court rules in favor of the medical office, the office still must collect the money from the defendant.

Special Collection Situations

Bankruptcy

Bankruptcy is defined as a legal declaration of an individual's inability to pay debts.

The number of individual bankruptcies filed in the United States continues to rise. The number of personal bankruptcies hit 117,060 in March 1997, a record for the month. In the first quarter of 1997, 312,699 individuals filed for protection, a 25 percent increase over the previous year's first quarter. These totals effectively put an end to any hope that they would recede or at least level off after breaking the one million mark for the first time in 1996. An estimated 1.44 million American consumers filed bankruptcy in 1997.

This increase has a significant impact on health care providers whose bills often make up a large portion of the debts discharged in the bankruptcy court. Because the physician's fee is an unsecured debt, it is one of the last to be paid. (GLA Collections, 1998, p.32)

Bankruptcy is governed under the Bankruptcy Act of 1978 and the Bankruptcy Amendment Act of 1984. There are different types or chapters of bankruptcy, usually determined by legal advice that can be voluntary or involuntary. The main objectives of a bankruptcy proceeding are the collection and distribution of a debtor's assets and the discharge of the debtor from obligations. The decree terminating the bankruptcy proceeding is called a "discharge," which releases the debtor from the debt. What should you do in the medical office when a patient files bankruptcy? When verbal or written notice is received that a debtor has filed bankruptcy, immediately discontinue all collection attempts. The United States Bankruptcy Court is now involved, and it will make the decision about who will receive any assets that are available. Any further contact with the debtor may constitute a violation of the protection of the bankruptcy court. If you have questions, contact your office attorney or the debtor's attorney. If an account has been turned over to a collection agency and you receive notice of a bankruptcy proceeding, contact the agency immediately. Copies of any bankruptcy notices received from the bankruptcy court should be sent to the agency so that appropriate action may be taken on the account.

Figures 10–21 and 10–22 are examples of notices from bankruptcy court.

B10 (Official Form 10)
(rev. 6/91)

United States Bankruptcy Court _____ District of _____	**PROOF OF CLAIM**
In re (Name of Debtor)	Case Number

NOTE: This form should not be used to make a claim for an administrative expense arising after the commencement of the case. A "request" of payment of an administrative expense may be filed pursuant to 11 U.S.C. § 503.

Name of Creditor _(The person or entity to whom the debtor owes money or property)_	☐ Check box if you are aware that anyone else has filed a proof of claim relating to your claim. Attach copy of statement giving particulars.
Name and Addresses Where Notices Should be Sent	☐ Check box if you have never received any notices from the bankruptcy court in this case.
	☐ Check box if the address differs from the address on the envelope sent to you by the court
Telephone No.	THIS SPACE IS FOR COURT USE ONLY

ACCOUNT OR OTHER NUMBER BY WHICH CREDITOR IDENTIFIES DEBTOR:	Check here if this claim: ☐ replaces ☐ amends a previously filed claim, dated: _____

1.   BASIS FOR CLAIM:

☐ Goods sold
☐ Services performed
☐ Money loaned
☐ Personal injury/wrongful death
☐ Taxes
☐ Other (Describe briefly)

☐ Retiree benefits as defined in 11 U.S.C. § 1114(a)
☐ Wages, salaries, and compensations (Fill out below)
    Your social security number _____
    Unpaid compensations for services, performed
    from _____ to _____
            (date)   (date)

2.   DATE DEBT WAS INCURRED:

3.   IF COURT JUDGMENT, DATE OBTAINED:

4.   CLASSIFICATION OF CLAIM. Under the Bankruptcy Code all claims are classified as one or more of the following: (1) Unsecured nonpriority, (2) Unsecured Priority, (3) Secured. It is possible for part of a claim to be in one category and part in another.
     CHECK THE APPROPRIATE BOX OR BOXES that best describe your claim and STATE THE AMOUNT OF THE CLAIM.

☐ SECURED CLAIM $_____
   Attach evidence of perfection of security interest
   Brief Description of Collateral:
   ☐ Real Estate   ☐ Motor Vehicel   ☐ Other (Describe briefly)

Amount of arrearage and other charges included in secured claim above, if any $_____

☐ UNSECURED NONPRIORITY CLAIM $_____
   A claim is unsecured if there is no collateral or lien on property of the debtor securing the claim or to the extent that the value of such property is less than the amount of the claim.

☐ UNSECURED PRIORITY CLAIM $_____

   Specify the priority of the claim.

   ☐ Wages, salaries, or commissions (up to $2000), earned not more than 90 days before filing of the bankruptcy petition or cessation of the debtor's business, whichever is earlier—11 U.S.C. § 507(a)(3)

   ☐ Contributions to an employee benefit plan—U.S.C. § 507(a)(4)

   ☐ Up to $900 of deposits toward purchase, lease, or rental of property or services for personal, family, or household use—11 U.S.C. § 507(a)(7)

   ☐ Taxes or penalties of governmental units—11 U.S.C. § 507(a)(7)

   ☐ Other—11 U.S.C. §§ 507(a)(2), (a)(5)—(Describe briefly)

5.   TOTAL AMOUNT OF CLAIM AT TIME CASE FILED: $_____ $_____ $_____ | $_____ |
                                                          (Unsecured)   (Secured)   (Priority)   (Total)

☐ Check this box if claim includes prepetition charges in addition to the principal amount of the claim. Attach itemized statement of all additional charges.

6.   CREDITS AND SETOFFS: The amount of all payments on this claim has been credited and deducted for the purpose of making this proof of claim. In filing this claim, claimant has deducted all amounts that claimant owes to debtor.

7.   SUPPORTING DOCUMENTS: _Attach copies of supporting documents,_ such as promissory notes, purchase orders, invoices, itemized statements of running accounts, contracts, court judgments, or evidence of security interests. If the documents are not available, explain. If the documents are voluminous, attach a summary.

8.   TIME-STAMPED COPY: To receive an acknowledgement of the filing of your claim, enclose a stamped, self-addressed envelope and copy of this proof of claim.

THIS SPACE IS FOR COURT USE ONLY

Date	Sign and print the name and title, if any, of the creditor or other person authorized to file this claim (attach copy of power of attorney, if any)

Page 35

Penalty for presenting fraudulent claim: Fine of up to $500,000 or imprisonment for up to 5 years, or both. 18 U.S.C. §§ 152 and 3571.

Figure 10–21 Notice of bankruptcy.

FORM B9A 12/94 United States Bankruptcy Court Southern District of Indiana Case Number: 97-90496-BHL-7	NOTICE OF COMMENCEMENT OF CASE UNDER CHAPTER 7 OF THE BANKRUPTCY CODE, MEETING OF CREDITORS, AND FIXING OF DATES (individual or Joint Debtor No Asset Case)

In re (Name of Debtor)	Addresses of Debtors	Soc. Sec./Tax ID Nos.
	Date Filed	
Addressee:	Address of the Clerk of the Bankruptcy Court	

Name and Address of Attorney for Debtor	Telephone Number	Name and Address of Trustee	Telephone Number

DATE, TIME, AND LOCATION OF MEETING OF CREDITORS
April 18, 1997, 11:00 A.M., 121 W. SPRING ST. ROOM 205 FEDERAL BUILDING, NEW ALBANY, IN 47150

DISCHARGE OF DEBTS
Deadline to File a Complaint Objecting to the Discharge of the Debtor or
to Determine Dischargeability of Certain Types of Debts: June 17, 1997

AT THIS TIME THERE APPEAR TO BE NO ASSETS AVAILABLE FROM WHICH PAYMENT MAY BE MADE TO UNSECURED CREDITORS. DO NOT FILE A PROOF OF CLAIM UNTIL YOU RECEIVE NOTICE TO DO SO.

COMMENCEMENT OF CASE. A petition for liquidation under chapter 7 of the Bankruptcy Code has been filed in this court by or against the person or persons named above as the debtor, and an order for relief has been entered. You will not receive notice of all documents filed in this case. All documents filed with the court, including lists of the debtor's property, debts, and property claimed as exempt are available for inspection at the office of the clerk of the bankruptcy court.

CREDITORS MAY NOT TAKE CERTAIN ACTIONS. A creditor is anyone to whom the debtor owes money or property. Under the Bankruptcy Code, the debtor is granted certain protection against creditors. Common examples of prohibited actions by creditors are contacting the debtor to demand repayment, taking action against the debtor to collect money owed to creditors or to take property of the debtor, and starting or continuing foreclosure actions, repossessions, or wage deductions. If unauthorized actions are taken by a creditor against a debtor, the court may penalize that creditor. A creditor who is considering taking action against the debtor or the property of the debtor should review § 362 of the Bankruptcy Code and may wish to seek legal advice. The staff of the clerk of the bankruptcy court is not permitted to give legal advice.

MEETING OF CREDITORS. The debtor (both husband and wife in a joint case) is required to appear at the meeting of creditors on the date and at the place set forth above for the purpose of being examined under oath. Attendance by creditors at the meeting is welcomed, but not required. At the meeting, the creditors may elect a trustee other than the one name above, elect a committee of creditors, examine the debtor, and transact such other business as may properly come before the meeting. The meeting may be continued or adjourned from time to time by notice at the meeting, without further written notice to creditors.

LIQUIDATION OF THE DEBTOR'S PROPERTY. The trustee will collect the debtor's property and turn any that is not exempt into money. At this time, however, it appears from the schedules of the debtor that there are no assets from which any distribution can be paid to creditors. If at a later date if appears that there are assets from which a distribution may be paid, the creditors will be notified and given an opportunity to file claims.

EXEMPT PROPERTY. Under state and federal law, the debtor is permitted to keep certain money or property as exempt. If a creditor believes that an exemption of money or property is not authorized by law, the creditor may file an objection. An objection must be filed not later than 30 days after the conclusion of the meeting of creditors.

DISCHARGE OF DEBTS. The debtor is seeking a discharge of debts. A discharge means that certain debts are made unenforceable against the debtor personally. Creditors whose claims against the debtor are discharged may never take action against the debtor to collect the discharged debts. If a creditor believes that the debtor should not receive any discharge of debts under § 727 of the Bankruptcy Code or that a debt owed to the creditor is not dischargeable under § 523(a)(2), (4), (6), or (15) of the Bankruptcy Code, timely action must be taken in the bankruptcy court by the deadline set forth above in the box labeled "Discharge of Debts." Creditors considering taking such action may wish to seek legal advice.

DO NOT FILE A PROOF OF CLAIM UNLESS YOU RECEIVE A COURT NOTICE TO DO SO

For the Court: _____ _____
                     Clerk of the Bankruptcy Court   Date

Figure 10–22 Bankruptcy court notice of discharge of debtor(s).

Billing Minors

Statements for services performed to minors must be addressed to a parent or guardian, as shown in Figure 10–23.

A statement addressed to a child, or patient under the legal age declared in that state, may prove difficult to collect payment if the parents take the attitude that they are not responsible because the statement is not addressed directly to them. If the parents are separated or divorced, the parent who brings the child to the office for medical services is responsible for payment. Financial agreements in these circumstances exist between the parents and should not involve the medical staff.

STATEMENT

Practon Medical Group, Inc.
4567 Broad Avenue
Woodland Hills, XY 12345-4700
Tel. 013/486-9002

JASON R. RUSSELL
2551 BROOKSIDE DR
RIDGEFIELD IN 47580

For: Adrian S. Russell

DATE	REFERENCE	DESCRIPTION	CHARGES	CREDITS		BALANCE
				PYMNTS.	ADJ.	
		BALANCE FORWARD ⟶				

RB40BC-2-96   PLEASE PAY LAST AMOUNT IN BALANCE COLUMN ⟶

THIS IS A COPY OF YOUR ACCOUNT AS IT APPEARS ON OUR RECORDS

Figure 10–23 Ledger card statement for billing of a minor.

In some circumstances, a child may be covered under two insurance policies. The **birthday rule** determines which policy is primary and which is secondary. The birthday rule states that the primary policy is the one taken out by the policyholder with the earliest birthday occurring in the calendar year.

> EXAMPLE: Tom Brown is a dependent child carried on both parents' policies. His father's policy is through his employment at General Motors. His mother's policy is a group policy through her employer, Good Samaritan Hospital.
>
> The father's birth date is June 6, 1950.
> The mother's birth date is February 1, 1955.
>
> February 1 is the earliest birth date in the year, and would be the primary policy for Tom, with his father's policy secondary.

If both policyholders have the same birth dates, the primary policy is the policy in effect the longest. The *year* of birth is not considered in the birthday rule.

Emancipated Minors

Minors cannot be held responsible for payment of a bill unless they are emancipated.

An **emancipated minor** is a person under the age of majority, usually 18 or 21 years old, as defined by state statute, who is one of the following:

■ Married
■ Self-supporting
■ Serving in the armed forces
■ Living separately from parents or a legal guardian

An emancipated minor who comes to the medical facility requesting treatment is responsible for the charges incurred.

EXERCISE 10–4

1. Explain the correct procedure to follow in billing a minor.

2. Define emancipated minor.

3. Jennifer Catz is a 9-year-old child carried on both her parents' health care policies. Her father's policy is through his employment at General Foods.

   Jennifer's mother is employed at National American Life Insurance Company with medical insurance coverage through her employer.

   Jennifer's father's birth date is September 2, 1960.

   Jennifer's mother's birth date is September 28, 1956.

4. Applying the birthday rule, which policy is primary?

Tracing Skips

A "skip" is a person who has apparently moved, leaving no forwarding address. If a statement is returned to your office "No Forwarding Address," or "Undeliverable," determine first if there are any errors made in addressing the envelope. Compare the address on the envelope with the one on the patient registration form in the chart. If the address is correct, the billing office may try to call the patient. The copy of the driver's license obtained during the patient registration process can be used as a tracking device to locate the patient. If all these efforts fail, a decision should be made on whether to pursue the debt. This usually depends on office policy and the amount that is owed. The unpaid account at this time could be turned over to a collection agency.

EXERCISE 10–5

1. Explain the **first** thing to do when a statement is returned to the office, "Moved—No Forwarding Address."

Billing for a Deceased Patient

Health care providers sometimes write off accounts of deceased patients simply due to lack of information on whom to bill and how to bill.

When the patient has Medicare, submit the claim with the physician accepting assignment by marking "X" in "Yes" box in Block 27. **Accepting assignment** means the physician or provider will accept what Medicare pays and not bill the difference between the cost of the service and the Medicare payment. For example, Medicare is billed for a service that cost $150. The Medicare payment is in the amount of $98. When the provider accepts assignment, the payment of $98 is accepted as payment in full. The remaining balance or difference of $52 is adjusted or written off. No signature is required by a family member. In Block 12 where the patient's signature is required, type in "Patient Died (date)".

If the physician does not accept assignment on a Medicare patient, the balance on the account will remain unpaid until the estate is settled. Individuals filing to receive benefits on behalf of a deceased beneficiary are encouraged to submit documentation to establish their entitlement, such as a letter of appointment, proof of executorship, and copies of receipted funeral bills.

When you receive word that a patient has died, show courtesy by not sending a statement in the first week or so after the death. Address the statement to "Estate of (name of patient)" and mail to the patient's last known address. If your office had a long-term relationship with the deceased, the surviving spouse or family member usually will notify the billing office if there is an estate and who is the executor or administrator.

A call to the Probate Court in the county clerk's office where the estate was entered can verify that the estate has been or will be probated. If there is a special form for the billing provider to complete, such as proof of claim, the clerk of the Probate Court, the executor, or the administrator will assist you in filing your claim.

PROFESSIONAL COURTESY

Historically, many physicians chose to treat some patients at no charge or for the amount covered by the patient's insurance. This courtesy is usually extended to other physicians and their families, the practice's personnel and their families, and other health care professionals such as dentists, pharmacists, and clergy members.

The AMA is reviewing their position on the practice of professional courtesy, based on legal and ethical concerns. A service or procedure cannot be billed as an "insurance only" fee. Co-payments, coinsurance and deductibles must be billed as contracted under the insurance plan. Physicians would be billed as other patients: perform the service, bill the insurance, bill the policyholder for co-insurance, co-pays, and deductibles, writing off only amounts when there is a contractual obligation to do so.

When billing non-physician patients such as family members of a physician, hospital employees or employees of other physicians, it is recommended the deductibles, co-pays and coinsurance be collected as indicated under the insurance plan. In the event of a true hardship, the balance can be safely adjusted.

EXERCISE 10–6

Match the term with its definition, placing the correct letter in the space provided.

_____ **1.** Bankruptcy

_____ **2.** Daysheet

_____ **3.** Receipt

_____ **4.** Superbill

_____ **5.** Posting

_____ **6.** Transaction

_____ **7.** Ledger card

_____ **8.** Pegboard system

_____ **9.** Accounts receivable

_____ **10.** Cycle billing

a. the patient's financial record

b. a record of payment received

c. a record or journal of daily financial transactions

d. the amount of money owed to a medical practice by its patients

e. a legal declaration of inability to pay debts

f. accounts divided into groups, usually alphabetically, with each group billed at a different time of the month

g. a "write-it-once" method of bookkeeping

h. transferring information from one record to another

i. a three-part form providing record of account information, charges, payments, CPT and ICD-9-CM codes

j. the occurrence of a financial activity to be recorded

SUMMARY

▪ Initial patient contact usually starts with a telephone call inquiring about the practice and scheduling the appointment.

- The initial face-to-face contact starts at the reception window with patient registration for preparation of the patient record.

- There must be an understanding of the patient registration process for both new and established patients.

- There must be a working knowledge of insurance regulations, especially those contracts with which the physician participates such as HMOs and federal programs.

- Billing procedures including deductibles, co-payments, and referrals, as well as the actual billing process must be accurately performed.

- The collection policy and how to handle various collection problems must be managed by understanding federal and state regulations mandating this process.

- Continuing education is required to keep up-to-date and current in changes relative to administrative skills. This is accomplished by attending seminars and reading newsletters, manuals, and bulletins.

REFERENCES

Altman, Larry. *How to increase your in-house collections.* GLA Collection Company Inc., Louisville, KY, 1998

Bonewit-West, Kathy. *Computer concepts & applications for the medical office.* Philadelphia: W.B. Saunders, 1993.

Fordney, Marilyn Takahashi. *Insurance handbook for the medical office,* 5th ed., Philadelphia: W.B. Saunders, 1997.

Lindh, Wilburta, Marilyn Pooler, Carol Tamparo, Joanne Cerrato. *Comprehensive medical assisting, administrative and clinical competencies.* Albany, NY: Delmar Publishers, 1998.

Rowell, JoAnn. *Understanding health insurance: A guide to professional billing.* Albany, NY: Delmar Publishers, 1998.

Taylor, Dorothy, Sandra Freeman, Keeling B. Lewis. *Medical pegboard procedures,* 3rd ed. Albany, NY: Delmar Publishers, 1996.

Module 11
Filing the Claim Form

Sandra L. Johnson, CMA

LEARNING OBJECTIVES

Upon successful completion of this module, you should be able to :

1. Abstract information from the patient medical record to complete the HCFA-1500 claim form.
2. Complete the HCFA-1500 for commercial and government carriers.
3. Recognize common guidelines to complete the HCFA-1500 claim form.
4. Differentiate between a participating (PAR) physician and a nonparticipating physician (nonPAR).
5. Define and explain the two parts of Medicare.
6. Define Medicaid and the regulations mandated for provider participation.
7. Define the regulations mandated for Worker's Compensation coverage.
8. Explain the functions of the Health Maintenance Organization (HMO).
9. Define CHAMPUS/TRICARE/CHAMPVA.
10. Identify various Blue Cross/Blue Shield policies and their benefits.

INTRODUCTION

Approximately 94% of patients seeking health care have some type of insurance coverage. This means completion of a claim form, an intricate part of the billing process, is necessary.

Each insurance program such as Medicare and Medicaid has terms pertinent to its particular program. The terminology that is common to all programs is discussed before each program is introduced.

What is really meant when the question is asked, "What kind of insurance do you have?" In the medical office, we are referring to health insurance. Health insurance is defined as a contract between the insured and an insurance company or government program designed to reimburse a portion of the cost of medically necessary treatment to those who are sick or injured, or preventive services as a means of preventing illness or injury, or to seek early diagnosis and treatment. Medical care and treatment can be rendered in many settings: physician's offices, clinics, hospitals, ambulatory care centers, nursing homes, just to name a few. More and more medical care today is performed in the outpatient setting as a means of reducing medical costs.

Medical practices today see patients with a variety of health insurance plans:

- Employer sponsored private plans
- Insurance plans
- Health maintenance organizations
- Medicare
- Medicaid
- Individual policies
- CHAMPUS/ TRICARE
- Worker's Compensation

Third-party payers involved in the reimbursement proceedings in the medical practice may be insurance companies and employers. A third-party payer is an individual or company that makes a payment on a debt, but is not a party involved in the creation of the debt. In the physician/patient contract, the first party is the patient who is seeking medical care; the second party is the physician or provider of the service or supply.

Due to the variety of health insurance plans, there will be various methods of reimbursement.

Fee-For-Service reimbursement is the traditional method of reimbursement. Each service performed has a price that is charged to the patient's account.

Capitation is the reimbursement method used by some HMOs and other managed care plans. This method pays the health care provider a fixed amount per person for a period of time regardless of whether expenses are incurred or not, rather than by the type or number of services performed.

Episode-Of-Care reimbursement is a payment method of issuing one lump sum for services rendered to a patient for a specific illness. Global surgical fee payment is an example of this reimbursement method for physicians who perform major surgeries. The global surgical fee payment includes the preoperative visit, the surgery, and the postoperative visit. Any surgical complications are usually paid on a fee-for-service basis.

When a policyholder has two or more medical insurance policies, **coordination of benefits** determines the plan of payment. Coordination of benefits (COB) is a ruling in an insurance policy or state law requiring insurance companies to coordinate reimbursement of benefits when a policyholder has two or more medical insurance policies. This is a legal attempt so that the benefits from the combined policies do not exceed 100% of the covered benefits of the combined policies for all medical expenses submitted.

EXERCISE 11–1

1. Define health insurance.

2. Name four types of health insurance plans presented to the health care facility.

    1. _____

    2. _____

3. _____

4. _____

3. Name four health care settings medical treatment can be given.

1. _____

2. _____

3. _____

4. _____

THE HEALTH INSURANCE CLAIM FORM

Claim forms can be submitted to the carrier electronically or on paper. In April 1975 the American Medical Association (AMA) approved a universal claim form called the health insurance claim form or HCFA-1500. This was a standardized form that could be used to submit both group and individual claims for physician services. In 1990, the HCFA-1500 was revised and printed in red so claims could be optically scanned using optical character readers (OCRs) by the insurance carriers. This universal claim form is now accepted by Medicare, Medicaid, CHAMPUS and private companies, although electronic claims submission is preferred to reduce the costs and expedite reimbursement. An example is shown in Figure 11–1.

The following guidelines are recommended in the preparation of claims for OCRs:

- Claim forms should be typed. Any handwritten data, with the exception of blocks requiring signatures, will have to be manually processed resulting in a delay in payment of the claim.
- Claim forms must be typed on the original red printed form. Photocopies of claims cannot be optically scanned.
- Proper printer alignment of claim forms is necessary.
- Do not interchange a zero with the alpha character O.
- Use pica type (10 characters per inch) and type all alpha characters in uppercase or capital letters.
- Leave one blank space between the patient/policyholder's last name, first name, and middle initial.
- Do not use punctuation in the patient/policyholder's name, except for a hyphen in a compound name.
- Do not use titles such as Sr., Jr., unless they appear on the patient's insurance ID card.
- Do not add dollar signs, decimals, or commas in any dollar field.
- Do not add the decimal in the diagnostic code number as it is imprinted on the form.
- List only one procedure per line.
- Do not add a dash in front of a procedure code modifier.

PLEASE
DO NOT
STAPLE
IN THIS
AREA

CARRIER

APPROVED OMB-0938-0008

PICA

HEALTH INSURANCE CLAIM FORM

PICA

1. MEDICARE MEDICAID CHAMPUS CHAMPVA GROUP FECA OTHER
   (Medicare #) (Medicaid #) (Sponsor's SSN) (VA File #) HEALTH PLAN (SSN or ID) BLK LUNG (SSN) (ID)

1a. INSURED'S I.D. NUMBER (FOR PROGRAM IN ITEM 1)

2. PATIENCE'S NAME (Last Name, First Name, Middle Initial)

3. PATIENT'S BIRTH DATE MM DD YY SEX M F

4. INSURED'S NAME (Last Name, Firts Name, Middle Initial)

5. PATIENT'S ADDRESS (No., Street)

6. PATIENT RELATIONSHIP TO INSURED Self Spouse Child Other

7. INSURED'S ADDRESS (No., Street)

CITY STATE

8. PATIENT STATUS Single Married Other
   Employed Full-Time Student Part-Time Student

CITY STATE

ZIP CODE TELEPHONE (Include Area Code)

ZIP CODE TELEPHONE (Include Area Code)

9. OTHER INSURED'S NAME (Last Name, First Name, Middle Initial)

10. IS PATIENT'S CONDITION RELATED TO:

11. INSURED'S POLICY GROUP OR FECA NUMBER

a. OTHER INSURED'S POLICY OR GROUP NUMBER

a. EMPLOYNMENT? (CURRENT OR PREVIOUS) YES NO

a. INSURED'S DATE OF BIRTH MM DD YY SEX M F

b. OTHER INSURED'S DATE OF BIRTH MM DD YY SEX M F

b AUTO ACCIDENT? PLACE (State) YES NO

b. EMPLOYER'S NAME OR SCHOOL NAME

c. EMPLOYER'S NAME OR SCHOOL NAME

c. OTHER ACCIDENT? YES NO

c. INSURANCE PLAN NAME OR PROGRAM NAME

d. INSURANCE PLAN NAME OR PROGRAM NAME

d. RESERVED FOR LOCAL USE

d. IS THERE ANOTHER HEALTH BENEFIT PLAN? YES NO If yes, return to and complete item 9 a-d.

READ BACK OF FORM BEFORE COMPLETEING & SIGNING THIS FORM.
12. PATIENT'S OR AUTHORIZED PERSON'S SIGNATURE I authorize the release of any medical or other information necessary to process this claim. I also request payment of government benefits either to myself or to the party who accepts assignments below.

SIGNED_____ DATE_____

13. INSURED'S OR AUTHORIZED PERSON'S SIGNATURE I authorize payment of medical benefits to the undersigned physician or supplier for services described below.

SIGNED_____

14. DATE OF CURRENT: MM DD YY ILLNESS (First sympton) OR INJURY (Accident)OR PREGNANCY (LMP)

15. IF PATIENT HAS HAD SAME OR SIMILAR ILLNESS. GIVE FIRST DATE MM DD YY

16. DATES PATIENT UNABLE TO WORK IN CURRENT OCCUPATION MM DD YY MM DD YY FROM TO

17. NAME OR REFERRING PHYSICIAN OR OTHER SOURCE

17a. I.D. NUMBER OF REFERRING PHYSICIAN

18. HOSPITALIZATION DATES RELATED TO CURRENT SERVICES MM DD YY MM DD YY FROM TO

19. RESERVED FOR LOCAL USE

20. OUTSIDE LAB? YES NO $ CHARGES

21. DIAGNOSIS OR NATURE OF ILLNESS OR INJURY. (RELATE ITEMS 1,2,3 OR 4 TO ITEM 24E BY LINE)
   1.|_____.___   3. I_____.___
   2.I_____.___   4. I_____.___

22. MEDICAID RESUBMISSION CODE ORIGINAL REF. NO.

23. PRIOR AUTHORIZATION NUMBER

24. A DATE(S) OF SERVICE		B Place of Service	C Type of Service	D PROCEDURES, SERVICES, OR SUPPLIES (Explain Unusual Circumstances) CPT/HCPCS MODIFIER	E DIAGNOSIS CODE	F $ CHARGES	G DAYS OR UNITS	H EPSDT Family Plan	I EMG	J COB	K RESERVED FOR LOCAL USE
From MM DD YY	To MM DD YY										
1											
2											
3											
4											
5											
6											

25. FEDERAL TAX I.D. NUMBER SSN EIN

26. PATIENT'S ACCOUNT NO.

27. ACCEPT ASSIGNMENT? (For govt. claims, see back) YES NO

28. TOTAL CHARGE $

29. AMOUNT PAID $

30. BALANCE DUE $

31. SIGNATURE OF PHYSICIAN OR SUPPLIER INCLUDING DEGREES OR CREDENTIALS (I certify that the statements on the reverse apply to this bill and are made a part thereof.)

SIGNED DATE

32. NAME AND ADDRESS OF FACULTY WHERE SERVICES WERE RENDERED (If other than home or office)

33. PHYSICIAN'S, SUPPLIER'S BILLING NAME, ADDRESS, ZIP CODE & PHONE#

PIN # GRP #

PATIENT AND INSURED INFORMATION

PHYSICIAN OR SUPPLIER INFORMATION

(APPROVED BY AMA COUNCIL ON MEDICAL SERVICE 8/88) **PLEASE PRINT OR TYPE**

FORM HCFA-1500 (U2) (12-90)
FORM OWCP -1500 FORM RRB-1500

Figure 11–1 HCFA 1500 Universal Claim Form.

- Do not add parentheses when designating the area code of the telephone number as they are imprinted on the form.
- **DO** use two zeros in the cent column when the fee is listed in whole dollars.
- All dates should be typed using eight-digit dates representing month, day and year, taking care to remain within the vertical dividers within the block.
  EXAMPLE: 01/01/2000

  Eight-digit dates are a new requirement by HCFA to accommodate the new millennium.
- Do not type anything in the upper right-hand corner of the claim form as indicated on the form, "Do Not Write In This Space".

The name and address of the insurance company to receive a paper claim can be typed in the upper left-hand corner of the form.

Completing the HCFA-1500

The patient information required to complete the top portion of the HCFA-1500 is retrieved from the patient's registration form found in the chart. Verify the patient has signed the release of medical information statement either by signing the claim form or a special form unique to the practice and retained in the patient's chart. This special form authorizes the processing of the claim form without the patient's signature on each form submitted. In Block 12 of each claim form filed for that patient, **"Signature On File"** must be typed or stamped, as in Figure 11–2.

Figure 11–3 shows an example of a special statement form adopted for use by a particular medical office.

This dated, signed statement to release information is generally considered to be valid for one year from the signature date. However, most offices update medical records yearly, including the statement to release medical information. Undated signed forms are assumed to be valid until revoked by the patient or guardian. HCFA allows government programs to accept both dated and undated authorizations.

There are exceptions to the need for a signed authorization for release of information. These exceptions are patients covered by Medicaid and those covered by Workers' Compensation. The federal government has mandated in these programs that the patient is a third-party beneficiary in a contract between the health care provider and the governmental agency that sponsors these programs. When the provider agrees to treat Medicaid patients or a Workers' Compensation patient, they agree to accept the program's payment as payment in full for covered procedures performed to those patients. The patient can only be billed for services that are not covered, or when the insurance carrier determines the patient was ineligible for benefits on the dates of services reported.

If the patient is physically or mentally unable to sign, the person representing the patient may sign for the patient. This is accomplished by indicating the patient's name on the signature line, followed by the representative's name, address, relationship to the patient, and the reason the patient cannot sign. Medicare and Medigap carriers accept this authorization indefinitely unless the patient or the patient's representative revokes this arrangement.

Figure 11–2 "Signature on File."

Lowery B. Johnson, M.D.
Hwy 311 Suite A31
Sellersburg, IN 47172
812-246-1234

ASSIGNMENT OF BENEFITS

I instruct my insurance company to pay benefits directly to Dr. Lowery Johnson for services rendered and that such payment should be mailed to this physician's office. A photocopy of this assignment shall be as valid as the original.

I also authorize this office to release such medical information as may be required to process my claim with the insurance company.

_____
Signature

_____
Date

Figure 11–3 Special form for authorization and assignment of benefits.

If the patient is illiterate or physically handicapped and unable to sign the authorization, an "X" can be made on the signature line. A witness must sign his/her name and address next to the "X".

Another exception to the signed authorization is when filing claims for medical services provided by a physician to patients seen at a hospital that are not expected to be seen in that physician's office for follow-up care. These patients are required to sign an authorization for treatment and release of medical information at the hospital before being seen by the health care provider. If the hospital's release form is written to include the release of information from the hospital and the physician's service in treating the patient, claims submitted by the physician's office for his/her charges do not require a separate release of medical information form from the patient. "Signature On File" can be typed or stamped in Block 12. The hospital can provide a copy of the signed authorization if it is needed at a later date for verification purposes.

Block 13 of the HCFA-1500 is the assignment of benefits authorization. The patient's signature here allows the insurance company to pay claim benefits directly to the physician or provider rather than to the patient. Obtaining this authorization can also be accomplished by an assignment of benefits to the physician statement as demonstrated in Figure 11–4.

12. PATIENT'S OR AUTHORIZED PERSON'S SIGNATURE I authorize the release of any medical or other information necessary to process this claim. I also request payment of government benefits either to myself or to the party who accepts assignment below.

SIGNED ___SIGNATURE ON FILE___   DATE _____

13. INSURED'S OR AUTHORIZED PERSON'S SIGNATURE I authorize payment of medical benefits to the undersigned physician or supplier for services described below.

SIGNED ___SIGNATURE ON FILE___

Figure 11–4 Payment authorization.

EXERCISE 11–2

1. What is the purpose of obtaining a signature on file form?

2. What are the two exceptions to the need for release of information.

3. What is the recommended procedure to obtain the signature for release of medical information when the patient is treated in the hospital and not expected to be seen for follow-up in the office?

The lower portion of the HCFA-1500 contains information abstracted from the patient's medical record.

The following instructions are generally recognized for filing commercial and health maintenance organization (HMO) fee-for-service claims. Some regional carriers may require information in special blocks based on local requirements; typically those blocks are marked "Reserved for Local Use."

PATIENT AND POLICY IDENTIFICATION

Block 1—Program Destination Boxes—Place "X" in the box of program for which you are submitting the claim form.

Block 1A—**Insured's Identification Number**—Enter the insurance identification number as it appears on the policyholder insurance card.

1. MEDICARE	MEDICAID	CHAMPUS	CHAMPVA	GROUP HEALTH PLAN	FECA BLK LUNG	OTHER	1a. INSURED'S I.D. NUMBER	(FOR PROGRAM IN ITEM 1)
(Medicare #)	(Medicaid #)	(Sponsor's SSN)	(VA File #)	(SSN or ID)	(SSN)	(ID)		
2. PATIENT'S NAME (Last Name, First Name, Middle Initial)			3. PATIENT'S BIRTH DATE MM DD YY	SEX M F			4. INSURED'S NAME (Last Name, First Name, Middle Initial)	

Figure 11–5 HCFA-1500 Blocks 1–1A.

Block 2—**Patient's Name**—Enter the full name, last name first, followed by first name and middle initial, of the patient listed on the insurance identification card. Incorrect format of name or nicknames could cause rejection of the claim.

Block 3—**Patient's Birth Date**—Enter birth month, date and year, using eight-digit dates. Place dates in between parallel lines.

Example: 01/01/1950

Block 4—**Insured's Name**—If insured is same as patient, enter "SAME". If different than patient, enter last name first, followed by first name, then middle initial as it appears on the insurance card.

Figure 11–6 HCFA-1500 Blocks 2, 3, 4.

BLOCK 5—Patient's Address—Enter patient's complete mailing address on line 1, city and two-letter initials of state on line 2, zip code, area code, and telephone number on line 3.

Block 6—Patient Relationship to Insured—Place "X" in the appropriate box for patient's relationship to insured.

Block 7—Insured's Address—If the insured's address is the same as the patient's address listed in Block 5, enter the word "SAME". If different, type in the mailing address of the insured.

Block 8—Patient Status—Place "X" in the appropriate boxes pertaining to the patient.

Note If the patient is between the ages of 19 and 23, is dependent on a family policy, and is a full-time student, the claim will not be paid unless the patient proves full-time student status at the time of the medical encounter. Written acknowledgment of the student's status from the school, college, or university should be filed with the first claim of each semester.

Figure 11–7 HCFA-1500 Blocks 5, 6, 7, 8.

Block 9—Other Insured's Name—If none, type in the word "NONE". If there is secondary or supplemental health care coverage, the insured's name of the secondary policy is entered, last name, first name, middle initial. In 9a, enter the policy number or group number of the secondary policy; 9b, date of birth and sex, employer of the insured, if the coverage is an employer-sponsored group policy or an organization/union as identified on the patient's identification card.

Figure 11–8 HCFA-1500 Block 9.

Block 10—Is Patient's Condition Related to—

Block 10a—Employment (Current or Previous)—In most cases mark "X" in "No" box. "YES" indicates the services reported in Block 24d are related to an on-the-job injury and the previously filed Workers' Compensation claim has been rejected. To file claim with commercial carrier in these circumstances, a copy of the Workers' Compensation Explanation of Benefits and/or letter indicating rejection of the claim must be attached to the commercial claim.

Block 10b—Auto Accident—Mark "X" in the appropriate box. "YES" indicates possible third-party liability. The commercial health insurance claim carrier will return the claim until the issue of third-party liability coverage is settled.

Block 10c—Other Injury—Mark "X" in the appropriate box. "YES" indicates possible third-party liability. If this is not the case, enter one or more E codes in Block 21 in addition to the code(s) for the type of injury to indicate cause of injury and its place of occurrence.

Block 10d—Reserved for Local Use—Leave blank.

9. OTHER INSURED'S NAME (Last Name, First Name, Middle Initial)	10. IS PATIENT'S CONDITION RELATED TO:	11. INSURED'S POLICY GROUP OR FECA NUMBER
a. OTHER INSURED'S POLICY OR GROUP NUMBER	a. EMPLOYMENT? (CURRENT OR PREVIOUS) ☐ YES ☐ NO	a. INSURED'S DATE OF BIRTH MM DD YY SEX M ☐ F ☐
b. OTHER INSURED'S DATE OF BIRTH MM DD YY SEX M ☐ F ☐	b. AUTO ACCIDENT? PLACE (State) ☐ YES ☐ NO	b. EMPLOYER'S NAME OR SCHOOL NAME
c. EMPLOYER'S NAME OR SCHOOL NAME	c. OTHER ACCIDENT? ☐ YES ☐ NO	c. INSURANCE PLAN NAME OR PROGRAM NAME
d. INSURANCE PLAN NAME OR PROGRAM NAME	10d. RESERVED FOR LOCAL USE	d. IS THERE ANOTHER HEALTH BENEFIT PLAN? ☐ YES ☐ NO *If yes*, return to and complete item 9 a-d.

Figure 11–9 HCFA-1500 Block 10.

Block 11—Insured's Policy Group or FECA Number—Enter the policy or group number if one is indicated on the card. Not all policies have FECA numbers. FECA (Federal Employees' Compensation Act) provides Workers' Compensation coverage to federal and postal workers including wage replacement, medical and vocational rehabilitation benefits for work-related injury and occupational illness. For example, coal miners afflicted with black lung disease and the federal workers injured in the 1995 Oklahoma City bombing tragedy are covered under FECA.

Block 11a—Insured's Date of Birth and Sex—Enter the birth date (using the eight-digit date) and sex of the insured, other than patient, named in Block 4.

Block 11b—Employer's Name or School Name—Enter the name of the employer if the coverage is an employer-sponsored group policy or an organization/union/school name, if one is identified on the patient's identification card.

Block 11c—Insurance Plan Name or Program Name—Enter the name of the carrier for the patient's policy.

Block 11d—Is There Another Health Benefit Plan—Mark "X" in "NO" box if patient is covered by only one insurance. If "YES" is marked, complete Block 9a–d to indicate a secondary policy.

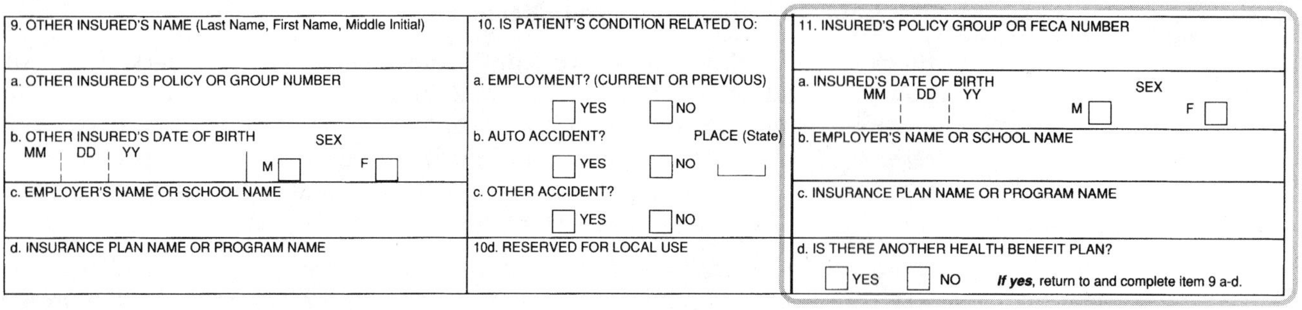

Figure 11–10 HCFA-1500 Block 11.

Block 12—Authorization for Release of Information—Patient can sign here or the words "SIGNATURE ON FILE" may be typed here.

Block 13—Authorization for Payment of Benefits to the Provider—The patient's signature authorizes direct payment to the physician for the benefits due the patient. "SIGNATURE ON FILE" is acceptable if an assignment statement has been previously signed and is on file.

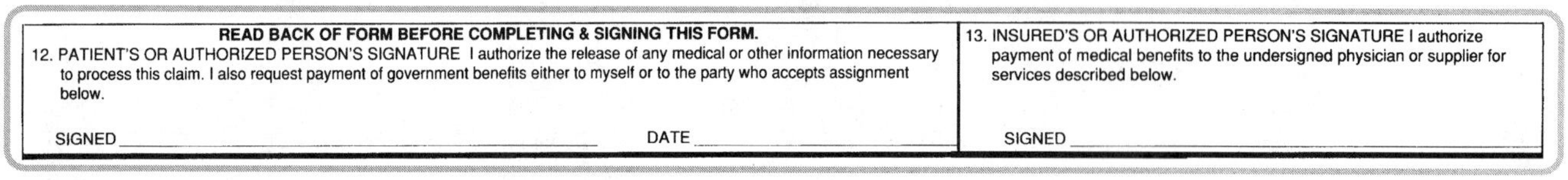

Figure 11–11 HCFA-1500 Blocks 12, 13.

DIAGNOSTIC AND TREATMENT DATA

Block 14—Date of Illness, First Symptom, Injury, Pregnancy, LMP (last menstrual period)—Enter data from the patient's medical record, if it is available. In cases where the history does not give the first date but does give an approximation, count back to the approximated date and enter it on the claim form.

Example: Today's date 1/9/2000, record states, "injured 2 months ago." The date typed would be 11/09/1999.

Block 15—If Patient Has Had Same or Similar Illness, Give First Date—Enter the data if applicable.

Block 16—Dates Patient Unable To Work in Current Occupation—Enter data if applicable.

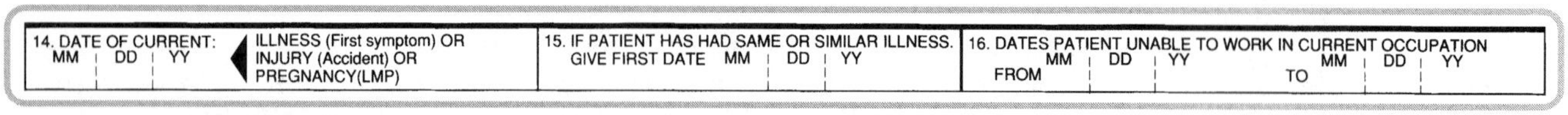

Figure 11–12 HCFA-1500 Blocks 14, 15, 16.

Block 17—Name of Referring Physician or Other Source—Enter the name of the referring/ordering physician(s) or other health care provider, if any of the following services are listed in Block 24d:

consultation, surgery, diagnostic testing, physical or occupational therapy, home health care, or durable medical equipment

For Assistant Surgeon claims, enter the name of the attending surgeon.

Block 17a—ID Number of Referring Physician—Enter the Social Security Number (SSN) of the provider named in Block 17. If there is no referring provider, leave blank.

Block 18—Hospitalization Dates Related to Current Services—Enter the admission date and the discharge date using eight-digit date, if any procedure/service is provided to a patient who is admitted to the hospital as an inpatient.

Block 19—Reserved for Local Use—Information to be entered is determined by regional carriers. Consult appropriate billing manual or the carrier to determine if any information is required for this block.

Block 20—Outside Lab—Mark "X" in NO box if all laboratory procedures included on this claim form were performed in the provider's office.

Mark "X" in YES box if laboratory procedures listed on the claim form were performed by an outside laboratory and billed to the referring health care provider. If YES is marked, enter the total amount charged for all tests performed by the outside laboratory. The charge for each test should be entered as a separate line in Block 24f and the name and address of the outside laboratory included in Block 32.

Note Some local carriers may have other specific instructions for completing this block.

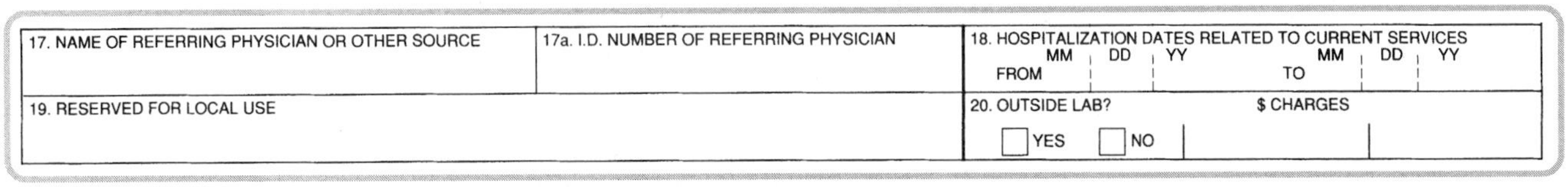

17. NAME OF REFERRING PHYSICIAN OR OTHER SOURCE	17a. I.D. NUMBER OF REFERRING PHYSICIAN	18. HOSPITALIZATION DATES RELATED TO CURRENT SERVICES MM DD YY MM DD YY FROM TO
19. RESERVED FOR LOCAL USE		20. OUTSIDE LAB? $ CHARGES ☐ YES ☐ NO

Figure 11–13 HCFA-1500 Blocks 17, 17a, 18, 19, 20.

Block 21—Diagnosis or Nature of Illness or Injury—Enter the ICD-9-CM code(s) for the diagnosis of conditions treated on this claim in this space. Four codes can be submitted per claim form.

Block 22—Medicaid Resubmission Code—Leave blank. Used for Medicaid claims only.

Block 23—Prior Authorization Number—Enter the assigned prior authorization number when the patient's insurance plan requires specific services to be authorized by the patient's primary physician or the carrier's managed care department before the procedure is performed. Some carriers may require written authorization to be attached to the claim form.

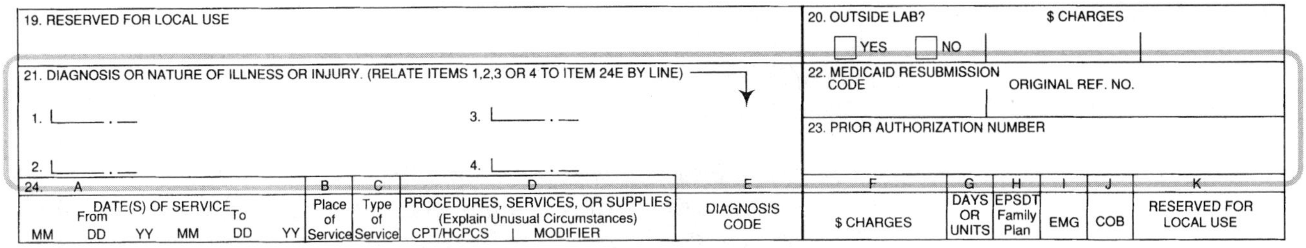

Figure 11–14 HCFA-1500 Blocks 21, 22, 23.

Block 24a—Date(s) of Service—Enter the date the procedure was performed in the "FROM" column. Do not fill in the "TO" column for a single procedure entry. To list similar procedures with same procedure codes and charges performed on consecutive dates, indicate the last day the procedure was performed in the "TO" column. In Block 24g, enter the number of consecutive days or units in the "days/units column."

Block 24b—Place of Service (POS)—Enter the correct POS code number from the following list of codes.

Provider's Office	11
Patient's Home	12
Inpatient Hospital	21
Outpatient Hospital	22
Emergency Room Hospital	23
Ambulatory Surgical Center	24
Birthing Center	25
Military Treatment Facility or	26
Uniformed Service Treatment Facility	26
Skilled Nursing Facility	31
Nursing Home	32
Custodial Care Facility	33
Hospice	34
Federally Qualified Health Center	50
Inpatient Psychiatric Center	51
Psychiatric Facility—Day	52
Community Mental Health Center	53
Intermediate Care Facility/Mental Retardation	54
Resident Substance Abuse Treatment Center	55
Psychiatric Residential Treatment Center	56
Comprehensive Inpatient Rehab Facility	61
Comprehensive Outpatient Rehab Facility	62
End-Stage Renal Disease Treatment Facility	65
State/Local Public Health Clinic	71
Independent Laboratory	81
Other unlisted facility	99

Block 24c—Type of Service Codes (TOS)—Enter the correct TOS code from the following list of codes. NOTE: Not all carriers use TOS codes.

Medical Care	1
Surgery	2
Consultation	3
Diagnostic X-ray	4
Diagnostic Laboratory	5
Radiation Therapy	6
Anesthesia	7
Assistant Surgeon	8
Other medical services	9
Pneumococcal Vaccine	V
Second surgical opinion	Y

Block 24d—Procedures, Services, or Supply Codes—Enter the correct five-digit CPT code or HCPCS Level II/III code number and any required modifiers for the procedure being reported in this block. No more than six procedures/services can be listed per claim.

Block 24e—Diagnosis Code—Enter the reference number (1 through 4) for the ICD-9-CM code listed in Block 21 that most closely justifies the medical necessity for each procedure listed in Block 24d.

Note Some carriers will accept more than one reference number on each line. If more than one reference number is used, the first number stated must represent the primary diagnosis that justifies the medical necessity for performing the procedures on that line. Do not use commas, dashes or slashes to separate multiple reference numbers.

Block 24f—Charges—Enter the fee for the procedure charged to the patient's account. If identical, consecutive procedures are reported on this line, enter the TOTAL fee charged for the combined procedures.

Block 24g—Days or Units—Enter the number of days/units or services reported on each line.

Block 24h—EPSDT (Early and Periodic Screening for Diagnosis and Treatment)—Leave blank. This block is used for identifying all services that are provided under the special Medicaid EPSDT program.

Block 24i—EMG (Emergency Treatment)—Check this box when the health care provider determines that a medical emergency existed and a delay in treatment would be injurious to the patient. This is especially important in a managed care situation and no prior authorization was obtained before the start of emergency treatment.

Block 24j—COB (Coordination of Benefits)—Leave blank.

Block 24k—Reserved for Local Use—Leave blank.

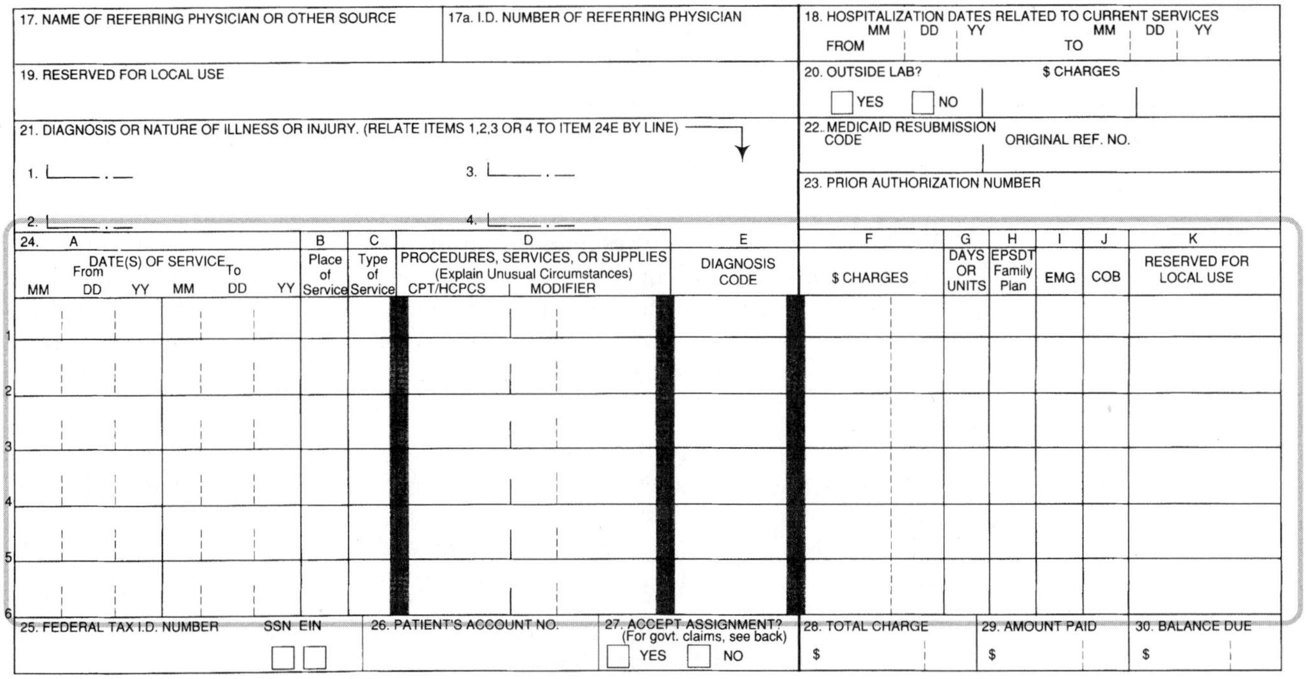

Figure 11–15 HCFA-1500 Blocks 24.

PROVIDER/BILLING ENTITY IDENTIFICATION

Block 25—Federal Tax ID Number—Enter the provider's Employer Tax Identification Number (EIN) and check the appropriate box.

Block 26—Patient Account Number—If a numerical identification is assigned to identify the patient's account or ledger card, enter that number here. Leave blank if the practice files patient accounts by patient name rather than number.

Block 27—Accept Assignment—Mark "X" when appropriate for Medicare claims. Participating physicians MUST accept assignment. Nonparticipating physicians may accept on a case-by-case basis. Assignment must be accepted for Medicare/Medicaid patients. **Accepting assignment** means the physician or provider will accept what Medicare pays and not bill the difference between the cost of the service and the Medicare payment. The difference is adjusted or written off.

Block 28—Total Charge—Add up all charges on this claim form and enter the total in this block. If multiple claims for one patient are completed because there are more than six services/procedures reported, the total charge recorded on each claim form must represent the total of the items on each separate claim form submitted.

Block 29—Amount Paid—Enter the amount the patient has paid toward the required annual deductible, or any co-payments collected from the patient for the procedures listed on this claim form.

Block 30—Balance Due—Enter the amount subtracted from the figure in Block 29 from the figure in Block 28.

25. FEDERAL TAX I.D. NUMBER SSN EIN	26. PATIENT'S ACCOUNT NO.	27. ACCEPT ASSIGNMENT? (For govt. claims, see back) YES NO	28. TOTAL CHARGE $	29. AMOUNT PAID $	30. BALANCE DUE $
31. SIGNATURE OF PHYSICIAN OR SUPPLIER INCLUDING DEGREES OR CREDENTIALS (I certify that the statements on the reverse apply to this bill and are made a part thereof.)	32. NAME AND ADDRESS OF FACILITY WHERE SERVICES WERE RENDERED (If other than home or office)		33. PHYSICIAN'S, SUPPLIER'S BILLING NAME, ADDRESS, ZIP CODE & PHONE #		
SIGNED DATE			PIN#	GRP#	

Figure 11–16 HCFA-1500 Blocks 25, 26, 27, 28, 29, 30

Block 31—Signature of Physician or Supplier—If arrangements have not been made with major health insurance carriers to permit either a signature stamp or a typed name and professional title, the provider must sign each claim. When transmitting claims electronically to an insurance company, a certification letter must be filed with the insurance company to replace the signature usually required in this space.

Block 32—Name and Address of Facility Where Services Rendered—Complete when the services listed on the claim form were performed at a site other than the provider's office or the home.

If the "YES" box in Block 20 is checked, enter the name and address of the laboratory that performed the laboratory procedures.

Block 33—Physician's Supplier's Billing Name, Mailing Address, Phone Number, Provider's Identification Number (PIN) and Group Number (GRP)—Type in the official name of the practice/clinic and the full mailing address on the next three lines. Do not put the zip code in the last line of this block where the words "PIN# GRP#" appear. The phone number, including the area code, are typed to the right of the phrase "& PHONE #." It may overlap into the above printing. Enter any carrier-assigned participating identification number (PIN) and/or group practice identification number (GRP) in the appropriate space.

25. FEDERAL TAX I.D. NUMBER SSN EIN	26. PATIENT'S ACCOUNT NO.	27. ACCEPT ASSIGNMENT? (For govt. claims, see back) YES NO	28. TOTAL CHARGE $	29. AMOUNT PAID $	30. BALANCE DUE $
31. SIGNATURE OF PHYSICIAN OR SUPPLIER INCLUDING DEGREES OR CREDENTIALS (I certify that the statements on the reverse apply to this bill and are made a part thereof.) SIGNED DATE	32. NAME AND ADDRESS OF FACILITY WHERE SERVICES WERE RENDERED (If other than home or office)		33. PHYSICIAN'S, SUPPLIER'S BILLING NAME, ADDRESS, ZIP CODE & PHONE # PIN# GRP#		

Figure 11–17 HCFA-1500 Blocks 31, 32, 33.

■ *When filing insurance claims for a medical practice, it is critical to obtain and read updated billing manuals, newsletters and brochures that contain changes, as they become effective.*

Figure 11–18 is an example of a completed HCFA-1500 form.

Common Errors That Delay Claims Processing

After checking the claim form for errors, retain a copy of the claim for office files, post the date of the claim filing on the patient's account/ledger, and mail to the insurance carrier. Some common errors that delay processing of the claim, or result in rejection of the claim are:

- Incorrect patient insurance identification number.
- Incorrect CPT code with failure to use modifier when valid.
- Incorrect ICD-9-CM code with failure to use fourth or fifth digits when required.
- ICD-9-CM code does not correspond with CPT code as a service performed or treatment provided by the physician to validate procedure was medically necessary.
- Failure to identify referring physician and the identification number.
- Incorrect charges and total amounts that do not equal total charges.
- Missing place-of-service code required for Medicare, Medicaid and CHAMPUS, and most commercial carriers.
- Missing type-of-service code required for CHAMPUS and some commercial carriers.
- Incorrect, missing or duplicate dates of service.
- Incomplete provider information such as name, address, identification numbers.

When the insurance company receives the insurance claim form, the computer first scans the claim form for patient and policy identification to match with subscriber name. CPT codes are checked with services determined as covered procedures contained in the policy. CPT codes are cross-matched with ICD-9-CM codes to certify the medical necessity of the claim. A preexisting condition clause may be checked in the policy. This is a medical condition under active treatment at the time application is made for an insurance policy. This could result in the disease or condition to be listed as an uncovered service not reimbursable in an insurance policy.

PLEASE
DO NOT
STAPLE
IN THIS
AREA

CIGNA

APPROVED OMB-0938-0008

CARRIER

| | PICA | | | | | | | | **HEALTH INSURANCE CLAIM FORM** | | PICA | | |

1. MEDICARE	MEDICAID	CHAMPUS	CHAMPVA	GROUP HEALTH PLAN	FECA BLK LUNG	OTHER	1a. INSURED'S I.D. NUMBER	(FOR PROGRAM IN ITEM 1)
(Medicare #)	(Medicaid #)	(Sponsor's SSN)	(VA File #) X	(SSN or ID)	(SSN)	(ID)	403082214	

2. PATIENT'S NAME (Last Name, First Name, Middle Initial)
PEARL OPAL J

3. PATIENT'S BIRTH DATE
MM 12 DD 24 YY 68 M F X

4. INSURED'S NAME (Last Name, First Name, Middle Initial)
PEARL BRUCE J

5. PATIENT'S ADDRESS (No., Street)
7775 SMITH RD

6. PATIENT RELATIONSHIP TO INSURED
Self Spouse X Child Other

7. INSURED'S ADDRESS (No., Street)
SAME

CITY
SMITHFIELD   STATE IN

8. PATIENT STATUS
Single Married X Other

CITY   STATE

ZIP CODE
47222   TELEPHONE (Include Area Code)
(513) 222-4773

Employed Full-Time Student Part-Time Student

ZIP CODE   TELEPHONE (INCLUDE AREA CODE)
(   )

9. OTHER INSURED'S NAME (Last Name, First Name, Middle Initial)

10. IS PATIENT'S CONDITION RELATED TO:

11. INSURED'S POLICY GROUP OR FECA NUMBER
EPN500

a. OTHER INSURED'S POLICY OR GROUP NUMBER

a. EMPLOYMENT? (CURRENT OR PREVIOUS)
YES X NO

a. INSURED'S DATE OF BIRTH
MM 07 DD 07 YY 67 M X SEX F

b. OTHER INSURED'S DATE OF BIRTH
MM DD YY M F

b. AUTO ACCIDENT? PLACE (State)
YES X NO

b. EMPLOYER'S NAME OR SCHOOL NAME
SMITHFIELD ELECTRICAL CO

c. EMPLOYER'S NAME OR SCHOOL NAME

c. OTHER ACCIDENT?
YES X NO

c. INSURANCE PLAN NAME OR PROGRAM NAME
CIGNA

d. INSURANCE PLAN NAME OR PROGRAM NAME

10d. RESERVED FOR LOCAL USE

d. IS THERE ANOTHER HEALTH BENEFIT PLAN?
YES NO If yes, return to and complete item 9 a-d.

READ BACK OF FORM BEFORE COMPLETING & SIGNING THIS FORM.
12. PATIENT'S OR AUTHORIZED PERSON'S SIGNATURE I authorize the release of any medical or other information necessary to process this claim. I also request payment of government benefits either to myself or to the party who accepts assignment below.

SIGNED SIGNATURE ON FILE   DATE _____

13. INSURED'S OR AUTHORIZED PERSON'S SIGNATURE I authorize payment of medical benefits to the undersigned physician or supplier for services described below.

SIGNED _____

14. DATE OF CURRENT: ILLNESS (First symptom) OR INJURY (Accident) OR PREGNANCY(LMP)
MM 05 DD 01 YY 9X

15. IF PATIENT HAS HAD SAME OR SIMILAR ILLNESS. GIVE FIRST DATE MM DD YY

16. DATES PATIENT UNABLE TO WORK IN CURRENT OCCUPATION
FROM MM DD YY TO MM DD YY

17. NAME OF REFERRING PHYSICIAN OR OTHER SOURCE

17a. I.D. NUMBER OF REFERRING PHYSICIAN

18. HOSPITALIZATION DATES RELATED TO CURRENT SERVICES
FROM MM DD YY TO MM DD YY

19. RESERVED FOR LOCAL USE

20. OUTSIDE LAB? $ CHARGES
YES NO

21. DIAGNOSIS OR NATURE OF ILLNESS OR INJURY. (RELATE ITEMS 1,2,3 OR 4 TO ITEM 24E BY LINE)
1. 599 0   3. |___ . ___
2. |___ . ___   4. |___ . ___

22. MEDICAID RESUBMISSION CODE ORIGINAL REF. NO.

23. PRIOR AUTHORIZATION NUMBER

24. A. DATE(S) OF SERVICE						B. Place of Service	C. Type of Service	D. PROCEDURES, SERVICES, OR SUPPLIES (Explain Unusual Circumstances)		E. DIAGNOSIS CODE	F. $ CHARGES	G. DAYS OR UNITS	H. EPSDT Family Plan	I. EMG	J. COB	K. RESERVED FOR LOCAL USE
From MM	DD	YY	To MM	DD	YY			CPT/HCPCS	MODIFIER							
05	01	9X				11		90213		1	46 00	1				
05	01	9X				11		81000		1	18 00	1				

25. FEDERAL TAX I.D. NUMBER SSN EIN
75-2166173 X

26. PATIENT'S ACCOUNT NO.

27. ACCEPT ASSIGNMENT? (For govt. claims, see back)
YES NO

28. TOTAL CHARGE
$ 64 00

29. AMOUNT PAID
$ 10 00

30. BALANCE DUE
$ 54 00

31. SIGNATURE OF PHYSICIAN OR SUPPLIER INCLUDING DEGREES OR CREDENTIALS (I certify that the statements on the reverse apply to this bill and are made a part thereof.)

SIGNED Lowery Johnson MD DATE 5/1/9X

32. NAME AND ADDRESS OF FACILITY WHERE SERVICES WERE RENDERED (If other than home or office)
SAME

33. PHYSICIAN'S, SUPPLIER'S BILLING NAME, ADDRESS, ZIP CODE & PHONE #
LOWERY JOHNSON MD
HWY 311 SUITE A31
SELLERSBURG IN 47172
PIN# 1948 GRP# (822) 752-9118

(APPROVED BY AMA COUNCIL ON MEDICAL SERVICE 8/88) **PLEASE PRINT OR TYPE**

FORM HCFA-1500 (U2) (12-90)
FORM OWCP-1500 FORM RRB-1500

PHYSICIAN OR SUPPLIER INFORMATION

PATIENT AND INSURED INFORMATION

Figure 11–18 HCFA-1500 completed for a commercial insurance carrier.

The common data file is checked to determine if the patient is receiving concurrent care for the same condition by more than one physician.

Charges submitted on the claim form are verified with the allowed charges of the policy. Determination is made of the patient's annual deductible obligation. The **deductible** is the total amount the patient must pay for covered services before insurance benefits are payable. Co-payment requirement is then determined. **Co-payment** is a specified dollar amount the patient must pay the provider for each visit or service. **Coinsurance** is a specified percentage of the insurance-determined allowed fee, for each service the patient must pay the health care provider.

The **Explanation of Benefits (EOB)** is a summary explaining how the insurance company determines its reimbursement, containing the following information (Figure 11-19):

■ A list of all procedures and charges submitted on the claim form.

■ A list of procedures submitted on the claim form but not covered by the policy.

■ A list of all allowed charges for each covered procedure.

■ The amount of the deductible, if any, subtracted from the total allowed charges.

■ The patient's financial responsibility for the claim, such as the co-payment.

■ The total amount payable on this claim by the insurance company.

■ Direct payment means the physician receives the insurance check and the EOB. Direct payment occurs when:

   1. The physician participates with an insurance carrier in a contract agreement.

   2. The patient signs Block 13 on the HCFA-1500, authorization of benefits statement to pay benefits directly to the physician.

   3. Box 27 on the HCFA-1500 is marked "Yes" to accept assignment.

An example of carrier's EOB is shown in Figure 11–19.

EXERCISE 11–3

Match the term with its definition, placing the letter of the correct answer in the space provided.

_____ **1.** explanation of benefits

_____ **2.** preexisting condition

_____ **3.** deductible

_____ **4.** co-payment

_____ **5.** coinsurance

a. a specified dollar amount the patient must pay the provider for each visit or service.

b. a summary outlining the insurance company's determination of reimbursement.

c. a medical condition under active treatment at the time application is made for an insurance policy.

d. the total amount the patient must pay for covered services before insurance benefits are payable.

e. a specific percentage of the insurance-determined allowed fee for each service the patient must pay the health care provider.

ID NO | 406-76-1759 | DATE | JUN 08, 1998

HEALTH CARE CLAIM SUMMARY

This summary shows claims processed for the insured of   SANDRA L JOHNSON   ID NUMBER   406-7
Any payments shown were made during the period of   JUN 01, 1998   through   JUN 08, 1998

TOTAL CHARGES PROCESSED	$400.00

TOTAL PAID TO YOU	$.00	TOTAL PAID TO PROVIDER	$360.00

TOTAL AMOUNT NOT PAID $40.00
This amount is the sum of the LESS DEDUCTIBLE column plus the AMOUNT NOT PAID column

PLEASE REFER TO THE CODES IN THE EXPL COLUMN AND THEIR EXPLANATIONS.

CLAIM NUMBER	PATIENT	PROVIDER (PROV)	TYPE OF SERVICE	SERVICE DATES FROM	TO	TOTAL CHARGES	BASIC PAYS YOU OR PROVIDER	ELIGIBLE CHARGES	MAJOR MEDICAL LESS DEDUCT-IBLE	PAYS YOU OR PROVIDER	AMOUNT NOT PAID
8138064538	SANDRA	GINGER Q MAGUIRE	ANESTHESIA	040398	040398	400.00		400.00		360.00PROV	40.00
						400.00	.00PROV	400.00	.00	360.00PROV	40.00

IF YOUR BENEFIT SUMMARY INCLUDES CHARGES YOU DON'T RECOGNIZE, IT COULD BE THE RESULT OF A MISHANDLED OR FRAUDULENT CLAIM. PLEASE NOTIFY YOUR CUSTOMER SERVICE REPRESENTATIVE.

EXPLANATION:
872 THIS AMOUNT IS THE COINSURANCE (SHARE) THAT IS YOUR RESPONSIBILITY UNDER YOUR POLICY

THIS IS NOT A BILL

FOR CUSTOMER ASSISTANCE CALL TOLL FREE 1-800-553-2084
SEND WRITTEN INQUIRIES TO: ANTHEM INSURANCE COMPANIES, INC, PO BOX 590, GREENWOOD IN 46142-0590

DEAR INSURED: This summary of claims received on behalf of you and any other persons covered under your policy. We are providing it to you to help you better understand how your coverage is working to protect you.

CONTACT US AT THE PHONE OR ADDRESS SHOWN ABOVE:
IF YOU HAVE MOVED; we will correct your address.
IF YOUR IDENTIFICATION CARD HAS BEEN LOST OR STOLEN; we will replace it.
IF YOU HAVE ANY QUESTIONS ABOUT THIS CLAIM SUMMARY OR YOUR COVERAGE; we will be glad to answer them.

ADDITIONAL REMINDERS:
• WE CANNOT RETURN ANY PAPERS YOU SEND US. If you need to send us this summary or any other papers, please make photocopies beforehand. You may need them for income tax purposes.
• YOU HAVE THE RIGHT TO APPEAL ANY CLAIM WE DON'T PAY OR PAY ONLY IN PART. Mail us a request to review your claim within sixty (60) days of the date you received this summary.   32N-0233 r3(09-90) D

Figure 11–19 One carrier's Explanation of Benefits.

MEDICAID

In 1965, Congress passed Title 19 of the Social Security Act establishing a jointly sponsored federal and state government medical assistance program to provide medical care for persons with incomes below the national poverty level. This assistance program is known as **Medicaid**. Individual states may have local names for their program, such as Medi-Cal in California. Coverage and benefits vary greatly from state to state since each state mandates its own program following federal guidelines. The current qualifications for Medicaid eligibility are as follows:

■ Medically indigent low-income individuals and families
■ Aged and disabled persons covered by Supplemental Security Income (SSI) and Qualified Medicare Beneficiaries (QMBs)
■ Persons covered by Aid to Families with Dependent Children (AFDC) funds. AFDC covers:
  1. Children and qualified family members who meet specific income eligibility requirements.
  2. Pregnant women who meet the income requirements and would qualify if their babies were already born.
■ Other pregnant women not covered by AFDC.
■ Persons receiving institutional or other long-term care in nursing and intermediate care facilities.

The patient must present a valid Medicaid identification card on each visit. Eligibility should be confirmed for each visit, since eligibility could fluctuate from month to month. Failure to check eligibility could result in a denial of payment.

note Medicaid is the payer of last resort. If there is other medical coverage or liability, this must be billed first.

Any provider who accepts a Medicaid patient must accept the Medicaid-determined payment as payment in full. It is against the law for a provider to bill a Medicaid patient for Medicaid-covered services. Some states require providers to sign formal Medicaid participation contracts; other states do not require contracts. However, because most Medicaid patients have income below the poverty level, collection of fees for uncovered services is difficult.

HCFA-1500 is the claim form used in most states to submit a provider's fees. Some states do use a state-developed special optical scanning form. The local Medicaid office can supply this information if there is uncertainty about what claim form to use.

The following instructions are for filing Medicaid claims using the HCFA-1500 form only.

Block 1	Check Medicaid.
Block 1a	Enter patient's Medicaid ID number.
Block 2	Enter patient's name (last name, first name, middl initial).
Block 3	Patient's date of birth (entering eight-digit dates).
Block 4	Enter "same" or leave blank.
Block 5	Enter patient's address.
Block 6	Check "self".
Block 7	Enter "same" or leave blank.
Block 8	Check appropriate marital status.
Block 9–9d	Leave blank.
Block 10–10d	Leave blank. 10d is regionally determined.
Block 11a–d	Leave blank.
Block 12	Patient's signature is not required on Medicaid claims.

Block 13–16	Leave blank.
Block 17	Enter the complete name and degree of referring, requesting, ordering or prescribing provider, if appropriate.
Block 17a	Enter the Medicaid ID number of the provider.
Block 18	Enter dates, if appropriate.
Block 19	Enter the Medicaid provider number of the practice rendering the service.
Block 20	Check "No" box. A Medicaid provider cannot bill for services performed by another provider.
Block 21	Enter ICD-9-CM code(s).
Block 22	Leave blank.
Block 23	Enter the prior authorization number if applicable. If written authorization was obtained, attach a copy to the claim.
Block 24a	Enter the date service was rendered using eight-digit dates.
Block 24b	Enter the appropriate HCFA Place of Service (POS) code listed. (Refer to page 380 for a complete listing.)
Block 24c	Enter the appropriate Type of Service (TOS) code listed below, if applicable. (Refer to page 380 for complete listing.)
Block 24d	Enter CPT code(s) and modifiers as appropriate.
Block 24e	Enter the diagnosis reference number from Block 21 that best proves the medical necessity for this service on this line.
Block 24f	Enter charge for service rendered.
Block 24g	Enter the number of units for service reported on this line.
Block 24h	Enter "E" if the service is rendered under the Early and Periodic Screening, Diagnosis, and Treatment program. Enter "F" if the service is for Family Planning. Otherwise, leave blank.
Block 24i	Enter "X" if the service was for a medical emergency and performed in an Emergency Room.
Block 24j	Leave blank.
Block 24K	Leave blank. Use if regionally determined.
Block 25	Enter provider's Federal Tax Employment Number. Check the "EIN" box.
Block 26	If applicable, enter the patient account number. This number will then be listed on the EOB, making it easier to identify when files are indexed numerically rather than alphabetically.
Block 27	Check "Yes" box. Providers treating Medicaid patients MUST accept assignment.
Block 28	Enter total charges.
Block 29	Leave blank.
Block 30	Enter total charges.
Block 31	The provider's signature or signature stamp is used.
Block 32	Enter the name, address, and Medicaid provider number of the facility where services were rendered, *if other than the provider's office or patient's home.*
Block 33	Enter the provider's billing name, address, and phone number. Next to "PIN" enter the Medicaid provider number.

Figure 11–20 is an example of a completed HCFA-1500 for a Medicaid patient.

APPROVED OMB-0938-0008

MEDICAID

HEALTH INSURANCE CLAIM FORM

PLEASE DO NOT STAPLE IN THIS AREA

PICA			PICA

1. MEDICARE (Medicare #) | MEDICAID [X] (Medicaid #) | CHAMPUS (Sponsor's SSN) | CHAMPVA (VA File #) | GROUP HEALTH PLAN (SSN or ID) | FECA BLK LUNG (SSN) | OTHER (ID)

1a. INSURED'S I.D. NUMBER (FOR PROGRAM IN ITEM 1)
257885301

2. PATIENT'S NAME (Last Name, First Name, Middle Initial)
JONES BONNIE L

3. PATIENT'S BIRTH DATE MM 10 DD 10 YY 90 SEX M □ F [X]

4. INSURED'S NAME (Last Name, First Name, Middle Initial)
SAME

5. PATIENT'S ADDRESS (No., Street)
7611 MORTON ST

6. PATIENT RELATIONSHIP TO INSURED
Self [X] Spouse □ Child □ Other □

7. INSURED'S ADDRESS (No., Street)
SAME

CITY TEMPLE   STATE IN

8. PATIENT STATUS
Single [X] Married □ Other □
Employed □ Full-Time Student □ Part-Time Student □

CITY   STATE

ZIP CODE 47555   TELEPHONE (Include Area Code) (822) 361-5678

ZIP CODE   TELEPHONE (INCLUDE AREA CODE) ( )

9. OTHER INSURED'S NAME (Last Name, First Name, Middle Initial)

10. IS PATIENT'S CONDITION RELATED TO:

11. INSURED'S POLICY GROUP OR FECA NUMBER

a. OTHER INSURED'S POLICY OR GROUP NUMBER

a. EMPLOYMENT? (CURRENT OR PREVIOUS) □ YES □ NO

a. INSURED'S DATE OF BIRTH MM DD YY SEX M □ F □

b. OTHER INSURED'S DATE OF BIRTH MM DD YY SEX M □ F □

b. AUTO ACCIDENT? PLACE (State) □ YES □ NO

b. EMPLOYER'S NAME OR SCHOOL NAME

c. EMPLOYER'S NAME OR SCHOOL NAME

c. OTHER ACCIDENT? □ YES □ NO

c. INSURANCE PLAN NAME OR PROGRAM NAME
MEDICAID

d. INSURANCE PLAN NAME OR PROGRAM NAME

10d. RESERVED FOR LOCAL USE

d. IS THERE ANOTHER HEALTH BENEFIT PLAN?
□ YES [X] NO   If yes, return to and complete item 9 a-d.

READ BACK OF FORM BEFORE COMPLETING & SIGNING THIS FORM.
12. PATIENT'S OR AUTHORIZED PERSON'S SIGNATURE I authorize the release of any medical or other information necessary to process this claim. I also request payment of government benefits either to myself or to the party who accepts assignment below.

SIGNED _____ DATE _____

13. INSURED'S OR AUTHORIZED PERSON'S SIGNATURE I authorize payment of medical benefits to the undersigned physician or supplier for services described below.

SIGNED _____

14. DATE OF CURRENT: MM 06 DD 25 YY 9X ILLNESS (First symptom) OR INJURY (Accident) OR PREGNANCY(LMP)

15. IF PATIENT HAS HAD SAME OR SIMILAR ILLNESS. GIVE FIRST DATE MM DD YY

16. DATES PATIENT UNABLE TO WORK IN CURRENT OCCUPATION FROM MM DD YY TO MM DD YY

17. NAME OF REFERRING PHYSICIAN OR OTHER SOURCE

17a. I.D. NUMBER OF REFERRING PHYSICIAN

18. HOSPITALIZATION DATES RELATED TO CURRENT SERVICES FROM MM DD YY TO MM DD YY

19. RESERVED FOR LOCAL USE

20. OUTSIDE LAB? □ YES □ NO $ CHARGES

21. DIAGNOSIS OR NATURE OF ILLNESS OR INJURY. (RELATE ITEMS 1,2,3 OR 4 TO ITEM 24E BY LINE)
1. 782 . 1
2. ___ . ___
3. ___ . ___
4. ___ . ___

22. MEDICAID RESUBMISSION CODE   ORIGINAL REF. NO.

23. PRIOR AUTHORIZATION NUMBER

24. A DATE(S) OF SERVICE From MM DD YY To MM DD YY	B Place of Service	C Type of Service	D PROCEDURES, SERVICES, OR SUPPLIES (Explain Unusual Circumstances) CPT/HCPCS | MODIFIER	E DIAGNOSIS CODE	F $ CHARGES	G DAYS OR UNITS	H EPSDT Family Plan	I EMG	J COB	K RESERVED FOR LOCAL USE
1 06 25 9X	11		90212	1	46 00	1				
2										
3										
4										
5										
6										

25. FEDERAL TAX I.D. NUMBER   SSN EIN
75-2166173   □ [X]

26. PATIENT'S ACCOUNT NO.

27. ACCEPT ASSIGNMENT? (For govt. claims, see back) [X] YES □ NO

28. TOTAL CHARGE $ 46 00

29. AMOUNT PAID $

30. BALANCE DUE $ 46 00

31. SIGNATURE OF PHYSICIAN OR SUPPLIER INCLUDING DEGREES OR CREDENTIALS (I certify that the statements on the reverse apply to this bill and are made a part thereof.)
SIGNED *Lowery Johnson MD* DATE 6/25/9X

32. NAME AND ADDRESS OF FACILITY WHERE SERVICES WERE RENDERED (If other than home or office)
SAME

33. PHYSICIAN'S, SUPPLIER'S BILLING NAME, ADDRESS, ZIP CODE & PHONE #
LOWERY JOHNSON MD
HWY 311 SUITE A31
SELLERSBURG IN 47172
PIN# 1948   GRP# (822) 752-9118

(APPROVED BY AMA COUNCIL ON MEDICAL SERVICE 8/88)   **PLEASE PRINT OR TYPE**
FORM HCFA-1500 (U2) (12-90)
FORM OWCP-1500   FORM RRB-1500

CARRIER

PATIENT AND INSURED INFORMATION

PHYSICIAN OR SUPPLIER INFORMATION

Figure 11–20 Completed HCFA-1500 for Medicaid.

The deadline for submitting Medicaid claims varies from state to state. Claims should be filed as soon as possible. With Medicare/Medicaid crossover claims, the deadline follows Medicare Guidelines of December 31 of the year following the date of service. A **crossover claim** occurs when the Medicare carrier will electronically transfer the information submitted on the Medicare claim form to Medicaid or Medigap carrier. Medicare will also process the patient's Medicare deductible and coinsurance responsibilities and any information regarding a noncovered service or procedure by Medicare.

MEDICARE

Medicare is a federal health insurance program authorized by Congress and managed by HCFA. Created in 1965 as Title 18 of the Social Security Act, it is the largest single medical program in the United States offering benefits in all fifty states.

Persons eligible for Medicare benefits include:

- People age 65 and over, retired, on Social Security Administration (SSA) benefits, railroad retirement, or civil service retirement.
- People who have received Social Security Disability Insurance (SSDI) benefits for two years.
- People with end-stage renal disease (ESRD).

Local Social Security Administration offices take applications for Medicare benefits. All persons who meet the eligibility requirements receive Medicare Part A Benefits (Hospital Insurance). Medicare Part A covers inpatient, institutional services, hospice and home health care.

Those persons eligible for full medical benefits may choose to take Medicare Part B (Medical Insurance), by paying an annual premium to the Social Security Administration or having the premium automatically deducted from the monthly social security check.

As previously discussed in Module 10, it is important to always check the patient's insurance card or cards and retain a photocopy in the patient's medical record. This is especially important with a Medicare patient as the card indicates whether the patient has both Medicare Parts A and B, and the effective dates. It will also verify the correct Medicare claim or identification number. A replica of a Medicare card is shown in Figure 11–21.

When a husband and wife both have Medicare, they receive separate cards and claim numbers. A patient whose Medicare claim number ends in "A" will have the same social security number and claim number. A patient whose Medicare claim number ends in "B" or "D" will have different social security and Medicare claim numbers.

Table 11–1 designates what some of the letters following a Medicare claim number represent.

A distinction from this Medicare format is Railroad Retirement Medicare. This Medicare claim number has one to three letters before the numbers, as shown in Figure 11–22. Railroad retirement beneficiaries have the same benefits and deductibles under Parts A and B as other Medicare recipients.

This chapter will focus on Medicare Part B, which is the part designed to cover such outpatient services as:

- Physician Office Services
- Physical Therapy
- Diagnostic Lab Testing

Figure 11–21 Example of a Medicare card, showing patient has Parts A & B.

TABLE 11–1

Code	Description
A	Wage Earner
B	Husband's Number when wife is 62 years or older
D	Widow
HAD	Disabled Adult
C	Disabled Child
J, J1 or K1	Special monthly benefits, Never worked under Social Security

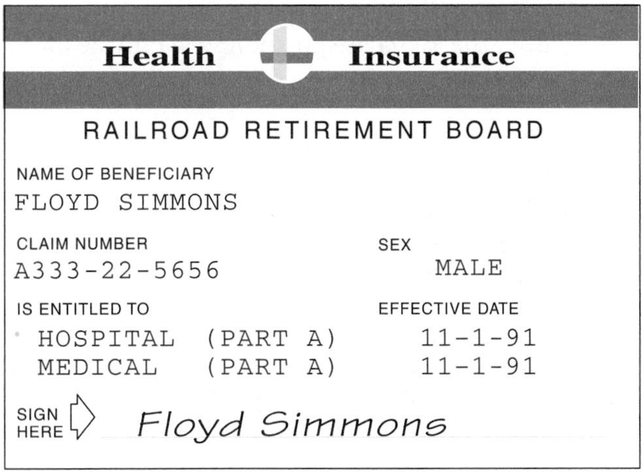

Figure 11–22 Example of a Railroad Medicare card, showing patient has Parts A & B.

- Radiology
- Periodic Pap Smears and Mammograms
- Influenza, Pneumonococcal and Hepatitis B Vaccines
- Drugs that are not self-administered
- Ambulance Services
- Durable medical equipment and supplies used in the home certified by a physician

Today the majority of physicians contract to be a Medicare **Participating Physician (PAR)** Incentives to increase the number of health care providers to sign PAR agreements include:

- Direct payment of all claims.
- Faster processing of claims resulting in quicker reimbursement.
- A five percent higher fee schedule.
- Annual PAR directories available to Medicare patients.
- All unassigned Remittance Advice (RA), formerly known as Explanation of Benefits (EOB) forms, to patients include a message making them aware of the reduced out-of-pocket expenses if they use a PAR.

Under the PAR agreement, the physician accepts assignment on all claims, agreeing to eighty percent of the allowable payment from Medicare plus the remaining twenty percent of reasonable charges after the deductible has been met.

Physicians electing not to participate as a contracted Medicare Provider **(a non-participating physician or NonPARs)** can accept assignment on a claim-by-claim basis, but there are restrictions.

- All Medicare claims must be filed by the provider.
- Fees are restricted to charging no more than the limiting fee charge on non-assigned claims, or no more than fifteen percent above the NonPAR Medicare fee schedule, which is five percent below the PAR fee schedule.
- Collections are restricted to only the deductible and coinsurance due at the time of service on assigned claims.
- NonPARs *must* accept *assignment* on clinical laboratory charges.

Table 11–2 gives an example of a NonPAR fee and payment rate.
Table 11–3 is an example of a PAR fee and payment rate.
NonPARs who accept assignment are not restricted to billing the limited fee. However, the Medicare payment will only be at the NonPAR approved rate. Non-

TABLE 11–2

NonPAR Charges Limiting Fee or Charge	$85.00
NonPAR Approved Rate	$70.00
The difference between Limiting Fee or Charge & NonPAR Rate	$15.00
Plus (+) 20% of NonPAR approved Rate $70.00	$14.00
Patient Owes	$29.00

TABLE 11–3

PAR charges usual fee	$100.00
PAR Medicare approved rate	$75.00
PAR adjusted difference between the usual charge and approved rate	$25.00
Patient pays PAR 20% of approved rate	$15.00

PARs submitting an assigned claim may collect any unpaid deductible and the twenty percent coinsurance of the Medicare schedule at the time the service is rendered. If the full fee is collected at the time of service, the assigned status of the claim becomes void.

Federal law requires all physicians and suppliers to submit claims to Medicare if they provide a Medicare-covered service to a patient enrolled in Medicare Part B. The HCFA-1500 is the form used to submit those claims.

Federal law also mandates accepting assignment on all clinical laboratory charges when the patient has lab services and other medical or surgical services. The NonPAR physician accepts assignment on only the lab services. In such a case two claim forms will need to be submitted, one for the lab procedures with Block 27 checked "Yes" to accept assignment, and one for other services.

Assignment must be accepted on all services performed by nurse practitioners, midwives, certified nurse anesthetists and physician assistants, as well as psychologists, clinical psychologists, and clinical social workers.

Medicare is only required to pay for services and supplies that are considered to be reasonable and medically necessary for the diagnosis stated on the claim form. Medicare will not cover procedures considered experimental or still under investigation or being tested. To be considered medically reasonable and necessary, the supply or service must:

- Be consistent with the symptoms or diagnosis of the illness or injury under treatment
- Be necessary and consistent with generally accepted professional medical standards
- Not be furnished primarily for the convenience of the patient, attending physician or other physician or supplier

In cases where the provider feels the treatments or services are justified, the options are explained to the patient with an agreement in writing to pay the full cost of the uncovered procedure. This Advanced Notice Medicare beneficiary agreement is signed by the patient prior to receiving the medical service. This advance notice must state a reason why the physician believes Medicare is likely to deny the claim. The notice must contain accurate information so the patient can make an informed decision on whether or not to receive the service and pay for it without Medicare reimbursement.

An acceptable advanced notice as determined by HCFA must include the following:

- Date of service
- A narrative of the particular service
- A statement that the physician/supplier believes Medicare is likely to deny payment for the particular service

- An accurate reason why the physician/supplier believes Medicare is likely to deny payment
- The beneficiary's signed and dated agreement to pay, obtained *BEFORE* the service is performed

Failure to obtain this Advanced Notice Medicare beneficiary agreement for services not reasonable and necessary will result in the following:

- Nonparticipating physicians who do not accept assignment must refund to the patient any amounts collected that have been denied by Medicare as considered not reasonable and necessary.
- The participating physician or nonparticipating physician accepting assignment may be held liable for services considered by Medicare to be not reasonable and necessary. If payment has been collected from the beneficiary for such services, the provider is required to refund the amount collected from the patient within thirty days of receiving Medicare's notice.

To avoid delay of claim processing, a copy of this notice may be submitted with the claim. An example of an HCFA-approved Advance Notice Medicare beneficiary agreement is outlined in Figure 11–23.

Medicare can be primary insurance coverage or a secondary payer or supplemental policy. It is important to know the Medicare status in order to correctly submit the claim form.

Circumstances under which Medicare may be secondary to other insurance include:

- Group health plan coverage such as the person who continues working after the age of 65.
- Liability coverage such as automobile accidents.
- Work-related illness and injury that falls under Workers' Compensation, veterans benefits, or black lung disease.

When Medicare is primary, additional insurance is often purchased to supplement the Medicare program by covering the patient's deductible and coinsurance obligations. This additional coverage can be:

1. Medigap
2. Employer Sponsored Medicare Supplemental Plan

A **Medigap** policy is a private, commercial insurance plan with the premiums paid directly by the patient, which is offered to persons entitled to Medicare benefits to supplement those benefits. It is designed to "fill in the gaps" in Medicare coverage by providing payment for some of the charges for which Medicare does not have responsibility due to deductibles, coinsurance amounts or other Medicare-imposed limitations. These policies must meet federal government standards for Medigap coverage. These claims are handled in one of two ways:

1. PAR—Medicare is filed first, then the Medicare carrier can electronically transfer claim information completed in Blocks 9 through 9D to the Medigap carrier.
2. NonPAR providers are not required to include Medigap information on the claim form, although many offices will file the Medigap claim for the patient. To do this, the patient must provide a copy of the Medicare **Remittance Advice (RA)** with the Medigap claim.

Lowery B. Johnson, M.D.
Hwy 311 Suite A31
Sellersburg, IN 47172
812-246-1234

ADVANCED NOTICE MEDICARE BENEFICIARY AGREEMENT

Medicare will only pay for services that it determines to be "reasonable and necessary" under Section 1662 (a) (1) of the Medicare law. If Medicare determines that a particular service, although it would otherwise be covered, is not "reasonable and necessary" under Medicare program standards, Medicare will deny payment for that service. I believe that in your case, Medicare is likely to deny payment for:

1. _____

2. _____

for the reason(s) checked below:

Medicare does not usually pay for this:

_____ many visits or treatments

_____ service or this many services within this period of time

_____ injection or this many injections

_____ because it is a treatment that is yet to be proved effective

_____ office visit unless it was needed because of an emergency

_____ same services by more than one doctor during the same time period

_____ equipment

_____ laboratory test

_____ visit since it is more than one visit per day

_____ extensive procedure

_____ same service by more than one doctor of the same specialty

_____ nursing home visit since only one is allowed per month

Medicare Beneficiary Agreement

I have been notified by my physician that he/she believes that, in my case, Medicare is likely to deny payment for the services identified above, for the reasons checked. If Medicare denies payment, I agree to be personally and fully responsible for payment.

_____   _____
Date   Beneficiary Signature

Figure 11–23 Advanced Notice Medicare Beneficiary Agreement

An employer-sponsored plan is a plan available to employees at the time of their retirement from the company. These plans are not regulated by the federal government but follow the guidelines established in the employer's regular health insurance plan. Premiums are paid to the insurance carrier via the employer. Health care providers are not required to file claims through employer-sponsored retirement plans, although many do, or the patient can file for benefits after the Medicare RA is received.

The following outlines step by step how to complete the HCFA-1500 for a primary Medicare claim, with Medigap supplemental policy.

Block 1	Enter "**X**" in Medicare box.
Block 1a	Enter **Medicare ID number including alpha suffix** for traditional Medicare, alpha prefix for Railroad Medicare.
Block 2	Enter **last name, first name, and middle initial** as they appear on the Medicare card. Use no punctuation.
Block 3	Enter **patient's date of birth using eight-digit dates**. (01/01/1929) Mark appropriate **gender** of the patient.
Block 4	Enter "**Same**" or leave blank.
Block 5	Enter **patient's address and telephone number**.
Block 6	Mark "**Self**" or leave blank.
Block 7	Enter "**Same**" or leave blank.
Block 8	Mark appropriate **marital and employment** status boxes. Mark "**Single**" if widowed or divorced.
Block 9	Enter last name, first name, middle initial to indicate Medigap Policy **if different** from patient's name in Block 2. If patient and insured are the same, enter "Same".
Block 9a	Enter "**Medigap**", followed by the policy and/or group number.
Block 9b	Enter the eight-digit **date of birth** of Medigap insured if different from patient.
Block 9c	If Medigap PAYERID is known and entered in block 9d **leave blank**. This is identified by the numbers "99" in the seventh and eighth positions of the nine-digit ID number. If the PAYERID is not known, enter abbreviated mailing address of the Medigap carrier as listed on the insured's identification card.

EXAMPLE: 231 Cannon Street
  Talltown, IN 12345
  Is entered as: "231 Cannon St IN 12345"

Block 9d	Enter **Medigap PAYERID nine-digit number**. If no number is available, enter the Medigap Plan name.

Note Information in Blocks 9, 9a, 9b, and 9d must be complete and accurate in order to transfer or cross over claim information to the Medigap insured.

Blocks 10a–10d	Mark "**No**". If any are checked "**Yes**", the Third-Party Liability or Worker's Compensation would be primary and filed first; Medicare would be secondary.
Block 11	Enter "**None**" or leave blank.
Block 11a–11c	**Leave blank**.
Block 11d	**Leave blank**. Not required by Medicare.
Block 12	Patient signature required or patient can sign a separate authorization for release of medical information retained in the patient's chart. **If authorization is on file, enter "Signature on File"**.
Block 13	PAR Providers—**Enter "Patient Signature on File"**, if the patient has a signed Medigap authorization on file.

Block 14	Enter **date** of the beginning of the illness reported on this claim, or date accident or injury occurred.
Block 15	Leave **blank**.
Block 16	If the patient is employed and unable to work in current occupation, enter the eight-digit dates. This entry may indicate employment-related insurance coverage.
Blocks 17&17a	Enter name of referring, requesting, ordering or supervising physician, and the Unique Provider Identification number (UPIN) of this physician.

The list below groups provider services differentiating referring, requesting, ordering and supervising physician:

Group 1—Physician Services

- Consultation
- Surgery
- Independent Diagnostic Radiology Provider
- Independent Diagnostic Laboratory Provider

All referrals need the name of the referring provider. Both the referring and the ordering physician's name must be included if the consultant personally orders and performs diagnostic testing on a patient.

Group 2—Nonphysician Services

- Physical therapy
- Audiology
- Occupational therapy
- Durable Medical Equipment (DME)
- Prosthesis
- Orthotic devices
- Parenteral and enteral nutrition
- Immunosuppressive drug claims
- Portable X-ray services

All claims need the name of the ordering physician.

GROUP 3—Physician Extender/Limited License Practitioners

- Physician Assistants
- Nurse Practitioners
- Other Limited License Practitioners referring patients for consultation services

All claims need the name of the supervising physician.

Blocks 17&17a	Leave blank if the physician reporting all the services is the attending physician.
Block 18	Enter **Dates of Admission and Discharge** when services relate to hospitalization.
Block 19	Required for the following:

- Chiropractor Claims: Enter eight-digit date required x-ray was taken.

- Global Surgery Claims: Two physicians sharing postop care. Enter appropriate eight-digit date care was assumed or relinquished.

- Unlisted CPT codes in Block 24d: Enter a description of the actual service. If the description does not fit, attach the narrative to the claim.

- Modifier "99" in Block 24d. Enter all modifiers covered in Block 24d by multiple modifiers "99". Enter the line number being reported followed by an equal sign listing all modifiers that apply to that line.

    Example: 1 = 25   58   80

- Independent Physical or Occupational Therapist and all podiatrist claims: Enter eight-digit date patient was last seen by the referring or ordering physician and the UPIN of attending physician.

- CPT Code for "Not Otherwise Classified Drug" in Block 24d: Enter **Name of the Drug**.

- Independent Laboratory Claim: When a portable EKG is performed or lab specimens are obtained from a patient at home or an institution enter "Homebound".

Block 20	"Yes" indicates an outside lab performed a diagnostic test listed on this claim form. The provider billing this claim form was billed for the test, and the provider is billing the patient.
Block 21	Enter ICD-9-CM code, primary code first. Up to four codes may be entered.
Block 22	Leave blank.
Block 23	Enter prior authorization number if required for procedure listed.
Block 24a	Enter date of service in "To" column.
	"From" is used only if billing for same service, same CPT code, on consecutive days. For consecutive dates, first date of service is in "To" block, last date of service in "From" block.
Block 24b	Enter appropriate Place of Service (POS) code. (Refer to page 380 for complete listing.)
Block 24c	Leave blank. Not required for Medicare.
Block 24d	Enter CPT or HCPCS code of service performed and any appropriate modifier. If more than two modifiers are required, use modifier "99" and follow instructions for Block 19 for multiple modifiers.
Block 24e	Enter the ICD-9-CM code from Block 21 that best proves medical necessity for this service.
Block 24f	Enter the amount charged for service performed. For consecutive services reported on one line, enter the charge for a single service, indicating number of units in 24g.
Block 24g	Enter number of units reported on this line.
Block 24h–24j	Leave blank.
Block 24k	Solo practices leave blank.
	Group practices enter PIN of the provider performing the service.
Block 25	Enter physician's federal tax employer ID number, marking the "EIN" box.
Block 26	If applicable, enter the patient account number. This number will then be listed on the RA for numerical identification of an account.

Block 27	"Yes" or "No" option must be marked.
	"Yes" must be marked for all PAR claims. NonPARs may mark either box. Assignment MUST be accepted on the following claims:

- Medicare/Medicaid crossover claims
- All Clinical Diagnostic Laboratory Services
- Services performed by Physician Assistants, Nurse Practitioners, Midwives, Nurse Anesthesiologists, Clinical Psychologists, and Social Workers
- Ambulatory Surgical Center claims

Block 28	Enter total charges submitted on this claim.
Block 29	Enter payments made by patients for covered services reported on this claim.
Block 30	Leave blank.
Block 31	Enter provider's name and credentials, either signature or signature stamp, and date claim was prepared.
Block 32	Enter the name and address of the facility where services are *if other than provider's office or patient's home.*
Block 33	Enter the official name of the practice, mailing address and phone number.
	Solo providers enter PIN number to the right of "PIN". Providers in group practices enter group PIN number to the right of "GRP".

Clarification Of PIN, UPIN, NPI, and PAYERID

PIN is the provider identification number assigned to a health care provider by an insurance company to be used on all claims filed by the provider.

UPIN is the unique provider identification number assigned by HCFA to a physician to be used as identification on claim forms.

NPI is the National Provider Identifier, scheduled to begin January 1999, assigned by HCFA as an identification number for Medicare claim forms, bills, and correspondence. The NPI is an eight-digit number to identify the provider with a two-digit location identifier. The objective of the NPI number is to develop a uniform system to standardize and simplify the use of provider identification number process. It will assist in detecting and tracing fraudulent and abusive submission of claim forms.

PAYERID is the payer identification number assigned to identify all third party payers of health care claims.

Figure 11–24 shows a completed claim form for a patient with Medicare Part B and Medigap coverage.

Medicare/Medicaid (Medi-Medi)

Medicare patients whose incomes are below the federal poverty level are also eligible for Medicaid, referred to as Medi-Medi. When a patient has both Medicare and Medicaid, the claim can be filed by "crossover" method. This means once the billing office has submitted the claim to Medicare, Medicare will automatically electronically transfer the Medicare claim and payment information to Medicaid for payment of any service that is covered by Medicaid but not Medicare.

It is important to remember that assignment must be accepted on Medi-Medi claims. Payment should be received by the billing office two to four weeks after the

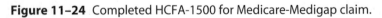

Figure 11–24 Completed HCFA-1500 for Medicare-Medigap claim.

Medicare payment has been received. If assignment is not taken, both Medicare and Medicaid payments may be sent to the patient, and a collection problem could exist due to State policy of not billing the patient for covered services.

A completed HCFA-1500 for Medicare-Medicaid services is shown in Figure 11–25. Note in Block 27, assignment MUST be accepted by marking the "Yes" box.

Figure 11–25 Completed HCFA-1500 for Medicare-Medicaid (Medi-Medi) claim.

Extra-coverage plans are insurance plans that cover a specific disease or special hospital indemnity policies. The specified disease plans pay only upon documentation and physician certification of the disease, such as cancer or AIDS. Special hospital indemnity plans are advertised as policies paying a specified amount for every day the patient is hospitalized. Payment for these claims is made directly to the patient and is not reportable to Medicare or any other primary health insurance plan.

MEDICARE AS SECONDARY PAYER

Medicare is a secondary payer when the patient is eligible for Medicare and also covered by one or more of the following plans:

- An employer-sponsored group health plan with more than twenty covered employees.
- Disability coverage through an employer-sponsored group health plan with more than 100 covered employees.
- A third-party liability policy if treatment is for an injury covered by automobile insurance and self-insured liability plans.
- Workers' Compensation injury or illness.
- End-stage renal disease covered by an employer-sponsored group health plan of any size during the first eighteen months of the patient's eligibility for Medicare.
- A Veterans Affairs (VA) pre-authorized service for a beneficiary eligible for both VA benefits and Medicare.
- Black lung disease.

All primary plans are filed first. Medicare is filed after the RA from the primary plan has been received. A copy of the RA must be attached to the Medicare claim when submitted. Providers are not required to file Medicare secondary claims unless the patient specifically requests it.

For clarification purposes of primary and secondary plans, when a Medicare patient is seen in the medical office, a Medicare secondary payer form can also be completed by the Medicare beneficiary. An example of this form is shown in Figure 11–26.

The deadline for filing Medicare claims is December 31 of the year following the date of service. However, all claims should be filed promptly to avoid potential problems with billing and collections.

HEALTH MAINTENANCE ORGANIZATIONS (HMOS)

Many physicians today are enrolled as participating physicians in health maintenance organizations, more commonly referred to as HMOs.

The term managed care is derived from the HMO concept of medical care. They manage, negotiate and contract for health care at the same time, keeping health care costs down. The goal of HMOs is to promote wellness and preventive medical care, covering the cost of annual examinations, routine X-rays, laboratory procedures, Pap smears, and mammograms. This encourages patients to undergo routine annual checkups, which can save costs by diagnosing medical problems before they become critical, therefore helping to lower medical costs.

Practon Medical Group, Inc.
4567 Broad Avenue
Woodland Hills, XY 12345
Telephone 013/486-9002

LIFETIME BENEFICIARY CLAIM AUTHORIZATION AND INFORMATION RELEASE

Patient's
Name_____Busaba McDermott_____Medicare I.D. Number___329-98-6745___

I request that payment of authorized Medicare benefits be made either to me or on my behalf to (name of physician/supplier) for any services furnished me by that physician/supplier. I authorize any holder of medical information about me to release to the Health Care Financing Administration and its agents any information needed to determine these benefits or the benefits payable to related services.

I understand my signature requests that payment be made and authorizes release of medical information necessary to pay the claim. If other health insurance is indicated in Item 9 of the HCFA-1500 claim form or elsewhere on other approved claim forms or electronically submitted claims, my signature authorizes releasing of the information to the insurer or agency shown. In Medicare assigned cases, the physician or supplier agrees to accept the charge determination of the Medicare carrier as the full charge, and the patient is responsible only for the deductible, co-insurance, and noncovered services. Co-insurance and the deductible are based upon the charge determination of the Medicare carrier.

_Busaba McDermott_____   ___May 15, 199X_____
Patient's Signature   Date

Figure 11–26 Medicare Special Authorization and Assignment Form.

To participate in an HMO plan, members and dependents must enroll in the plan. Most HMOs charge their members a co-payment (specified dollar amount) for office visits, emergency room visits, and other services. Most insurance cards for HMO patients indicate these co-pay amounts on the card. The patient is responsible for this fee and it should be collected at the time of the visit. If it is not paid, the patient is billed directly for the co-pay amount. Physicians participating in an HMO are listed in a directory published by the HMO that is distributed to its members. The member chooses a physician from the list as a primary care physician (PCP), also referred to as a gatekeeper, to manage the health care of the member. This management requires the patient to contact the PCP for referrals to hospitals, emergency rooms and specialists.

The following is an example of how the PCP manages the health care of an HMO patient:

A patient makes an appointment with the primary care physician to discuss symptoms possibly related to allergies: headaches, nasal drainage, cough. Oral medications alleviate the symptoms but side effects from the medications occur:

daytime drowsiness, insomnia at night, dry mouth. The PCP refers the patient to an allergist for consultation and allergy testing. The referral form states how many visits may be required (consultation, allergy testing, and allergy vaccine if indicated).

Figure 11–27 is only one example of a referral form.

Prior authorization or preapproval is required by HMOs for hospital admissions and surgeries.

CHAMPUS/TRICARE/CHAMPVA

CHAMPUS/TRICARE/CHAMPVA are federal government programs to provide health care benefits to families of personnel currently serving in the armed forces, retired military personnel, and veterans of the armed forces.

CHAMPUS stands for **C**ivilian **H**ealth **A**nd **M**edical **P**rogram of the **U**niformed **S**ervices. **TRICARE** was recently established within CHAMPUS to provide a managed care program. The name TRICARE comes from the formation of a three-part health care system adding HMOs and PPOs to the standard CHAMPUS program.

CHAMPUS/TRICARE is a program designed to benefit the dependents of personnel serving in the armed forces: Army, Navy, Air Force, Coast Guard, public health services and National Oceanic & Atmospheric Administration (NOAA), and the North Atlantic Treaty Organization (NATO).

These families are offered three choices of health care benefits:

1. TRICARE Prime—operates as a managed care program of a full service health maintenance organization.
2. TRICARE Extra—is a network of health care providers that dependents can use on a case-by-case basis, without a required enrollment.
3. TRICARE Standard—provides the same benefits as the original CHAMPUS program allowing freedom to choose a health care provider but with greater out-of-pocket expenses than TRICARE Prime and Extra plans.

CHAMPVA stands for **C**ivilian **H**ealth **A**nd **M**edical **P**rogram of the **V**eterans **A**ffairs. CHAMPVA covers the expenses of dependent spouses and children of veterans with total, permanent service-connected disabilities. It also covers surviving spouses and dependent children of veterans who died in the line of duty or as a result of disabilities connected to the uniformed service.

Medical services and treatment for CHAMPUS/TRICARE/CHAMPVA patients are usually provided in a military-related facility. CHAMPVA patients are not eligible to receive medical care at a military medical facility but are eligible for treatment in a veterans hospital. Emergency services or nonemergency care that a military facility cannot provide may be seen by the civilian provider. CHAMPUS/TRICARE/CHAMPVA must authorize all nonemergency inpatient care in a civilian medical facility before admission. Failure to obtain this authorization will result in nonpayment of the claim. A nonavailability statement (Form DD1251) documents the authorization. This requirement is waived if the patient lives 40 miles or more from a military base. No advance authorization is required in an emergency. CHAMPVA patients do not need availability statements for outpatient medical care in a civilian facility.

The CHAMPUS definition of a medical emergency as stated in *CHAMPUS NEWS No 95-17* is a:

> "sudden and unexpected onset of a medical condition, or the acute worsening of a chronic condition, that is treating of life, limb or sight, and which required

PRIMARY CARE PHYSICIAN REFERRAL

Ætna US Healthcare®

DATE

3219154

PLEASE IMPRINT OR FURNISH MEMBER INFORMATION

ID NO./S.S. NO.

NAME

DATE OF BIRTH

PRIMARY OFFICE NAME AND ADDRESS

OFFICE NO.

PRIMARY DR. NO.

PRIMARY DR. SIGNATURE

Plan Type
- ❑ Select Choice (HMO)
- ❑ Senior Choice
- ❑ Managed Choice (POS)
- ❑ Motor Vehicle Accident
- ❑ Managed Choice II (POS)
- ❑ Worker's Compensation
- ❑ Elect Choice (POS)

REFERRAL SECTION

Participating Specialist/Address | Provider No.

Specialty

Diagnosis (Print Clearly) | ICD-9 or DX Group

Procedures to be Performed (Print Clearly) | CPT-4
1.
2.

Participating Facility/Address | Provider No.

Place of Service

(01) ❑ Inpatient   (02) ❑ Outpatient

Consult: ❑ No ❑ Yes
Follow-Up Visits: ❑ No ❑ Yes   No. of Visits _____
Hospital Care: ❑ No ❑ Yes   If Blank, 1 visit

INSTRUCTIONS TO THE PRIMARY CARE OFFICE

1. Referrals for HMO Members should be transmitted electronically through either telephone voice response unit, point-of-service device, or computer link.

2. If not transmitted electronically (see #1 above), mail or fax Aetna U.S. Healthcare™ referral copy to:
   P.O. Box 9107, Tyler, TX 75711-9894.
   Fax: 1-800-588-2386. Please submit daily.

3. Referrals must be completed with specific instructions to participating specialist or facility (date of referral, member information, PCP office information, specialist/facility name and provider number, place of service if facility, PCP signature).

4. Inpatient admissions and outpatient surgery cases must be precertified by the admitting physician. Reference the back of the member's ID card for the specific 800# to call, or contact your local Aetna U.S. Healthcare office.

5. If the patient listed above has been in an automobile accident, under the automobile insurance law, bills for customary medical expenses should be sent to the automobile insurance carrier. If it is found that automobile insurance coverage does not exist for all or some of these expenses, return this form with bills attached to Aetna U.S. Healthcare along with a copy of the auto carrier's rejection and it will be processed appropriately.

FREQUENTLY REFERRED SERVICES (PLEASE CHECK BOXES)

Allergy
- ❑ 11 Allergy Serum
- ❑ 10 Allergy Testing (Work Up)

Cardiac
- ❑ 01 CABG
- ❑ 02 Cardiac Cath
- ❑ 03 Cardiac Valve Procedure
- ❑ 16 Echocardiogram
- ❑ 12 EKG
- ❑ 15 Holter Monitor
- ❑ 04 Pacemaker
- ❑ 05 PTCA
- ❑ 13 Stress Test

ENT
- ❑ 18 Audiogram/Tympanometry
- ❑ 55 Bony Impacted Tooth Extraction
- ❑ 21 Laryngoscopy
- ❑ 51 Major ENT Procedure
- ❑ 52 Maxillofacial Procedure
- ❑ 20 Myningotomy/Tympanostomy
- ❑ 58 Nasal/Sinus Endoscopy
- ❑ 62 Sinus/Mastoid Procedure
- ❑ 73 Thyroid Procedure
- ❑ 63 Tonsil/Adenoid Procedure

Eye
- ❑ 78 Cataract/Lens Procedure
- ❑ 39 Cornea Procedure
- ❑ 79 Glaucoma Procedure
- ❑ 22 Refraction/Routine Eye Care
- ❑ 37 Retinal Procedure
- ❑ 38 Strabismus Procedure
- ❑ 23 Visual Field

GI
- ❑ 06 Cholecystectomy
- ❑ 07 ERCP
- ❑ 08 Inguinal Herniorrhaphy
- ❑ 25 Lower GI Endoscopy
- ❑ 09 Major Bowel Procedure
- ❑ 48 Rectal/Anal Procedure
- ❑ 24 Upper GI Endoscopy

GU
- ❑ 67 Kidney Stone Procedure
- ❑ 83 Major Kidney/Bladder/Ureter Procedure
- ❑ 33 Male Infertility
- ❑ 85 TURP/Prostatectomy
- ❑ 27 Urologic Endoscopy (includes Cystoscopy)
- ❑ 84 Vasectomy

GYN
- ❑ 32 Colposcopy
- ❑ 41 Dilation & Curettage
- ❑ 42 Endometrial Biopsy
- ❑ 43 Excision Fibroid Tumor
- ❑ 44 Female Birth Control (includes Tubal Ligation)
- ❑ 33 Female Infertility
- ❑ 81 Gynecologic Endoscopy
- ❑ 86 Gynecologic Lesion Excision/Biopsy
- ❑ 47 Hysterectomy
- ❑ 49 Ovarian/Tubal Procedure

Mental Health Therapy
- ❑ 28 Mental Health Visit

Neurologic
- ❑ 61 Craniectomy/Craniotomy
- ❑ 29 EEG
- ❑ 30 EMG/Nerve Conduction
- ❑ 64 Peripheral Nerve Procedure
- ❑ 65 Sleep Study

Oncologic
- ❑ 50 Chemotherapy
- ❑ 68 Lymph Node Procedure
- ❑ 69 Radiation Therapy

Orthopedic
- ❑ 35 Arthroscopy
- ❑ 53 Back/Neck Procedure
- ❑ 54 Foot/Ankle Procedure
- ❑ 34 Fracture Care
- ❑ 56 Hand/Wrist Procedure
- ❑ 57 Hip Arthroplasty
- ❑ 40 Injection, Joint
- ❑ 59 Knee Arthroplasty
- ❑ 95 Major Shoulder/Elbow Procedure

Other Therapeutic Procedures
- ❑ 98 Physician Consult
- ❑ 60 Rehabilitation/Physical Therapy

Pregnancy
- ❑ 31 Pregnancy/Delivery

Pulmonary
- ❑ 71 Bronchoscopy
- ❑ 72 Major Thoracic Procedure
- ❑ 36 Spirometry/PFT

Renal
- ❑ 70 Dialysis

Skin/Breast
- ❑ 74 Breast Lesion Biopsy/Excision
- ❑ 75 Incision/Drainage Skin Abscess
- ❑ 76 Laceration Repair
- ❑ 77 Lumpectomy/Mastectomy
- ❑ 80 Skin Graft
- ❑ 45 Skin Lesion Biopsy/Excision

Vascular
- ❑ 66 Carotid Endarterectomy
- ❑ 96 Major Vascular Procedure
- ❑ 97 Varicose Vein Procedure

Lab
- ❑ 88 Laboratory Studies
  Specific Study:
  _____
  _____

Radiology
- ❑ 91 CT Scan
- ❑ 92 Magnetic Resonance Imaging
- ❑ 93 Mammography
- ❑ 87 Ultrasound (not Obstetric)
- ❑ 94 X-ray/Nuclear Imaging
  Specific Study:
  _____
  _____

GR-67347   AETNA U.S. HEALTHCARE COPY   (6-97)   CAT. 2000868400   © 1997 Aetna U.S. Healthcare Inc.

Figure 11–27 One carrier's primary care physician referral.

immediate medical treatment or which required treatment to relieve suffering from painful symptoms. Pregnancy-related medical emergencies must involve a sudden and unexpected medical complication that puts the mother, the baby, or both at risk."

An urgent medical problem is defined in the same *CHAMPUS NEWS* article as a:

"medical situation that isn't life threatening, but you need medical care."

Pre-authorization is required for civilian community medical treatment for urgent medical problems.

In the civilian medical facility treating the CHAMPUS/TRICARE/CHAMPVA patient, follow these guidelines to process a HCFA-1500 claim for services rendered:

1. Check the patient's identification card for name, ID number, issue date, effective date and expiration date. Make a copy of the front and back of the card.

Note *CHAMPUS/TRICARE/CHAMPVA uses the term "sponsor" instead of insured or subscriber. The sponsor is the service person—active duty, retired, deceased—whose relationship to the patient provides eligibility for the program.*

In Block 1a, enter the following:

CHAMPUS/TRICARE:	Sponsor's social security number.
CHAMPVA:	Patient's veterans affairs file number.
NOAA/NATO:	Type "NOAA" or "NATO" and sponsor's ID number.
Block 7:	Active duty sponsor: Sponsor's duty station address.
Blocks 17–17a:	Name of referring physician and EIN or SSN. If patient is referred from a military treatment facility, enter name of facility and attach form DD 2161 "Referral for civilian medical care"
Block 27:	Mark appropriate box. NonPARs may elect to accept assignment on a case-by-case basis.

2. If a patient has other insurance, including Workers' Compensation and liability policies, CHAMPUS/TRICARE/CHAMPVA are secondary payers.
3. CHAMPUS/TRICARE is primary when the other insurance is Medicaid or a supplemental policy to CHAMPUS/TRICARE.

The deadline for filing CHAMPUS/TRICARE/CHAMPVA claims is one year from date of service.

Figure 11–28 is an example of a completed HCFA-1500 claim form for a CHAMPUS patient.

WORKERS' COMPENSATION

Workers' Compensation is a program covering on-the-job accidents and injuries or illness related to employment. This program is mandated by federal and state governments. Premiums are paid by employers to a statewide fund to cover medical expenses and a portion of lost wages directly related to the employee's injury or illness. This premium is determined by the number of employees and the degree of risk posed by the job.

APPROVED OMB-0938-0008

CHAMPUS

CARRIER

| PICA | | **HEALTH INSURANCE CLAIM FORM** | PICA | |

1. MEDICARE   MEDICAID   CHAMPUS   CHAMPVA   GROUP HEALTH PLAN   FECA BLK LUNG   OTHER

(Medicare #)   (Medicaid #) [X] (Sponsor's SSN)   (VA File #)   (SSN or ID)   (SSN)   (ID)

1a. INSURED'S I.D. NUMBER (FOR PROGRAM IN ITEM 1)
300543030

2. PATIENT'S NAME (Last Name, First Name, Middle Initial)
DUCHANE PATRICIA S

3. PATIENT'S BIRTH DATE MM DD YY   SEX
07 01 92   M [ ] F [X]

4. INSURED'S NAME (Last Name, First Name, Middle Initial)
DUCHANE WILLIAM T

5. PATIENT'S ADDRESS (No., Street)
2510 NORTH ST APT 21B

6. PATIENT RELATIONSHIP TO INSURED
Self [X] Spouse [ ] Child [ ] Other [ ]

7. INSURED'S ADDRESS (No., Street)
ZION AIR FORCE BASE

CITY
DUVALL

STATE
IN

8. PATIENT STATUS
Single [X] Married [ ] Other [ ]

CITY
APPLACHIA

STATE
NY

ZIP CODE
47232

TELEPHONE (Include Area Code)
(511) 293-2190

Employed [ ] Full-Time Student [ ] Part-Time Student [ ]

ZIP CODE
22330

TELEPHONE (INCLUDE AREA CODE)
( )

PATIENT AND INSURED INFORMATION

9. OTHER INSURED'S NAME (Last Name, First Name, Middle Initial)

10. IS PATIENT'S CONDITION RELATED TO:

11. INSURED'S POLICY GROUP OR FECA NUMBER
NONE

a. OTHER INSURED'S POLICY OR GROUP NUMBER

a. EMPLOYMENT? (CURRENT OR PREVIOUS)
YES [ ] NO [X]

a. INSURED'S DATE OF BIRTH MM DD YY   SEX
M [ ] F [ ]

b. OTHER INSURED'S DATE OF BIRTH MM DD YY   SEX   M [ ] F [ ]

b. AUTO ACCIDENT?   PLACE (State)
YES [ ] NO [X]

b. EMPLOYER'S NAME OR SCHOOL NAME

c. EMPLOYER'S NAME OR SCHOOL NAME

c. OTHER ACCIDENT?
YES [ ] NO [X]

c. INSURANCE PLAN NAME OR PROGRAM NAME

d. INSURANCE PLAN NAME OR PROGRAM NAME

10d. RESERVED FOR LOCAL USE

d. IS THERE ANOTHER HEALTH BENEFIT PLAN?
YES [ ] NO [X]   *If yes*, return to and complete item 9 a-d.

READ BACK OF FORM BEFORE COMPLETING & SIGNING THIS FORM.
12. PATIENT'S OR AUTHORIZED PERSON'S SIGNATURE I authorize the release of any medical or other information necessary to process this claim. I also request payment of government benefits either to myself or to the party who accepts assignment below.

SIGNED SIGNATURE ON FILE   DATE 6/25/9X

13. INSURED'S OR AUTHORIZED PERSON'S SIGNATURE I authorize payment of medical benefits to the undersigned physician or supplier for services described below.

SIGNED SIGNATURE ON FILE

14. DATE OF CURRENT: MM DD YY
06 25 9X   ILLNESS (First symptom) OR INJURY (Accident) OR PREGNANCY(LMP)

15. IF PATIENT HAS HAD SAME OR SIMILAR ILLNESS. GIVE FIRST DATE MM DD YY

16. DATES PATIENT UNABLE TO WORK IN CURRENT OCCUPATION MM DD YY   MM DD YY
FROM   TO

17. NAME OF REFERRING PHYSICIAN OR OTHER SOURCE

17a. I.D. NUMBER OF REFERRING PHYSICIAN

18. HOSPITALIZATION DATES RELATED TO CURRENT SERVICES MM DD YY   MM DD YY
FROM 03 11 9X   TO 03 15 9X

19. RESERVED FOR LOCAL USE

20. OUTSIDE LAB? $ CHARGES
YES [ ] NO [ ]

21. DIAGNOSIS OR NATURE OF ILLNESS OR INJURY. (RELATE ITEMS 1,2,3 OR 4 TO ITEM 24E BY LINE)

1. 870 . 0
2. E884 . 0
3. L___ . ___
4. L___ . ___

22. MEDICAID RESUBMISSION CODE   ORIGINAL REF. NO.

23. PRIOR AUTHORIZATION NUMBER

24. A DATE(S) OF SERVICE						B Place of Service	C Type of Service	D PROCEDURES, SERVICES, OR SUPPLIES (Explain Unusual Circumstances) CPT/HCPCS MODIFIER	E DIAGNOSIS CODE	F $ CHARGES	G DAYS OR UNITS	H EPSDT Family Plan	I EMG	J COB	K RESERVED FOR LOCAL USE
From MM	DD	YY	To MM	DD	YY										
06	25	9X				23	1	99282	1	185 00	1				
06	25	9X				23	2	12051	1	110 00	1				

PHYSICIAN OR SUPPLIER INFORMATION

25. FEDERAL TAX I.D. NUMBER   SSN EIN
75-2166173   [ ] [X]

26. PATIENT'S ACCOUNT NO.

27. ACCEPT ASSIGNMENT? (For govt. claims, see back)
YES [ ] NO [X]

28. TOTAL CHARGE
$ 295 00

29. AMOUNT PAID
$

30. BALANCE DUE
$ 295 00

31. SIGNATURE OF PHYSICIAN OR SUPPLIER INCLUDING DEGREES OR CREDENTIALS (I certify that the statements on the reverse apply to this bill and are made a part thereof.)

SIGNED *Lowery Johnson MD*   DATE 6/25/9X

32. NAME AND ADDRESS OF FACILITY WHERE SERVICES WERE RENDERED (If other than home or office)
DOGOOD COMMUNITY HOSPITAL
8080 FIFTH AVE
TEMPLE IN 47555

33. PHYSICIAN'S, SUPPLIER'S BILLING NAME, ADDRESS, ZIP CODE & PHONE #
LOWERY JOHNSON MD
HWY 311 SUITE A31
SELLERSBURG IN 47172
PIN# 1948   GRP# (822) 752-9118

(APPROVED BY AMA COUNCIL ON MEDICAL SERVICE 8/88)   ***PLEASE PRINT OR TYPE***   FORM HCFA-1500 (U2) (12-90)
FORM OWCP-1500   FORM RRB-1500

Figure 11–28 Completed HCFA-1500 for CHAMPUS claim.

A claim form is completed for the job-related illness or injury and sent to the insurance carrier or the state Workers' Compensation Fund for reimbursement. The injured worker receives no bills, pays no deductible or coinsurance, and is covered 100 percent for medical expenses related specifically to that injury or illness. Figure 11–29 is a sample Workers' Compensation claim form.

INSTRUCTIONS

1. Type answers to All questions and file original with the Workers' Compensation Commission within 72 hours after first treatment.
2. DO NOT FAIL to forward to the Workers' Compensation Commission PROGRESS REPORTS and FINAL REPORT upon discharge of patient.

DO NOT WRITE IN THIS SPACE

WCC CLAIM #

EMPLOYER'S REPORT Yes ☐ No ☐

WORKERS' COMPENSATION COMMISSION

This is First Report ☐ Progress Report ☐ Final Report ☐

EVERY QUESTION MUST BE ANSWERED AND FORM SIGNED

1. Name of Injured Person: Maureen A. Santega | Soc. Sec. No. 610-98-7432 | D.O.B. 7/19/69 | Sex M ☐ F ☑
2. Address: (No. and Street) 905 Raymond Lane | (City or Town) Atlanta | (State) GA | (Zip Code) 30385-8893
3. Name and Address of Employer: Majors Concrete Company, 238 Leaf Lane, Atlanta, GA 30342-3329
4. Date of Accident or Onset of Disease: 4/9/XX | Hour: A.M. ☑ P.M. ☐ | 5. Date Disability Began: 4/9/XX
6. Patient's Description of Accident or Cause of Disease: Concrete truck struck and backed over patient's foot while she was pouring concrete at job site
7. Medical description of Injury or Disease: Massive bruising to left foot, no broken bones, great deal of pain associated with bruises
8. Will Injury result in: (a) Permanent defect? Yes ☐ No ☑ If so, what? | (b) Disfigurement Yes ☐ No ☑
9. Causes, other than injury, contributing to patients condition: None
10. Is patient suffering from any disease of the heart, lungs, brain, kidneys, blood, vascular system or any other disabling condition not due to this accident? Give particulars: No
11. Is there any history or evidence present of previous accident or disease? Give particulars: No
12. Has normal recovery been delayed for any reason? Give particulars: No
13. Date of first treatment: 4/10/XX | Who engaged your services? patient
14. Describe treatment given by you: Darvon, 100 mg q4h prn for pain
15. Were X-Rays taken: Yes ☑ No ☐ | By whom? — (Name and Address) Edwin Gordon, M.D. 802 Manor Lane, Atlanta 30303 | Date 4/10/XX
16. X-Ray Diagnosis: No broken bones
17. Was patient treated by anyone else? Yes ☐ No ☑ | By whom? — (Name and Address) | Date
18. Was patient hospitalized? Yes ☐ No ☑ | Name and Address of Hospital | Date of Admission: Date of Discharge:
19. Is further treatment needed? Yes ☐ No ☑ | For how long? | 20. Patient was ☑ will be ☐ able to resume regular work on: 4/14 Patient was ☐ will be ☐ able to resume light work on:
21. If death ensued give date: | 22. Remarks: (Give any information of value not included above)
23. I am a qualified specialist in: orthopedics | I am a duly licensed Physician in the State of: Maryland | I was graduated from Medical School (Name) Johns Hopkins | Year 1967

Date of this report: 6/21/XX | (Signed) *John N. Sparks, M.D.*

Address: 8504 Capricorn Drive Atlanta GA 30312 | Phone: (404) 544-0078 | (This report must be signed PERSONALLY by Physician)

Figure 11–29 An example of a Workers' Compensation claim form (adapted from Comprehensive Medical Assisting, Lindh, Pooler, Tamparo, Cerrato).

BLUE CROSS/BLUE SHIELD

Blue Cross/Blue Shield (BC/BS) is a nationwide federation of local nonprofit service organizations that provide health care services to its subscribers. BC/BS is undoubtedly one of the more popular insurance plans in the United States. Typically Blue Cross covers hospital expenses, Blue Shield covers physician services. The patient may have a Blue Cross plan only, a Blue Shield plan only, or a combined BC/BS plan.

Coverage plans vary under BC/BS coverage. Two basic types of policies are offered: service benefit and indemnity benefit. A service benefit policy may have higher premiums but lower out-of-pocket expenses for the patient. An indemnity benefit policy may feature lower premiums with a deductible and coinsurance amount payable by the subscriber.

Some patients may present a Blue Shield card that has a double-headed arrow with an "N" and a three-digit number signifying membership in a permanent reciprocity plan (see Figure 11–30). The plan allows the insured to be treated anywhere in the United States with treatment expenses covered, whether the treatment is an emergency or not. The "N" and three-digit number must be entered on the claim form when filing for services rendered.

Blue Shield plans vary greatly; therefore, deductibles, co-payments, and specific coverages will differ from patient to patient. Because of the different plans, reimbursement will depend upon the specific plan. For example, the patient may pay the physician directly with a Blue Shield claim filed for reimbursement. A physician's office may file a claim and bill the patient for the difference between the payment and fee charged. The payment is usually sent to the insured for services provided by nonparticipating physicians. Participating physicians are paid directly. Various methods are used by BC/BS to determine payment:

■ Primary method of payment is usual, customary, and reasonable (UCR) fees.

■ Relative Value Scale (RVS). A five-digit number and a unit value are assigned to each procedure based on the procedure's relative value compared to that of other common procedures. A conversion factor is applied to the unit value to determine payment.

■ Diagnosis Related Groups (DRGs). This pays a fixed fee based on the patient's diagnosis rather than actual services performed.

As with many other health insurance companies, Blue Shield negotiates participating contracts with providers. A Blue Shield PAR must submit claims for its patients, and adjust the difference between the amount charged and the approved

Figure 11–30 Example of a Blue Cross/Blue Shield card showing reciprocity.

fee on all covered services included in a policy written by the local corporation. Blue Shield agrees to make direct payments to PARs, and provide assistance and educational means.

Providers who have not signed a participating contract (nonPAR) can bill the entire amount of the fee charged for services performed. The claim can be filed by the billing office or the patient. In either case, the payment will be sent directly to the patient.

BC/BS has unique features that set them apart from other commercial health insurance groups:

- A patient's policy cannot be cancelled by BC/BS due to poor health or greater-than-average benefit payments.

- Any rate increase and/or benefit changes must get approval from the state insurance commissioner.

- BC/BS plans can be converted from group to individual coverage and can be transferred from state to state.

- In negotiating contracts with health care providers, Blue Shield agrees to make prompt, direct payment of claims, provide assistance with claim filing, and provide training seminars, manuals, and newsletters to keep personnel current and up-to-date in billing and claim filing.

In some states BC/BS assists in the administration of government programs such as Medicaid, Medicare and CHAMPUS/TRICARE. Many patients have BC/BS as supplemental coverage to Medicare. One of the largest national plans is the Federal Employee Health Benefit Program (FEP) serving federal government employees. These cards will have the words "Government-Wide Service Benefit Plan", and the identification number begins with an "R" followed by eight digits. On the front of the card is a three-digit enrollment code. There are four enrollment options the government employee can select when applying for the program:

101 Individual, high option plan
102 Family, high option plan
103 Individual standard, (low) option plan
104 Family standard, (low) option plan

Figure 11–31 shows the FEP Blue Shield card. The FEP is primary when a patient also has CHAMPUS or MEDICAID. It coordinates benefits with Medicare Parts A and B, and any other employer group policy.

The deadline for filing Blue Shield claims is one year from the date of service.

Figure 11–32 is an example of a Blue Shield claim form.

Figure 11–31 Example of a Blue Cross/Blue Shield Federal Employee Plan (FEP) card.

APPROVED OMB-0938-0008

BLUE CROSS / BLUE SHIELD

CARRIER

PICA | **HEALTH INSURANCE CLAIM FORM** | PICA

| 1. MEDICARE (Medicare #) | MEDICAID (Medicaid #) | CHAMPUS (Sponsor's SSN) | CHAMPVA (VA File #) | GROUP HEALTH PLAN (SSN or ID) | FECA BLK LUNG (SSN) | OTHER ☒ (ID) | 1a. INSURED'S I.D. NUMBER (FOR PROGRAM IN ITEM 1) 404883124 XEP |

| 2. PATIENT'S NAME (Last Name, First Name, Middle Initial) ANTON JEREMY D | 3. PATIENT'S BIRTH DATE MM 12 DD 24 YY 55 | SEX M ☒ F ☐ | 4. INSURED'S NAME (Last Name, First Name, Middle Initial) SAME |

| 5. PATIENT'S ADDRESS (No., Street) 6702 MOUNTAINTOP RD | 6. PATIENT RELATIONSHIP TO INSURED Self ☒ Spouse ☐ Child ☐ Other ☐ | 7. INSURED'S ADDRESS (No., Street) SAME |

| CITY SMITHFIELD | STATE IN | 8. PATIENT STATUS Single ☐ Married ☒ Other ☐ | CITY | STATE |

| ZIP CODE 47222 | TELEPHONE (Include Area Code) (822) 273-0880 | Employed ☐ Full-Time Student ☐ Part-Time Student ☐ | ZIP CODE | TELEPHONE (INCLUDE AREA CODE) ( ) |

| 9. OTHER INSURED'S NAME (Last Name, First Name, Middle Initial) | 10. IS PATIENT'S CONDITION RELATED TO: | 11. INSURED'S POLICY GROUP OR FECA NUMBER PPD8021 |

| a. OTHER INSURED'S POLICY OR GROUP NUMBER | a. EMPLOYMENT? (CURRENT OR PREVIOUS) YES ☐ NO ☒ | a. INSURED'S DATE OF BIRTH MM DD YY SEX M ☐ F ☐ |

| b. OTHER INSURED'S DATE OF BIRTH MM DD YY SEX M ☐ F ☐ | b. AUTO ACCIDENT? PLACE (State) YES ☐ NO ☒ | b. EMPLOYER'S NAME OR SCHOOL NAME TIPTON SUPPLY CO |

| c. EMPLOYER'S NAME OR SCHOOL NAME | c. OTHER ACCIDENT? YES ☐ NO ☒ | c. INSURANCE PLAN NAME OR PROGRAM NAME BLUE SHIELD |

| d. INSURANCE PLAN NAME OR PROGRAM NAME | 10d. RESERVED FOR LOCAL USE | d. IS THERE ANOTHER HEALTH BENEFIT PLAN? YES ☐ NO ☒ **If yes**, return to and complete item 9 a-d. |

READ BACK OF FORM BEFORE COMPLETING & SIGNING THIS FORM.
12. PATIENT'S OR AUTHORIZED PERSON'S SIGNATURE I authorize the release of any medical or other information necessary to process this claim. I also request payment of government benefits either to myself or to the party who accepts assignment below.

SIGNED SIGNATURE ON FILE DATE

13. INSURED'S OR AUTHORIZED PERSON'S SIGNATURE I authorize payment of medical benefits to the undersigned physician or supplier for services described below.

SIGNED

| 14. DATE OF CURRENT: MM 06 DD 25 YY 9X ILLNESS (First symptom) OR INJURY (Accident) OR PREGNANCY(LMP) | 15. IF PATIENT HAS HAD SAME OR SIMILAR ILLNESS. GIVE FIRST DATE MM DD YY | 16. DATES PATIENT UNABLE TO WORK IN CURRENT OCCUPATION FROM MM DD YY TO MM DD YY |

| 17. NAME OF REFERRING PHYSICIAN OR OTHER SOURCE | 17a. I.D. NUMBER OF REFERRING PHYSICIAN | 18. HOSPITALIZATION DATES RELATED TO CURRENT SERVICES FROM MM DD YY TO MM DD YY |

| 19. RESERVED FOR LOCAL USE | 20. OUTSIDE LAB? YES ☐ NO ☐ $ CHARGES |

| 21. DIAGNOSIS OR NATURE OF ILLNESS OR INJURY. (RELATE ITEMS 1,2,3 OR 4 TO ITEM 24E BY LINE) 1. 870.0   3. 2. E884.0   4. | 22. MEDICAID RESUBMISSION CODE   ORIGINAL REF. NO. 23. PRIOR AUTHORIZATION NUMBER 1239011-1 |

24. A DATE(S) OF SERVICE From MM DD YY To MM DD YY	B Place of Service	C Type of Service	D PROCEDURES, SERVICES, OR SUPPLIES (Explain Unusual Circumstances) CPT/HCPCS	MODIFIER	E DIAGNOSIS CODE	F $ CHARGES	G DAYS OR UNITS	H EPSDT Family Plan	I EMG	J COB	K RESERVED FOR LOCAL USE
1 03 11 9X	11		99242		1	65 00	1				
2 04 03 9X	23		46060	80	2	287 50	1				
3											
4											
5											
6											

| 25. FEDERAL TAX I.D. NUMBER 75-2166173 SSN ☐ EIN ☒ | 26. PATIENT'S ACCOUNT NO. | 27. ACCEPT ASSIGNMENT? (For govt. claims, see back) YES ☐ NO ☒ | 28. TOTAL CHARGE $ 352 50 | 29. AMOUNT PAID $ | 30. BALANCE DUE $ 352 50 |

| 31. SIGNATURE OF PHYSICIAN OR SUPPLIER INCLUDING DEGREES OR CREDENTIALS (I certify that the statements on the reverse apply to this bill and are made a part thereof.) SIGNED *Lowery Johnson MD* DATE 4/3/9X | 32. NAME AND ADDRESS OF FACILITY WHERE SERVICES WERE RENDERED (If other than home or office) DOGOOD SURGICAL CENTER 8080 FIFTH AVE TEMPLE IN 47555 | 33. PHYSICIAN'S, SUPPLIER'S BILLING NAME, ADDRESS, ZIP CODE & PHONE # LOWERY JOHNSON MD HWY 311 SUITE A31 SELLERSBURG IN 47172 PIN# 12001   GRP# (822) 752-9118 |

(APPROVED BY AMA COUNCIL ON MEDICAL SERVICE 8/88)   **PLEASE PRINT OR TYPE**   FORM HCFA-1500 (U2) (12-90) FORM OWCP-1500   FORM RRB-1500

Figure 11–32 Completed HCFA-1500 for Blue Shield claim.

EXERCISE 11–4

Match the term with its definition, placing the letter of the correct answer in the space provided.

_____ **1.** Workers' compensation

_____ **2.** Medicaid

_____ **3.** Blue Cross/Blue Shield

_____ **4.** Medicare Part A

_____ **5.** Medicare Part B

_____ **6.** CHAMPUS/TRICARE/ CHAMPVA

a. a nationwide federation of local nonprofit service organizations providing health care to all its subscribers.

b. hospital insurance for persons age 65 and over, disabled, or with end-stage renal disease.

c. federal program providing health care benefits to families of armed forces and retired military personnel and veterans.

d. an assistance program to provide medical care for persons with incomes below the national poverty level.

e. medical coverage optional for persons age 65 and over, disabled, or with end-stage renal disease.

f. coverage for work-related illness or injury.

ELECTRONIC CLAIM FILING

One function of a computerized office system is the preparation and generation of insurance claims. Almost 90 percent of all insurance companies participate in electronic submission of claims. It is quicker, cost-effective, and does improve cash flow in the practice. The billing program first scans the medical practice database to obtain the information necessary to complete each block on the claim form. The computer will then group the claim forms by the insurance carrier.

When this preparation phase is complete, the computer will then generate the insurance claim forms by printing a paper claim form or transmitting electronically directly to the insurance carrier. When printing the paper claim, the HCFA-1500 forms can be purchased as a continuous-feed, single- or multiple-part form. Once printed, they are separated at the perforation and mailed to the insurance company. A copy should always be retained for the office.

To file insurance claims electronically, the medical office must have the ability in the computer program to perform this task. The computer must be connected to a modem. A modem is a device that changes data into a form that allows transmission over telephone lines to be received by the computer at the insurance companies.

When the preparation phase is completed, a message will appear on the screen of the terminal to indicate the claims are ready for transmission to the insurance carrier. During the time of transmission, a message remains on the screen that transmission is in progress as that computer cannot be used for any other functions. When all prepared claims have been transmitted, a final message is displayed on the screen relaying the transmission process has been completed. This process is repeated until all claims have been filed with each individual insurance carrier.

There are two types of computer systems to process claims: carrier-direct and clearinghouse. Medicare, Medicaid, Blue Cross/Blue Shield, CHAMPUS, and many private insurance carriers use the carrier-direct system. The medical office enters the claim form data and transmits via the modem over the telephone line directly to the insurance company. A distinct advantage of the carrier-direct system is the error-edit process. In the event an error is made during the electronic filing process, the error is known and can be corrected immediately.

A clearinghouse, also known as third-party administrator, separates the paper or electronic claims submitted to them by the medical office and sends each one to the insurance carrier indicated. The claim is checked for completeness and accuracy and then processed for reimbursement. Claims that are inaccurate are manually reviewed. Rejected claims are returned by mail or to the physician's computer terminal.

Processing claims electronically does occasionally present problems. Static in the telephone line can delay or reject claims when information may be lost in the transmission. Delays may occur when too many offices are trying to transmit data and the insurance carrier's computer becomes backlogged. Sometimes computers malfunction and are down, allowing no transmission or communication. And sometimes there may be errors or "bugs" in the hardware or software that must be removed. It is important to update software as ICD-9-CM and CPT codes are added, deleted or changed annually. Failure to do so can result in rejected claims.

Other transactions can be communicated via the computer. Inquiries as to the status of a claim can be made, and payment or denial can be checked. The patient's eligibility can be verified as well as deductibles and other coverage. Other information such as fee schedules, limiting charges, and procedures codes can be accessed. These transactions save time that would otherwise be spent on the telephone on hold or resubmitting a claim by mail.

INSURANCE CLAIMS FOLLOW-UP

A system must be developed in order to follow up insurance claims. A tickler file can be set up as a manual system or in a computer system as a reminder to telephone or send inquiries to insurance carriers about unpaid claims. A copy of the claim form can be filed in the tickler file then retrieved when the remittance advice (RA) or explanation of benefits (EOB) and check are received. Review the RA or EOB and compare with the claim form. A copy of the RA or EOB is attached to the claim form copy and filed in a folder for paid claims. Copies of claim forms remaining in the tickler file past the time limit for processing of payment denial can be resubmitted to the insurance carrier, indicating on the copy that this is a second request.

An insurance claims register can also be used to follow status of claim forms. This can be a three-ring binder using indexes identifying various insurance companies. A copy of the claim form can be filed under the index of the insurance carrier and the submission information is recorded in the insurance claims register. The register as demonstrated in Figure 11–33 contains columns to note the date the claim was submitted, the amount of the claim, and the date payment was received. When payment is received and posted to the patient's account, the copy of the claim is removed from the binder and placed in the patient's chart or a separate file maintained for audit purposes. A line is drawn through the information on the register to indicate claim status is complete.

INSURANCE CLAIM REGISTRY						
Date Filed	Patient Name	ID Number	Insurance Company	Amount Filed	Amount Paid	Follow-up Date
05/11/9X	Opal Pearl	403-08-2214	CIGNA	$ 54.00		06/30/9X
06/25/9X	Patricia Duchane	300-54-3030	CHAMPUS	$ 295.00	$ 236.00	

Figure 11–33 An insurance claim registry can be used to follow status of claim forms.

Problem Claims

No matter how accurate, complete and efficient the medical office may be, there will still be problem claims that require some type of action. Some of these problems are claims that are denied, rejected, or lost, incorrect payment, down coding, and pending claims.

When claims are delinquent or pending, this means payment is overdue due to the claim being reviewed or additional information required or an error has been made. An insurance tracer form can be used to follow up these problem claims as indicated in Figure 11–34.

State laws require insurance companies to notify the insured when a claim is denied and the reason for the denial. Federal laws require Medicare to issue an explanation for each denied service.

Claim forms are stamped the date received by the insurance carrier. A claim number is assigned and logged into the payer system. If the claim has not been received and logged in or has been lost, a copy of the original claim can be resubmitted indicating this is a copy of the original claim submitted on (date).

Earlier in this module the most common reasons why claim forms are rejected were listed. When claim forms are rejected, make the necessary corrections or provide additional information, and resubmit the claim for regular processing. Do not send a corrected claim for review or appeal.

When a claim is denied, it is usually denied due to medical coverage policy or program issues. These issues may be:

▪ The procedure was not a covered service in the policy.
▪ Treatment submitted was for a preexisting condition.
▪ Patient was no longer covered by policy when service was rendered, or service was performed before coverage was in effect.
▪ Service was not medically necessary.

When notice of denial is received, notify the patient by telephone or mail so he/she is aware of the denial. An appeal is then made with a request for a review in writing. Figure 11–35 is an example of a Request for Review of Part B Medicare Claim Form HCFA-1964. This is further discussed in Module 12.

Occasionally claims are processed by an insurance carrier resulting in lowered reimbursement due to down coding. Down coding occurs in the following situations:

▪ Insufficient diagnostic information submitted on the claim form.
▪ Conversion of a CPT or ICD-9-CM code submitted on a claim form by the insurance carrier.
▪ Routine use of unspecified ICD-9-CM codes with the number "9" as the fourth or fifth digit.

INSURANCE COMPANY_____ DATE _____

ADDRESS:_ _____

PATIENT NAME_____ NAME OF INSURED_____

IDENTIFICATION NUMBER_____

EMPLOYER NAME & ADDRESS_____

DATE CLAIM FILED_____ CLAIM AMOUNT_____

Attached is a copy of the original claim submitted to you on _____. We have not yet received a request for additional information and still await payment of this claim. Please review the attached duplicate and process for payment.

If there are any questions regarding this claim, please answer the following and return this letter to our office.

IF CLAIM HAS BEEN PAID:

          Date of payment   _____

          Amount of payment   _____

          Payment made to: _____

IF CLAIM HAS BEEN DENIED:

          Reason for denial   _____

                                _____

          Has the patient been notified: ☐ Yes   ☐ No

IF CLAIM IS STILL PENDING:

          Please state reason why?

                  _____

                  _____

Please return this insurance claim tracer in the enclosed envelope or you may fax to (222) 663-2211.

Thank you in this request.

Sincerely,

Judy Jolly, **CMA**
Insurance Specialist

Figure 11–34 An example of an insurance claim tracer used to follow up delinquent claims.

DEPARTMENT OF HEALTH AND HUMAN SERVICES
HEALTH CARE FINANCING ADMINISTRATION

Form Approved
OMB No. 0938-0033

REQUEST FOR REVIEW OF PART B MEDICARE CLAIM
Medical Insurance Benefits - Social Security Act

NOTICE—Anyone who misrepresents or falsifies essential information requested by this form may upon conviction be subject to fine and imprisonment under Federal Law.

1 Carrier's Name and Address

2 Name of Patient

3 Health Insurance Claim Number

4 I do not agree with the determination you made on my claim as described on my Explanation of Medicare

Benefits dated:

5 MY REASONS ARE: (Attach a copy of the Explanation of Medicare Benefits, or describe the service, date of service, and physician's name—NOTE.—If the date on the Notice of Benefits mentioned in item 3 is more than six months ago, include your reason for not making this request earlier.)

6 Describe Illness or Injury:

7 ☐ I have additional evidence to submit. (Attach such evidence to this form.)

☐ I do not have additional evidence.

COMPLETE ALL OF THE INFORMATION REQUESTED. SIGN AND RETURN THE FIRST COPY AND ANY ATTACHMENTS TO THE CARRIER NAMED ABOVE. IF YOU NEED HELP, TAKE THIS AND YOUR NOTICE FROM THE CARRIER TO A SOCIAL SECURITY OFFICE, OR TO THE CARRIER. KEEP THE DUPLICATE COPY OF THIS FORM FOR YOUR RECORDS.

8 SIGNATURE OF <u>EITHER</u> THE CLAIMENT <u>OR</u> HIS REPRESENTATIVE

Representative	Claimant
Address	Address
City, State, and ZIP Code	City, State, and ZIP Code
Telephone Number Date	Telephone Number Date

Form HCFA-1964 (8-85)   (over)

CARRIER'S COPY

Figure 11–35 Request for Review of Part B Medicare Claim can be used to request a review of a submitted claim.

The impact of down coding is lowered reimbursement. Review the EOBs and RAs to identify reasons a claim may be down coded. Use appropriate codes, indicate the medical necessity of the ICD-9-CM and CPT codes, and code to the highest level of specificity. Module 12 gives detailed steps in the review and appeals process.

Figure 11–36 is a summary linking the cycle that occurs from the patient visit to payment.

INSURANCE CLAIM FORM SUMMARY

Charge Slip/Superbill

1. Charge slip or superbill is attached to the outside of the patient's chart.

2. Physician sees patient, completes charge slip/superbill by marking service and diagnosis, signs charge slip/superbill, and indicates if patient needs an appointment to return.

3. Patient "checks out" at reception desk, makes return appointment if indicated by physician, and pays co-pay or other charges.

Ledger Card/Account

4. Charge slip/superbill is used to post services, charges and payments to the patient's account.

Insurance Claim Form

5. Claim form is completed and submitted to insurance carrier.

Insurance Claims Register

6. Copy of claim form is filed in pending file. Date of submission is posted on ledger card/account and recorded in the insurance claims register.

Payment

7. Payment is received and posted to patient's ledger card/account. Check is endorsed and recorded on bank deposit slip.

Patient Statement

8. Bill the patient for any balance due.

Patient or Paid File

9. Claim form copy is retrieved from the pending file and attached to the EOB and filed in patient's chart or paid file for audit.

Figure 11–36 An Insurance Claim Form Summary shows the billing and claim form cycle from the time the patient is first seen in the office until the claim is paid.

EXERCISE 11–5

Match the term with its definition, placing the correct answer in the space provided.

_____ **1.** Capitation

_____ **2.** Workers' Compensation

_____ **3.** Medicaid

_____ **4.** Medicare Part A

_____ **5.** Medicare Part B

_____ **6.** Co-payment

_____ **7.** Deductible

_____ **8.** Third-party payer

_____ **9.** Assignment of benefits

_____ **10.** CHAMPUS/TRICARE/ CHAMPVA

a. authorization to pay benefits directly to the physician

b. federal program providing health care benefits to families of armed forces and retired military personnel and veterans

c. an individual or company making a payment on a debt

d. a reimbursement method that pays a fixed amount per person

e. hospital insurance for persons age 65 and over, disabled, or have end-stage renal disease

f. medical insurance optional for persons age 65 and over, disabled, or have end-stage renal disease

g. the total amount the patient must pay for covered services before benefits are payable

h. a specified dollar amount a patient must pay for each service or procedure

i. coverage for work-related illness or injury

j. an assistance program to provide medical care for persons with incomes below national poverty level

EXERCISE 11–6

In the following exercises, complete a HCFA-1500 claim form for each patient's insurance plan as indicated on the patient registration form. Remember to:

- Refer to the patient registration form for patient information.
- Refer to the patient's medical record to complete the medical information.
- Refer to the patient's ledger card to complete charges.

PROVIDER BILLING INFORMATION

Physician: Lowery Johnson, M.D.
             Internal Medicine

Address: Hwy 311 Suite A31
Sellersburg, IN 47172

Phone: (822) 752-9118

Employer ID Number: 75-2166173

PIN: 1948

Provider is a PAR with Medicare.

Hospital services performed at: Dogood Community Hospital
8080 Fifth Avenue
Temple, IN 47555

Case #1—Phila G. Badd

Welcome

Thank you for selecting our healthcare team! We will strive to provide you with the best possible healthcare. To help us meet all your healthcare needs, please fill out this form completely in ink. If you have any questions or need assistance, please ask us – we will be happy to help.

1 Personal Information

Date ___8/2/9x___
Birth date ___9/10/32___   Soc. Sec. # ___406-26-8683___
Name ___Phila G. Badd___   Wishes to be called _____
❑ Male ☒ Female ❑ Minor ❑ Single ❑ Married ❑ Divorced ☒ Widowed ❑ Separated
Address ___4515 Wildwood Circle___
City, State, Zip ___Sellersburg, IN 47172___
Employer ___Retired___   Occupation ___Social Worker___
Referred by ___Dr. Jeff Roe___

2 Responsible Party

Who is responsible for the account? _____
Name ___Phila G. Badd___
Relationship to patient ___Self___
Birth date ___9/10/32___   Driver's License ___R406-26-8683001___
Soc. Sec. # ___406-26-8683___
Address ___4515 Wildwood Circle___
City, State, Zip ___Sellersberg, IN 47172___
Employer ___Retired – Magna Services___
Occupation ___Social Worker___
Work Phone ___None___   Ext # _____
Home Phone ___(822) 266-5403___

3 Telephone

Home Phone ___(822) 266-5403___
Work Phone ___N/A___   Ext # _____
Car Phone _____
Where do you prefer to receive calls ☒ Home ❑ Work ❑ Car
When is the best time to reach you?   Time ___Any___ Days ___Any___
In the event of emergency, who should we contact?
Name ___Ellen Sipps___ Relationship ___Daughter___ Work # ___–___ Home # ___322-8121___

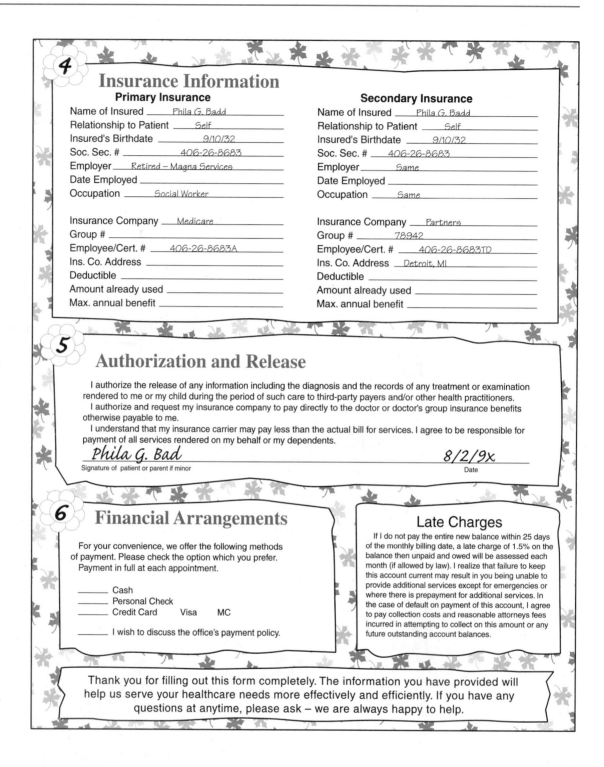

④ Insurance Information

Primary Insurance

Name of Insured _____ Phila G. Badd _____
Relationship to Patient _____ Self _____
Insured's Birthdate _____ 9/10/32 _____
Soc. Sec. # _____ 406-26-8683 _____
Employer _____ Retired – Magna Services _____
Date Employed _____
Occupation _____ Social Worker _____

Insurance Company _____ Medicare _____
Group # _____
Employee/Cert. # _____ 406-26-8683A _____
Ins. Co. Address _____
Deductible _____
Amount already used _____
Max. annual benefit _____

Secondary Insurance

Name of Insured _____ Phila G. Badd _____
Relationship to Patient _____ Self _____
Insured's Birthdate _____ 9/10/32 _____
Soc. Sec. # _____ 406-26-8683 _____
Employer _____ Same _____
Date Employed _____
Occupation _____ Same _____

Insurance Company _____ Partners _____
Group # _____ 78942 _____
Employee/Cert. # _____ 406-26-8683TD _____
Ins. Co. Address _____ Detroit, MI _____
Deductible _____
Amount already used _____
Max. annual benefit _____

⑤ Authorization and Release

I authorize the release of any information including the diagnosis and the records of any treatment or examination rendered to me or my child during the period of such care to third-party payers and/or other health practitioners.

I authorize and request my insurance company to pay directly to the doctor or doctor's group insurance benefits otherwise payable to me.

I understand that my insurance carrier may pay less than the actual bill for services. I agree to be responsible for payment of all services rendered on my behalf or my dependents.

Phila G. Bad _____   _8/2/9x_ _____
Signature of patient or parent if minor   Date

⑥ Financial Arrangements

For your convenience, we offer the following methods of payment. Please check the option which you prefer. Payment in full at each appointment.

_____ Cash
_____ Personal Check
_____ Credit Card   Visa   MC

_____ I wish to discuss the office's payment policy.

Late Charges

If I do not pay the entire new balance within 25 days of the monthly billing date, a late charge of 1.5% on the balance then unpaid and owed will be assessed each month (if allowed by law). I realize that failure to keep this account current may result in you being unable to provide additional services except for emergencies or where there is prepayment for additional services. In the case of default on payment of this account, I agree to pay collection costs and reasonable attorneys fees incurred in attempting to collect on this amount or any future outstanding account balances.

Thank you for filling out this form completely. The information you have provided will help us serve your healthcare needs more effectively and efficiently. If you have any questions at anytime, please ask – we are always happy to help.

INTERNAL MEDICINE	PROGRESS NOTES	**Formedic**

NAME PHILA G. BADD   S M Ⓦ D   DATE OF BIRTH 09/10/32   AGE 67   PAGE NO. 1

DATE	HISTORY & PHYSICAL
4/4/9X	Weight 133–1/3 lbs. Blood pressure 180/92.
	CC: Lump in right breast
	Established patient is in the office today stating she has found a
	"lump" in her right breast. Breast exam today reveals a 1.5 x 2 cm
	nodule in the right breast around 1 o'clock. It is movable and
	nontender. Patient is referred to Dogood Community Hospital for
	bilateral mammograms tomorrow morning. She will call later
	tomorrow for results and further orders. *Lowery B. Johnson, M.D.*
4/5/9X	Telephone Call with patient today: The bilateral mammograms done
	this morning confirm the presence of a nodule in the right breast
	as noted on breast exam yesterday, 4/4/9X. Patient will return to
	the office tomorrow for a breast biopsy and referral to Dr. Steven
	Jones for surgical consultation. *Lowery B. Johnson, M.D.*
4/6/9X	Office visit: Patient has returned today for biopsy of the nodule
	in the right breast. Blood pressure continues to be elevated –
	today it is 192/98 in the left arm; 190/96 in right arm.
	RECOMMENDATIONS: 1. Increase Norvasc to 10 mg each day for
	hypertension. *Lowery B. Johnson, M.D.*
4/7/9X	The breast biopsy obtained yesterday, 4/6/9X, reveals breast
	carcinoma. She is referred to Dr. Steven Jones for surgical
	consultation.. *Lowery B. Johnson, M.D.*

120 WORLD'S FAIR DR. SOMERSET N.J. 08873   PRINTED IN CANADA   FORMEDIC 1982. IM PN LE

STATEMENT

Lowery B. Johnson, M.D.
Hwy 311 Suite A31
Sellersburg, IN 47172
812-246-1234

PHILA G BADD
4515 WILDWOOD CIRCLE
SELLERSBURG IN 47172

DATE	REFERENCE	DESCRIPTION	CHARGES		CREDITS PYMNTS.	CREDITS ADJ.		BALANCE
		BALANCE FORWARD ⟶						
4/4/9x		OS – EPF	42	00				42	00
4/6/9x		OS – DETAILED	58	00				100	00
4/6/9x		NEEDLE BIOPSY – BREAST	155	00				255	00

RB40BC-2-96

PLEASE PAY LAST AMOUNT IN BALANCE COLUMN ⟶ ▲

THIS IS A COPY OF YOUR ACCOUNT AS IT APPEARS ON OUR RECORDS

PLEASE
DO NOT
STAPLE
IN THIS
AREA

APPROVED OMB-0938-0008

CARRIER

☐☐ PICA

HEALTH INSURANCE CLAIM FORM

PICA ☐☐

1. MEDICARE MEDICAID CHAMPUS CHAMPVA GROUP HEALTH PLAN FECA BLK LUNG OTHER	1a. INSURED'S I.D. NUMBER (FOR PROGRAM IN ITEM 1)

☐ (Medicare #) ☐ (Medicaid #) ☐ (Sponsor's SSN) ☐ (VA File #) ☐ (SSN or ID) ☐ (SSN) ☐ (ID)

2. PATIENT'S NAME (Last Name, First Name, Middle Initial)

3. PATIENT'S BIRTH DATE MM | DD | YY   SEX   M ☐ F ☐

4. INSURED'S NAME (Last Name, First Name, Middle Initial)

5. PATIENT'S ADDRESS (No., Street)

6. PATIENT RELATIONSHIP TO INSURED   Self ☐ Spouse ☐ Child ☐ Other ☐

7. INSURED'S ADDRESS (No., Street)

CITY   STATE

8. PATIENT STATUS   Single ☐ Married ☐ Other ☐

CITY   STATE

ZIP CODE   TELEPHONE (Include Area Code) (   )

Employed ☐   Full-Time Student ☐   Part-Time Student ☐

ZIP CODE   TELEPHONE (INCLUDE AREA CODE) (   )

9. OTHER INSURED'S NAME (Last Name, First Name, Middle Initial)

10. IS PATIENT'S CONDITION RELATED TO:

11. INSURED'S POLICY GROUP OR FECA NUMBER

a. OTHER INSURED'S POLICY OR GROUP NUMBER

a. EMPLOYMENT? (CURRENT OR PREVIOUS)   ☐ YES ☐ NO

a. INSURED'S DATE OF BIRTH MM | DD | YY   SEX   M ☐ F ☐

b. OTHER INSURED'S DATE OF BIRTH MM | DD | YY   SEX   M ☐ F ☐

b. AUTO ACCIDENT?   PLACE (State)   ☐ YES ☐ NO

b. EMPLOYER'S NAME OR SCHOOL NAME

c. EMPLOYER'S NAME OR SCHOOL NAME

c. OTHER ACCIDENT?   ☐ YES ☐ NO

c. INSURANCE PLAN NAME OR PROGRAM NAME

d. INSURANCE PLAN NAME OR PROGRAM NAME

10d. RESERVED FOR LOCAL USE

d. IS THERE ANOTHER HEALTH BENEFIT PLAN?   ☐ YES ☐ NO   *If yes*, return to and complete item 9 a-d.

READ BACK OF FORM BEFORE COMPLETING & SIGNING THIS FORM.
12. PATIENT'S OR AUTHORIZED PERSON'S SIGNATURE I authorize the release of any medical or other information necessary to process this claim. I also request payment of government benefits either to myself or to the party who accepts assignment below.

SIGNED _____ DATE _____

13. INSURED'S OR AUTHORIZED PERSON'S SIGNATURE I authorize payment of medical benefits to the undersigned physician or supplier for services described below.

SIGNED _____

PATIENT AND INSURED INFORMATION

14. DATE OF CURRENT: ◀ ILLNESS (First symptom) OR INJURY (Accident) OR PREGNANCY(LMP)
MM | DD | YY

15. IF PATIENT HAS HAD SAME OR SIMILAR ILLNESS. GIVE FIRST DATE MM | DD | YY

16. DATES PATIENT UNABLE TO WORK IN CURRENT OCCUPATION
FROM MM | DD | YY TO MM | DD | YY

17. NAME OF REFERRING PHYSICIAN OR OTHER SOURCE

17a. I.D. NUMBER OF REFERRING PHYSICIAN

18. HOSPITALIZATION DATES RELATED TO CURRENT SERVICES
FROM MM | DD | YY TO MM | DD | YY

19. RESERVED FOR LOCAL USE

20. OUTSIDE LAB? $ CHARGES   ☐ YES ☐ NO

21. DIAGNOSIS OR NATURE OF ILLNESS OR INJURY. (RELATE ITEMS 1,2,3 OR 4 TO ITEM 24E BY LINE)

1. L___.___   3. L___.___
2. L___.___   4. L___.___

22. MEDICAID RESUBMISSION CODE   ORIGINAL REF. NO.

23. PRIOR AUTHORIZATION NUMBER

24. A DATE(S) OF SERVICE From MM DD YY To MM DD YY	B Place of Service	C Type of Service	D PROCEDURES, SERVICES, OR SUPPLIES (Explain Unusual Circumstances) CPT/HCPCS MODIFIER	E DIAGNOSIS CODE	F $ CHARGES	G DAYS OR UNITS	H EPSDT Family Plan	I EMG	J COB	K RESERVED FOR LOCAL USE
1										
2										
3										
4										
5										
6										

25. FEDERAL TAX I.D. NUMBER   SSN ☐ EIN ☐

26. PATIENT'S ACCOUNT NO.

27. ACCEPT ASSIGNMENT? (For govt. claims, see back)   ☐ YES ☐ NO

28. TOTAL CHARGE $

29. AMOUNT PAID $

30. BALANCE DUE $

31. SIGNATURE OF PHYSICIAN OR SUPPLIER INCLUDING DEGREES OR CREDENTIALS (I certify that the statements on the reverse apply to this bill and are made a part thereof.)

SIGNED _____ DATE _____

32. NAME AND ADDRESS OF FACILITY WHERE SERVICES WERE RENDERED (If other than home or office)

33. PHYSICIAN'S, SUPPLIER'S BILLING NAME, ADDRESS, ZIP CODE & PHONE #

PIN#   GRP#

PHYSICIAN OR SUPPLIER INFORMATION

(APPROVED BY AMA COUNCIL ON MEDICAL SERVICE 8/88)

PLEASE PRINT OR TYPE

FORM HCFA-1500 (U2) (12-90)
FORM OWCP-1500   FORM RRB-1500

Case #2—Katrina C. Burton

Welcome To Our Office   NEW PATIENT INFORMATION   DATE _JUNE 10, 199X_

PATIENT'S NAME (PLEASE PRINT)	S.S. #	MARITAL STATUS	SEX	BIRTH DATE	AGE	RELIGION (OPTION)
KATRINA C. BURTON	*302-15-4478*	(S) M W D SEP	M (F)	*1/3/80*	*18*	

STREET ADDRESS PERMANENT TEMPORARY	CITY AND STATE	ZIP CODE	HOME PHONE #
1005 MAIN ST.	*TEMPLE IN*	*47555*	*NONE*

PATIENT'S OR PARENT'S EMPLOYER	OCCUPATION (INDICATE IF STUDENT)	HOW LONG EMPLOYED	BUS. PHONE # EXT. #
NONE	*NONE*		

EMPLOYER'S STREET ADDRESS	CITY AND STATE		ZIP CODE

DRUG ALLERGIES, IF ANY
PENICILLIN

SPOUSE OR PARENT'S NAME	S.S. #	BIRTHDATE
ANNA BURTON	*404-32-7719*	*10/3/70*

SPOUSE OR PARENT'S EMPLOYER	OCCUPATION (INDICATE IF STUDENT)	HOW LONG EMPLOYED	BUS. PHONE #
NONE	*NONE*		

EMPLOYER'S STREET ADDRESS	CITY AND STATE		ZIP CODE

*SPOUSE'S STREET ADDRESS, IF DIVORCED OR SEPARATED	CITY AND STATE	ZIP CODE	HOME PHONE #

PLEASE READ: ALL CHARGES ARE DUE AT THE TIME OF SERVICES. IF HOSPITALIZATION IS INDICATED, THE PATIENT IS RESPONSIBLE FOR FURNISHING INSURANCE CLAIM FORMS TO THE OFFICE PRIOR TO HOSPITALIZATION.

PERSON RESPONSIBLE FOR PAYMENT, IF NOT ABOVE	STREET ADDRESS, CITY, STATE	ZIP CODE	HOME PHONE #

BLUE SHIELD (GIVE NAME OF POLICYHOLDER) ☐	EFFECTIVE DATE CERTIFICATE #	GROUP #	COVERAGE CODE

OTHER (WRITE IN NAME OF INSURANCE COMPANY) ☐	EFFECTIVE DATE	POLICY #

OTHER (WRITE IN NAME OF INSURANCE COMPANY) ☐	EFFECTIVE DATE	POLICY #

MEDICARE # ☐	RAILROAD RETIREMENT # ☐	☐ VISA or ☐ MASTERCARD #	EXP. DATE /

MEDICAID ☒ *100100536201*	EFFECTIVE DATE *4/1/97*	PROGRAM #	COUNTY #	CASE #	ACCOUNT #

INDUSTRIAL ☐	WERE YOU INJURED ON THE JOB? ☐ YES ☐ NO	DATE OF INJURY	INDUSTRIAL CLAIM #

ACCIDENT ☐	WAS AN AUTOMOBILE INVOLVED? ☐ YES ☐ NO	DATE OF ACCIDENT	NAME OF ATTORNEY

WERE X-RAYS TAKEN OF THIS INJURY OR PROBLEM? ☐ YES ☐ NO	IF YES, WHERE WERE X-RAYS TAKEN? (HOSPITAL, ETC.)	DATE X-RAYS TAKEN

HAS ANY MEMBER OF YOUR IMMEDIATE FAMILY BEEN TREATED BY OUR PHYSICIAN(S) BEFORE? INCLUDE NAME OF PHYSICIAN AND FAMILY MEMBER.
MOTHER, ANNA BURTON, HAS SEEN DR. JOHNSON

REFERRED BY	STREET ADDRESS, CITY, STATE	ZIP CODE	PHONE #

ALL PROFESSIONAL SERVICES RENDERED ARE CHARGED TO THE PATIENT. NECESSARY FORMS WILL BE COMPLETED TO HELP EXPEDITE INSURANCE CARRIER PAYMENTS. HOWEVER, THE PATIENT IS RESPONSIBLE FOR ALL FEES, REGARDLESS OF INSURANCE COVERAGE. IT IS ALSO CUSTOMARY TO PAY FOR SERVICES WHEN RENDERED UNLESS OTHER ARRANGEMENTS HAVE BEEN MADE IN ADVANCE WITH OUR OFFICE BOOKKEEPER.

INSURANCE AUTHORIZATION AND ASSIGNMENT

Name of Policy Holder _____ HIC Number _____

I request that payment of authorized Medicare/Other Insurance company benefits be made either to me or on my behalf to _____ for any services furnished me by that party who accepts assignment/physician. Regulations pertaining to Medicare assignment of benefits apply.

I authorize any holder of medical or other information about me to release to the Social Security Administration and Health Care Financing Administration or its intermediaries or carriers any information needed for this or a related Medicare claim/other Insurance Company claim. I permit a copy of this authorization to be used in place of the original, and request payment of medical insurance benefits either to myself or to the party who accepts assignment. I understand it is mandatory to notify the health care provider of any other party who may be responsible for paying for my treatment. (Section 1128B of the Social Security Act and 31 U.S.C. 3801-3812 provides penalties for withholding this information).

Signature *Katrina Burton* _____   Date *6/10/9X* _____

NEW PATIENT INFORMATION

INTERNAL MEDICINE	PROGRESS NOTES	**Formedic**

NAME Katrina C. Burton (S) M W D   DATE OF BIRTH 01/03/80   AGE 18   PAGE NO. 1

DATE	HISTORY & PHYSICAL
6/10/9X	Office Service: Weight 125–3/4 lbs. B/P 102/70 T 100F. R 18.
	She was seen in the ER on 6/8/9X with symptoms of chest congestion,
	dyspnea, hemoptysis, with a T at that time of 102F. Chest x-ray
	in the ER demonstrated bronchopneumonia right lung field.
	Today in the office she continues to complain of cough productive of
	yellow-green sputum with some blood streaks. Chest x-ray in the
	office today shows patchy consolidation right lung field representative
	of bronchopneumonia. CBC reveals an elevated WBC of 18.5.
	DIAGNOSIS: Bronchopneumonia.
	RECOMMENDATIONS: 1. Keflex 250 mg q.i.d. x 2 weeks.
	2. Aspirin for temp. elevation q 4 hrs.
	She is to return one week for recheck and repeat chest x-ray.
	Lowery B. Johnson, M.D.
6/17/9X	Office Service–Recheck: Patient continues to be quite ill with
	T 100F or greater. Continues to have productive cough with some
	blood occurring mostly at night and early a.m. She has remained on
	the Keflex as prescribed on 6/10/9X.
	RECOMMENDATIONS: 1. Outpatient admission to Dogood Community
	Hospital for 24-hour observation, repeat chest x-ray, bronchoscopy,
	collection of sputum x 2 for acid fast stains and cultures.
	Lowery B. Johnson, M.D.
6/17/9X	Admission to hospital observation bed, 24-hour. P/A 42003698–1
6/22/9X	Office Service–Follow-up: Patient is in today for follow-up after
	24-hour observation 6/17/9X. She has improved. Temp. today is
	99F. Lab/x-ray studies on 6/17/9X revealed the bronchopneumonia;
	no underlying disease or neoplasm. Repeat chest x-ray today shows
	pneumonia resolving. She will continue Keflex one more week and
	then discontinue. Repeat chest x-ray will be made at that time.
	Lowery B. Johnson, M.D.

12D WORLD'S FAIR DR., SOMERSET N.J. 08873   PRINTED IN CANADA   FORMEDIC 1982: IM PN LE

STATEMENT

Lowery B. Johnson, M.D.
Hwy 311 Suite A31
Sellersburg, IN 47172
812-246-1234

KATRINA C. BURTON
1005 MAIN ST
TEMPLE IN 47555

DATE	REFERENCE	DESCRIPTION	CHARGES		CREDITS PYMNTS.	ADJ.	BALANCE	
		BALANCE FORWARD ———————▶						
6/10/9x		OS – Comp. – NP	55	00			55	00
6/10/9x		CBC (AUTO)	22	00			77	00
6/10/9x		CHEST X-RAY (2 VIEWS)	118	00			195	00
6/17/9x		OS	N/C				195	00
6/17/9x		OBSV – INITIAL – DET	125	00			320	00
6/22/9x		OS – P.F.	46	00			366	00
6/22/9x		CHEST X-RAY (2 VIEWS)	118	00			484	00

RB40BC-2-96   PLEASE PAY LAST AMOUNT IN BALANCE COLUMN ———▲

CBC—Complete Blood Count   INJ—Injection
OS—Office Service   UA—Urinalysis
OBSV—Observation Bed   EKG—Electrocardiogram

THIS IS A COPY OF YOUR ACCOUNT AS IT APPEARS ON OUR RECORDS

PLEASE
DO NOT
STAPLE
IN THIS
AREA

APPROVED OMB-0938-0008

←——— CARRIER ———→

| | PICA | | **HEALTH INSURANCE CLAIM FORM** | | PICA | |

1. MEDICARE ☐ (Medicare #)   MEDICAID ☐ (Medicaid #)   CHAMPUS ☐ (Sponsor's SSN)   CHAMPVA ☐ (VA File #)   GROUP HEALTH PLAN ☐ (SSN or ID)   FECA BLK LUNG ☐ (SSN)   OTHER ☐ (ID)

1a. INSURED'S I.D. NUMBER   (FOR PROGRAM IN ITEM 1)

2. PATIENT'S NAME (Last Name, First Name, Middle Initial)

3. PATIENT'S BIRTH DATE   MM | DD | YY   SEX   M ☐   F ☐

4. INSURED'S NAME (Last Name, First Name, Middle Initial)

5. PATIENT'S ADDRESS (No., Street)

6. PATIENT RELATIONSHIP TO INSURED   Self ☐   Spouse ☐   Child ☐   Other ☐

7. INSURED'S ADDRESS (No., Street)

CITY   STATE

8. PATIENT STATUS   Single ☐   Married ☐   Other ☐

CITY   STATE

ZIP CODE   TELEPHONE (Include Area Code)   ( )

Employed ☐   Full-Time Student ☐   Part-Time Student ☐

ZIP CODE   TELEPHONE (INCLUDE AREA CODE)   ( )

9. OTHER INSURED'S NAME (Last Name, First Name, Middle Initial)

10. IS PATIENT'S CONDITION RELATED TO:

11. INSURED'S POLICY GROUP OR FECA NUMBER

a. OTHER INSURED'S POLICY OR GROUP NUMBER

a. EMPLOYMENT? (CURRENT OR PREVIOUS)   ☐ YES   ☐ NO

a. INSURED'S DATE OF BIRTH   MM | DD | YY   SEX   M ☐   F ☐

b. OTHER INSURED'S DATE OF BIRTH   MM | DD | YY   SEX   M ☐   F ☐

b. AUTO ACCIDENT?   PLACE (State)   ☐ YES   ☐ NO

b. EMPLOYER'S NAME OR SCHOOL NAME

c. EMPLOYER'S NAME OR SCHOOL NAME

c. OTHER ACCIDENT?   ☐ YES   ☐ NO

c. INSURANCE PLAN NAME OR PROGRAM NAME

d. INSURANCE PLAN NAME OR PROGRAM NAME

10d. RESERVED FOR LOCAL USE

d. IS THERE ANOTHER HEALTH BENEFIT PLAN?   ☐ YES   ☐ NO   **If yes**, return to and complete item 9 a-d.

READ BACK OF FORM BEFORE COMPLETING & SIGNING THIS FORM.

12. PATIENT'S OR AUTHORIZED PERSON'S SIGNATURE I authorize the release of any medical or other information necessary to process this claim. I also request payment of government benefits either to myself or to the party who accepts assignment below.

SIGNED _____ DATE _____

13. INSURED'S OR AUTHORIZED PERSON'S SIGNATURE I authorize payment of medical benefits to the undersigned physician or supplier for services described below.

SIGNED _____

←——— PATIENT AND INSURED INFORMATION ———→

14. DATE OF CURRENT: ◀ ILLNESS (First symptom) OR INJURY (Accident) OR PREGNANCY(LMP)   MM | DD | YY

15. IF PATIENT HAS HAD SAME OR SIMILAR ILLNESS. GIVE FIRST DATE   MM | DD | YY

16. DATES PATIENT UNABLE TO WORK IN CURRENT OCCUPATION   MM | DD | YY   FROM   MM | DD | YY   TO

17. NAME OF REFERRING PHYSICIAN OR OTHER SOURCE

17a. I.D. NUMBER OF REFERRING PHYSICIAN

18. HOSPITALIZATION DATES RELATED TO CURRENT SERVICES   MM | DD | YY   FROM   MM | DD | YY   TO

19. RESERVED FOR LOCAL USE

20. OUTSIDE LAB?   ☐ YES   ☐ NO $ CHARGES

21. DIAGNOSIS OR NATURE OF ILLNESS OR INJURY. (RELATE ITEMS 1,2,3 OR 4 TO ITEM 24E BY LINE)

1. L___.___   3. L___.___

2. L___.___   4. L___.___

22. MEDICAID RESUBMISSION CODE   ORIGINAL REF. NO.

23. PRIOR AUTHORIZATION NUMBER

24. A					B	C	D		E	F	G	H	I	J	K
DATE(S) OF SERVICE					Place of Service	Type of Service	PROCEDURES, SERVICES, OR SUPPLIES (Explain Unusual Circumstances)		DIAGNOSIS CODE	$ CHARGES	DAYS OR UNITS	EPSDT Family Plan	EMG	COB	RESERVED FOR LOCAL USE
From MM	DD	YY	To MM	DD	YY			CPT/HCPCS	MODIFIER							
1															
2															
3															
4															
5															
6															

25. FEDERAL TAX I.D. NUMBER   SSN ☐ EIN ☐

26. PATIENT'S ACCOUNT NO.

27. ACCEPT ASSIGNMENT? (For govt. claims, see back)   YES ☐   NO ☐

28. TOTAL CHARGE $

29. AMOUNT PAID $

30. BALANCE DUE $

31. SIGNATURE OF PHYSICIAN OR SUPPLIER INCLUDING DEGREES OR CREDENTIALS (I certify that the statements on the reverse apply to this bill and are made a part thereof.)

SIGNED _____ DATE _____

32. NAME AND ADDRESS OF FACILITY WHERE SERVICES WERE RENDERED (If other than home or office)

33. PHYSICIAN'S, SUPPLIER'S BILLING NAME, ADDRESS, ZIP CODE & PHONE #

PIN# _____ GRP# _____

←——— PHYSICIAN OR SUPPLIER INFORMATION ———→

(APPROVED BY AMA COUNCIL ON MEDICAL SERVICE 8/88)   **PLEASE PRINT OR TYPE**   FORM HCFA-1500 (U2) (12-90)   FORM OWCP-1500   FORM RRB-1500

SUMMARY

- Today's insurance specialists, medical billers and coders, and medical assistants must have current knowledge of deductibles, co-payments, and referrals.

- Skill is required for CPT and ICD-9-CM coding and the medical necessity documented for reimbursement.

- There must be an understanding of the HCFA-1500 claim form and the filing process in the practice, whether it is paper or electronic.

- There must be a working knowledge of Medicaid, Medicare and its secondary payers, as well as all participating provider agreements, and what information is required to submit claim forms.

- In addition to understanding what amounts can be billed to the patient is also knowing when amounts are to be adjusted.

- When claims are rejected, denied, or payment is not received, it is important to know how to request a review of the claim or pursue an appeal.

- It is essential to remain current in the profession by attending training and continuing education seminars, reading newsletters and bulletins published by the insurance carriers as proposed changes become implemented: ICD-10, APGs and E/M documentation guidelines.

REFERENCES

AdminaStar Federal, Inc. *Medicare B Special Bulletin.* SB97-08, August 1997. Indianapolis, IN.

Fordney, Marilyn Takahashi. *Insurance handbook for the medical office,* 5th ed., Philadelphia: W.B. Saunders, 1997.

Health Care Financing Administration (HCFA) Available from http://www.hcfa.gov/medicare/ncarpti.htm.

Lindh, Wilburta, Marilyn Pooler, Carol Tamparo, Joanne Cerrato. *Comprehensive medical assisting: administrative and clinical competencies.* Albany, NY: Delmar Publishers 1998.

Rowell, JoAnn. *Understanding health insurance: A guide to professional billing.* Albany, NY: Delmar Publishers, 1998.

Module 12
Reimbursement and Auditing/Appeals

Gay Boughton-Barnes, CPC, MPC

KEY TERMS:

Advanced Beneficiary Notice (ABN)
Allowable
Audit
Balance Billing
Balanced Budget Act
Budget Neutrality
Capitation
Covered Service
Direct Contract
Down-coding
False Claims Act
"Hold harmless" Clause
Indemnity Insurer
IPA
Medical Necessity
Non-participating Provider (NonPAR)
OIG (Office of the Inspector General)
Overpayment
Participating Provider (PAR)
PPO
POS Insurance Plan
Prepayment Review
Postpayment Review
R&C (Reasonable and Customary)
Reimbursement
RBRVS
Up-coding
Unbundling
UCR (Usual, Customary and Reasonable)
U&P (Usual and Prevailing)
Waiver of Liability
Withhold

LEARNING OBJECTIVES

Upon successful completion of this module, you should be able to:

1. Define and distinguish HCPCS Level I, II, III; CPT; and ICD-9-CM coding systems.
2. Recognize multiple mechanisms of reimbursement.
3. Explain components for payment calculation and reimbursement strategy.
4. Describe Medicare participating, nonparticipating and direct contract status.
5. Recognize internal and external obstacles to accurate and timely reimbursement.
6. Pinpoint discrepancies in billing and documentation (e.g., dates, performing provider, site of service, etc.).
7. Recognize and identify audit flags, compliance concepts, documentation deficit and E&M guidelines for documentation.

INTRODUCTION

This module discusses the overall reimbursement concept. This section defines and distinguishes multiple payment methods and pinpoints internal and external payment obstacles. It also introduces United States coding systems as well as the most recent laws, regulations, requirements and guidelines for billing, coding and documentation purposes. Waivers, balance billing, and adjustments are also covered, as well as prepayment and post-payment audits, review cycles and the compliance process. Table 12–1 includes some common healthcare acronyms and their meanings for reference.

REIMBURSEMENT AND CODING SYSTEMS

Reimbursement refers to the action of being paid back or the receipt of remuneration in exchange for goods or services. In the physician

TABLE 12–1 **Table of Acronyms**

HMO	Health maintenance organization
PPO	Preferred provider organization
BBA	Balanced Budget Act
HIPAA	Health Insurance Portability and Accountability Act
OIG	Office of the Inspector General
RBRVS	Resource based relative value system
IPA	Independent Provider Association
HCFA	Health Care Financing Administration
FCA	False Claims Act
HCPCS	Health Care Financing Administration's Procedural Coding System (pronounced 'hick-picks')
CPT	Current Procedural terminology
ICD	International Classification of Diseases

office setting, reimbursement occurs after professional services are rendered. Reimbursement may come directly from the patient or from a third-party payer or insurer. Reimbursement is received after a request for payment in the form of a statement to the patient or an insurance claim to the payer has been issued and processed. In either case, complex medical terminology describing the problem, diagnosis, illness or injury of the patient along with a technical description of what services and/or procedures were required for the stated problem(s) is submitted on a request for payment document. A document submitted for reimbursement in the physician office is known as a HCFA-1500 form or a health insurance claim form (see Figure 12–1). Later in this module, we will examine the necessary elements that must appear on a health insurance claim form to ensure appropriate reimbursement for healthcare services provided to patients.

Medical terminology is required to correctly describe the patient's condition, injury or problem. Additionally, specific medical terms are required to accurately describe surgical procedures, diagnostic tests and/or medical services provided. With the passage of the Medicare Catastrophic Coverage Act of 1988, the Health Care Financing Administration (HCFA) has mandated that physicians must use numeric or alphanumeric codes to report diagnoses for which treatment is provided and services and supplies provided relative to those diagnoses. The correct linkage of the diagnosis to the procedures validates the necessity of the physician's work and ensures that services are correctly reported to the insurer.

PLEASE
DO NOT
STAPLE
IN THIS
AREA

APPROVED OMB-0938-0008

CARRIER

[ ] [ ] PICA

HEALTH INSURANCE CLAIM FORM

PICA [ ] [ ]

1. MEDICARE [ ] (Medicare #) MEDICAID [ ] (Medicaid #) CHAMPUS [ ] (Sponsor's SSN) CHAMPVA [ ] (VA File #) GROUP HEALTH PLAN [ ] (SSN or ID) FECA BLK LUNG [ ] (SSN) OTHER [ ] (ID)   1a. INSURED'S I.D. NUMBER   (FOR PROGRAM IN ITEM 1)

2. PATIENT'S NAME (Last Name, First Name, Middle Initial)

3. PATIENT'S BIRTH DATE   MM | DD | YY   SEX   M [ ]   F [ ]

4. INSURED'S NAME (Last Name, First Name, Middle Initial)

5. PATIENT'S ADDRESS (No., Street)

6. PATIENT RELATIONSHIP TO INSURED   Self [ ] Spouse [ ] Child [ ] Other [ ]

7. INSURED'S ADDRESS (No., Street)

CITY   STATE

8. PATIENT STATUS   Single [ ]   Married [ ]   Other [ ]

CITY   STATE

ZIP CODE   TELEPHONE (Include Area Code) (   )

Employed [ ]   Full-Time Student [ ]   Part-Time Student [ ]

ZIP CODE   TELEPHONE (INCLUDE AREA CODE) (   )

9. OTHER INSURED'S NAME (Last Name, First Name, Middle Initial)

10. IS PATIENT'S CONDITION RELATED TO:

11. INSURED'S POLICY GROUP OR FECA NUMBER

a. OTHER INSURED'S POLICY OR GROUP NUMBER

a. EMPLOYMENT? (CURRENT OR PREVIOUS)   YES [ ]   NO [ ]

a. INSURED'S DATE OF BIRTH   MM | DD | YY   SEX   M [ ]   F [ ]

b. OTHER INSURED'S DATE OF BIRTH   MM | DD | YY   SEX   M [ ]   F [ ]

b. AUTO ACCIDENT?   PLACE (State)   YES [ ]   NO [ ]

b. EMPLOYER'S NAME OR SCHOOL NAME

c. EMPLOYER'S NAME OR SCHOOL NAME

c. OTHER ACCIDENT?   YES [ ]   NO [ ]

c. INSURANCE PLAN NAME OR PROGRAM NAME

d. INSURANCE PLAN NAME OR PROGRAM NAME

10d. RESERVED FOR LOCAL USE

d. IS THERE ANOTHER HEALTH BENEFIT PLAN?   YES [ ]   NO [ ]   If yes, return to and complete item 9 a-d.

READ BACK OF FORM BEFORE COMPLETING & SIGNING THIS FORM.

12. PATIENT'S OR AUTHORIZED PERSON'S SIGNATURE I authorize the release of any medical or other information necessary to process this claim. I also request payment of government benefits either to myself or to the party who accepts assignment below.

SIGNED _____   DATE _____

13. INSURED'S OR AUTHORIZED PERSON'S SIGNATURE I authorize payment of medical benefits to the undersigned physician or supplier for services described below.

SIGNED _____

PATIENT AND INSURED INFORMATION

14. DATE OF CURRENT: ILLNESS (First symptom) OR INJURY (Accident) OR PREGNANCY(LMP)   MM | DD | YY

15. IF PATIENT HAS HAD SAME OR SIMILAR ILLNESS. GIVE FIRST DATE   MM | DD | YY

16. DATES PATIENT UNABLE TO WORK IN CURRENT OCCUPATION   MM | DD | YY   FROM   TO   MM | DD | YY

17. NAME OF REFERRING PHYSICIAN OR OTHER SOURCE

17a. I.D. NUMBER OF REFERRING PHYSICIAN

18. HOSPITALIZATION DATES RELATED TO CURRENT SERVICES   MM | DD | YY   FROM   TO   MM | DD | YY

19. RESERVED FOR LOCAL USE

20. OUTSIDE LAB?   YES [ ]   NO [ ] $ CHARGES

21. DIAGNOSIS OR NATURE OF ILLNESS OR INJURY. (RELATE ITEMS 1,2,3 OR 4 TO ITEM 24E BY LINE)

1. |___.___| 3. |___.___|
2. |___.___| 4. |___.___|

22. MEDICAID RESUBMISSION CODE   ORIGINAL REF. NO.

23. PRIOR AUTHORIZATION NUMBER

24. A DATE(S) OF SERVICE From MM DD YY To MM DD YY	B Place of Service	C Type of Service	D PROCEDURES, SERVICES, OR SUPPLIES (Explain Unusual Circumstances) CPT/HCPCS	MODIFIER	E DIAGNOSIS CODE	F $ CHARGES	G DAYS OR UNITS	H EPSDT Family Plan	I EMG	J COB	K RESERVED FOR LOCAL USE
1											
2											
3											
4											
5											
6											

25. FEDERAL TAX I.D. NUMBER   SSN [ ] EIN [ ]

26. PATIENT'S ACCOUNT NO.

27. ACCEPT ASSIGNMENT? (For govt. claims, see back)   YES [ ]   NO [ ]

28. TOTAL CHARGE $

29. AMOUNT PAID $

30. BALANCE DUE $

31. SIGNATURE OF PHYSICIAN OR SUPPLIER INCLUDING DEGREES OR CREDENTIALS (I certify that the statements on the reverse apply to this bill and are made a part thereof.)

SIGNED _____   DATE _____

32. NAME AND ADDRESS OF FACILITY WHERE SERVICES WERE RENDERED (If other than home or office)

33. PHYSICIAN'S, SUPPLIER'S BILLING NAME, ADDRESS, ZIP CODE & PHONE #

PIN#   GRP#

PHYSICIAN OR SUPPLIER INFORMATION

(APPROVED BY AMA COUNCIL ON MEDICAL SERVICE 8/88)

PLEASE PRINT OR TYPE

FORM HCFA-1500 (U2) (12-90)
FORM OWCP-1500   FORM RRB-1500

Figure 12–1 HCFA-1500 Claim Form (Revised 12–90).

EXERCISE 12–1

1. How does a physician request payment for services to a third-party payer or insurer? _____

2. Define reimbursement. _____

3. Name the document sent to patients requesting payment for services.

_____

GOVERNMENT PAYMENT MECHANISMS

Insurers make payments to providers of health care services depending on a number of different methods of calculation, payment strategies and timetables. Medicare has relied upon the resource-based relative value system (**RBRVS**) for payment determination for physician services since the implementation of RBRVS in January 1992. This conversion of payment method represented the most drastic change in the Medicare program since its 1965 inception under the Lyndon Johnson administration.

This payment system employed a relative value unit for work (RVUw), practice expense (RVUpe) and malpractice (RVUm) combined with a geographic cost index (GPCI) for a given area and multiplied by an annual conversion factor (CF). In 1998, the **Balanced Budget Act** required **budget neutrality** and thus decreased payment for surgical services while providing for increased payment to medicine and primary care services. This internal and self-adjusting calculation was designed to prevent increased expenditure for Medicare services for 1998. Many private payers have adopted the RBRVS strategy but have modified the annual stated conversion factor to coincide with internal budgetary constraints.

Prior to implementation of the RBRVS, Medicare payment consisted of 80% of the maximum **allowable** Medicare fee schedule for covered and approved services. Beneficiaries were required to pay an annual deductible and a 20% coinsurance on the remaining approved amount for covered services. Covered services are those determined to be the generally accepted treatment for a specific problem, consistent with standard medical practice within the appropriate specialty, reasonably provided according to the provider's expertise, and medically necessary for the patient's condition (see Figure 12–2). In examining this figure, you can see

1998 CONVERSION FACTOR UPDATE

1997 Conversion Factors	*Dollar Amount Change from 1997 to 1998*	*Percentage Change from 1997 to 1998*
Primary Care = $35.7671	$ .9202 increase	2.57% increase
Surgical Services = $40.9603	$4.273 decrease	10.43% decrease
Non-surgical Services = $33.8454	$2.8419 increase	8.40% increase

Figure 12–2 1998 Conversion Factor Update.

the annual alterations that are made to the previous year's calculations. Each year the proposed changes are published at mid-year in the *Federal Register*. At the end of the calendar year, in late November or early December, the final rule is published which states the formula by which the coming year's calculations will be made.

EXERCISE 12–2

1. Budget neutrality refers to the concept of self-adjusting federal payment for mechanisms by which some areas show increased revenue and others show decreased revenue. When averaged together, there is no increase in outlay from the federal arena. (True or False.) _____

2. The acronym GPCI denotes the geographic practice cost index. (True or False.) _____

3. Medicare was begun in 1965 under the Lyndon Johnson administration. (True or False.) _____

Participation Status with Medicare

As discussed in previous modules, **participating providers (PARs)** are those who have agreed to be enrolled in the Medicare program. Medicare remits payment directly to the provider's office and not to the beneficiary. Such providers agree to accept assignment on Medicare patients. This requires that the provider files claims for services with Medicare, accepts the Medicare allowable payment for 80% of the approved amount, and only bills the patient for the remaining 20% of the allowable amount. Providers are allowed and expected to collect the patient's annual deductible.

Provider offices are not allowed to **balance bill** beneficiaries. This means that patients cannot be billed for the difference between Medicare's allowable amount and the provider's usual fee for the service. For example, a provider's fee may be $150 for a consultation. Medicare's participating-provider allowable may be $100. Medicare would, therefore, pay 80% or $80 to the provider. The provider office would then bill the patient $20 for the 20% coinsurance due. The provider office would adjust off the bill the unpaid $50, leaving the patient with a -0- balance. Medicare expects its beneficiaries to share in the cost of healthcare. It also imposes strict penalties against providers who routinely "forgive" the 20% coinsurance. Providers are expected to make a "reasonable effort" to collect the 20% amount, which consists of at least 90 days of billing effort from the provider standpoint. If no payment has been made, the provider office can elect to adjust off or write off the remainder due at that point.

The only exception to this rule is for indigent patients who have signed an inability to pay form. This form details income vs. expenditures and illustrates graphically that the patient has no financial reserve with which to pay the co-insurance amount for services received. Part B carriers will furnish such forms upon request.

Nonparticipating (nonPAR) providers in the Medicare program are restricted to a designated limiting charge, which prevents billing above that stated annual amount. "NonPAR" providers do not receive direct reimbursement from Medicare. Beneficiaries submit claims for reimbursement and receive payment, which then must be made to the provider of service.

A 1998 payment scheme, known as **direct contracting**, allows providers to drop out of Medicare participation status for at least two years. In direct contracting, providers contract directly with patients for predetermined services and predetermined fees. Providers may not see other Medicare patients not directly contracted with them during the two-year time period.

EXERCISE 12–3

1. The government can change conversion factors each in the RBRVS calculations to comply with budget constraints. (True or False.) _____

2. Prior to RBRVS, Medicare payments were based on 80% of the maximum allowable for each service. (True or False.) _____

3. If a Medicare patient visits a participating provider, he should expect to pay a coinsurance of 20% of the Medicare allowable fee for the service plus any unpaid deductible. (True or False.) _____

Waiver of Liability or Advanced Beneficiary Notice

Waiver of liability or **advanced beneficiary notice (ABN)** statements require patient signatures. These notices inform patients that Medicare (or other insurers) generally do not pay for the service planned for the patient. It states that the provider will bill the patient directly and not the insurer for the service. The language of the waiver or notice states that the patient has been informed that Medicare usually does not pay for a service or procedure and further states that the patient agrees to the service and agrees to being billed for the service. Medicare requires such informed consent to ensure protection of beneficiaries against illegal or excessive billing from providers. Figure 12–3 presents sample language found in waivers of liability or advanced beneficiary notice to Medicare beneficiaries.

MANAGED CARE PAYMENT METHODS

Health maintenance organizations (HMOs) and preferred provider organizations (**PPOs**) may use a variety of payment methods. HMOs often pay according to **capitation** schemes. Such a scheme pays an allotted amount at a predetermined point in the fiscal year to providers in the HMO/PPO network. Providers receive a fixed amount multiplied by the number of patients who specify a certain physician as their caregiver when enrolled in the insurance plan. HMOs may be **IPAs** or independent physician associations in which physicians retain free-standing offices or group model HMOs where providers have offices together in a facility constructed and maintained by the corporation.

Preferred provider organizations or PPOs may pay with capitation schemes, with-

---

SAMPLE ADVANCED BENEFICIARY NOTICE
(Waiver of Liability)

Medicare will only pay for services that it determines to be "reasonable and necessary" under Section 1862 (a)(1) of the Medicare law. If Medicare determines that a particular service, although it would otherwise be covered is "not reasonable and necessary" under Medicare program standards, Medicare will deny payment for that service. I believe, in your case, Medicare is likely to deny payment for: _____

_____

for the following reason(s): _____

_____

SAMPLE BENEFICIARY AGREEMENT

I have been notified by my physician that he or she believes that in my case, Medicare is likely to deny payment for the services identified above for the reasons stated. If Medicare denies payment, I agree to be personally and fully responsible for payment.

_____   _____
Medicare Beneficiary   Date Signed

Examples of reasons for the advance notice:

Medicare usually does not pay for this many visits or treatments.

Medicare does not usually pay for this service.

Medicare usually does not pay for this shot.

Medicare does not pay for this because it is a treatment that has yet to be proved effective.

Medicare usually does not pay for like services unless it was needed because of an emergency.

Medicare usually does not pay for this many services within this period of time.

Medicare usually does not pay for more than one visit a day.

Medicare usually does not pay for like services by more than one doctor during the same time period.

Medicare usually does not pay for this lab test.

Figure 12–3 Sample Advanced Beneficiary Notice (Waiver of Liability).

holds, fee-for-service arrangements, maximum allowable fee schedules, risk-sharing pools or any combination of strategies. A withhold consists of the insurer holding back a designated portion (such as 20%) of the usual payment due the provider. If the provider works well within the designated fiscal structure of the provider network by keeping referrals, admissions and administrative costs contained, the withhold amount is returned, with interest, to the provider. If the provider exceeds the cost ceiling, the withhold is retained by the insurer to cover the deficit. Risk-sharing pools, like withholds, place the burden of cost-containment on all providers within the provider network. There is a measurable financial incentive for providers who abide by the plan strategy, limit referrals, screen and restrict admissions and elective surgeries, monitor access to and utilization of ancillary services.

A risk-sharing pool works similarly to a withhold without a stated percentage being withheld from each reimbursement. In a risk-sharing arrangement, network physicians team with the managed care organization to designate a set amount of dollars to be spent on consultative referrals (referrals to specialists), admissions to the hospital and other ancillary services (laboratory, radiology, physical therapy, etc.) within a fiscal year. Primary care physicians, designated as the gatekeeper for the patient's care, attempt to limit specialty referrals by managing problems without asking for routine specialty consultations.

Specialty physicians attempt to limit admissions and referrals to ancillary resources to ensure that the stated aggregate dollar amount for the fiscal year is not exceeded. By ensuring that all network physicians enter the agreement, the HMO and the physicians share the same risk or part in controlling healthcare costs. If the network providers meet the goal and hold costs at or below the agreed-upon dollar amount, a bonus or incentive is awarded to the network providers.

By distributing the cost-containment risk among the primary care as well as specialty physicians, the HMO ensures that all physician providers share equal risk for penalty or profit by managing patients in the most cost-efficient manner possible.

More recently, **POS (point of service) insurance plans** have become popular. This payment strategy pays a greater benefit percentage to subscribers or patients who utilize services at designated provider sites. Patients accessing medical services outside the network incur greater out-of-pocket expense. Patients have a greater choice of providers and sites of service, but pay substantially more for services rendered by non-network providers at non-network sites.

Even with managed care plans, patients are generally required to pay co-payments for specific services and procedures. Some plans also have annual deductibles and ceilings on payments for specific types of care such as mental health, chiropractic, podiatry or physical medicine.

In managed care payment arrangements, beneficiaries are covered under a **"hold harmless" clause**. This clause prevents the provider from balance billing the patient for the difference between the provider's standard fee and the approved amount from the payer. "Hold harmless" means that patients are not held liable for differences between standard and insurer-approved fees.

EXERCISE 12–4

1. Fee-for-service refers to the fee a physician is paid without discounts, withholds or fee schedule reductions. (True or False.) _____

2. Risk-sharing pools are found only in traditional insurance plans. (True or False.) _____

3. POS plans require that patients utilize services at designated provider sites. (True or False.) _____

Indemnity (Traditional) Insurance Plans

Traditional health insurance plans have typically been based on an actuarial-based methodology. Payment was calculated to the provider on a **U&P (usual and prevailing)**, **R&C (reasonable and customary)** or **UCR (usual, customary and rea-**

sonable) payment strategy. Eighty percent of the approved or allowable amount was remitted to the provider. In these scenarios, a percentage of what is considered to be the usual payment in a specific geographic area is considered the maximum payment available for designated covered services. In the 80/20 payment scheme, the patient or subscriber was expected to remit the remaining 20% of the unpaid balance plus any additional monies between the physician's fee and the insurance allowable.

Before the creation and acceptance of managed care organizations, insurers often paid the actual fee-for-service or standard fee amount of the provider. Due to increasing health care costs, however, few insurers even consider fee-for-service payments to providers and facilities.

Covered services include those not specifically excluded in writing by the insurer's contract with the subscriber or dependent. Non-covered services would include those specifically designated as not covered, such as treatment for infertility, weight control, cosmetic surgery, etc.

Some indemnity insurers, also termed traditional insurance companies, use a maximum allowable fee schedule for capping the dollar amount on professional service payments. Regardless of the reimbursement mechanism, patients potentially incur greater expense but retain greater mobility with fewer restrictions through traditional insurance as compared to managed care access.

EXERCISE 12-5

1. Indemnity insurers are also known as _____ insurance plans.

2. Traditional insurance is based on an _____% _____% formula.

3. "Hold harmless" refers to a clause that protects that patient from paying more than the contracted fee for a defined service. (True or False.) _____

PAYER CONSIDERATIONS: EXTERNAL PAYMENT OBSTACLES

Third-party payers receive an insurance claim form either via the mail or through electronic claim submission. Claim forms request payment from the insurer for professional services and procedures provided the patient for treatment and/or management of the patient's illness, injury or condition. Payers depend upon properly completed paper forms or electronic templates ("clean claims") when making decisions for reimbursement to physicians. Because there is limited space for data entry in either format, billers must follow specific guidelines when entering diagnosis, procedure/service, demographic and identification data. Additionally, billers must link procedures/services to the diagnoses that best illustrate medical necessity for the action. The step-by-step process of filing a claim form is outlined in Module 11. Payers must then process claims based on fee schedules, payment arrangements, discounts, withholds, risk-sharing pools, U&P, R&C and UCR payment strategies.

▬ *Highlight*

Together with payment schemes, conflicting or incomplete information can jeopardize the percentage of reimbursement the physician ultimately receives.

Another consideration in billing is global payment rules. Surgical procedures have global payment periods, which preclude payment for services related to the surgery during the stated follow-up period. Major surgeries encompass a 90-day follow-up period. For services unrelated to the surgery, payment can be made provided services are billed with the correct modifier and an unrelated diagnosis. Unskilled or non-compliant physicians or office staff may incorrectly report and bill services by inadvertently **unbundling** surgical procedures. By itemizing services related to the surgery itself or those performed during the normally accepted postoperative follow-up period, physician offices may be accused of billing abuse. This itemization or "a la carting" results in higher initial payment if not uncovered in **prepayment** or **postpayment review** audits. However, this practice can also have serious financial and legal consequences and should be avoided.

Some insurers have a lifetime maximum payment for specific catastrophic illnesses or conditions. That is, a predetermined amount or cap is stated. The insurer refuses to pay beyond that set dollar amount for services on the patient. This may occur with heart disease, renal, blood, lung or liver disorders. Benefit caps may apply for patients who frequently and repeatedly access the same type of care or treatment. For example, patients with chronic mental conditions may frequently utilize mental health benefits. The payer may have a stated cap or ceiling on mental health benefits. They can, therefore, refuse payment of claims for services that exceed the stated cap.

Preexisting conditions refer to problems the patient had prior to enrollment with the insurer. Problems may be congenital or acquired but are ongoing. There is usually a six-month moratorium on payment for services related to the preexisting condition. A veritable maze of external obstacles can prevent, delay or reduce reimbursement to the provider.

EXERCISE 12–6

1. Define unbundling. _____

2. Differentiate a prepayment and a postpayment review or audit. _____

3. Describe a "clean claim". _____

INTERNAL PAYMENT OBSTACLES

Aside from insurer payment discounts, physician office or medical staff may unwittingly set the stage for delayed payment, **down-coded** or discounted payments, and/or total denial of payment. It is not uncommon to find oversights, omissions, errors or incomplete portions of health insurance claim forms.

Figure 12–4 identifies the "who, what, where, when, and why" components of claim preparation for reimbursement. Each of the five "Ws" represents a vital component in consistent and accurate reporting of services and completion of the request for reimbursement to the insurer, resulting in a "clean claim" status: timely processing of the claim that is free of errors with all information completed.

CONSISTENT BILLING AND MEDICAL RECORD DOCUMENT	
WHERE:	Place of service (POS)
WHEN:	Date of service by physician to patient (DOS)
WHO:	Provider and recipient of medical service
WHAT:	Services, procedures, supplies and/or diagnostics furnished to patients
WHY:	Rationale for services, procedures, diagnostics provided to patient (stated diagnoses reflect medical necessity of physician services)

Figure 12–4 Consistent billing and medical record document.

"Where" the service occurred must also match the area of CPT from which the "what" or services/procedures, and so forth took place.

In other words, if you report that a patient was seen for an ER consultation, the place of service reported should be the hospital ER.

The "what" refers to the CPT code(s) and modifier(s) used to report the physician's actions, interventions, services or supplies.

"Who" identifies the patient and the provider of services. The "when" component refers to the date the service was rendered. "Why" the service is rendered is entirely dependent on the diagnosis or diagnoses reported as well as the accurate placement of ICD-9-CM code(s). These diagnoses serve as justification or **medical necessity**, which validates the need for the service to be performed.

■ *Highlight*

Aside from the five "Ws" being correct on the claim form, this information must also be discoverable and consistent with the information found in the patient's medical record. Discrepancies between claim forms and patient charts have resulted in large pay-back requests, fines and loss of participation status for providers.

Other areas that should be carefully scrutinized for completion pertain to patient demographics, insurance (primary and secondary) information, ordering/performing physician information, insurer address information, site where service was provided, provider of services, etc.

The E/M (evaluation and management) code must agree with the place in which the service was rendered. Ensure that the place of service code matches the procedure code. In other words, do not bill an inpatient admission for an office consultation. Also, make sure that there is a clear understanding between the rules for consultation and the description of new/established patients.

Consultations occur when one physician requests that another physician see a particular patient. The consulting and the requesting physician should document the request for consultation. The consultant may initiate diagnostics or therapeutics at the encounter. The consultant must provide opinions or advice to the requesting physician. The consultant's findings must be documented and communicated to the requesting physician. The consultant should encourage the return of the patient to the requesting physician for routine or future care.

Care should be taken to differentiate between new and established patients. CPT clearly states that patients are new to a practice at the first encounter. Patients who have not been seen in the practice or specific specialty for a period of three continuous years are considered a new patient again after three years without treatment. Established patients are those seen more frequently than three-year intervals or on a cyclical basis. A patient seen once every two years and 11 months is still, technically, treated as an established patient in the practice.

EXERCISE 12–7

1. Code linkage relates to _____ the correct procedure or service code (CPT) with the accurate diagnosis (ICD-9-CM) code.

2. Patients are considered new or established if they have not been seen regularly in the practice within a three-year period. _____

3. _____ occur when one physician requests that another physician sees a patient and offers an opinion.

Discrepancies in Data

Often, discrepancies appear in data within the medical record and charge documents such as the superbill (fee slip, encounter form or charge ticket) and the health insurance claim form. In the majority of cases, no criminal or deliberate intent to over-bill or defraud is the culprit. The charge document or superbill may go through a number of personnel as it passes from the encounter with the patient and physician to the business office for charge entry. In many offices, the nurse or medical assistant selects the level of service, the ancillary services used and even the patient's diagnosis(es). The physician may dictate or make notes on the patient record at a later time or place. Because two separate individuals are handling data, there may be inconsistency between procedures and diagnoses selected on the superbill and documentation found in the medical record.

In the hospital setting, physicians may not always dictate or make notes on the medical record immediately after an encounter with or service to the patient. A delay in time may result in discrepancy between what is documented in the medical record and what the physician submits to the business office on hospital billing or productivity devices. Another error that may be discovered in hospital reporting and billing occurs between the date service was rendered as reported by the physician and the date service was rendered as noted in the actual medical record.

In some practices, physicians do not submit hospital charges to billing staff until the patient is discharged from the facility. Billing staff then rely on the hospital discharge summary, consultation reports, operative reports, admission history and physical reports and diagnostic test findings to serve as a resource for the diagnoses and procedures rendered to the patient. Some practices, however, submit daily rounding or productivity lists for interim billing on hospitalized patients. Billers often find discrepancies between diagnoses or services submitted on the daily form and those stated on the more "official record" documents such as discharge summary, consultation note, daily hospital encounter, etc.

EXERCISE 12–8

1. Medical necessity is determined by the physician before treating the patient or ordering tests. Can the insurer question medical necessity if the physician orders a test for a diagnosis that does not validate the need for a certain procedure? _____

2. Do billers find discrepancies between diagnoses or services found on the physician's daily hospital production sheet and official record documents? _____

3. Do physicians always provide daily information to the coding/billing department on hospitalized patients? _____

Conflicts in Procedure/Service Reporting

In the process of extracting information from physician source documents for surgical or diagnostic procedures, billers may inadvertently submit incorrect CPT code information. Depending upon the routine for reporting in a practice, physicians often supply abbreviated versions or acronyms for procedures or diagnostics performed.

Unless the billing staff has a medical background, is proficient in coding and completely understands all components of the procedures commonly performed by the practice, errors in selection of procedure codes (CPT) can easily occur. Additionally, special circumstances or events may have occurred which would require application of a CPT modifier for correct reporting and reimbursement consideration. If physicians do not furnish the complete picture to billers, that important data will not be communicated to the payer.

Some practices delay coding and billing of interventional services until the operative or diagnostic intervention report is received. They feel more confident abstracting data from the full report than relying on the physician's abbreviated format for billing purposes. Additionally, operative or interventional reports describe special circumstances such as repeat procedures, multiple procedures, use of surgical assistants, additional difficulty, multiple incisions or vessels, route of access to surgical site, staged procedures, etc.

The billing staff, unless very experienced or medically trained, will require access to the medical staff for questions and clarification of specific issues that affect code and modifier selection. Physicians or medical staff unfamiliar with CPT language, may have difficulty in translating surgical or interventional services into existing CPT codes and modifiers. Information sharing from both areas is vital to correct billing, coding and reporting.

Diagnosis Errors

Errors in documenting diagnoses can occur at many points along the office paper trail. A medical staff member, even the physician, may inadvertently enter a vague or non-applicable diagnosis on the patient encounter form. A billing clerk may transpose a number, thus assigning an incorrect, obsolete or non-existent diagnosis (ICD-9-CM) code. A coder may use an outdated code book resulting in a deleted or revised code or a code without the required additional digits for specificity. ICD-9-CM codes contain three, four or five digits. The fourth and fifth digits may be required to specifically report an injury, accident or condition. A data entry clerk may link an incorrect diagnosis to a procedure. The place-of-service code on the claim screen may be incorrect and inconsistent for the type of service performed.

At the insurer level, the claims processor may transpose codes, dates, identification numbers or demographics in the entry process. Additionally, the information submitted by the provider might provoke edit screens that prevent release of payment. Circumstances that might trigger such payment denial are: non-covered services; services not medically necessary; invalid diagnosis; procedure performed too frequently within stated time period; service that is a component of a greater procedure and not billable separately; service provided outside provider's specialty area; fees exceed allowable payment margin; expensive diagnostics when a less expensive test would suffice, for example, MRI rather than CT scan.

EXERCISE 12–9

1. CPT codes require three, four or five digits. (True or False.) _____

2. ICD-9-CM codes may require modifiers. (True or False.) _____

3. The use of an outdated code book can interfere with correct submission of information to the insurer on the claim form. (True or False.) _____

DOCUMENTATION ISSUES

Along with the drastic change in payment strategy, RBRVS provoked a revamping of physician encounters. In restructuring physician-patient encounters, new terminology was developed to better represent typical physician patterns of service. A re-valuing of services was done to give credit for counseling, coordination of care, formulation and update of patient history, detail and effort required in the physical exam, complexity of risk for death and impairment, amount of data reviewed, number of problems managed and treated along with the overall time expended in the total process. HCFA has developed documentation guidelines to ensure that physician documentation supports the evaluation and management code reported.

Physicians are offered a choice of either a general multi-system exam or a single organ system specialty exam as the criterion for measuring the intensity of the examination process. The history component of an encounter was also greatly expanded to include not only a history of the present illness, but also a review of systems as well as past, family and social history as applicable to the patient's condition. As in previous years, the decision-making process was broken down into number of treatment/management options for the presenting problems; risk of death or impairment; amount/complexity of data reviewed.

The stricter language found within the proposed documentation guidelines represents an added burden for physician and billing staff. Because the guidelines result in a change in physician documentation style and format, HCFA and AMA have agreed to extend the implementation date of the guidelines indefinitely. Physician specialty groups, various study groups within the AMA and HCFA representatives continue to study the impact and the practicality of the proposed guidelines. The rationale is that the added time frame gives office and physician staff time to change behaviors, modify internal documents and to be in compliance by the official date of implementation. In the interim, HCFA has announced that physicians may choose either the proposed guidelines, the 1993 or 1997 guidelines as a documentation model. The enhanced and expanded guidelines are displayed in Figures 12–5 and 12–6.

GENERAL MULTI-SYSTEM EXAMINATION

Constitutional:
- Measurement of **any three** of the following **seven** vital signs:
  Sitting/Standing blood pressure
  Supine blood pressure
  Pulse rate and regularity
  Respiration
  Temperature (or lack of temperature)
  Height
  Weight
- General appearance of the patient (development, nutrition, body habitus, deformities, attention to grooming)

Eyes:
- Inspection of conjuctivae and lids
- Examination of pupils and irises (reaction to light and accommodation, size and symmetry)
- Ophthalmoscopic exam of optic discs (size, C/D ratio, appearance) and posterior segments (vessel changes, exudates, hemorrhages)

Ears, Nose, Mouth & Throat
- External inspection of ears and nose (overall appearance, scars, lesions, masses)
- Otoscopic exam of external auditory canals and tympanic membranes
- Assessment of haring (whispered voice, finger rub, tuning fork)
- Inspection of nasal mucosa, septum and turbinates
- Inspection of lips, teeth and gums
- Examination of oropharynx: oral mucosa, salivary glands, hard and soft palates, tongue, tonsils and posterior pharynx

Neck:
- Examination of neck (masses, overall appearance, symmetry, tracheal position, crepitus)
- Examination of thyroid (enlargement, tenderness, mass)

Respiratory:
- Assessment of respiratory effort (intercostal retractions, use of accessory muscles, diaphragmatic movement)
- Percussion of chest (dullness, flatness, hyperresonance)
- Palpatation of chest (tactile fremitus)
- Auscultation of lungs (breath sounds, adventitious sounds, rubs)

continues

Figure 12–5 General multi-system examination.

Cardiovascular:
- Palpation of heart (location, size, thrills)
- Auscultation of heart with notation of abnormal sounds and murmurs

Examination of:
- Carotid arteries (pulse amplitude, bruits)
- Abdominal aorta (size, bruits)
- Femoral arteries (pulse amplitude, bruits)
- Pedal pulses (pulse amplitude)
- Extremities for edema and/or varicosities

Chest (breasts):
- Inspection of breasts (symmetry, nipple discharge)
- Palpation of breasts and axillae (masses or lumps, tenderness)

Gastrointestinal (abdomen):
- Examination of abdomen with notation of presence of masses or tenderness
- Examination of liver and spleen
- Examination for presence or absence of hernia
- Examination of anus, perineum and rectum, including sphincter tone, presence of hemorrhoids, rectal masses
- Obtain stool sample for occult blood test when indicated

Genitourinary (male):
- Examination of the scrotal contents (hydrocele)
- Examination of the penis
- Digital rectal examination of prostate gland (size, symmetry, nodularity, tenderness)

Genitourinary (female):

Pelvic examination (with or without specimen collection for smears and cultures) including:
- Examination of external genitalia (general appearance, hair distribution, lesions) and vagina (general appearance, estrogen effect, discharge, lesions, pelvic support, cystocele, rectocele)
- Examination of the urethra (masses, tenderness, scarring)
- Examination of the bladder (fullness, masses, tenderness)
- Cervix (general appearance, lesions, discharge)
- Uterus (size, contour, position, mobility, tenderness, consistency, descent or support)
- Adnexa/parametria (masses, tenderness, organomegaly, nodularity)

Lymphatic:

Palpation of lymph nodes in **two or more** areas:
- Neck
- Axillae
- Groin
- Other

Musculoskeletal:
- Examination of gait and station
- Inspection and/or palpation of digits and nails (clubbing, cyanosis, inflammatory conditions, petechiae, ischemia, infections, nodes)

Examination of joints, bones and muscles of **one or more of the following six** areas:
- Head and neck
- Spine, ribs and pelvis
- Right upper extremity
- Left upper extremity
- Right lower extremity
- Left lower extremity

Figure 12–5 General multi-system examination. (*Continued*)

(The exam of a given area includes:)

- Inspection and/or palpation with notation of presence of any misalignment, asymmetry, crepitus, defects, tenderness, masses, effusions
- Assessment of range of motion with notation of any pain, crepitation or contracture
- Assessment of stability with notation of any dislocation (luxation), subluxation of laxity
- Assessment of muscle strength and tone (flaccid, cog wheel, spastic) with notation of any atrophy or abnormal movements

Skin:
- Inspection of skin and subcutaneous tissue (rashes, lesions, ulcers)
- Palpation of skin and subcutaneous tissue (induration, subcutaneous nodules, tightening)

Neurologic:
- Test cranial nerves with notation of any deficits
- Examination of deep tendon reflexes with notation of pathological reflexes (Babinski)
- Examination of sensation (by touch, pin, vibration, proprioception)

Psychiatric:
- Description of patient's judgment and insight

Brief assessment of mental status including:
- Orientation to time, place and person
- Recent and remote memory
- Mood and affect (depression, anxiety, agitation)

How to score the General Multi-system Exam according to the 1998 HCFA documentation guidelines:

Content and Documentation Requirements:

Exam Level	_Perform and Document_
Problem-Focused	**One to five** elements identified by a bullet
Expanded Problem-Focused	**At least six** elements identified by a bullet
Detailed	**At least two** elements identified by a bullet from **each of six areas/systems** OR **at least twelve** elements identified by a bullet **in two or more areas/systems**
Comprehensive	**At least two** elements identified by a bullet **from each of nine areas/systems**

Figure 12–5 General multi-system examination. (_Continued_)

SINGLE ORGAN SYSTEM EXAMINATION **(Cardiovascular)**	
Constitutional:	■ Measurement of **any three of the following seven** vital signs: Sitting/Standing blood pressure Supine blood pressure Pulse rate and regularity Respiration Temperature (or lack of temperature) Height Weight ■ General appearance of the patient (development, nutrition, body habitus, deformities, attention to grooming)
	continues

Figure 12–6 Single organ system examination (Cardiovascular).

Eyes:	▪ Inspection of conjuctivae and lids (xanthelasma)
Ears, Nose, Mouth & Throat:	▪ Inspection of teeth, gums and palate ▪ Examination of oral mucosa with notation of presence of pallor or cyanosis
Neck:	▪ Examination of jugular veins (distention, a, v or cannon a waves) ▪ Examination of thyroid (enlargement, tenderness, mass)
Respiratory:	▪ Inspection of respiratory effort (intercostal retractions, use of accessory muscles, diaphragmatic movement) ▪ Auscultation of lungs (breath sounds, adventitious sounds, rubs)
Cardiovascular:	▪ Palpation of heart (location, size and forcefulness of the point of maximal impact; thrills, lifts; palpable S3 or S4) ▪ Auscultation of heart including sounds, abnormal sounds and murmurs ▪ Measurement of blood pressure in two or more extremities when indicated (aortic dissection, coarctation) Examination of: ▪ Carotid arteries (waveform, pulse amplitude, bruits, apical-carotid delay) ▪ Abdominal aorta (size, bruits) ▪ Femoral arteries (size, bruits) ▪ Pedal pulses (pulse amplitude) ▪ Extremities for peripheral edema and/or varicosities
Gastrointestinal (abdomen):	▪ Examination of abdomen with notation of presence of masses or tenderness ▪ Examination of liver and spleen ▪ Obtain stool sample for occult blood from patients who are being considered thrombolytic or anticoagulant therapy
Musculoskeletal:	▪ Examination of the back with notation of kyphosis or scoliosis ▪ Examination of gait with notation of ability to undergo exercise testing and/or participation in exercise programs ▪ Assessment of muscle strength and tone (flaccid, cog wheel, spastic) with notation of any atrophy and abnormal movements
Extremities:	▪ Inspection and palpation of digits and nails (clubbing, cyanosis, inflammation, petechiae, ischemia, infections, nodes)
Skin:	▪ Inspection and/or palpation of skin and subcutaneous tissue (stasis dermatitis, ulcers, scars, xanthomas)
Neurologic/ Psychiatric:	Brief assessment of mental status including: ▪ Orientation to time, place and person ▪ Mood and affect (depression, anxiety, agitation)
	continues

Figure 12–6 Single organ system examination (Cardiovascular). (*Continued*)

How to score the Single Organ System Exam according to the 1998 HCFA documentation guidelines:

Content and Documentation Requirements:

Exam Level	_Perform and Document_
Problem-Focused	**One to five** elements identified by a bullet
Expanded Problem-Focused	**At least six** elements identified by a bullet
Detailed	**At least twelve** elements identified by a bullet
Comprehensive	Perform **all** elements identified by a bullet; document **every** element in a shaded box and **at least one** element in an unshaded box

Figure 12–6 Single organ system examination (Cardiovascular). (_Continued_)

EXERCISE 12–10

1. HCFA and AMA have worked together to develop documentation guidelines. (True or False.) _____

2. Documentation guidelines are designed to standardize the amount and type of data found in medical records. _____

3. Stricter documentation guidelines result in more detailed patient records. (True or False.) _____

GENERAL GUIDELINES TO ENSURE ADEQUATE DOCUMENTATION

There are guideposts for ensuring that each medical record document has been thoroughly and fully completed. The following ten steps should assist in evaluating medical records.

1. Make sure all medical records are complete and legible.
2. Make sure each encounter includes: date of service, rationale for encounter, history and physical appropriate to the problem, lab, x-ray, review, assessment, treatment (and/or) discharge plan.
3. Ensure that all records contain both current and past diagnoses.
4. Make sure a clear rationale is stated for any and all diagnostics ordered.
5. Ensure that each document includes the patient's response to treatment, notation of new or discontinued treatments or medication(s), and evidence of non-compliance (if applicable).
6. Ensure that each narrative is signed or authenticated by the provider of service.

Auditors agree that initials and stamps do not suffice as signatures. Electronic signatures, however, are acceptable as they are password-protected and unique to the physician provider.

7. Make sure that each record clearly states the intensity of the patient's evaluation and/or treatment, including the clinical or diagnostic pathway plus the complexity of the decision-making.

8. Make sure that risk factors are stated relevant to the patient's problems, injuries or conditions.

9. Ensure that each record contains a care plan including medication (frequency and dosage); suggestions for testing, referrals or education; and appropriate follow-up instructions.

10. Make sure that the diagnosis and procedure codes chosen reflect the specificity and complexity of the patient's condition(s) and the services and treatments rendered are appropriate to those conditions.

E&M CODING CHECKLIST

Coders and billers together with the medical staff should institute internal controls and devices to assist in choosing appropriate E&M codes. Since auditors from Medicare as well as the private sector have announced that physician encounters (especially in the office setting) will be carefully reviewed, preventive maintenance can certainly improve the accuracy ratio of code selection at the office level. Although each specialty and each office will develop its own checklist, some routine and pertinent questions on the checklist may include the following suggestions:

1. Is this a Medicare patient?
2. Is this a routine (non-acute) encounter?
3. Did our physician admit the patient?
4. Is this a new or established patient?
5. Were we called to the ER to see this patient?
6. Is this patient here for consultation or as a new patient?
7. Will we see this patient in follow-up if needed or return them to their family physician?
8. What should this service or procedure be called?
9. Where was the procedure done (site service was rendered)?
10. Was care or partial patient management assumed?
11. What diagnosis(es) support this service or procedure?
12. Were there unusual, complex or complicating circumstances surrounding the encounter?
13. Were any procedures done at the time of the encounter?
14. Could any additional services be considered incidental to the visit?
15. Is the patient in a global or postoperative follow-up period from a major or minor surgical procedure?
16. Did the patient seek medical care as a result of a postoperative complication?
17. Is the patient seeking a second or third opinion?

AUDIT AND RECOVERY PROCESS

Expenditures for healthcare in the United States equal more than 14% of our gross national product (GNP). Americans are obsessed with health and demand complete access to healthcare providers and institutions. With the advent of high-tech equipment for diagnostic and surgical procedures, equipment and supply costs have skyrocketed. Facilities scramble to update equipment and technical staff to ensure state-of-the-art detection and treatment resources. Some facilities even contract directly with employer group insurance plans to deliver preventive health packages at competitive rates. Despite the national preoccupation with access to healthcare, medical necessity remains the deciding factor in determining amount and potential for reimbursement from the insurance industry.

When payers request refunds for **overpayments**, reimbursement is no longer controlled in the practice. In this scenario, the physician has essentially provided service free of charge. The payer is recouping the reimbursement plus any other assessments, percentages or fines, and the provider has lost payment for professional services rendered.

Insurers, especially Medicare, conduct **audits** to monitor efficacious billing and reimbursement patterns. Audits can occur at various points during the reimbursement cycle. A concurrent or prepayment or a postpayment audit or review may occur. With concurrent or prepayment reviews, payers review necessity of services, procedures or admissions, fees, dates of services, and diagnoses submitted prior to releasing reimbursement to the providers of services. In postpayment review, an audit is conducted after the payment has been released to the provider. If it is determined that the provider was overpaid because the fees, services, procedures or diagnoses did not merit the amount paid according to their reviewer's standard, an overpayment request or denial will be forthcoming.

As stated previously, audits may result in the discovery of overpayments, documentation errors, date and diagnosis discrepancies, and incorrectly billed procedures. In some instances, audits may provoke fines, civil monetary penalties and even incarceration for providers found guilty of fraudulent billing. Providers can be forced to pay back reimbursement plus fines and interest on the overpayment in the event that an audit detects improprieties.

Previously, this module has discussed internal errors and omissions which prove to be internal payment obstacles, as well as detailing insurer payment strategies, benefits caps, preexisting condition exceptions, and lifetime maximum payments for certain diagnoses. In the discussion of external obstacles to reimbursement, however, either prepayment or postpayment audit must figure into the big picture as it can negatively impact the provider's "bottom line".

EXERCISE 12–11

1. An audit is only done because a physician has been accused of fraud or abusive billing practices. (True or False.) _____

2. Define overpayment. _____

3. A concurrent or prepayment review is conducted prior to release of reimbursement. (True or False.) _____

Articles Examined in Audit

Many documents or tools may be used in the monitoring and auditing function. Charge documents such as billing sheets (superbills, fee slips, encounter forms, charge tickets, etc.), patient record documentation, insurance claim forms, and appointment lists may be used in the review process.

Audit Flags

Errors, omissions and discrepancies, as previously stated, can lead to problems when audits are conducted. Certain services, procedures and billing patterns flag auditors to scrutinize billing documents and medical records. Problematic areas exist in the billing and reporting of the following:

1. Length and size of lesions excised or wounds repaired
2. Layers of fascia, muscle and skin involved in repair
3. Wound debridement for major infections or contamination
4. Complications encountered during or following a service or procedure
5. Evaluation and management services (primarily in the office setting)

Audit Statistics

HCFA sources state that 30% of all claims paid in fiscal year 1996 contained errors. fourteen percent of Medicare fee-for-service payments or $23.2 billion annually is accounted for in this 30% error ratio. The greatest percentage of error occurred on inpatient services reported. Strictly speaking, then, hospitals billed in error for their facility an average of 22.59% of the time. Physician providers, however, followed closely with a 21.68% error ratio for their services.

Home health providers constitute nearly 16% of the errors made in billing services to HCFA, while outpatient hospital and ancillary service errors amount to 12% of the aggregate. Skilled nursing services billing errors equaled nearly 11%, and laboratories billed in error nearly 6% of the time. Nearly 12% of the remaining total represented a miscellaneous or multiple provider reporting error ratio. See Figure 12–7 for more details.

HIPAA

The Health Insurance Portability and Accountability Act of 1996 is merely an amendment to the Internal Revenue Code of 1986. The portion of this act, which most impacts coders and billers is found in the section concerning the prevention of healthcare fraud and abuse. Title II, Subtitle A, Section 201 states the program is established to: "(1) Coordinate federal, state and local law enforcement programs to control fraud and abuse with respect to health plans, (2) to conduct investigations, audits, evaluations, and inspections relating to the delivery of and payment for health care services in the United States, (3) to facilitate the enforcement of the provisions of sections 1128, 1128A, and 1128B and other statutes applicable to health care fraud and abuse, (4) to provide for the modifications and establishment of safe harbors* and to issue advisory opinions and special fraud alerts pursuant to section 1128B, and (5) to provide for the reporting and disclosure of certain final adverse actions against health care providers, suppliers, or practitioners pursuant to the data collection system established under section 1128E."

RESULTS OF 1996 HCFA PROVIDER BILLING REVIEW

Inpatient provider errors	22.59%
Physician provider errors	21.68%
Home health provider errors	15.74%
Outpatient provider errors	12.12%
Skilled nursing provider errors	10.45%
Laboratory provider errors	5.76%
Other provider errors	11.66%
TOTAL	100.00%

Figure 12–7 Results of 1996 HCFA Provider Billing Review.

Providers have voiced concern about the lack of discernment in the act between honest coding errors and deliberately fraudulent billing practices. The amendment states that a $10,000 fine, an imprisonment of five years or both can be applied to even an "honest" coding error. In Subtitle D, Section 231, the act states that the term "should know" means that a person "(A) acting in deliberate ignorance of the truth or falsity of the information; or (B) acts in reckless disregard of the truth or falsity of the information and no proof of specific intent to defraud is required." Under a section of this document entitled "Claim for Item or Service Based on Incorrect Coding or Medical Unnecessary Services", fraudulent actions are defined as those by "any person who engages in a pattern or practice of presenting or causing to be presented a claim for item or service that is based on a code that the person knows or should know will result in greater payment than the code the person knows or should know is applicable to the item or service actually provided".

Kickbacks are another area for review and result from agreements through which a physician or group of physicians and another entity enter into a mutual and exclusive referral agreement. In other words, a hospital might propose to furnish all the supplies, equipment, personnel, rent and overhead for a physician who refers patients exclusively to that hospital. In some areas, hospitals may offer membership to exclusive clubs or organizations in exchange for admissions or provide cash bonuses to physicians with the largest admission census. Other examples, for illustration purposes, may consist of an ancillary provider such as a laboratory or radiology clinic owned by physicians who, in turn, refer all of their patients only to that facility for lab or x-ray services.

A "safe harbor" is a legal mutual referral agreement wherein physicians are allowed to invest in and profit from ancillary businesses or to refer to specific hospitals by limiting the number of patients referred or the number of admits. Physicians, then, may admit to or refer to several available and appropriate entities or institutions instead of limiting all patients to a facility in which they have a financial stake or from which compensation or a bonus will be derived.

EXERCISE 12–12

1. HIPAA deals with a new type of third-party payment plan. (True or False.)
   _____

2. Safe harbors are a provision of the HIPAA legislation. (True or False.)
   _____

3. Can fines be levied for so-called "honest" coding errors? _____

OIG 1998 Work Plan

In view of this legislation, the **Office of the Inspector General (OIG)** has developed a work plan for areas of specific review. Areas under the greatest scrutiny will be: Physicians at teaching hospitals (PATH), outside billing services, DRG (diagnosis related group) coding, modifier -25, issues relevant to Medicare's correct coding initiative (CCI), monitoring (by the carrier) of coding accuracy for physician visits, and utilization of diagnosis codes by physicians and other providers.

HCFA's Action Plan

HCFA has a plan of its own to assist in the investigation and audit process. Plans are to increase prepayment reviews, increase postpayment reviews, increase review of E&M claims, increase number of random prepayment E&M claims audits by 10/1/98 and increase security to prevent claim submission from improper providers.

HCFA plans to identify audit sites through providers selected because of submission of improper claims. They plan to target providers who submit such claims and to conduct extensive investigation. The final point of the action plan is to demand more documentation from all providers submitting claims for reimbursement. Many providers report that they have already noticed an increase in the volume of letters from Medicare requesting additional information prior to the adjudication of claims for reimbursement.

EXERCISE 12–13

1. HCFA is working with the OIG and FBI to target fraudulent physicians. (True or False.) _____

2. HCFA plans to increase the number of claims reviewed in the coming years. (True or False.) _____

3. HCFA and the OIG's final point in their action plan calls for demanding more documentation from providers submitting claims for reimbursement. (True or False.) _____

ABUSIVE BILLING PATTERNS AND TENDENCIES

Up-coding and **down-coding** are common and often innocent habits in the physician office. Up-coding is the tendency to submit codes at a higher level than substantiated by the medical record. Very few providers or offices deliberately up-code for greater reimbursement. Most are either ignorant or careless about the application of documentation and procedure guidelines in the code selection process.

Down-coding, though not necessarily fraudulent, occurs when more work or intensity was required than the chosen code describes. Some physicians deliberately down-code encounters with patients to avoid fulfilling the documentation requirements for the higher levels of service. Some providers feel that it is better to under-code and draw less attention to the practice. Unfortunately, consistent use of low codes presents as much jeopardy as does up-coding or high-level service reporting.

Too many visits reported at the same level of service by a provider can provoke closer examination by an outside payer. Such a pattern implies that all patients have similar needs, treatments and management options. In truth, however, each patient encounter is somewhat unique and requires differing levels of intervention for treatment and management.

Evaluation and management guidelines specifically outline how much data should be recorded for each level of service. Examples can be found within CPT to illustrate correct application and selection of codes for billing and reporting services. Additionally, HCFA instructs regional Medicare carriers to provide instruction to providers of medical service. Medicare bulletins and seminars promote correct coding and appropriate billing practices.

CPT codes define components inherent in surgical and interventional procedures. There are ample resources for clarification of procedure codes to prevent under-coding or over-coding of a surgical or interventional procedure. Many professional societies such as the American College of Cardiology, American Academy of Orthopedic Specialists and the American Academy of Family Physicians publish guidelines and detailed descriptions to assist physicians, billers and coders with code selection. Additional reference sources are newsletters, books, how-to manuals, seminars and workshops.

Because so much information has been made readily available and updated annually, the Office of the Inspector General (OIG) has stated that "ignorance is no excuse" or defense in cases where fraudulent billing is discovered.

EXERCISE 12–14

1. Up-coding is not as severe as down-coding in the eyes of the outside auditors. (True or False.) _____

2. Too many instances of reporting the same date of service may provoke an audit. (True or False.) _____

3. E/M guidelines offer suggested types of data that should be documented in the patient medical record to satisfy criteria for a level of service. (True or False.) _____

Potential Fraud Risk Areas

Specific faults, omissions, errors and oversights are considered traps for audit jeopardy. As stated repeatedly in this module, coding issues are extremely critical. "Gray areas", unspecified or undefined coding or billing practices; lack of training for coding and billing personnel; poor internal communication; improper or inaccurate application of modifiers; poor documentation; poor diagnosis coding; discrepancies between dates of service and performance; missing documentation; and itemization or unbundling of procedure codes can provoke intense review in the audit context.

Prepayment vs. Postpayment Review

Medicare plans to continue and increase the current number of prepayment reviews it conducts. Prepayment review, though resulting in payment delay to the provider, may ultimately save overpayment interest and fines if errors are uncovered. This type of review, as implied by the name, occurs before payment consideration is made and reimbursement is forwarded to the physician. Prepayment review may provoke a request for additional documentation such as an operative or encounter report. Auditors will compare billed charges, diagnoses, procedures to the medical record for consistency, accuracy, errors or omissions.

In postpayment review, which means the claim is reviewed after the reimbursement is made to the provider, the same documents may be compared. If errors are found, an overpayment amount is assessed which can include up to twice the overpayment amount, up to $10,000 per error, plus overpayment interest. Furthermore, the audit may apply the overpayment amount to all instances of reporting a specific code within a defined period of review. In other words, if a practice has submitted claims for established patient office visits-level four 230 times during the period under audit, all those visits will be reviewed and evaluated. The percentage of incorrect usage of the code will be analyzed. If 90% of the time the practice chose the code in error, the assessment will be applied to 90% of the dollars paid during the review period.

The Audit Process

Audits may be conducted either on-site, by mail, at the carrier office or electronically. Audits can be random or focused. A focused medical review occurs because the provider has exhibited a trend or pattern of billing that triggers closer scrutiny by the payer. A random audit is a "spot check" device designed to test general billing practices and uncover undiscovered errors or omissions in provider billing.

Mail audits occur when records and documents are solicited through a letter from the regional carrier as seen in Figure 12–8. Good documentation and appropriate billing practices and diagnoses will go far to ensure that the office is not required to pay back or be fined in such a review.

On-site audits occur when carriers have strong suspicions or have received tips about questionable billing practices. Such audits may be carried out by special agents working for the Federal Bureau of Investigation (FBI) or the OIG. Often a "search and seize" warrant accompanies the agent(s). In such cases, the agent has the authority to search for and seize all medical, billing, and insurer records contained in the practice that are considered pertinent to the investigation. Such a massive seizure can paralyze daily operations within a medical practice. Providers are, therefore, instructed to seek immediate legal counsel before submitting to interrogation and to cooperate fully with the agent's document requests.

Medicare Part B
Any Region
4503 Abernathy Road
Anytown, USA

Joe Q. Hazard, MD
1190 S. 48th Place
Suite 520
Anytown, USA

Dear Dr. Hazard:

We have completed our review of the information you submitted in response to my January 10, 1997 letter. We were able to revise a portion of the sampled claims as reflected on the attached itemization. The results of the sample have once again been projected to assigned claims paid from July 1, 1996 to September 1, 1996. A final overpayment amount of $153,778.92 has been determined.

We have determined that you were not "without fault" in causing the overpayment. Therefore, we are not waiving your obligation to repay this amount in full. We cannot find you without fault because you are responsible for being aware of correct claim filing procedures and must use care when billing and accepting payment. Therefore, you will be responsible for the repayment of the overpayment amount.

Applicable authorities are: Section 1870(b) of the Social Security Act; SS 405.350-405.359 of Title 42 and SS 404.506-404.509, 404.510 and 404.512 of Title 20 of the United States Code of Federal Regulations.

Please return the overpaid amount to this office no later than January 31, 1997. No interest charge will be assessed if we receive your payment in full. Should you be unable to remit in full, payment arrangement will be made to include an interest charge.

Your prompt attention to this matter will be appreciated.

Sincerely,

Martha J. Wilson
Overpayment Audit Chief

Figure 12–8 Sample "Dear Doctor" letter from Medicare.

Such audits should be taken very seriously. Outcomes in such audits rarely vindicate the physician and generally uncover major documentation deficits as well as billing errors, conflicts and omissions.

Despite the fact that a government source may have instigated the audit, fraud and abuse units exist within all insurance companies. Federal investigators share information with the private sector. Most formal audits result in recovery of both federal and private payments. Physicians found liable can be prosecuted under the RICOH Act, which was enacted to combat money-laundering, mail fraud and anti-racketeering cases. Settlements, plea bargains and other arrangements are sometimes made which prevent or reduce terms of incarceration for providers (see Figure 12–9). By studying this figure, you will become familiar with common terms and abbreviations used in regard to issues of compliance.

Internal audits initiated by the practice should also be supported with external contracted audits. Such outside influence provides a fresh and objective assessment of the billing and coding practices within the provider setting. Additionally, comparisons and evaluations from an outside source serve as a quality indicator

---

GLOSSARY OF COMPLIANCE TERMINOLOGY

BBA—Balanced Budget Act of 1997. A bipartisan agreement adding new penalties for combating fraud while providing budget neutral modifications to the RBRVS for subsequent years.

Corporate integrity agreement—A governmentally mandated compliance program between a healthcare corporation and the government in the settlement of a fraud and abuse investigation.

DHHS/HHS—The Department of Health and Human Services or HHS. HCFA and the OIG are part of this department of the federal government.

FCA—False Claims Act. This act prohibits "knowingly" submitting false or fraudulent claims to government payers and/or submission of false records or statements to conceal, avoid, or decrease an obligation to pay money or property to the government. "Knowingly" is defined by this act as having actual knowledge of false information, acting in deliberate ignorance of the truth and/or falsity of information, and/or acting in reckless disregard of the truth or falsity of information.

Healthcare compliance—Ensuring that a healthcare provider or facility is providing and billing for services according to the laws, regulations and guidelines governing that organization.

HIPAA—Health Insurance Portability and Accountability Act. Legislation designed to fight healthcare fraud by a broader expansion of HHS-OIG jurisdiction along with substantial increases in the investigative resources available to the OIG and FBI for healthcare enforcement. This law also clarifies and increases the number of healthcare fraud and abuse offenses while significantly increasing administrative and criminal penalties.

OIG—Office of the Inspector General. An enforcement arm of the DHHS responsible for investigation and enforcement of fraud and abuse cases and legislation.

ORT—Operation Restore Trust. A federal Medicare/Medicaid pilot program targeted at combating fraud, waste and abuse. The ORT focus is presently on home health agencies, nursing homes, and DME (durable medical equipment) suppliers. At its inception, the five largest Medicare states were enrolled in the pilot program. Currently, twelve more states have been added to the program.

Qui tam action—A lawsuit usually brought by an employee (often referred to as a "whistleblower") in regard to specific employer activities that employee believes to be fraudulent or abusive.

Figure 12–9 Glossary of compliance terminology.

for the practice personnel. Bi-annual reviews, at a minimum, are recommended. This prevents the passage of too much time should an abusive or fraudulent trend develop. Both random and focused reviews are suggested to sample records in general as compared to high-dollar or frequently performed procedures or encounters. It is further recommended that codes from all areas of the facility as well as hospital or other outpatient services should weigh heavily in the audit selections.

Compliance in the Physician Office

What constitutes compliance by Medicare standards? Compliance is not limited to coding and billing but covers corporate ethics, internal operating procedures, fraud and abuse laws, coding and billing processes, ethical marketing techniques and ethical management styles. Within each of these subdivisions, the following elements must exist: standards of conduct, education, auditing, monitoring and plan development and update.

It is suggested that in analyzing coding and billing compliance, office staff follow the simple steps in the plan shown in Figure 12–10.

Managers can assist with the development of an awareness of the necessity of care in coding and billing functions. By internal monitoring and auditing documentation, employees and physicians become accustomed to the cycle of review. Supervisors should require that only qualified or credentialed employees perform coding, billing and claim submission operations. Processes and procedures within the practice should be documented and readily available to internal employees and external auditors. Problems, opportunities and solutions for billing operations should be explored and implemented. Ideas for improvement should be solicited from the billing and coding staff and employed if feasible. Information should be accessible to all employees to assist with and expedite compliance within the department.

Coding and Billing Compliance Basics

Educating personnel through attendance at outside seminars and workshops as well as internal in-services is highly recommended for updating and enhancing the knowledge base of billing personnel. Written job descriptions detailing minimum standards should be accessible to all personnel within the practice. The latest coding books, newsletters, and billing aids should be available to employees in this area.

CODING AND BILLING COMPLIANCE POINTS

- Procedures and policies governing coding and billing should be formulated.

- Actively seek education for all staff directly or indirectly involved with coding, documentation and/or billing, and claims submission.

- Require and clearly communicate minimum competency level for all staff.

- Establish non-punitive mechanisms for reporting violations.

- Involve (as needed or appropriate) outside legal counsel.

Figure 12–10 Coding and billing compliance points.

For monitoring purposes, periodic review of coders and billers should occur. Additionally, cyclical physician provider reviews should be scheduled and conducted. A checklist can be used for medical record completion to ensure proper maintenance and retention of medical records.

Communication through weekly meetings of the coding and billing staff has proven helpful in many practices. Access to medical records is a must for confirmation and reference when billing or coding questions or problems arise. Frequent and routine communication between billing, coding, ancillary and insurance personnel is valuable in working through hindrances and internal obstacles to billing or coding. Published results of audit findings are extremely beneficial to this department. Tendencies and patterns cannot be corrected if not communicated to the responsible party.

Initiating the Process for Compliance

To initiate the compliance process, first familiarize the practice with the necessity, the work plan, the basics and the "big picture." The first step is the completion of a comprehensive internal billing/coding and records audit. Share the audit findings with the staff. Risk areas should be isolated upon identification. Internal billing and coding patterns should be compared to national and regional norms. Information regarding OIG investigations, HCFA work plans, and so forth, should be shared with target staff and providers. Educational material should be shared with pertinent staff, management and physicians. Model compliance plans may be used as examples for the practice plan development. Upon completion of the initial steps, a compliance draft should be drawn up for review by appropriate management and physician personnel.

EXERCISE 12–15

1. Internal audits can be conducted to uncover billing problems within the practice setting. (True or False.) _____

2. Documenting that the practice has a compliance program will vindicate an office in a fraud investigation. (True or False.) _____

3. Agents of the FBI and/or OIG may possess search and seize warrants, which give them authority to search the premises and seize medical and financial documents pertaining to the investigation. (True or False.) _____

PERFORMING THE ON-SITE INTERNAL AUDIT

Although each practice operates uniquely under the direction of the managing physician, administrator or managers, there are standard steps in an internal audit that will enable discovery of billing, coding and documentation errors, omissions and deficits. The twenty-one step work plan that follows is one such "road map" that can be used for personnel attempting to develop an internal audit program (see Figure 12–11). In this step-by-step work plan, office staff is presented clear direction as to the tasks required to begin the on-site audit process.

PERFORMING AN ON-SITE AUDIT
A 21-Step Work Plan

1. Randomly select five evaluation and management encounters (both inpatient and outpatient) for review of each physician audited.

2. Is the medical record complete and legible?

3. Attempt to locate the following:

   A. Reason for encounter (medical necessity issues)

   B. Relevant history

   C. Examination findings

   D. Prior diagnostic findings (if applicable)

   E. Assessment of the patient

   F. Clinical impression or diagnosis(es)

   G. Plan of care, treatment or further disposition of the patient

   H. Date and legible identity of performing provider

4. If not documented, is the rationale for ordering further diagnostics or workup implied?

5. Are past and present diagnoses accessible to the treating or consulting physician?

6. Are appropriate health risk factors identified/stated?

7. Is there documentation regarding the patient's progress, response to and/or changes in treatment, and/or revision of diagnosis(es)?

8. Are billing services/procedures and diagnoses supported within the medical record?

9. Compare billed procedures to performed date of service. Are these dates consistent?

10. Compare billed diagnosis(es) to documented diagnosis(es). Are these consistent?

11. Are the billing and performing provider the same?

12. Analyze and evaluate documentation by reviewing required components for each billed service.

13. Score documentation according to audit tools provided.

14. Complete audit analysis sheet on each service level reviewed:

    A. Tally points scored and compare to billed services

    B. Show discrepancies, insufficiencies, omissions, etc.

    C. Make needed recommendations

    D. Make constructive suggestions and appropriate comments

    E. Illustrate missing components for satisfaction of service level requirements

15. Sign and date each analysis sheet with name and title of reviewer/auditor as well as the date of the review.

16. Analyze level-of-service patterns billed by each physician.

17. Compare/contrast individual physician billing patterns within the practice.

18. Consult with the managing partner before presenting findings to determine whether results should be presented to the group or individually to the specific physician.

19. Furnish each physician with his/her individual results.

20. Prepare a summary of findings both on an individual and group basis. Furnish this summary to each physician reviewed along with individual findings and results.

21. Retain an indexed file or binder (per provider) labeled with date of review, reviewer's name and title, practice name (at the time of the review).

Figure 12–11 Performing an on-site audit: a 21-step work plan.

UNCOVERING ERRORS AND OMISSIONS

Many staff members and physicians are unsure as to how to proceed when internal audits uncover glaring errors, omissions and overpayments. The following steps are recommended should this occur in the practice:

1. Inform payers of overpayments.
2. Follow instructions for return of incorrect reimbursement and resubmission of corrected claims.
3. Scrutinize, analyze and redesign internal processes and procedures to prevent recurrence of errors and/or omissions.
4. Ensure that coders, billers and insurance claims personnel cannot independently alter codes, billing procedures or fees for professional services.

PROTECTING REIMBURSEMENT

Compliance with federal billing and coding guidelines is obviously the best protection against audit recovery. Not only does careful adherence to the guidelines prevent payback of reimbursement, it ensures the completeness and integrity of the medical record. Many physicians feel that too much regulation and too many requirements prevent the delivery of quality healthcare as well as the receipt of appropriate reimbursement for their services. They feel that the Balanced Budget Act, the HIPAA, the **False Claims Act**, RBRVS have nothing to do with the way they conduct the business of delivering healthcare within the community.

As in any other industry, however, a few "bad apples" have brought intense scrutiny to the profession as a whole. Physician services are often intangible and difficult to qualify and quantify. Because it is difficult to capture the essence of a physician's activities and services to a patient, documentation is often the only criteria for validation of necessity or performance.

Proactive practices are appointing compliance officers within the practice to perform internal audits, to measure and publish results, to educate and update providers, and to periodically monitor and assess compliance. Additionally, forward-thinking offices contract with outside auditors, at least annually, to provide an outside and objective assessment of reimbursement, coding and billing operations. HCFA guidelines support such actions and recommend such proactive programs and cycles.

REIMBURSEMENT DENIAL: THE APPEALS PROCESS

When claims are correctly filed, insurers often refer to such documents as "clean claims" because they are quickly processed, error-free and straightforward in detail. No conflicts exist in the five "Ws" found earlier in this module. All demographic and insurance data is correct. The insurer has not selected the claim randomly for audit, and the CPT (procedure) codes link and match the ICD-9-CM (diagnosis) codes.

When all components fit and are correctly entered, a remittance is issued either in paper form (a check with remittance advice attached) or an electronic deposit is made. In either case, an explanation of benefits (EOB) will accompany the remittance to explain payments and/or denial of payment. When a denial occurs, a reason for denial code is also provided. Denials may result from a number of reasons, which may or may not result from the fault of the physician office.

Such denials may occur due to lack of patient eligibility, patient's failure to pay premiums, cancellation of the patient's policy (by either party), termination of patient or guarantor's employment, exhaustion of a lifetime benefit maximum, etc. Possession of an insurance card does not guarantee insurance benefits or payment! Verification of benefits is one method of preventing denials, especially with expensive treatments or procedures.

Occasionally, however, denials do occur because of office-related errors. Such denials may result from too many procedures performed within a stated time, services not covered under the patient's contract with the insurer, billing for services related to a preexisting condition for which the insurer has refused to pay, not billing within the stated filing time limit, or services provided by a non-network provider or at a non-network facility.

Yet another reason for denial may occur within the insurer and be unrelated to the patient or the physician office. Unless the denial occurs because of the patient-related issues stated above, a physician office may have the right to appeal a denial of reimbursement. Most insurers have an appeal process that should be carefully followed in order to be considered for an appeal.

Medicare has a strictly structured review and appeal process for denials. Enhanced by amendments to the 1986 Social Security Act, multiple levels of review and appeal exist for physicians (known as suppliers) paid under Part B, and for hospitals (called providers) paid under Part A of the Medicare program.

As defined in previous modules, HCFA is the national regulatory office for Medicare and Medicaid. This entity publishes federal guidelines and works with the states to regulate pricing, payment, allowable and non-allowable procedures, services, etc. Carriers are individual private insurers or HMOs contracted with the health care authority within a defined state or region headed by a carrier medical director (CMD). The CMD works through the administrative process of that company to issue local policies and guidelines and to authorize or deny payment of claims in a specifically defined locale. Carriers are contracted for Medicare Part B services only.

For Medicare Part A services, carriers are called Fiscal Intermediaries (FIs). Carriers and FIs are usually not from the same company. In other words, HFCA receives bids from independent insurers and HMOs for administering Part B and/or Part A payments and claims within a defined geographical area. When a carrier or FI receives the contract for Medicare Part A or Part B, they designate a separate division or entity dedicated only to the processing and payment of Medicare claims.

With the increased number of prepayment and postpayment audits underway, it is vitally important that physician suppliers understand their rights and privileges when denials occur.

In general, almost any payment dispute with the carrier over payment or coverage can be appealed administratively. All levels of review and appeal must be exhausted before bringing a case to court, in fact. This is known as an "exhaustion of remedies rule."

Coverage issues that result in dispute occur most frequently because of the vague language found in the coverage statutes. Such appeals are answered on two levels: at the HCFA level, and at the carrier level. At the HCFA level, coverage determinations are (a) formal national coverage determinations and (b) more informal coverage determinations HCFA plans to implement nationally.

At the formal national coverage level, decisions are extremely difficult to reverse because of the careful planning and research carried out prior to the issuance of the formal policy. HCFA's *Coverage Issues Manual* spells out such national coverage issues in detail. Most coverage issues, however, are determined at the carrier level. Suppliers have the greatest opportunity to appeal and overturn decisions made at this level. *Ad hoc* notice and comment procedures involving input from committees within the carrier's region are part of the policy development process. Since a committee approach is used to formulate coverage policy, this less formalized body is more receptive to challenge and appeal.

Issues regarding payment or reimbursement to a physician supplier may include payment methods, adequacy of documentation, calculation of allowable amounts, calculations of payment limits to nonparticipating physicians, payment calculations based on RBRVS formulae, payment rates on new procedures for which no established or published allowables exist, computation of physician payments, fairness of audit samplings and projected disallowed payment amounts.

To initiate the Part B Medicare appeal process, an "initial determination" must be made. First, a claim for reimbursement must be forwarded to the Part B carrier. The carrier's first reaction and determination on that claim constitutes the initial determination phase of appeal. This first determination is communicated to the physician supplier by means of an EOB or Medicare Part B Benefit form sent out by the carriers to the beneficiary regarding a claim submitted by the physician. Upon reopening, if an initial determination is changed (as can happen in post-payment audit scenarios), and provided the total claim in question totals $100 or more, the claim is placed at a carrier fair hearing level. Claims totaling less than $100 result in a review-level of appeal.

Occasionally, suppliers may not receive a determination that can be appealed. Such determinations are termed consent settlement demands. These documents resemble initial determination documents but are not appealable determinations. Carriers may also choose to deny payment based on technical deficiencies in records accompanying the claim request for reimbursement. Missing documentation, incorrect signatures or illegible documents all may fall into this category of denial.

An additional review device is triggered when 60 days or more have passed without the carrier acting upon the request for payment. The physician supplier can request a fair hearing under such situations as stated in the *Medicare Carrier's Manual* §§ 12005 and 12015.

Under RBRVS, certain issues may not be appealed according to the Social Security Act § 1848 (I); 42 U.S.C. §1395 w-4. Such issues include relative value components, conversions factors, adjusted historical payment bases, geographic adjustments, and the actual RBRVS coding system.

Medicare retains a separate initial process for questions or entitlement of beneficiaries. Such questions which may deal with age, disability or beneficiary eligibility determination come under the Social Security Administration for appeals, not under the Medicare appeals process.

In studying the appeals process, the first question you should ask is in regard to who can request an appeal. For Part B purposes, beneficiaries or their assignees may appeal. Assignees are defined as the supplier who takes "assignment" on the claim for reimbursement. Under the rules, the assignee or supplier is entitled to the same rights as the beneficiary as outlined in 42 C.F.R. §§ 405.802 and 405.805.

Prior to initiating an appeal, a physician supplier who receives a denial or adverse ruling should first attempt negotiation with the carrier. Although the carrier is not required to negotiate, many will agree in order to avoid a protracted review and appeal process. When negotiating, it is wise for the physician practice to not only negotiate the issue in dispute but a repayment schedule if large sums are potentially due the carrier. Suppliers should be aware, however, that the six-month limitation period for appeal expires while negotiations are ongoing.

The next step the physician supplier should take is to obtain information as to why the claim was denied. Under the Freedom of Information Act (*Medicare Carrier's Manual* § 12010.2) the physician supplier can obtain the carrier's work sheets;

screening criteria; HCFA directives and policies; as well as the identity and qualifications of peer reviewers, consultants or experts.

Suppliers would do well to take advantage of the negotiation phase to supplement the medical record documentation. Although it is fraudulent to alter or enhance existing medical records, the addition of supplementary reports, findings or explanatory narratives may be used to clear up questions or insufficiencies in the initial submission of documents.

Private parties may agree to a stated dollar amount in settlement of a court hearing or settlement case. Carrier settlements are substantially more complex, however, because individual carriers do not have the authority to compromise Medicare principles and statutes by agreeing to a monetary settlement. For this reason, negotiations for settlement require that the supplier persuade the carrier that Medicare principles require the reversal of an adverse ruling and not just the stated amount that the supplier is required to repay.

In looking at all the weapons in the supplier's arsenal, special defenses should be summoned as critical bargaining points. Establishing liability limitation for medical necessity denials; without fault limitations for non-medical necessity denials; challenges to peer review member's qualifications; invalid sampling or coverage determination methods, and so forth, may be important tools in the supplier's defense during such review processes.

While an appeal is pending, reopening of the case is not permitted. Once the appeal rights period has expired, a physician can request a reopening of a specific disputed claim. Carriers retain the discretion to grant or deny such requests.

Five levels of appeal are built into the Part B Medicare Appeals Process. This process is only one of several distinct appeal processes in the Medicare program. Each process is integrated into a separate phase of the program. Other processes include Part B beneficiary-derived, Part A beneficiary-derived, civil monetary penalties, PRO (peer review organization) sanctions, PRO determinations for medical necessity on Part B claims, Part A cost report, fraud or abuse exclusions, and provider agreement and conditions of participation.

Time and Dollar Limits for Appeals

Type of Appeal	Time Limit	Minimum Dollar
Review	Must be filed within 6 months of the date of the processing notice (EOMB), voucher or remittance advice	No limit
Fair Hearing	Within 6 months of the informal review decision	$100
Administrative Law Judge (ALJ) Hearing	Within 60 days of the Fair Hearing decision	$500
Appeals Council	Within 60 days of the final ALJ decision	$500
Federal District Court	Within 60 days of the Appeals Council decision	$1000

Five levels of the Part B Medicare appeals process

Appeal level one is entitled "Request for Review." At this level, the appeal is addressed to the carrier (under 42 C.F.R. § 405.807–.817). This appeal must be submitted within six months of receipt of the initial determination. Extensions may be granted, at the carrier's discretion, if "good cause" can be shown. (MCM § 12007.) This level of appeal must be presented to a carrier or a Social Security office. The tool used for the appeal may be HCFA Form 1964 or a clearly written legible letter of request for review.

If such requests are not particularly time-sensitive, physician suppliers may invoke the Freedom of Information Act and request working papers, consultant reports, and the initial determination file pertinent to the claim in dispute. At this level, no hearing is granted. The review is based entirely on the record and any additional information submitted by the requestor. According to MCM § 12010.2, a decision should be issued within 45 days of receipt of the request for review.

At the next appeal level, termed a "Carrier Fair Hearing," the appeal is directly to a hearing officer. This officer is an employee of the carrier or independent contractor employed by the carrier. Requests at this level are made for claims totaling $100 or more.

Timely submission of request must occur within six months of the review determination by the carrier. If such a determination is the result of a reopened dispute, the timely submission must occur within six months of that determination. By the submission of either HCFA Form 1965 or a clear and legible letter, suppliers may request an appeal at the second level. Suppliers must appear either in person, by telephone or by written argument on the record (OTR). The hearing officer has the authority to prepare an OTR decision and to propose this decision as a resolution to the matter in dispute. Suppliers can either accept the officer's offer or decline and request an in-person hearing. The manual guarantees the supplier the right to request and be granted such a hearing, which will be conducted by another hearing officer.

Any party subjected to the review determination or whose rights to benefit are affected by the ruling may attend the second appeal level hearing. This fair hearing is considered *de novo*, and therefore, formal courtroom rules of evidence do not apply. In other words, rules for labeling and submitting evidence in court is not strictly followed in an informal setting such as an appeal hearing. Part 3, Chapter XII of the *Medicare Carrier's Manual* outlines instructions for the carrier and the hearing officer. Suppliers should attempt to attend any pre-hearing meetings to establish procedural and evidence issues as well as to become familiar with the background and "track" record of the actual hearing officer.

This hearing is considered non-adversarial because the carrier is not represented except for the hearing officer's presence. Direct or cross-examination cannot occur. Carrier representatives serve only as witnesses at this level of appeal. The physician in the dispute or some other expert should represent the supplier's case to ensure the most knowledgeable presentation of facts in the dispute.

HCFA binds carrier fair hearing officers to its interpretations of the law as set forth in the carrier manual. Therefore, even if a supplier presents a valid, factual and legal case, the hearing officer may not be able to rule for the physician supplier due to limitations or conflicts found within the *Medicare Carrier Manual* or in HCFA directives, policies or instructions. If physician suppliers have offices in multiple states and/or carrier regions, they can petition an out of area hearing if needed. To conserve resources of the carrier and the physician supplier, carriers can consolidate claims from different carriers into one hearing process.

After receipt of request for a fair hearing, the carrier should schedule such a hearing to permit the delivery of a decision within 120 days. When a decision is made, it should be issued in writing to the physician supplier. The findings of the hearing officer should take effect within 15 days of the hearing. Determinations made in favor of the physician supplier not paid within 30 days of the ruling should result in added interest paid by the carrier to the physician practice.

The third appeal level, known as an administrative law judge (ALJ) appeal, is available to appeal the adverse rulings of a carrier fair hearing. Section 1869 of the

Social Security Act gave beneficiaries and their assignees the right to appeal denials to an administrative law judge, to the appeals council and, finally, to federal court.

To initiate an appeal at this level, the amount in dispute must equal or surpass $500. ALJs are employed by the Social Security Administration's Office of Hearings and Appeals (OHA). Approximately 800 ALJs are employed by the Social Security Administration and roughly 200 specialize in Part B appeal judges. Such a hearing will usually be held in a nearby location to the physician supplier; however, other locations may be arranged to include Washington, D.C.

Within 60 days of receipt of a review determination, this level of appeal hearing should occur. HCFA Form 501 1B U6 may be used to request this sort of appeal or a clear and legible written request will suffice for request. Within 10 days of the receipt of the request for ALJ hearing, the carrier should forward that request to the Office of Hearings and Appeals at the *Medicare Part B Development Center* in Falls Church, Virginia under direction of the MCM § 12027. A docket number is assigned and the claim file is forwarded to the appropriate ALJ. The supervising attorney of the development center may be contacted to provide information to expedite complex cases in dispute.

Hearings at this level are also considered non-adversarial. HCFA and the carrier are not considered as parties to the appeal. Therefore, they are not allowed to directly examine or cross-examine witnesses. As in the Fair Hearing appeal level, this is considered a *de novo* hearing, and rules of evidence do not apply. If constitutional issues are in question, an expedited review is available.

The ALJ's discretionary power is broad and extensive. HCFA's instructions do not bind the judge to carrier instructions, interpretations, regulations, national coverage issues or HCFA rulings under 42 C.F.R. § 401.108. Within 15 days of receipt from the HCFA regional office of an ALJ ruling, carriers are required to act upon the ruling. Carriers must pay interest on claims not paid within 30 days of the ALJ decision.

The Medicare Appeals Council represents the fourth level of Medicare Part B appeal. This appeal must be initiated within 60 days of receipt of an ALJ ruling. Form HA 520 or a clear and legible written request must be received by the appeals council. The Part B Development Center docket number as well as individual Medicare numbers of impacted beneficiaries must be included in the request. ALJ ruling on its "Own Motion" must occur within 60 days of the date of the ruling. No extension is available for this sixty day time period. Set limits to the Own Motion Review of the record include errors requiring reversal, discretionary abuses, unsupported conclusions, and issues of broad or vague policy. Although the council has the authority to grant a hearing, most reviews are on record only.

The appeals council has the authority to decline the review of an ALJ decision. In such cases, the ALJ ruling stands and the final route of appeal, federal court appeal, is available to the beneficiary or supplier. The appeals council may choose to remand or return a case to the ALJ for further consideration or action. The council has the right to reopen a case for one year for any reason. For four years, the council can choose to reopen a case for "good cause". In cases of fraud, there is no time limit restricting the reopening of a case.

The HCFA regional offices periodically review ALJ rulings. Should HCFA disagree with an ALJ ruling, HCFA may send a letter of protest requesting that the appeals council review the decision. Such a request must be filed within 60 days for the appeals council to accept the case on its own motion for reconsideration.

At the fifth and final appeal level, a federal court review occurs. Within 60 days of an appeals council ruling such an appeal can be heard. $1,000 is the minimum monetary amount for fifth-level appeals cases. The federal court review will either take place in the supplier or beneficiary's district or in Washington, D.C. In cases at this level, the defendant is the Secretary of Health and Human Services. Unlike appeals at lower levels, substantial evidence rules apply. Because of the formality and the extensive preparation and resource allocation for a review at this level, physician suppliers and beneficiaries must be extremely determined and willing to wait out such an intense and protracted process.

As Benjamin Franklin noted, "an ounce of prevention is worth a pound of cure." Billers and physician suppliers should take to heart previous sections regarding audits, compliance, documentation and coding/billing compliance. The best defense is to prevent denials and, therefore, the need for navigating the appeals process. You have been given carefully formulated plans to conduct on-site and proactive reviews as well as tips for protecting reimbursement within the medical practice.

In the following sections, you will discover a number of tools designed to capture accurate and specific diagnosis (ICD-9-CM) and procedure/service (CPT) data from the medical staff. Billing staff should use every available instructional and educational device to ensure compliance.

EXERCISE 12–16

1. There are _____ levels of appeal within the Medicare program.

2. Evidence is required at every level of appeal. (True or False.) _____

3. A carrier employs a hearing officer or contracts with an outside officer to perform this duty. (True or False.) _____

DESIGNING TOOLS TO ASSIST WITH REIMBURSEMENT

A variety of tools are used and can be streamlined and developed to accurately capture charges for services performed by the practice physicians.

Superbills, Fee Slips, Encounter Forms or Charge Tickets

One important device that assists with potential reimbursement capture is the charge slip or superbill. This vital piece communicates from the medical area to the business office what services or procedures and diagnoses the physician dealt with as well as what level of service was rendered at the encounter. Properly completed charge slips are the key to "clean" an accurate data entry and, subsequently, to insurance claim submission.

There are no standards or mandates for superbill design. Therefore, office practices can be as creative or as focused as is practical and beneficial to the capture and reporting of data. There are some required data fields for demographics that should appear on the charge slip. These include patient name; name of responsible party if different than the patient; address, insurance data and co-pay (if applicable). Optional fields are insurance identification numbers, social security numbers, and signature of the patient and/or provider.

Some hints for design include the use of categories with bold headings; an alphabetic list of procedures, services, diagnoses; single or double column entries; multipart forms (with NCR carbons); color-coding for various departments or insurers; and front and back design to maximize information and selection options.

It is crucial that the business office staff work closely with the medical staff in the design of a "user-friendly" billing tool. Ensure that categories, data, diagnoses, and services are worded in language used by and familiar to the medical area of the office. Since both areas of the practice will use this tool daily, both areas need to feel comfortable and capable of using the form effectively and easily. Additionally, in many practices, this tool is the only access the coding and/or data entry staff have to medical data. It is, therefore, crucial that this tool provide as much accurate and complete information as is possible for billing and reporting purposes.

Just as the coding system requires annual updating, so does the physician's office billing tools. CPT, HCPCS, and ICD-9-CM codes must be updated on the form to prevent data/charge entry personnel from submitting obsolete or incomplete codes. As discussed under the HIPAA section, submission of incorrect codes can be construed as fraud by investigators. Therefore, compliance with coding updates must occur in all aspects of the practice each year.

Billing "Cheat" Sheets

Many offices furnish "cheat sheets" or diagnosis and procedure coding lists that represent the majority of conditions or services reported by the medical office. As insurance uses an 80/20 rule in determining payment, it is often true that 80% of the time, physicians see the same 20% of conditions. Also, 80% of the time, they perform the same 20% of services. It is then, therefore, productive and wise to funnel that routinely used data into a list that is easy to use and access. Some practices have such sheets laminated and made into convenient sizes for the medical staff. Other offices create notebooks for billers and nursing staff that contain the most commonly used codes. Either way, the sheets are only beneficial if they are also annually updated as the new codes are available. Care should be followed in designing such sheets that ICD-9-CM codes used include all applicable digits and are specific to the cases being billed.

Progress Notes

With the announcement and publication of the enhanced evaluation and management requirements, many offices are designing internal progress notes, new patient forms, and history forms to accommodate the newly required components. HCFA has pushed the implementation date of this new language into a future date. However, since the new documentation guidelines are straightforward, clearly defined and easy to use, many office administrators and managers are taking the information and inserting it directly into the working medical documents. By facilitating the capture of this information on the working documents, medical staff are automatically prompted to ask the additional questions, examine the additional body area or organ system and better quantify their decision-making processes. Such documentation aids also assist with internal and external audits because no doubt can exist about whether the required information is present in the medical record.

Hospital Production Sheets

Various methods for charge capture and productivity reporting are used in the hospital setting. Some offices use small cards that fit in the physician's lab coat for this purpose. Others use full-size sheets that are either handwritten or computer-generated. Some use multi-part forms that can be brought back to the office for routing. Some even carry notebooks or daybooks in which the provider enters the hospital activities for a particular date of service.

In the information and automation age, more offices have converted to electronic medical records and charge tools. Physicians carry notebook or palm-top computers and enter data directly as patients are seen in rounds. Software and hardware vendors have teamed up to facilitate billing by developing data download through radio wave transmission as well as the more common modem transmission mechanisms. Harvard HMO has developed a paperless environment as a prototype for a totally automated large multi-specialty practice. Electronic medical and billing records are used exclusively in the managed care facility. Most veteran office billing and coding staff shudder at the thought of the crippling effect a "down-day" for the computer would have in such an environment!

Regardless of the way in which the information is communicated, many lost dollars can potentially occur between the hospital and office. Some reasons for this are: the provider fails to write down a procedure or encounter performed; the provider misses a patient on the list when entering data against the room number; the provider fails to note an ER or critical care encounter, etc. Physicians are famous for doing more work than is documented. Because shortened formats are used for capturing this data, information can easily be omitted or entered in error.

Ancillary Technical Charge Slips

Many practices have separate billing tools for their strictly technical areas. Lab, x-ray, physical/occupational therapy, diabetic counseling/management, pacemaker/AICD evaluation and reprogramming, venous/arterial diagnostics, stress testing, and so forth, all may be a routine part of the daily-practice activity. Designing specialized and streamlined tools to facilitate charge and data capture is helpful in these areas as well. In this way, only the services and the diagnoses most frequently seen by these technicians appear on their billing tools. This further assists the charge/data entry personnel in focusing on potential codes limited to the particular technical area. Fewer choices or options can narrow the focus of the data entry operator, and, therefore, reduce the error ratio in entry and claim submission errors.

EXERCISE 12–17

1. Office managers should update their billing forms on an _____ basis.

2. Billing cheat sheets may contain commonly used _____ and _____ codes.

3. _____ documents can be designed to capture charge information required to select a CPT or ICD-9-CM code.

PIECING TOGETHER THE REIMBURSEMENT PUZZLE

The United States healthcare delivery system is truly one of the most technologically sophisticated systems in the modern world. Billions of annual dollars and research hours have brought us to the cutting edge of the latest and greatest systems, devices and processes for patient care, health intervention and wellness/preventive medicine. Unfortunately, the billing tools and systems for reimbursement have not necessarily grown and expanded at the same lighting speed as the technology we furnish.

Though the United States is not a national-health-service country like Great Britain, Australia, Canada and the Scandinavian countries, government bureaucracy and "red tape" figure heavily in our reimbursement potential due to the federal and state entitlement programs such as Medicare, Medicaid and CHAMPUS/CHAMPVA. Healthcare is strictly governed, regulated and paid through legislative reform and budget consciousness.

Additionally, managed care has become a daily reality as an alternative reimbursement and insurance option. In many states even the federal and state programs such as Medicare and Medicaid are administered on an HMO/PPO platform. It has been predicted that in the near future, all such public programs may become managed care delivery services.

The custodians of the billing, coding and medical record organization and retention functions in the physician office are integral parts of the reimbursement picture. These positions are challenged to stay abreast of and current on the latest rules, regulations and requirements on a federal, state, regional and local level in order to keep their practices competitive, solvent and in compliance.

By understanding all the potential payers in the world of medicine as well as the multiple payment systems, a small piece of the reimbursement puzzle takes shape. Learning about internal and external payment obstacles further fills in the important center section of the jigsaw. Becoming familiar with the coding systems, their significance and function establishes the puzzle's border.

Being proactive enough to take compliance efforts seriously and to react accordingly places the central puzzle picture into perspective. Designing user-friendly tools that capture data and charges effectively finish the outer edges of the puzzle picture.

SUMMARY

- The five "Ws" represent a vital component in consistent and accurate reporting of services and completion of the request for reimbursement to the insurer.

- An audit can occur at any time to monitor the effectiveness of billing and reimbursement patterns.

- The 21-Step Work Plan outlines the process for preparation and performance of an on-site audit.

- There are many reasons a claim may be denied for payment. When the reason for denial occurs within the insurer and is not related to the patient or physician's office, the physician's office may have the right to appeal a denial of reimbursement, carefully following the insurer's appeal process.

- The ability to receive and retain appropriate reimbursement for the services and procedures rendered is more important than ever to deliver quality health care.

REFERENCES

Balanced Budget Act of 1997, HR 2015.

Becker, Scott. "OIG Issues Model Compliance Plan for Clinical Laboratories." *Bender's Health Care Law Monthly* 12 (4): 3–5 (1997).

Bolinger, Roxanne. *Coding Answer Book.* United Communications Group; December 1997.

Budeiri, Priscilla R. "The Return of Qui Tam." *The Washington Lawyer* 11, no. 1 (1996): 24.

Department of Health and Human Services. *1997 Office of Inspector General Workplan.* Washington, D.C.: Office of the Inspector General, 1997.

Department of Health and Human Services. *1998 Office of Inspector General Workplan,* Washington, D.C.: Office of the Inspector General 1998.

Department of Health and Human Services. *Model Compliance Plan for Clinical Laboratories.* Washington, D.C.: Office of the Inspector General, 1997. (Available online at *http://www.os.dhhs.gov/progorg/oig/cpcl.html.*)

Department of Health and Human Services. *Model Compliance Plan for Hospitals (Draft).* Washington, D.C.: Office of the Inspector General, 1997.

Documentation Guidelines for Evaluation & Management Services. Marshfield Clinic. MGMA (1997)

False Claims Act, 31 USC 3729.

"HCFA Assigns Required Level of Supervision to Diagnostic Tests." *Part B News* 11 (22): 3–4 (1997).

"HCFA Backs Off the Actual Charge Proposal." *Part B News* 11 (22): 1–2 (1997).

Health Insurance Portability and Accountability Act 42 USC 201, 110 Stat. 1936. August 21, 1996.

"HHS IG Issues Model Clinical Lab Compliance Plan, Settles with SmithKline." *BNA's Health Law Reporter,* vol. 6 (1997): 328.

King, Ellen, (Healthcare Fraud Unit, Financial Crimes Section, Criminal Investigative Division, FBI). "Playing a Part: The FBI's Role in Healthcare Fraud Investigations." *Journal of AHIMA* 69 (1) 43 (1998).

Kloss, Linda. "A Hot Topic, A New Year." *Journal of AHIMA* 69 (1) 22 (1998).

Manning, Susan C. "Configuring Compliance: A Professional Fit." *Journal of AHIMA* 69 (1): 36–38 (1998).

Peoples, Paula. "Medicare's Final Rule Spells Out What's Done, What's Left to Discuss." *St. Anthony's Cardiovascular Newsletter* 7 (12.84): 1–3 (1998).

Peoples, Paula. "Refined E/M Documentation Guidelines Tell You What's the 'Bare Minimum'." *St. Anthony's Cardiovascular Coding Newsletter* 9 (8.80): 1–2 (1997).

Pontius, C. Anne. "New Test Profiles, Model Compliance Plan for Clinical Laboratories, Prothrombin Time Self-Testing." *Medical Laboratory Observer* 29 (6): 20, 22 (1997).

Prophet, Sue and Cheryl Hammen. "Coding Compliance: Practical Strategies for Success." *Journal of AHIMA* 69 (1) 50–61 (1998).

Prophet, Sue. "Fraud and Abuse: What You Can Do." *Journal of AHIMA* 69 (1): 68–70 (1998).

Reiling, Michael P. and David M. Glaser. "Compliance Plans: The Closest Thing to a 'Get-Out-Of-Jail-Free' Card You Will Ever Have." *Partners Integration Advisor* 5(2): 1–3 (1997).

Russo, Ruthann and Joseph J. Russo. "Healthcare Compliance Plans: Good Practice for the New Millennium." *Journal of AHIMA* 69 (1): 24–31 (1998).

Ryan, Elizabeth. "Building an Effective Corporate Compliance Plan." *Healthcare Financial Management* 51 (9): 60–63 (1997).

Seare, Jerry G., MD. *Medical Documentation.* Medicode 2nd Edition (1996).

Snell, Roy and Marc Dettmann. "Putting Teeth Into a Compliance Program." *Medical Group Management Journal* 44 (5): 17–18, 20, 22 (1997).

Stratton, Kathleen M. and Margit H. Nahra. "Managed Care Under Siege: How an Effective Compliance Program Can Protect Your Company." *Managed Care Quarterly* 4 (1): 80–85 (1996).

"The Nuts and Bolts of an Effective Compliance Program." *HR Focus* 74(8): 13–14 (1997).

U.S. v. Krizek, 111 F.3d 934, 324 US. App. D.C. 175 (May 2, 1997).

"Use OIG's Model Compliance Plan to Steer Clear of Lab Fraud Problems." *Professional Practice Today* 8(2): 6–8 (1997).

Vincze, L. Stephan. "Compliance, Medical Records, and the FBI: Preventing Fraud and Abuse." *Journal of AHIMA* 69 (1): 40–42 (1998).

Whitehead, Trudy and Robert Salcido. "Coding Component Important Element of Compliance Plan." *Healthcare Financial Management* 51(8): 56–58 (1997).

Whitley, Joe D., et al. "Healthcare Provider Compliance Plans." *Bender's Health Care Law Monthly* 11(9): 3–11 (1996).

Glossary

abnormal uterine bleeding   excessive menstrual flow or too frequent menstruation.

abortion   termination of a pregnancy before the fetus is viable. Spontaneous abortion occurs naturally; also called miscarriage. Therapeutic abortion is induced and is a deliberate interruption of pregnancy.

abruptio placenta   separation of the placenta from the wall of the uterus.

abscess   skin or cutaneous abscesses are collections of pus caused by a bacterial infection. This is usually caused when a minor skin injury allows skin bacteria to penetrate and cause an infection.

account aging   a method of identifying how long an account is overdue by the length of time it has been unpaid.

accounts receivable (A/R)   the amount of money owed to the medical practice by its patients.

achalasia   the inability of muscles to relax.

actinic keratoses   also known as solar or senile keratoses, they are caused by the sun and occur in areas exposed to the sun. These are considered precancerous, which means they can develop into a malignant skin cancer.

ACVD   arteriosclerotic cardiovascular disease. Laymen may refer to this condition as "hardening of the arteries" or heart disease. It consists of scleroses or hardened plaque deposits that may block blood flow within a vessel. As a result, blood circulation is poor. In advanced cases, comprised coronary vessels may result in ischemia or oxygen starvation to the heart muscle, which can result in necrosis or tissue death within the muscle of the heart (myocardium).

adjustment   a reduction made in a patient's account not related to the charge incurred or payment received; (also known as write-off).

advanced beneficiary notice (ABN)   notice to Medicare beneficiaries that the program will probably not pay for a service. The patient assumes financial responsibility for paying the provider directly for the service.

age analysis   a summary listing all patient account balances and when the charges were made.

AHA   American Hospital Association, one of the four cooperating parties for ICD-9-CM.

AHIMA   American Health Information Management Association, one of the four cooperating parties for ICD-9-CM. Professional association for over 38,000 Health Information Management Professionals throughout the country.

AICD   automatic implantable cardioverter-defibrillator devices are designed as self-contained and automatic systems capable of identifying and treating life-threatening arrhythmias, most commonly ventricular tachycardia (VT) or ventricular fibrillation (VF). The device is surgically implanted and battery-operated similar to a pacemaker. Two-lead electrodes and a pulse generator make up the system. An electrical countershock fires during an arrhythmic event directly into the heart to restore a normal sinus rhythm.

allowable   the fee the insurer has determined is the maximum payable amount for the service or procedure.

alphabetic index   Volume 2 of ICD-9-CM, the alphabetic listing of diagnoses.

ambulatory patient groups (APGs)   an outpatient classification system for Medicare patients where payment is based on procedure rather than on the diagnosis.

amenorrhea   no menstrual flow.

AMI   acute myocardial infarction. Known by laymen as a "heart attack" or "coronary," acute myocardial infarctions result from a sudden decrease of oxygen (hypoxia) to the heart muscle or a sudden decrease in blood circulation (perfusion) to the heart muscle. MIs are characterized and described by the area of muscle or muscle layer involved in the infarction or tissue death. Three zones surround the injured tissue. The first zone is an area made up of dead muscle cells, vessels and connective tissue. The second zone is composed of injured muscle cells, connective tissue and vessels. If proper circulation is restored quickly, these cells and tissues may recover. The last zone is called the ischemic area and may also recover unless the ischemia or decreased blood and/or oxygen supply has persisted long enough to starve the tissues and cells, and therefore, became necrotic (dead).

amniocentesis   percutaneous transabdominal puncture of the uterus to obtain amniotic fluid for diagnostic studies.

anemia   reduction below normal in the number of erythrocytes, in the quantity of hemoglobin, or in the volume of packed red blood cells; common in pregnancy.

anesthesia   partial or complete loss of sensation with or without loss of consciousness.

anesthesia   the pharmacological suppression of nerve function.

angioplasty   a medical cardiology procedure in which a catheter with an inflatable balloon on the tip is passed through a vessel and inflated at the site of an obstruction within the vessel wall. As the balloon inflates, any soft plaque is flattened against the vessel wall to prevent obstruction of blood flow and to open up the vessel for blood passage.

antepartum   time of pregnancy from conception to onset of delivery.

anteverted   tipped forward; in gynecology, this term is used to describe the normal position of the uterus.

aorta   the main arterial trunk within the circulatory system. All other arteries, except the pulmonary artery, are branches off of this main channel. This vessel originates in the left ventricle of the heart and passes upward toward the neck. The carotid (major artery to the brain) and the coronary (major artery to the heart) are branches of the aorta. Blood that has been cleaned and freshly oxygenated flows through the aorta to the various body organs.

aortic valve   the aortic valve is found between the aorta and the left ventricle. It prevents backflow or regurgitation of blood from the aorta into the heart. This is also called a semilunar or moon-shaped valve.

aphakia   absence of the crystalline lens of the eye.

approved service   a service approved for payment in situations where medical necessity is satisfied to support the service or procedure.

arthropathy   a vague, general term meaning pathology affecting a joint.

ASHD   Atherosclerotic heart disease. A condition similar to ACVD.

atopic dermatitis   a chronic itchy inflammation of the skin that often occurs in persons with hay fever or asthma or in family members with the same condition.

atrium   right and left upper chambers of the heart are known as the atria. Individual upper chambers are known as either the right or left atrium. Blood carrying waste products and very little oxygen circulates from the vena cava into the right atrium. The blood continues downward through the right ventricle and into the lungs. Waste products are deposited in the lungs, and the blood is infused with a fresh supply of oxygen. The fresh blood flows through the pulmonary vein into the left atrium, downward to the left ventricle and then out into general circulation through the aorta.

atypical moles   flat or raised dark skin growths bigger than moles. These are sometimes considered a precancerous state before malignant melanoma develops; also known as dysplastic nevi.

audit   an evaluation of the billing practices within a medical office. Medical records, billing and insurance records are abstracted and compared to investigate proper billing, coding and documentation technique and practices.

automated   laboratories that assay large numbers of samples mechanically.

balance billing   the action of billing a patient the difference between the physician's standard customary fee for a service and the insurance reimbursement for the service.

Balanced Budget Act   legislation designed to balance the federal budget in the Clinton-Gore administration.

bankruptcy   a legal declaration of an individual's inability to pay debts.

beneficiary   a person eligible to receive benefits of a specific insurance policy or program.

benign lesion   a noncancerous injury, wound, or infected patch of skin.

birthday rule   guideline for determination of the primary insurance policy when dependents are covered on two or more policies.

bookkeeping   the recording of daily transactions in a business.

BP   blood pressure is measured during two phases: systole and diastole. Systole results from the squeeze effect of the heart's left ventricle, and diastole is a result of the heart's chambers at a relaxed and expanded state. The force of blood on arterial walls as a result of the squeezing and relaxing effort of the heart and vessels is what is measured with a sphygmomanometer when assessing a patient's blood pressure reading.

brachytherapy   a natural or man-made radioactive element that is applied in or around a particular treatment field.

Braxton-Hicks contractions   light, usually painless, irregular uterine contractions beginning in the first trimester of pregnancy and increasing in frequency, duration, and intensity as the pregnancy progresses.

bruit   an abnormal "whooshing" sound heard through a stethoscope; this condition is the result of turbulence of the blood flow within a major artery. Often heard in the carotid artery, bruits may be the result of vessel obstruction.

budget neutrality   the self-adjusting process of increasing and decreasing cost centers within the federal program's budget to net a -0- increase in expenditures.

bundled   term used to indicate the inclusion of more than one procedure or service into one comprehensive procedure code.

Bundle of His   a fibrous band of highly specialized heart tissue that serves as a conductor for cardiac electrical impulses from the AV node to the heart's ventricles.

burns a burn is an injury to tissue resulting from heat, chemicals, or electricity. The depth or degree of burns are identified as first degree, second degree, and third degree.

CABG coronary artery bypass graft is a surgical "open heart" procedure. Vessels are harvested from the saphenous veins in the legs or the mammary arteries or veins within the chest and affixed around a blocked or occluded coronary vessel to reestablish blood flow or circulation to the heart and other body organs and tissues. Collateral circulation develops and blood and oxygen-starved tissues are once again perfused and oxygenated via the bypassed vessel grafts.

CAD coronary artery disease is also known as atherosclerosis. See ASHD or ACVD.

calculus a stone.

capitation represents a common managed care payment strategy by which providers are paid according to the number of patients choosing a physician as primary caregiver. The capitation payment is made for a predetermined amount at a predetermined time each quarter or year.

cardiogenic shock an abnormal and often critical body state resulting in inadequate supplies of oxygen to the body's organs and tissues because of heart failure.

cardiomegaly enlargement of the heart, sometimes known as an athletic heart, occurs because of increased oxygen demand brought on by obesity or strenuous sports activity or prolonged hypertension or cardiovascular disease.

cardiomyopathy a condition or general term describing a problem with the heart muscle.

cardioversion an electric shock to the heart muscle, which helps to convert an arrhythmia into a normal or sinus rhythm.

category categories are three-digit representations of a single disease or group of similar conditions, such as category 250, Diabetes Mellitus. Many categories are divided further into subcategories and subclassifications.

cellulitis bacteria spreads from a localized abscess to surrounding superficial tissues causing acute inflammation. It may also affect nearby lymph nodes. Necrotizing fasciitis is an extreme form of cellulitis caused by *Streptococcus* that destroys infected tissue under the skin.

cephalopelvic disproportion disproportionate relationship of the fetal head to the maternal pelvis.

certification the process of evaluating an individual's knowledge of a certain skill set to verify that the person meets predetermined standards as set by an organization.

cervical referring to the seven cervical vertebrae, C1–C7. The first and second cervical vertebrae are also known as the atlas and axis respectively.

charge slip, superbill, encounter form a three-part form with a record of account information for services performed including charges and payment; can also serve as an insurance reporting form.

CHF congestive heart failure is a condition in which circulatory congestion occurs due to retention of water (fluids) and salt by the kidneys. Shortness of breath, fluid accumulation in the lungs and edema or retention of swelling in the legs, hands and feet are characteristic of the problem. Diuretics (water/fluid medications), bed rest, elevation of lower extremities, oxygen, vasodilators and digitalis may all be used in the treatment regimen.

chief complaint a subjective statement made by a patient describing his or her most significant or serious symptoms or signs of illness or dysfunction.

chorionic villus sampling procedure using a catheter, which is inserted through the cervix to aspirate fetal tissue from the villous area of the chorion that surrounds the fetus; usually performed during the end of the first trimester for diagnoses of genetic disorders.

cicatrix   an area where the dermis layer of normal skin has been destroyed and forms fibrous tissue or a scar.

circumflex artery   a branch of the LCA (left coronary artery), this artery supplies the left atrium of the heart, the rear surfaces of the left ventricle and the rear portion of the heart's dividing wall or septum.

closed fracture   one in which the fracture site does not communicate with the outside environment.

closed reduction   the physician manually or through the use of traction devices, realigns the bone ends or fragments, without surgically exposing the fracture or dislocation site.

coccyx   referring to a single fused bone at the end of the spinal column made up of three to five segments.

coinsurance   a specified amount of insurance determined for each service the patient must pay the health care provider.

colposcopy   procedure in which an instrument (colposcope) with a magnifying lens and a bright light is used to examine vaginal and cervical tissue; biopsy and endometrial curettage may be done with the assistance of a colposcope after an abnormal Pap smear.

compliance   assuring that proper procedures and rules are followed; complying with the government's requirements for proper coding and sequencing.

comprehensive   extensive, broad, complete; used in reference to history and physical examination to include all relevant multi-system or single organ system information.

Computerized Axial Tomography (CAT)   this type of radiological procedure is used to scan any part of the body; most useful in scanning brain, lung, mediastinum, retroperitoneum, and liver.

concurrent care   the provision of similar services, for example, hospital visits, to the same patient by more than one physician on the same day.

congenital anomaly   condition or abnormality from birth.

consciousness   a general state of wakefulness and the ability to perceive oneself, one's acts, and one's environment.

consultation   a type of service provided by a physician (usually a specialist) whose opinion or advice regarding evaluation and management of a specific problem is requested by another physician or other appropriate source.

contact dermatitis   an inflammation caused by contact with a particular substance where the rash is confined to a specific area. Common causes of this allergic reaction are cosmetics, metal compounds, plants, drugs in skin cream, and chemicals.

cooperating parties   four agencies who share responsibility for maintaining and updating ICD-9-CM.

coordination of benefits (COB)   coordination of payment of services submitted on the claim form when a patient is covered by two or more primary medical insurance policies.

coordination of care   the arrangement and/or organization of patient care to include all healthcare providers.

co-payment   a specified dollar amount the patient must pay the provider for each visit or service per contract agreement with insurance carrier.

copulation   act of sexual intercourse.

counseling   the act of providing advice and guidance to a patient and his or her family. It is a therapeutic technique that helps the patient recognize and manage stress and that facilitates interpersonal relationships between the patient and the family, significant others or the health care team.

covered service   a contracted benefit from the insurer to the provider and patient. While infertility treatment may not be a covered service, testing and treatment until infertility is diagnosed may be a covered service with the insurer.

CPR (cardiopulmonary resuscitation)   A life-saving attempt in which the cardiac muscle is compressed externally (or manually squeezed internally) and artificial respiration is administered either via mouth-to-mouth breathing, AMBU bag or ventilator. The purpose of the chest compression and artificial breathing is to prevent brain and organ death due to cardiac and/or respiratory arrest. CPR in a medical setting may not only consist of internal manipulation of the heart, IV and intracardiac drug therapy, and also external or internal electric fibrillation to "shock" the heart into beating or into restoring normal cardiac rhythm.

cycle billing   accounts divided alphabetically into groups with each group billed at a different time.

daysheet   a record of daily financial transactions including posting of charges, payments, credits and adjustments, giving daily accounts receivable status.

debridement   a procedure where foreign material and contaminated or devitalized tissue are removed from a traumatic or infected lesion or wound until the surrounding healthy tissue is exposed.

deductible   a specified amount of covered medical expense that must be paid by the insured to a health care provider before benefits will be reimbursed by the insurance company.

dermatitis   an inflammation of the upper layers of the skin (eczema). Drugs taken internally can also cause skin reactions, which are considered adverse reactions. Sunburn is classified as dermatitis in ICD-9-CM.

detailed   chief complaint with extended history of present illness; problem pertinent system review extended to include a review of a limited number of additional systems; pertinent past, family and/or social history directly related to the patient's problems.

dilation   stretching and opening of the cervix during labor to facilitate the baby's passage through the pelvis; measured in centimeters; also called dilatation.

direct contract   an agreement with a third-party payer, such as Medicare, by which patients contract with the physician for a set fee for a defined service.

dislocation   a disarrangement of two or more bones from their articular processes.

DOE   dyspnea on exertion describes shortness of breath, labored breathing or difficulty in breathing with mild to strenuous exertion or activity. Lung disorders, hypertension, stress or heart disease may produce this symptom.

down-coding   selecting a lower code than the one billed due to poor or non-existent documentation, poor coding and linking choices or failure to satisfy the components required for a certain service level.

DRG   Diagnosis Related Groups, method of prospective payment used by Medicare and other third-party payers for hospital inpatients.

DVT   deep vein thromboses or "blood clots" may form within the deep vessels in the extremities, usually the lower legs. Venous stasis (blood pooling) in the lower extremities, damage to the vein interior or hypercoagulation of blood may aid in this formation. Patients on long-term IV therapy, patients bedridden for long periods or surgical patients are prime candidates for this problem. Treatment may include elevation of the affected extremity plus warm, moist heat pack application; anticoagulant, antiplatelet or fibrinolytic drug therapy; or surgical removal of the clot.

dysmenorrhea   painful or difficult menstruation.

echo or echocardiography   a non-invasive test that evaluates the interior of the heart and its major vessels by means of ultrasonic beams bouncing images off the structures and vessels in the heart via a transducer. The echoes or beams are transmitted to a monitor for the mapping of the heart's function, size, shape, blood flow, etc. Three common techniques are used: Doppler ultrasound, color-flow mapping and 2D/M Mode.

echography   use of ultrasound to obtain a diagnosis.

eclampsia   condition occurring between the 20th week of pregnancy and the end of the first week of postpartum marked by convulsions and coma.

effacement   obliteration of the cervix during labor as it shortens from one or two centimeters in length to paper thin, leaving only the external os; expressed as a percentage.

emancipated minor   a person under the age of majority, usually 18 to 21 years of age as defined by state statute, who is self-supporting, married, serving in the armed forces, and/or living separate from parents.

embryo   stage of human development from the time of fertilization to the eighth week of life.

employer-sponsored plan   insurance benefits available to persons employed within a company or corporation, or retired from a company or corporation.

endocardium   the innermost layer of cardiac muscle, the endocardium is found in the lining of the heart's chambers, the valves, and other cardiac internal structures.

endoscopy   inspection of organs or cavities by use of a tube through a natural body opening or through a small incision.

enthesopathy   pathology occurring at the site where muscle tendons and ligaments attach to bones or joint capsules.

epicardium   the outermost layer of cardiac muscle, the epicardium covers the surface of the heart and vessels.

epidural   located over or upon the dural.

episiotomy   surgical incision in the perineum to enlarge the vaginal opening and prevent tissue from tearing during childbirth.

episode of care   a reimbursement method of issuing one lump sum for services rendered for a specific illness. An example is global surgical fee payment.

EST or ETT   exercise stress or exercise tolerance test is a diagnostic tool used to evaluate the heart's response to exercise or activity loads. The test provides measurement of increasing oxygen demands on the heart and determines the amount and integrity of cardiac blood flow. Stress is either induced by exercise on a treadmill or bicycle or induced by a pharmacological agent such as Persantine, Dobutamine, etc.

established patient   one who has received professional services from the physician or another physician of the same specialty who belongs to the same group practice, within the past three years.

etiology   cause of the disease or illness.

evaluation and management section codes   the first section of the CPT coding manual that describes office visits, hospital visits, nursing facility visits, and consultations.

examination   a critical inspection and investigation, usually following a particular method, performed for diagnostic or investigational purposes.

exostosis a bony growth arising from the surface of the bone.

expanded problem focused chief complaint; brief history of present illness; problem pertinent system review.

explanation of benefits (EOB) a summary explaining an insurance company's determination for reimbursements of benefits; for Medicare claims, this is referred to as a Remittance Advice (RA).

face-to-face time the time that the physician spends face-to-face with the patient and/or family, performing such tasks as history, examination and counseling.

Fair Credit Reporting Act guidelines for reporting and collecting credit background information to businesses to use in evaluation of an individual's application for credit, insurance or employment.

Fair Debt Collection Practices Act a consumer protection policy against abusive collection practices by debt collectors.

False Claims Act a federal legislation that prohibits submission of claims for services not rendered or for any services considered fraudulent upon investigation.

fee-for-service the traditional method of charge or reimbursement in which each visit or service rendered is itemized, priced and charged.

fee schedule a list of fees of common services and procedures performed by a physician. It also means the listing in an insurance policy stating the maximum dollar amount the insurance company will allow for specific medical procedures performed.

first degree burn the skin is red (erythema), painful, sensitive, and moist areas become swollen. The burned area whitens (blanches) when touched.

fissure a groove, split, or natural division.

fistula an abnormal tubelike passage from a normal cavity to another cavity or surface.

fixation (fracture) a procedure where the fractured bones or bone fragments are secured in their normal anatomical alignment.

fracture a structural break in the continuity of bone as a result of physical forces exerted upon the rigid bone tissue beyond its ability to accommodate by resistance, elasticity, or bending.

gangrene tissue death usually associated with loss of blood supply to the affected area and followed by bacterial invasion. This skin necrosis is most often caused by anaerobic bacteria, which only grow in the absence of oxygen.

gatekeeper term applied to primary care physicians since they "open the gate" to specialist referrals.

gatekeeper the primary care physician providing or managing the patient's medical care.

general anesthesia a state of unconsciousness, produced by anesthetic agents, with absence of pain sensation over the entire body.

general multi-system examination a physical examination that includes several organ systems or body areas.

gestation time in which a woman is pregnant and fetal development takes place.

gestational diabetes glucose intolerance with onset of pregnancy.

global surgical fee in surgical cases, the fee includes the preoperative visit, the surgical procedure, the postoperative visit, provided there are no complications.

gravidity term used to indicate the number of pregnancies a woman has had; gravida is used with numerals (e.g., 0, I, II).

HCFA-1500 the standardized insurance reporting form to submit outpatient services to private and government insurance carriers.

HCFA Health Care Financing Administration, one of the four cooperating parties for ICD-9-CM.

HDL high density lipoprotein or "good" cholesterol is a protein product of blood plasma that contains more protein than fat. It transports the "bad" or LDL (low density lipoprotein) cholesterol from plasma to the tissues, thus acting as a clean-up crew for lipids in the blood circulation.

Health Care Financing Administration (HCFA) the government agency responsible for the administration of governmental health care plans.

Health Maintenance Organization (HMO) a managed care concept of health care delivery focusing on wellness and preventive medicine in an attempt to reduce health care costs.

heart catheterization a diagnostic test designed to examine the heart via a catheter placed within a major artery in the arm (brachial) or a major groin artery (femoral). The catheter passes through the vessels into the heart's arterial system. Dye is injected to trace blood circulation through the heart. Obstruction in flow indicates the presence of thrombi, plaque, stenosis or collapsed vessels. This procedure may also be called angiography or an angiogram.

history a record of past events; a systematic account of the medical, emotional and psychosocial occurrences in a patient's life and of factors in the family, ancestors and environment that may have a bearing on the patient's condition.

"hold harmless" clause a managed care clause that holds the patient/subscriber harmless from balance billing.

HR heart rate is the pulse or actual number of beats per minute measured.

HTN or HPN hypertension is commonly called high blood pressure. This is assessed by several successive and persistent measurements in which the blood pressure of the patient exceeds 140/90 mm Hg.

hydramnios excess of amniotic fluid.

hyperthermia this procedure uses heat to raise the temperature of a specific area of the body to try to increase cell metabolism and increase the destruction of cancer cells.

hypoxia oxygen starvation in the blood supply is called hypoxia. Symptoms produced by this deprivation may include: cyanosis (blue-tinged coloration of the skin, nails or lips), high blood pressure, mental confusion or rapid pulse rate. In severe or prolonged cases, cardiac and/or respiratory failure may occur.

ICD-10-CM International Classification of Diseases, 10th Revision, Clinical Modification.

ICD-10-PCS International Classification of Diseases, 10th Revision, Procedure Classification System.

immunizations series of injections and oral medications that assist the body in developing immunity to specific antigens; also called vaccinations.

indemnity insurer traditional 80%/20% insurance payment mechanism that also requires satisfaction of an annual deductible. In general, the higher the deductible, the lower the premiums are for the patient.

infarction also called a heart attack, an infarction refers to tissue or heart muscle death or necrosis.

injections a parenteral route of administration during which a needle penetrates the skin or muscle; subcutaneous injection; intramuscular injection.

insured, subscriber, policyholder the person obtaining the insurance policy, whether by purchasing an individual policy, or as a benefit of an employer-sponsored plan.

internal derangement   a range of injuries of the joint involving the soft tissues such as the synovium, cartilage, and ligaments.

intracavitary   within a cavity.

IPA   Independent Practice Association is a physician group working together for a PPO or HMO in free-standing clinics and offices.

ischemia   decreased blood supply to a specific area, which may occur due to obstruction from an occlusion, thrombosis or constriction of a blood vessel.

kerotoses   non-cancerous growths on the skin.

lactation   process of secreting milk from the breasts.

LAD   left anterior descending refers to one of the major coronary arteries.

LBBB   left bundle branch block is a specific type of left-sided heart block occurring due to a defect in the heart's electrical conduction system.

ledger card   the patient's financial record in a medical practice including date and description of service, charge(s), payment, and balance.

lesion   skin lesions are growths that can be either benign or malignant.

level of service   the extent to which services are provided, taking into consideration the components of history, examination, medical decision making, counseling, coordination of care, nature of presenting problem and time.

limiting charge   a percentage limitation on fees that nonparticipating physicians are allowed to bill Medicare patients above the fee schedule amount.

lipomas   deposits of fatty material that grow under the skin causing lumps.

local anesthesia   anesthesia confined to one part of the body.

lumbar   referring to the five lumbar vertebrae, L1–L5.

lumbosacral   referring to one or more lumbar vertebrae in conjunction with the sacrum.

LV   left ventricle of the heart which is the lower left heart chamber.

LVH   left ventricular hypertrophy is an enlargement of the left ventricle of the heart.

Magnetic Resonance Imaging (MRI)   this type of radiological procedure is used to scan brain, spinal cord, soft tissues, adrenal and renal masses. More superior scan than the (CAT).

main term   the patient's illness or disease. In ICD-9-CM the main term is the primary way to locate the disease in the alphabetic index. Main terms are printed in boldface type, even with the left margin on each page.

malignant melanoma   a mole that turns cancerous.

managed care   a method of delivering health care that places a priority on cost savings.

managed health care   a health insurance program that utilizes primary care physicians and case managers to oversee hospital admissions, surgeries and referrals in an effort to reduce health care costs.

manual   performing something by hand or with the hands.

mastitis   disturbances in lactation due to abnormalities of parts of the mammary glands, anemia, emotional disturbances, malnutrition, and inflammation of the breast.

Medicaid   a jointly sponsored federal and state government medical assistance program to provide medical care for persons with incomes below the national poverty level.

medical decision making   the complexity of establishing a diagnosis and/or selecting a management option.

medical necessity   the justification for an action or service based on the patient's condition, problem or illness.

medically necessary   a procedure considered needed and necessary for the proper treatment of the documented diagnosis for reimbursement.

Medicare fee schedule (MFS)   a listing of allowable charges for services rendered to Medicare patients.

Medicare Part A   the portion of Medicare covering hospital inpatient, institutional, home health, and hospice services.

Medicare Part B   the optional portion of Medicare covering outpatient services.

Medicare   a federal health insurance program for persons over 65 years of age, retired, on social security benefits, receiving social security disability benefits, or end-stage renal disease coverage.

medicine section codes   the last section of the CPT coding manual that covers a wide variety of non-surgical physician services.

Medigap   a private, commercial insurance plan purchased by a patient as a supplementary plan to Medicare coverage.

medi-medi   a combined claim form for a patient eligible for both Medicare and Medicaid.

menarche   time when the first menstruation begins.

menopause   time when menstruation ceases.

mitral valve   a two-leafed or cusped valve shaped like a bishop's miter (head covering), this valve is located between the left atrium and left ventricle. Considered an atrioventricular valve, the mitral opens when the atria contract and sends blood into the ventricles. When the ventricles contract, pressure is exerted on the leaflets causing them to balloon upward toward the atria.

modifier   a two-digit number placed after the usual procedure number, separated by a hyphen, which represents a particular explanation to further describe the procedure or circumstances involved with the procedure.

moles   small, dark skin growths that develop from pigment-producing cells in the skin (melanocytes); also called nevi.

monthly billing   billing patients at one designated time of the month.

MUGA   cardiac blood pool imaging; nuclear and multigated ventriculogram is referred to as a MUGA. This diagnostic tool evaluates left ventricular function, ventricular aneurysms, intracardiac shunting or other wall motion abnormalities. Technetium radioisotopes "tag" the blood's red cells or serum albumin. With the uptake of the radioactive isotope, a scintillation camera records the radioactivity on its primary left ventricular pass. The second pass includes an EKG and a gated camera used while the patient is manipulated to view all segments of the ventricle. Additional views may be obtained and observed after administration of sublingual (under the tongue) nitroglycerin or initiation of physical exercise.

muscle flap   a layer of muscle is dissected and is moved to a new site.

MVP   Mitral valve prolapse is the bulging or upward billowing of the cusps or leaflets of the mitral valve during the systolic phase of the heart. Such bulging occurs with an overgrowth or redundancy of valve tissue making the valve too large for the ventricular space. Connective tissue or skeletal abnormalities may be the precursor to such a condition. Mitral regurgitation or back wash may occur when the leaflets prolapse to such an extent that the cusps fail to meet and form a seal.

myelopathy   pathology of the spinal cord due to the arthritic changes of the vertebrae. Paresthesia, loss of sensation, and loss of sphincter control are the most common forms of myelopathy.

myocardium   the center layer of heart muscle is termed the myocardium. It is the major "workhorse" of the muscle layers because it is responsible for the pumping action of the ventricles.

myocutaneous flap   a muscle flap which contains overlying skin.

NCHS   National Center for Health Statistics, one of the four cooperating parties for ICD-9-CM.

necrosis   pathologic death of cells, tissue, or organ.

new patient   one who has not received any professional services from the physician or another physician of the same specialty who belongs to the same group practice, within the past three years.

nonparticipating physician (nonPAR)   a health care provider who has not signed a contract with an insurance company (also known as an out-of-network provider).

nonparticipating provider (nonPAR)   providers not participating with the Medicare program must not exceed the limiting charge when billing beneficiaries.

NTG   Nitroglycerin is a vasodilator for coronary vessels. Its rapid action is counted on with patients experiencing chests pain, angina pectoris, unstable angina, etc.

occlusion   blockage or obstruction by thrombus or plaque deposits within a blood vessel or passageway.

open fracture   one in which the fracture site communicates with the outside environment.

open reduction   the fracture site is exposed during the reduction procedure, and it is normally performed in an operating room.

orthopedics   a medical specialty concerned with the prevention, investigation, diagnosis and treatment of diseases, disorders, and injuries of the musculoskeletal system.

osteomyelitis   infection or inflammation of the bone or bone marrow. It may be acute, subacute, or chronic.

ova   female sex cell; also called gamete, ovum, or egg.

overpayment   excess amount paid in error by the insurer for codes or documentation used to support the claim for payment.

ovulation   release of the ovum from the ovary; usually occurs every twenty-eight days.

pacemaker   electrical (battery-powered) device that helps maintain normal sinus heart rhythm by stimulating cardiac muscles to contract or pump. Pacemakers come in single or dual chamber models and are programmed to sense and correct low heart rates or abnormal rhythms. The devices can be set a fixed number of beats per minute.

Paget's disease   a rare type of skin cancer that originates under the skin and resembles dermatitis. This should not be confused with another Paget's disease, which is an unrelated metabolic bone disease.

Papanicolaou test (Pap smear)   study of cells that are shed from the body (vagina and cervix) for the early detection of cancer.

parity   term used to indicate the number of pregnancies in which the fetus has reached viability; approximately twenty-two weeks of gestation. May also be used with a series of numerals to indicate the number of full-term infants, pre-term infants, abortions, and living children (e.g. Para 0-1-0-1).

participating physician (PAR)   a health care provider who has signed a contract with an insurance company to provide medical services to subscribers in the contract plan (also known as an in-network provider).

participating provider   Medicare participating physician who accepts assignment (receives payment directly) from the federal program.

parturition   labor and delivery.

pathological fracture   any fracture through diseased bone without any identifiable trauma or following only minor trauma.

pedicle   in skin grafting, it is the stem that attaches to a new growth.

pedicle flap   a flap of skin that is lifted from a healthy site, a portion of which is grafted to a new site, but remains attached to its blood supply.

pelvic inflammatory disease (PID)   inflammation of the entire female reproductive tract (uterus, fallopian tubes, and broad ligaments) usually caused by a bacteria ascending from the vagina or cervix; most common cause is sexually transmitted disease.

pelvic relaxation   weakened condition of supporting ligaments of the uterus and bladder; caused by aging, trauma, or excessive stretching from the act of childbirth.

pericardiocentesis   the withdrawal of fluid from the outer covering (pericardium) of the heart is called pericardiocentesis. This can be used as either a diagnostic or therapeutic tool. When used for diagnostics, a fluid analysis is performed to detect bacteria, blood accumulation or foreign body infiltration. As therapeutic management, this procedure liberates the heart's beating action by ridding the constricting fluid built up around the heart's surface.

peritonitis   inflammation of the peritoneum (the serous membrane that lines the abdominal cavity) produced by bacteria or irritating substances introduced into the abdominal cavity.

physical status modifier   a two-digit amendment to the anesthesia CPT codes that describes the physical status of the patient who is receiving anesthesia.

placenta accreta   condition where the placenta grows deep into the muscle tissue of the uterus.

placental anomalies   abnormalities in the size, shape, or function of the placenta, placental membranes and cord, and the amniotic fluid.

placenta previa   implantation of the placenta anywhere in the lower segment of the uterus; partial blockage is referred to as partial placenta previa and full blockage is referred to as full placenta previa.

plaque   soft deposits of fatty substances that harden with time and produce rock-like obstructions within vessels. Plaque production occurs due to high-fat dietary intake, sedentary lifestyles and hereditary tendencies in patients with progressive atherosclerosis.

POS insurance plan   Point Of Service insurance plans encourage members to use network facilities by financially penalizing the patient using services outside the plan.

postpartum   time after giving birth.

postpayment review   this review process is conducted after payment has been sent to the provider. If reimbursement was incorrect based on the reviewed data, providers are asked to pay back the overpayment amount plus interest if applicable.

PPO   Preferred Provider Organization is a group of physicians affiliated through a network with a managed care organization. If patients use physicians in network, the insurer pays at the highest possible level.

preeclampsia   toxemia of pregnancy marked by hypertension, headache, proteinuria, and edema.

preexisting condition   a medical condition under active treatment at the time application is made for an insurance policy, possibly resulting in an exclusion of that disease or illness.

prepayment review a review process conducted by insurers prior to reimbursement. Such a review process may solicit medical and billing records used to support the insurance claim for payment.

presentation manner in which the fetus appears to the examiner during delivery (e.g., breech, cephalic, transverse, vertex).

primary care the initial care rendered to an individual who exhibits a health problem.

primary care physician a physician who is responsible for the overall evaluation and management of an individual's health care; also known as family practice physicians, internal medicine physicians, general practitioners, or gatekeepers.

primary (first) diagnosis in the outpatient setting, the primary diagnosis is the main reason for the visit. It is usually the diagnosis taking the majority of resources for the visit.

principal diagnosis the reason, after study, which caused the patient to be admitted to the hospital.

problem focused chief complaint; brief history of present illness or problem.

professional courtesy medical treatment free of charge or at a reduced rate, or accepting what insurance pays as full payment to physicians and their families, office employees and their families, and other health care professionals, such as dentists, pharmacists and clergy, as determined by office policy.

prolapse falling or dropping down of an organ from its normal position or location such as the uterus, bladder, vagina, or rectum.

prospective payment payment system where the amount of payment to the hospital is fixed in advance of the patient's hospitalization based on the discharge diagnosis and other factors.

provider the physician, hospital or others that provide medical services and/or supplies.

PT prothrombin time is a laboratory diagnostic tool designed to evaluate the blood's coagulation status. This test also measures the efficacy of anti-coagulation drug therapy. Elevated prothrombin time may indicate "free bleeding" and require adjustment of drug therapy.

PTCA percutaneous transluminal coronary angioplasty is also referred to as balloon angioplasty (See reference for angioplasty).

puerperal time immediately following childbirth; puerperium.

puerperium time after delivery that it takes for the uterus to return to its normal size; usually three to six weeks.

pulmonary artery a major blood vessel that transports blood between the heart and the lungs for oxygenation. Deoxygenated blood is carried from the right ventricle via this vessel, which forks into the right and left lungs. The pulmonary vein then carries freshly oxygenated blood into the left atrium of the heart for passage into the left ventricle and, subsequently, into systemic circulation.

pulmonic valve a three-leaflet valve, the pulmonic is another semilunar valve. It is situated between the right ventricle and the pulmonary artery. During heart contractions, internal pressure forces this valve to open. Loss of pressure during diastole (heart relaxation) allows the valve to close.

PVD peripheral vascular disease is a common problem in cardiology offices. This atherosclerotic disease process affects peripheral vessels such as those found in the hands, legs and feet. Patients who are also diabetic have a greater tendency toward this problem and the after-effects of long-term circulatory deficits to the vessels furthest from the body's midline.

pyogenic arthritis   arthropathy due to a specific bacterial organism known to produce suppuration.

qualitative   tests that detect a particular analyte.

quantitative   expresses specific numerical amounts of an analyte.

RA   the right atrium is the upper right chamber of the heart responsible for receiving systemic venous or deoxygenated blood from the superior vena cava (which drains the upper body) and from the inferior vena cava (which drains the lower body). The coronary sinus also empties into the right atrium above the tricuspid valve. Pressure during filling of the right atrium may vary with respiration. Right atrial filling primarily occurs during inspiration or the taking in of air.

R & C   Reasonable and Customary. An indemnity insurance payment strategy for determining what is considered reasonable and customary payment in a specific area for a service or procedure.

Radiation Absorbed Dose   a unit of measure in radiation.

radiculitis   inflammation of the spinal nerve roots.

radiculopathy   disease of the spinal nerve roots.

RBBB   right bundle branch block is a clearly defined right-sided heart block due to a defect in the heart's electrical conduction system.

RBRVS   Resource Based Relative Value System is Medicare's payment strategy basis since 1992.

RBRVS   resource based relative value scale. Method of payment used by the government to reimburse physician's services.

RCA   the right coronary artery supplies the right atrium and the anterior right ventricle. The posterior portion of the septal wall, the posterior papillary muscle, the inferior left ventricle, the coronary sinus and the AV node all depend on this vessel for blood supply.

receipt   a form given to show payment received in cash.

reduction (fracture)   a procedure where the physician aligns fractured bones and bone fragments back into their normal anatomical alignment.

referral   the transfer of a patient's medical care to another physician for treatment of a specific disorder.

referring physician   the physician who sends or refers the patient to another physician for consultation or treatment.

regional anesthesia   the production of insensibility of a part by interrupting the sensory nerve conductivity from that region of the body.

reimbursement   the act of being paid back or payment in exchange for goods or services.

remittance advice   a summary explaining the insurance company's determination for reimbursement of benefits; (also referred to as Explanation of Benefits).

removal   removal of lesions can be by excision, destruction, shaving, or ligation. A biopsy only removes a portion of a lesion.

repair   repair of open wounds or lacerations are classified as simple, intermediate, or complex.

Resource-Based Relative Value System (RBRVS)   a Medicare fee schedule that ranks services and procedures performed by physicians by units based on service performed, practice expenses, and professional liability insurance.

retroverted   tipped back; in gynecology, this term is used to describe the backward displacement of the uterus.

ribbons   temporary interstitial placement in clinical brachytherapy.

rotablator   one of three established methods for atherectomy or removal of an arterial occlusion, a rotational device is inserted into the vessel for removal of plaque deposits. A balloon angioplasty and/or a stent may or may not be used following the rotablator to achieve and maintain an open vessel.

RV   the right ventricle is situated in the most anterior chamber of the heart in congenitally anatomically correct patients. It lies directly behind the sternum or rib cage and can be divided into an inflow and outflow tract. The tricuspid area and the trabeculations that embody the ventricular inner surface make up the inflow tract. The outflow tract consists of the infundibulum and extends to the pulmonary artery.

sacral   referring to a single fused bone made up of five segments, S1.

SBE   subacute bacterial endocarditis is a chronic bacterial infection of the heart valves often subsequent to dental and/or surgical procedures or heavy drug abuse. Heart murmur, fever, splenomegaly and abnormalities of the cardiac tissue are slow-developing but prominent signs and symptoms. Treatment involves long-term antibiotic administration, bed rest, increased fluid intake and pain relievers.

seborrheic dermatitis   an inflammation of the skin causing scales on the scalp, face, and other areas.

seborrheic keratoses   flesh-colored, brown, or black growths that can appear anywhere on the skin.

second degree burn   the burned area blisters. The blisters may be filled with a clear, thick fluid.

semilunar valve   named for its resemblance to the shape of the moon, the pulmonic and aortic valves are semilunar in shape.

septicemia   condition of bacteria in the bloodstream.

sequencing   arranging codes in the proper order according to the definitions of principal or primary diagnosis.

signature on file   a statement typed or stamped on the claim form for authorization purposes, indicating the patient has signed a release of medical information retained in the patient's chart.

single organ system examination   a physical examination that includes topics that are related to a specific organ system; e.g., cardiovascular, respiratory, eyes, or musculoskeletal.

skin graft   a plastic repair of a defect caused by either an open wound or from lesion removal that involves using skin from the patient or other source. Skin grafts can be split-thickness, full-thickness, adjacent tissue transfer, or free.

skin tags   small, soft, flesh-colored skin flaps that appear mostly on the neck, armpits, or groin.

skip   a person who has apparently moved without leaving a forwarding address.

SOB   shortness of breath, also known as dyspnea, occurs with heart-lung malfunction, congestive heart failure (CHF), chronic obstructive pulmonary disease (COPD), and other lung disorders such as pneumonia, pneumonitis and asthma. Cardiac patients often verbalize and exhibit this symptom in conjunction with greater than average exertion.

sources   intracavitary placement or permanent interstitial placement in clinical brachytherapy (e.g., simple management is a single treatment area single—port or parallel opposed ports or simple blocks).

sphincter   muscles that constrict an orifice.

sprain   a severe stretching of a ligament with minor tears and hemorrhage, without subluxation, dislocation or fracture.

squamous cell carcinoma   cancer that originates in the middle layer of the epidermis. Bowen's disease is a form of this cancer that is confined to the epidermis and has not invaded the underlying dermis.

stasis dermatitis   a chronic redness, scaling, warmth, and swelling (inflammation) on the lower legs, often causing dark brown skin.

stent   following the dilation of an artery, usually by means of balloon angioplasty, the stent is loaded on a special catheter with an expandable balloon. Both devices are threaded into a guide catheter and threaded to the occlusion site. The cardiologist then positions and deploys the stent by expanding the balloon. The stent is composed of a meshlike material that assists in keeping the vessel open and clear of future occlusions.

strain   an imprecise term that applies to any soft tissue injury (joint capsule, ligament, muscle, tendon) occurring from overexertion.

subcategory   four-digit subcategories are subdivisions of categories to provide greater specificity regarding etiology, site, or manifestations.

subclassification   fifth-digit subclassifications are subdivisions of subcategories to provide even greater specificity regarding etiology, site, or manifestation of the illness or disease.

tabular list   Volume One of ICD-9-CM is a tabular listing (numerical order) of diseases.

third degree burn   causes damage due to injury of the nerve endings in the skin, therefore there may be little feeling nor does skin blanch when touched. The burned surface may be white and soft or black, charred, and leathery. Scarring usually occurs. Deep third degree burns have an underlying necrosis with thrombosed vessels and may have loss of a body part.

third-party payer   a payment made by an employer, insurance company, or anyone other than the patient, to a health care provider for medical expenses.

thoracic   referring to the twelve thoracic vertebrae, T1–T12.

toxemia   group of pathologic conditions, essentially metabolic disturbances, occurring in pregnant women and manifested by preeclampsia and fully developed eclampsia.

toxoplasmosis   acute or chronic widespread disease of animals and humans caused by the obligate intracellular protozoon *Toxoplasma gondii* that can infect a fetus transplacentally as a result of maternal infection.

transient   short-term or disappearing after a short amount of time.

tricuspid valve   diametrically larger and thinner than the mitral valve, three separate leaflets or cusps are found in this critical valve. The anterior, posterior and septal leaflets are competent only if the right ventricle's lateral wall functions correctly. The septal leaflet is attached to the interventricular septum and is in close proximity to the AV node.

trimester   first, second, and third three month period of which the pregnancy is divided.

Truth-In-Lending Act   a consumer protection act requiring a written statement when there is a bilateral agreement between the physician and patient to pay for a procedure in more than four installments, disclosing finance charges, if any.

U&P   Usual and Prevailing, like R&C and UCR is a traditional insurance payment method by which usual and prevailing fees are averaged and paid at a percentage by the insurer.

UCR   Usual, Customary, and Reasonable is an alternate indemnity payment mechanism by which insurers attempt to pay a percentage of what is usual, customary or reasonable payment in a defined area.

ulcer loss of a portion of the skin, penetrating the dermis. Gangrene can be associated with skin ulcers. These are usually due to a vascular disease, as in diabetes. Decubitus ulcers are also known as bedsores or pressure sore. These result from a lack of blood flow and irritation to the skin over a bony projection. As the name indicates, decubiti occur in bedridden or wheelchair-bound patients or from a cast or splint.

ultrasound diagnostic technique using inaudible sound waves to produce an image or photograph of an organ or tissue (e.g., uterus or baby).

unbundling itemization of services for maximizing reimbursement for surgical or office procedures.

unbundling practice of billing multiple procedure codes for a group of procedures that are covered by a single comprehensive CPT code.

unit/floor time the time that the physician is present on the patient's hospital unit, establishes and/or reviews the chart, examines the patient, communicates with other health professionals and the patient's family and reviews diagnostic testing that may be located in another area of the facility; associated with the total work done before, during and after the patient visit.

upcoding the action of selecting a higher level of service or procedure code than the documentation or diagnoses support for the purpose of receiving higher reimbursement.

usual, customary, reasonable (UCR) a method used to average fee profiles to determine what is allowable for reimbursement. **usual** a physician's average fee for a service or procedure; **customary** the average fee for the service or procedure based on national trends rather than regional or local customs; **reasonable** a fee that is acceptable for a service that is unusually difficult or complicated, requiring more time and effort to perform.

VAD ventricular access devices are implanted for assistance with ventricular circulation. Whether used for single or dual chamber failure, the device is used during the weaning of patients from cardiopulmonary bypass devices. For long-term ventricular assistance, this pump device may be implanted in a body pocket created just outside the thoracic cavity.

ventricles the two lower chambers of the heart are called the ventricles. The right ventricle is two to three times thinner in muscle tissue than the left ventricle. The greater thickness and muscle mass of the left chamber is necessary to exert enough pressure and force to propel blood into systemic circulation.

VSD ventricular septal defect is a congenital (abnormality from birth) anomaly characterized by an abnormal opening (communication) between the right and left cardiac ventricles. Blood is shunted from the left to the right ventricle. Large defects create a volume overload for both ventricles and may produce pulmonary hypertension. If this occurs, the shunting action may reverse itself causing systematic cyanosis (blue discoloration). The defect may be found either in the (lower) muscular portion of the ventricles or the (upper) membranous portion.

waiver of liability another term for the advanced beneficiary notice.

wheal swelling in the skin that produces an elevated, soft, spongy area that appears suddenly most commonly due to an allergic reaction. Wheals are also known as hives.

withhold a percentage held out by the managed care organization as an incentive to keep costs, admissions and referrals low each year. If the provider follows the plan strategy, the withhold percentage is returned with interest at a predetermined time.

Workers' Compensation coverage for work-related illnesses or injuries.

WPW Wolff-Parkinson-White syndrome is also called pre-excitation disorder. This condition prompts the heart to use an accessory (substitute) pathway between the atria and ventricles. This substitution produces tachycardia or rapid heart beat. This condition can produce atrial fibrillation or it can degenerate into a ventricular fibrillation that may culminate in cardiac arrest.

X used in Module 1 to show that varying fourth and fifth digits may be used, depending on the specific diagnosis. For example, 250.XX shows that the diabetes category of 250 is used with appropriate fourth and fifth digits to further identify the type and manifestations of the disease.

Appendix

Prepared by Karen S. Scott, MEd, RRA

INTERNET SITES OF INTEREST TO CODERS

E Mail Lists

A discussion "list" is one that is designed to address specific issues by people with similar interests. Members of a list receive electronic mail from the list and can submit questions or comments regarding the topic. For example, on the Part-B list, people interested in physician's office issues address topics such as coding and billing. Subscribers may also submit questions to the list. Other subscribers can then respond to messages or submit messages of their own. E-mail lists that might provide information for coders are as follows:

Name of List	Address to Sign On	Summary of Discussion
Part-B list	Listserv@USA.NET Type "subscribe Part-B list your name"	Physician's office personnel discuss items of interest including coding.
HIM-list	Listserv@lists.umsmed.edu Type "subscribe your name"	HIM professionals from throughout the country on a wide variety of topics.
St. Anthony's Coding List	Coding-request@st-anthony. com Type "subscribe coding your e-mail address"	Mostly hospital coding discussion.

*To join a list, an e-mail message must be sent to the appropriate "list server," which is a separate address set up to be responded to by a computer. For example, to join the Part-B list, Joe Snow would send an e-mail message to the address listserv@USA.NET that reads "subscribe Part-B list Joe Snow." Joe Snow would then receive a message back from the list server confirming his subscription.

WEB SITES

Web sites are added and changed continuously. The coder may want to review some of the following:

Web Site	Internet Address	Types of Information Available
American Academy of Professional Coders (AAPC)	http://aapcnatl.com	AAPC membership, CPC, CPC-H Coding Certification Exams
American Health Information Management Association (AHIMA)	http://www.ahima.org	AHIMA member services, Clinical Coding Society, CCS, CCS-P Coding Certification Exams
American Medical Association (AMA)	http://www.ama-assn.org	CPT, publications, links to other medical web sites
Health Care Financing Administration (HCFA)	http://www.hcfa.gov	ICD-10-PCS information, Medicare rules and laws, proposed and final changes, ICD-9-CM procedure updates
National Center for Health Statistics (NCHS)	http://www.cdc.gov/nchswww/nchshome.htm	ICD-9-CM diagnosis updates, ICD-10-CM, vital statistics
Merck Manual Online	http://www.merck.com/	Provides information on diseases including cause, diagnostic tests, symptoms, and treatment

CODING CERTIFICATION AND CERTIFYING ORGANIZATIONS

Two organizations currently certify coders by providing examinations that test coding skills. Professional coders may wish to become certified to acknowledge their expertise in the coding field. After passing a coding certification exam, they sometimes receive promotions, raises or qualify for a better coding position.

The American Health Information Management Association has two certifications available.

> **CCS-Certified Coding Specialist** exam is given once per year and covers all aspects of coding in the hospital, outpatient clinic and physician's office settings. A coder must have three years experience in a hospital setting to qualify to take the CCS exam.

> **CCS-P Certified Coding Specialist-Physician** is a newer certification to test the knowledge of physician-based coders. Coders with at least three years experience in a doctor's office, group practice, or managed care who are experts in physician-based ICD-9-CM and the CPT/HCPCS coding systems are qualified to take the CCS-P exam.

AHIMA can be reached at 312-787-2672 and their address is 919 Michigan Avenue, Suite 1400, Chicago, IL 60611-1683. Their web site on the Internet is http://www.ahima.org.

The American Academy of Professional Coders has two certifications available.

> **CPC-Certified Procedural Coder**

> The CPC is a five hour, 150 question exam designed to test the skills of physician practice coders. The exam tests knowledge of medical terminology, anatomy, and CPT and ICD-9-CM coding.

CPC-H—Certified Procedural Coder-Hospital

The CPC-H exam is a five hour, 150 question exam designed to test the knowledge of outpatient facility coders. The exam covers medical terminology, anatomy, the UB-92 claim form, Medicare guidelines, ASC facility coding, reimbursement issues, and rules on modifiers.

The AAPC requires coders to have at least two years of coding experience prior to taking the exam. If the exam is taken successfully without two years of experience, an initial designation of Apprentice will be awarded.

The AAPC can be contacted at 145 W. Crystal Avenue, Salt Lake City, Utah 84115. The AAPC can be reached at 800-626-2633. This information was obtained from their web site on the Internet at http://www.aapcnatl.org.

Both the AHIMA and AAPC offer Independent Study type programs to prepare coders for the certification exams.

TOOLS TO HELP THE CODER

CPT Assistant—a monthly newsletter published by the American Medical Association

Coding Clinic for ICD-9-CM—contains the official ICD-9-CM coding guidelines and is available through the American Hospital Association.

Coding & Medicare Updates—a monthly publication by the medical management institute (800-334-5724)

Medical Dictionary—A medical dictionary is a must for every coder. This can be used to look up unfamiliar terms, procedures, anatomy of the human body, and diagnoses.

Medical Terminology Textbook—If the coder does not have a strong background in medical terminology and human anatomy, a good medical terminology textbook is essential. There are many that are "self-help"; i.e., they provide practice exercises and answers so that students can work at their own paces and obtain feedback on their progress. Some of these also contain computer software for additional practice.

Encoders—Encoders are computer software programs that help the coders assign correct codes. There are two types of encoders. One type, called a "branching logic", asks the coder several questions until it receives enough information to provide a code. The second type is simply an automated code book where the computer screen looks similar to the pages in the manual code book. When purchasing an encoder, it is helpful to have the coders test both types of encoders to see which one is preferred. An encoder is just a tool. Coders need to understand the logic and fundamentals of coding to use encoders effectively.

The Society for Clinical Coding is a specialty group affiliated with the American Health Information Management Association. According to the AHIMA web site on the Internet, membership is open to credentialed and noncredentialed parties interested in "advancing the quality of coded data, contributing to the education of the coding population, and promoting the recruitment of new coders." A bimonthly newsletter *CodeWrite* is published by this group, and coding roundtables are sponsored in many states to address coding issues. Interested parties may reach AHIMA at 312-787-2672 and their address is 919 Michigan Avenue, Suite 1400, Chicago, IL 60611-1683. AHIMA's web site on the Internet is http://www.ahima.org.

Index